Cost–benefit analysis

COST–BENEFIT ANALYSIS

Second edition

edited by
RICHARD LAYARD
and
STEPHEN GLAISTER

CAMBRIDGE
UNIVERSITY PRESS

CAMBRIDGE UNIVERSITY PRESS
Cambridge, New York, Melbourne, Madrid, Cape Town, Singapore, São Paulo

Cambridge University Press
The Edinburgh Building, Cambridge CB2 2RU, UK

Published in the United States of America by Cambridge University Press, New York

www.cambridge.org
Information on this title: www.cambridge.org/9780521461283

© Cambridge University Press 1994

First published 1994
Reprinted 1996, 2001, 2003

A catalogue record for this publication is available from the British Library

Library of Congress Cataloguing in Publication data
Cost benefit analysis / edited by Richard Layard and Stephen Glaister.
– 2nd ed.
   p. cm.
ISBN 0–521–46128–6. – ISBN 0–521–46674–1 (pbk.)
1. Cost effectiveness.
I. Layard, R. (Glaister, S.) II. Glaister, Stephen.
HD47.4C668 1994
658.15′52–dc20   93–37740   CIP

ISBN-13 978-0-521-46128-3 hardback
ISBN-10 0-521-46128-6 hardback

ISBN-13 978-0-521-46674-5 paperback
ISBN-10 0-521-46674-1 paperback

Transferred to digital printing 2005

To Molly Meacher and Michael Beesley

CONTENTS

PART III   CASE STUDIES

INTRODUCTION

Should Chicago build a new airport, or India a new steel mill? Should higher education expand, or water supplies be improved? How fast should we consume non-renewable resources and what are the costs and benefits of protecting the environment? These are typical of the questions on which cost–benefit analysis has something to say. However, there is no problem, public or personal, to which its broad ideas could not be applied.

The chapters in this book concentrate on those issues that are common to all cost–benefit appraisals. We have cast this introduction in a form that is theoretical and also shows how one might tackle a particular problem.[1] We take an imaginary project and show how the chapters throw light on the analysis of this project. But first a few remarks are needed on the general ideas involved.

The basic notion is very simple. If we have to decide whether to do A or not, the rule is: Do A if the benefits exceed those of the next best alternative course of action, and not otherwise. If we apply this rule to all possible choices, we shall generate the largest possible benefits, given the constraints within which we live. And no one could complain at that.

Going on a step, it seems quite natural to refer to the 'benefits of the next best alternative to A' as the 'costs of A'. For if A is done those alternative benefits are lost. So the rule becomes: do A if its benefits exceed its costs, and not otherwise.

So far so good. The problems arise over the measurement of benefits and costs. This is where many recoil in horror at the idea of measuring everything on one scale. If the objection is on practical grounds that is fair enough; and many economists have swallowed hard before making a particular quantification, or have refused to make one. But if the objection is theoretical it is fair to ask the objector what he means by saying that A is better than B, unless he has some means of comparing the various dimensions along which A and B differ. There are some people who believe that one particular attribute of life, such as the silence of the countryside, is of absolute importance. For them cost–benefit analysis is easy: the value of all other benefits and costs is negligible. More problematical are those people who believe in the absolute importance of two or more items, for they are doomed to intellectual and spiritual frustration. Whenever A is superior to its alternative on one count and inferior on another, they will feel obliged to do both. Choices between such alternatives have to be made only too often. However, rational choice may be possible even if not every item has a unique price. Often it will be sufficient to know that the prices lie within some finite range; the answer will be unaffected by exact values. The only basic principle is that we should be willing to assign numerical values to costs and benefits, and arrive at decisions by adding them up and accepting those projects whose benefits exceed their costs.

But how are such values to be arrived at? If we assume that only people matter, the analysis naturally involves two steps. First, we must find out how the decision would affect the welfare of each individual concerned. To judge this effect we must ultimately rely on the individual's own evaluation of his mental state. So the broad principle is that 'we measure a person's change in welfare as he or she would value it'. That is, we ask what he or she would be willing to pay to acquire the benefits or to avoid the costs. There is absolutely no need for money to be the numeraire (i.e., the unit of account) in such valuations. It could equally well be bushels of corn but money is convenient.

The problems of inferring people's values from their responses to hypothetical questions or from their behaviour are clearly acute and present a central problem in cost–benefit analysis.

The second step is to deduce the change in social welfare implied by all the changes in individual welfare. Unless there are no losers, this means somehow valuing each person's £1. If income were optimally distributed, £1 would be equally valuable regardless of whose it was; that is what 'optimally distributed' means. Each person's £1 has equal weight. And if income is not optimally distributed most economists would argue that it should be redistributed by cash transfers rather than through the choice of projects. But what if we think that cash will not be distributed, even if it should be? Then we may need to value the poor person's extra £1 more highly than the rich person's.

However, this raises the kind of question that underlies almost all disputes about cost–benefit analysis, or indeed about moral questions generally: the question of which constraints are to be taken as given. If a government agency knows for certain that cash will not be redistributed to produce a desirable pattern of income, even if it should be, then the agency should allow for distributional factors when evaluating the project. Equally, it should not allow for these factors if it can ensure that redistribution is achieved by some more appropriate method. In practice it may not know whether this can be ensured, or it may decide that the issue is outside its competence. Until this is settled a rational project appraisal is impossible.

Likewise, in the personal sphere it is reasonable to take unalterable features of one's character into account in deciding what is right. But which features are unalterable? In each case the issue is which constraints are exogenous to the decision maker.

This brings us to the relation between cost–benefit analysis and the rest of public policy. The government's overall aim is presumbly to ensure that social welfare is maximized subject to those constraints over which it has no control such as tastes, technology and resource endowments. In any economy this objective requires some government activity owing to the failure of free markets to deal with the problems of externality, economies of scale, imperfect information and inadequate markets for risky outcomes, and also because of the problem of the maldistribution of wealth.

Three main methods of intervention are open: regulation, taxes and subsidies, and public direction of what is to be produced, be it *via* public enterprise or purchase from private firms. Each of these types of government activity can be subjected to cost–benefit analysis, as the case studies in this volume illustrate. In the case of public production the great strength of cost–benefit analysis is that it permits decentralized decision making. This is needed because, even if the public sector is small, no one office can hope to handle the vast mass of technical information needed to decide on specific projects. Decentralization deals with that problem, just as the price mechanism does, but it raises the obverse problem that the right decisions will only result if the prices used by the decision makers correctly reflect the social values of inputs and outputs at the social optimum: what are usually called their 'shadow prices'.

In a mixed economy market prices often do not do this. So the main problem in cost–benefit analysis is to arrive at adequate and consistent valuations where market prices fail in some way. If production is to take the form of public enterprise, government will generally lay down some of the prices (like the discount rate) to be used by public-sector enterprises, as well as their decision rules. A similar adjustment is to be made in the price quoted when purchase is from private firms. In a more planned economy the government will lay down more of the prices and might, in principle, by iterative search find a complete set of prices, which, if presented to producers, would lead to their production decisions being consistent with each other and with consumers' preferences.[2] However, in practice no government has tried this and most rely in part on quantitative targets or quotas, as well as taxes and subsidies, to secure consistency in at any rate some areas of production.

If any of the activities of government agencies are non-optimal, the cost–benefit analysis is faced with a second source of difficulty in finding relevant prices: whether and how to allow for those divergences between market prices and social values that arise from the action or inaction of government itself.

Broadly the valuations to be made in any cost–benefit analysis fall under four main headings:

1   The relative valuation of costs and benefits at the time when they occur.
2   The relative valuation of costs and benefits occurring at various points in time: the problem of time preferences and the opportunity cost of capital.
3   The valuation of risky outcomes.
4   The valuation of costs and benefits accruing to people with different incomes.

Part I of this book deals with the various issues of principle involved in cost–benefit analysis. Part II shows how to evaluate time savings, safety, the environment and exhaustible resources. Part III contains case studies which illustrate some of the problems to which the techniques of cost–benefit analysis have been applied.

1 THE OVERALL APPROACH

Suppose there is a river which at present can only be crossed by ferry. The government considers building a bridge, which, being rather upstream, would take the traveller the same time to complete a crossing. The ferry is a privately owned monopoly and charges £0.20 per crossing, while its total costs per crossing are £0.15. It is used for 5,000 crossings per year. The bridge would cost £30,000 to build but would be open free of charge. It is expected that there will be 25,000 crossings a year with the bridge and that the ferry would go out of business. The government send for the cost–benefit analyst to advise them on whether to go ahead with the bridge.

In any cost–benefit exercise it is usually convenient to proceed in two stages:

(a) Value the costs and benefits in each year of the project;
(b) Obtain an aggregate 'present value' of the project by 'discounting' costs and benefits in future years to make them commensurate with present costs and benefits, and then adding them up.

At each stage the appraisal differs from commercial project appraisal because (i) costs and benefits to all members of society are included and not only the monetary expenditures and receipts of the responsible agency, and (ii) the social discount rate may differ from the private discount rate. The main work goes into step (a) and we shall concentrate on this for the present.

Consumers' surplus and willingness to pay

We need to avoid logical errors in deciding which items are to be included as costs and benefits and to value those that are included correctly. The guiding principle is that we list all parties affected by the project and then value the effect of the project on their welfare as it would be valued in money terms by them. In this case there are four parties: taxpayers, ferry owners, existing travellers and new travellers (who previously did not cross but would do so at the lower price).

1   The taxpayers lose £30,000, assuming the bridge is financed by extra taxes.
2   The ferry owners lose their excess profits of £250 [i.e., 0.05 × 5,000] in each future year for ever (area A on figure 1).

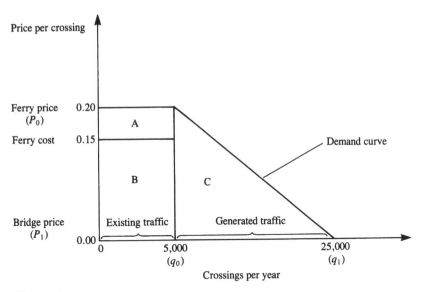

Figure 1

3   The existing travellers gain £1,000 [0.20 × 5,000] in each future year for ever, due to the fall in price (areas A + B).

4   The new travellers: to evaluate their gains is more difficult. We know that the new journey which is most highly valued was nearly made by ferry, and is therefore worth very nearly £0.20; while the journey which is least highly valued is valued only marginally more than its price of £0.00. For the intermediate journeys we have to make some arbitrary assumption and will assume that the value per journey falls at a constant rate from £0.20 to zero. In other words we are assuming that the demand curve is a straight line. So the average gain to new travellers is £0.10 per crossing and the total gain £2,000 [0.10 × 20,000] per year for ever. This figure corresponds to the gain in consumers' surplus on the part of the new travellers, since it represents the sum of the differences between the maximum they would be willing to pay for their journeys and the amount they actually pay, which in this case is zero.[3] Geometrically it is represented by area C, the area under the demand curve and above a horizontal line at the final price (which here is zero). In this special case where the demand curve is a straight line the value of generated sales will always equal $\frac{1}{2}(p_0 - p_1)(q_1 - q_0)$, i.e., half the price fall times the quantity increase. This is a formula which is used over and over again in cost–benefit analysis, especially for small changes in prices so the linearity assumption is a reasonable approximation to *any* actual demand curve.

5

Criteria for a welfare gain

We can now tabulate (table 1) the overall picture of net benefits (benefits minus costs), discounting all the future permanent flows of net benefits by an arbitrary 10 per cent per annum to obtain their present values.[4]

Can these now be added up? It depends entirely on our approach to the problem of income distribution. If we wish to use the very restrictive Pareto criterion of a welfare improvement, we shall support a project only if some people gain and nobody loses. But if some people gain while others lose, the Pareto criterion provides no guidance. If we follow it we must add up the net receipts of all the parties concerned. Then we only support the project if the sum is positive and compensation is paid to the losers. However, there is in practice almost no case where it is feasible to compensate everybody and if the Pareto rule were applied no projects would ever get done. Therefore many cost–benefit analysts have fallen back on the Hicks–Kaldor criterion, which says that a project can be supported provided the gainers could, in principle, compensate the losers even if they do not.[5]

In this case net receipts can always be added. However, there is no ethical justification for the Hicks–Kaldor criterion; where compensation will not be paid there seems no alternative to interpersonal comparisons of the value of each person's gains and losses.

This brings us to a second case for unweighted adding up – where interpersonal comparisons are made but it is judged that in the prevailing income distribution £1 is equally valuable to all the parties concerned. This may in some cases be quite a reasonable procedure. If not, there are only two alternatives: to use some system of distributional weights or simply to show the net benefits to each party and let the policy maker apply his own evaluation. If distributional weights are used they need not be unique: it may be that the weights can take a wide range of alternative values and yet provide an unambiguous verdict on a project. Viewed from this angle the Pareto criterion is just an extreme case where the distributional weights are allowed to vary infinitely.

For the time being we shall assume, as many cost–benefit analysts do, that unweighted adding up is permissible. We now learn an important lesson: that the area A disappears from the calculation. The reason is of course that it was a transfer payment (monopoly rent) rather than a payment for real goods and services; and if everybody's £1 is equally valuable transfers cannot change social welfare. Consumers used to pay this rent and now they do not, but there is no saving in resource cost as a result of the non-payment after the bridge is built. The economic cost–saving from the demise of the ferry comes from the liberation of resources worth B for production elsewhere in the economy. The only other economic change is the value of the additional consumption (C) – the real value of the first 5,000 journeys is neither more nor less than it was before. Thus, if one had wanted to take a short cut to estimating future net benefits (granted all

Table 1

	Future net benefits per year for ever		Present value at 10% discount rate
	£	Area in figure 1	
Ferryowners	− 250	− A	− 2,500
Existing consumers	+ 1000	A + B	+ 10,000
New consumers	+ 2000	C	+ 20,000
Taxpayers	—	—	− 30,000
Society			?

pounds equally valuable) one could have straightaway identified only the changes of real economic significance, i.e., the cost–saving on the ferry (B) and the consumers' surplus on the generated traffic (C).

Suppose the shares of the ferry company, which were previously worth £2,500, fall to zero. Should this also be included as a cost? Clearly not, since when we calculated the capitalized value of the ferry's profits we were in fact approximating the change in welfare of the shareholders, which is measured by changes in the value of their equity. We can use one measure or the other but not both, and it may generally be easier to measure the yield and to ignore changes in asset values.

So let us bravely add up the table. The present value turns out to be negative (− £2,500) and the project should be turned down. At this point someone might suggest that the project could be made 'viable' by charging a toll on the bridge. This is nonsense – all that it does is to reduce the number of journeys and hence reduce the gain in the real value of additional consumption, without any corresponding reduction in cost. The reader might like to confirm his understanding of the argument so far by recalculating the table for the case where the government levies a toll of £0.05 per crossing. The moral of this is that the prices charged for the output of a project may profoundly affect its economic desirability.[6] The correct price is the marginal social cost per unit of output, which is zero in the case of journeys across an uncongested bridge.

2 MEASURING COSTS AND BENEFITS WHEN THEY OCCUR

The concept of a shadow price

The concept of the shadow price associated with a constraint is of fundamental importance.

Consider first a simple example: you are to find two numbers, each greater than or equal to zero, which maximizes the sum of their squares. The *objective* is clear enough, but, as stated, this problem is ill defined. There is no solution because one can make the sum of the squares as big as one wishes by simply increasing the numbers themselves without bound. The problem can be made well defined by adding a *constraint*: for example, the sum of the first number and twice the second number must be less than or equal to ten. The solution is easy to see. One wants to make both numbers as large as possible, but for each unit subtracted from the second number, the first number can be increased by two units whilst remaining within the constraint, with a net gain to the sum of the squares. Therefore the solution is that the first number should be 10, the second number should be zero and the sum of the squares will be 100. So 100 is the value of the objective at the solution of the problem.

Now, suppose the constraint is relaxed by one unit. The first number plus twice the second number must be less than or equal to 11. Clearly, the solution will be to put the first number at 11 and leave the second number at zero. The objective will increase to 121 at the new solution.

> The shadow price on the constraint is the increase in the maximized objective when the constraint is relaxed by one unit.

In this case the shadow price is $121 - 100 = 21$.

The shadow price therefore measures how much better we could do, measured by the stated objective, if the constraint were relaxed by one unit: it is the penalty of having to observe the constraint. Put another way, it is the maximum we should be willing to pay to secure a relaxation of the constraint.

In practical work we have to face a series of constraints. If there were no constraints then there would be few interesting problems! Each constraint will have its own shadow price. It will be apparent how very useful that information is. It tells us which are the most important (or damaging) constraints and therefore where it would be most productive to direct effort towards relaxing constraints.

Consider now a simplified economic example which illustrates the way in which these concepts arise in planning.

A planner in a developing country has to set the outputs of two commodities: manufactured goods and food. He values a unit of manufactured goods at US \$4 and a unit of food at US \$7. To produce a unit of manufactured goods requires two units of trained labour and one unit of capital equipment. To produce a unit of food requires three units of trained labour and one unit of capital equipment. Twelve units of labour and five units of capital are available. What output levels should be set in order to maximize the value of the plan?

This is a simple Linear Programming problem. It is linear because the objective and the technical constraints all have coefficients which are independent of the volumes produced: doubling all outputs doubles the value of the plan and also doubles the input requirements.

Denote the quantity of manufactures by M and the quantity of food by F. Then the objective is to

Maximize $4M + 7F$

The constraints say that the consumption of each of the two factors cannot exceed the total amounts available

Capital constraint $M + F \leq 5$
Labour constraint $2M + 3F \leq 12$
and $M \geq 0$ and $F \geq 0$

This problem can be solved using the diagram in figure 2. The diagram shows the line representing points such that

$M + F = 5$ or equivalently $F = 5 - M$

The capital constraint dictates that the planner must choose a point on that line or below it. The line representing the labour constraint is similarly shown. Since the constraints must be observed simultaneously the *feasible region* is the area bounded by all the constraints.

The diagram also shows the lines representing

$4M + 7F = 42$ and $4M + 7F = 49$

These are sometimes referred to as 'iso-revenue lines'. If they were feasible then all points on these lines would yield a value to the plan of 42 and 49 respectively. The problem is solved by finding a point on a line parallel to these two lines, as far away to the north east of the origin as possible whilst being within the feasible region.

This must occur at one of the three vertices and these are the only points we need to consider. $M = 5$ and $F = 0$ yields a value of $20; $M = 3$ and $F = 2$ yields a value of $26; $M = 0$ and $F = 4$ yields a value of $28. As is obvious from the relative slopes of the lines in the diagrams, this last point is the solution to the problem: produce no units of manufactures, four units of food, giving a value of $28.

Now, what of the shadow prices of the constraints? Note that the solution point lies inside the capital constraint. The capital constraint turns out to be 'non-binding', that is, irrelevant! Therefore the value to the plan of an extra unit of capital is zero – this is its shadow price. This is a general result. *Any resource which is in excess supply at an optimum allocation of resources will have a social value of zero.* In the context of our example note that this shadow price may be quite different from the international market price of capital (denominated in US $). So we see that there may be a distinction between the market price of a resource and its 'true' value measured relative to the objective. Note also that the shadow price is a marginal concept – we say that the value of an extra unit of capital is zero, *on the margin.* This is not to deny the value of intra-marginal units.

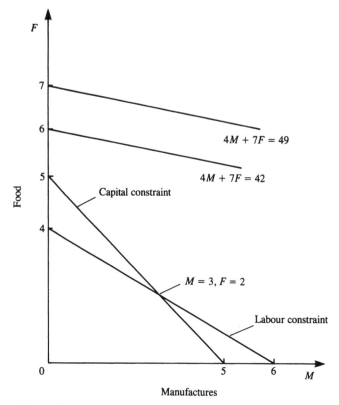

Figure 2

The technology dictates that we cannot produce anything unless we have some capital. It is just that too much is available, so it is not worth paying anything to get some more. Indeed, it would be sensible to sell the one unit of surplus capital on the international market for whatever positive price it would fetch, providing that it were feasible to do so at a sufficiently low selling and transport cost.

Finally, note that the shadow price is only meaningful in relation to the particular objective. For instance, if the relative valuations of the two products changed from the present ratio of 4:7 then the slope of the iso-revenue line would change. It might become sufficiently steep for the optimum point to shift to $M = 3$ and $F = 2$, or even to $M = 5$ and $F = 0$. In either case the capital constraint binds and the shadow price is definitely positive. So shadow prices depend upon the nature of the technical constraints, the quantities of resources available *and* the particular objectives.

What is the shadow price of skilled labour? If the quantity of skilled labour that is available increases from 12 to 13 then the intercept of the labour constraint on the vertical axis of figure 2 will increase from $12/3 = 4$ to $13/3$. Therefore the output of food can increase by $1/3$. The value of this incremental output is $7/3 and so that is the shadow price of the skilled labour constraint.

In order to facilitate the reading of Drèze and Stern's survey in this volume it is worth expressing these results more formally. Suppose the problem is to

Maximize $f(x_1, x_2, \ldots, x_n)$

subject to a constraint

$g(x_1, x_2, \ldots, x_n) \leq b$

Imagine that this problem has been solved. If the value of b is increased then the solution values for each of the x_i will vary and so will the maximized value of the objective. Let $V(b)$ describe the relationship between the maximized value of the objective and b. Then the shadow price of the constraint is given by

$\partial V(b)/\partial b$

In words, the shadow price on the constraint is the rate of change of the maximized objective with respect to a unit relaxation of the constraint.

Many readers will be aware that a standard approach to solving problems of this kind is to introduce a new variable, λ, known as a Lagrangean multiplier, and to maximize the Lagrangean function

$L = f(x_1, x_2, \ldots, x_n) + \lambda\{b - g(x_1, x_2, \ldots, x_n)\}$

with respect to the x_i. This procedure will provide the optimal values for the x_i and also a value for $\lambda \geq 0$. It can be shown that this value for λ at the optimum is precisely the shadow price on the constraint.

An elementary result is now apparent which essentially justifies the existence of cost–benefit analysis as a subject. Suppose that, in some economy, an objective function has been specified. A 'project' is proposed which will consume some goods and services and produce others. An age-old question is whether the 'market test' is a good test of whether the project is worthwhile: is it the case that the project is worthwhile if and only if it is predicted that the money values of the revenues will exceed the money values of the costs? It is almost a tautology that the answer is 'yes', but if and only if the prices used in calculating values are the correct shadow prices. By definition the shadow prices measure the 'worth' of a unit of each of the commodities as measured by the objective function. This is demonstrated formally by Drèze and Stern. Therefore a correct measure of the value of a nation's net national product must use shadow prices, see Dasgupta and Maler in this volume. As a corollary, if market prices differ significantly from market prices then a simple commercial, financial appraisal of the project will not give a correct answer. Therefore, if one believes that market prices always reflect shadow prices there is no reason to carry out cost–benefit analysis: straight financial appraisal will suffice. Cost–benefit analysts earn their living through the proposition that this is not the case.

Market prices and shadow prices

As a practical matter it is necessary to start with market prices as our first estimate of shadow prices where they exist. Very often they will be immediately acceptable as shadow prices. But it is not just a matter of convenience to use market prices as a starting point. Under certain circumstances market prices have desirable properties. In fact relative market prices are often excellent approximations to relative shadow prices. This result is one of the oldest and most famous results in economics. It has come to be known as 'the fundamental theorem of welfare economics'. Roughly speaking this states that, under the right conditions, a competitive market equilibrium will be an efficient allocation of resources and, conversely, any particular allocation of resources can be achieved as the outcome of competitive equilibrium if the initial distribution of assets to consumers is appropriate.

The bones of the first part of the fundamental theorem can be seen from the familiar, partial equilibrium, demand and supply model. Consider figure 3 which represents the market for a particular commodity. By definition the demand curve represents the number of units consumers *would like* to purchase at each price. The supply curve is the number of units the producing industry *would like* to sell at each price. We are particularly interested in the point of intersection of the two curves. This is an equilibrium because at this price the wishes of the two sets of agents are consistent with one another. The elementary analysis of markets predicts that there will be a tendency for this price to become established in a freely competitive market.

There is another way to look at this analysis. The demand curve can be thought of as the price that consumers are willing to pay for each quantity of the product. It therefore represents their marginal valuation of the product as we have already noted in the context of our bridge example (figure 1). In a competitive industry the supply curve is derived as the 'horizontal sum' of individual firms' marginal cost curves. It therefore represents the marginal cost of producing one more unit. Therefore, the point of intersection is special in that the value to consumers of an extra unit coincides with the cost of producing it. On the face of it the market price is the shadow price, providing that the objective is to maximize the value to consumers net of costs of supply.

To illustrate how this argument may break down, consider the case of environmental pollution by producers. (The following argument applies equally to other negative externalities like congestion, and, with an obvious modification, to positive externalities such as education.) If a firm creates pollution then we have to recognize a distinction between the cost to firms of their production (the *private cost*) and the total cost to society (the *social cost*). Consider figure 3.[7]

The additional feature here is the new curve representing the marginal social cost of supply. At any level of output the vertical distance between this and the supply curve is the money value of the additional social pollution cost of the

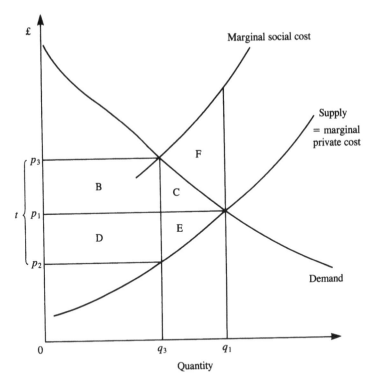

Figure 3

marginal unit produced. Therefore, the area $C + E + F$ is the total social cost of pollution attributable to increasing production from q_3 to q_1.

The free market will set demand equal to supply; i.e., marginal private cost equal to the marginal willingness to pay, p_1. But this price does not equal the shadow price of the commodity. Consider a proposal to impose a tax t equal to $p_3 - p_2$. Consumers pay p_3 but producers now receive p_2.

Let us appraise this from the point of view of the consumers. They face a unit price increase of $p_3 - p_1$. The area B represents extra cash paid for the same units. The area C represents the loss to consumers because of the deterred consumption. These areas correspond to the areas $(A + B)$ and C respectively of figure 1.

Now consider the point of view of producers. Since the supply curve is the marginal cost curve, the area below it is the total variable cost. Therefore the area $D + E$ is the loss of profit due to the tax.

The area $B + D$ is the product of t and the quantity traded, q_3, so it is the tax revenue. This represents benefits for others in the economy perhaps because it facilitates reduction in taxation elsewhere.

Taking all these items we find that there is a net loss from the tax of $(B + C) + (D + E) - (B + D) = (C + E)$. If there were no pollution then that would be the end of it. We would have demonstrated that the imposition of a tax creates a net economic loss represented by the two triangles. This is known as the *deadweight loss*. It comes about because of the 'wedge' which is driven between marginal producer costs and producer benefits. For all units between q_3 and q_1 the benefits exceed the (private) costs.

However, in this case the situation is complicated by the presence of pollution. By reducing output from q_1 to q_3 social benefits of C + E + F are created. These exceed the deadweight loss to give a net gain represented by area F.

Notice that at the solution the tax has the property that the price paid by consumers is just equal to the total marginal social cost of their consumption. This is the correct shadow price for this commodity. Notice also that a proposal to impose this tax is silent on the issue of the distribution of the costs and benefits.

Incidentally, we can immediately see the solution to the classical problem of what charge to make for crossing an uncongested bridge – one of the first problems to be subject to this kind of analysis (Dupuit, 1844). If there is no congestion and if there are no other significant externalities, then the optimum price is the marginal cost. If the marginal cost of an extra crossing is zero, as in the situation illustrated in figure 1, then the optimum price is zero, as previously noted.

The matter, however, is not usually as easy as it has been made to appear so far. There are two main problems that arise in valuing net benefits when they occur.

1   For market items, market prices may not represent the true social value of the items. They may be either distorted (e.g., by taxes or monopoly) or there may be a market disequilibrium (e.g., unemployment or balance of payments troubles).

2   We need to devise methods of valuation (e.g., for time, recreational amenities, life and so on) for non-market items including public goods and the external effects of market items.

Both problems are handled by the use of shadow prices. The fundamental importance of shadow prices is shown by Drèze and Stern in this volume. In all economies the price structure is so distorted that it is impossible to estimate with precision the price for each item which would lead to the 'second-best optimum' choice and scale of projects, given the constraints. All that is possible is a partial approach in which the adjustments made to market prices make it more likely that the right decision is made than would be the case using unadjusted prices.

Some examples of market failures

Monopoly

Suppose first that our bridge project uses cement produced by a monopolist and sold at well above its marginal cost. Should we use its market price or its marginal production cost? The answer, as to all questions in shadow pricing, is that it depends on how one expects the rest of the economy to adjust when the project is undertaken. If the national production of cement is expected to increase by the full amount used by the project, then clearly it should be charged at marginal cost. If, on the other hand, no extra cement will be produced, then the project should value its cement at its alternative use value, which is given by its (market) demand price. If we expect a mixture of the two responses we use a weighted average of price and marginal cost.[8]

Indirect taxes

Similar principles apply when an input is subject to indirect tax. We use the producer's supply price if we expect production to increase by the full amount of the project's demand, and the demand price if we expect no growth in output. For a mixture of the two responses the relevant weighting depends on the elasticities of supply and demand as explained in Harberger (1969). Thus if the project consumes $a + b$ units of the input, where b is the number of extra units produced as a result of the project, the relevant price becomes approximately $a/(a + b)$ times the demand price (p^D) plus $b/(a + b)$ times the supply price (p^S), see figure 4.

This whole argument assumes of course that there is no economic rationale for the indirect tax other than the need to raise revenue. Where there is a rationale, such as the correction of external diseconomies (e.g., via fuel tax), the discouragement of 'merit bads' (like smoking) or the redistribution of income, no adjustment may be called for.

Unemployment

Suppose that the bridge is built by workers who would otherwise be unemployed. If there are no macroeconomic costs of employing them (such as more inflation, or reductions in private investment) the cost is not their wage but the value of their lost leisure. This is less than their wage, if they were involuntarily unemployed. Employing people on the project may mean reducing employment and output elsewhere, and the cost of a worker is then measured by his wage. However, in most countries there is a degree of structural unemployment, and the inflationary effects of employing an extra worker depend on who he is and where he lives. So different costing procedures are needed, relevant to the particular circumstances. In countries worried by sub-optimal investment, the effects on

15

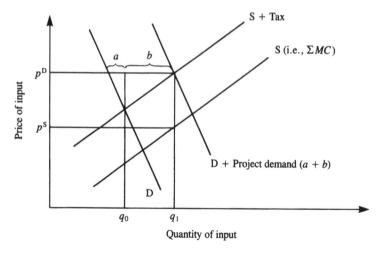

Figure 4

consumption of employing more people must also be allowed for (see Sen in this volume).

Pearce in this volume on investment in forestry illustrates how a shadow wage can be estimated and how the value chosen can affect the outcome of an evaluation.

Property rights

A market can only function if it is clear who owns what. Dasgupta and Mäler in this volume show how inadequate specification of property rights and lack of trust between potential traders can lead to important failures in environmental economics. For example, if a timber merchant purchases the right to deforest an upland then he will take no account of the fact that in doing so he may reduce the ability of the forest to restrain heavy rain, thereby increasing the risk of damaging floods to farmers in the lowlands. In principle the lowland farmers could get together and compensate the timber merchant for not damaging their interests. However, as the authors say, 'when the cause of the damages is hundreds of miles away and when the victims are thousands of impoverished farmers, the issue of a bargained outcome usually does not arise'. The result may be overharvesting of the forest which would be socially inefficient. They show how, because of this kind of market failure, different institutional arrangements for assigning property rights can lead to differing outcomes, some of which are less socially efficient than others.

Foreign exchange

Another thorny problem arises over the foreign exchange component of cost and benefits. This is often considerable, especially when indirect effects are allowed

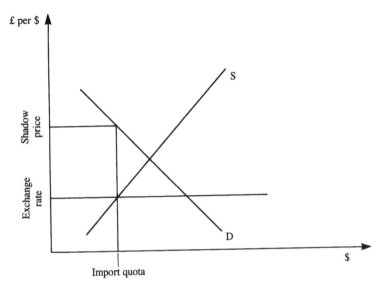

Figure 5

for. On our bridge, for example, the steel used may be imported; or, if produced at home, it may be made by imported equipment or it could be exported. Similarly, the extra journeys over the bridge may carry goods to the ports.

Now suppose that the country has an overvalued currency, causing a balance of payments problem which is handled by exchange controls. This means that the demand price for foreign exchange is greater than the official price which the recipients of import licences pay (see figure 5). How then should we price imports and exports? The standard approach is to use a shadow price of foreign exchange corresponding to the demand price rather than the official price. In this way imports and exports receive prices higher than their nominal prices, so as to measure their social value in terms of the prices of domestic (non-traded) goods. It is easy to see why imports have to be raised in value – their scarcity value is indicated by the demand price for foreign exchange. Export prices have to be raised *pari passu*, assuming that £1 worth of extra exports would be used to pay for £1 worth of extra imports.

However, Little and Mirrlees (1969) argue that it is far preferable to price exports and imports (and indeed all goods which in *optimal conditions* would be traded internationally) at their unadjusted prices, and to adjust downwards the value of 'non-traded' goods. (Strictly, imports are to be valued at their marginal import cost and exports at their marginal export revenue.) Their proposal really has two elements. The first is to take as numeraire the bundle of goods which a unit of domestic currency will buy on the world market rather than on the domestic market. This is a matter of convenience rather than of principle which Little and Mirrlees justify on the grounds that there are more traded than non-traded goods, which is probably the case for industrial projects with which their *Manual of Industrial Project Analysis* is concerned.

The second element of their proposal is that all goods which are 'tradable', that is that would be traded in optimal conditions, ought generally to be valued at world prices, even if they are not currently being traded freely because of non-optimal government policies. The purpose here is moralistic: to ensure that countries have the least possible excuse for overlooking the possible gains from trade. As is well known, a price-taking country producing two traded outputs maximizes its welfare by maximizing the value of its output valued at world prices and thus expanding its consumption possibly set to the maximum (OAB in figure 6). If the world price of guns is one ton of butter and a country has an import quota of guns raising their domestic price to 1.1 tons of butter, it should still not produce guns at any cost above one ton of butter unless it is determined to maintain the quota. Doing cost–benefit at world prices is intended to focus planners' minds on the cost of such distorted trading policies. Drèze and Stern demonstrate this point clearly.

Not surprisingly, the Little–Mirrlees proposals aroused a minor hornets' nest. Some critics consider them to have the wrong ideals. For example, Stewart and Streeten (1971) accuse them of an unduly piecemeal approach to development and of ignoring the linkages in the economy which necessitate a strategy of growth in which free trade may not be optimal. Sen, in this volume, though more in favour of the open economy approach to development, points out that, if this aim is not shared by other government agencies, that constraint should be allowed for in project appraisal. For example, if it would be rational to import a certain input but this is banned by the government, the input should in his view be valued not at its world price but rather at its domestic cost of production.[9] In the final chapter in part I of this volume Little and Mirrlees review the debate and discuss the impact that it has had on actual project appraisal.

Pricing of non-market items

With non-market goods and services, we do not even have a market price as a starting point. The marginal value which people place on a good (A), for which they do not directly pay money, has therefore to be inferred from the money they would have to pay for a good (B) which they show themselves to value equally. In this book we illustrate this approach to a few examples of the many items to which it can be applied.

Time

Suppose that our bridge will in fact save travellers time (say ten minutes) as well as money (the ferry charges). We have a good deal of evidence on how to value

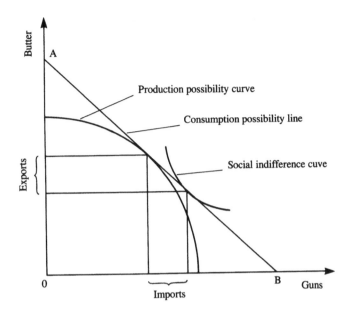

Figure 6

savings of time. Take leisure time first. A crude approach would be based on the theory of labour supply. This asserts that if a worker has freedom to vary his hours of work, the marginal value of one hour's leisure can be inferred from his gains from one hour's work, since at the margin he must be indifferent between the two. So one hour's leisure is worth the post-tax wage rate minus the marginal psychic disvalue of one hour's work.

One problem with this approach is that the disvalue of work has to be guessed. Equally problematical, an hour's travelling during one's leisure hours does not deprive one of an hour's leisure; it merely involves using leisure one way rather than another. We want to know the difference in value between an hour's leisure travelling and an hour's leisure in its alternative use.

We have therefore to find cases where individuals can choose to save travelling time at the cost of spending money. Such choices frequently arise in the choice between two methods of transport (say bus versus rail, on the journey to work). Suppose that everybody equally dislikes spending time travelling (T), in the sense that they agree on the money equivalent (say b) of a marginal minute spent at home rather than travelling. Then we can describe the costs (C) of the bus and underground journeys by the following expressions

$$C_B = a_B + bT_B + M_B$$

$$C_R = a_R + bT_R + M_R$$

where a_B and a_R are parameters reflecting the intrinsic pleasures of bus and rail respectively and T and M represent the time and money costs involved. The difference in these costs (ΔC) depends on where a person lives, and turns out to be a good predictor of the probability (P_B) of his travelling by bus rather than rail. One can for example fit a function such as the following

$$\log\left(\frac{P_B}{1 - P_b}\right) = B\Delta C = B(a_U - a_B + b\Delta T + \Delta M)$$

From it we can estimate b and hence the cost of commuting time in terms of its money equivalent.

In fact, if data can be obtained on the options facing *individuals* and the choices they actually make then it is more efficient in the statistical sense to develop models of individual behaviour. 'Behavioural (binary, disaggregate) choice modelling' has developed considerably over the 1970s and 1980s both in the theory and in the techniques available for collecting suitable data.

Of particular note has been the development of 'Stated Preference' techniques, where individuals respond to hypothetical questions, as distinct from 'Revealed Preference' techniques, where actual behaviour is observed. Stated preference methods have considerable cost advantages and allow the exploration of future options where no present-day analogue can be found.

Other advances have been in the fall in the cost of computing, the development of statistical models and the associated software. These have made easy things which would have been prohibitively expensive a few years ago.

These matters are explored in detail in this volume by MVA *et al*. It is shown how they have been applied in the context of value of time studies to derive estimate values for savings in leisure time in many different circumstances.

For time saved in the course of work the problem is simpler because the main cost is the loss of the worker's output, measured roughly by his wage. However, we should still take into account the worker's excess psychic (dis)satisfaction from travelling rather than working.

Recreational facilities

For recreational facilities too, attempts have been made to infer valuations from behaviour. Following the method developed by Clawson (1959), Mansfield (1971) estimated the value to the community of the English Lake District National Park countryside viewed as a recreational facility. For this we need to know the excess of the total value which people put upon their visits over the costs they incur in making them. Thus we need to know the demand curve for visits. Since people come to the Lake District from differing distances they incur differential costs in getting there. It seems reasonable to suppose that the number of visits from an area would be proportional to the population of the area, but that this proportion would depend on the costs (and also on car ownership per head of population in the area). Mansfield fits a demand curve using these variables for each area from which visitors come. For visitors from each area the surplus can be readily computed as the area under the implied demand curve. The total surplus is simply the sum of these surpluses.

There are many problems with the method, in particular its failure to include the price of substitute recreational facilities in the regression analysis. (The reader may like to work out for himself the direction of bias which would result in the estimated surplus, supposing, as seems likely, that the price of substitutes rises as the cost of reaching the Lake District rises.) In addition, as Mansfield points out, it is very difficult to use evidence on existing facilities to evaluate new and potentially competitive ones, such as a lake trapped by a barrage across nearby Morecambe Bay.

Cost-effectiveness analysis

There is a wide range of non-market items which can be valued in one way or another. For example, the cost of noise is discussed in Mishan (1970). Nevertheless, there remain other goods for which no meaningful valuation can be made especially pure public goods, which can jointly benefit many people and where it is difficult to exclude people from the benefits. Owing to the difficulty of exclusion, there is no way of getting people to reveal their valuations of such goods. Whenever cost–benefit analysis becomes impossible, since the benefits cannot be valued, it is still useful to compare the costs of providing the same beneficial outcome in different ways. This is called cost-effectiveness analysis and is regularly used in defence, public health and other fields.

Avoiding the problem of the value of saving life

Perhaps the most difficult item of all to value is human life. Yet it is quite clear that countless policy decisions affect the incidence of death. So each decision implies some valuation of human life.

Since valuation of life is a difficult and controversial subject it is worthwhile asking how far one can go in analysing safety without having to make this judgement. The answer is: quite a long way!

Consider the following simplified problem. A manager in a health service is given a fixed budget. There are several quite different ways in which that budget might be spent: renal dialysis units, heart surgery, hip replacements, preventative screening, health education, etc. Assume that accurate estimates are available of the number of lives that would be saved by each kind of expenditure, related to each level of expenditure. The following objective is set – 'allocate the budget so as to maximize the total number of lives saved'. (Wagstaff in this volume discusses some more sophisticated objectives that have been applied in practice.)

The reader may wish to reflect on the characterstics of the solution to this problem. At first sight it might seem attractive to spend a large proportion of the budget on areas of treatment of conditions which cause a large number of deaths.

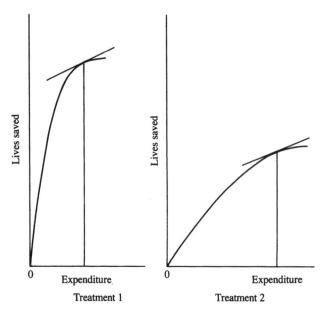

Figure 7

This is not necessarily correct. It may be that increasing expenditure on such a treatment would have little effect on the death rate. Or to put it another way, it may be that the expenditure per life saved is very high. There may be other ways of spending the money which will save more lives per £1 saved.

If the problem has been solved it must be the case that the number of extra lives saved per £1 of extra expenditure is the same for every kind of treatment. Otherwise it would be possible to spend less on one treatment, transfer the funds to another treatment and end up with a net increase in lives saved with the same total expenditure budget.

The solution is illustrated in figure 7 in a case where there are two treatments. The slopes of the curves must be equated to each other and to a value such that the implied expenditures exhaust the total available.

Several points emerge from this simple analysis. If we observe areas of public policy where these margins are not equated then it must be the case that there are more lives being lost than necessary, given the overall level of public expenditure. Yet it is a commonplace that safety regulations and other public expenditure decisions imply very widely varying valuations per life saved. Moody (1977) cites values ranging from £50 per life, implied by the decision not to spend on a particular medical screening programme to £20,000,000 per life saved by a change in building regulations following the collapse of a block of flats caused by a gas explosion.

Second, in many fields it is not even possible to investigate the subject simply because the technical relationships – like those drawn out in figure 7 – have not been established. For instance, design engineers in the transport industries will often say that they have worked in accordance with professional guidelines and standards which assure safety. Yet, it is not possible to evaluate the safety of the designs because no one is able to state the change in accident rate and the change in cost as the various characteristics of the designs are changed.

If our problem has been solved then we know how many lives would be saved if an extra £1 were spent. This is the shadow price on the budget constraint for this problem. It gives us a way of judging whether a proposed *new* way of spending money is going to be worthwhile – it must offer at least as many lives saved per £1 of expenditure as the established shadow price.

A great deal can be achieved by cost-effectiveness analysis. Note that all of this discussion has avoided the need to specify an *ex ante* value of life. But *ex post* a value is implied – the shadow price. It is this which should be considered when decisions are made about whether the overall budget should be increased. However, sooner or later we have to face up to the fact that we cannot work out the overall worth of projects which affect safety (and most of them do) without deciding what value to give to saving lives and avoiding injuries.

The value of saving life

Suppose that each worker on our bridge has a 1 per cent probability of being killed on the job, and there are twenty-five workers. One approach would be to cost the risk of loss of life at 25 per cent times the (average) human capital value per worker. But this immediately raises the question of 'value to whom?' Weisbrod (1961) distinguishes two measures, without committing himself to saying which is relevant to public decision. The first consists of the present (discounted) value of a person's future lifetime production, measured by his earnings. This measure implies that production is equally valuable, regardless of how many people there are to consume the fruits of it. Alternatively he assumes that all that matters is consumption per living person, in which case the value of someone's life is measured by the effects of his death on the welfare of those who would survive him. This equals the excess of his expected future production over his future consumption, again discounted to the present.

However, neither of these approaches is very satisfactory. The former would, in most countries, support population policies which maximized the birthrate, while the latter would support policies which minimized it. An alternative that has been proposed is the use of life insurance values, but these could only reflect, if anything, a view of what dependants would need in the event of the death of the insured. It does not tell us anything about the benefits of a change in the probability of death occurring – and that is what a project does change.

Mishan (1971b), after reviewing the methods that have been used, concluded that there are three cost consequences of a policy decision which affects the probability of a person's (Jack's) death: First, there is the way in which Jack himself values the extra risk. If he voluntarily assumes the risk, this value is already included in the price he requires for accepting it. This is why bridge builders get relatively high wages, and there is no need to make any additional allowance for the risk cost to them of their work. If, on the other hand, the labour was conscript we should have to find a way of valuing the risk. Likewise, we should allow for any risk imposed on people living beneath the bridge who might get killed. The second item is the value which others put on the financial consequences for them of Jack's increased risk of death. This may bear some relation to the measure of his future production less consumption. Where Jack has allowed for this in the terms on which he accepted the risk, it should not of course be double counted. Finally, there is the psychic value to others of the increased risk of Jack's death, for which again any double counting must be avoided.

The key feature of this approach is that it does not value death (or life) as such, but only change in the probability of death. All the valuations are thus *ex ante* and no attempt is made to value the suffering which will actually (*ex post*) be caused if a typical worker dies.

Is this right? Suppose, for example, that the suffering which a worker's partner will experience if he or she dies is equivalent to $-£x$. The expected *ex post* suffering in our example is then $-£0.25x$. What is the *ex ante* valuation of it? If the partner values risky outcomes in terms of expected utility and knows that the probability of the partner's death is 0.01 and that its utility would be $-£x$, then his or her *ex ante* valuation of the risk is $-£0.01x$ and the overall *ex ante* valuation (of all twenty-five partners) is $-£0.25x$. The *ex ante* valuation is thus the same as the *ex post* one quoted above. But individuals may instead be ill-informed about the probability of death or may not make a realistic estimate of the suffering they would experience in the event of their partner's death. In this case what does the planner put into his calculation: his own expected *ex post* evaluation or the *ex ante* one expressed by the individuals? The answer to this quite general question depends on the degree of paternalism the planner is willing to exercise. If he supports the prohibition of taxation of 'merit bads', like cigarette smoking, on the grounds that the government can foresee the suffering these will cause better than the individual can, then it seems quite logical to adopt the same approach in cost–benefit analysis. The present valuations of the parties affected are then disregarded in favour of their future valuations. How often one would be willing to do this is debatable, but it seems absurd to argue that one should always regard people's present preferences as decisive.

Reverting to the valuation of life, it remains clear that *ex ante* states of mind are relevant in the sense that, if a husband's life is blighted by the fear of his wife's death, this needs to be taken into account, quite independently of how he would value the actual event of her death. As far as the individual who may die is concerned this fear of death is in fact the only element that enters the calculation, since she will feel nothing once she is dead.

So where does this leave us? How could we calculate the various magnitudes? The answer is that it is very difficult, but, as Mishan points out, it is better to know what it is one should know, even if one cannot know it, than to know something that is irrelevant.

Rosen, in this volume, shows how to interpret labour market data as a reflection of differences in risk. Jones-Lee gives a comprehensive survey and critique of the various estimates that have been made. He reports some of his pioneering work in developing stated preference techniques in this area in the book from which the extract in this volume is taken. In an area where there is so much doubt and room for debate it is not surprising that there is a range of estimates to choose from. What *is* surprising is that the evidence, taken as a whole, strongly suggests an order of magnitude for the value of saving a life: a 'reasonable' value (at 1992 prices) might be £500,000 per life or £2 million per life, but it would not be consistent with the evidence to use a value of £20 million per life saved. In safety appraisal getting the correct orders of magnitude is often all one can aspire to. The literature can now offer a solid contribution to that.

3 THE SOCIAL TIME PREFERENCE RATE AND THE SOCIAL OPPORTUNITY COST OF CAPITAL[10]

Suppose we have satisfactorily computed the net benefits of a project in each future year. So we know $B_0 - C_0$, $B_1 - C_1$, ..., $B_n - C_n$, where B indicates benefits, C costs and n is the number of periods during which the project produces its effects. We still have the problem of aggregating these, to see if they are positive in total. If we have done the job properly, these net benefits represent the changes in consumption brought about by the project, for it is only consumption (rightly defined) that ultimately affects human welfare. So we need to know the value of next year's consumption relative to this year's, and so on for all future years. This relative value is expressed in terms of a time preference rate, or (the same thing) a discount rate. If this rate is 5 per cent per annum, this means that £1 of next year's consumption is worth only about £0.95 of this year's. More generally, if r is the rate, we value each £1 of next year's consumption the same as £1$/(1 + r)$ of this year's, r being from this point of view the rate at which we discount next year's benefits. Or, to put the matter the other way round, £1 of this year's consumption is worth £$(1 + r)$ of next year's, r being the rate by which present consumption is preferred to future consumption. As Feldstein (1964) points out, there is no *a priori* reason why the rate at which we discount 1994s pounds to make them equivalent in value of 1993s should equal the rate at which we discount 2004s pounds to make them equivalent to 2003s. But his assumption is almost invariably made. If we make it, the value of a project (valued in terms of today's consumption) becomes

$$PV = B_0 - C_0 + \frac{B_1 - C_1}{1 + r} + \frac{B_2 - C_2}{(1 + r)^2} + \ldots + \frac{B_n - C_n}{(1 + r)^n}$$

and the project should be undertaken if it has a positive value. The project could, of course, be valued in terms of pounds in year n (by multiplying the present value by $(1 + r)^n$) or in any other year, but this makes no difference to the decision, since if the value is positive in one year it is positive in all other years and vice versa.

The problem is: How do we choose the discount rate? This is an issue of considerable practical importance. In poor countries in particular, the choice between present and future consumption is truly agonizing. How far is it legitimate to depress present levels of living for the sake of the future? The horizon for a road scheme might well extend to forty years into the future. A benefit valued at £100 in forty years' time will have a present value of £14.2 at a discount rate of 5 per cent, £4.6 at 8 per cent and only £2.2 at 10 per cent! A high rate of discount will count against projects which take a long time to gestate. For instance, the case of forestry is discussed by Pearce in this volume. As Pearce notes, it is not legitimate to use an artificially low discount rate just because of this consideration.

To think about this question it is most useful to begin with a single-person economy (Robinson Crusoe) and to apply to his situation the tools of capital theory developed by Irving Fisher.[11]

Suppose that Crusoe's consumption consists only of fish and that he knows he will live for only two years. At present he spends all his time fishing with his existing equipment and catches 100 fish a year. He will do the same next year unless he takes time off to improve his equipment. If he does some investment of this type, he opens up the production possibility curve shown in figure 8. This schedule consists of a series of projects arrayed from right to left in order of their rate of return – the cost in year 0 is the sacrifice of consumption involved and the return is the gain of consumption in year 1. Only one of these projects is shown separately in the diagram – the most profitable project, costing two fish now and yielding six in the following year.

Crusoe chooses from the various production possibilities so as to reach his highest inter-temporal indifference curve. In other words he calculates the amount by which he can increase future consumption by sacrificing a further unit of present consumption and invests until this is equal to the minimum amount of extra future consumption required to induce him to sacrifice a further unit. The first of these amounts is the (absolute) slope of the production possibility curve. If B_1 is the benefit of the marginal investment project and C_0 is its cost then its value corresponds to B_1/C_0. This can be written as $[(B_1 - C_0)/C_0] + 1$, or $\rho + 1$, where ρ is the (marginal) rate of return on investment. The second is the slope of the indifference curve. Its value is MU_0/MU_1, which can be written $(MU_0 - MU_1)/MU_1 + 1$, or $r + 1$, where r is the (marginal) rate of time preference. So the

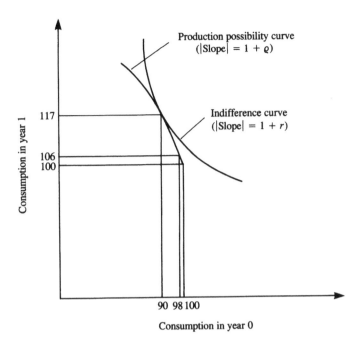

Figure 8

process of choice involves equating the rate of return on capital to the rate of time preference.

This choice simultaneously determines not only the discount rate but also the rate of saving of the economy (here 10 per cent, 10/100) and its rate of growth (here 17 per cent, 17/100).[12] Any reader who thinks it is right to maximize the rate of growth of an economy should think again. That is done by nearly starving. The real problem is to decide on the right rate of growth.

If the level of investment and its consumption is determined simultaneously with the discount rate, one might well ask what is the use of the discount rate in individual project appraisal? The answer, as mentioned earlier, is that in the real world there are many potential decision makers who, though they cannot see the overall scene, have, taken together, a much clearer view of the detailed poss-ibilities than could possibly be comprehended in a central planning agency. There is therefore a strong case for decentralized decision making, provided the central government sets prices (including the discount rate) and decision rules to the individual agencies which ensure consistency in their decisions.

There remains, however, the acute problem of finding a figure for the discount rate. Three main approaches have been suggested.

1 Use post-tax interest rates on long-term risk-free bonds.
2 Make assumptions about the desired growth rate and the inter-temporal indifference map.

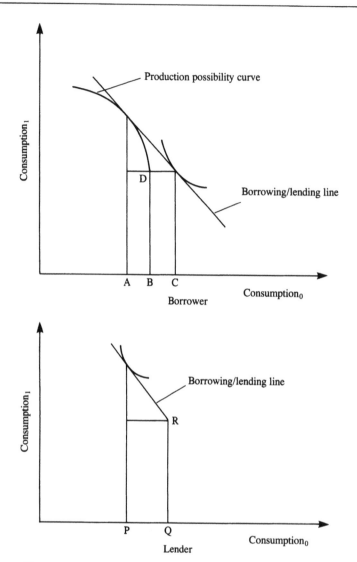

Figure 9

3   Make assumptions about the desired growth rate and the production
     possibility curve.

The market rate of interest

In a mixed economy the most obvious indicator of time preference is the market
rate of interest. To see how this is determined in a perfectly competitive Walras-
ian system of general equilibrium we modify the economy of Robinson Crusoe in
two ways only: we multiply the human species, and we allow for the possibility of

borrowing and lending. The interest rate then adjusts until it equals simultaneously the rate of time preference of all individuals in the society and the rate of return on productive investment (see Stigler, 1966, or Stiglitz in this volume). This is illustrated in figure 9. The representative borrower, with initial endowment indicated by point D, invests AB and borrows AC and thereby increases the consumption available in year 0 whilst leaving consumption in period 1 unchanged. The representative lender, initially endowed at point R, lends PQ. If there are as many borrowers as lenders, QP must equal AC – the function of the interest rate is to equate the two, and it varies until they are equal (compare Dasgupta in this volume).[13] At their equilibrium levels of consumption the borrowers' and lenders' rates of time preference are equated to the interest rate. So does this mean that the interest rate indicates the true rate of social time preference?

This is a subject of controversy, but before we embark on the controversy there is one point on which everyone is agreed. If there is inflation the money rate of interest will be adjusted to some extent to allow for the expected rate of change of prices. But we are interested in the subjective rate of substitution between real consumption in one period and another, and so we need to find a 'real' rate of interest which reflects this.[14]

If the money interest rate indicates that people are indifferent between £1 now and $£1 + i$ next year, it follows that, if I expect prices to rise by a proportion p during the year, I must be indifferent between £1 worth of goods now (at today's prices) and the goods which $£(1 + i)/(1 + p)$ would buy tomorrow if today's prices still prevailed. This last figure equals approximately $£1 + i - p$, so that the $i - p$ is the real rate of time preference and the real rate of interest. How price expectations are formed is something we only partially understand. If expectations equalled actual rates of price change, one would have to conclude that the real rate of interest in Britain in 1971 was negative! What can be said quite dogmatically is that money interest rates must be substantially reduced in inflation to obtain a measure of the real rate of interest.

This much is agreed, but there remain many problems with using even an adjusted interest rate as a measure of society's time preference.

Uncertainty and imperfect capital markets

The future is uncertain and this leads to a multiplicity of interest rates depending on the credit risks involved. Which rate should be used in cost–benefit analysis? It would of course be possible to vary the discount rate according to the riskiness of the net returns of the project, but it is preferable to express all net returns in terms of their certainty equivalent. We then need a standard discount rate relevant to certainly known levels of consumption. This is why the most commonly used estimate of private (and social) time preference is the rate on long-term government bonds (reduced to allow for expected inflation and income tax payments).

These bonds are generally considered free of risk. However, since the future price level is uncertain, there is in fact no truly risk-free rate of interest, nor are there any long-term bonds whose nominal yield is independent of unknown future interest rates, unless they are held to maturity (Arrow, 1969). Nevertheless it remains true that, for the ordinary lender, the adjusted long-term bond rate probably gives as good evidence as we are likely to get on his risk-free time preference.[15]

But whether this is what his time preference would be, given an optimal allocation of resources, is another matter. The fact of uncertainty means that, in the absence of a complete system of futures markets, market prices are of limited welfare significance. For the savings and investment decisions of each individual depend upon his forecast of future incomes and prices, yet these will themselves depend on the decisions made by others. This some believe to be a potent source of underinvestment.[16]

Moreover, the imperfections of the capital market mean that the time preferences of borrowers will almost always exceed those of lenders. In principle, the discount rate for each project should be a weighted average of the time preferences of all those affected by the project (Musgrave, 1969).[17]

The influence of money on interest rates

Interest rates have also been criticized on the grounds that they reflect monetary as well as real forces, and therefore should not be used for decisions of real resource allocation. There are, of course, some who maintain that money cannot alter real rates of interest except where there are unanticipated changes in the rate of change of money creation. But most economists would accept that money creation can change real interest rates, through its effect on prices and thus on the public's perception of its real wealth (Metzler, 1951; Mundell, 1963). Given these influences, do interest rates retain any normative significance?

This, as usual, is a question of which constraints are to be taken as given. There must, in principle, be an optimum quantity of money, which could be solved for simultaneously with all the other magnitudes in the economic system, including the implied rate of interest. However, in all probability we do not have the optimum quantity, and project planners, unless they are trying to secure changes in monetary policy, must accept whatever preferences the monetary authorities have helped to create.

Myopic (or 'pure time preference')

A third problem with interest rates is that they reflect each individual's *ex ante* anticipation of the relative value of his future consumption. But individuals may underestimate the pleasure which future consumption will in fact give them, if, as Pigou (1920) alleged, they are victims of 'defective telescopic faculty'. According to Pigou, an individual with the same commitments in both years must, in fact, be as well off if he consumes £100 in year 0 and £150 in year 1 or the reverse. That is to say, his indifference map in figure 8 ought to look the same whichever year's consumption is measured along the horizontal axis. So the indifference curves should be symmetrical about the 45° line from the origin, with the time preference rate being zero when consumption in the two periods is equal. But in fact Pigou surmises that people have 'pure time preference': they value present consumption more highly than future consumption even on the 45° line.

The problem with myopia lies partly in telling whether people have it, though there are certainly stagnant economies with higher interest rates than can be readily explained by risk and capital market imperfections. But even if people do have it and their *ex ante* evaluations fail to equal what the planner knows they will feel *ex post*, there is still the question of how far the planner should impose his own long sight upon the myopic multitude. Marglin (1963a) adopts the view that it is undemocratic for him to do so. But cost–benefit analysis is not in itself a 'democratic' process. It is a thought process which attempts to throw light on what is right, given our knowledge of the consequences of certain actions. If the planners really knew there was myopia they should surely use this knowledge. The main argument against overriding current preferences is that planners may be unlikely to know better than the individuals actually affected, and this argument is a strong one.

External effects in consumption

The problems discussed so far relate to the ability of interest rates to produce an optimum, assuming that all that matters is the welfare of individuals now living and that each individual's welfare is affected only by his own family's consumption stream. But, the reader may say, what about the welfare of future generations? After all, public investments may augment or reduce the consumption of people yet unborn. Surely this should be taken into account?

There are two approaches to this problem. In the first we continue to value only the welfare of those now living, but recognize that this is affected by the consumption available to future generations. Now if my welfare depended only on the consumption available to me and my own heirs, there would be no problems. But most of us do in fact derive pleasure from contemplating the welfare of others and their heirs, and this poses a classic case of externality. For in a free market these external effects are ignored and individuals maximize their own utility, taking the savings decisions of others are exogenous to their own decisions. But if they could bargain or take a collective decision *via* the political process a better outcome could be obtained.

The originial argument about this 'isolation paradox' was propounded by Sen (1961), developed by Marglin (1963a), criticized by Lind (1964) and reformulated in a more general form by Sen (1967). His argument is this.

Suppose each individual in society makes the following valuation of one unit of consumption according to who consumes it:

consumed by him now 1
consumed by his heir γ
consumed by others now β
consumed by others' heirs a

Suppose also that one unit of consumption foregone by the present generation leads to k units extra of consumption by the next.

(a) Consider the equilibrium of a competitive market in which each individual makes his own independent saving decision. Assume that, if an individual saves one unit, his heir will benefit by λk and others' heirs by $(1 - \lambda)k$, λ depending on the level of taxes, such as death duties. The individual will save till his future return from saving equals his present sacrifice, so that in equilibrium

$$\lambda k\gamma + (1 - \lambda)ka = 1$$

The marginal rate of return on capital $(k - 1)$ is thus given by

$$k = \frac{1}{\lambda\gamma + (1 - \lambda)a}$$

(b) Now suppose that whenever one individual saves one unit, every other individual does the same. This could be the case for example if all investment was financed by taxes and all individuals were equally rich. And suppose the decision on whether everyone shall save one more unit is taken by referendum. Then each individual will vote for more saving until the future return (in terms of his own utility) from such saving equals his present sacrifice. If there are N members of the community, each with one heir, each individual's heir can expect to get a $(1/N)$th share of the Nk units of extra future consumption; so in equilibrium

$$k\gamma + (N - 1)ka = 1 + (N - 1)\beta$$

In this case the marginal rate of return on capital $(k - 1)$ is given by

$$k = \frac{1 + (N - 1)\beta}{\gamma + (N - 1)a}$$

The vital question is whether this equilibrium rate is the same as under competition (i.e., as in (a)). Sen's argument is that it would be pure chance if it was and in fact he thinks it is lower. It certainly would be if both $\lambda < 1$, as it would if inheritance taxes spread the proceeds of saving, and $1/\beta > \gamma/a$, as it would be if people were more egoistic when comparing their own consumption with their own contemporaries' than when comparing their heir's consumption with their heirs' contemporaries'. And in this case a free market will produce underinvestment and an excessive interest rate. Whatever one thinks of the values of the various parameters, the approach at least draws attention to the issues raised by external effects in consumption. However, none of those who have argued on these lines has suggested how one would actually get a social discount rate which did allow for these external effects.

The welfare of future generations per se

Nor have we yet considered what allowance should be made for the welfare of future generations *per se*. Is it really right that projects should be judged exclusively in terms of their effects on the welfare of those now living? Most economists would say 'Yes' on the grounds that cost–benefit analysis should be democratic.[18] However, if one takes the alternative view that cost–benefit analysis aims to throw light on what is right, it is difficult to think of any ethical justification for ignoring future generations.[19] Suppose, for example, that one were to subscribe to the widely held ethical position that the best course of action is that which has consequences one would prefer if one had an equal probability of being each of the people affected by the action.[20] Then clearly future generations must be taken into account in so far as they are affected by the action. But how would one do this by means of a discount rate, when it is essentially a problem of income distribution? The answer is that conceptually the discount rate is an untidy way of proceeding. We should really work out the value of the project to each of the people affected (including the unborn), choosing as the unit for each person £1 of his consumption at some specified point in his life. We should then aggregate across persons using as weights for each individual the relative social value of his consumption at that point in his life. However, suppose that we regard 'me today' as a different person from 'me tomorrow'. Then all inter-temporal problems become distributional. If we can find a satisfactory general solution to the problem of distribution we shall also have solved the inter-temporal problem. This, in a sense, is the approach of 'optimal growth theory' to the discount rate problem.

Making assumptions about the social inter-temporal utility function

The theory of optimal growth, stemming from the seminal work of Ramsey (1928),[21] assumes that there is a cardinal utility-of-consumption function $U(C)$ common to all persons, and that total inter-temporal welfare consists of an aggregation of the utilities enjoyed by each person in each period. So, beginning again with Robinson Crusoe, his total inter-temporal welfare is[22]

$$W = U(C_0) + U(C_1)$$

The absolute slope of the indifference curve is

$$\frac{\partial W/\partial C_0}{\partial W/\partial C_1} \quad \text{or} \quad \frac{U'(C_0)}{U'(C_1)}$$

Now, suppose we assume that the marginal utility of consumption falls steadily, in such a way that for each 1 per cent increase in consumption the marginal utility falls by ϵ per cent. Then $U'(C) = C^{-\epsilon}$.

The slope of the indifference curve is now

$$\frac{U'(C_0)}{U'(C_1)} = \frac{C_0^{-\epsilon}}{C_1^{-\epsilon}} = [C_1/C_0]^{\epsilon} = (1+g)^{\epsilon} \simeq 1 + g\epsilon$$

where g is the proportional rate of growth of consumption.[23] So the discount rate equals $g\epsilon$, which is the rate of growth of consumption times the elasticity of the marginal utility of consumption with respect to consumption. If our economy were growing at 2 per cent a year and the elasticity of marginal utility with respect to consumption were, say, 1.5, the discount rate would be 3 per cent. The faster the rate of growth of the economy the higher the appropriate discount rate, since future income is that much higher than present income and therefore that much less valuable at the margin.

To many people this approach seems to provide the only valid rationale for discounting, rather than investing until the marginal rate of return is zero.[24] Geometrically, it provides an explanation for the convexity of the indifference curves in figure 8, if one remembers that the rate of growth of the economy is indicated by the slope of a ray through the origin to the point in question on the curve.

Dasgupta, in this volume, illustrates the ethical problems posed by the utilitarian approach. He shows that on certain assumptions any positive rate of impatience, no matter how small, will imply that it will be optimal to allow an economy with exhaustible resources to decay in the long run, even though it would be feasible to avoid the decay. Current generations will not accumulate sufficient capital in the early years to offset the declining resource use inevitable in later years, at the costs of later generations' welfare.

The practical importance of these arguments is illustrated by Pearce in this volume. In the context of renewable resources he records the view held by some that 'sustainability' is somehow an ideal to strive for in determining the rate of extraction. But as Dasgupta and Dasgupta and Mäler (both in this volume) note, there will, in principle, be an optimal rate of depletion and there is generally no reason to think that the historically determined stocks of renewable resources happen to be at an optimal level or that the level should be sustained at its present level: 'Whether or not policy should be directed at expanding environmental resource bases is something we should try and deduce from considerations of population change, intergenerational well-being, technological possibilities, environmental regeneration rates and the existing resource base.'

So much for Robinson Crusoe. If we turn to an economy of many persons we should presumably calculate social welfare as some aggregation of individual utilities. Supposing, however, that at each point in time income is equally distributed. Then social welfare in a particular period depends on the utility of consumption per head. But is this all or does it also depend on the number of people enjoying that consumption per head? This is a matter of controversy, which profoundly affects one's approach to the problem of optimal population. However, as far as the discount rate goes, it is enough to note that with a static population the discount rate is the same whichever we assume. With a population growing at rate n the time preference rate is $(g - n)\epsilon + n$, if welfare depends only on the utility of consumption per head; if it depends on that times the number of people, the rate is $(g - n)\epsilon$.[25] Which ever assumption we make, the discount rate is lower the faster the rate of population growth, provided ϵ exceeds unity.

How can we determine the magnitude of ϵ? It can be regarded in two separate lights. One can take the view that there is no place in positive economics for a utility function which says by what proportion a person prefers A to B. And if the same utility function is held to apply to more than one person, this is said to be even more unreasonable, involving as it does inter-personal comparisons of utility. From this point of view therefore the utility-of-consumption function becomes a purely normative device for representing one's ethical position – it is, if you like, a particular form of Bergsonian social welfare function (see Bator, 1957).

Alternatively, it can be argued that we have, from the fact of insurance, some positive evidence that individuals do compare the psychic loss from losing their insurance premium with the psychic loss from losing their houses (Friedman and Savage, 1948). The trouble is that, though the fact of insurance provides evidence of a diminishing marginal utility of income over some range, the fact of gambling suggests that for some people the marginal utility is increasing over some range. We can therefore get no estimate of ϵ from behaviour towards risk. An alternative approach is one in which the static utility function of the individual is assumed to be additive in two of the items of consumption, such as food and other goods, i.e., the marginal utility of food is independent of the quantity of other goods and vice versa. If this highly questionable assumption is made, the elasticity of the marginal utility of consumption can be calculated from the price and income elasticities of food and from its share in income. The kind of values which are found for ϵ in this way tend to fall between 1 and 2.5 (Fellner, 1967).[26]

Clearly, the use of any single value of ϵ is exceedingly arbitrary. Some people's marginal utility of income may indeed rise over some ranges making ϵ negative; and inter-personal comparisons, though they conform to some of our deepest intuitions about the human situation, are bound to be based on the most intuitive of judgements. Most of those who use the utility-of-consumption function would regard it as having some basis in positive reality, but as being so incapable of empirical investigation that the value assumed for ϵ is essentially normative: the larger ϵ the more egalitarian the approach.

And what of the rate of growth of consumption (g)? The problem here is that this is one of the variables which in principle we want to optimize at the same time as the discount rate (see figure 8). It is of course true that once we have chosen the growth rate we have settled the rate of time preference. But then, assuming our initial decision was correct, we have also settled the marginal rate of return on capital, making it equal to the rate of time preference.

Making assumptions about the production possibility curve

This has led Marglin (1963a) to put forward as an alternative approach the following strategy of decision. First decide on the growth rate you want and then see what investment that would require (see figure 8). If this is unacceptable, consider different combinations of investment and growth till you have found the one you prefer. This will imply a marginal rate of return on capital, which, since the choice is optimal, must by definition equal the rate of time preference. Use this rate as the discount rate. Critics have argued that this approach is impractical (Prest and Turvey, 1965) but it is less likely to produce inconsistent decisions than the above approach, where the rate of growth (g) and the discount rate ($g\epsilon$) are separately decided, independently of the production possibilities which must in fact link them.

So we are left with two main alternatives. The first allows adjusted market interest rates to determine the government's discount rate and hence the rate of investment and the rate of growth of the economy. The other starts by deciding on the rate of growth and infers from it the appropriate discount rate for use in decentralized decision making. The latter is widely regarded as in-feasible, and most cost–benefit analysts have followed some procedure where interest rates are taken as starting points for a measure of the social rate of time preference.

The social opportunity cost of capital

However, all the discussion so far has been based on the assumption that the government can bring the economy somehow to the optimal rate of saving and investment, either by inducing the private sector to act or by acting itself. But this may be impossible for various reasons, in which case the cry will be heard, as it is in so many countries: too little growth. We now have a problem in that capital investment, and hence investment displaced by the current project, is socially more valuable than consumption of equivalent monetary value. So if the resources used on the current project would otherwise have been producing investment goods valued at £x in the market, the cost of these resources is greater than £x, since £1 of investment is worth more than £1 of consumption and we choose to measure values in units of consumption.

Let us take a concrete example. Suppose certain products (say shirts) are only produced in the private sector and the government is not permitted to invest funds in the private sector. Suppose too that long-term lending rates (after income tax) accurately reflect private time preference. Nevertheless, owing to Income Tax and Corporation Tax, investors will require from investments in shirts a pre-tax rate of return (ρ) that far exceeds their rate of time preference. The government now considers building our bridge, financing it by borrowing on the capital market, and this borrowing will displace an equal amount of investment in the shirt industry. At what discount rate should the bridge project be evaluated?

The answer is simple. The stream of benefits (consumption generated) and cost (consumption displaced) should (by definition) be discounted at the rate which represents the social value of consumption in different periods, i.e., at the rate of social time preference (r). But what is the consumption stream foregone when £1-worth of resources are diverted from investment in the shirt industry to bridge building? The investment would have had a rate of return of ρ, so the stream of consumption from an investment of £1 can be approximated by the 'permanent' income stream, ρ, ρ, ρ and so on for ever. The present value of this stream when discounted at the time preference rate (r) is ρ/r.[27] So each £1 of cash spent on the bridge should now be costed at £ρ/r (Marglin, 1963b). But the social discount rate remains r, and the present value of the project, where C is the initial money cost and B the additional consumption generated per year for ever, is

$$V = -C\frac{\rho}{r} + \frac{B}{r}$$

The project should be undertaken if this is greater than zero.

The reader will see that this requires that

$$-C + \frac{B}{\rho} > 0$$

In other words, if the costs are counted in money terms (unadjusted), we get the correct decision if we then compute the present value, using ρ as the discount rate. It can, however, be confusing to do so and is sometimes incorrect; and the reader is recommended to hold on to the notion of discounting by the time preference rate. We shall revert to this point later.

The case we have just quoted, where any government investment displaces an investment of equal monetary cost in the private sector, occurs when there is an absolute savings constraint (i.e., total overall capital rationing). This is sometimes regarded as the standard position in underdeveloped countries, and in such a case the social time preference rate assumed will make little difference to the selection of projects.

However, the most general case is where the government is subject to some constraints – it cannot ensure that all projects which ought to be undertaken are, but equally it does have power to alter the overall rate of investment in the economy. Suppose, for example, that it finances the bridge by taxes, and each

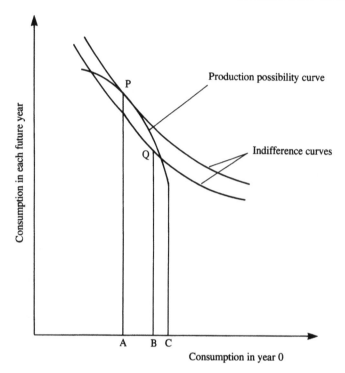

Figure 10

£1 spent reduces private saving and investment by £θ and consumption by £$(1 - \theta)$. Then the cost per pound of bridge building is $\theta p / r + (1 - \theta)$ pounds.

The crucial issue, as usual, concerns which constraints are considered binding. For clarity let us briefly repeat the argument, using the basic Fisher diagram in figure 10.

1   If the government can ensure that all projects which ought to be done are done (i.e., B is invested) the time preference rate is the (absolute) slope of the indifference curve at P and the opportunity cost of capital is £1 per pound spent.

2   If there is an absolute savings constraint CB, the time preference rate is the slope of the indifference curve at Q; the opportunity cost of capital is the slope of the production possibility curve at Q divided by the time preference rate.

3   If the private sector will undertake no projects less profitable than the marginal project at Q but the public sector can undertake projects falling within AC, then the time preference rate is the slope of the indifference curve at the final point chosen in consumption space (call it *r*) and the opportunity cost of capital is $\theta p / r + (1 - \theta)$, where p is the final marginal rate of return on private investment and θ is the rate of displacement.[28]

An even more constrained position is where the volume of private investment and of public investment are regarded as being separately constrained. In this case, the relevant opportunity cost of capital for public-sector projects is p'/r where p' is the marginal rate of return in the public sector.

If the disequilibrium at Q is caused by Corporation Tax, Income Tax, or the like, an alternative to public-sector operation of projects AC (where these produce private goods) would be a cut in the tax or the equivalent use of investment grants or allowances. This broad approach is preferred by Musgrave (1969). Monetary policy could also be used to reduce interest rates. But the final cost–benefit decision must be consistent with whatever other arrangements are finally decided on, and the calculation of opportunity cost should proceed as indicated.

The approach outlined above has been frequently criticized. Pioneered by Krutilla and Eckstein (1958), and formalized by Marglin (1963b), it was sharply attacked by Baumol (1968) in a celebrated article which begins by arguing in favour of using the social opportunity cost rate (p) as the social discount rate. However, as Arrow (1969, p. 58) points out, he seems here to be dealing with the case of an absolute savings constraint, where, as we have shown, it may in practice be all right to discount by p. When, later, he allows for a variable savings rate, he agrees that we have a second-best problem and, given this, the Marglin approach seems correct (Diamond, 1968; James, 1969; Usher, 1969). Mishan (1967) has also argued in favour of using the social opportunity cost rate, provided the government has the power to invest in the private sector. This again seems consistent with the approach outlined above.

There remain three problems. First there is the question of the 'synthetic discount rate'. We saw before that where the cost of capital is p/r the correct decisions could sometimes be obtained by valuing all costs and benefits at their nominal value and discounting by p. Similarly, if the cost of capital were $\theta/r + (1 - \theta)$ we could use a synthetic discount rate $\theta p + (1 - \theta)r$. This is the approach used by some economists (Diamond, 1968; Usher, 1969) and practised by many governments. However, there are many cases where the approach breaks down, and Feldstein (1974) makes out a cogent case against it.

The second problem is of course the assessment of the actual borrowing. Harberger (1969) outlines a fruitful approach to the problem in the case of borrowing, even though it is couched in terms of the search for a synthetic discount rate. Feldstein (1974) argues that it is by no means self-evident that the cost of £1 financed by taxes is less than that of £1 financed by borrowing, once one has allowed for the possible reinvestment of tax-financed interest on the part of those from whom the government borrows.

The third problem is that of reinvestment of the benefits of a project. If savings are sub-optimal, reinvested benefits of nominal value £1 are worth more than benefits which are consumed. In underdeveloped countries one of the arguments put forward for public-sector rather than private-sector production has been that the rate of reinvestment out of profits may be higher. Marglin (1963b) shows how the rate of reinvestment can be allowed for by adjusting the cost of capital, but the same result could equally well be achieved by adjusting the benefit stream. Marglin has been criticized by Arrow (1966) for treating the rate of reinvestment as exogenous, rather than as something optimized over time simultaneously with current investment. One should also, in a full treatment, allow for the possibility that p and r would change over time and optimally tend to converge (Little and Mirrlees, 1969).

We can now apply the notions we have been developing to our original simple problem of the bridge. Suppose the risk-free rate on government bonds is 10 per cent per annum, the rate of inflation in recent years 4 per cent per annum and the marginal tax rate 0.33. Then we might put the rate of time preference at 4 per cent $[(10 - 4)0.66]$. (This assumes a fairly perfect market for borrowing and lending.) But the pre-tax nominal rate of return on private investment is, say, 14 per cent, or 10 per cent in real terms. If the bridge is financed by taxation, each £1 spent may reduce private investment by approximately the marginal propensity to save (or rather more) – by say £0.2. Thus the opportunity cost of the bridge is £30,000 times $(0.2 \times 0.10/0.04 + 0.8) = £39,000$. The present value of the perpetual stream of future benefits, assuming none is reinvested, now becomes £2,750/0.04 = £68,750. So the project should be done.

The cost of capital under structural unemployment

Before leaving the question of opportunity cost we must look briefly at a special case which is important in economies suffering from structural unemployment. When we consider the cost of doing something we are normally interested in the value of the activities we shall have to give up, if the general level of economic activity is to be held constant. This corresponds to the procedure, advocated by Musgrave (1959), of making the 'allocation branch' assume that the 'stabilization branch' is doing its job properly. In this case, if resources costing £1 are used in this project, there must be a corresponding reduction of £1's worth in the output of other investment or consumption goods (valued at market prices).[29]

But, especially in underdeveloped countries, there may often be resources which are unemployed, even though there are no reasons from a stabilization policy point of view why they need be. In such cases of non-demand–deficient unemployment, the spending of £1 which displaces £θ of private investment may displace less than £$(1 - \theta)$ of consumption. It may even increase consumption by, say, £φ. In this case we subtract from the cost because it is a positive gain to have this consumption being undertaken. The cost per pound is now £$\theta p/r - \varphi$, which may or may not exceed £1.

The most obvious relevance of this is to the shadow wage of previously underemployed rural labourers now employed in urban industry. Suppose their marginal product in agriculture was zero. If no output of investment or consumer goods elsewhere in the economy were displaced by employing them, the cost of employing them would be zero. But the very act of employing them will probably raise their consumption, because they now receive a positive wage. This extra consumption could, of course, be provided by cutting down the consumption of other workers by the same amount (by stiffer taxes, for example); and if this were done the cost of employing them remains zero – there is no change elsewhere in the output of investment or consumption goods. But more likely there will be some increase in the output of consumption at the expense of investment. Suppose in fact that the gain in consumption equalled the full wage (W) and that the project itself produced none of these extra consumption goods. Then each £1 spent in wages would reduce investment by the same amount and the shadow wage would be $W(\rho/r - 1)$ (Marglin, 1967, pp. 56–7). This is clearly a special case and a general presentation of the problem can be found in Sen (1972).

But the basic point is that, when unemployed resources exist in the presence of sub-optimal saving, we have the dual problem that, while the resources can be employed with little loss of output elsewhere, the act of employing them is likely to raise the demand for consumption. Thus, a project may displace other investment, not only through its method of finance, but through the payments which it makes to the hitherto unemployed factors it employs.

It will be apparent from this discussion that the choice of a discount rate is always going to be a tricky matter. Spackman (1991) gives a practitioner's account of how the problem has been approached by the UK Treasury.

By way of summary we cannot do better than quote from the final paragraph of Stiglitz's survey in this volume:

The value of the social rate of discount depends on a number of factors, and indeed I have argued it might vary from project to project depending, for instance, on the distributional consequences of the project.[30] . . . The decision on the appropriate rate of discount thus inevitably will entail judgements concerning what are the relevant constraints. I have suggested . . . that the distortionary consequences of taxation and the implications of imperfect risk markets are significant. Both lead to social rates of discount that normally exceed the consumer rate of interest. Indeed, under not unreasonable circumstances, they may exceed the producer rate of interest.

Present value versus internal rate of return rules

So far we have assumed that the most convenient way to maximize the present value of consumption is to choose all projects having positive present values or, where there are two or more mutually exclusive projects, to choose the one with the highest present value. However, there is an alternative approach which has often been advocated and even more often used: the rate of return approach. The

Table 2

Stream		IRR	PV at $r = 0.05$
A	− 100, 110	0.10	5
B	− 10, 12	0.20	1.5
C	− 100, 6, 6, (for ever)	0.06	20

rate of return is that rate (p) which sets the present value of the project at 0. Thus we solve for p in

$$0 = B_0 - C_0 + \frac{B_1 - C_1}{1 + p} + \ldots + \frac{B_n - C_n}{(1 + p)^n}$$

The rule then is: undertake the project if p exceeds the discount rate r.

In very many cases the two approaches give the same answer, and often the rate of return is an interesting and suggestive statistic. However, there are three main arguments against using the rate of return rule for specific decisions. First, it is not the intrinsically correct rule: it is merely a procedure which often gives the same answer.[31] In cases where the discount rate changes from period to period (e.g., falls over time) there is no one value of r with which p can be compared, while the present value rule remains well defined. Ignoring this, a second problem arises in the case of mutually exclusive projects, where the internal rate of return may provide the wrong ranking. For example, the table above compares two projects of different size, A and B, in which this is the case. It also compares two projects of different length, A and C, where again the rate of return gives the wrong ranking.

As Feldstein and Flemming (1964) point out, this problem can, in principle, be overcome by calculating not the separate internal rates of return for each project but the rate of return on the difference between each project being considered (say A) and each of its alternatives. For example, taking A and B above, this is the rate of return on − 90, 98 which at nearly 9 per cent is well above the discount rate of 5 per cent. However, the more projects there are the more pairs of projects have to be considered.

Moreover, there remains a third objection. The rate of return calculations may not give a unique answer and in fact may give as many solutions which could have economic meaning as there are sign changes in the stream of net returns (this is an application of Descartes' 'rule of signs'). For example, if we take the stream − 1, 5, − 6 and plot its present value this becomes zero at both 100 per cent and 200 per cent (see figure 11). At any discount rate on either side its present value is, not surprisingly, negative. Each calculated rate of return tells us that at that discount rate the present value is moving from negative to positive or vice versa, and nothing more. However, if a project can be terminated at will at

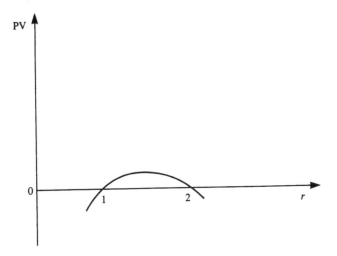

Figure 11

any point in time, it will have a unique internal rate of return, assuming that for each possible discount rate we choose the optimal life of the project (Arrow and Levhari, 1969). But it is not clear how often projects can be usefully regarded as terminable in this way. In real life there may of course be few projects for which the net returns stream changes sign more than once, except in industries where there may be heavy terminal costs (such as filling in mines, decommissioning nuclear power stations and so on). But the differences in net returns between projects may change signs frequently, and thus for mutually exclusive projects the internal rate of return rule may frequently break down.

Finally, there is the problem of capital rationing, where the correct approach is to select projects in order of their present value per unit of constrained cost until the cost constraint is exhausted.[32] Selection in order of rate of return provides a less general approach.

The first year rate of return

A project may pass the test of showing a positive net present value; but might it be a better project if it were delayed by one year? By delaying we would defer the capital expenditures but lose a year's benefit.

Suppose that the initial cost in the coming year is C_0 and the net benefits in following years are $N_1, N_2, \ldots, N_T$, where T is the horizon. Then the PV of the scheme would be

$$- C_0 + N_1/(1 + r) + N_2/(1 + r)^2 + \ldots + N_T/(1 + r)^T$$

However, if we delay by one year then the PV of the scheme would be

$$-C_0/(1+r) + N_2/(1+r)^2 + \ldots + N_{T+1}/(1+r)^{T+1}$$

If we can ignore the present value of the benefits in the final year, N_{T+1} then the gain from delay is

$$-C_0/(1+r) + C_0 - N_1/(1+r)$$

This will be positive if

$$N_1/C_0 < r$$

The quantity on the left of this expression is known as the first year rate of return. We conclude that if the first year rate of return is less than the rate of discount then the benefits of one year's delay exceeds the costs and the project should be delayed, and in doing so we will increase the overall worth of the project. Of course, delay may have other advantages in that more information may become available in the meantime or some adverse and unforeseen factor may emerge.

In practice it is rare for this test to be applied. The question posed is usually 'whether' rather than 'when?'.

4 THE TREATMENT OF RISK

We have so far studiously avoided the problem of risk. But suppose that we really do not know how much the bridge will cost. It could cost £25,000, but equally well £35,000. How do we proceed? If the project were being undertaken by a private firm, which bore all costs and reaped all benefits, and whose discount rate for certainly known income streams was 5 per cent, it would be likely to cost the bridge at its 'expected' (average) cost of £30,000 and then use a higher discount rate than 5 per cent. The reason is simply that the owners of the firm are averse to risk and to anyone who is risk averse a certain prospect of receiving £b is worth more than a 50–50 chance of £$0.5b$ and £$1.5b$.

Much of human behaviour towards risk can be explained by the hypothesis that people maximize their expected utility, using a cardinal utility-of-income function of the kind we have already discussed. Thus if a person is a risk averter, whose marginal utility of income falls as income rises, we can see from figure 12 that the utility of £b exceeds the expected utility of a 50 per cent chance of £$0.5b$ plus a 50 per cent chance of £$1.5b$. The latter is

$$E(U) = 0.5U(0.5b) + 0.5U(1.5b)$$

that is, a weighted sum of the possible utilities resulting, the weights being the probabilities attaching to each.[33] The cost of risk is the difference between the mean or 'expected value' of the prospect (here $0.5 \times 0.5b + 0.5 \times 1.5b = b$) and

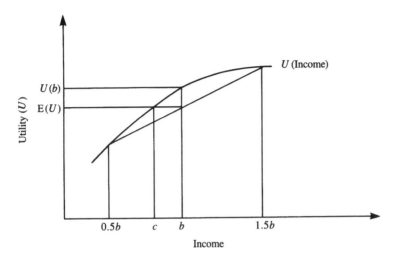

Figure 12

the value which the individual actually places on the uncertain prospect (i.e., the certain prospect which he rates as of equal value, here *c*).[34]

Now, if there were perfect (and costless) markets for insurance, the firm would not need to bear the cost of risk and could happily discount this project at 5 per cent. But, largely because of the problem of 'moral hazard' such markets generally exist in only a limited form. The securities market makes possible a good deal of pooling of risk among ultimate wealth owners (Pauly, 1970), but even so private firms generally use discount rates much higher than the rate applying to certainly known costs and returns, the excess depending largely on the degree of risk of the project.[35]

Should the public sector follow suit? It has been argued that, unless it does, it will be led to undertake projects identical in their net returns to those which the private sector would have rejected, and this is sub-optimal. However, Arrow and Lind in this volume argue otherwise.

They start with our standard assumption that net returns should be valued as they would be valued by the people to whom they accrue. Thus a risky project undertaken by one person ought to be valued at less than its expected value. If insurance is impossible it is absolutely right for a one-man firm with a certainty discount rate of 5 per cent not to undertake a project with only a 5 per cent rate of return and he ought not to be subsidized to encourage him to do so – the subsidy cannot reduce the social cost of risk.

However, the public sector (or indeed General Motors) is a very large firm with very many shareholders. Our difference between £35,000 and £25,000 when averaged over, say, ten million taxpayers amounts to no more than £1/1,000. The question is: Is a spread of possible project costs of this order sufficient to make us value the cost of the project to each taxpayer at something higher than its expected value of £3/1,000 (assuming each taxpayer pays the same)? Arrow and Lind prove that as the number of taxpayers tends to infinity the cost of the risk tends to zero. The verbal part of their article should be comprehensible to any reader, but the proof of this proposition is presented in formal mathematics and it may be helpful here to provide an intuitive illustration of it. Suppose that ignoring the cost of the bridge my income is y. If the bridge is built and paid for out of taxes, my income will fall to an expected value of $y - 0.003$. However, there is in fact a 50–50 chance that it will be either $y - 0.0025$ or $y - 0.0035$. Do I value this uncertain prospect significantly less than a certain prospect of $y - 0.003$? The answer is that it depends on whether my marginal utility of income falls significantly as y rises from $y - 0.0035$ to $y - 0.0025$. It seems unlikely that the fall is significant. Moreover, if my share in the cost were halved, my cost of risk would be more than halved. So the more taxpayers a given risky project is spread over, the smaller is the total cost of risk. In practice it seems reasonable, for most investment projects, to assume that the costs and benefits accruing to taxpayers have no risk cost and should therefore be discounted at the risk-free rate of time preference.[36]

However, not all the benefits or costs of public projects do accrue to taxpayers as a whole. In the case of our bridge, the cost accrues to the taxpayers but the benefits accrue to the travellers. Whether or not the benefits are sufficiently large and uncertain for any one traveller for them to be valued at less than their expected value is an empirical question.

For some projects it is unquestionably the case that the projects impose substantial risk cost. Suppose that the bridge was designed to be safe in all normal weathers but would collapse under the influence of a tidal wave of a kind that has happened once in the last 100 years. If one assumed that the probablility of disaster in each future year was 1 per cent and one knew the consequences of disaster, one could in principle make an evaluation along the lines we have been discussing if some utility-of-income function were assumed.

However, sometimes the probabilities attaching to the outcomes of a project may not even be guessable. This provides a case of what Knight called uncertainty and here the only approach is to fall back on game theory. The various possible strategies are discussed in Dorfman (1962). No one of them can be said to be correct, but they do at any rate provide a way of marshalling one's thoughts.

5 THE TREATMENT OF INCOME DISTRIBUTION

Finally, we revert to the problem of the distribution of income. Suppose that travellers over our bridge are on average twice as rich as taxpayers but half as rich as ferry owners. Clearly the project will redistribute income. Should this be taken into account in deciding whether to build the bridge? And if so, how?

As we saw earlier, there is no need to allow for distribution if lump-sum transfers will be made so as to compensate the losers. For in that case, if the present value of the project to the gainers exceeds its cost to the losers, the gainers will still be better off than before, even after they have compensated the losers.

But in practice redistribution cannot be effected by lump-sum transfers. It normally requires taxation which imposes an 'excess burden' upon those taxed, representing a loss of efficiency in the economy. Moreover, there may be political objections to cash redistribution, and it is often administratively difficult to devise a tax which falls specifically on the beneficiaries of a project and a transfer which goes specifically to the losers. If redistribution to offset the losses due to the project is not implemented, then the project cannot be justified on the grounds that it is a Pareto-improvement, since at least some people are worse off.

Then a wider criterion has to be introduced to decide whether or not the project increases social welfare – a criterion in which the changes of income to each of the parties affected are weighted by the marginal social values attaching to the income of each group. The criterion is thus that the project should be undertaken if $\Sigma a_i \Delta Y_i$, is positive, where ΔY_i, is the present value of the project to the ith person and a_i is the marginal social value of the ith person's wealth.

However, we need to distinguish between two separate cases. The first is the regular situation where there is a possibly profitable project available, which yet has distributional implications. Musgrave (1969) argues that the excess burden of most taxes is small and therefore one should in general judge projects on efficiency grounds and leave taxation to perform the redistributional objective. But it is hard to see how in our illustrative project or in many others specific taxes and transfers could be devised which actually compensated the losers; and to say that the government undertakes many projects and everyone will therefore come out better off in the end is to put excessive trust in princes. So, for many specific projects that have been devised for other reasons, there seems no alternative to looking at their distributional implications.

It is quite another matter, however, to devise projects specifically as a means of redistributing income. There is always a strong argument for redistribution in cash rather than kind, when redistribution in kind may lead individuals to consume more of any good than they would if given the equivalent command over resources in the form of cash. However, even here there may be cases where redistribution in kind may be essential if it is to avoid humiliating its recipients or to benefit children rather than adults; any such projects to redistribute in kind need to be evaluated using some system of weights (a_i).

The obvious system of weights come from a utility-of-income function of the kind we have used in discussing discount rates and risk. If social welfare (W) is the sum of individual utilities, and the ith individual's utility depends on his income Y_i, then $W = \Sigma U(Y_i)$ and $\partial W/\partial Y_i = U'(Y_i)$.[37] So the appropriate weight (a_i) is $U'(Y_i)$ and the project should be undertaken if $\Sigma U'(Y_i)\Delta Y_i$ is positive. The simplest assumption as before would be that $U'(Y_i) = Y_i^{-\epsilon}$. If some value of ϵ is assumed we can now proceed to recompute the present value of our bridge project. For example, if (for convenience of computation) $\epsilon = 1$, then, on our hypothesis about the relative incomes of the groups, the present values to taxpayers, travellers and ferry owners are weighted in the ratios 4:2:1 and the total present value of the project (in units of ferry owners' present value) is now proportional to $4(-39,000) + 2(75,000) + 1(6,250) = 250$.[38] It is just worth doing.

The problem as usual is in determining ϵ. Eckstein (1961) argued that the government's estimate of ϵ should be implicit in the structure of marginal income tax rates. However, as Freeman (1967) has pointed out, this is not the case if the government seeks to maximize the sum of individual utilities. To do this a government with a given national income to distribute would need to equalize the marginal utility of income of all individuals, i.e., it would aim at complete income equality, by setting taxes equal to $y - \bar{y}$, where y is individual income and $\bar{y}$ is average income.[39]

Weisbrod (1968) has therefore suggested that the government's weights for different income groups should be inferred from its previous decisions on whether or not to adopt the various projects open to it. This involves the solution of a set of simultaneous equations. There is an obvious logical objection to this approach: either the government's decisions so far have been consistent; in which case why worry about helping it continue to be consistent, or they have been inconsistent, in which case why pretend they were consistent. There is much force in this criticism, especially when it is linked to the difficulties of estimation that arise. However, Weisbrod's article is important in stressing that from now on government decisions should embody some consistent set of distributional weights.

A third, and more limited, approach has been suggested by Marglin (1967). In this, total consumption is maximized subject to some minimum consumption being secured to a given underprivileged group or region. Alternatively, the consumption of the underprivileged may be maximized subject to some minimum total consumption. Any constrained maximization of this kind implies in its solution a relative weight attaching to consumption of the underprivileged as against consumption in general. This is measured by the shadow price on the constraint. But this value is determined *ex post*.

It is a less general approach to the income distribution problem, but, if no other is available, it is one way of allowing for an important dimension of public policy.[40] The only alternative is that pursued by the Roskill Commission on the Third London Airport (1970), which is to show the costs and benefits of different groups in society separately and let the policy makers decide their own weights.[41]

The question of the criteria for a welfare improvement is discussed in more detail by Layard and Walters in this volume. This shows how welfare changes for individuals can be estimated, but that the question of whether a social gain has occurred cannot be separated from the issue of the social valuation of benefits to the rich compared with benefits to the poor.

NOTE TO P. 35

If welfare depends on consumption per head, we can write

$$W = \frac{1}{1-\epsilon}\left[\frac{C_0}{N_0}\right]^{1-\epsilon} + \frac{1}{1-\epsilon}\left[\frac{C_1}{N_1}\right]^{1-\epsilon},$$

$$\frac{\partial W/\partial C_0}{\partial W/\partial C_1} = \frac{(C_0/N_0)^{-\epsilon}(1/N_0)}{(C_1/N_1)^{-\epsilon}(1/N_1)}$$

$$\simeq (1+g-n)^\epsilon(1+n)$$

$$\simeq \{1+(g-n)\}\epsilon(1+n)$$

Even if consumption per head is going to be roughly constant, additional consumption will be less useful in period 1 than in period 0 because it is spread over more people. (In this respect Eckstein's approach (1957, p. 75) seems inappropriate. The expression given above is taken from Sen (1968, p. 16, footnote 16) where, however, C should refer to total rather than per capita consumption.)

If welfare depends on population times the utility of consumption per head, we can write

$$W = \frac{N_0}{1-\epsilon}\left[\frac{C_0}{N_0}\right]^{1-\epsilon} + \frac{N_1}{1-\epsilon}\left[\frac{C_1}{N_1}\right]^{1-\epsilon},$$

$$\frac{\partial W/\partial C_0}{\partial W/\partial C_1} = \frac{(C_0/N_0)^{-\epsilon}}{(C_1/N_1)^{-\epsilon}}$$

$$\simeq (1+g-n)^\epsilon$$

$$\simeq 1+(g-n)\epsilon$$

If consumption per head is going to be roughly constant, the effect on welfare per head of a unit gain in consumption per head is equal in the two periods. Additional consumption sufficient to produce a unit gain in consumption per head in period 0 will produce a $1-n$ gain in consumption per head in period 1 and therefore a gain in utility per head $1-n$ as large as the gain in period 0. But this gain is spread over a population $1+n$ as large. So if consumption per head is constant the discount rate is zero.

As to which assumption is reasonable see Meade (1955, ch. 6). The discussion in Feldstein (1964) is more general and assumes simply that

$$W = f\left(\frac{C}{N}, N\right)$$

NOTES

We are extremely grateful to P. Dasgupta, C.D. Foster, A.K. Sen and A.A. Walters for detailed comments and suggestions and to E. Basenden and N.J. Krafft for help in preparing the first edition of this book for publication. We are also indebted to D. Anderson, P. Dasgupta, R. Turvey, A. Wagstaff and the publisher's advisors for suggestions for this edition.

1 Good textbooks are Mishan (1971a), UNIDO (1972) and Pearce and Nash (1981). Comprehensive survey articles are Prest and Turvey (1965), Henderson (1965) reprinted in R. Turvey (1968) and Eckstein (1961) reprinted in R.W. Houghton (1970).

2 This proposition assumes no increasing returns to scale.

3 This statement is true if the marginal utility of income is constant. In this case the statistic also measures the 'compensating variation' in income – i.e., the amount by which these consumers would have to be taxed after the price fall to make them no better off than before – and the 'equivalent variation' – i.e., the amount which consumers would need to be given if the price fall did not occur to make them as well off as if it did. Opinions differ on which of these measures is the most relevant indicator of welfare gain. Mishan (1971a, pp. 48–9) favours the compensating variation, assuming, as he does, that the Hicks–Kaldor criterion is used in aggregating the gains of different consumers. See Layard and Walters in this volume for a discussion of these issues.

4 The reasons for discounting and the choice of discount rate are discussed by Stiglitz in this volume. Below we explain why the present value of a stream of £a per year for ever at a 10 per cent discount rate equals £$10a$.

5 On welfare criteria see Mishan (1971a) or Layard and Walters in this volume. For a passionate plea in favour of the Hicks–Kaldor criterion see Harberger (1971). Mishan (1971a) argues that if this criterion is used, as he believes it should be, this is because it corresponds to the 'virtual constitution' of the society.

6 See for example Beesley and Foster (1965), and Newbery and Morrison and Winston in this volume.

7 This figure and the analysis in the text is based closely on Alasdair Smith's (1982) excellent text, p. 129.

8 This, and what follows, assumes strictly that other goods are competitively produced and untaxed. It also ignores questions of income distribution. In general if other goods are taxed an average rate t marginal factor cost (MC) should be replaced by $MC(1 + t)$.

9 For reply to criticisms of their approach see Little and Mirrlees (1972) and their chapter in this volume. On other approaches to the problem see Dasgupta (1972) and Bacha and Taylor (1971).

10 For a full survey of this topic, with a special emphasis on the point that the rate to be used must depend upon which constraints have to be accepted as binding, see Stiglitz in this volume.

11 For an excellent exposition of Fisherian capital theory see Hirshleifer (1958) reprinted in B.V. Carsberg and H.C. Edey (1969).

12 A savings rate of 10 per cent would not normally produce a growth rate of 17 per cent; this results from the use of the two-period model.

13 This diagram is extremely partial and does not bring out the simultaneous need for aggregate saving to equal aggregate investment.

14 In principle, it makes no difference whether we use a money rate of interest and nominal consumption valued at forecast rates of inflation, or a real rate of interest and real consumption at constant prices. However, it is difficult to forecast inflation, so C–B analysis is normally done in constant prices.

15 Spackman (1991) contains a review of the long-term history of these rates in the UK experience.

16 For a good discussion of the optimality or otherwise of saving/investment decisions in a market economy see Phelps (1965, ch. 4), reproduced in A.K. Sen (1970b).

17 Strictly the only correct procedure is to evaluate, separately for each individual, the present value of his net benefit stream, discounted at his own time preference rate.

18 This view is held most strongly by those who would also use the Hicks–Kaldor welfare criterion in project evaluation. It is easy to see why the two approaches are natural bedfellows. The Hicks–Kaldor criterion aims, as far as possible, to separate decisions about production and investment from those about distribution, and acquires whatever plausibility it has from the thought that we could always alter the income distribution by cash transfers. However, distribution between non-overlapping generations in a closed economy can only be altered by decisions about investment. It is therefore convenient if future generations need not be considered.

19 A practical argument is sometimes put forward for ignoring them, in that we cannot know their preferences. However, there are many items (like life) where we do not know how they are valued by present generations, and many (like bread) where we can be fairly sure what future generations will feel.

20 On possible ethical approaches to the question of fairness, see Sen (1971).

21 This is reproduced in A.K. Sen (1970a). See also Dasgupta in this volume.

22 Compare Dasgupta in this volume, equation 4.

23 The reader will find this approach presented in Eckstein (1957, pp. 75ff.) and in Eckstein (1961), which is reproduced in R.W. Houghton (1970) where, however, the printing of ϵ on p. 232 is in some places misplaced. For a more elaborate application of optimal growth theory to the choice of discount rate, see Arrow (1966 and 1969); Arrow however discounts future utilities to allow for some element of pure time preference. See also Arrow and Kurtz (1970), Stiglitz in this volume and Dasgupta in this volume.

24 For a full discussion of the rationale of discounting, along these lines, see Feldstein (1964). Feldstein does not, however, assume a constant ϵ and therefore provides no actual formula. The reader should note that in optimal growth theory it is necessary for optimality, but not sufficient, that the marginal rate of return equal the proportional rate of decline of marginal utility.

25 For proof of these propositions see the note at the end of the Introduction.

26 Harberger (1969) argues that such values are too high to be consistent with the limited amount of insurance purchased by most individuals.

27 If the rate of interest is r per annum, this means that 1 now has the same value as r per year for ever. Therefore $1/r$ now is equivalent to 1 per year for ever and p/r is equivalent to p per year for ever.

28 In an open economy there are possibilities of lending and borrowing abroad which need to be added to the production possibility curve of figure 10, before we can claim to have society's true consumption possibility frontier. Thus, in principle, we might need to allow for the effect of a project in displacing foreign lending. Equally, if the country

is a net borrower, the cost of capital is the present value of the debt service at the margin.

29 As Baumol (1968, p. 792) points out, this need not imply that for a tax-financed project the extra taxes should equal the expenditure on the project. This depends on the propensities to consume of all the parties affected. If the MPC is uniform for all, more taxes need to be raised than expenditure incurred if employment is to be held constant.

30 On the distributional consequences see later in this introduction.

31 Hirschleifer (1958) shows why the present value rule is intrinsically correct for the private investor or for a society which can borrow or lend abroad. In the case of a closed economy the optimum occurs at a direct tangency between the indifference surface and the production possibility surface. Hirschleifer also sets out the main problems with the IRR approach. For a simplified exposition of some of these points see Baumol (1965, pp. 422–7 and 437–47).

32 At the level of the economy this is the problem of the savings constraint. Here the problem can be handled in the simplified case by costing capital at ρ/r (where ρ is the rate of return on the marginal project within the constraint) and then doing all projects with positive present values. The rule given above in the text is a general rule which should be used also by separate agencies subject to budget constraints.

33 More generally $E(U) = \Sigma p_i U(Y_i)$, where p_i is the probability of obtaining income Y_i. Thus in the example we should, strictly, be concerned with the utilities of $y + 0.5b$ and $y + 1.5b$, where y is normal income. For a full analysis see Friedman and Savage (1948).

34 See Layard and Walters (1978) for a full treatment which relates the cost of risk to the degree of risk and aversion and the variability of the prospect.

35 This is partly because, unlike the stockholder, a manager cannot insure against the personal risk associated with a project which he initiates.

36 This assumes that the returns to each separate project are independent of national income, that is, that stabilization policy is successful.

37 In fact it is much more satisfactory to assume that $W = W[U_1(Y_1), \ldots, U_n(Y_n)]$, in which case $\partial W/\partial Y_i = (\partial W/\partial U_i)U_i'(Y_i)$. This satisfies the notion of fairness, that additional happiness for a miserable man is more desirable than additional happiness for someone who is already happy. However, it renders the problem of quantification even more intractable, even if we assume that all individuals have the same utility-of-income function.

38 The present values to each party are those computed on p. 40.

39 (i) Put another way, the government equalizes the marginal sacrifice (of utility) per dollar of tax. By contrast, the Eckstein approach implies that governments equalize the marginal sacrifice per dollar of income due to tax; if so, a man with a marginal tax rate of 0.25 could then be assumed to have a marginal utility of income double that of a man with a marginal tax rate of 0.50. However, there is no reason to think that governments do or should pursue this principle – nor the principles of equiproportional sacrifice or equal absolute sacrifice used by Mera (1969) – to derive implicit utility-of-income functions.

(ii) If the government maximizes the sum of individual utilities but tax rates affect production, it should equalize the marginal rates of transformation between pairs of individual incomes to the ratios of marginal utilities of income (Freeman, 1967).

40 For a strong plea to exclude income distribution from formal economic welfare analysis see Harberger (1971).
41 Roskill Commission on the Third London Airport (1970, ch. 29). Separate calculations are not shown in the final report. The Roskill Commission treated foreigners on the same footing as British nationals, whereas some cost–benefit analyses assign them a distributional weight of zero (often without even discussing the issue).

REFERENCES

Arrow, K.J. (1966), 'Discounting and public investment criteria', in A.V. Kneese and S.C. Smith (eds.), *Water Research*, Johns Hopkins Press, pp. 13–32.
    (1969), 'The social discount rate', in G.G. Somers and W.D. Wood (eds.), *Cost–Benefit Analysis of Manpower Policies*, Proceedings of a North American Conference, Industrial Relations Centre, Queen's University, Kingston, Ontario, pp. 56–75.
Arrow, K.J. and M. Kurtz (1970), *Public Investment, the Rate of Return, and Optimal Fiscal Policy*, John Hopkins.
Arrow, K.J. and D. Levhari (1969), 'Uniqueness of the internal rate of return with variable life of investment', *Economic Journal*, 79: 560–6.
Arrow, K.J. and R.C. Lind (1970), 'Uncertainty and the evaluation of public investment decisions', *American Economic Review*, 60: 364–78.
Bacha, E. and L. Taylor (1971), 'Foreign exchange shadow prices: a critical review of current theories', *Quarterly Journal of Economics*, 85(2): 197–224.
Bator, F.M. (1957), 'The simple analytics of welfare maximisation', *American Economic Review*, 47 (March): 22–59.
Baumol, W.J. (1965), *Economic Theory and Operations Analysis*, 2nd edn, Prentice-Hall.
    (1968), 'On the social rate of discount', *American Economic Review*, 58: 788–802.
Beesley, M.E. and C.D. Foster (1965), 'The Victoria line: social benefit and finances', *The Journal of the Royal Statistical Society*, series A (General), 128: 67–88.
Blaug, M. (ed.) (1968), *Economics of Education*, Penguin.
Buchanan, C. (1971), 'Note of dissent', Roskill Commission on the Third London Airport, Report, HMSO, pp. 149–60.
Carsberg, B.V. and H.C. Edey (eds.) (1969), *Modern Financial Management*, Penguin.
Chase, S.B. (ed.) (1968), *Problems in Public Expenditure Analysis*, Brookings Institution.
Clawson, M. (1959), *Methods of Measuring the Demand for and Value of Outdoor Recreation*, Resources for the Future, Inc., Washington, DC.
Dasgupta, P. (1972), 'A comparative analysis of the UNIDO Guidelines and the OECD Manual', *Bulletin of the Oxford University Institute of Economics and Statistics*, 34: 33–52.
Diamond, P. (1968), 'The opportunity cost of public investment: comment', *Quarterly Journal of Economics*, 82: 682–8.
Dorfman, R. (1962), 'Basic economic and technologic concepts: a general statement', in A. Maass *et al.*, *Design of Water Resource Systems*, Macmillan.
Dupuit, J. (1844), 'On the measurement of the utility of public works', *Annales des Ponts et Chaussées*, 2nd series, vol. 8.
Eckstein, O. (1957), 'Investment criteria for economic development and the theory of intertemporal welfare economics', *Quarterly Journal of Economics*, 71: 56–85.

(1961), 'A survey of the theory of public expenditure criteria', in R.W. Houghton (ed.), *Public Finance*, Penguin.

Feldstein, M.S. (1964), 'The social time preference discount rate in cost benefit analysis', *Economic Journal*, 74: 360–79.

(1974), *Financing in the Evaluation of Public Expenditures*, in W.C. Smith and J.M. Culbertson (eds.) essays in honour of Richard A. Musgrave, North Holland.

Feldstein, M.S. and J.S. Flemming (1964), 'The problem of time stream evaluation: present value versus internal rate of return rules', *Bulletin of Oxford University Institute of Economics and Statistics*, 26: 79–85.

Fellner, W.J. (1967), 'Operational utility: the theoretical background and a measurement', in W.J. Fellner *et al.*, *Ten Economic Studies in the Tradition of Irving Fisher*, Wiley.

Freeman, A.M. (1967), 'Income distribution and planning for public investment', *American Economic Review*, 57: 495–508.

Friedman, M. and L.J. Savage (1948), 'The utility analysis of choices involving risk', *Journal of Political Economy*, 56: 279–304, reprinted in Richard D. Irwin, G.J. Stigler and K.E. Boulding (eds.), *Readings in Price Theory*, American Economic Association.

Hall, P. (1971), 'The Roskill argument: an analysis', *New Society*, January, pp. 145–8.

Harberger, A.C. (1969), 'Professor Arrow on the social discount rate', in G.G. Somers and W.D. Wood (eds.), *Cost–Benefit Analysis of Manpower Policies*, Queen's University, Kingston, Ontario, pp. 76–88.

(1971), 'Three basic postulates for applied welfare economics: an interpretative essay', *Journal of Economic Literature*, 9: 785–97.

Harrison, A.J. and D.A. Quarmby (1969), 'The value of time in transport planning: a review', in *Theoretical and Practical Research on an Estimation of Time Saving*, European Conference of Ministers of Transport, Economic Research Centre.

Henderson, P.D. (1965), 'Notes on public investment criteria in the United Kingdom', in R. Turvey (ed.), *Public Enterprise*, Penguin.

Hirshleifer, J. (1958), 'On the theory of the optimal investment decision', *Journal of Political Economy*, 66.

Houghton, R.W. (ed.) (1970), *Public Finance*, Penguin.

James, E. (1969), 'On the social rate of discount: comment', *American Economic Review*, 59: 912–16.

Krutilla, J.V. and O. Eckstein (1958), *Multiple Purpose River Development*, Studies in Applied Economic Analysis, Johns Hopkins.

Layard, P.R.G. and A.A. Walters (1978), *Microeconomic Theory*, McGraw-Hill.

Lind, R.C. (1964), 'The social rate of discount and the optimal rate of investment: further comment', *Quarterly Journal of Economics*, 78: 336–45.

Little, I.M.D. and J.A. Mirrlees (1969), *Manual of Project Analysis in Developing Countries*, vol. I, Social Cost Benefit Analysis, Development Centre of the Organization for Economic Cooperation and Development.

(1972), 'A reply to some criticisms of the OECD manual', *Bulletin of the Oxford University Institute of Economics and Statistics*, 34: 153–68.

Maass, A. (ed.) (1962), *Design of Water Resource Systems*, Macmillan.

McKean, R.N. (1958), *Efficiency in Government Through Systems Analysis*, Wiley.

(1968), 'The use of shadow prices', in S.B. Chase (ed.), *Problems in Public Expenditure Analysis*, Brookings Institution, pp. 33–65.

Malinvaud, E. (1969), 'Risk-taking and resource allocation', in J. Margolis and H. Guitton (eds.), *Public Economies*, Macmillan.

Mansfield, N.W. (1971), 'The estimation of benefits from recreation sites and the provision of a new recreation facility', *Regional Studies*, 5(2): 55–69.

Marglin, S.A. (1963a), 'The social rate of discount and the optimal rate of investment', *Quarterly Journal of Economics*, 77: 95–111.

(1963b), 'The opportunity costs of public investment', *Quarterly Journal of Economics*, 77: 274–89.

(1967), *Public Investment Criteria*, Allen & Unwin.

Meade, J.E. (1955), *Trade and Welfare*, Oxford University Press.

Mera, K. (1969), 'Experimental determination of relative marginal utilities', *Quarterly Journal of Economics*, 83: 464–77.

Metzler, L.A. (1951), 'Wealth, savings, and the rate of interest', *Journal of Political Economy*, 59: 93–116.

Mishan, E.J. (1967), 'Criteria for public investment: some simplifying suggestions', *Journal of Political Economy*, 75: 139–46.

(1970), 'What is wrong with Roskill?', *Journal of Transport Economics and Policy*, 4(4): 221–34.

(1971a), *Cost–Benefit Analysis*, Unwin University Books.

(1971b), 'Evaluation of life and limb: a theoretical approach', *Journal of Political Economy*, 79: 687–705.

Moody, G.H. (1977), *The Valuation of Human Life*, Macmillan.

Munby, D. (ed.) (1968), *Transport*, Penguin.

Mundell, R. (1963), 'Inflation and real interest', *Journal of Political Economy*, 71: 280–3.

Musgrave, R.A. (1959), *The Theory of Public Finance*, McGraw-Hill.

(1969), 'Cost–benefit analysis and the theory of public finance', *Journal of Economic Literature*, 7: 797–806.

Pauly, M.V. (1970), 'Risk and the social rate of discount', *American Economic Review*, 60: 195–8.

Pearce, D.W. and C.A. Nash (1981), *The Social Appraisal of Projects*, Macmillan.

Peters, G.H. (1968), *Cost Benefit Analysis and Public Expenditure*, Eaton paper 8, 2nd edn, The Institute of Economic Affairs.

Phelps, E.S. (1965), *Fiscal Neutrality Toward Economic Growth*, McGraw-Hill.

Pigou, A.C. (1920), *The Economics of Welfare*, 4th edn, Macmillan.

Prest, A.R. and R. Turvey (1965), 'Cost–benefit analysis: a survey', *Economic Journal*, 75: 683–735.

Ramsey, F.P. (1928), 'A mathematical theory of saving', *Economic Journal*, 38: 543–59.

Rosenberg, N. (ed.) (1971), *The Economics of Technological Change*, Penguin.

(Roskill) Commission on the Third London Airport (1970), *Papers and Proceedings*, vol. 7, HMSO.

(1971), *Report*, HMSO.

Self, P. (1970), 'Nonsense on stilts: the futility of Roskill', *New Society*, July, pp. 8–11.

Sen, A.K. (1961), 'On optimizing the rate of saving', *Economic Journal*, 71: 479–96.

(1967), 'Isolation, assurance and the social rate of discount', *Quarterly Journal of Economics*, 81: 112–24.

(1968), *Choice of Techniques*, 3rd edn, Basil Blackwell.

(1970a), *Growth Economics*, Penguin.

(1970b), 'Interrelations between project, sectoral and aggregate planning', United Nations' *Economic Bulletin for Asia and the Far East*, 21: 66–75.

(1971), *Collective Choice and Social Welfare*, Oliver Boyd.

(1972), 'Control areas and accounting prices: an approach to economic evaluation', *Economic Journal*, 82(325 S): 486–501.

Smith, Alasdair (1982), *A Mathematical Introduction to Economics*, Blackwell.

Spackman, M. (1991), 'Discount rates and rates of return in the public sector; economic issues', Government Economic Service Working Paper No. 113, HM Treasury, London.

Stewart, F. and P. Streeten (1971), 'Little–Mirrlees methods and project appraisal', *Bulletin of the Oxford University Institute of Economics and Statistics*, 34: 75–92.

Stigler, G.J. (1966), *The Theory of Price*, 3rd edn, Macmillan.

Turvey, R. (ed.) (1968), *Public Enterprise*, Penguin.

UNIDO (United Nations Industrial Development Organisation) (1972), *Guidelines for Project Evaluation*, United Nations. Authors: P. Dasgupta, S.A. Marglin and A.K. Sen.

Usher, D. (1969), 'On the social rate of discount: comment', *American Economic Review*, 59: 925–9.

Walsh, H.G. and A. Williams (1969), *Current Issues in Cost–Benefit Analysis*, CAS occasional paper no. 11, HMSO.

Weisbrod, B.A. (1961), 'The valuation of human capital', *Journal of Political Economy*, 69: 425–36.

(1968), 'Income redistribution effects and benefit cost analysis', in S.B. Chase (ed.), *Problems in Public Expenditure Analysis*, Brookings Institution, pp. 177–209.

Williams, A. (1972), 'Cost–benefit analysis, bastard science? and/or insidious poison in the body politick', *Journal of Public Economics*, 1(2) July.

PART I

THEORETICAL ISSUES

1

SHADOW PRICES AND MARKETS:

Policy reform, shadow prices and market prices

Jean Drèze and Nicholas Stern

1 INTRODUCTION

1.1 The objectives of the paper

Economists are often asked to give policy advice in situations where, it is claimed, prices give distorted or misleading signals. And many of them are fond of suggesting that governments should leave more to the market so that private agents can respond effectively to price incentives. While these positions are not necessarily contradictory, their juxtaposition should lead us to ask some questions. What do we mean by misleading signals? Can we define satisfactorily an index of scarcity or value which is not misleading? How do we identify the social opportunity cost or shadow price of a commodity? How do these shadow prices compare with market prices and under what circumstances will they coincide? Should governments leave decisions to the market when prices give impaired signals? How can the government improve price, tax, or regulatory incentives? How can concern with income distribution be integrated systematically with measures to improve efficiency? Generally, how can shadow prices and market prices be combined in the understanding and implementation of the reform of government policies?

The purpose of this paper is to suggest a framework for the analysis of these issues and to provide the practitioner with a structured and productive way of thinking about the problems of how market distortions should influence proposals for reform. In so doing we attempt to provide help in identifying the empirical questions that should be raised and the judgements that need to be made before deciding on a particular line of policy.

We shall begin the analysis (in section 2) by defining shadow prices. We shall argue that there is only one sensible way to approach the definition of shadow prices if those shadow prices are to be used to evaluate the net impact on welfare of public-sector projects. The shadow prices are the social opportunity costs of the resources used (and correspondingly for outputs generated). Having defined

This chapter previously appeared in the *Journal of Public Economics*, 42 (1990). We would like to thank Elsevier Science Publisher B.V. (North-Holland) for their kind permission to reproduce it here.

shadow prices in this rather general way, we then set out a formal exposition of their properties in a model of an economy where markets need not be perfectly competitive. Such models are generally more difficult to analyse than those with well-functioning competitive markets, but we shall try to make the discussion accessible and avoid unnecessary technicalities. The literature on shadow prices has been somewhat bewildering in its different definitions, methods and models, and we shall attempt to provide a unified analysis within which many of the apparently disparate results and propositions can be understood. The theory and discussion are microeconomic in form but a macroeconomy is, of course, implied. We make the link explicit in section 3 where we focus on government revenue and the macroeconomy.

Shadow prices are defined for public-sector projects but they are readily extended to the private sector. This extension is provided in section 4 where we also bring out relationships between shadow and market prices and show how the ideas of the paper can be applied to problems concerning efficiency of supply including privatization and price reform. In this last application we provide some new results concerning basic questions of market reform which appear to have received insufficient analytic attention. Given current concerns for the reform of socialist economies the particular question of when one should raise the price of a good in excess demand (or lower price for excess supply) is of special interest. A summary and concluding comments are provided in section 5.

The paper is mainly expositional. We attempt to present a way of thinking coherently about policy reform in second-best economies, without pretending to supply general formulae that can blindly be applied to specific problems. The formulation and many of the results draw on our earlier, more detailed and technical survey (Drèze and Stern, 1987). The interested reader is referred to that survey for a more comprehensive and rigorous discussion.

1.2 The motivation for using shadow prices

In the remainder of this section we shall review briefly the lessons of the standard theory of prices and policy for competitive economies and then identify some complications that may invalidate the use of prices as indicators of social opportunity costs or values. This will help to explain our choice of model for section 2 and indicate which types of complication are considered and which are not.

It is convenient to approach the discussion of the social value of commodities in distorted economies by defining an undistorted system where shadow prices would coincide with market prices. A 'distorted economy' is *defined* here as one where market prices and shadow prices do not coincide. This reflects our concern with distortions in (price) *signals*, rather than with deviations in economic organization from some allegedly 'undistorted' or 'perfect' system (such as that of competitive markets). Two further remarks are necessary. First, a competitive economy may well be 'distorted' in this sense, e.g., if the distribution of income fails to be optimum (see below). Second, there is no general presumption that price distortions, as defined here, should be systematically removed, in the sense that market prices and shadow prices should be brought as close as possible to each other (see sub-section 4.4). Whether they should be removed or not depends, in fact, on the kind of policy tools that are available for this purpose.

It is a well-known result of classical welfare economics that, under standard conditions (particularly the presence of all markets and the absence of externalities), a perfectly competitive equilibrium is Pareto efficient. In order for market prices to reflect the social value of commodities, the distribution of income should also be optimum according to the ethical judgements underlying the shadow price system. This additional requirement is often swept under the carpet, but this attitude is really hard to defend. Indeed, it is arguable that an essential role of government is to ensure that the standard of living of poorer groups receives some protection. Many would go further than this; indeed, redistribution is a commonly articulated concern of (and demand on) governments. Incorporating this objective typically requires sustained attention to the distributional consequences of government policies. To achieve an optimum distribution of income without interfering with the price system one needs to be able to redistribute resources and raise government revenue by lump-sum taxes and transfers (i.e., taxes and transfers which cannot be altered through the behaviour of agents). Since appropriate fiscal instruments of this kind are typically not available, shadow prices are liable to deviate substantially from market prices even in perfectly competitive economies.

Further distortions arise when the economy does not have the necessary features for Pareto efficiency described above. Possible sources of interference with the marginal equalities which are necessary for efficient allocation include: (i) indirect or income taxes; (ii) uncorrected externalities; (iii) quantity controls; (iv) controlled prices; (v) tariffs and trade controls; (vi) oligopoly; and (vii) imperfect information, transaction costs and missing markets. The first five of these sources of imperfection are either included in whole or in part in the models that follow or can be easily added. The last two are more problematic.

2 THE BASIC THEORY

We want to derive a set of shadow prices reflecting the social value of commodities, in order to guide policy reform and the choice of public-sector projects. To this end, the shadow price of a commodity is defined as its social opportunity cost, i.e., the net loss (gain) associated with having one unit less (more) of it. The losses and gains involved have to be assessed in terms of a well-defined criterion or objective, which is referred to as 'social welfare'. The evaluation of social welfare is naturally based (at least partly) on assessments of the well-being of individual households, supplemented by interpersonal comparisons of well-being. The latter are embodied in what we shall call 'welfare weights'. This is not the place to debate which weights should be used – they should be discussed responsibly and intelligently but are ultimately value judgements depending, *inter alia*, on one's views of inequality and poverty.

It is difficult, however, to dispense with the reliance on the notion of social welfare. Most practical examples of policy reform or public projects make some people better off and some worse off and we have to take a decision which trades off these gains and losses. Implicitly or explicitly we shall be using weights. In our judgement, attempts to produce cost–benefit tests for policy appraisal that avoid inter-personal comparisons have not got very far. For example, hypothetical transfers of the Hicks–Kaldor variety that could yield Pareto improvements are not relevant when such transfers will not take place; and if such transfers do take place systematically it is straightforward to incorporate them in the present framework. Also, assertions that 'a dollar is a dollar is a dollar' – that money values across households can be simply added up – do not avoid value judgements but invoke a specific one which says that all welfare weights (in terms of social marginal utilities of income) are equal. This is not an ethical position we would find attractive and, like other ethical statements, it would require explanation and discussion rather than a simple assertion. Furthermore, it risks serious logical inconsistencies (see, for example, Roberts, 1980).

In this paper we shall make extensive use of the Bergson–Samuelson social welfare function. This amounts, in effect, to assuming that (1) individual well-being depends only on the fixed characteristics of individuals and on their consumption of commodities (so that social welfare can be defined on the commodity space), and (2) the marginal rate of substitution between two commodities going to the same individual are the same in the social welfare function and in the individual 'utility function' (see Drèze and Stern, 1987) for further discussion and note that, to keep things simple, we are excluding externalities). We shall not be constrained to any particular form of the social welfare function (the choice of which would involve additional assumptions and arguments) but shall present results in relation to a general function of the Bergson–Samuelson variety. Much of the theory would go through with a more general social objective although a number of the results which link social welfare to market choices would have to be modified.

When the social opportunity cost or shadow price of a good is defined in terms of the marginal effect on social welfare of the availability of an extra unit, it leads directly to a 'cost–benefit test', i.e., projects which make positive profits at shadow prices should be accepted because they increase welfare. Indeed, it should be clear (and see below) that no other definition of a shadow price can have this property. Thus, in this paper there will be one single definition of shadow price – it is the increase in social welfare resulting from the availability of an extra unit of the specified commodity. Strictly speaking, one also has (generally) to state from which agent the extra unit comes. For specificity, and because the interest here is primarily in public-sector decisions, this agent will be understood to be the public sector. The shadow prices themselves will depend on the social welfare function and on how the economy, including the government, functions. But there is nevertheless essentially only one definition of the concept which allows their systematic link to cost–benefit tests.

In sub-section 2.1 we provide a formal definition of shadow prices and illustrate the basic ideas with simple examples. The model we shall use is set out and discussed in sub-section 2.2, and in sub-section 2.3 we describe the relationship between optimum policies, shadow prices and policy reform. Guidelines for reforming policy, and the rules satisfied by shadow prices, are analysed in sub-section 2.3.

2.1 Definitions and simple examples

Our definition of shadow prices requires us to calculate the effect of an extra unit of net public supplies (the latter are represented by the vector z) on social welfare. The public supplies are to be interpreted as outputs of and (negative) inputs in public production, rather than as public consumption (or what is conventionally termed 'public goods'). Thus, they do not impinge directly on social welfare but only affect it through the variables that influence household welfare and demands: prices, wages, rations and so on.[1] We shall think of these variables as being of two types: 'control variables', s, and parameters or 'predetermied variables', ω. The former are determined within the system, subject to the scarcity constraints that usages of goods cannot exceed availability, and to any other constraints that may be relevant. The variables ω are fixed as parameters of the system. We shall, however, examine the consequences of shifts in these parameters.

We shall refer to the person or agency responsible for the evaluation of public decisions as the 'planner'. This does not imply that we think of the government as a well-tuned, harmonized whole, acting coherently and consistently in pursuit of a well-defined set of objectives, captured by a single social welfare function. The planner will usually be operating in a particular agency and may have to treat the responses of other government agencies (e.g., taxes set by the finance ministry or quotas specified by a trade ministry) as outside its control. This causes no problems for the analysis since such items can be included among the list of predetermined variables, ω. We shall assume that the planner chooses those variables which are in its control with respect to the same social welfare or objective function that is being used to evaluate changes in public supplies. This is simply an assumption of consistency for the planner in the selection of those variables which are within the range of control (and this basic consistency is indeed what the adviser may recommend). The planner's range of control may, however, be so limited that there is essentially no choice at all. Crudely, there may be exactly the same number of constraints as there are control variables. This is the approach typically adopted in cost–benefit theory and practice. It does not disturb the analysis and is retained as an important special case throughout. We shall refer to this case as one where the model is 'fully determined'. Our analysis represents therefore a generalization of the standard approach.

The problem then is one of an optimizing planner, but where that planner may have little (or negligible) scope in the selection of policies. The planner may well be asked, however, to decide on, or appraise, new opportunities in the form of new (small) projects, dz, or in the form of marginal reforms, or shifts, dω, in variables which were initially regarded as predetermined.

It is important to note here that our list of 'control variables' includes what one may wish to call the 'endogenous variables' of the system, i.e., the variables whose value is determined by the constraints of the problem. To put it crudely again, when there are I constraints, a vector of K control variables can often be interpreted as consisting of I 'endogenous variables', and $(K - I)$ variables under the effective and direct control of the planner. We shall, however, want to consider all K variables together, and the distinction between endogenous variables and control variables will often be somewhat arbitrary. For instance, in a model where the only constraints are the scarcity constraints and the control variables consist of prices and indirect taxes, it does not matter whether we choose to describe prices as being determined by the market-clearing process and taxes by the planner, or the other way round. From a formal point of view, it is enough to note that *both* prices and taxes should be treated as 'control variables', given that the scarcity constraints enter the model explicitly. This point is important for a correct interpretation of the models analysed in this paper.

We are now in a position to define shadow prices. We write social welfare $V(s;\omega)$ as a function of s and ω, and think of the 'planner's problem' as that of choosing s to solve

$$\text{maximize } V(s;\omega) \text{ subject to } E(s;\omega) - z = 0 \qquad (2.1)$$

where $E(s;\omega)$ is the vector of net demands arising from the private sector, z is (as indicated earlier) the vector of net supplies from the public sector, and 0 is a vector of zeros. The constraints expressed by (2.1) are the *scarcity constraints*, which say that available supplies must match demands. There may in practice be additional constraints. Often it will be possible to capture these constraints by considering some variables as predetermined, and to this extent they are included in our formulation; but where they cannot be modelled in this way they should be included as constraints additional to the scarcity constraints. To keep things simple, we shall avoid including them in the analysis that follows (see Drèze and Stern, 1987, for a more general treatment).

Given z and ω, the solution of (2.1) gives a level of social welfare which we write as $V^*(z;\omega)$ – the maximum level of social welfare associated with the production plan z (given ω). The shadow price v_i of the ith good is defined by

$$v_i \equiv \partial V^* / \partial z_i \tag{2.2}$$

Thus, v_i is precisely the increase in social welfare associated with a unit marginal increase in z_i; or the social opportunity cost in terms of social welfare of a marginal unit reduction in z_i. Alternatively, relative shadow prices represent marginal rates of substitution in the social utility function $V^*(\cdot)$ defined on the space of commodities.

A *project* is a small change in public supplies, dz (private projects are discussed in section 4). We can see from equation (2.2) that the value of a project dz at shadow prices, vdz (i.e., $\Sigma_i v_i dz_i$), is equal to dV^*, so a project increases social welfare if and only if it makes a profit at shadow prices. Thus, the cost–benefit test 'accept the project if it is profitable at shadow prices' correctly identifies all those projects that are desirable in the sense of increasing social welfare.[2] Our definition of shadow prices is, of course, designed with precisely this property in view, and it can be seen that any set of relative prices that fails to coincide with the relative shadow prices defined by equation (2.2) cannot possess the same property. Notice, on the other hand, that it is only relative shadow prices that matter and we can always scale the vector v up or down by a positive factor without changing anything of substance. We have not assumed that public production has been chosen optimally. This is, of course, retained as a special case since the analysis can be applied at any z. The planner, however, might be unaware of the detail of production possibilities and therefore unable to go straight to the best point in the production possibility set. Indeed, the role of shadow prices is precisely to evaluate those production possibilities of which he becomes aware. Finally, it must be stressed that the shadow prices discussed in this paper are appropriate only for the evaluation of *small* projects: for large changes, differential techniques based exclusively on first-order terms are no longer adequate.[3]

The change in welfare from an extra unit of public supplies comes about through the resultant change in the variables which affect household welfare. These changes will, of course, be determined by the structure of the economy including, in particular, the policy instruments available to the government.[4] The link between shadow prices and the tools at the government's disposal may be illustrated using two simple examples.

Consider an economy with a single consumer who supplies labour to produce corn. The only firm is owned entirely by the government. In the first example the government can control the economy fully in the sense that it can allocate labour and corn in both production and consumption subject only to the availability of each good. The control variables are the quantities of corn and labour in both production and consumption. In the second example the government has to work through the price system and can only obtain labour by hiring at each wage the amount the worker-consumer wishes to supply at that wage. Furthermore, it cannot levy lump-sum taxes, i.e., a poll tax or subsidy is ruled out. It is clear that in the second case the powers of the government are more limited than in the first and that the overall level of welfare it can achieve will be lower. It is also true that the marginal rates of substitution in terms of social welfare, or relative shadow prices, will be different in the two cases.

The problem is illustrated in figures 1.1 and 1.2. In the first case (figure 1.1) the government has complete control over the economy and chooses the first-best allocation, X. The relative shadow prices are given by the loss of labour (i.e., extra labour required of the worker) that would hold social welfare constant if an extra unit of corn became available. The changes envisaged in response to the increased availability of a unit of corn must be achievable making the best possible use of the tools at the government's disposal and observing the scarcity constraints. If an extra unit of corn becomes available, then utility could be held constant by a marginal increase in labour from X along the line DE towards D. The gradient of the line DE gives the marginal rate of substitution in social welfare and hence relative shadow prices.

In the second case the government can choose only points along the offer curve OF in figure 1.2(a). Since utility increases as we move up the offer curve (higher real wages) the optimum will be at Z where the offer curve cuts the production frontier OG. Relative consumer prices (the real wage to the consumer) are represented by the gradient of the line OZA and the marginal rate of trans-formation in production (the marginal product of labour here) is given by the gradient of BC. Thus, marginal rates of substitution for the consumer and marginal rates of transformation for the producer are not equal. The former is equal to the consumer–price ratio and we may think of the latter as the producer–price ratio. The difference is a tax, or if it is negative, a subsidy. Here it is a subsidy that is financed by the profits of the firm (at the given producer price ratio) of OB in terms of corn. If we now have an extra unit of corn, what will be the increase in labour requirement which will maintain utility constant given the tools at the government's disposal, i.e., when we are restricted to movements along the offer curve? It is clear that constant utility must involve a return to Z since any other point on the offer curve involves higher or lower utility. Thus, the consumer–price ratio must remain unchanged after the adjustment and the accommodation to the changes must be on the production side. This means that the change in labour in response to an extra unit of corn must be one that takes us back to the production frontier so that production can adjust to take us back to Z. The increase in availability of one unit is represented in figure 1.2(b) by the move to Z′ and the increase in labour to regain the frontier by the move Z′ to Z″. Production can then be adjusted to bring us back to Z with no utility change. The marginal rate of substitution in social welfare is now seen to be given by the gradient of BC or relative *producer* prices.

It is straightforward to generalize these results to higher dimensions and several consumers, and some related results are discussed below. These simple

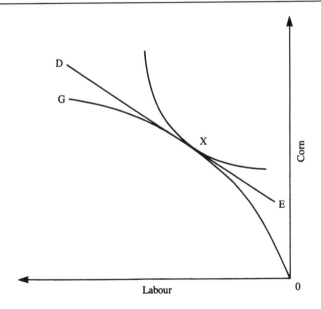

Figure 1.1 Shadow prices equal to consumer prices

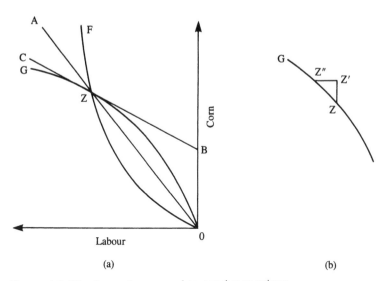

Figure 1.2 Shadow prices equal to producer prices

examples, however, illustrate the important point that shadow prices depend on the tools at the government's disposal: we have seen that there will be cases where they are equal to consumer prices and others where they are equal to producer prices. We are also going to find examples where they are averages of the two, or obey more complicated formulae.

2.2 The model

We shall now set out the basic model in which the properties of shadow prices will be investigated. This model is, in effect, a mixture of fix-price and flex-price models (in the language of Hicks) where prices in some markets are free to adjust but in others are not. Households and firms are price takers, but may be subject to quantity rationing in certain markets. This formulation will allow us to capture at once the important phenomena of price responses as well as quantity rationing. In particular, the familiar themes of the literature on temporary equilibrium with quantity rationing, such as Keynesian unemployment, are firmly within our framework.

We have H consumers (indexed by $h = 1, \ldots, H$), one private firm and one public firm. It is straightforward to extend the model to allow for an arbitrary number of private and joint public–private firms (see Drèze and Stern, 1987), but we are trying to keep the model as simple as possible whilst retaining its essential features. In a similar spirit we shall ignore externalities. There are I goods, indexed by $i = 1, \ldots, I$ (distinguished, if necessary, by time and contingency). The private firm trades at prices given by the vector p and its net supply vector is y. We follow the usual convention that a negative supply by a firm represents a demand for an input and a negative demand by a household represents a supply by that household. The firm may be subject to quantity constraints on its choice of inputs or outputs. These are represented by an I vector of lower bounds $\bar{y}_-$ and a similar vector of upper bounds $\bar{y}_+$; the $2I$ vector $(\bar{y}_-, \bar{y}_+)$ is called $\bar{y}$. When the firm has maximized profits subject to the constraints it faces, its output of the ith good will be equal to the ith component of $\bar{y}_-$ or of $\bar{y}_+$, or will lie between them. If it is equal to the lower bound or the upper bound we say that the corresponding bound is the 'binding constraint'. The binding constraint for good i, if any, is referred to as $\bar{y}_i$ (the upper and lower bounds cannot both be binding unless they are equal). The firm's profit-maximizing supply $y(p, \bar{y})$ is then a function of the prices and quotas which it faces. Its pretax profits, $\pi(p, \bar{y})$, are also a function of p and $\bar{y}$ and are distributed to households according to the shares θ^h. We denote $1 - \Sigma_h \theta^h$ by ζ, which represents the government's share in the profits of the private firm, including any profits tax.

Households face prices $q \equiv p + t$, where t is the vector of indirect taxes (linear factor taxes are included within the components of t but there are no taxes on intermediate transactions). The hth household receives lump-sum income $m^h \equiv r^h + \theta^h \pi$, where r^h is a lump-sum transfer from the government (positive, zero, or negative). Each household chooses a utility-maximizing consumption vector x^h subject to its budget constraint and quantity constraints which are represented by vectors of quotas, $\bar{x}^h_-, \bar{x}^h_+$, as with the firm. We denote the $2I$ vector $(\bar{x}^h_-, \bar{x}^h_+)$ by $\bar{x}^h$ and the relevant binding constraints by $\bar{x}^h_i$. The demands x^h of household h are functions of q, $\bar{x}^h$, and m^h. They are written as $x^h(q, \bar{x}^h, m^h)$, but the identities $q \equiv p + t$ and $m^h \equiv r^h + \theta^h \pi$ should be kept in mind throughout.

The vector of net government supplies is z as before, and the vector of net imports is denoted by n. There is a given endowment F of foreign exchange, and world prices are fixed at p^w. F has an analogous status to z in the analysis in that it is exogenous to the optimization but will be amongst those variables for which exogenous shifts will be examined. The scarcity constraints are then

$$\sum_h x^h - y - n - z = 0 \tag{2.3}$$

$$p^w n - F = 0 \tag{2.4}$$

We have chosen to write (2.4) separately from (2.3) to bring out the role of foreign trade more sharply. A more unified treatment, dispensing with (2.4), can be obtained by treating foreign exchange as a separate commodity and net imports as the net supplies of a separate firm. However, for greater transparency we shall treat foreign exchange and net imports explicitly.

The constraints are written as equality constraints without loss of generality, since they simply trace what happens to each unit of each commodity – disposal activities (with or without cost) could be included in a straightforward way (see Drèze and Stern, 1987, for details). To keep things simple we have supposed that the only constraints which arise are the scarcity constraints (2.3) and (2.4) and those which can be expressed in the form that a variable is 'predetermined'.

The vector s of control variables consists of K variables drawn from the following list

$$(p_i), (t_i), (r^h), (\bar{x}_i^h), (\bar{y}_i), (\theta^h), (n_i) \tag{2.5}$$

where $i = 1, 2, \ldots, I$ and $h = 1, 2, \ldots, H$.

The variables included in s are under the planner's control, but they must be chosen subject to the constraints (2.3) and (2.4). The more variables s contains, the larger the degree of freedom for the planner. Crudely speaking, if there are just $(I + 1)$ control variables, then the planner has no real choice since (2.3) and (2.4) represent $(I + 1)$ constraints – this is the 'fully determined' case to which we have already referred. If there are more than $(I + 1)$ variables in the list s, then the planner has a genuine choice which it exercises so as to maximize social welfare. The variables in (2.5) which are not in s are predetermined, or are parameters, and denoted as before by ω.

Finally, the social welfare function takes the Bergson–Samuelson form $W(u^1, u^2, \ldots, u^H)$, where u^h is the level of utility of the hth household. This can also be written as

$$V(s; \omega) \equiv W(\ldots, v^h(q, \bar{x}^h, m^h), \ldots,) \tag{2.6}$$

where v^h is the indirect utility function relating individual welfare to prices, rations, and income.

In the remainder of this paper we shall assume some familiarity with the elementary properties of the functions $x^h(q, \bar{x}^h, m^h)$, $y(p, \bar{y})$, $v^h(q, \bar{x}^h, m^h)$, and

$\pi(p, \bar{y})$, i.e., with the basic theory of competitive demand and supply in the presence of quantity constraints or rationing. We also assume knowledge of simple optimization techniques using Lagrange multipliers.

2.3 Optimum policies, shadow prices and policy reform

Nearly all our results are derived from the first-order conditions for the maximization of social welfare subject to the scarcity constraints (2.3) and (2.4). We shall examine, in particular, the Lagrange multipliers associated with the scarcity constraints. It should be clear that this is a natural way to proceed since these Lagrange multipliers will tell us precisely how much social welfare goes up if we have a little extra of public supply, and this corresponds exactly to our definition of shadow prices. To see this, let us write the Lagrangian L of the social welfare maximization problem as

$$L(s; \omega, z, F, \lambda, \mu) \equiv V(s; \omega) - \lambda[E(s; \omega) - z] - \mu[p^w n - F] \tag{2.7a}$$

where μ is a Lagrange multiplier on the foreign exchange constraint, λ a vector of Lagrange multipliers on the other scarcity constraints, and

$$E(s; \omega) \equiv \sum_h x^h - y - n \tag{2.7b}$$

Now let $V^*(z, F; \omega)$ denote, as before, the maximum social welfare associated with given values of z, F, and ω. A standard result of optimization theory (the 'envelope theorem') states that the gradient of the 'maximum value function', V^*, is identical to the gradient of the Lagrangian, L. Therefore we have

$$\lambda \equiv \frac{\partial L}{\partial z} \equiv \frac{\partial V^*}{\partial z} \equiv v \tag{2.8a}$$

which confirms our assertion that the Lagrange multipliers on the scarcity constraints can be interpreted as 'shadow prices' in the sense defined earlier.[5] Similarly we can at once derive

$$\frac{\partial V^*}{\partial F} \equiv \frac{\partial L}{\partial F} \equiv \mu \tag{2.8b}$$

so that μ can be interpreted as the *marginal social value of foreign exchange*: it measures the increase in social welfare resulting from the availability of an extra unit of foreign exchange. Notice that the shift in V^* following a change in z works through the effect of a change in s on household utilities. However, the shift in L is at *constant* s (see the arguments of L in (2.7a); we can ignore any effects operating on L through s precisely because s has been chosen optimally – this is the 'envelope property').

Our writing of (2.3) and (2.4) separately to replace the constraint in (2.1) means that the evaluation of a project (dz, dF) is now given by whether or not

$$\sum_{i=1}^{I} v_i dz_i + \mu dF > 0 \tag{2.9}$$

where we accept the project if (2.9) holds. Note that the foreign exchange component, dF, will be zero unless the project is tied to a direct gift of foreign exchange: the (direct and indirect) effects of a project on foreign exchange will be captured by the first term in the left-hand side of (2.9), and should not be counted again through the component dF.

As we have already pointed out, it is only the relative shadow prices in the vector $(v_1, v_2, \ldots, v_I, \mu)$ that matter. In other words, we are free to choose a unit of account for our shadow prices. One common practice in the literature has been to do the accounting in terms of foreign exchange so that μ is set equal to one (see Little and Mirrlees 1974).

The control variables are chosen to maximize social welfare subject to the scarcity constraints. The first-order conditions for maximization are

$$\frac{\partial L}{\partial s_k} \equiv \frac{\partial V}{\partial s_k} - v \frac{\partial E}{\partial s_k} = 0 \tag{2.10}$$

if the kth control variable is any element in the list (2.5) excluding n_i. The first-order conditions for n_i are discussed below. The conditions (2.10) have a very natural interpretation: they tell us that at an optimum the direct effect on social welfare of a marginal adjustment in any control variable should equal the marginal social cost of the extra net demands generated. Thus, the shadow prices are picking up the welfare effects of the full general equilibrium adjustments in the system. In this sense they are sufficient statistics for the general equilibrium responses: they summarize what we need to know about those consequences for the purpose of policy evaluation.

The first-order conditions (2.10), together with those for net imports, n_i, where relevant, give us a set of K first-order conditions, where K is the number of control variables. These K conditions, together with the $(I + 1)$ scarcity constraints (2.3) and (2.4), determine the values of the K control variables, s_k, at the optimum and the $(I + 1)$ shadow prices. Thus, we can see that to speak of 'rules determining shadow prices' and 'rules determining optimum policies' is to describe the same set or a sub-set of the same set of conditions but from a different viewpoint. Moreover, we retain the 'fully determined' case, with $K = (I + 1)$, as a special case – here the scarcity constraints uniquely determine the controls and the condition (2.10) represents a set of equations which we must solve for the shadow prices given these values of the controls.

As we have already emphasized, when K is greater than $(I + 1)$ one could think of a particular sub-set of control variables, $K - (I + 1)$ in number, as the variables directly under the control of the planner, and the remaining $(I + 1)$ as determined endogenously from the general equilibrium system. This dichotomy may occasionally be helpful in interpretation and to fix ideas but, analytically, it is somewhat artificial because one could in principle think of any particular $(K - (I + 1))$ subset of the controls, s_k, as being directly controlled by the planner. Unless otherwise stated, therefore, we shall simply speak of the s_k being K controls chosen subject to $(I + 1)$ constraints.

We can now discuss the value of a shift in one of the parameters, ω_k, i.e., a 'reform'. Suppose, for example, that we can contemplate a marginal shift in some tax or grant, ω_k, that was previously outside the control of the planner. To evaluate such a prospect, we want to know its effect on social welfare, i.e., $\partial V^*/\partial \omega_k$. Applying the 'envelope theorem' once again we find that

$$\frac{\partial V^*}{\partial \omega_k} \equiv \frac{\partial L}{\partial \omega_k} \tag{2.11}$$

or, using (2.10)

$$\frac{\partial V^*}{\partial \omega_k} \equiv \frac{\partial V}{\partial \omega_k} - v \frac{\partial E}{\partial \omega_k} \tag{2.12}$$

when ω_k is one of the variables in (2.5) (excluding (n_i)). This tells us that we evaluate whether the change is welfare-improving by first taking the direct effect $(\partial V/\partial \omega_k)$, and then comparing it with the cost at shadow prices of the extra demands $(\partial E/\partial \omega_k)$ generated by the change. Again, the partial derivatives involved are calculated for constant s and the shadow prices capture for us the relevant general equilibrium consequences of the change.

The result (2.12) is of great generality, and it will be used repeatedly in the remainder of this paper. It is convenient, as well as natural, to refer to the gradient of L (or, equivalently, of V^*) with respect to any parameter ω_k as the *marginal social value* of that parameter (MSV for short). By analogy, and for presentational purposes, we shall also speak of the gradient of L with respect to a control variable s_k as its 'marginal social value' (MSV). The first-order conditions (2.10) thus simply require that the MSV of a control variable should be zero.

2.4 Rules for policies and shadow prices

We shall now examine the particular form of the rules for optimum policies and shadow prices which arise from the model with objective function as in (2.6) and constraints as in (2.3) and (2.4). For this purpose it may be helpful to rewrite the Lagrangian (2.7a) explicitly as

$$L(\cdot) \equiv W(\ldots, v^h(p + t, \bar{x}^h, r^h + \theta^h \pi(p, \bar{y})), \ldots)$$
$$- v \left[\sum_h x^h(p + t, \bar{x}^h, r^h + \theta^h \pi(p, \bar{y})) - y(p, \bar{y}) - n - z \right] - \mu[p^w n - F] \tag{2.13}$$

We can now consider, for variables in the list (2.5), the first-order conditions (2.10) as well as the marginal social values (2.12).

Transfers to households, r^h

$$\frac{\partial L}{\partial r^h} = \frac{\partial W}{\partial v^h} \frac{\partial v^h}{\partial r^h} - v \frac{\partial x^h}{\partial r^h} \tag{2.13a}$$

This tells us that the marginal social value of a transfer to household h is the direct effect (the private marginal utility of income of household h, $\partial v^h/\partial r^h$, multiplied by the rate of change of social welfare with respect to the utility of household h, $\partial W^h/\partial v^h$) less the cost at shadow prices of meeting the extra demands by the household ($\partial x^h/\partial r^h$) arising from the extra income. We shall refer to ($\partial W^h/\partial v^h$)·($\partial v^h/\partial r^h$) as the social marginal utility of income or *welfare weight* of household h and denote it by β^h; we also write

$$b^h \equiv \beta^h - v \frac{\partial x^h}{\partial r^h} \tag{2.13b}$$

so that b^h stands for the marginal social value of a transfer to household h. If b^h is greater than zero, we would want to increase the transfer if an upward adjustment were possible, and if b^h is less than 0, we would want to decrease it. If the transfer to household h is a control variable, then the first-order conditions (2.10) require that b^h should be equal to zero.

Net imports, n_i

$$\frac{\partial L}{\partial n_i} = v_i - \mu p_i^w \tag{2.14}$$

Recalling our earlier discussion of control variables and 'endogenous' variables, it can be seen that the variable n_i will be a control variable either if it is set by the planner as an optimum quote on net trade, or if the level of net imports for that commodity is determined endogenously within the system (as when trade in the commodity is unrestricted – although possibly subject to tariffs – and net imports meet the gap between domestic demand and supply). From the formal point of view there is no difference between these two situations. Where n_i is a control variable, the first-order conditions (2.10) imply

$$v_i = \mu p_i^w \tag{2.15}$$

This says that the shadow price of good i is equal to its world price multiplied by the marginal social value of foreign exchange. Thus, relative shadow prices within the set of goods for which n_i is a control variable are equal to relative world prices.

We have, therefore, derived a standard rule for relative shadow prices of traded goods in cost–benefit analysis – they are equal to relative world prices. The model we have constructed allows us to see clearly the conditions under which this result holds. The crucial feature is that public production of any of the commodities under consideration can be seen as displacing an equivalent amount of net imports, and moreover the general equilibrium repercussions involved are mediated exclusively by the balance of payments constraint. Formally, this can be seen from the fact that, in equation (2.13), the vector n enters the Lagrangian in exactly the same capacity as the vector z, except for its presence in the balance of payments constraint.

That this is the crucial condition should be intuitively clear from the economics of the problem. An extra demand for an imported good will generate a foreign exchange cost and thus create a cost given by its world price multiplied by the marginal social value of foreign exchange. If there is *no other* direct effect in the system, then all the relevant general equilibrium repercussions are captured in the marginal social value of foreign exchange and we have found the shadow price of the good. If, however, there is a direct effect of increasing net imports somewhere else in the system, then the world price (multiplied by μ) will no longer be equal to the shadow price.

One example of the latter complication would arise with an exported good for which world demand was less than perfectly elastic. One might think it sufficient in this case simply to replace the world price by the marginal revenue in the shadow price formula (2.15). This is correct if the domestic price of the good can be separately controlled. If it cannot (because, say, the indirect tax on the good is predetermined and cannot be influenced by the planner) then the calculation of the shadow price should take into account the effects on private-sector supplies and profits of the fall in the world price as a result of extra public production.

A second example would arise if there were separate foreign exchange budgets for different sectors which were set outside the control of the planner. If a sector is identified by its group of commodities, then within a sector relative shadow prices of traded goods would be equal to relative world prices, but across sectors this would not apply since the marginal social value of foreign exchange across sectors would no longer be equal. This is a further example of the importance for shadow prices of being clear as to just what the planner controls. If the planner also controlled the allocation of foreign exchange across sectors then the correct rule would be to allocate across sectors so that the marginal social value of foreign exchange across sectors would be equal, and then relative shadow prices for traded goods would be equal to relative world prices for all goods.

Producer rations, $\bar{y}_i$

$$\frac{\partial L}{\partial \bar{y}_i} = v \frac{\partial y}{\partial \bar{y}_i} + b \frac{\partial \pi}{\partial \bar{y}_i} \tag{2.16}$$

where

$$b \equiv \sum_h \theta^h b^h \tag{2.17}$$

and b^h is as in equation (2.13b). The expression (2.16) is most easily interpreted if we think of good i as the output of the firm and of $\bar{y}_i$ as the amount it is required to produce. Then an increase in the required output will require extra inputs and the overall change in the production vector will be $\partial y / \partial \bar{y}_i$ with value at shadow prices given by the first term on the right-hand side of (2.16). The increase in required output will also affect the profits of the firm and this is captured in the second term on the right-hand side of (2.16) – b is the weighted sum of the marginal social values of transfers to households with weights given by the shares of the households in the profits of the firm. Using the properties of the functions y and π, and noting in particular that $\partial y_i / \partial \bar{y}_i \equiv 1$, we can rewrite (2.16) as

$$\frac{\partial L}{\partial \bar{y}_i} = v_i - MSC_i + b(p_i - MC_i) \tag{2.18}$$

where

$$MC_i \equiv - \sum_{j \neq i} p_j \frac{\partial y_j}{\partial \bar{y}_i} \tag{2.18a}$$

is the marginal (private) cost of good i (i.e., the value at market prices of the inputs required to produce an extra unit), and

$$MSC_i \equiv - \sum_{j \neq i} v_j \frac{\partial y_j}{\partial \bar{y}_i} \tag{2.18b}$$

is its 'marginal social cost' (i.e., the value at shadow prices of the same inputs).

If $\bar{y}_i$ is a control variable, then the expression in (2.18) must be zero and we have

$$v_i = MSC_i - b(p_i - MC_i) \tag{2.19}$$

This states that the shadow price of good i is its marginal social cost, corrected by the marginal social value of the relevant profit effects.

As in the earlier discussion of trade, we can interpret the fact that $\bar{y}_i$ is a 'control variable' in two different ways. First, the private firm may be subjected to a quota which is directly (and optimally) set by the planner. Second, the output of the private firm may be determined endogenously, with the private firm adjusting to demand (this is sometimes called a 'Keynesian equilibrium' for the firm). In both cases, the intuition behind the shadow price rule (2.19) is that a change in public production of the relevant good results in a corresponding displacement of private production. Equation (2.19) provides a starting point for our discussion in sub-section 4.5 of the net benefits from lowering the price of a good in excess supply.

Producer prices, p_i

If a small change in the public production of a commodity is accommodated by a change in its market price p_i, complicated adjustments in both consumption and private production will follow. The corresponding shadow price expression will then be quite complicated as well. Roughly speaking, the main result here is that the shadow price of a good whose market clears by price adjustment can be seen as a weighted average of the shadow prices of its complement and substitute commodities, the weights being given by the relevant price elasticities (in addition, the social value of income effects has to be taken into account). Under simplifying assumptions, short cuts can be obtained, such as more elementary 'weighted average rules' involving marginal social costs on the production and consumption sides. The correct expressions can be derived from the first-order conditions for maximization with respect to the producer price, p_i. They involve a little more technicality than we would want in this paper and are therefore not pursued here (for details, see Drèze and Stern, 1987; see also Guesnerie, 1980, on 'Ramsey–Boiteux' pricing rules).

Consumer rations, $\bar{x}_i^h$

The social value of adjusting a consumer ration can be analysed in an analogous manner to producer rations. The details will not be presented here. One can show that, if preferences are such that the ith good is (weakly) 'separable' from the others (i.e., a change in the consumption of the ith good does not affect marginal rates of substitution amongst the others), then the first-order condition for an optimum ration of that good to household h reduces to

$$v_i = \beta^h p_i^h - b^h q_i \tag{2.20}$$

where p_i^h is the 'marginal willingness to pay' for good i by household h (the marginal utility of good i divided by the marginal utility of income).

The expression (2.20) for the shadow price of a rationed good clearly brings out the two components of the gain in social welfare associated with extra public production of that good. First, the consumer who benefits from the extra ration available enjoys an increase in utility measured (in money terms) by his or her marginal willingness to pay, p_i^h, and the social valuation of this change in private utility is obtained by using the usual 'welfare weights', β^h. Second, a transfer of income occurs, as the same individual is required to pay the consumer price, q_i, for the extra ration; the social evaluation of this second effect relies on the marginal social value of a transfer to the concerned consumer, b^h.

This formulation can be adapted to give us shadow prices for important special cases, e.g., public goods and the hiring of labour in a rationed labour market (see section 3). Public goods, for instance, can be modelled here as a rationed commodity – everyone has to consume the same amount, i.e., that which is made available – with a zero price. Analogously to expression (2.20), and under the same assumption of 'separability', we then obtain the shadow price of a public good as $\Sigma_h \beta^h \rho_i^h$, the aggregate, welfare-weighted, marginal willingness-to-pay.

If the separability assumption is violated, expression (2.20) will involve an extra term that captures the marginal social value of the resulting substitution effects. Alternatively, this extra term can be seen as reflecting the effect on the 'shadow revenue' of the government – a notion explored in detail in section 3.

Indirect taxes, t_i

$$\frac{\partial L}{\partial t_i} = -\sum_h \beta^h x_i^h - v \frac{\partial x}{\partial q_i} \tag{2.21}$$

This can be reformulated after decomposing $\partial x / \partial q_i$ into an income and a substitution effect (and using the symmetry of the Slutsky terms) to give

$$\frac{\partial L}{\partial t_i} = -\sum_h b^h x_i^h + (q - v) \frac{\partial \hat{x}_i}{\partial q} \tag{2.22}$$

where $\hat{x}_i^h(q, \bar{x}^h, u^h)$ is the *compensated* demand of consumer h for good i, and $\hat{x}_i \equiv \Sigma_h \hat{x}_i^h$. Thus, the jth component of the vector $\partial \hat{x}_i / \partial q$ is the compensated response in aggregate consumption of good i to the price of good j. If t_i is a control variable, then we have

$$\tau^c \frac{\partial \hat{x}_i}{\partial q} = \sum_h b^h x_i^h \tag{2.23}$$

where $\tau^c \equiv q - v$ is a vector of 'shadow consumer taxes' equal to the difference between consumer prices and shadow prices. If, under a suitable normalization rule, shadow prices, v, are equal to producer prices, p, then τ^c reduces to the indirect tax vector, t, and expression (2.23) precisely amounts to the familiar 'many-person Ramsey rule' (see, for example, Diamond, 1975 and Stern, 1984).

We see, therefore, that expression (2.23) gives us a remarkably simple generalization of the standard optimum tax rules. The kind of economies where the standard rules are derived happen, in fact, to be economies for which shadow prices are proportional to producer prices (as in Diamond and Mirrlees, 1971). What we have now seen is that the same rules apply in much more general economies if we simply replace producer prices by shadow prices.

Much of the discussion of the structure of indirect taxes and the balance between direct and indirect taxation also carries through on replacing actual taxes by shadow taxes. One can show, for example, that if there is an optimum poll tax, households have identical preferences with linear Engel curves, and labour is separable from goods, then shadow taxes should apply at a uniform proportionate rate (see Drèze and Stern, 1987 and Stern, 1987). Note that if shadow prices are not proportional to producer prices, this means that actual indirect taxes should *not* be uniform.

3 SHADOW PRICES AND THE MACROECONOMY

We shall now investigate the relation between the theory developed so far and more familiar considerations of public finance and macroeconomic policy. These two themes are treated in sub-sections 3.1 and 3.2, respectively.

3.1 Public finance and the shadow revenue

If the public sector trades at prices p we can calculate its net revenue, R_p, as the sum of profits in the public sector, pz, the value of the foreign exchange sold, φF (where φ is the exchange rate), revenue from indirect taxes, tx, tariff revenue, $(p - \varphi p^w)n$, the government's share of private profits, $\zeta\pi$, which includes profits taxes, and lump-sum taxes, $- \Sigma_h r^h$

$$R_p \equiv pz + \varphi F + tx + (p - \varphi p^w)n + \zeta\pi - \sum_h r^h \qquad (3.1)$$

It is important to recognize that this expression for R_p gives us the net revenue for the government in a way that is different from the standard procedures in published government accounts in a number of important respects. First, it takes the revenue and expenditure accounts together. If we were to separate the elements of R_p in (3.1) we might think of $(-pz + \Sigma_h r^h)$ as government expenditure and of the remaining terms as revenue, with the net revenue being the difference between the two. However, there is nothing compelling in this particular way of making the distinction since, in fact, many different components of R_p could turn out to be either positive or negative. Second, R_p represents net government revenue expressed in present value terms – expenditures and revenues occurring in the future are taken together with those occurring now and the use of present value prices converts them to a common unit of account. Thus, the government may actually run a deficit this year and this will be covered by surpluses at some stage in the (possibly distant) future. Third, there is no difference here between current and capital accounts for the government. This is an aspect of the inter-temporal nature of the net revenue R_p – purchases and receipts are noted as and when they occur irrespective of whether they might be labelled 'current' or 'capital'. This approach is essentially standard in theoretical treatments of optimum taxation although it is usually implicit.

Now using the identity

$$py \equiv (1 - \zeta)\pi + \zeta\pi \qquad (3.2)$$

and the aggregate budget constraint for consumers

$$qx \equiv \sum_h r^h + (1 - \zeta)\pi \qquad (3.3)$$

we easily obtain

$$R_p \equiv p(z + y + n - x) + \varphi(F - p^w n) \tag{3.4}$$

This gives us Walras' law for this economy, i.e., the government budget constraint is balanced ($R_p = 0$) if and only if the value of the net excess demands at producer prices (including the excess demand for foreign exchange) is zero. This value of net excess demands at producer prices can be zero whether or not markets clear, but if they do clear then it must be zero. Hence, in this economy the government's budget is balanced as soon as the scarcity constraints are met and we do not have to impose budget balance as a separate constraint.

On the other hand, we do have to ask about the process by which the government budget is balanced because we must specify the control variables, i.e., we must say which of the taxes, transfers, quotas and so on are under the control of the planner. As we have seen, we get different rules for shadow prices depending on which variables are controlled and which are exogenous. Notice also that we are treating all government activities – projects, transfers and the like – as being financed out of a common 'pot' of general revenue. Where there are separate budget constraints applying to specific government activities, they have to be incorporated explicitly into the analysis (see section 4).

Note also, however, that there are many alternative ways of defining 'government revenue'. Indeed, when a transaction takes place between two agents, the prices which they respectively face can be arbitrarily split between the 'transaction price' and agent-specific taxes. In the earlier definition of government revenue, producer prices were implicitly taken as 'transaction prices', but any other vector of prices could be considered. In particular, if we use shadow prices as transaction prices, we obtain an alternative and – it turns out – an extremely useful definition of government revenue which we shall call *shadow revenue* (denoted by R_v)

$$R_v \equiv vz + \mu F + (q - v)x + (v - \mu p^w)n + \zeta \pi - \sum_h r^h + (v - p)y \tag{3.5}$$

This definition is analogous to (3.1), with v and μ, respectively, replacing p and φ, and the natural addition of the extra term $(v - p)y$. As in section 2, the components of the vector $q - v$ (also denoted by τ^c) are referred to as 'shadow consumer taxes', and similarly the components of the vector $v - p$ (also denoted by τ^p) are referred to as 'shadow producer taxes'. Clearly, if $v = p$ then $\tau^p = 0$ and $R_v = R_p$.

Using expressions (3.2) and (3.3) again we have

$$R_v \equiv v(z + y + n - x) + \mu(F - p^w n) \tag{3.6}$$

much as in (3.4). It follows, in particular, that $R_v = 0$ when the scarcity constraints are satisfied. Moreover, from (3.6) and (2.7) or (2.13) we may rewrite the Lagrangian L as

$$L \equiv V + R_v \tag{3.7}$$

and, therefore, for shifts in parameters ω_k

$$\frac{\partial V^*}{\partial \omega_k} \equiv \frac{\partial L}{\partial \omega_k} \equiv \frac{\partial V}{\partial \omega_k} + \frac{\partial R_v}{\partial \omega_k} \tag{3.8}$$

This last expression provides us with an interesting and important way of evaluating policy reforms. We can evaluate such reforms by first assessing the direct effect on households, as evaluated through the social welfare function, and then adding the increase in *shadow* revenue (or equivalently subtracting the loss in shadow revenue) resulting from the reform.

This simple result shows us that a very common method of costing a policy change, i.e., asking about its effect on the government deficit, is mistaken in a distorted economy. In the United Kingdom, for example, in the last few years measures to reduce unemployment – tax cuts, public expenditure programmes, employment subsidies and the like – have been extensively discussed and it has been common practice to evaluate their cost in terms of the implied savings or losses of public revenue. This is, indeed, the spirit of many simplistic applications of the fashionable 'cost-effectiveness' criterion. Equation (3.8) shows us that this approach is incorrect. If we are to cost our policies correctly we should be using shadow revenue and not actual revenue. We should emphasize again that this does not neglect issues of financing since Walras' law tells us that satisfying the scarcity constraints will imply budget balance by whatever methods have been incorporated into the specification of the model.

This example, and (3.8), indicate that there is no need in this framework for a separate concept of the shadow price of government revenue. Government revenue (unlike foreign exchange) is not a separate good here. The shadow prices take account systematically of all the repercussions of a project including those which operate via the readjustment of public finances.

3.2 Some macroeconomic considerations

We now turn to some important macroeconomic aspects of shadow price systems: savings, foreign exchange, shadow wages and shadow discount rates. In discussing the concepts of savings and discount rates we must give the model an inter-temporal interpretation by indexing commodities by the date at which they appear. Prices and budget constraints are to be interpreted in present value terms.

It is often argued that developing countries should place a special premium on savings, i.e., that for some reason savings are too low and that it is important to provide measures to increase them. This position is not always clearly argued. The statement that savings are too low implies a judgement on the inter-temporal allocation of consumption (since to increase savings is to increase the welfare of the future generations relative to current ones) which may not be easy to make. Moreover, savings rates in developing countries are now commonly around 20 per cent, which does not suggest immediately that savings are 'too low'.

It is possible, within our framework, to give precision to the notion of a premium on savings. We can write the expression for b^h (2.13b) as

$$b^h = \beta^h - \sum_{i,\tau} \frac{v_{i\tau}}{q_{i\tau}} MPC_{i\tau}^h \tag{3.9}$$

where, $MPC_{i\tau}^h$ is the marginal propensity of household h to spend on the ith good in period τ

$$MPC_{i\tau}^h \equiv q_{i\tau} \frac{\partial x_{i\tau}^h}{\partial m^h} \tag{3.10}$$

We can then see that the marginal social value, b^h, of a transfer to household h is higher, the higher is its propensity to spend on goods in periods when the shadow price is low relative to the market price (low $v_{i\tau}/q_{i\tau}$). If current period commodities are relatively more valuable than future period commodities, then, other things being equal, there will be a higher value attached to transfers to those with a higher propensity to save. In this context we should think of a household as representing a dynasty which takes full account of the future welfare of descendants in its own utility function. If the government thinks it has a responsibility to give weight to future generations over and above that which arises from households' concern for their own descendants, then this might induce a separate argument for a premium on savings.

The model we have described so far contains a shadow price on foreign exchange, μ, and it is tempting to compare it with the exchange rate, φ, i.e., the price of a unit of foreign exchange. The simple comparison, however, contains no information since we can choose any absolute level of μ by rescaling the shadow price vector (v, μ) without changing anything real. The marginal social value of foreign exchange will also depend on the way in which the balance of payments is secured; an example will both illustrate this and provide a possible definition of a premium on foreign exchange which would be of substance.

Suppose that an import quota applies to the first good and that this quota can be set by the planner, or (equivalently for our purposes) that it adjusts endogenously to ensure the balance of payments. Then n_1 is a control variable and from (2.14) we have

$$v_1 - \mu p_1^w = 0 \tag{3.11}$$

Suppose further that the producer price for the good is simply the import price (φp_1^w in domestic prices) plus a tariff t_1^f so that

$$p_1 = \varphi p_1^w + t_1^f \tag{3.12}$$

Then

$$\frac{\mu}{\varphi} = \left(\frac{\varphi p_1^w + t_1^f}{\varphi p_1^w}\right)\frac{v_1}{p_1} \tag{3.13}$$

using expressions (3.11) and (3.12). Therefore, if the tariff is positive we have

$$\frac{\mu}{\varphi} \quad \text{is greater than} \quad \frac{v_1}{p_1} \tag{3.14}$$

or the shadow price of foreign exchange as a proportion of the market price is greater than the corresponding ratio for good 1. We may then say that there is a premium on foreign exchange in the sense of expression (3.14), and that this premium can be measured by the term in parentheses in (3.13), i.e., the extent to which the producer price of good 1 is above the world price. The analysis may be generalized in a straightforward way if the balance of payments is achieved not solely through the first good but by adjusting the quotas for a fixed bundle of goods – the premium is then given by the ratio between the value at producer prices and the value at world prices of that bundle. This idea is commonly embodied in manuals on cost–benefit analysis (see, for example, Dasgupta, Marglin and Sen (1972) who use a shadow exchange rate along these lines, or Little and Mirrlees (1974) who work in terms of a standard conversion factor for converting the value of broad groups of commodities from market prices to shadow prices).

The appropriate cost of labour is a further topic that has received great attention in discussions of policies and shadow prices in developing countries. It is often argued, for example, that if market wages are kept above the marginal product of labour elsewhere in the economy, then there will be a bias against employment and techniques of production will be more capital intensive than they 'should' be. The model that we are using embodies fixed prices and rationing and can, therefore, be used to derive an expression for shadow wages in the context just described.

The shadow wage will depend on just how the market for labour (indexed hereafter by ℓ) functions. For a simple but important example we shall think of a model where total labour is fixed and residual labour not employed in the formal sector is absorbed in self employment. We can think of a peasant farm or family firm owned by a single household. We shall index this firm by g and it is to be distinguished from the single private firm of the model as previously defined which we shall think of as being a formal-sector firm employing labour at a wage p_ℓ. We consider the suppliers of labour to be rationed in the amount of work they can sell to the formal sector (i.e., they would like to work more). Under these assumptions, we can regard employment in firm g, the peasant farm (owned by a single household h), as being determined by an endogenous quota $\bar{y}_\ell^g$. The corresponding first-order condition (just as in expression (2.16)) is then

$$0 = v\frac{\partial y^g}{\partial \bar{y}_\ell^g} + b^h\frac{\partial \pi^g}{\partial \bar{y}_\ell^g} \tag{3.15}$$

where π^g is the profit in the gth firm (which goes entirely to the hth household). We can rewrite the right-hand side of expression (3.15) (as in (2.19)) to give

$$v_\ell = MSP_\ell^g - b^h(p_\ell - MP_\ell^g) \tag{3.16}$$

where MP_ℓ^g is the marginal product of labour in firm g ($-\Sigma_{j\neq\ell}p_j(\partial y_j^g/\partial y_\ell^g)$) and MSP_ℓ^g is its marginal social product of ($-\Sigma_{j\neq\ell}v_j(\partial y_j^g/\partial y_\ell^g)$). This is precisely the shadow wage of Little–Mirrlees (1974, pp. 270–1).

The interpretation of expression (3.16) should be intuitively clear. The social cost of employing labour is the social value of what it would otherwise have produced less the marginal social value of the gains in income for household h. One can also consider different types of alternative activity where, for example, those who are not employed in the formal sector do not work but receive unemployment benefit. Then MSP_ℓ^g is replaced by the value of leisure, or reservation wage, adjusted by the welfare weight, and the income change is now the difference between the market wage and the unemployment benefit. The model can be adapted to deal with several interesting examples of unemployment. Migration equilibria can also be captured through extra constraints of the form, say, $v^R(\cdot) = v^U(\cdot)$, where R and U are indices for rural and urban households, respectively.

The last example of a broad macroeconomic issue that we shall discuss here is the shadow discount rate. In order to define this we must make the inter-temporal features of the problem more explicit. Assuming the project does not come along with a gift of foreign exchange ($dF = 0$) we can think of its social value, S, as $v\,dz$. Indexing now explicitly on time we have

$$S \equiv v\,dz \equiv \sum_\tau v_\tau dz_\tau = \sum_i \sum_\tau v_{i\tau} dz_{i\tau} \tag{3.17}$$

where $dz_{i\tau}$ is the change in public supplies of good i in period τ, dz_τ is the vector $(dz_{i\tau})$, and similarly for $v_{i\tau}$ and v_τ. When we discuss discounting we focus on the shadow price (or marginal social value) of the numeraire commodity in year τ relative to its shadow price in other years. This, of course, requires the specification of a numeraire relative to which social profitability is measured in each year. Formally we may write

$$v_{i\tau} \equiv \bar{v}_{i\tau} a_\tau \tag{3.18}$$

where $\bar{v}_{i\tau}$ is the vector of shadow prices for year τ normalized relative to the numeraire and a_τ is the shadow discount factor. The shadow discount rate, ρ_τ, is then defined as

$$\rho \equiv \frac{a_\tau - a_{\tau+1}}{a_{\tau+1}} \tag{3.19}$$

The process of going through expressions (3.17)–(3.19) is essentially unavoidable in defining the social discount rate since the notion precisely concerns the rate at which the marginal social value of the numeraire is falling over time. If we take commodity i as the numeraire, then the shadow discount rate simply becomes

$$\rho_\tau = \frac{v_{i\tau} - v_{i,\tau+1}}{v_{i,\tau+1}} \tag{3.20}$$

It is clear from equation (3.20) that the choice of numeraire will affect the shadow discount rate unless the relative shadow prices of alternative numeraire commodities are constant over time, i.e., if ρ_τ is the shadow discount rate using i as numeraire and ρ'_τ is the shadow discount rate when j is used as numeraire, then

$$\rho_\tau \equiv \rho'_\tau, \quad \text{if and only if} \quad \frac{v_{i\tau}}{v_{j\tau}} = \frac{v_{i,\tau+1}}{v_{j,\tau+1}} \tag{3.21}$$

We cannot, therefore, answer the question, 'What should be the shadow discount rate?' without being told, or without our choosing, what the numeraire is to be. And the apparent difference between the shadow discount rates proposed in alternative methods of cost–benefit analysis should not mislead us into thinking that the differences are necessarily real – alternative methods may simply involve different units of account.

One particularly easy and transparent choice for the numeraire in each year is foreign exchange. Trading in foreign exchange from one year to the next (i.e., borrowing and lending on world capital markets) can be seen as a form of production activity which we can think of as being undertaken by a public-sector firm. If this firm is maximizing its profits at shadow prices, as it should (see section 4), then its marginal rate of transformation of foreign exchange in the future into foreign exchange now will be given by the relevant interest rates ruling in the world capital markets. The rate of fall of the social value of a unit of foreign exchange is then equal to the interest rate on world capital markets. Therefore, the shadow discount rate will be equal to the rate of interest on world capital markets when foreign exchange in each year is the numeraire. Notice that the numeraire in this example is foreign exchange in the hands of the government. As we saw in our discussion of the marginal social value of transfers and the net social marginal utility of income (see (2.13a) and (2.13b)) the valuation of income in the hands of other agents will differ from that in the hands of the government.

The values of the broad variables we have been examining here may be seen as major determinants of the appropriate level of investment, its allocation across industries, and its intensity in different factors of production. But it would not be correct to see these variables as exogenous so that the chain of causation flows from them to the appropriate level of investment. One should think of the shadow prices and the investment level as being determined simultaneously within the same model. And neither would it be correct to think of just one of these variables, say the shadow discount rate, as determining or being determined by the size of the investment budget. Whether or not a project should be accepted depends on the whole vector of shadow prices and not on one single aspect of them, so that the overall level of investment as determined by this method of project selection depends on all the shadow prices.

4 SHADOW PRICES, MARKET PRICES AND THE PRIVATE SECTOR

Our concern in the previous section was with public revenue and macroeconomic considerations; we now examine the implications of our theory for policy towards the private sector. We shall be particularly concerned with the relationship between public and private production, and with defining the circumstances and sense in which certain market prices may be reliable guides to policy making even in distorted economies. We begin the discussion by examining (in subsection 4.1) the relation between projects and plans; we then look (in sub-section 4.2) at efficiency in the public sector and between public and private sectors; project appraisal for private firms, and for public firms with separate budget constraints, are examined in sub-section 4.3. In sub-section 4.4 we discuss the relation between shadow prices and market prices. Finally, in sub-section 4.5 we ask about price reform and, in particular, examine the question of whether the price of a good in excess demand should be increased.

4.1 Projects and plans

So far, our examination of public production decisions has been confined to small projects defined as changes dz undertaken from an arbitrary initial public production plan. In particular, while we have assumed that (subject to the scarcity constraints) the levels of control variables available to the planner were chosen optimally, we have *not* assumed that the public production plan itself had been optimized. Thus, our theory of shadow prices and policy appraisal does not assume either the optimization of public production or even the knowledge of public production possibilities.

It is clear, therefore, that since the theory we have presented applies to an arbitrary public production plan, it applies in particular to the situation where the initial public production also happens to be a socially optimum one. Of course, the *values* taken by shadow prices are generally different if evaluated at a different public production plan; but the *rules* determining them will not change as long as the controls available to the planner are the same. This point is worth emphasizing, because it has caused confusion in the literature (see Drèze and Stern, 1987 and Dinwiddy and Teal, 1987, for further elaboration).

Moreover, while shadow prices have been defined for an arbitrary public production plan, it is important to realize that they provide crucial signals for the improvement and optimization of public production decisions. This is so not only because, as we have seen, shadow prices allow a straightforward identification of socially desirable projects; in addition, it can be shown that under fairly general conditions a socially optimum public production plan is one that maximizes profits at shadow prices. To see this, let Z represent the set of feasible public production plans. Let also z^* be a socially optimum production plan (formally, a production plan which maximizes $V^*(z;\omega)$ within Z), and v^* the corresponding vector of shadow prices. If, at z^*, some feasible project dz existed with $v^* dz$ greater than 0, then z^* would not be optimum, since $v^* dz$ greater than 0 indicates that dz increases welfare; hence, it must be true that at z^* no feasible project dz shows a profit at shadow prices. If Z is convex, this in turn implies that z^* maximizes shadow profits (in Z) at the shadow prices v^*, since otherwise a small move in the direction of some production plan with greater shadow profits would represent a feasible project. Thus, when public production possibilities are convex, a socially optimum public production plan is one that maximizes shadow profits.

4.2 Public efficiency and private efficiency

Given some initial public production plan, we have a set of shadow prices, v. These shadow prices should be used by all public-sector firms except (i) public-sector firms facing an independent revenue constraint (this is discussed in the next sub-section) and (ii) public-sector firms that generate externalities. All public-sector firms to which these two qualifications do not apply should, moreover, choose a production plan that maximizes shadow profits (if they know their production set and the latter is convex). For those firms taken together, therefore, production should be efficient. This may seem an unremarkable result, but it can have quite strong implications – see, for example, sub-section 4.4.

There is no general reason to suppose that public-sector and private-sector firms taken together should be efficient, although under certain circumstances this may be desirable. For example, we can show that when we make some quite strong assumptions, shadow prices v will be proportional to producer prices p and government and private firms taken together should be efficient (see sub-section 4.4).

4.3 Private firms and budget-constrained public firms

The projects dz we have considered so far have been explicitly in the public sector. The government may also wish to appraise private-sector projects – for example, for the purpose of granting licenses. The essential difference in the model between a public and a private project representing the same change in net supplies lies in who receives the profits; this difference is reflected in the nature of the prices appropriate for appraising public and private projects.

Formally, we can introduce into the model a private firm (indexed by 0) whose production plan, y^0, is regarded as a vector of predetermied variables. A private project, dy^0, then induces a change in welfare, dV, where

$$dV = \frac{\partial L}{\partial y^0} dy^0 = v\,dy^0 + b^0(p\,dy^0) \tag{4.1}$$

where b^0 is the average of the marginal social values of transfers (b^h) for the shareholders of the firm, weighted by their shares in the firm's profits ($b^0 \equiv \Sigma_h \theta^{0h} b^h$, where θ^{0h} is the share of the hth household). Thus

$$dV = (v + b^0 p)dy^0 \tag{4.2}$$

The appropriate price vector for the evaluation of private projects is therefore a straightforward weighted sum of shadow prices for public projects and of market prices, with weights reflecting the marginal social value of private profits. It should be noted that it is possible, or even likely for some firms, that b^0 will be negative; indeed, shareholders are rarely regarded as priority targets for income transfers from the government.

A similar result arises if the firm belongs to the public sector but is subject to a budget constraint of the form

$$py^0 = \bar{\pi}^0 \tag{4.3}$$

for some price vector p. The analysis proceeds much as in the previous problem. The Lagrangian now includes a term $b^0(py^0 - \bar{\pi}^0)$, where b^0 is the Lagrange multiplier on constraint (4.3), and for a project dy^0 we have

$$dV = (v + b^0 p)dy^0 \tag{4.4}$$

The appropriate price vector for evaluating projects in this public firm is then a weighted sum of the shadow price vector and the vector of prices defining the firm's budget constraint – the latter may, of course, be the vector p of market prices. Note, however, that for a feasible project dy^0 preserving (4.3), i.e., a project satisfying $p\,dy^0 = 0$, expression (4.4) reduces to $dV = v\,dy^0$. In other words, an alternative and simpler way of formulating socially desirable production decision rules for budget-constrained public firms is to state that such firms should seek to improve profits at *ordinary* shadow prices *within* the possibilities compatible with their budget constraint. Budget constrained public firms are quite common in practice where public firms have performance criteria related to profit, or are separately organized, and this case is therefore of some importance.

We can use the analysis of this section to examine the issue of 'privatization'. Suppose it is suggested that some production be transferred to the private sector in the sense that the public-sector production plan is modified by dz and a private-sector firm is relied upon to make a compensating adjustment. If the private sector does things differently from the public sector, then the private firm's production change, dy^0, may not be exactly the converse of dz. The social value of the change is then, using expression (4.2)

$$dV = (v + b^0 p)dy^0 - v\,dz \tag{4.5}$$

which may be written

$$dV = v(dy^0 - dz) + b^0 p\,dy^0 \tag{4.6}$$

The social value of the change then consists of an efficiency effect associated with the difference in the production changes, dy^0 and dz, evaluated at *shadow* prices, and a distributional effect associated with the transfer of profits. If the marginal social value of the income of profit receivers is negative, then the second term in expression (4.6) will be negative. This will have to be adjusted if there is a *payment* from the purchasers of the privatized activity since this represents a transfer to the government. If the payment is less than the (discounted) value of the profits stream, then there is a net outflow of public funds which would probably count negatively.

One then has to ask whether this loss of funds is outweighed by any efficiency gain. Leaving aside the empirical evidence on private versus public efficiency (which appears ambiguous), it must be emphasized that the difference in production vectors should be evaluated at shadow prices. There are, moreover, no incentives for private firms to economize on inputs at shadow prices, whereas government firms can, in principle, be directed to do so. The issues included in this analysis do not therefore provide a strong presumption that privatization will yield net social benefits. There are obviously wider and important issues that this analysis omits, including difficulties of information, organization and incentives in public relative to private firms, but they should be set carefully against those we have succeeded in capturing here.

4.4 Market prices and shadow prices

We derived in section 2 a number of rules which should be satisfied by shadow prices, and saw that these rules varied according to which variables could be controlled by the planner. We now focus on the relationship between shadow prices and market prices. Throughout this section it must be borne in mind that we are concerned with relative prices – thus, when we speak (say) of shadow prices and market prices being 'equal', we really mean 'proportional'.

It is fair to say that the conditions that ensure that (relative) shadow prices are equal to (relative) producer prices are, generally, rather restrictive. Perhaps the most important example of a set of conditions that ensures this equality is given by the well-known model of Diamond and Mirrlees (1971), where (i) all goods can be taxed and indirect taxation is fully under the control of the planner; (ii) private production is competitive and production sets are convex; (iii) private profits, if any, are fully taxed; and (iv) no quantity rationing applies to private producers (the only exception being that a quantity signal may determine the production plan of industries with constant returns within their supply correspondence). Roughly speaking when these assumptions are satisfied the private sector is effectively under full government control: by setting the appropriate set of producer prices the government can induce the private firm to produce at any relevant point that it wishes, and this has no direct repercussions on the consumer sector since profits are fully taxed and consumer prices can be manipulated separately. The optimum will therefore be the same as if the private firm were part of the public sector, and the marginal rates of transformation in the private firm will therefore be equal to shadow prices. They are also equal to market prices (since private production is competitive) and therefore shadow prices are equal to market prices.

An alternative set of conditions ensuring the equality of shadow prices and producer prices, which does not involve the restrictive assumption of optimum indirect taxation, consists of the conditions underlying the so-called 'non-substitution theorem': constant returns to scale, a single scarce factor, no joint production, and competition (without rationing) among private producers. See Diamond and Mirrlees (1976) and Drèze and Stern (1987) for further discussion of this result and those of the preceding paragraph.

Apart from restrictive models of the kind involved in these two examples, one would not usually expect to find shadow prices equal to producer prices. But we can still ask whether shadow prices, or a sub-set of them, will coincide with other kinds of market prices. The principal case of this coincidence is where shadow prices for traded goods are equal to world prices. We saw in section 2 that the conditions for this to be true are fairly general, and basically involve the relevant goods being traded without quota, or the quotas being optimally selected.

Where shadow prices are not equal to world prices, we can in many cases see them as a weighted average of marginal social costs of goods drawn from production and from consumption (see sub-section 2.4), with weights reflecting quantities drawn from each side. This will not be the same, however, as a weighted average of consumer and producer prices. One can derive rules along these lines (see Drèze and Stern, 1987), but the weighting procedure is much more complicated and involves averaging (using matrices of demand derivatives) across all markets taken together.

A case where market prices and shadow prices have a strong link, although they do not coincide, is related to the existence of constant-returns-to-scale firms. If there are no quantity constraints on such firms (other than the 'scale factor', determining a firm's production plan within its supply correspondence) and they make zero profits, then one can show that they should also make zero profits at shadow prices. Intuitively, one can understand the result as follows. A small public project using the same input and output proportions as a private firm operating under constant returns could be accommodated in the general equilibrium if the production plan of the private firm were correspondingy displaced. This public project would then have no effect on social welfare since no household welfare level has changed. It should therefore 'break even' at shadow prices. But this project was simply a scaled down version of the activity of the private firm and therefore that firm would also break even at shadow prices. From a formal point of view this result can be derived by examining the first-order conditions for the scale factor of the firm, which may be regarded as a control variable.

The result does not allow us to say that producer prices are equal to shadow prices since the condition on one firm provides only one linear constraint on the I vector of shadow prices. If it holds for several constant-returns-to-scale firms, then it can narrow down considerably the difference between shadow and producer prices. It must be remembered, however, that the condition is only relevant if the constant-returns firms should be operating at a strictly positive scale at the optimum level of the controls. We would not expect to find producer prices equal to shadow prices unless the conditions of one of the two examples above are met.

When there is a binding quota on the output of a firm, the question naturally arises whether the corresponding good should be devalued in the shadow price system relative to the producer price system. From expression (2.19) one can show (abstracting from distributional considerations) that the accounting ratio, v_i/p_i, of a good i in excess supply is lower than a weighted average of the accounting ratios of its inputs by a fraction measuring the discrepancy between price and marginal cost (see (4.7)). Hence, the intuitive presumption that a good in excess supply is overvalued in the producer price system does have some content. A discussion of how prices should be reformed in this context is provided in the next sub-section.

We have seen, therefore, that while it is not usually true that shadow prices coincide with market prices in a distorted economy, quite a lot can be said about how they might diverge.

4.5 Price reform

Should we lower the price of a good in excess supply and increase the price of a good in excess demand? The average economist's first reaction would be 'yes', but it would or should also be acknowledged that a whole range of factors may invalidate this recommendation. The basic principles of policy analysis in distorted economies can point us to what might go wrong and direct any empirical enquiry that is necessary to check whether the economist's initial response is reliable. We provide in this sub-section an analysis which both gives an example of how the approach can guide applied analysis and judgement, and yields some results on the important problem of the reform of controlled economies. As with privatization we focus on those aspects of rationing and price reform which can be illuminated by the theory. There is no discussion here, for example, of attempts to influence rations – we do not discuss rent seeking.

We begin with the case of excess supply and rationed producers and then look at excess demand and rationed consumers. We consider the producer price of good i, p_i, to be an exogenous parameter, which is currently fixed at a level which is 'too high' in the sense that the consumers (who are not rationed for this good) demand less at the price they face, q_i, than the firm would like to supply at the price p_i. This is captured by the existence of a binding constraint $\bar{y}_i$, applying to the firm's production of good i. The variable $\bar{y}_i$ acts as the equilibrating variable on the ith market.

Since $\bar{y}_i$ is an endogenous variable we have equation (2.19). To reiterate the latter

$$v_i = MSC_i - b(p_i - MC_i) \tag{2.19}$$

where MSC_i is the value at shadow prices of the marginal inputs required to produce an extra unit of the ith good (see (2.18b)). If b is small enough, i.e., profit taxes are not too far from optimum, then given $p_i > MC_i$, we may write

$$\frac{v_i}{p_i} \simeq \sum_{j \neq i} \left[a_j \frac{v_j}{p_j} \right] \left(\frac{MC_i}{p_i} \right) < \sum_{j \neq i} a_j \frac{v_j}{p_j} \tag{4.7}$$

where a_j is the share of the jth input in the marginal cost (the a_j sum to one for $j \neq i$). Equation (4.7) says that, under the given assumption, the accounting ratio, v_i/p_i, for the ith good is less than a weighted average of the accounting ratios of the inputs, the weights being given by the respective shares in marginal cost. In this sense the good in excess supply is devalued in the shadow price system relative to the market price system.

We want now to look at the marginal social value of lowering the market (producer) price, p_i, of a good which is in excess supply. The 'standard reaction' is justified if $\partial V^*/\partial p_i < 0$. From (2.11) we have

$$\frac{\partial V^*}{\partial p_i} = \frac{\partial L}{\partial p_i} \tag{2.11'}$$

which gives us, using (2.13) and (2.17)

$$\frac{\partial V^*}{\partial p_i} = -\sum_h \beta^h x_i^h - v \left(\frac{\partial x}{\partial q_i} - \frac{\partial y}{\partial p_i} \right) + by_i \tag{4.8}$$

If we decompose $\partial x_j/\partial q_i$ into income and substitution effects we have

$$\frac{\partial V^*}{\partial p_i} = v \left(\frac{\partial y}{\partial p_i} - \frac{\partial \hat{x}}{\partial q_i} \right) - d_i \tag{4.9}$$

where $\partial \hat{x}/\partial q_i$ is the vector of aggregate substitution effects, s_{ij}, and d_i is a 'net distributional characteristic', defined by $d_i \equiv \Sigma_h b^h x_i^h - by_i$. The latter captures the pure income effects associated with an increase in the ith price. If, as we are assuming, the ith output is rationed, then $\partial y/\partial p_i$ is zero and $\partial V^*/\partial p_i$ is given by

$$\frac{\partial V^*}{\partial p_i} = -\left(v\frac{\partial \hat{x}}{\partial q_i} + d_i\right) \tag{4.9a}$$

The sign of d_i depends on how far the consumers and shareholders are seen as transfer deserving. More precisely, d_i will be more likely to be positive the poorer are the consumers and the more they spend their income on goods with low shadow prices (and conversely with shareholders). If we use the index $h = 0$ for the government, with $b^0 \equiv 0$ (since a transfer from the government to the government naturally has zero marginal social value) we can also write d_i as

$$d_i \equiv H\,\mathrm{cov}(b^h, e_i^h)$$

where, using the earlier notation $\zeta \equiv 1 - \Sigma_h \theta^h$,

$$e_i^h \equiv x_i^h - \theta^h y_i \quad (h \neq 0)$$

$$e_i^0 \equiv \zeta y_i - z_i$$

and notice that $\sum_{h=0}^{H} e_i^h$ is zero (for each i) from the scarcity constraint. We can think of e_i^h as that part of net excess demand 'arising' from the hth household and then d_i is given by the covariance across households between net excess demand and the marginal social value of income. In particular, if no strong correlation between these two is expected, the distributional characteristic can be ignored.

It remains to examine the sign of $v(\partial \hat{x}/\partial q_i)$. We have, from the homogeneity of the compensated derivatives

$$-v\frac{\partial \hat{x}}{\partial q_i} = (q - v)\frac{\partial \hat{x}}{\partial q_i} \tag{4.10}$$

$$= (s_{ii}q_i)\left[\left(\frac{q_i - v_i}{q_i}\right) - \sum_{j \neq i}\gamma_j\left(\frac{q_j - v_j}{q_j}\right)\right] \tag{4.11}$$

where $s_{ii} < 0$ and

$$\gamma_j = -\frac{s_{ij}q_j}{s_{ii}q_i} \tag{4.12}$$

(from the homogeneity of the compensated derivatives $\sum_{j \neq i}\gamma_j = 1$). Thus, when d_i is 'small', we can say that the price p_i should be lowered ($\partial V^*/\partial p_i < 0$), i.e., the standard reaction is correct if

$$\left[\frac{q_i - v_i}{q_i}\right] > \sum_{j \neq i}\gamma_j\left[\frac{q_j - v_j}{q_j}\right] \tag{4.13}$$

This can be usefully compared with (4.7) which already tells us that

$$\left(\frac{p_i - v_i}{p_i}\right) > \sum_{j \neq i}a_j\left[\frac{p_j - v_j}{p_j}\right] \tag{4.14}$$

The basic economic issues embodied in our question, 'Should we raise the price of a good in excess supply?', are now embodied in (4.9)–(4.14). We have already indicated the determinants of the sign of the distributional term in (4.9a), $-d_i$. We may call $(q - v)(\partial \hat{x}/\partial q_i)$ the allocative term in $\partial V^*/\partial p_i$ (but see below). The own-price effect, $\partial \hat{x}_i/\partial q_i$, will be negative and we think intuitively of the shadow price v_i of the good being 'low' since it is in excess supply. This leads us to suppose that $(q - v)(\partial \hat{x}/\partial q_i)$ will indeed be negative provided the own-price term is now swamped by cross-price effects. Condition (4.14) tells us that the shadow producer tax rate on good i is greater than a weighted average of the shadow producer tax rates applying to the inputs. In order for the allocative term to be negative we need the shadow *consumer* tax rate on good i to be greater than a weighted average of the consumer tax rates applying to the other goods (see (4.13)). The former condition being true militates in favour of the latter being true as well. For example, if there are only two goods, so that a_j and γ_j are both 1, and taxes are proportional (q_j is proportional to p_j), then (4.14) implies (4.13).

The formal analysis of this section lends some support to the simple idea that we should lower the price of a good in excess supply but also gives us an understanding of the conditions under which this conclusion might be overturned. It is tempting to regard the distributional considerations as summarized in the term $-d_i$ and the allocative in the term $-v(\partial \hat{x}/\partial q_i)$. If, for example, the producers (shareholders) of good i are regarded as deserving, then this would weaken (through $-d_i$) the case for lowering the price. The distributional aspect, however, is not captured solely in $-d_i$ since from (2.19) we see that the valuation, b, of marginal transfers to the firm enters v_i, and thus $\partial V^*/\partial p_i$. On substituting from (2.19) into (4.8) and examining the coefficient on b, one can immediately see (using $\partial y/\partial p_i = 0$) that the coefficient on b in the resulting expression for $\partial V^*/\partial p_i$ is $(p_i - MC_i)\partial x_i/\partial q_i + y_i$. If we assume all extra supplies came from domestic production, then this is simply the effect of the price increase on the firm's profits (note that the demand response comes in here precisely because the producer cannot choose the output level). Hence, if we were to regard producers as more deserving (higher b) then this would militate in favour of a price increase (i.e., would increase $\partial V^*/\partial p_i$) provided that the elasticity of demand is not so high that profits are thereby reduced. If the good is predominantly consumed by households with low welfare weights, β^h, e.g., the rich, then we can see from (4.8) or (4.9) that this works to increase $\partial V^*/\partial p_i$ and is a factor against the standard reaction (which involves $\partial V^*/\partial p_i < 0$). From the allocative viewpoint, we may wish to raise the price if this would lead consumers to substitute towards goods with low shadow prices.

Faced with a practical question the formal analysis tells us where to look to check whether the presumption that the price should be lowered is sound, i.e., at the incomes of producers and consumers and at the substitution behaviour of the consumers. For example, if cotton weavers are poor, consumers of cotton cloth are rich, and the shadow price of polyester (cotton substitute) is low, then there might be an argument for raising the price of cotton cloth even though it is in excess supply, provided demand is not thereby so reduced that the net incomes of cotton weavers fall. The example, however, points in two important directions. First, it is not very easy to find plausible counterexamples to the standard presumption, and second the problems generating the counterexamples can sometimes be solved in other ways. Thus, one could try to support the incomes of cotton weavers by retraining them to other jobs. And one could shift consumption towards goods with low shadow prices by changing the prices of those goods themselves rather than of substitutes. Of course if these steps are actually taken, this will be reflected in the value of $\partial V^*/\partial p_i$ itself.

A similar kind of analysis can be used to examine the question of whether the price of a good in excess demand should be raised. In this case we can think of suppliers being unrationed and producing and selling as much as they wish at a controlled price p_i, but consumers, buying at q_i, are rationed. We have (4.8) and (4.9) as before but now $\partial \hat{x}/\partial q_i$ is zero. The standard answer that the price should be raised is supported if $\partial V^*/\partial p_i$ is *positive*. The relevant contributions are d_i and $v(\partial y/\partial p_i)$. We have indicated previously the determinants of d_i; this is more likely to be positive the less 'deserving' the producers and the more 'deserving' the consumers.

The sign of $v(\partial y/\partial p_i)$, which can also be written as $(v - p)(\partial y/\partial p_i)$, is more likely to be positive the more producers switch towards goods with a high shadow price. The effect through the ith good would point in this direction since $\partial y_i/\partial p_i$ is positive (the basic 'law' of supply) and one would expect the shadow price of the good in excess demand to be high. In an analogous manner to the previous analysis we can discuss whether $v(\partial y/\partial p_i)$ will, in fact, be positive by examining the condition for the optimum (i.e., endogenous) consumer rations. The rations are adjusted to clear the market given the supply. If the ration which clears the market operates on a single consumer (i.e., $\bar{x}_i^h$ adjusts) then the first-order condition is

$$0 = \beta^h(\rho_i^h - q_i) - v_i - \sum_{j \neq i} v_j \left(\frac{\partial x_j^h}{\partial \bar{x}_i^h} \right) \tag{4.15}$$

where ρ_i^h is the marginal willingness to pay for good i

$$\rho_i^h \equiv \frac{\partial u^h}{\partial \bar{x}_i^h} \bigg/ \frac{\partial v^h}{\partial m^h}$$

We are supposing that the good is rationed to the hth household so that $\rho_i^h > q_i$ and we therefore have (using (4.15))

$$\frac{v_i}{q_i} > \sum_{j \neq i} \frac{v_j}{q_j} \hat{a}_j \tag{4.16}$$

where $\hat{a}_j$ is $[-(q_j/q_i)(\partial x_j^h/\partial \bar{x}_i^h)]$ so that $\sum_{j \neq i} a_j = 1$. Expression (4.16) is the counterpart, in the analysis of consumer rationing, of (4.7) (or, equivalently,

(4.14) in the earlier analysis of production rationing). Analogously to (4.10)–(4.13) we have

$$v\frac{\partial y}{\partial p_i} = p_i \frac{\partial y_i}{\partial p_i}\left(\frac{v_i}{p_i} - \sum_{j\neq i}\hat{\gamma}_j\frac{v_j}{p_j}\right) \qquad (4.17)$$

where

$$\hat{\gamma}_j = \frac{-p_j\partial y_j/\partial p_i}{p_i\partial y_i/\partial p_i} \quad \text{and} \quad \sum_{j\neq i}\hat{\gamma}_j = 1 \qquad (4.18)$$

from profit maximization.

The analysis of (4.17) proceeds (using (4.16)) in a similar manner to that of (4.11). A valid general presumption exists to the effect that raising the price of a good in excess demand is beneficial. One can establish this result for the one-consumer economy where taxes are proportional. But there are exceptions as well. Exceptions may arise where the good is primarily consumed by those who are particularly 'deserving' or produced by the 'less deserving' and the price increase leads to a greater use of inputs which have high shadow prices. Again, these exceptions may be fairly rare in practice, and arise in circumstances where the problems generating them might be tackled in other ways. Nonetheless, the possibility that the standard rule is a mistake is a real one and should be checked.

We have analysed here the validity of the simple reform of adjusting the producer price with a constant tax rate so that the consumer price is also raised. It is also natural to think of other possible reforms such as adjusting the producer price but holding the consumer price constant. In the case of lowering the price of a good in excess supply this amounts to increasing the tax by the same amount that the producer price is lowered. Hence, the change in welfare is $-\partial V^*/\partial p_i + \partial V^*/\partial t_i$. One can consider a variety of possibilities of producer price and tax changes as well as changes in the rationing rules.

5 SUMMARY AND CONCLUDING COMMENTS

Our purpose has been to examine the theory of public policy in an economy with distortions. We have seen that the use of shadow prices, defined as social opportunity costs, can provide both a unifying theme for that theory and a simplification of results, in the sense that they summarize rather complicated general equilibrium effects. The social opportunity cost of a good is the net loss (gain) in social welfare associated with increasing its use (reducing its production) in the public sector. The rules satisfied by shadow prices are derived from the maximization of social welfare with respect to the policy tools under the control of the planner or decision maker, and subject to all the constraints restricting the choices involved including in particular the scarcity constraints. The choice involved in this optimization may or may not be broad depending on how many control variables there are relative to the number of constraints; at one extreme, there may be no real choice at all if the constraints are so restrictive that only one feasible option is really available to the planner. Whatever the degree of freedom involved, shadow prices and optimum policies are determined together by the scarcity constraints and by the conditions for optimum policies. Thus, shadow prices and the theory of policy are part and parcel of the same problem and theory.

We saw in section 2 that shadow price rules can be very different depending on which are the controls at the planner's disposal; to put it another way, shadow prices can be very sensitive to the way in which the economy responds to a change in public production. This is hardly surprising but it is, nevertheless, a crucial point to bear in mind. On the other hand, the rules for shadow prices do *not* depend on whether or not public production is itself optimized. The *values* taken by shadow prices do, of course, depend on the public production levels at which they are evaluated; but the *rules* (or formulae) involved in the computation remain the same.

A marginal policy reform may be assessed by calculating the direct effect on households of the policy change and subtracting the cost at shadow prices of meeting the extra demands generated. Moreover, and this is very important, we have seen (in sub-section 3.2) that for any policy change the social value of excess demands generated is precisely equal to the implied loss of 'shadow revenue' to the government. Roughly speaking, shadow revenue is to nominal revenue what shadow prices are to market prices. This important concept brings the notion of government revenue firmly within the general theory, and provides a theoretical underpinning to fashionable but often poorly understood analytical tools, such as that of 'cost effectiveness', which gives government revenue a central role.

Among the rules derived in section 2, those concerning the use of world prices for traded goods and the marginal social costs of production for non-traded goods were of particular importance. The first of these is very robust and general, and would apply in any model where an increase in the public production (use) of a traded commodity results in an equivalent reduction of net imports (exports), and where the general equilibrium effects operate entirely through the balance of payments. This is generally true if there are no quotas on the commodity itself and world prices are fixed. The second rule is much less general, and will usually depend on the assumption that an extra unit of the relevant commodity comes exclusively from extra production. If this is not true, then we have to look at the social opportunity costs applying to different sources, and only exceptionally (with extensive optimization of taxes and production) will the shadow values associated with the different sources be the same.

The generalizations of the rules for optimum taxation were also of importance to an understanding of appropriate tax policy. Many of the standard rules for optimum taxes in economies where shadow prices are equal to producer prices can be straightforwardly extended to a distorted economy provided actual taxes are replaced by the difference between consumer prices and *shadow prices* (rather than producer prices). This suggests that we use the tax system to compensate for differences between market prices and shadow prices generated by distortions elsewhere in the system. Thus, *ceteris paribus*, we should have a lower tax on non-traded labour-intensive goods if the shadow price of the relevant type of labour is judged to be particularly low relative to its market price.[6]

The ideas and theory developed in section 2 and in the first part of section 3 were applied in the second half of the paper to show, first, how important shadow prices should be calculated. We were able to give precise meaning to the notion of a premium on saving and to show how the standard treatment of shadow wages in a one-good model could survive transplantation to a more general framework. The idea of a premium on government revenue as such played no separate role but the relative weights on incremental incomes to different households or groups, including the government, were an integral part of the whole analysis.

In section 4 we showed how the approach could be used to structure the analysis of important applied problems. Two critical issues in the appraisal of privatization fit neatly into the framework. Privatization involves a transfer of profits from the public to the private sector and also typically involves changes in production techniques and levels. The first aspect is evaluated as any other income transfer taking into account the welfare weights for recipient groups and the marginal propensity to spend on goods with high or low shadow prices. The second is evaluated by calculating the value at shadow prices of the production change.

Our final application was concerned with the question of whether the price of a good in excess demand should be raised (or that of a good in excess supply lowered). We saw that the answer depended on the distributional pattern of consumption and production and whether net demand was switched to or from goods with high shadow prices. If producers of a good are poor and consumers rich, then the distributional consequences of increasing the price of a good in excess demand would be favourable. There is some validity in the general presumption that the shadow price of a good in excess demand is 'high' (relative to its consumer price) so that the effect of raising its price to producers is to switch production towards a good with a high shadow price. One has reason, therefore, to suppose that the policy of raising the price would be justified. Analysis has, however, warned us to check the distributional effects and whether the inputs involved in increasing production might be at an even higher premium in the shadow price system than the rationed good itself.

In distorted economies it is possible to provide counterexamples to most propositions concerning shadow prices. This does not, however, mean that nothing can be said, that anything goes, and that there are no rules. We have tried to show in this paper how structured argument can define social values, provide rules for their calculation, and integrate cost–benefit analysis and the theory of policy. Shadow prices should not therefore be seen narrowly as tedious tools of the lowly project appraiser. They are part of an approach to policy analysis which is founded on the notion of opportunity cost and which allows analytic and practical discussion of a whole range of policy questions.

NOTES

This paper was partly written during a visit by Stern to the Fiscal Affairs Department (FAD) of the International Monetary Fund in July and August 1987. He is grateful to FAD and its Director, Vito Tanzi, for the invitation and hospitality. Support from the Suntory–Toyota International Centre for Economics and Related Disciplines and from the ESRC Programme on Taxation, Incentives and the Distribution of Income is gratefully acknowledged. We have been strongly influenced by the work of Roger Guesnerie on second-best theory. For helpful discussion and comments, we would also like to thank Tony Atkinson, Lans Bovenberg, Angus Deaton, Peter Diamond, Peter Heller, Mervyn King, Partho Shome, Richard Stern, Alan Tait, Vito Tanzi and two referees. The paper draws on our 1987 survey (Drèze and Stern, 1987), which is more technical and may be consulted by the reader who wishes to pursue the subject in greater depth.

1 Household welfare depends on individual consumption and not on aggregate supplies as such, and the link between consumption and supplies will be provided by the scarcity constraints of the model. Public goods and, more generally, externalities can be included in the model in a straightforward way although they will not be a central concern in what follows.
2 Strictly speaking, if a project makes exactly zero profit at shadow prices, one should examine second-order terms to see whether it is socially desirable or not. If $v\,dz$ is zero, then the change in welfare to second-order is $dz'A\,dz$, where A is the matrix of second derivatives of V^* with respect to z.
3 See, for example, Hammond (1983) for a discussion of the problems raised by the analysis of large projects.
4 Notice that the project will generally imply some changes in policy instruments and it is clear, and illustrated in what follows, that the form of adjustment will be critical to the welfare implications of the project. However, some projects may be directly linked to changes to parameters in the vector ω. For example, a foreign donor might link support for a project to a change in a quota. In this case we should appraise the project by considering the welfare effects of $(dz, d\omega)$. This would be given by $v\,dz + (\partial V^*/\partial\omega)\,d\omega$. We discuss $(\partial V^*/\partial\omega)$ in the next sub-section; see, in particular, equations (2.11) and (2.12).
5 Notice that there are, generally speaking, many equivalent ways of expressing a set of constraints in an optimization problem. In this context, rewriting the constraints in an equivalent manner would change the Lagrange multipliers but not the shadow prices. Thus, it is important to recognize that our definition of shadow prices comes first, and we have shown that they happen to be equal to Lagrange multipliers *if* the constraints on the problem are written in an appropriate way.
6 It does *not* mean that the correct tax is simply the difference between market and shadow price.

REFERENCES

Dasgupta, P., S. Marglin and A.K. Sen (1972), *Guidelines for Project Evaluation*, UNIDO, New York.

Diamond, P.A. (1975), 'A many-person Ramsey tax rule', *Journal of Public Economics*, 4: 335–42.

Diamond, P.A. and J.A. Mirrlees (1971), 'Optimal taxation and public production I: Production efficiency and II: Tax rules', *American Economic Review*, 61: 8–27 and 261–78.

   (1976), 'Private constant returns and public shadow prices', *Review of Economic Studies*, 43: 41–7.

Dinwiddy, C. and F. Teal (1987), 'Shadow prices for non-traded goods in a tax-distorted economy: Formulae and values', *Journal of Public Economics*, 33(2).

Drèze, J.P. and N.H. Stern (1987), 'The theory of cost–benefit analysis', in A.J. Auerbach and M.S. Feldstein (eds.), *Handbook of Public Economics*, vol. II, Amsterdam, North-Holland, ch. 8.

Guesnerie, R. (1979), 'General statements on second-best Pareto optimality', *Journal of Mathematical Economics*, 6: 169–94.

   (1980), 'Second-best pricing rules in the Boiteux tradition', *Journal of Public Economics*, 13: 51–80.

Hammond, P.J. (1983), 'Approximate measures of the social welfare benefits of large projects', Technical report no. 410, Institute for Mathematical Studies in the Social Sciences, Stanford University, California.

Little, I.M.D. and J.A. Mirrlees (1974), *Project Appraisal and Planning for Developing Countries*, London, Heinemann.

Roberts, K.W.S. (1980), 'Price independent welfare prescriptions', *Journal of Public Economics*, 13: 277–97.

Stern, N.H. (1984), 'Optimum taxation and tax policy', *IMF Staff Papers*, 31(2): 339–78.

   (1987), 'Uniformity versus selectivity in tax structure: Lessons from theory and policy', presented at the World Bank Conference on Political Economy: Theory and Policy Implications, June 1987, and circulated as Development economics research programme discussion paper no. 9, STICERD, LSE, July. Forthcoming in *Economics and Politics*.

2

SHADOW PRICES AND MARKETS:

Feasibility constraints: foreign exchange and shadow wages

A.K. Sen

A prerequisite of a theory of planning is an identification of the nature of the State and of the government. The planner, to whom much of planning theory is addressed, is part of a political machinery and is constrained by a complex structure within which he has to operate. Successful planning requires an understanding of the constraints that in fact hold and clarity about precise areas on which the planners in question can exercise effective control. The limits of a planner's effective control depend on his position *vis-à-vis* the rest of the government as well as on the nature of the political, social and economic forces operating in the economy. This paper is concerned with an analysis of some aspects of these inter-relationships in the specific context of project appraisal and benefit–cost evaluation.

In section 1, the problem is posed. In section 2, the OECD *Manual of Industrial Project Analysis*, prepared by Professors Little and Mirrlees (1969), is critically examined in the light of the approach outlined in section 1. In section 3, the approach is illustrated in the specific context of fixing a shadow price of labour in benefit–cost analysis.

1 SPHERES OF INFLUENCE AND CONTROL VARIABLES

For any planning agent the act of planning may be viewed as an exercise in maximizing an objective function subject to certain constraints. In the absence of non-convexities it is relatively easy to translate the problem into a framework of shadow prices. Corresponding to the maximizing 'primal' problem one could define a 'dual' problem involving the minimization of a function where there will be one shadow price (acting as a value-weight) corresponding to each constraint in the original problem. All this is straightforward and mechanical and there is not really very much to argue about. The interesting questions arise with the *selection* of the objective function and the constraints.

If $W(x)$ is the objective to be maximized through the selection of choice

This chapter previously appeared in *The Economic Journal*, 82(1972): 486–501. We would like to thank Basil Blackwell Publishers for their kind permission to reproduce it here.

variables in the form of a vector x subject to a set of m constraints, $F_i(x) \leq R_i$, for $i = 1, \ldots, m$, then the dual related to any particular constraint F_i will correspond to the additional amount of maximized W that would be generated by relaxing the constraint by one unit, i.e., by raising R_i by a unit. Thus, the dual p_i corresponding to F_i can be viewed as the marginal impact of R_i on W, the objective, and if R_i is the amount of a given resource then p_i is the marginal contribution of R_i to W (not necessarily corresponding to the marginal product in terms of market evaluation). It may be convenient to view p_i as the shadow price of resource i. Since the value of p_i is essentially dependent on the objective function $E(x)$ and on the other constraints, the shadow price of any resource clearly depends on the values of the planner reflected in the objective function W and on his reading of the economic and other constraints that bind his planning decisions.

Consider now a project evaluator. What does he assume about other agents involved in the operation of the economy, e.g., the private sector (if any), the households and the other government agencies? Presumably, in so far as he can influence the private sector and households directly or indirectly he builds that fact into his description of the exercise, but except for this the operation of the private sector and households will constrain his exercise. He may express this either in the form of specific constraints or in the form of implicit relations embodied in other constraints or even in the objective function. The actual form may not be very important but the inclusion of these elements is, of course, a crucial aspect of realistic planning. In principle, the position outlined above may be fairly widely accepted, though I would argue later that the implications of this position are frequently overlooked.

What about the relation between the project evaluator and other planning agents and how does his role fit in with the rest of the government apparatus? This question has several facets, one of which is the problem of coordination, teamwork, decentralization and related issues. This basket of problems has been discussed quite a bit in the literature and will not be pursued here.[1] Another facet is the problem of conflict between the interests of the different government agencies. This is particularly important for a federal country since the relation between the state governments and the centre may be extremely complex. But even between different agencies of the central government there could be considerable conflict of interests, e.g., between the road authorities and the nationalized railways, to take a narrow example, or between the department of revenue and the public enterprises, to take a broader one. Whenever such conflicts are present a question arises about the appropriate assumption regarding other agencies of the government in the formulation of the planning exercise by any particular agency.

A third facet is the question of the impact not of government policy on the private business sector but of the private business sector on government policy. The control variables are affected by such influences but they are often not affected in a uniform way. For example, a public-sector project evaluator may think that certain taxes cannot be imposed because of political opposition, but somewhat similar results could be achieved through variations in the pricing and production policy of the public sector.

In a very broad sense, taxes, tariffs, quotas, licences, prices and outputs of the public sector are all control variables for the government as a whole. But they are each constrained within certain ranges by administrative, political and social considerations. For a project evaluator, therefore, it is important to know which variables are within his control and to what extent, and in this respect a feeling of oneness with the totality of the government may not be very useful. This aspect of the problem has been frequently lost sight of because of the concentration in the planning models on a mythical hero called 'the Planner', and unitarianism is indeed a dominant faith in the theory of economic planning.

2 THE USE OF WORLD PRICES

A distinguishing feature of the Little–Mirrlees *Manual* (henceforth, LMM) is its advocacy of the use of world prices in the evaluation of commodities. For 'traded' goods produced in the economy the evaluation is at the import price (c.i.f.) or the export price (f.o.b.) depending on whether it would potentially replace imports or be available for exports; and a traded good used up is valued at the import price if its source (direct or indirect) is imports and at the export price if it comes from cutting out potential exports. When opportunities of trade are present these values reflect the opportunity costs and benefits. The non-traded goods are also related to trade indirectly since they may be domestically produced by traded goods, and the non-tradables involved in their production can be traced further back to tradables. 'Following the chain of production around one must end at commodities that are exported or substituted for imports.'[2]

This is not the place to discuss or evaluate the nuances of the LMM. Problems such as imperfections of international markets are taken into account by replacing import and export prices by corresponding marginal cost and marginal revenue considerations. Externalities are somewhat soft-pedalled partly on the grounds that there is 'little chance, anyway, of measuring many of these supposed external economies',[3] and also because a discussion of the main types of externalities generally emphasized makes the authors 'feel that differences in those external effects, which are not in any case allowed for in our type of cost–benefit analysis, will seldom make a significant difference'.[4] These and other considerations may be important in practical decisions but I do not want to discuss them here. These problems are essentially factual in nature and can only be resolved by detailed empirical work.

The crucial question lies in deciding on what is to be regarded as a 'traded' good. The LMM proposes two criteria, *viz.* '(a) goods which are actually imported or exported (or very close substitutes are actually imported or exported)', and '(b) goods which would be exported or imported if the country had followed policies which resulted in an optimum industrial development'.[5] It is the second category that relates closely to the question we raised in section 1 of this paper.

Suppose it appears that project *A* would be a worthwhile investment if a certain raw material *R* needed for it were to be imported but not if *R* were to be manufactured domestically (assuming that *R* is not economically produced in the economy). 'Optimal industrial development' requires that *R* be not manufactured in the economy but be imported. Suppose the project evaluator examining project *A* finds that the country's trade policies are not 'sensible', and *R* would in fact be manufactured, no matter what he does. It does not seem right, in these circumstances, to recommend that project *A* be undertaken on the grounds that 'if the countries had followed policies which resulted in an optimal industrial development' then *R* would not in fact have been domestically produced; the question is whether or not *R* will be domestically produced *in fact*.

The question at issue here is the theory of government underlying the planning model of the LMM. Little and Mirrlees explain their approach thus:

Sometimes, our guess about whether a commodity will be imported or not may be almost a value judgement: we think that a sensible government would plan to import some, so we assume that it will do so. Of course, if one of our assumptions required government action in order to be fulfilled, this should be drawn to the attention of the appropriate authorities.[6]

The judgement would readily become a fact if the appropriate authorities would do the 'sensible' thing whenever their attention is drawn to such action. There is no logical problem in this approach; the only question is: *Is this a good theory of government action?*

One could doubt that this is a good theory on one of many grounds.[7] Some people may doubt whether governments typically do think sensibly. Often enough, evidence of sensible thinking, if present, would appear to be very well concealed. But more importantly, something more than 'sensible thinking' is involved in all this, and it is necessary to examine the pressures that operate on the government. There would certainly be some interest groups involved, e.g., those who would like to produce good *R* under the protection of a quota, or an enhanced tariff, or some other restriction. By choosing project *A* and thus creating a domestic demand for *R* (or by augmenting the demand that existed earlier) one is opening up this whole range of issues involving protection and domestic production. If the project evaluator thinks that the pressures for domestic production of good *R* will be successfully crushed by the government agencies responsible for policies on tariff, quota, etc., it will certainly be fair to choose project *A*. But what if the project evaluator thinks that it is very likely that if project *A* is chosen then there will be irresistible pressure for domestic production of good R inside the economy? Similarly, what should the project evaluator do if he finds that there already exists a quota restriction on the import of good R so that the additional demand for R will be met by domestic production unless the trade policies are changed, and he does not believe that they will change because of political pressures in favour of the continuation of these policies? It is not a question of *knowing* what is the 'sensible' policy in related fields but of being able to *ensure* that these policies will in fact be chosen. This would depend on one's reading of the nature of the state and of the government and on one's analysis of the influences that affect government action. And on this should depend the appropriate set of accounting prices for cost–benefit analysis.

It is possible to argue that if one uniform assumption has to be made about the actions to be undertaken by other government agencies, then the LMM assumption is as good as any. It may well be better to assume that the actions taken by the other agencies will be all 'sensible' in the sense defined rather than be 'distorted' in a uniform way in all spheres of decision taking. But there is, in fact, no very compelling reason for confining oneself artificially to assumptions of such heroic uniformity. The correct assumption may vary from country to country and from case to case, and may also alter over time, since the projects sometimes have a long life and the political and social influences on the tax and trade policies may change during the lifetime of the project. What the LMM approach seems to me to do is to assume implicitly that either the project evaluator is very *powerful* so that he can ensure that the rest of the government machinery will accept his decisions in other fields as well (and the political acceptance of 'sensible' tax, tariff and quota policies is ensured), or that he is very *stupid* so that he cannot be trusted to make a realistic appraisal of the likely policies and would be better advised to assume a role of uniform simplicity.

3 COST OF LABOUR IN PROJECT ANALYSIS

This section will be concerned with the valuation of labour cost and will be divided into six sub-sections. In 3.1 a general expression for the social cost of labour will be suggested, and in 3.2 some of the other formulae will be compared and contrasted with the one proposed here. In the subsequent sub-sections the problem of evaluation of specific value weights will be discussed in the line of the general questions raised earlier in the paper.

3.1 Social cost of labour: an expression

Let w be the wage rate of the kind of labour with which we are concerned and let these labourers be drawn from a peasant economy. The reduction of output in the peasant economy as a consequence of someone being withdrawn from there is m, and the value of income which the person thus drawn away would have received had he stayed on in the rural area may be y. If there is surplus labour, we have $m = 0$, but y is, of course, positive. Even when m is positive and there is no surplus labour, it will often be the case that $y > m$ since the marginal product of a labourer may be considerably less than the average income per person. When the peasant in question moves away as a labourer in the urban area, his income goes up from y to w, and those remaining behind experience an increase in income equal to $(y - m)$. However, as a consequence of the departure of one member of the family those remaining behind may also work harder, and the value of more sweat is a relevant constituent of the social cost of labour. Let z^1 and z^2 be the increase in work effort respectively for the peasant family and for the person who moves to the project in question.[8]

A part of the respective increases in income may be saved, and we may assume that the proportions saved out of the marginal earnings of the peasant family and of the migrant worker are respectively s^1 and s^2. The proportion of project profits that are saved[9] may be denoted s^3. The marginal impact on project profits of the employment of one more man is given by $(q - w)$, where q is the relevant marginal product. Thus the total impact on the different groups can be summarized as follows:

Category	1 Increase in income	2 Increase in savings	3 Increase in efforts
1 Peasant family	$y - m$	$(y - m)s^1$	z^1
2 Labourer migrating	$w - y$	$(w - y)s^2$	z^2
3 Project	$q - w$	$(q - w)s^3$	

Taking v^{ij} to be the relevant marginal weight for the jth item in the ith row in the social welfare function W, we obtain the following expression for the change in social welfare as a consequence of the employment of one more man in the project

$$U = v^{11}(y - m) + v^{12}(y - m)s^1 + v^{13}z^1 + v^{21}(w - y) + v^{22}(w - y)s^2$$
$$+ v^{23}z^2 + v^{31}(q - w) + v^{32}(q - w)s^3 \tag{1}$$

If there is no other restriction on the use of labour, the optimal policy would be to expand the labour force as long as U is positive, and making the usual divisibility assumptions, the optimal position will be characterized by $U = 0$.

U is in one sense the social cost of labour, and indeed the shadow price of labour in this sense must be zero since there is no binding constraint on labour in addition to the relations that have already been fed into the expression of social welfare. However, the shadow price is frequently used in the sense of *that* value of labour which, if equated to the marginal product of labour, will give the optimal allocation of labour.[10] In this sense the shadow price of labour (w^*) is the value of q for $U = 0$. This is readily obtained from (1)

$$w^* = [w\{(v^{31} - v^{21}) + (v^{32}s^3 - v^{22}s^2)\} - y\{(v^{11} - v^{21}) + (v^{12}s^1 - v^{22}s^2)\}$$
$$+ m(v^{11} + v^{12}s^1) - (v^{13}z^1 + v^{23}s^2)]/(v^{31} + v^{32}s^3) \tag{2}$$

3.2 Some other expressions

In the basic model in my *Choice of Techniques* (Sen, 1968), henceforth COT, I made the following assumptions which are here translated into the terminology used in sub-section (3.1) above:

(i) all current consumption is equally valuable, i.e., $v^{11} = v^{21} = v^{31}$;
(ii) all saving is equally valuable and marginally more valuable than consumption, i.e., $v^{12} = v^{22} = v^{32} = \lambda > 0$;[11]
(iii) marginal disutility of efforts are negligible, i.e., $v^{13} = v^{23} = 0$;
(iv) the peasant economy has surplus labour, i.e., $m = 0$;
(v) the savings propensity of the workers and peasants are equal at the margin, and less than that out of project profits, i.e., $s^1 = s^2 < s^3$.

Taking consumption as the numeraire, i.e., putting $v^{11} = 1$, we can obtain from (2)

$$w^* = \frac{w\lambda(s^3 - s^2)}{1 + \lambda s^3} \tag{3.1}$$

Certain distinguished cases may be commented on. First, in the Polak–Buchanan–Kahn–Tinbergen criterion the shadow price of labour is taken to be zero in a surplus labour economy. This follows from taking consumption and savings to be equally valuable at the margin, i.e., $\lambda = 0$.

$$w^* = 0 \tag{3.2}$$

The case associated with the names of Dobb (1960) and Galenson and Leibenstein (1955) corresponds to the assumption that the growth rate should be maximized, which amounts to maximizing the savings rate with no weight on consumption, i.e., taking λ to be infinitely large, and this leads to

$$w^* = \frac{w(s^3 - s^2)}{s^3} \tag{3.3}$$

With the further assumption of no savings out of wages, i.e., $s^2 = 0$, we get

$$w^* = w \tag{3.3*}$$

The case of using taxes in a manner such that the savings propensities of the different classes are equated, as put forward by Bator (1957), will lead to (3.2), as is readily checked by putting $s^3 = s^2$ in (3.1).

The LMM takes a set of assumptions that are equivalent to (i)–(iii) and (v) above, but omits the assumption (iv) of surplus labour, and in addition assumes:

(vi) $s^1 = s^2 = 0$;
(vii) $s^3 = 1$.

This yields from (3.1) the following expression[12]

$$w^* = \frac{w\lambda + m}{1 + \lambda} \tag{3.4}$$

The following aspects of the problem will now be discussed:

(a) the premium on investment, i.e., λ being positive;
(b) the question of distributional weights, reflected in v^{11}, v^{21}, v^{31}, etc.;
(c) the valuation of efforts, i.e., the choice of v^{13} and v^{23}; and
(d) the question of the relation between the intake of labour into the project and the outflow of labour out of the peasant economy.

These are not the only problems that deserve comment, but they do seem to be related closely to the general issues raised in the earlier sections of the paper.

3.3 Premium on investment

The question of whether λ should be positive depends on whether at the margin investment is regarded as more important than consumption. It is assumed to be so in the COT as well as in the LMM. The underlying assumption is one of sub-optimality of savings. The question is why should such an assumption be made?

The tendency for market savings to be below optimal has been argued from various points of view. One reason is the presence of an externality in the form of members of the present generation having some concern for the well-being of the future generations which is, therefore, like a public good in the Samuelsonian sense. Another reason is the presence of a tax system which makes the private after-tax rate of return lower than the social rate of return to investment. In the underdeveloped countries with surplus labour it can also be argued that the private rate of return falls short of the social since wages are a cost for the individual investor whereas the social opportunity cost of labour may be much lower so that the market underestimates the rate of return. There are other possible arguments and Phelps (1970) has provided a critical survey of the literature.

All these, however, amount merely to demonstrating that the level of market-determined savings may be sub-optimal. But this is not a good enough reason for taking λ to be positive, because that would require us to assume that savings are sub-optimal *even after* any possible government policy that could be used to change the rate of saving. If the savings as given by the market are too low, why not raise their level through taxation, subsidies, deficit spending, etc., to make it optimal and then proceed to do the project selection exercise without having to bother about raising the rate of savings through project evaluation itself? This is precisely where the argument relates to the main question with which this paper is concerned. We have to look at the relevant constraints that restrict the planners.

The project evaluator may find the savings rate to be sub-optimal for one of two different reasons. First, his judgements about the relative importance of present consumption *vis-à-vis* future consumption may be different from that of the planners in charge of taxes and other policies that influence the national rate of savings. He may wish to attach a higher weight on savings than that which is reflected in the government policy concerned with macroeconomic planning. Second, the planners in charge of taxes, etc., may themselves regard the savings level to be sub-optimal but be unable to set it right through taxes, etc., because of political constraints on taxation and other instruments.

In putting an extra weight on savings in the determination of the shadow price of labour one is essentially exploring the possibility of raising the savings rate through project selection and the choice of capital-intensity of investment.[13] It raises the question as to whether such a means of savings generation can be utilized when there are constraints that prevent the savings rate from being raised through more taxes. In one case savings are raised by income being taxed away and in the other savings are raised by choosing a lower level of employment in the project design thereby reducing disposable wage income and cutting down consumption. I have tried to discuss elsewhere the mechanism as well as the plausibility of using choice of techniques as a means of raising savings (Sen, 1968, chapter 5), so that I shall not go into the problem further here. I would only point out that the question rests on two propositions, viz. (i) the project evaluator finds the savings rate to be sub-optimal which implies more than finding that the *market-determined* savings rate is sub-optimal since the possibility of government action (through taxes, etc.) is present, and (ii) the project evaluator believes that the political or other constraints that rule out raising savings through taxes would not rule out raising savings indirectly through an employment policy. The whole problem turns on the precise reading of the area of control for the project evaluator.

3.4 Income distributional considerations

Should there be differences in the weights attached to different kinds of income on grounds of distribution? In expressions (1) and (2) this will take the form of v^{11}, v^{21} and v^{31} being not necessarily equal, and similarly v^{12}, v^{22} and v^{32} being different. The simplicity of expressions (3.1)–(3.4) arose partly from neglecting these differences. What could be said in defence of such a procedure?

The most common argument is that income distributional changes are best brought about by taxes and subsidies and other general policy measures and not by affecting project designs. If lump-sum transfers were permitted then the force of this argument is obvious, but in an important paper it has been demonstrated by Diamond and Mirrlees (1971) that even in the absence of the possibility of lump-sum transfers social welfare maximization requires that production efficiency be preserved, given some assumptions, including constant returns to scale. If the incomes of two factors of production are valued differently in making production decisions it could conceivably violate production efficiency. The rate of substitution between the factors in the production process to be decided on may then be different from that in the rest of the economy, and this will amount to production inefficiency.

Once again the question turns on the possibilities of taxation. While Diamond and Mirrlees (1971) do not necessarily assume the availability of any taxes other than commodity taxes, they do assume that there are no constraints on the quantum of such taxes, e.g., there will be no political difficulty in having a tax rate of, say, 1,000 per cent on some commodity if the optimization exercise requires this. This may or may not be a good assumption, but what is our concern here is to note that the question relates once again to the identification of political and other influences on the operation of the government machinery; and also that the result depends on the ability to tax *all* commodities if necessary. There is a clear link here with the problem discussed in the last section. If wages could be taxed and the rise in income of the peasant family could also be taxed, then the question of using employment policy as a vehicle of savings adjustment will diminish in importance; COT, LMM and other frameworks do imply a certain inability to tax all commodities (including labour). It may in fact turn out that this is not a limiting constraint for the problem of income distribution, but the question will have to be posed in the context of commodity taxes *with* some constraints even in that sphere and not in terms of a model where any tax rate on any commodity is possible.

In addition to this aspect of the problem viewed from the angle of the totality of the planning set-up, there is, of course, also the problem of the project evaluator being constrained by the operation of the tax system on which he may not have more than a small amount of control. *Given* the tax system he might feel the necessity to violate efficiency by introducing income distributional considerations even though he might have preferred to do the adjustment through changing the tax system rather than affecting the project selection. The question relates again to the identification of areas of control.

This problem may also arise in the context of location planning. In many developing countries an important constituent of planning is the regional allocation of investment. To take an illustration from India, in spite of the higher rate of return (in the absence of distributional considerations) from investment in fertilizers to be used on wet land *vis-à-vis* that from investment in irrigation in the dry areas, the appropriateness of the policy of emphasizing fertilizers and ignoring irrigation is open to question on distributional grounds. The problem would disappear if inter-regional transfers could be arranged so that more income might be generated through an appropriate production policy and the distribution were looked after through transfers. But the question of inter-state transfers in a federal country like India has important political limits and the choice of agricultural policy must, therefore, depend on a reading of the areas of control.

Another set of illustrations from India relates directly to the question of social cost of labour for projects. Given the limitations of regional transfers there are considerable social pressures on the location of big industrial projects, and this seems to have been an important consideration in a number of locational decisions. The inoptimality of it has been well discussed by Manne (1967) and others. The question does, however, depend on the constraints that bind. By attaching a higher weight on the income of workers from the backward regions it is possible to alter substantially the benefit–cost balance sheet. But there remains the question of the control that the project evaluator can, in fact, exercise on the actual choice of manpower for projects. It is not uncommon for a project evaluator to decide to locate a project in a backward region on the grounds of income distribution, and then for project managers to recruit labour from outside. When project selection is guided by one set of shadow prices and the performance of the project manager judged by profits in the commercial sense at market prices, this can easily happen. In some of the major industrial projects in India local labour has not really been much absorbed; project managers have seen considerable advantage from the point of view of 'performance' in using labour from areas with earlier industrial experience. However, from the point of view of the project evaluator the ranking may be in descending order: (1) project *A* in the backward region with the use of local labour, (2) project *A* in a non-backward region closer to the traditional sources of supply of industrial labour, and (3) project *A* in the backward region with importation of labour from traditional sources. If the area of control of the project evaluator extends to the location of the project but not to the exact recruitment policy, the use of shadow prices with distributional weights may conceivably make the situation worse from every point of view than ignoring distribution altogether. This complex range of issues is involved in the choice of appropriate weights and much depends on a clear perception of the exact sphere of the project evaluator's influence.

3.5 Valuation of sweat

Neither the COT model nor the LMM model attaches any value to greater effort on the part of the peasant family in cultivation after the departure of the labourer for the project. In the COT model it is assumed that the disutility of labour up to a point is zero, and this feature produces surplus labour in that model.

A similar assumption about no disutility of labour may have been implicitly made by Little and Mirrlees (1969) since the 'plausible simplified utility function' for the labouring community as presented in the *Appendix for Professional Economists* takes individual utility to be a function only of individual income without any account of efforts. But if this is really so then there clearly must be surplus labour in the peasant economy, since the marginal rate of substitution between income and leisure will be constant at zero; and constancy (at zero or not) is known to be the necessary and sufficient condition for the existence of surplus labour (Sen, 1966). However, surplus labour is not assumed in the LMM model, and unlike in the COT model the value of m (alternative marginal product of a labourer) is not assumed to be zero.

It would, thus, appear that in the LMM model the peasants do dislike more work in the relevant region but this dislike is not to be reflected in the social objective function. That is, the peasant's attitude to work is accepted in the LMM model as a constraint that binds the planner but not as an element that directly enters the objective function.

If, on the other hand, it is assumed that if the peasants dislike more sweat then it must be reflected in the social objective function, then the problem will require reformulation. The positivity of m will imply that v^{13} must be positive. It should also be added that even if m is zero, i.e., even if there is surplus labour, it does not follow that v^{13} should not be positive. Surplus labour will exist whenever the marginal rate of substitution between income and leisure is constant in the relevant region and this rate need not necessarily be zero. Thus the existence of surplus labour may still require a positive shadow price of labour even in the absence of a premium on investment, i.e., even if $\lambda = 0$. The movement of labour from the peasant economy may not reduce the output there since those who remain behind may work harder, but then the enhanced effort of the remaining members requires some valuation in the planning exercise. In this view the peasants' attitude to work will be treated not merely as a constraint but also as a constituent of the social welfare measure.

3.6 Control of migration

The point has been raised that when there is a wage differential between a protected urban labour market and the average earning in the rural sector from which the labourers come, there will be a tendency for more people to move than the number of jobs created.[14] Migration from the rural to the urban sector may equate the expected value of earnings in the urban area with that in the rural area, and if w is the urban wage rate, p the probability of employment in the urban area and m the level of rural marginal product, then the migration will be up to the point that would guarantee

$$pw = m \tag{4}$$

Further, if the probability of employment p equals the proportion of urban labour force that is employed, then the migration equilibrium will exactly equate the wage rate of the employed people to the alternative marginal product sacrificed in the rural sector as a consequence of the movement of labour. For every employed man with w wage rate there will be $1/p$ men in the urban labour pool (including the employed and the unemployed), and m/p will be the amount of output sacrificed in the rural sector. And thanks to (4), w must equal m/p.

Thus in the absence of considerations of savings premium, income distribution and effort variation, the market wage rate will be the appropriate shadow wage rate for project evaluation in spite of the existence of dualism and the wage gap, i.e., in spite of $w > m$. There is much force in this argument. Professor A.C. Harberger, who is responsible for this form of the argument, has also extended it to the case where the migrant labourers may not maximize the expected value of earnings.[15] Suppose they are risk averse and pw exceeds m at equilibrium, it could still be argued that they regard the probability p of w income to be equivalent to the certainty of m, so that for project choice w is still the right measure of labour cost if social welfare must be based on the individual's measure of expected utility. There is scope for dispute in this, since it is arguable that social welfare should be based not on the *expected* utility of the labour force (all of whom had probability p of getting a job) but on the *realized ex post* utility of all of them (making a distinction between those who got the job and those who did not). And when pw is not equated to m by expected utility calculus it will make a difference whether *ex ante* expected utility (von Neumann–Morgenstern type) or *ex post* realized utility (certainty type) is taken.

There is also the question as to whether the migrant regards m or y as the value of income that he is sacrificing by moving. His income while in the peasant economy was y and his marginal product m, which might or might not have been zero depending on whether surplus labour existed or not. If he acts from the point of maximizing *family welfare* then m is the cost that he should consider, but if he wants to maximize his personal welfare then the relevant cost is y. The equilibrium condition will then be

$$pw = y \tag{5}$$

In explaining the gap between the urban wage rate and the marginal product of labour in the rural sector, it has often been suggested that the migrant views his loss in terms of his income rather than in terms of the income of the previously joint family, and it is even possible to take a model[16] where $w = y > m$. This type of personal motivation will, of course, reduce the incidence of urban unemployment as a device of marginal equilibrium, and in the case where $w = y$, the problem will disappear altogether. Also, the correctness of the thesis that the market wage rate is the right wage rate even in the presence of a gap between w and m depends on these considerations.

4 CONCLUDING REMARKS

One of the most complex aspects of the exercise of project appraisal is the precise identification of the project evaluator's areas of control. This will affect the nature of the exercise that he has to solve and the shadow prices that will be relevant for his evaluation. Much of the paper was concerned with demonstrating how variations in the assumptions about areas of control will radically alter the nature of the appropriate shadow prices.

The important approach to project evaluation developed by Professors Little and Mirrlees was studied in this context. The procedure of using world prices for project evaluation was critically examined and it was argued that that procedure required a rather extraordinary assumption about the project evaluator's areas of control.

The relation between the project evaluator's control areas and the appropriate shadow prices was illustrated in terms of the question of labour cost. The relevance of a premium on savings over consumption, weights based on income distributional considerations, valuation of efforts by the peasant family and the labourers, and the impact of employment creation on migration, were analysed in this context. The determination of the appropriate shadow price of labour is impossible without a clear understanding of the extent of influence that the planner exercises over the relevant variables in each category. There was an attempt in the paper to relate differences among schools of thought on the accounting price of labour to differences in assumptions (often implicit) about the areas of control and the motivations of the relevant economic agents.

NOTES

1 I have tried to discuss the relation of this range of issues to the exercise of project evaluation (Sen, 1970).
2 Little and Mirrlees (1969, p. 93).
3 *Ibid.*, p. 37.
4 *Ibid.*, p. 219.
5 *Ibid.*, p. 93.
6 *Ibid.*, p. 106.
7 See also Sen (1969) and Dasgupta (1970). Further, Dasgupta and Stiglitz (1974).
8 If project work is more or less backbreaking than peasant farming an adjustment for this may be included in z^2.
9 It is conventional to assume that $s^3 = 1$ if it is a public project. But there are problems of group consumption for project employees and they may be tried to project profits.
10 See Sen (1968), Little and Mirrlees (1969) and Stern (1972).
11 λ is a 'premium' since savings get a weight anyway as part income.
12 See Little and Mirrlees (1969, p. 167). Their formula is the same as (3.4) but for notational differences.

13 The problem of optimal development in an economy with constraints on taxation and savings and with a wage gap (i.e., in a dual economy) is, of course, a complex one, and the precise determination of q must be posed as a variational problem involving inter-temporal optimality. On this question see Marglin (1966), Dixit (1968), Lefeber (1968), Stern (1972) and Newbury (1972).

14 See Todaro (1969) and Todaro and Harris (1970).

15 Presented in a seminar in Nuffield College, Oxford, in May 1970.

16 See Lewis (1954). See also Jorgenson (1961).

REFERENCES

Bator, F. (1957), 'On capital productivity, input allocation and growth', *Quarterly Journal of Economics*, 71.

Dasgupta, P. (1970), 'Two approaches to project evaluation', *Industrialization and Productivity*.

Dasgupta, P. and J. Stiglitz (1974), 'Benefit–cost analysis and trade policies', *Journal of Political Economy*, 82(1): 1–33.

Diamond, P. and J. Mirrlees (1971), 'Optimal taxation and public production: I and II', *American Economic Review*, 60.

Dixit, A.K. (1968), 'Optimal development in the labour-surplus economy', *Review of Economic Studies*, 35.

Dobb, M.H. (1960), *An Essay in Economic Growth and Planning*, Routledge.

Galenson, W. and H. Leibenstein (1955), 'Investment criteria productivity and economic development', *Quarterly Journal of Economics*, 69.

Jorgenson, D.W. (1961), 'The development of a dual economy', *Economic Journal*, 71.

Lefeber, L. (1968), 'Planning in a surplus labour economy', *American Economic Review*, 58.

Lewis, W.A. (1954), 'Economic development with unlimited supplies of labour', *Manchester School*, 22.

Little, I.M.D. and J.A. Mirrlees (1969), *Manual of Industrial Project Analysis in Developing Countries*, vol. 2, OECD.

Manne, A.S. (1967), *Investment for Capacity Expansion: Size, Location and Time-Phasing*, Allen & Unwin.

Marglin, S.A. (1966), 'Industrial development in the labor-surplus economy', mimeo.

Newbury, D.M.G. (1972), 'Public policy in the dual economy', *Economic Journal*, 82.

Phelps, E.S. (1970), *Fiscal Neutrality Toward Economic Growth*, reproduced in A.K. Sen (ed.), *Growth Economics*, Penguin, ch. 4.

Sen, A.K. (1966), 'Peasants and dualism with or without surplus labour', *Journal of Political Economy*, 74.

(1968), *Choice of Techniques*, 3rd edn, Blackwell.

(1969), 'The role of policy-makers in project formulation and evaluation', *Industrialization and Productivity*, bulletin 13.

(1970), 'Interrelations between project, sectoral and aggregate planning', *United Nations Economic Bulletin for Asia and the Far East*, 21: 66–75.

Stern, N.H. (1972), 'Optimum development in a dual economy', *Review Economic Studies*, 118: 171–85.

Todaro, M.P. (1969), 'A model of labor migration and urban employment in less developed countries', *American Economic Review*, 59(118): 171–85.

Todaro, M.P. and J.R. Harris (1970), 'Migration, unemployment and development: a two-sector analysis', *American Economic Review*, 60.

UNIDO (1972), *Guidelines for Project Evaluation*, United Nations.

3

DISCOUNT RATES:

The rate of discount for benefit–cost analysis and the theory of the second best

Joseph E. Stiglitz

INTRODUCTION

In this paper I wish to present a way of thinking about what the rate of discount ought to be for evaluating projects within the public sector. The conclusion of my analysis is that there is not a convincing case that the social rate of time reference ought to be used. Nor is there a convincing case that the marginal rate of transformation in the private sector ought to be used. Neither of these rates is, in general, appropriate; indeed, the appropriate rate of discount may not even lie between the two.

Interest in the problems of benefit–cost analysis arises from the belief that in a variety of circumstances one does not want to use market prices for evaluating a project; implicitly, there is some market failure, which leads market prices not to reflect social evaluations. Thus, intrinsically, benefit–cost analysis is concerned with second-best situations. We assume, for one reason or the other, that the failure giving rise to a discrepancy between market prices and social evaluations cannot be attacked directly

It seems fundamental that the first stage in any analysis of the relation between market prices and shadow prices is the analysis of the structure of the economy and the constraints on government that lead to the persistence of a non-optimality. That is, we must begin with an explanation of why market prices do not reflect social evaluations and of why the given set of distortions cannot be better corrected by government policy.

I hope to show that use of explicit but simple models of the economy, in which the appropriateness of alternative second-best constraints can be discussed, will eliminate much of the controversy over the choice of a discount rate for use in benefit–cost analysis.

In the remainder of this introduction, I wish to summarize the results of the paper. First, however, it may be useful to review certain terms that will be used throughout the analysis.

This chapter previously appeared in R. Lind *et al.* (1982), *Discounting for Time and Risk in Energy Policy*. We would like to thank Resources for the Future, Washington, DC for their kind permission to reproduce it here.

We consider a project that has net consumption benefits of $\Delta C_1, \Delta C_2, \ldots, \Delta C_t,$ $\ldots$ at each date; ΔC_t could easily be a vector, but it is convenient for the moment to think of it as a single commodity. We wish to know whether the project should be undertaken. We cannot simply add $\Delta C_1 + \Delta C_2 + \ldots + \Delta C_t + \ldots$ because consumption at one date is a different commodity from consumption at another date. Rather, we normally assign less weight to future benefits and costs than to present benefits and costs. We form the weighted sum

$$\Sigma v_t C_t$$

If the economy is in some kind of long-run steady state, we have

$$v_t = \left(\frac{1}{1+\rho}\right)^t$$

We refer to $1/(1 + \rho)$ as the *social discount factor*. It is more convenient, however, to express our results in terms of ρ. This is called the social *rate* of discount.

There are some analysts who believe that the social discount factor ought to be equal to *consumers' marginal rate of substitution*, the amount of income they require at time t to compensate for a decrease in income at $t + 1$. If there are perfect capital markets, this will be equal to

$$\frac{1}{1+i}$$

where i is the *consumer rate of interest*, the real rate at which individuals can borrow and lend.

There are others who believe that the social discount factor ought to be equal to producers' marginal rate of transformation, the inverse of the increase in output next period generated by an increase in input this period. If firms can borrow and lend at the rate r, then the producers' marginal rate of transformation will be equal to $1 + r$. We refer to r as the *producer* rate of interest.

Finally, there are those analysts who postulate a social welfare function, of the form

$$\sum_t U(C_t) \frac{1}{(1 + \delta)^t} \tag{1}$$

(where C_t is total consumption at time t and δ is the rate at which future utility is discounted). They believe that the social discount factor should not be the individual consumer's marginal rate of substitution but the social marginal rate of substitution defined by the welfare function (1). Thus, they believe that the social rate of time discount should equal the *social rate of time preference*

$$\frac{\dfrac{U'(C_t)}{U'(C_{t+1})} - 1}{1 + \delta}$$

In the steady state, in which $C_t = C_{t+1}$, this is equal to δ, which is referred to as the *social rate of pure time preference*.

Thus, the three major 'extreme views' hold that (dropping for the moment the t subscripts)

$\rho = r$, the social rate of discount should equal the producer rate of interest;
$\rho = i$, the social rate of discount should equal the consumer rate of interest; and
$\rho = \delta$, the social rate of discount should equal the social rate of time preference

In addition to these extreme views, there is the more common, eclectic view that it should be a weighted average of the producer and consumer rates of interest.

Our analysis casts doubt on the *general* validity of any of these simplistic approaches; we identify some important cases in which, for instance, the social rate of discount may not lie between the producer and consumer rates of interest. We find other cases in which, even in the long run, the social rate of discount is not equal to the pure social rate of time preference. These results should not, however, be looked upon as simply negative results, contradicting so much of the conventional wisdom. For in each of the models we present, we are able to derive precise formulas determining the appropriate social rate of discount. Our analysis shows that one must specify what one thinks are the critical sources of market imperfection; then one can infer the correct rate of discount to use.

In this paper, I shall discuss briefly six important reasons that market rates of interest for private consumption goods might not be appropriate for evaluating public projects.

The first is that the outputs of public projects are often public consumption goods, and the marginal rate of substitution between the consumption of public goods at different dates will in general differ systematically from the marginal rate of substitution of private goods at different dates. I shall argue that this systematic difference implies that the discount rate that should be used for public consumption ought to differ (perhaps by a considerable amount) from that for private goods.[1]

The second and third reasons arise from limitations on the set of taxes that the government can impose. If the government must raise revenue through distortionary taxation, then in general it will be desirable to impose an interest income tax. But if the government produces only private goods, and there are no other constraints on taxation, then the discount rate that should be used is equal to the marginal rate of transformation in the private sector. I shall show that, in effect, under these circumstances a unit of public investment displaces exactly a unit of private investment.

On the other hand, if the government produces public capital goods, and if some part of the returns to the public capital goods are appropriated by private firms and are not taxed away, then an increase in public investment will in general displace some private investment. Accordingly, the social rate of discount will not in general be equal to the private return to capital. The precise relationship between the rate of discount and the producer rate of interest, the rate of social time preference and the consumer rate of interest depends critically on the constraints that are imposed on the government. Specifically, the relationship depends on the government's ability to (1) impose a 100 per cent tax on profits, (2) control the real debt supply freely and (3) differentiate tax rates among individuals and across classes of income. If the government cannot control the real debt supply, the social rate of discount, though equal to the social rate of time preference, will not in general be equal to the producer rate of interest, and, indeed, will not necessarily lie between the producer and the consumer rates of interest.

If the government cannot impose a 100 per cent tax on profits, then in general, the social rate of discount will not be equal to the social rate of time preference but all projects within the public sector should use the same rate of discount.

If the government has constraints on its ability to differentiate the tax rates imposed on different kinds of income, then different projects within the public sector should have different rates of discount. The distributional impact of various projects needs to be taken into account. Thus, the Diamond–Mirrlees result, seeming to reverse the long-standing presumption that, within public projects, distributional effects need not be taken into account, is seen to be very special – a consequence of the extremely strong assumptions concerning the government's taxing powers.

One of the more widely discussed explanations for why the social rate of time discount ought to differ from market rates of interest is that there are constraints on savings. I shall attempt to show that the case for such a constraint is far from persuasive. Indeed, I shall argue that, if there is a constraint on savings, the effect is not that too little saving occurs but that the level of consumption is less than is socially desirable. If this argument is accepted, it implies that the rate of discount to be used in public projects exceeds the private return to capital.

The fifth explanation for the use of social rates of discount that differ from market rates of interest relates to unemployment and the indirect effect of public expenditure on unemployment. This provides an argument for using social rates of time discount differing from market rates of interest only if the unemployment rate is changing. But if the unemployment rate is changing, inputs and outputs need to be valued with different rates of discount.

The final explanation I shall discuss for the use of social rates of discount differing from market rates is concerned with the imperfections in the risk markets. I will show that there may be a discrepancy between the marginal rates of transformation and substitution in the private sector (even in the absence of taxation) and that the social rate of discount lies between the two.

This paper focuses on a centralized governmental structure. There is a single decision-making unit, which sets all taxes, controls monetary policy and allocates all public expenditures. It calculates shadow prices, including the social rate of discount, which it transmits to project managers, who use these prices to decide whether to accept or reject various projects.

Most governmental structures are not this centralized; those people who make decisions concerning monetary policy may be different from those who make decisions about taxation, and there may be yet a third group of decision makers allocating revenues among alternative projects. These different decision makers may have different objective functions, there may be limited coordination between them, and the relationship between their objectives and the preferences of the populace may be very weak. In such a situation, should a project manager use the project to pursue his own social goals if there are agencies of the government that are better suited to pursue those goals, but do not? To what extent should he take into account the consequences of his actions on other agencies and their responses to his actions? These are important questions, but I shall not be able to deal with them here. At the same time, it should be emphasized that these may be central questions in the political debate about the appropriate rate of discount. If the inter-temporal distribution of income is inappropriate, I shall argue that there are better instruments for correcting the distribution than distorting the choice of projects. But if those people who have control of these instruments refuse to use them, what is the project manager to do? Should it be assumed that these better instruments are not used because there is some not usually recognized constraint on their use and, hence, that what would appear to be a better instrument is not really available? Or should it be assumed that there is not social consensus concerning the social goal in question, and that 'direct instruments' are not used because to do so would require a clearer statement of social objectives, or, indeed, that those people who control these direct instruments have different judgements concerning social objectives? If that is the case, is it appropriate for the project manager to attempt to use the instruments he controls (project selection) to pursue his interpretation of social objectives? Unfortunately, the approach taken in this paper casts little light on these important questions.

THE NATURE OF THE PROBLEM AND THE APPROACH

Any project can be viewed as a perturbation of the economy from what it would have been had some other project been undertaken instead. To determine whether the project should be undertaken, we first need to look at the levels of consumption of all commodities by all individuals at all dates under the two different situations. If all individuals are better off with the project than without it, then clearly it should be adopted (if we adopt an individualistic social welfare function). If all individuals are worse off, then clearly it should not be adopted. If some individuals are better off and others are worse off, whether we should adopt it or not depends critically on how we weight the gains and losses of different individuals.

Although this is obviously the 'correct' procedure to follow in evaluating projects, it is not a practical one; the problem of benefit–cost analysis is simply whether we can find reasonable shortcuts. In particular, we are presumed to have good information concerning the direct costs and benefits of a project, that is, its inputs and its outputs. The question is, Is there any simple way of relating the total effects, that is, the total changes in the vectors of consumption, to the direct effects? Then, having calculated the total effects, is there any way of relating the relative evaluations of different effects to market prices? For instance, if consumers are not rationed in the market, it is reasonable to assume that their relative evaluation of different commodities is equal to the relative (consumer) prices. If all total effects were simply proportional (say by a factor k) to the direct effects, then the net social benefit of the project would be simply k times the net benefit of the project, evaluated using consumer prices.

To ascertain the relationship between the total effects and the direct effects, one needs to have a theory of the structure of the economy, including statements about governmental behaviour. Although a full-blown theory of government and a fully specified model of our economy are probably beyond what we can expect soon, we can specify scenarios about government policy (for instance, how it responds to any balance of payments deficit resulting from undertaking the project) and make reasonable assumptions about the structure of the economy to reach some conclusions for broad classes of public projects.[2]

In the first-best world, in which there are no distortions and there is lump-sum redistributive taxation, then, with an individualistic welfare function, there exists a general result relating direct and total effects: If the project is 'profitable' on the basis of its direct effects using market prices, it is socially desirable. Thus the problem of finding the correct shadow prices (incuding the social rate of discount) for benefit–cost analysis arises from the existence of market imperfections and failures. The problem concerns situations in which one cannot necessarily infer social desirability on the basis of the profitability of the project.

The question of the appropriate rate of discount for public projects is simply a question of how we evaluate outputs and inputs at different dates. If we could always calculate the total effects, there is a trivial sense in which we would always wish to use the social rate of time preference for evaluating the benefits and costs accruing in different periods. The problem is that we normally do not calculate total effects and there is no reason to believe that the total effects are simply proportional to the direct effects. Indeed, if the ratio of total effects to direct effects systematically changes over time, then we would not wish to use the social rate of time discount in evaluating a project when looking only at direct costs and benefits.

Even if we could calculate the total effects, saying that we should use the social rate of time discount may not be very helpful. Who is to determine the social rate of time discount? And how is the social rate of time discount related to observed (consumer and producer) market rates of interest?

Thus the analysis of the social rate of discount needs to focus on the inter-temporal structure of the economy; that is, the analysis should focus on the constraints on individual and governmental behaviour and how these constraints are changing over time. This, as I have suggested, is the focus of this paper.

An example may help clarify the issue. Consider a simple project costing $I today and yielding a benefit $B in private consumption goods in the next period. To raise the revenue for the project, bonds will have to be floated, taxes will have to be raised, or money must be printed. The 'indirect effects' for each of these ways of financing the project may be quite different. The complete specification of the project ought to include all of the perturbations to which it gives rise. Assume, for instance, that the government raises the revenue by floating bonds and that, as a consequence, $I less of private investment has occurred. The private investment yielded a return of r (the before-tax marginal rate of return), and hence the loss in consumption next period from the reduction in private investment is $(1 + r)I$. The total change in consumption during the first period is zero and during the second period, $B - (1 + r)I$. Hence, the project should be undertaken only if

$$\frac{B}{I} > 1 + r \tag{2}$$

so the return on the project exceeds the *producer* rate of interest. But note that there is no inter-temporal evaluation involved in this project. The question is simply, What is the effect on consumption in the second period?

In contrast, had the project been financed out of taxation in such a way that consumption during the first period had been reduced (but private investment had been unchanged), then the project would have lowered consumption during the first period by I and raised it in the second period by B. Assume that we use an individual's own marginal (relative) evaluations of consumption in each period. Clearly, then, the project should be undertaken only if

$$\frac{B}{I} > \text{marginal rate of substitution} \tag{3}$$

If there is a perfect capital market, the marginal rate of substitution will be equal to the consumer (after-tax) rate of interest.

Thus, we have determined, under two different hypotheses concerning the total effects of the project, that we should either use the consumer or the producer rate of interest. Clearly, as we have stated the problem, the decision depends on what the public project displaces; but this is just another way of saying that it depends on the relationship between the total effects and the direct effects.

A two-period model, however, really cannot provide an adequate framework within which to analyse the problem of inter-temporal evaluation of different projects. A two-period model cannot distinguish between situations in which the shadow price on investment in the public sector differs from the market price on investment and situations in which the relative social evaluation of consumption at different dates in the future differs from the market rate of interest. To see this most clearly, return to the first example, in which public investment is financed by bonds and displaces private investment, and assume that both the private project and the public project yield returns over two periods. Thus, if the investment occurs at time 0, and we denote the output of the public project in the two periods by $C_1{}^g$ and $C_2{}^g$ and the output of the private project by $C_1{}^p$ and $C_2{}^p$, then the net changes in consumption are $C_1{}^g - C_1{}^p$ and $C_2{}^g - C_2{}^p$. If i is the after-tax return (the marginal rate of substitution), the project should be undertaken only if

$$C_1{}^g - C_1{}^p + \frac{C_2{}^g - C_2{}^p}{1 + i} > 0 \tag{4}$$

where, for the marginal project in the private sector costing I

$$I = \frac{C_1{}^p}{1 + r} + \frac{C_2{}^p}{(1 + r)^2} \tag{5}$$

Rewriting equation (4), we require

$$\frac{C_1{}^g}{1 + i} + \frac{C_2{}^g}{(1 + i)^2}$$
$$> I + C_1{}^p \left(\frac{1}{1 + i} - \frac{1}{1 + r} \right) + C_2{}^p \left(\frac{1}{(1 + i)^2} - \frac{1}{(1 + r)^2} \right) \tag{6}$$

The left-hand side of the equation gives the present discounted value of benefits using the consumer rate of interest. Different public projects with the same displacement effect can be ranked simply by their present discounted value, using consumers' marginal rates of substitution. But the criterion for accepting the project is not just a benefit–cost ratio exceeding unity. There is, in effect, a shadow price on investment, caused by the divergence between the producer and the consumer rates of interest.

Figure 3.1 illustrates how using the producer rate of interest – even when there is complete displacement of private production – leads to incorrect decisions. The line BB is the locus of points at which equation (6) is satisfied, while line AA provides the acceptance criterion using the producer's rate of interest, that is,

$$C_1{}^g - C_1{}^p + \frac{C_2{}^g - C_2{}^p}{1 + r} > 0 \tag{7}$$

Thus in region I, both criteria lead to acceptance of the project, while in region III both lead to rejection. Using the producer's rate of interest in region II leads to rejection when the project should have been accepted; the converse occurs in region IV.

Most of this paper is, in fact, concerned with the relationship between the direct effects and the total effects of a project and with exploring simple models in which the relationship between the two classes of effects can be easily calculated.

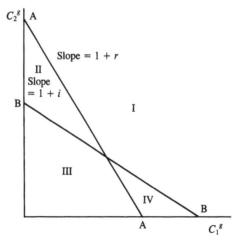

Figure 3.1

However, as we noted in the previous section, there are two aspects of benefit–cost analysis – first, calculating the total effects, and second, *evaluating* them. The first calculation requires a specification of the structure of the economy, the responses of firms and individuals to the particular project, and the constraints on individual and government behaviour. The evaluation entails somewhat different considerations and is the focus of the next section.

PROBLEMS OF EVALUATION

In this section, we assume that we have (somehow) correctly calculated all the effects, direct and indirect, of the project. As I suggested earlier, there is a trivial sense in which we can now say, 'evaluate the projects' total effects using relative marginal social evaluations'. Though correct, this evaluation is relatively uninformative. What we would like to know is: Is there any systematic relationship between market prices and this marginal social evaluation? In the first-best world, with an individualistic social welfare function and optimal lump-sum redistributive taxes, the answer is, generally: Yes. Prices will reflect relative marginal social valuations. Thus a project is desirable if its net present discounted value is positive. In the second-best situations with which we are concerned, there are at least three reasons that using market prices to evaluate total effects may not be appropriate:

1   Individuals may be constrained in their purchases or sales, and thus prices are not equal to marginal rates of substitution. For instance, if there is involuntary unemployment, the marginal rate of substitution between leisure and consumption goods is not necessarily equal to the real wage. If individuals are constrained in borrowing, then the marginal rate of substitu-

tion between consumption today and consumption tomorrow may not be equal to the market rate of interest.

2   There does not exist optimal lump-sum redistribution, so that the distributional consequences of projects have to be taken into account. The marginal social utility of an increase in consumption to one individual may not be the same as that to another. There are two distinct aspects of this situation: intra-temporal redistribution, that is, the effects on different groups at a particular date, and inter-generational distribution, that is, the effects on the relative welfare of different generations. For instance, the question of whether the savings rate is optimal is really a question of whether the distribution of income among different generations is optimal. Thus, questions of what rate of discount should be used for public projects almost inevitably will involve some discussion of these distributional issues, although there is at least one important situation in which, even in the absence of optimal redistribution taxes, the distributional implications of a project can be ignored. (See the section on optimally chosen taxes, below.)

3   The output of the project may be a pure public good, for which there are no market prices. The question is: Is it reasonable to use, for evaluating public consumption at different dates, the same discount rate one uses for evaluating private consumption at different dates? What I wish to show here is that the answer to this question is: No.

More formally, assume we have a social welfare function of the form

$$W = \int U(c_t, g_t, N_t)e^{-\delta t} dt \tag{8}$$

where c_t = per capita private consumption at time t,
 g_t = public goods consumption at time t,
 N_t = population at time t,
 δ = pure rate of (utility) time preference.

That is, we have assumed that there is inter-temporal separability of utility and that the instantaneous utility at each date is a function of the level of public goods, private goods and the size of the population at that date. There is considerable controversy about the appropriate specification of the social welfare function; the precise specification may affect the relationship between the inter-temporal marginal rate of substitution for public goods and for private goods.

Assume there are no constraints on the allocation of output between public goods expenditure and private goods expenditure, that is, if Q is total output, we have

$$Q = pg + cN$$

where p is the marginal rate of transformation between public and private goods (assumed to be given at each date but changing over time). Then, if the allocation between private and public goods has no effect on total output (this is a pure consumption good) and no effect on the size of the population, optimality requires

$$\frac{NU_g}{U_c} = p \tag{9}$$

which is equivalent to the familiar condition that the sum of the marginal rates of substitution equal the marginal rate of transformation.[3]

Differentiating equation (9) logarithmically, we obtain

$$\frac{d\ln U_c}{dt} = n + \frac{d\ln U_g}{dt} - a \tag{10}$$

where $a = (\dot{p}/p)$, the rate of change of the marginal rate of transformation, and

$n = \dfrac{d\ln N}{dt}$, the rate of change of population

The left-hand side of equation (10) is the marginal rate of substitution between consumption of private goods at different dates, while $n + (d\ln U_g/dt)$ is the corresponding marginal rate of substitution for public goods. Clearly, the two rates are the same if and only if the marginal rate of transformation remains unchanged, that is, if relative prices of public and private goods remain unchanged. Notice that what is relevant is really the marginal economic rate of transformation; that is, if distortionary taxation is required to raise the revenue for financing the public good, it is the total amount of private goods that have to be foregone to increase public expenditure by a unit that is relevant to the public investment decision. This might change even if the marginal physical rate of transformation remained unchanged (see Stiglitz and Dasgupta, 1971).

Thus, even if all the consequences of the project being undertaken can be calculated, and even if there is complete agreement on the use of an individualistic social welfare function for evaluating projects, there can still be disagreement concerning the relationship between market prices and social evaluations.

However, most of the debate about the appropriate rate of discount arises not from these considerations but, rather, from incomplete specification of the structure of the economy and the constraints on the behaviour of various agents within it. These are the questions to which we turn in the following sections.

TAX-INDUCED DISTORTIONS

Introduction

The question of what rate of discount to use for benefit–cost analysis is often presented as, Should we use the producer rate of interest or the consumer rate of interest? The examples we have already given suggest that this way of looking at the question is oversimplified. Indeed, this way of posing the question suggests that if there were no difference between the producer and the consumer rates of interest, there would be no problem. In fact, I shall show that this is not the case.

First, however, we turn to the analysis of the consequences of the major alleged source of distortion between consumer and producer rates of interest – the interest income tax.

Does the corporation tax introduce a distortion?

There are two questions to be addressed in an examination of the effects of the corporation tax. First, is there an important wedge imposed by the tax structure between the marginal rate of substitution and the marginal rate of transformation, that is, between consumer and producer rates of interest? There is undoubtedly a wedge, but how important it is is another matter. I have suggested that, because of the interest deductibility provision, the corporation tax can best be viewed as a tax on pure profits (Stiglitz, 1973, 1976); the marginal cost of capital to the firm is the before-tax rate of interest.[4] Moreover, because of the special provisions for pension funds and the special treatment of capital gains, a large fraction of interest income is exempt from taxation. Of course not all returns to capital receive such favourable treatment, so the wedge cannot be neglected.

Second, if there is a wedge, what implications does it have for the prices to be used in benefit–cost analysis? The answer depends in part on how the tax rate is determined.

I shall present two important cases in which, despite distortionary taxation, we can see that the correct rate of discount to use is the producer rate of interest. The cases, though important, are still special. In the following discussion of optimally chosen taxes, we see that, in general, with governmental budget constraints and distortionary taxation, the appropriate rate of discount need not even fall between the producer and consumer market rates of interest.

Optimally chosen taxes

First, consider the case in which all tax rates are optimally chosen, there are no untaxed profits or rents, and there is no exogenously imposed budgetary constraint for the public sector. Then an immediate application of the theory of optimal taxation and production (see Diamond and Mirrlees, 1971) is that producer prices, that is, marginal rates of transformation, ought to be used in benefit–cost analysis.

There are two alternative intuitive explanations of this result. Assume that government controlled all of production. Then it obviously would want to be productively efficient; by the usual theorems, this would imply the same marginal rates of transformation in all producing units in the economy. Now, assume that some of the firms are called private but that they have no profits because they are constant returns to scale or because their profits are fully taxed away. Obviously, calling them private makes no difference; the equilibrium will be sustained if the 'private firms' face relative producer prices equal to the marginal rates of transformation in the optimal allocation. For a formalization of this interpretation, see Stiglitz and Dasgupta (1971).

Alternatively, we can approach the problem using the concept of 'displacement' introduced earlier. We know that, for each commodity

$$q_i = p_i + \tau_i$$

the consumer price q_i is equal to the producer price p_i plus the (specific) tax τ_i. In our optimal-tax problem, it is usual to take q, the set of consumer prices, as one set of control variables. Having chosen the optimal q, we then choose the level of private and public production, subject of course to the feasibility constraint. In this formulation, once q is chosen, consumption levels are fixed; hence, a unit of public investment must exactly displace a unit of private investment.

Fixed tax rates

The same line of reasoning leads to another result. So long as the interest income tax rate (and all other tax rates) are fixed and unaffected by the project undertaken, and so long as the country involved is small and able to borrow and lend at the international market rate of interest (or so long as the production technology is a hyperplane), then it is producer prices, or international interest rates, that should be used for benefit–cost analysis. Again, the argument can be put simply. Assume we had a representative individual with an indirect utility function

$$V(q, Y)$$

where q represents the consumer price vector dated commodities – so (q_{t+1}/q_t) equals $1/1 + i$, where i is the consumer rate of interest – and Y represents the total value of the individual's endowment.

$$Y = \Sigma p_t Y_t$$

where p_t represents the producer price vector of dated commodities Y_t. With fixed taxes, for a small price-taking country, p and hence q are given and utility depends simply on Y. Maximizing Y maximizes welfare, and it is clear that in evaluating income we should use producer prices. For other applications of this kind of result, see Dasgupta and Stiglitz (1974), and Blitzer, Dasgupta and Stiglitz (1981).

These are the two conditions in which producer prices, or before-tax rates of interest, *clearly* should be used to evaluate projects. Note that these results hold for a quite general model, for example, a model including growth or many commodities.

But when the conditions assumed are not satisfied, the calculation of shadow prices becomes far more complicated. A full catalogue of the possible ways in which these conditions might not be satisfied would be laborious; we choose to mention here only those conditions that appear to be the most important.

Budgetary constraints, non-optimally chosen taxes and finite supply elasticities

Assume that the magnitude of the tax distortion is fixed at τ and assume that there are profits taxes at the rate τ_c. For simplicity (the results can easily be generalized), we employ a partial-equilibrium analysis; we assume demand and supply functions only of the price in that market. Let z be the purchase of the good by the government and x be the purchase by consumers. As before, let q be the consumer price, p be the producer price, and τ be the commodity tax, so $q = p + \tau$. Let $\mathcal{D}(q)$ and $\mathcal{S}(p)$ be the demand and supply functions, respectively. Let μ be the shadow price associated with government revenue. Then, market clearing requires[5]

$$\mathcal{D}(p + \tau) + z = \mathcal{S}(p) \tag{11}$$

from which we can immediately calculate the effect of an increase in the government's purchase of z.

$$\frac{dp}{dz} = \frac{1}{\mathcal{S}' - \mathcal{D}'} = \frac{p/x}{\left(\dfrac{x + z}{x}\right)\epsilon + \left(\dfrac{p}{p + t}\right)\eta} \tag{12}$$

where $x \equiv \mathcal{D}(q)$, private consumption,

$\eta = -\mathcal{D}' q/x$, elasticity of demand,

$\epsilon = \mathcal{S}' p/\mathcal{S}$, elasticity of supply.

Let γ equal the fraction of the good consumed in the private household sector

$$\gamma = \frac{x}{x + z}$$

Then we can rewrite equation (12) as

$$\frac{dp}{dz} = \frac{1/x}{\eta/q + \epsilon/\gamma p} \tag{12'}$$

The representative individual's indirect utility function can be written as

$$V[p + \tau, \pi(p)(1 - \tau_c)] \tag{13}$$

where π is the profits generated by a profit-maximizing firm when the price of its output is p. Hence, the effect that an increase in z has on utility can be written as

$$\frac{dp}{dz}[V_q + V_y(1 - \tau_c)\pi_p] = V_y\{-x + (1 - \tau_c)(x + z)\}\frac{dp}{dz} \tag{14}$$

where $V_q = -V_y x$ and $\pi_p = x + z$.

The government's budget is also affected by the increase in z. Besides the direct cost of z, there is an increase in costs of earlier purchases of z

$$z\frac{dp}{dz}$$

and a loss of tax revenue from the excise tax

$$\frac{d\tau\mathcal{D}(q)}{dz} = -\frac{\tau}{q}\eta\frac{xdp}{dz} \tag{15}$$

and finally, a gain in tax revenue from the increased profits of the firm

$$\frac{d\tau_c\pi(p)}{dz} = \tau_c(x + z)\frac{dp}{dz} \tag{16}$$

Thus, the total effect that an increase in z has on welfare is given by

$$-(1 + \rho) = \frac{dp}{dz}\left\{V_y[z(1 - \tau_c) - \tau_c x] + \mu\left[-z - \frac{\tau x}{p + \tau}\eta + \tau_c(x + z)\right]\right\} - \mu p \tag{17}$$

where $1 + \rho$ represents the shadow price of the given good and μ is the shadow price associated with government revenue. Then, using equation (12'), we obtain

$$1 + \rho = \frac{\mu(\eta + \epsilon/\gamma)}{\eta/q + (\epsilon/\gamma p)}\left[1 + \frac{\mu + V_y}{\mu}\left(\frac{1 - \gamma - \tau_c}{\epsilon + \gamma\eta}\right)\right] \tag{18}$$

Equation (18) provides a general formula from which a number of special cases may be identified:

1   If there are infinite supply elasticities, relative shadow prices are just equal to relative producer prices, as we asserted earlier.
    Take the limit of the right-hand side of equation (18) as $\epsilon \to \infty$ to obtain (provided $(\mu - V_y)/\mu$ is bounded)

$$1 + \rho = \mu p$$

Relative shadow prices for commodities i and j are

$$\frac{1 + \rho_i}{1 + \rho_j} = \frac{p_i}{p_j}$$

that is, equal relative producer prices, as asserted.[6]

2　If there are no profits tax and no government consumption, or purchases, of the given good, that is, $1 - \gamma = \tau_c = 0$, or if there is no budgetary constraint, in the sense that a dollar in the public sector has the same value as a dollar in the private or consumer sector, that is, $\mu = V_y$, then shadow prices are just a weighted harmonic average of p and q, that is, of producer and consumer prices.

Thus, the relative shadow price of commodities i and j is given by

$$\frac{1 + \rho_i}{1 + \rho_j} = \frac{\lambda_j/q_j + (1 - \lambda_j)/p_j}{\lambda_i/q_i + (1 - \lambda_i)/p_i}$$

where $\lambda_i = \eta_i/(\eta_i + \epsilon_i/\gamma_i)$

3　If there is a budgetary constraint ($\mu > V_y$), then the shadow price need not lie between the producer and consumer prices. Because of the budget constraint on the public sector, we have to value resources used in the public sector more highly; but because of their indirect effects on profits, different commodities may have different budgetary implications.

4　The effect of the budgetary constraint is dominant if $\tau = 0$, that is, $p = q$. Then, again from equation (18)

$$\frac{(1 + \rho_i)/p_i}{(1 + \rho_j)/p_j} = 1 + \left(\frac{\mu - V_y}{\mu}\right)\left(\frac{1 - \gamma_i - \tau_c}{\epsilon_i + \gamma_i\eta_i}\right) \bigg/ 1 + \left(\frac{\mu + V_y}{\mu}\right)\left(\frac{1 - \gamma_i - \tau_c}{\epsilon_j + \gamma_j\eta_j}\right)$$

If there is a fixed *ad valorem* tax, we obtain[7]

$$1 + \rho = \mu\left\{\bar{p} + \frac{\mu - V_y}{\mu}\frac{p}{\epsilon + \gamma\eta}[(1 - \gamma) - \gamma\tau - \tau_c]\right\}$$

where $\bar{p} = \dfrac{p\epsilon/\gamma + q\eta}{\epsilon/\gamma + \eta}$

Again, without a budgetary constraint, the shadow price is just a weighted average of the consumer and producer prices. With a budgetary constraint, the shadow price may not be between the two; for example if $p = q$

$$\frac{1 + \rho_i}{1 + \rho_j} = \frac{p_i}{p_j}\frac{1 + \dfrac{\mu - V_y}{\mu}(1 - \gamma_i - \tau_c - \tau_i\gamma_i)/(\epsilon_i + \gamma_i\eta_i)}{1 + \dfrac{\mu - V_y}{\mu}(1 - \gamma_j - \tau_c - \tau_j\gamma_j)/(\epsilon_j + \gamma_j\eta_j)}$$

The application of these results to discounting for public projects is immediate if we interpret τ_c as the corporate profits tax rate and τ as the tax on consumption in the second period.

Alternatively, if we have an interest income tax we need to interpret x as savings, so η is the interest elasticity of the supply of savings by individuals and ϵ is the interest elasticity of the demand for savings, or investment, by firms.

The fundamental non-decentralizability theorem

One of the interesting implications of the above analysis is that it may not be optimal to leave the determination of the correct set of shadow prices, including the social rate of time discount, to decentralized units. There are two reasons for this. Assume we divide the economy into a large number of sub-units; then the elasticity of supply facing each sub-unit would be infinite, that is, each would be a price taker. This implies, using the results of the previous discussion of budgetary constraints, that the social rate of discount should be the producer rate of interest or, more generally, that producer prices should be used. But if the decision is made centrally, then, except under the stringent conditions noted in the preceding discussion, producer prices should not be used.

Moreover, even if larger units are used, so that the elasticity of supply is finite, each of the sub-units would have to be instructed to take into account its effect on the tax revenues of all other sub-units; the correct determination of its shadow prices cannot depend simply on its own demand and supply functions and tax rates. This presents serious problems for the determination of shadow prices in non-centralized economies.

SAVINGS CONSTRAINTS[8]

Introduction

Traditional discussions of the choice of the correct social rate of discount have focused on constraints on savings. I find most of the arguments that the savings rate is too low unpersuasive; indeed, I shall argue that, if anything, there is some presumption that to the extent there is a deviation between socially desirable savings and market savings, the social rate of discount ought to exceed the market rate of interest.

We need to ask three questions:

1   What can the government do that individuals cannot do?
2   What can the government do that individuals cannot (or will not) undo?
3   If there are arguments that the social rate of time discount is not equal to the market rate of interest, is there any reason to believe that the appropriate remedy can, or ought to, involve an alteration in the choice of techniques in public projects?

In the subsequent discussion, we shall consider these questions.

The problem of inter-temporal redistribution

So far we have treated the goods 'consumption today' versus 'consumption tomorrow' just like any other two goods and have adapted the standard theory of the second best to the problems at hand. There are, however, some peculiar features of our inter-temporal problem to which some special attention should be devoted; in particular, it should be noted that the individuals who consume goods on different dates are different individuals. Thus, the problem of inter-temporal allocation is essentially a problem of the distribution of income across generations.

The rate of interest has two effects. It affects the allocation of consumption over the lifetime of an individual, and it affects the allocation of consumption among generations. The modelling we have done so far has treated the problem as if there were a single generation. So long as each generation considers the utility of the next generation entering its utility function, and so long as there are some bequests (that is, there is some altruism), then the above analysis is applicable. Any attempt by the government to alter the inter-generational distribution of income by lump-sum transfers will be offset by a change in bequests. Hence, to alter the inter-generational distribution of income, the government would have to introduce distortionary measures. There is no reason, in such a context, that concern for future generations ought to enter more strongly into the social welfare function than it does in the individual's own utility function.

There is an asymmetry, however. The present generation might like to increase its consumption at the expense of future generations but cannot so long as negative bequests are not allowed. Thus, it is conceivable that the present generation will attempt to use public means to increase its consumption in excess of its lifetime earnings, for example, by an unfunded social security scheme.

In short, if individuals would like to save more for future generations, they can do so; if they would like to borrow from future generations, they might not be able to. Thus, there is no natural constraint that would lead to too little savings, but there may be a constraint that could lead to excessive savings.

An objection may be raised to this argument. So long as children are earning income at the same time as their parents are alive, the children could transfer income to their parents, and in many cultures they do. Again, if the family has optimized its inter-generational family welfare, any lump-sum redistribution on the part of the government will be undone by the individuals.

The analysis, however, is not necessarily perfectly symmetric; we could postulate utility functions of the form

$$V^t = V(c_t, V^{t+1}, V^{t+2}, \ldots)$$

where V^t is the tth generation's utility, which depends on the welfare of descendants but not antecedents. Children may show no altruism towards their parents even though the parents show altruism towards their children. Thus, one generation may be able to redistribute towards itself from succeeding generations only by coercion, that is, taxation.

Even if there were perfect symmetry in the utility function between antecedents and descendants, there still may be constraints on the private transfer of income, or wealth, among generations. These constraints follow from the fact that perfect annuity, rental and mortgage markets do not exist. (The analysis of Rothschild and Stiglitz (1976) provides an argument for why, with imperfect information, one should not expect to find perfect annuity, rental and mortgage markets.)

The consequence of this, and the unpredictable timing of death, is that individuals may leave more to their heirs than they would have left had there been perfect markets. In the limit, if there had been no bequest motive, they would have left nothing. Accordingly, if the government leaves more to one's heirs in the form of public projects, it is likely that the government's action will not be completely undone. But at the same time, the presumption is that one's heirs are already, on average, better off than they would have been with perfect markets, and hence the presumption is that the social rate of discount is greater than the market rate of interest.[9]

In short, if individuals are concerned for their descendants, and if the government's attitudes towards inter-generational distribution are identical to those of the representative individual within his or her own family, then:

1   There is no convincing case that the savings rate is too low;
2   Because of certain market imperfections, there is some presumption that the savings rate is too high; and
3   Except in those cases in which the savings rate is too high, any attempt by the government to redistribute income to future generations by non-distortionary means will be undone by changes in individual actions.

However, we must enter an important caveat to the above analysis. The presumption that future generations will be better off than the present one, though certainly consistent with the history of the past few hundred years, ignores certain critical aspects of the energy and environmental problem. The essence of the argument that there is a long-term energy and resource problem and that there are likely to be serious long-term environmental problems is that the future will be less prosperous than the present. The critical issue, as has been discussed elsewhere (Solow, 1974; Stiglitz, 1979) is whether capital accumulation and technical change can offset the decreasing stock of natural resources and prevent environmental problems from becoming more serious. This remains a moot question.

It is apparent, however, that, aside from the unintentional positive bequests to heirs, there are probably unintended negative bequests in the form of nuclear wastes, lower air quality and general environmental degradation. Although this may redress the balance, it does so in an extremely inefficient way. (See the discussion below on alternative instruments for changing the inter-generational distribution of income.)

Plausibility of the existence of a savings constraint

There is, of course, in this argument one crucial assumption: individual and public attitudes towards inter-generational equity are at least roughly congruent. There is an alternative assumption that is, in my judgement, at least equally plausible as a working hypothesis: individuals have no altruistic feelings towards their descendants. In this case, the problem of redistribution across generations is identical to that of redistribution within a generation. Although private charity does exist, it is not so great that there is any presumption that public transfers will be offset significantly by a change in private transfers.

If we take this view, there is no more reason to believe that the distribution of income among generations is socially desirable than there is to believe that the intra-generational distribution of income resulting from the competitive process is socially optimal. But recognizing this, we need to ask: Is it likely that the market economy yields an inter-generational distribution of income which excessively favours the present generation or excessively disfavours it? There are strong reasons to believe, if the experience of the last hundred years is any guide, that the benefits of technical change will so improve the standards of living of our descendants that, under reasonable sets of value judgements, our present savings rate is probably too high. These benefits of technical change more than offset the disadvantages we bequeath to future generations in the form of a smaller stock of natural resources (see Stiglitz, 1979).

More formally, we ask: For what ethical beliefs about the optimal inter-generational distribution of income would the present savings rate be significantly too low? That is, we postulate that we wish to maximize a social welfare function of the form

$$\int_0^\infty U(c)e^{(n-\delta)t}\,dt$$

and we assume we have complete control of the economy. What would this imply about the long-run rate of interest, or social rate of discount for public projects? And how does this contrast with the long-run rate of interest that would emerge in a market economy with a savings rate of the kind ordinarily observed?

It is well known that the economy will converge to a steady state in which the long-term rate of interest r^* is equal to the rate of growth divided by the savings-to-profit ratio s, that is

$$r^* = \frac{n+\lambda}{s}$$

where n = rate of growth of population and λ is the rate of technical change.

On the other hand, the long-run social rate of time preference ρ is given by

$$\frac{-d\ln U'(c)e^{-\delta t}}{dt} = \frac{-U''c}{U'}\left(\frac{\dot{c}}{c}\right) + \delta$$

$$= v\lambda + \delta$$

where $v = -U''c/U'$

Hence $r^* \gtrless \rho$ as $v\lambda + \delta \lessgtr \dfrac{n + \lambda}{s}$

or $s \lessgtr \dfrac{n + \lambda}{v\lambda + \delta}$

Assume, for instance, that the elasticity of marginal utility is approximately -2 (see Stern, 1977, for an extensive discussion of arguments for alternative values of the elasticity of marginal utility), the rate of labour augmenting technical progress is 2 per cent, and the rate of population growth is 1 per cent. Assume that $\delta = 3$ per cent. Then, if the savings-to-profit ratio is, say, 0.8, the long-run rate of interest is 3.75 per cent, while the long-run social rate of discount is 7 per cent.

There is no presumption that the market rate of interest will be greater than the long-run social rate of discount for reasonable values of the parameters.

Alternative instruments for changing the inter-generational distribution of income

Finally, even if we were convinced that the social rate of discount is less than the market rate of interest, a question would remain. Why does not the government directly attack the problem, by using, for example, monetary-debt policy or social security policy to change the inter-generational distribution of income? Why should the government approach the problem of altering the inter-generational distribution of income in such a piecemeal way by affecting particular public projects? One needs to identify economic or political constraints, binding on a more general policy of inter-generational redistribution, that are not binding on the choice of technique for a public project. One obvious reason for pursuing inter-generational redistribution through public projects rather than by implementing a general policy of redistribution is that the redistribution through public projects is less open, less public, and therefore, less subjected to the same kinds of political pressures than a clearly articulated redistributional policy. However, this seems to be a questionable basis for public policy in a democratic society.

An alternative explanation, based on constraints facing the government in its tax and debt policy, is discussed in the next section.

PUBLIC CAPITAL GOODS, DISTORTIONARY TAXATION AND THE INTER-GENERATIONAL DISTRIBUTION OF INCOME

The preceding section argued that there is no convincing case for the existence of a savings constraint, at least not in a developed economy such as the United

States. On the other hand, the market obviously will provide an insufficient supply of pure public goods, including pure public capital goods. The government must necessarily be involved in deciding how much of these goods to produce. Because the revenues for these public capital goods are generally raised at least partially by distortionary taxation, the problem of the second best is unavoidable. Moreover, since the benefits accrue over time to different generations, we inevitably face a problem of inter-generational distribution. We explicitly assume that the individuals are non-altruistic, that is, they care only for their own consumption. Thus, to decide on the level of public goods to be produced, we need to introduce a social welfare function. We postulate that we are concerned with maximizing the expression

$$\sum_t \sum_j U_t^j \left(\frac{1}{1+\delta} \right)^t \tag{19}$$

where U_t^j is the utility of the jth individual in the tth generation, and δ is the pure social rate of time preference; that is, if $\delta > 0$, we weight future generations' utility less than that of the present generation. If $\delta = 0$, we simply add the individual, unweighted utilities. If the horizon is infinite, this criterion may not be well defined, but there are standard techniques for handling this difficulty. Expression (19) is just a weighted sum. As Ramsey argued, there is no convincing reason for setting $\delta > 0$ (except, perhaps, that associated with the probability of the world ending in finite time). Although I find the arguments against discounting persuasive, I shall continue the analysis without restricting δ to be zero.

The problem now is a standard *indirect* control problem. The government wishes to choose, at each date, for the instruments under its control (taxes, investments in public goods, levels of debt, etc.) a set of levels that are feasible, satisfy the government's budgetary constraints, and optimize social welfare. The government does not directly control private capital accumulation or labour supply, but its decisions affect private decisions, and the government must take that into account. We assume that the government does this. The solution to this problem yields, at each date, a set of shadow prices from which we can calculate the appropriate rate of discount to use at each date for each kind of expenditure.

Our problem is to find a simple way of characterizing the solution to this complicated indirect control problem, a characterization that provides some insight into the relationship between the rate of discount to use on public projects and markets rates of interest.

We can obtain a fairly complete characterization of the steady-state equilibrium of the economy. Under quite weak conditions, the economy will eventually converge to a balanced growth path. In the balanced growth path, we can make strong statements about the relationship between the rate of discount for public projects and market rates of interest. The relationship, as I suggested in the introduction, depends critically on the set of instruments available to the government.[10]

The basic model

The particular model (formulated by Pestieau) that has been examined in some detail is the following.[11] We assume each generation lives for two periods but works only in the first and that each generation saves in the first to provide for its retirement. Thus we have a utility function of the form

$$U_t = U_t(C_{1t}, C_{2t}, L_t) \tag{20}$$

where C_{1t} is the tth generation's consumption in the first period of life,
  C_{2t} is the tth generation's consumption in the second period of life,
  L_t is the tth generation's supply of labour.

If there are different individuals alive in each generation, we simply add superscripts j's to all variables. For this part of the analysis, we simplify by assuming all individuals are identical. For simplicity we assume the size of the population is fixed, and for the moment we normalize it to unity.
  Each generation earns a wage w_t and can invest savings at an interest rate i_t. The individual chooses (C_{1t}, C_{2t}, L_t) to maximize his utility subject to the budget constraint

$$C_{2t} = (1 + i_{it})(w_t L_t + I_t - C_{1t}) \tag{21}$$

where I_t is a lump-sum transfer, or tax, to the tth generation. For most of the analysis, we assume $I_t = 0$, that is, lump-sum taxes, or transfers, are not feasible.
  The solution to the individual's maximization problem yields his labour supply

$$L_t = L(w_t, i_t, I_t) \tag{22a}$$

and his first-period consumption

$$C_{1t} = C_{1t}(w_t, i_t, I_t) \tag{22b}$$

from which we can immediately calculate the value of his savings S_t, which is given by

$$S_t = S_t(w_t, i_t, I_t) = w_t L_t + I_t - C_{1t} \tag{22c}$$

The level of utility attained by the individual will thus be a function of the wage, the interest rate, and his exogenous income (lump-sum transfers). This is given by the indirect utility function

$$V_t = V_t(w_t, i_t, I_t) \tag{23}$$

We describe the production possibilities of the economy by an aggregate production function of the form

$$Y_t = F(K_t, G_t, L_t) \tag{24}$$

where G_t is the supply of the public capital good,
K_t is the supply of the private capital good,
L_t is the *aggregate* supply of labour.

We assume F has constant or decreasing returns to scale in the private factors (K, L) but may exhibit increasing returns in all three factors together.[12]
The aggregate labour supply L_t is given by the solution to the utility maximization problem stated in equation (22a). The determination of K_t, however, is somewhat more complicated. The solution to the individual's utility maximization problem gives a value to total savings. To relate K_t to S_t, we have to make specific assumptions concerning depreciation and the existence of alternative stores of value. The simplest depreciation assumption is that all capital lives for only one period. Then, if there exists no alternative store of value,

$$S_t = K_{t+1} \tag{25}$$

Output is allocated to three uses: consumption, public investment and private investment. We simplify the analysis by assuming that

$$Y_t = C_{1t} + C_{2t-1} + K_{t+1} + G_{t+1} \tag{26}$$

That is, we asume the production possibilities schedule is a hyperplane.
We are now prepared to formalize our maximization problem. We wish to maximize the present discounted value of social welfare

$$\max \sum_{t=0}^{\infty} V_t \frac{1}{(1+\delta)^t} \tag{27}$$

subject to the national income constraint

$$F(K_t, G_t, L_t) = C_{1t} + C_{2t-1} + G_{t+1} + K_{t+1} \tag{28}$$

where $K_{t+1} = S_t$, and where S_t is given by equation (22c) and L_t is a function of the wage rate and the consumer rate of interest given by equation (22a). The instruments available to the government are the wage rate, the consumer interest rate, and the expenditures on public investment goods. There are numerous other equivalent formulations; this one is particularly simple to work with, as will be evident shortly. Note that in this formulation we do not treat the level of taxation as a control variable, but it is implicitly defined in the solution. From equation (25) we will be able to find the level of capital in each period, and from equation (22a) we can find the labour supply. This, combined with knowledge of G_t, gives us

$$1 + r_t = F_1(K_{t+1}, G_{t+1}, L_{t+1})$$

where r is the producer rate of interest. From this expression we can easily calculate the producer rate of interest. Since we know the consumer rate of interest, the difference between the consumer and the producer rates of interest is simply the interest income tax. Similarly we calculate F_3 and the difference between that and the wage is the wage tax.

By directly substituting equations (25) and (26) into equation (28), we can obtain a simple formulation of the Lagrangian for our maximization problem.

$$\mathcal{L}_1 = \sum_t \left(V_t \frac{1}{(1+\delta)^t} \right) + \sum_t \lambda_t [F(S_{t-1}, G_t, L_t) - C_{1t} - C_{2t-1} - S_t - G_{t+1}] \tag{29}$$

An immediate result is that, in the steady state

$$\lambda_{t+1} = \frac{\lambda_t}{1+\delta} \tag{30}$$

and, differentiating equation (29) with respect to G_t, we have

$$\lambda_{t+1} F_2 = \lambda_t \tag{31}$$

Combining equations (30) and (31) we obtain

$$F_2 = 1 + \delta \tag{32}$$

Equation (32) tells us that, in the steady state, the marginal return to public investment, F_2, should be equal to $1 + \delta$; that is, the social rate of discount is equal to the pure rate of social time preference. The relationship between F_2 and the market rates of interest, however, is not so obvious. After some manipulation of the first-order conditions, it can be shown that (see Pestieau, 1974)

$$1 + \delta \equiv F_2 = \frac{F_1(1 - \epsilon_i) + (1 + i)\epsilon_i}{1 - \dfrac{t_w}{w} \epsilon_w} \tag{33}$$

where $\epsilon_w = \left(\dfrac{dL}{dw} \right)_0 \dfrac{w}{L}$ = total compensated variation elasticity of labour,

$$\epsilon_i = \left(\frac{dC_2}{di} \right)_0 \frac{i}{C_2} = \text{total compensated variation elasticity of} $$
second-period consumption.

That is, $\left(\dfrac{dL}{dw} \right)_0 = \dfrac{\partial L}{\partial w} - \dfrac{Lr^2}{C_2} \left(\dfrac{\partial L}{\partial i} \right)$,

$$\left(\frac{\partial C_2}{\partial i} \right)_0 = \frac{\partial C_2}{\partial i} - \frac{C_2}{L \cdot i^2} \left(\frac{\partial C_2}{\partial w} \right)$$

where t_w is the tax on wages.

If there were no tax on wages, the social rate of discount would be simply a weighted average of producer and consumer interest rates. But closer inspection shows that p does not have to lie between the two market rates, because of the wage tax and because ϵ_i is not constrained to lie in the interval $(0, 1)$.

Restrictions on profits taxes

The above formulation includes the assumption that the implicit returns to the pure public capital good were appropriated by the government, that is, there were 100 per cent pure profits taxes. If such taxes are not levied, firms will have an equity value E_t given by

$$E_t = \frac{(F - F_1 K_{t+1} - F_3 L_{t+1})(1 - \tau_c)}{1 + i_t} + \frac{E_{t+1}}{1 + i_t} - \frac{\tau_g(E_{t+1} - E_t)}{1 + i_t} \tag{34}$$

where τ_c is the total tax on rents, that is, corporation profits tax plus personal income tax, and τ_g is the capital gains tax. F is output, F_1 is the producer rate of interest, and hence $F_1 K$ is payment to capital owners, or bond holders. Similarly, F_3 equals the wage that the firm pays, so $F_3 L$ is total wage payment. The expression $F - F_1 K - F_3 L$ thus represents the profits of the producing sector. The amount that individuals would be willing to pay (in the aggregate) for the equity in the producing sector at the end of period t is the rent they will receive during period $t + 1$ discounted back to t at the consumer rate of interest, plus what they can sell the equity for at the end of the period (after taxes). Equation (34) defines a difference equation for E as a function of the control variables $\{i, w, G\}$, which we write (in backward form) as

$$E_\tau = \varphi[E_{\tau+1}, G_{\tau+1}, S_\tau(i_\tau, \omega_\tau), \omega_{\tau+1}, i_{\tau+1}, i_\tau] \tag{34'}$$

Clearly, now there are two stores of values, capital and equity, and we need to replace equation (25) with

$$S_{t-1} = K_t + E_{t-1} \tag{25'}$$

Using equation (25') we obtain a new Lagrangian

$$\mathcal{L}_2 = \sum_t V_t \frac{1}{(1 + \delta)^t} + \sum \lambda_t [F(S_{t-1} - E_{t-1}, G_t, L_t)$$

$$- C_{1t} - C_{2t-1} - S_t + E_t - G_{t+1}] + \sum Z_\tau(E_\tau - \varphi) \tag{29'}$$

where Z_τ is the Lagrange multiplier associated with constraint (34'), from which we immediately derive, for the steady state

$$F_2 - (1 + \delta) = [F_1 - (1 + \delta)] \frac{\varphi_G}{1 - \varphi_E/(1 + \delta)} \tag{35}$$

The right-hand side represents the displacement effect, the reduction in private investment induced by the increase in equity values from an increase in public capital.

The social rate of discount should be equal to the pure rate of time preference δ if and only if either

1 The private rate of return is also equal to the pure rate of time preference, a first-best situation that is not very interesting in our present context, or

2 There is no displacement effect, a situation that is equivalent to assuming that the public investment good has no effect on private profits that are not taxed away. This, too, is an unlikely situation. Indeed, if the effect on private profits is large, so that, for example

$$\frac{\varphi_G}{1 - \varphi_E/(1 + \delta)} = 1$$

the social rate of discount equals the private return to capital. For reasons that we shall set out shortly, we believe there is some presumption that the effect on equity values is smaller with the result that the social rate of discount lies between $1 + \delta$ and F_1.

It may be useful to consider two polar cases. First, assume the production function has constant returns in K and L, the private factors; then $E = 0$ and there is no displacement effect.

With $\tau_g = 1$ and constant returns to scale in all factors

$$E_t = \frac{F_2 G_{t+1}(1 - \tau_c)}{i}$$

and

$$\frac{\varphi_G}{1 - \varphi_E/(1 + \delta)} = \frac{(F_{22}G + F_2)(1 - \tau_c)}{i}$$

Hence

$$\frac{F_2 - (1 + \delta)}{F_2} = [F_1 - (1 + \delta)]\frac{(1 - \tau_c)}{i}\left(1 + \frac{F_{22}G}{F_2}\right) \tag{36}$$

Hence, provided $-1 < (F_{22}G/F_2) < 0$, either both F_1 and F_2 are less than $1 + \delta$, or both are greater than $1 + \delta$. But F_2 may be greater or less than F_1. With a Cobb–Douglas production function with the share of G being a_2

$$\frac{F_2 - (1 + \delta)}{F_2} = \frac{[F_1 - (1 + \delta)]}{F_1}\frac{(1 + i)}{i}a_2$$

Hence, if $i > a_2/(1 - a_2)$, either

$$F_1 < F_2 < (1 + \delta) \quad \text{or} \quad F_1 > F_2 > (1 + \delta)$$

if $i < a_2/(1 - a_2)$

$$F_2 > F_1 > (1 + \delta) \quad \text{or} \quad F_2 < F_1 < (1 + \delta)$$

while if $i = a_2/(1 - a_2)$

$$F_1 = F_2$$

On the selection of appropriate constraints in second-best tax models

The model I have described imposes one constraint on the behaviour of the government which I think is at least questionable; on the other hand, it ignores a number of other constraints, the effects of which ought to be taken into account. The questionable constraint is that the government must raise all the revenues for the public good by taxation; it cannot use debt. Obviously governments do use debt. Therefore, at first sight, this would appear to be an extremely artificial constraint. However, few governments have deliberately used debt policy to effect an inter-generational redistribution of income – an essential element in our analysis. Rather, debt and monetary policy are more a part of stabilization and balance of payments policy than they are of inter-generational redistribution policy.

The constraints we should have taken into account involve the ability of the government to impose an unrestricted set of taxes, except for lump-sum taxes and 100 per cent profits taxes. In particular, the above analysis requires that we be able to tax labour and capital at different rates, which is difficult within the unincorporated sector, and, even more important, that we be able to tax every kind of labour at different rates, clearly an absurd assumption.

In the following discussion, I show how the model may be modified to handle these cases.

Taxation constraints

First, assume we do not have complete control over all wage and interest income taxes; that is, we impose constraints, such as a requirement that the ratio of the after-tax wage to the marginal product be the same for all individuals. Then our new Lagrangian becomes

$$\mathcal{L}_3 = \sum_t \left(\sum_j V_i^j \frac{1}{(1+\delta)^t} \right) + \sum \lambda_t [F(K_t, G_t, L_t)$$

$$- C_{1t} - C_{2t-1} - K_{t+1} - G_{t+1}] \tag{29''}$$

$$+ \sum_t \sum_j \mu_{tj} \left(\frac{F_L^j}{F_L^0} - \frac{w^j}{w^0} \right)$$

where $C_{1t} = \sum C_{1t}^j$, aggregate first-period consumption,
$\qquad\ C_{2t} = \sum C_{2t}^j$, aggregate second-period consumption,
$\qquad\ L_t = \sum L_t^j$, aggregate labour supply
and where F_L^j = marginal product of the jth type of labour.

Hence, instead of equation (35), we obtain (assuming for simplicity a 100 per cent pure profits tax)

$$F_2 - (1 + \delta) = \sum_j \left(\frac{\mu_{ij}}{\lambda}\right) \frac{d(F_L^j/F_L^0)}{dG} \tag{32'}$$

Even with a 100 per cent profits tax, the social rate of time discount equals the pure rate of social time preference if and only if public expenditures have no distributive effects.

Debt

Assume the government can control the real money supply. Equation (25) becomes

$$S_{t-1} = E_{t-1} + K_t + M_{t-1} \tag{25''}$$

where M_{t-1} is the real money supply. Then from our Lagrangian, we obtain

$$F_1 - (1 + \delta) = \sum_j \left(\frac{\mu_{ij}}{\lambda}\right) \frac{d(F_L^j/F_L^0)}{dK} \tag{37}$$

If there are no distributive effects of capital, or if there are no constraints on redistribution, then the private return on capital is equal to the pure rate of social time preference. Thus we obtain the result referred to earlier in the discussion of alternative instruments for changing the inter-generational distribution of income, that is, with appropriate monetary policy and in the absence of problems concerning *intra-generational* distribution, the rate of discount should equal the producer's market rate of interest. In general, the discount rate will not be equal to the consumer's market rate of interest because of the necessity of taxing interest income.

With constraints on the government's ability to tax different groups at different rates, the appropriate rate of discount to use will depend on the distributional impact of the particular project. Different types of projects will have different distributional effects, and hence should use different discount rates. Production efficiency is not desirable, and the 'distribution branches' and the 'allocation branches' of the public sector cannot be separated.

Further constraints

The implications of other constraints may be analysed similarly. Assume, for instance, that the government cannot choose the tax rate but can decide only how much of the tax revenue to spend on public (production) goods or on social security (lump-sum payments to the aged). Then, instead of the Lagrangian given by equation (29''), we have

$$\mathcal{L}_4 = \mathcal{L}_1 + \sum_t \mu_{3t}[w - (1-\tau)F_3]$$

$$+ \sum_t \mu_{1t}[(1+i) - (1-\tau)F_1] \qquad (29''')$$

where $V = V(w, i, I)$; I is the lump-sum transfer $(I > 0)$; L_t, C_{1t}, and C_{2t} are all functions of I; and τ is the tax rate, which is assumed to be fixed.

Again for simplicity, we assume the government imposes a 100 per cent tax on pure profits, so there are no equities. The government budget constraint is thus[13]

$$\frac{I_{t-1}}{1+i} + G_t = \tau F + (1-\tau)F_2 G$$

Then, differentiating equation (29''') with respect to G, we obtain, letting b_τ be the Lagrange multiplier associated with the government's budget constraint

$$F_2 - (1+\delta) = \frac{(1-\tau)}{\lambda}[\mu_3 F_{32} + \mu_1 F_{12}] + b[F_2 + (1-\tau)F_{22}G - 1]$$

The deviation between the social discount rate and the pure rate of time preference depends on the complementarity of the public good with labour and private capital; it also depends on the effect of social security on private savings.[14]

Comparison of results with standard 'efficiency' results

There are two reasons for the difference between these results and those in the section on tax-induced distortions. That section suggested that the economy ought to be productively efficient and hence $F_1 = F_2$. First, the result of the desirability of productive efficiency of the economy required having only one restriction on the set of taxes that could be imposed, that is, there could be no lump-sum taxes. In Stiglitz and Dasgupta (1971) it is shown that, if any restriction is imposed, production efficiency is, in general, not desirable.

Second, the Diamond–Mirrlees efficiency result required that the government be able to produce or purchase all commodities. In our first model, the government is not allowed to sell bonds, which are one of the 'commodities' in our economy. We have already shown how the ability to sell bonds led the economy to a situation in which

$$1 + p = F_1 = F_2 = (1+\delta)$$

That is, the economy is productively efficient, and both the private and public rates of return are equal to the pure rate of time preference. As we noted earlier, without debt the amount of private capital is completely determined by consumers' savings decisions. Although the government can affect those decisions by altering wages w and interest rates i, it cannot alter consumers' savings decisions by any production or purchase decision.

Conclusion

In this section we have analysed the implications of a variety of restrictions on the set of instruments available to the government within a context in which the inter-generational distribution of welfare is explicitly taken into account.

In the first-best situation, in which the government has complete control over all taxes, including lump-sum taxes, there is obviously no question. The social rate of discount should equal the pure rate of social time preference, which in turn equals the private producer rate of interest, which in turn equals the consumer rate of interest.

In the second-best situation where the government can impose 100 per cent taxes on profits and use debt policy but can impose only interest income and wage taxes on individuals, with different rates for different individuals, it is still true that the social rate of discount is equal to the pure rate of social time preference, which in turn is equal to the private producer rate of interest. The economy is (in a particular sense) productively efficient, but the social rate of discount will not, in general, equal the consumer rate of interest.

The third-best situation in which the government cannot impose 100 per cent taxes on profits (we have imposed *two* constraints on the government) turns out to be equivalent to the second-best situation. The social rate of discount is equal to the pure rate of time preference, which equals the private producer's rate of interest. However, the third-best situation in which the government cannot freely control debt, that is, the real money supply, but can impose 100 per cent taxes on profits, is markedly different. The social rate of time discount is equal to the pure rate of social time preference. It is not, however, in general equal to either the consumer or the producer rate of interest, nor does it necessarily lie between the two.

In the third-best situation in which the government can freely control debt (the real money supply), can impose 100 per cent taxes on profits, but cannot impose lump-sum individual taxes and cannot differentiate the tax rate (for example, between skilled and unskilled labourers), in general, the social rate of discount will be different from project to project. For any particular project, the social rate of discount may be either larger or smaller than the pure rate of social time preference, and the private producer's rate of interest may be either larger or smaller than the pure rate of social time preference or the social rate of discount.

In the fourth-best situation, in which three constraints are imposed on the government, and the fifth-best situation, in which four constraints are imposed, similar results obtain. Since it is precisely these situations that appear to be relevant, the search for a single social rate of discount would seem to have been a misdirected effort. Rather, the questions should have been, What are the determinants of the social rate of discount? What are the characteristics of the project and the constraints on government action that affect the determination of the social rate of discount?

The results of this section are summarized in table 3.1.

Table 3.1 *Implications of various constraints on the determination of the social rate of discount*

Constraints		
	A	No lump-sum individual tax
	B	100 per cent pure profits tax not allowed
	C	Restrictions on government's control of real money supply (debt)
	D	Restrictions on the government's ability to differentiate tax rates (e.g., different types of labour must be taxed at the same rate)
	E	Restrictions on the government's ability to choose the tax rate

First-best (no restriction)	A	$\rho = i = r = \delta$
Second-best (one restriction)		$\rho = r = \delta \neq i$
Third-best (two restrictions)		
	A, B	$\rho = r = \delta \neq i$
	A, C	$\rho = \delta$, ρ need not lie between i
	A, D or E	and r
		$\rho \neq d$, $r \neq \delta$
Fourth-best (three restrictions)		
	A, B, C	either $\delta < \rho < r$ or $r < \rho < \delta$
	A, B, D or E ⎫	ρ need not lie between i and r,
	A, C, D or E ⎭	or r and δ; different ρ for different projects
Fifth-best (four restrictions)		
	A, B, C, D or E	ρ need not lie between i and r, or r and δ; different ρ for different projects

MARKET DISEQUILIBRIA

A major reason that market prices might not reflect social values is that the *equilibrium* assumptions, under which the two are the same, are not satisfied. The prevalence of unemployment equilibria is evidence that the competitive equilibrium model is deficient in some important respects. Whether this has an important effect on the appropriate rate of discount for benefit–cost analysis is not obvious, but it is clear that arguments based on a competitive equilibrium model are, at least, suspect.

In a disequilibrium situation, the analysis of the effect of an increased expenditure on one commodity requires a detailed specification of how the government and economy respond to the new situation. Some examples may help illustrate the point. Assume we have a situation in which the price in some market is fixed below the market clearing price. There must, in effect, be rationing in this market. Now an increase in government demand for the commodity shifts the demand curve upward. The government could respond by letting the price rise; alternatively, it could respond by forcing a reduction in the ration that is available to the private sector. In that case, the opportunity cost of increased government expenditure is not the price but the value of the displaced consumption. If rations are allocated to those who have the highest consumer surplus, the loss is just $U'(x)$, where $U(x)$ is the social utility from consuming quantity x. The term $U'(x)$ is the *implicit* demand price, which greatly exceeds the market price. For other rationing schemes the opportunity cost will be still higher. For example, in a random rationing scheme in which each individual consumes only one unit of the commodity and all individuals for whom $v > p$, where v is the individual's utility, apply for a ration, the opportunity cost is (indexing individuals by θ, with $v'(\theta) > 0$)

$$\int_{v(p)}^{\infty} v(\theta)\, dF(\theta) \Big/ \int_{v(p)}^{\infty} dF(\theta)$$

where $F(\theta)$ is the distribution function of individuals according to the utility they derive from the commodity.

If there is rationing in the market for a certain good during this period and the next, then the relative opportunity costs will depend on the magnitude of rationing or, more importantly, on changes in the degree of rationing. Thus, if the good in question is an investment good, so that the demand functions represent demand of the input during this period and the next, the ratio of opportunity costs is equal to the ratio of the marginal productivities if the ration is allocated in order of marginal productivities. Again the rate of discount ought to be the marginal rate of transformation.

This partial-equilibrium analysis gives us some insight into the problem of how to proceed with a general-equilibrium analysis, which is vastly more complicated in that a disequilibrium in one market may make itself evident in another market. The following simple macromodel will illustrate the nature of the calculations involved.

Continuing in the spirit of the previous example, let us consider a macromodel that uses the following assumptions:

1   The goods market clears.
2   The capital market clears but the rate of interest is arbitrarily fixed at an interest rate different from that which would be market clearing at full employment. This is, we assume that the interest rate is fixed too high.
3   There are rigid money wages.
4   The money supply is homogeneous of degree one in prices and wages.
5   The demand and the supply of savings may depend on current income, but the supply of savings is more elastic.

The implication of these assumptions is that, if we let $C(Y,r)$ and $I(Y,r)$ be the consumption and the investment functions, that is, functions of current income Y and the interest rate r, then in the goods market, we have

$$Y = F(N) = C + G + I \tag{38}$$

where F is the production function, N is the level of employment, and G is public expenditure. Output is equal to consumption plus investment plus government expenditure.

Equilibrium in the product market requires that the real wage be equal to the marginal productivity of labour

$$w = pF'(N)$$

where w is the money wage and p the price of output. This can be inverted to obtain the demand function for labour

$$N^d = N^d(w/p) \tag{39}$$

while the supply function for labour is found by maximizing utility ($Z(N)$ is the disutility of work)

$$\max W \equiv U(C) - Z(N)$$

$$\text{subject to } pC = wN$$

plus a constant if there is non-wage income. Hence

$$\frac{Z'}{U'} = \frac{w}{p} \tag{40}$$

If q is the shadow price of investment, the opportunity cost of the government's investing a unit today financed by debt is

$$\frac{dW}{dG} = U' \left[\frac{dC}{dY} + q\frac{dI}{dY} - \frac{Z'}{U'}\frac{dN}{dY} \right] \frac{dY}{dG}$$

$$= \frac{U'}{s} \left[\frac{dC}{dY} + q\frac{dI}{dY} - \frac{Z'/U'}{w/p} \right] \tag{41}$$

where

$$1 - s = \frac{dC}{dY} + \frac{dI}{dY}$$

Note that if the labour market were in equilibrium, that is, if w were set at the full-employment market clearing level, and the market price of investment equalled the shadow price, then the relative price of government expenditure today and government expenditure tomorrow is just the marginal rate of substitution, which equals the marginal rate of transformation. If, however, there is unemployment, then there is a correction factor. If the unemployment gap, as measured by the ratio of Z'/U' to w/p, remains constant, then the social rate of discount is still the interest rate. But if the unemployment rate is increasing, then the social rate of discount should be less than the market rate of interest. Conversely, if the unemployment rate is decreasing, then the social rate of discount should be greater than the market rate of interest. Note that if the unemployment rate is high enough the opportunity cost may be negative.

Equation (41) gave the opportunity cost of a government investment, an input, at different dates. On the other hand, the value of outputs of the public sector at different dates may not be affected in quite the same way. Assume, for instance, that national production is a function of labour and the supply of public capital goods K^p. The supply of public capital goods is, of course, a function of previous expenditure on public investment. Thus we have

$$Y = F(N, K^p) \tag{42}$$

We then ask, How will an increase in the output of public capital goods affect welfare, keeping total government expenditure, or inputs, unchanged? First, we observe that in a demand-constrained equilibrium

$$\frac{dY}{dK^p} = 0 \tag{43}$$

so that, since Y is unchanged,[15] equation (44) requires that employment must decrease by an amount

$$\frac{dN}{dK^p} = -\frac{F_{K^p}}{F_N} \tag{44}$$

Hence

$$\frac{dW}{dK^p} = U' F_{K^p} \frac{Z'/U'}{w/p} \tag{45}$$

Again, if $(Z'/U')/(w/p)$ remains constant, we should use the market rate of interest for public projects. But if the unemployment gap as measured by $(Z'/U')/(w/p)$ is changing, the market rate of interest and the social rate of discount differ in precisely the opposite way from which they differ in evaluating inputs.

IMPERFECT RISK MARKETS

We now come to perhaps the most important reason that market prices might differ from shadow prices: imperfect risk markets. It used to be conventional to argue that the appropriate way of treating risk is to add a 'risk discount factor', but that is obviously unsatisfactory. It implies, for instance, that an increase in uncertainty about a future cost makes that cost less important as viewed today.

The best way to approach the problem is, I think, within the special context of the mean-variance model. Then, at each date, we can calculate the certainty equivalent of any risky stream of returns. Under certain circumstances entailing separability of the utility functions, an appropriate way of evaluating a risky project would be to take the present discounted value of these certainty equivalents. If the ratio of the certainty equivalent to the mean is decreasing systematically over time, then an appropriate way of evaluating a risky project is to take the present discounted value – where the discount rate is augmented by the rate at which the ratio of the certainty equivalent to the mean is decreasing – of the *expected* net benefits. The ratio of the certainty equivalent to the mean will decline systematically if the risk discount factor is increasing (for which there is no obvious argument in a static population) or if risks in the future are greater than they are now. Such would be the case if the random variable is described, say, by a Wiener process.

There are some other special cases in which risk is appropriately treated by adding a risk discount factor. One such case, in particular, is that in which people have an uncertain lifetime.

Although this provides the basic procedure, it leaves unanswered the question of the relationship between observed market rates of return and the rate of discount that ought to be used for public projects. The imperfections of the risk markets may have an effect both on the aggregate level of savings and on the allocation of savings among alternative projects.

Uncertainty does not necessarily mean that the level of savings is smaller than it would have been otherwise; it might actually be larger, but to some extent this is irrelevant. What we wish to know is how we ought to evaluate, say, a safe project with a known increment in consumption at time t, of ΔC_t. If we have a separable utility function, it follows that we should calculate $\Sigma \Delta C_t EU'_t$, where U'_t is the marginal utility of consumption at time t as viewed today. The question is, What is the relationship between EU'_t and EU'_{t+1}? If there exists a perfectly safe asset in the economy, with return r, an individual will adjust his savings–consumption profile so that

$$EU'_t = EU'_{t+1}(1 + r_t)$$

It follows immediately that the presence of imperfect risk markets does not alter the basic result of discounting safe streams of return by the 'safe' rate of interest. This is true regardless of whether that rate of interest is larger or smaller than it would have been had there been a perfect risk market.

The matter becomes more complicated for risky projects. Assume we have a two-period project costing a fixed amount today, C_t, and yielding a benefit stream $\tilde{C}_{t+1}$ in the next period. We wish to calculate

$$EU'_{t+1}\tilde{C}'_{t+1} - U'_t C_t$$

Assume that in the private economy there is a risky stream that is perfectly correlated with $\tilde{C}$. Let $1 + \tilde{p}$ be the return per dollar yielded by the risky stream. Clearly

$$EU'_{t+1}(1 + \tilde{p}) = U'_t$$

and it follows that we can calculate the net benefits as

$$\frac{\bar{C}_{t+1}}{1 + \bar{p}} - C_t$$

by discounting at the mean rate of return for the same risk class.

This calculation does not require that the market be efficient in handling risk. It requires only that the private returns be perfectly correlated with the total social return $\tilde{C}$. We use only the private returns to estimate the attitudes towards risk.

There is one important implication of imperfect risk markets. If an individual has a considerable proportion of his or her wealth held in the assets of a particular risk class, he or she will act in a more risk-averse manner than if only an infinitesimal proportion of his or her wealth is held in that risk class. As a result, the return per dollar on that risk class, in equilibrium, will be larger. Since the government in effect spreads the risk among the entire population, a particular small risk class in which only a small proportion of the population invests considerable amounts of wealth should be discounted at a lower rate than the observed mean return. How important that is, however, is debatable. For although ownership of particular assets may be quite concentrated, what is required here is concentration of ownership of particular risk classes.

The procedure described above does not work if individuls are not identical and the project has an effect on the distribution of relative prices or if we do not calculate the total consumption flows, including indirect displacements. That is, it can be shown that the stock market does not attain even a constrained Pareto optimum when individuals differ and relative prices are affected by the allocation of investment (see Hart, 1975; Stiglitz, 1975). Shadow prices must take into account the changes in the price distribution and their distributional implications not taken into account by the above calculations. This is true even when there are optimal lump-sum redistributions, so long as those redistributions are not state-dependent. The conditions under which this implies a higher rate of discount or a lower rate of discount than the corresponding market rate are not known.

It is important to emphasize that the displacement effects may not be inconsiderable. If the government provides one unit of a stream of returns of a particular risk class, consumers will reallocate their portfolios to hold less of private assets of that particular risk class, lowering the demand for that risk class and thus investment in that risk class. For a constant-absolute-risk-aversion utility function, for instance, the demand for risky assets is independent of wealth and hence the provision of a risky asset publicly is exactly offset by a reduction of private holdings of the risky asset in the same risk class. This is important because if private returns are less than social returns (for example, because of bankruptcy), the social value of the displaced private holdings may exceed the value of the public project. Thus, even if we believe there is insufficient investment in risky assets, increased government expenditure on risky assets may not actually lead to an increased amount of total risk taking.

The magnitude of the displacement effect depends on one's model of investment in the stock market. Consider, for instance, a situation in which a number of firms have returns that are independently normally distributed. The firms maximize their net stock market value taking the risk discount factor k and the rate of interest r as given; that is

$$\max \frac{\bar{x}I - k\sigma^2 I^2}{1 + r} - I$$

where $\bar{x}$ is the mean return per dollar invested and σ^2 is the variance per dollar invested.

Assume that the government supplies I_g units of the risky asset at a cost $h(I)$. Firms now

$$\max \frac{\bar{x}I_p - kI_p(I_p + I_g)\sigma^2}{1 + r} - I_p \equiv V - I_p$$

that is

$$I_p = \frac{\bar{x} - (1 + r) - kI_g\sigma^2}{2k\sigma^2}$$

Hence

$$\frac{\partial I_p}{\partial I_g} = -\tfrac{1}{2}$$

A unit increment in the government's provision of the risky asset leads to a reduction of half a unit in the provision of that asset by private firms.

Thus, the net cost for a unit of increased output of the given type of risky assets is $2h' - 1$, and hence optimality implies that

$$V/I_p = 2h' - 1$$

where V/I_p is the market value of the private firm, per dollar invested.

Hence

$$h' = \frac{V/I_p + 1}{2}$$

The discount factor to use is between the present value of the risky stream (per dollar invested) in the private sector, V/I, and what that present value would be if firms assumed that their market value were proportional to their scale. To put it another way, h' would equal 1 if productive efficiency were desired, and h' would equal V/I if the displacement effect were ignored. In this model the correct discount factor is halfway between those values of h'. Thus, if equities sell at a 20 per cent premium over the value of the assets, the discount factor for public projects ought to be approximately 1.1.

It hardly needs to be emphasized that other models of investment behaviour may lead to quite different displacement effects.

Much of the discussion on the rate of discount for benefit–cost analysis seems to be motivated by a concern to obtain a lower value than the mean return observed on market assets. However, those mean returns are not risk free. The real return observed on riskless assets, or more generally, on assets uncorrelated with the business cycle, is in fact quite small – of the order of magnitude of 1 per cent to 2 per cent – which seems not inconsistent with the kinds of rates of discount expected on the basis of the simple savings models discussed earlier in the section on savings constraints.

For one important class of projects in natural resources it is probably the case that a still smaller discount rate ought to be used. The payoff to an invention of a substitute will be high when the price of the resource, in the absence of the discovery, would have been high. If $V(p, y)$ is the indirect utility function giving utility as a function of the price of the resource and income, then if $V_{py} > 0$, the returns to the invention are positively correlated with marginal utility of income.

In this section, I have argued that imperfect risk markets provide less reason for lowering the rate of discount from the observed market rates of return for risky assets than has sometimes been supposed. The extent to which the discount rate should be lowered depends on how well the stock market performs its function of risk sharing and the extent to which investment in risky assets is restricted below its Pareto optimum level.

CONCLUSION

The question of the appropriate rate of discount to use for public projects has been a subject of extensive controversy. The reason for this controversy is that the number of projects for which there is an acceptable benefit–cost ratio is critically dependent on the value of this rate. The object of this paper has been to present a framework within which the scope of such controversies may be limited. We can at least hope to identify whether the disagreements are due to (1) differences in views about the structure of the economy; (2) differences in views about the relevant constraints; or (3) differences in values, for example, attitudes towards inter-generational distribution.

We have identified some of the more important constraints on the economy, which lead market prices – in particular, market rates of interest – not to reflect social values. There are some important constraints that we have not discussed: those arising from imperfections of information and imperfections of competition. For the most part, we have treated one constraint at a time, ignoring the possible important interaction among constraints. I have argued throughout that a careful specification of the nature of the constraints and the structure of the economy is required in order to obtain the correct rate at which to discount public projects. Although for several specifications we obtained a 'weighted average' formula of the traditional kind, in several other important instances we obtained the result that the marginal rate of transformation ought to be used as the social rate of discount. In still other instances, the appropriate rate of discount did not even lie between the marginal rate of substitution and the marginal rate of transformation.

The value of the social rate of discount depends on a number of factors, and indeed I have argued it might vary from project to project depending, for instance, on the distributional consequences of the project. These results may be frustrating for those who seek simple answers, but such are not to be found. The decision on the appropriate rate of discount thus inevitably will entail judgements concerning what are the relevant constraints. I have suggested, for instance, that the savings constraint is probably not important but that the distortionary consequences of taxation and the implications of imperfect risk markets are significant. Both lead to social rates of discount that normally exceed the consumer rate of interest. Indeed, under not unreasonable circumstances, they may exceed the producer rate of interest.

NOTES

The author is greatly indebted to R. Lind and H. Wan for detailed comments on the paper. I also wish to acknowledge helpful discussions with D. Bevan, J. Flemming, K. Roberts, R. Arnott and J. Mirrlees on various parts of the paper.

Financial support from the National Science Foundation is gratefully acknowledged.

1 Here, as elsewhere, we have to be careful about specifying precisely what it is that is being discounted. Assume, for instance, that we are evaluating an aircraft carrier, and for simplicity, assume its performance characteristics are identical for N years, after which it falls apart (the conventional one-hoss shay assumption). Assume that we can ascertain the value, say in terms of foregone consumption today, of the services of the aircraft carrier this year. Assume, moreover, there is no technological change, so we can avoid the problem of obsolescence. How do we discount the future output of each of the next N years (assumed to be identical)?

One reader of an earlier draft suggested that it is benefits that should be discounted, not outputs. But then, how are we to evaluate these benefits? If we evaluate them using their net marginal change in social utility, we have simply begged the question, for then we need no discount factor at all.

2 This approach was first developed, in the context of the question of shadow foreign exchange rates, by Blitzer, Dasgupta and Stiglitz (1981).

The critical effect of constraints on government policy on the shadow prices used in the public sector had earlier been brought out by Boiteux (1956), Stiglitz and Dasgupta (1971), Dasgupta and Stiglitz (1974). Indeed, in his classic paper, Boiteux established that shadow prices in the public sector should equal those in the private sector only under special conditions.

The critical role of assumptions concerning the structure of the economy in determining shadow prices has been emphasized by the author in a series of papers on the shadow price of labour in less-developed countries (Stiglitz, 1974, 1977). It was shown that an implicit assumption in most of the benefit–cost analyses (for example, Little and Mirrlees, 1968) was that there was no migration from the rural to the urban sector, at least no migration induced by additional jobs within the urban sector. If there were such migration, then the shadow wage would, in general, be larger than if there were none; indeed, if migration continued until the expected wages in the urban sector equalled the rural wage, which was fixed, then the shadow wage in the urban sector was equal to the market wage.

3 It is not even always the case that, with a separable utility function, we can use a myopic decision rule for the allocation of public consumption goods as in equation (9). For instance, if, as in the section on public capital goods, the government is restricted in imposing lump-sum taxes and does not have complete control over private capital supply (for example, it does not have complete freedom in its debt policy), then changing the level of consumption goods at any date may affect the level of savings, and hence the level of (private) capital at subsequent dates. These 'dynamic' effects need to be taken into account and would lead to a modification in equation (9).

4 Indeed, under certain circumstances it can be established that the cost of capital is less than the before-tax rate of interest. If the firm does not invest the funds, it will distribute them and they will be immediately subjected to taxation. If the firm invests them, the taxes can, in effect, be permanently postponed.

5 If we drop the assumption of separability of demand and supply functions, we can reinterpret equation (11) as a set of vector equations.

6 This assumes the same kind of analysis can be applied to each market separately.

7 Instead of equation (12') we have

$$\frac{dp}{dz} = \frac{1}{\mathcal{G}' - \mathcal{D}'(1 = \tau)} = \frac{p/x}{\epsilon/\gamma + \eta} \tag{12''}$$

Instead of equation (14) we obtain

$$\frac{dp}{dz}\{(1 = \tau)V_q + V_y(1 - \tau_c)\pi_p\} = \frac{dp}{dz}V_y\{-\tau x - x + (1 - \tau_c)(x + z)\} \tag{14'}$$

and instead of equation (15) we have

$$\frac{d\tau p \mathcal{D}(q)}{dz} = \tau x \frac{dp}{dz}(1 - \eta) \tag{15'}$$

Hence equation (17) becomes

$$-(1 + p) = \frac{dp}{dz}\{V_y[z(1 - \tau_c) - (\tau_c + \tau)x]$$

$$+ \mu[-z + \tau x(1 - \eta) + \tau_c(x + z)]\} - \mu p \tag{17'}$$

or

$$1 + \rho = p\mu\left[1 + \frac{\tau\eta}{\epsilon/\gamma + \eta} - \frac{\mu - V_y}{(\epsilon/\gamma + \eta)\mu}\left(\tau + \tau_c - \frac{(1 - \gamma)}{\gamma}(1 - \tau_c)\right)\right]$$

8 This section owes much to David Bevan and John Flemming.

9 The importance of these considerations for the distribution of wealth has also been emphasized in recent work by Flemming (1976) and Bevan and Stiglitz (1979).

10 It is important to recognize that the way we have formulated the problem is not equivalent to asking what is the best steady state, that is, the steady state that maximizes utility. One can show that, in general, unless the discount rate is zero, the two formulations yield quite different results. The best steady-state question is not a meaningful question, since one cannot go from one steady state to another without cost, and one must evaluate the utility levels of intervening generations (see Stiglitz, 1970, and Atkinson and Stiglitz, 1980).

11 The model is an extension of Samuelson's consumption loan life-cycle model. The first application of the life-cycle model to the problem of determining the social rate of discount is contained in Diamond (1974), but no clear results are obtained.

The result contained in equation (32), that even with a full set of excise taxes we do not want the return on private and public capital to be equal, is contained in Pestieau's paper, as is the result on the effect of government debt.

The generalization of Pestieau's results to diverse consumers is contained in Stiglitz (1978); this also contains a more detailed discussion of the role of restricted taxation. The formulation presented here follows that of Stiglitz (1978).

The pioneering work of Arrow (1966) and Arrow and Kurz (1970) analyses the problem of the choice of discount rates as a control problem. However, it differs in several important ways from Pestieau's treatment. First, savings are arbitrarily given and not related directly to the utility function of consumers. Second, labour supply is inelastic. Third, there is no explicit treatment of different generations. The result is that there is no clear connection between the social welfare function and consumers' preferences, and there exists the possibility of non-distortionary taxation. The modelling of both the structure of the economy and the nature of the second-best constraints is less persuasive than that of Pestieau and the extensions presented here.

12 When the government can impose 100 per cent rent or profits taxes, in order for distortionary taxation to be required to finance the public good, there will, in general, have to be increasing returns to scale.

13 The lump-sum payment is made to the aged. The term I is the value of that lump-sum payment in the first period of the individual's life. See the discussion on the selection of appropriate constraints in second-best tax models.

14 This affects the value of b.

15 By our assumptions, C and I do not depend on K^p.

REFERENCES

Arrow, K.J. (1966), 'Discounting and public investment criteria', in A.V. Kneese and S.C. Smith (eds.), *Water Research*, Baltimore, Johns Hopkins University Press for Resources for the Future, pp. 13–32.

Arrow, K. and M. Kurz (1970), *Public Investment, the Rate of Return and Optimal Fiscal Policy*, Baltimore, Johns Hopkins University Press for Resources for the Future.

Atkinson, A. and J.E. Stiglitz (1980), *Lectures on Public Finance*, London, New York, McGraw-Hill.

Bevan, D. and J.E. Stiglitz (1979), 'Intergenerational transfers and inequality', *Greek Economic Review*, 1(1): 8–26.

Blitzer, C., P. Dasgupta and J.E. Stiglitz (1981), 'Project evaluation and the foreign exchange constraint', *Economic Journal*, 91: 58–74.

Boiteux, M. (1956), 'Sur le Gestion des Monopoles Publics Astreints à l'Équilibre Budgétaire', *Econometrica*, 24: 22–40.

Dasgupta, P. and J.E. Stiglitz (1974), 'Benefit–cost analysis and trade policies', *Journal of Political Economy*, 82 (January–February): 1–33.

Diamond, P. (1974), 'Taxation and public production in a growth model', in J.A. Mirrlees and N.H. Stern (eds.), *Models of Economic Growth* (presented at the International Economic Association Conference on the Essence of a Growth Model, 1970).

Diamond, P. and J.A. Mirrlees (1971), 'Optimal taxation and public production I and II', *American Economic Review*, 61: 8–27 and 261–78.

Flemming, J.S. (1976), *In Selected Evidence Submitted for Report No. 1. Royal Commission on the Distribution of Income and Wealth*. London, HMSO.

Hart, O.P. (1975), 'On the optimality of equilibrium when the market structure is incomplete', *Journal of Economic Theory*, 11: 418–43.

Little, I.M.D. and J.A. Mirrlees (1968), *Manual of Industrial Project Analysis, vol. II*, Paris, OECD Development Centre.

Pestieau, P.M. (1974), 'Optimal taxation and discount rate for public investment in a growth setting', *Journal of Public Economics*, 3: 217–35.

Rothschild, M. and J.E. Stiglitz (1976), 'Equilibrium in competitive insurance markets: the economics of markets with imperfect information', *Quarterly Journal of Economics Symposium*, 90: 629–49.

Solow, R.M. (1974), 'The economics of resources or the resources of economics', *American Economic Review* Papers and Proceedings (May): 1–14.

Stern, N.H. (1977), 'The marginal valuation of income', in M.J. Artis and A.R. Nobay (eds.), *Studies in Modern Economic Analysis*, Oxford, Basil Blackwell, Proceedings of 1976 AUTE Conference in Edinburgh, pp. 209–58.

Stiglitz, J.E. (1970), 'Factor price equalization in a dynamic economy', *Journal of Political Economy*, 78 (May–June): 456–89.

(1973), 'Taxation, corporate financial policy, and the cost of capital', *Journal of Public Economics*, 2 (February): 1–34.

(1974), 'Wage determination and unemployment in LDC's. I: the labor turnover model', *Quarterly Journal of Economics*, 88(2) (May): 194–227.

(1975), 'The efficiency of market prices in long run allocations in the oil industry', in G. Brannon (ed.), *Studies in Energy Tax Policy*, Cambridge, MA, Ballinger.

(1976), 'The corporation tax', *Journal of Public Economics*, 5: 303–11.

(1977), 'Some further remarks on cost–benefit analysis', in H. Schwartz and R. Berney (eds.), *Social and Economic Dimensions of Project Evaluation*, Proceedings of the Symposium on The Use of Socioeconomic Investment Criteria in Project Evaluation, Inter-American Development Bank, 1973.

(1978), 'The social rate of time preference and the rate of discount for cost–benefit analysis', Oxford, mimeo.

(1979), 'A neoclassical analysis of the economics of natural resources', in V.K. Smith (ed.), *Scarcity and Growth Reconsidered*, Baltimore, Johns Hopkins University Press.

(1982), 'The Inefficiency of the Stock Market Equilibrium', *Review of Economic Studies*, 49: 241–61.

Stiglitz, J.E. and P. Dasgupta (1971), 'Differential taxation, public goods, and economic efficiency', *The Review of Economic Studies*, 37(2): 151–74.

4

RISK AND UNCERTAINTY:

Uncertainty and the evaluation of public investment decisions

K.J. Arrow and R.C. Lind

The implications of uncertainty for public investment decisions remain controversial. The essence of the controversy is as follows. It is widely accepted that individuals are not indifferent to uncertainty and will not, in general, value assets with uncertain returns at their expected values. Depending upon an individual's initial asset holdings and utility function, he will value an asset at more or less than its expected value. Therefore, in private capital markets, investors do not choose investments to maximize the present value of expected returns, but to maximize the present value of returns properly adjusted for risk. The issue is whether it is appropriate to discount public investments in the same way as private investments.

There are several positions on this issue. The first is that risk should be discounted in the same way for public investments as it is for private investments. It is argued that to treat risk differently in the public sector will result in overinvestment in this sector at the expense of private investments yielding higher returns. The leading proponent of this point of view is Jack Hirshleifer.[1] He argues that in perfect capital markets, investments are discounted with respect to both time and risk and that the discount rates obtaining in these markets should be used to evaluate public investment opportunities.

A second position is that the government can better cope with uncertainty than private investors and, therefore, government investments should not be evaluated by the same criterion used in private markets. More specifically, it is argued that the government should ignore uncertainty and behave as if indifferent to risk. The government should then evaluate investment opportunities according to their present value computed by discounting the expected value of net returns, using a rate of discount equal to the private rate appropriate for investments with certain returns. In support of this position it is argued that the government invests in a greater number of diverse projects and is able to pool risks to a much greater extent than private investors.[2] Another supporting line of argument is that many of the uncertainties which arise in private capital markets are related to what may be termed moral hazards. Individuals involved in a given trans-

This chapter previously appeared in the *American Economic Review*, 60 (1970): 364–78. We would like to thank the American Economic Association for their kind permission to reproduce it here.

action may hedge against the possibility of fraudulent behaviour on the part of their associates. Many such risks are not present in the case of public investments and, therefore, it can be argued that it is not appropriate for the government to take these risks into account when choosing among public investments.

There is, in addition, a third position on the government's response to uncertainty. This position rejects the notion that individual preferences as revealed by market behaviour are of normative significance for government investment decisions, and asserts that time and risk preferences relevant for government action should be established as a matter of national policy. In this case the correct rules for action would be those established by the appropriate authorities in accordance with their concept of national policy. The rate of discount and attitude towards risk would be specified by the appropriate authorities and the procedures for evaluation would incorporate these time and risk preferences. Two alternative lines of argument lead to this position. First, if one accepts the proposition that the state is more than a collection of individuals and has an existence and interests apart from those of its individual members, then it follows that government policy need not reflect individual preferences. A second position is that markets are so imperfect that the behaviour observed in these markets yields no relevant information about the time and risk preferences of individuals. It follows that some policy as to time and risk preference must be established in accordance with other evidence of social objectives. One such procedure would be to set national objectives concerning the desired rate of growth and to infer from this the appropriate rate of discount.[3] If this rate were applied to the expected returns from all alternative investments, the government would in effect be behaving as if indifferent to risk.

The approach taken in this paper closely parallels the approach taken by Hirshleifer, although the results differ from his. By using the state-preference approach to market behaviour under uncertainty, Hirshleifer demonstrates that investments will not, in general, be valued at the sum of the expected returns discounted at a rate appropriate for investments with certain returns.[4] He then demonstrates that using this discount rate for public investments may lead to non-optimal results, for two reasons. First, pooling itself may not be desirable.[5] If the government has the opportunity to undertake only investments which pay off in states where the payoff is highly valued, to combine such investments with ones that pay off in other states may reduce the value of the total investment package. Hirshleifer argues that where investments can be undertaken separately they should be evaluated separately, and that returns should be discounted at rates determined in the market. Second, even if pooling were possible and desirable, Hirshleifer argues correctly that the use of a rate of discount for the public sector which is lower than rates in the private sector can lead to the displacement of private investments by public investments yielding lower expected returns.[6]

For the case where government pooling is effective and desirable, he argues that rather than evaluate public investments differently from private ones, the government should subsidize the more productive private investments. From this it follows that to treat risk differently for public as opposed to private investments would only be justified if it were impossible to transfer the advantages of government pooling to private investors. Therefore, at most, the argument for treating public risks differently than private ones in evaluating investments is an argument for the 'second best'.[7]

The first section of this chapter addresses the problem of uncertainty, using the state-preference approach to market behaviour. It demonstrates that if the returns from any particular investment are independent of other components of national income, then the present value of this investment equals the sum of expected returns discounted by a rate appropriate for investments yielding certain returns. This result holds for both private and public investments. Therefore, by adding one plausible assumption to Hirshleifer's formulation, the conclusion can be drawn that the government should behave as an expected-value decision maker and use a discount rate appropriate for investments with certain returns. This conclusion needs to be appropriately modified when one considers the case where there is a corporate income tax.

While this result is of theoretical interest, as a policy recommendation it suffers from a defect common to the conclusions drawn by Hirshleifer. The model of the economy upon which these recommendations are based presupposes the existence of perfect markets for claims contingent on states of the world. Put differently, it is assumed that there are perfect insurance markets through which individuals may individually pool risks. Given such markets, the distribution of risks among individuals will be Pareto optimal. The difficulty is that many of these markets for insurance do not exist, so even if the markets which do exist are perfect, the resulting equilibrium will be sub-optimal. In addition, given the strong evidence that the existing capital markets are not perfect, it is unlikely that the pattern of investment will be Pareto optimal. At the margin, different individuals will have different rates of time and risk preference, depending on their opportunities to borrow or to invest, including their opportunities to insure.

There are two reasons why markets for many types of insurance do not exist. The first is the existence of certain moral hazards.[8] In particular, the fact that someone has insurance may alter his behaviour so that the observed outcome is adverse to the insurer. The second is that such markets would require complicated and specialized contracts which are costly. It may be that the cost of insuring in some cases is so high that individuals choose to bear risks rather than pay the transaction costs associated with insurance.

Given the absence of some markets for insurance and the resulting sub-optimal allocation of risks, the question remains: How should the government treat uncertainty in evaluating public investment decisions? The approach taken in this paper is that individual preferences are relevant for public investment decisions, and government decisions should reflect individual valuations of costs and benefits. It is demonstrated in the second section of this paper that when the risks associated with a public investment are publicly borne, the total cost of risk bearing is insignificant and, therefore, the government should ignore uncertainty in evaluating public investments. Similarly, the choice of the rate of discount should in this case be independent of considerations of risk. This result is obtained not because the government is able to *pool* investments but because the government distributes the risk associated with any investment among a large number of people. It is the *risk-spreading* aspect of government investment that is essential to this result.

There remains the problem that private investments may be displaced by public ones yielding a lower return if this rule is followed, although given the absence of insurance markets this will represent a Hicks–Kaldor improvement over the initial situation. Again the question must be asked whether the superior position of the government with respect to risk can be made to serve private investors. This leads to a discussion of the government's role as a supplier of insurance, and of Hirshleifer's recommendation that private investment be subsidized in some cases.

Finally, the results obtained above apply to risks actually borne by the government. Many of the risks associated with public investments are borne by private individuals, and in such cases it is appropriate to discount for risk as would these individuals. This problem is discussed in the final section of the paper. In addition, a method of evaluating public investment decisions is developed that calls for different rates of discount applied to different classes of benefits and costs.

MARKETS FOR CONTINGENT CLAIMS AND TIME-RISK PREFERENCE[9]

For simplicity, consider an economy where there is one commodity and there are I individuals, S possible states of the world, and time is divided into Q periods of equal length. Further suppose that each individual acts on the basis of his subjective probability as to the states of nature; let π_{is} denote the subjective probability assigned to state s by individual i. Now suppose that each individual in the absence of trading owns claims for varying amounts of the one commodity at different points in time, given different states of the world. Let $\bar{x}_{isq}$ denote the initial claim to the commodity in period $q + 1$ if state s occurs which is owned by individual i. Suppose further that all trading in these claims takes place at the beginning of the first period, and claims are bought and sold on dated commodity units contingent on a state of the world. All claims can be constructed from basic claims which pay one commodity unit in period $q + 1$, given state s, and nothing in other states or at other times; there will be a corresponding price for this claim, $p_{sq}(s = 1, \ldots, S; q = 0, \ldots, Q - 1)$. After the trading, the individual will own claims x_{isq}, which he will exercise when the time comes to provide for his consumption. Let $V_i(x_{i1,0}, \ldots, x_{i1,Q-1}, x_{i2,0}, \ldots, x_{iS,Q-1})$ be the utility of individual i if he receives claims $x_{isq}(s = 1, \ldots, S; q = 0, \ldots, Q-1)$. The standard assumptions are made that V_i is strictly quasi-concave $(i = 1, \ldots, I)$.

Therefore each individual will attempt to maximize

$$V_i(x_{i1,0}, \ldots, x_{i1,Q-1}, x_{i2,0}, \ldots, x_{iS,Q-1}) \tag{1}$$

subject to the constraint

$$\sum_{q=0}^{Q-1} \sum_{s=1}^{S} p_{sq} x_{isq} = \sum_{q=0}^{Q-1} \sum_{s=1}^{S} p_{sq} \bar{x}_{isq}$$

Using the von Neumann–Morgenstern theorem and an extension by Hirshleifer,[10] functions $U_{is}(s = 1, \ldots, S)$ can be found such that

$$V_i(x_{i1,0}, \ldots, x_{iS,Q-1}) = \sum_{s=1}^{S} \pi_{is} U_{is}(x_{is0}, x_{is1}, \ldots, x_{iS,Q-1}). \tag{2}$$

In equation (2) an individual's utility, given any state of the world, is a function of his consumption at each point in time. The subscript s attached to the function U_{is} is in recognition of the fact that the value of a given stream of consumption may depend on the state of the world.

The conditions for equilibrium require that

$$\pi_{is} \frac{\partial U_{is}}{\partial x_{isq}} = \lambda_i p_{sq} \quad (i = 1, \ldots, I; s = 1, \ldots, S; q = 0, \ldots, Q-1) \tag{3}$$

where λ_i is a Lagrangian multiplier.

From (3) it follows that

$$\frac{p_{sq}}{p_{rm}} = \frac{\pi_{is}(\partial U_{is}/\partial x_{isq})}{\pi_{rm}(\partial U_{ir}/\partial x_{irm})} \quad (i = 1, \ldots, I; r,s = 1, \ldots, S; m,q = 0, \ldots, Q-1) \tag{4}$$

Insight can be gained by analysing the meaning of the price in such an economy. Since trading takes place at time zero, p_{sq} represents the present value of a claim to one commodity unit at time q, given state s. Clearly

$$\sum_{s=1}^{S} p_{s0} = 1$$

since someone holding one commodity unit at time zero has a claim on one commodity unit, given any state of the world. It follows that p_{sq} is the present value of one commodity at time q, given state s, in terms of a certain claim on one commodity unit at time zero. Therefore, the implicit rate of discount to time zero on returns at time q, given state s, is defined by $p_{sq} = 1/(1 + r_{sq})$.

Now suppose one considers a certain claim to one commodity unit at time q; clearly, its value is

$$p_q = \sum_{s=1}^{S} p_{sq}$$

and the rate of discount appropriate for a certain return at time q is defined by

$$\frac{1}{1 + r_q} = \sum_{s=1}^{S} \frac{1}{1 + r_{sq}} = \sum_{s=1}^{S} p_{sq} \tag{5}$$

Given these observations, we can now analyse the appropriate procedure for evaluating government investments where there are perfect markets for claims contingent on states of the world.[11] Consider an investment where the overall effect on market prices can be assumed to be negligible, and suppose the net return from this investment for a given time and state is $h_{sq}(s = 1, \ldots, S; q = 0, \ldots, Q - 1)$. Then the investment should be undertaken if

$$\sum_{q=0}^{Q-1} \sum_{s=1}^{S} h_{sq} p_{sq} > 0 \tag{6}$$

and the sum on the left is an exact expression for the present value of the investment. Expressed differently, the investment should be adopted if

$$\sum_{q=0}^{Q-1} \sum_{s=1}^{S} \frac{h_{sq}}{1 + r_{sq}} > 0 \tag{7}$$

The payoff in each time-state is discounted by the associated rate of discount. This is the essential result upon which Hirshleifer bases his policy conclusions.[12]

Now suppose that the net returns of the investment were (a) independent of the returns from previous investment, (b) independent of the individual utility functions, and (c) had an objective probability distribution, i.e., one agreed upon by everyone. More specifically, we assume that the set of all possible states of the world can be partitioned into a class of mutually exclusive and collectively exhaustive sets, E_t, indexed by the subscript t such that, for all s in any given E_t, all utility functions U_{is} are the same for any individual i ($i = 1, \ldots, I$), and such that all production conditions are the same. Put differently, for all s in E_t, U_{is} is the same for a given individual, but not necessarily for all individuals. At the same time there is another partition of the states of the world into sets, F_u, such that the return, h_{sq}, is the same for all s in F_u. Finally, we assume that the probability distribution of F_u is independent of E_t and is the same for all individuals.

Let E_{tu} be the set of all states of the world which lie in both E_t and F_u. For any given t and u, all states of the world in E_{tu} are indistinguishable for all purposes, so we may regard it as containing a single state. Equations (3) and (5) and the intervening discussion still hold if we then replace s everywhere by tu. However, $U_{is} = U_{itu}$ actually depends only on the subscript, t, and can be written U_{it}. From the assumptions it is obvious and can be proved rigorously that the allocation x_{isq} also depends only on t, i.e. is the same for all states in E_t for any given t, so it may be written x_{itq}. Finally, let π_{it} be the probability of E_t according to individual i, and let π_u be the probability of F_u, assumed the same for all individuals. Then the assumption of statistical independence is written

$$\pi_{itu} = \pi_{it}\pi_u \tag{8}$$

Then (3) can be written

$$\pi_{it}\pi_u \frac{\partial U_{it}}{\partial x_{itq}} = \lambda_i p_{tuq} \tag{9}$$

Since p_{tuq} and π_u are independent of i, so must be

$$\frac{\pi_{it}(\partial U_{it}/\partial x_{itq})}{\lambda_i}$$

on the other hand, this expression is also independent of u and so can be written u_{tq}. Therefore

$$p_{tuq} = u_{tq}\pi_u \tag{10}$$

Since the new investment has the same return for all states s in F_u, the returns can be written h_{uq}. Then the left-hand side of (6) can, with the aid of (10), be written

$$\sum_{q=0}^{Q-1}\sum_{s=1}^{S} h_{sq}p_{sq} = \sum_{q=0}^{Q-1}\sum_{t}\sum_{u} h_{uq}p_{tuq}$$

$$= \sum_{q=0}^{Q=1}\left(\sum_{t}\mu_{tq}\right)\sum_{u}\pi_u h_{uq} \tag{11}$$

But from (10)

$$p_q = \sum_{s=1}^{S} p_{sq} = \sum_{t}\sum_{u}p_{tuq}$$

$$= \left(\sum_{t}\mu_{tq}\right)\left(\sum_{u}\pi_u\right) = \sum_{t}\mu_{tq} \tag{12}$$

since of course the sum of the probabilities of the F_us must be 1. From (11)

$$\sum_{q=0}^{Q-1}\sum_{s=1}^{S} h_{sq}p_{sq} = \sum_{q=0}^{Q-1}\frac{1}{1+r_q}\sum_{u}\pi_u h_{uq} \tag{13}$$

Equation (13) gives the rather startling result that the present value of any investment which meets the independence and objectivity conditions, equals the expected value of returns in each time period, discounted by the factor appropriate for a certain return at that time. This is true even though individuals may have had different probabilities for the events that governed the returns on earlier investments. It is also interesting to note that each individual will behave in this manner so that there will be no discrepancy between public and private procedures for choosing among investments.

The independence assumption applied to utility functions was required because the functions U_{is} are conditional on the states of the world. This assumption appears reasonable, and in the case where U_{is} is the same for all values of s, it is automatically satisfied. Then the independence condition is simply that the net returns from an investment be independent of the returns from previous investments.

The difficulty that arises if one bases policy conclusions on these results is that some markets do not exist, and individuals do not value assets at the expected value of returns discounted by a factor appropriate for certain returns. It is tempting to argue that while individuals do not behave as expected-value decision makers because of the non-existence of certain markets for insurance, there is no reason why the government's behaviour should not be consistent with the results derived above where the allocation of resources was Pareto optimal. There are two difficulties with this line of argument. First, if we are to measure benefits and costs in terms of individuals' willingness to pay, then we must treat risk in accordance with these individual valuations. Since individuals do not have the opportunities for insuring assumed in the state-preference model, they will not value uncertainty as they would if these markets did exist. Second, the theory of the second best demonstrates that if resources are not allocated in a Pareto optimal manner, the appropriate public policies may not be those consistent with Pareto efficiency in perfect markets. Therefore, some other approach must be found for ascertaining the appropriate government policy towards risk. In particular, such an approach must be valid, given the non-existence of certain markets for insurance and imperfections in existing markets.

THE PUBLIC COST OF RISK BEARING

The critical question is: What is the cost of uncertainty in terms of costs to individuals? If one adopts the position that costs and benefits should be computed on the basis of individual willingness to pay, consistency demands that the public costs of risk bearing be computed in this way too. This is the approach taken here.

In the discussion that follows it is assumed that an individual's utility is dependent only upon his consumption and not upon the state of nature in which that consumption takes place. This assumption simplifies the presentation of the major theorem, but it is not essential. Again the expected utility theorem is assumed to hold. The presentation to follow analyses the cost of risk bearing by comparing the expected value of returns with the certainty equivalent of these returns. In this way the analysis of time and risk preference can be separated, so we need only consider one time period.

Suppose that the government were to undertake an investment with a certain outcome; then the benefits and costs are measured in terms of willingness to pay for this outcome. If, however, the outcome is uncertain, then the benefits and costs actually realized depend on which outcome in fact occurs. If an individual is risk averse, he will value the investment with the uncertain outcome at less than the expected value of its net return (benefit minus cost) to him. Therefore, in general the expected value of net benefits overstates willingness to pay by an amount equal to the cost of risk bearing. It is clear that the social cost of risk bearing will depend both upon which individuals receive the benefits and pay the costs and upon how large is each individual's share of these benefits and costs.

As a first step, suppose that the government were to undertake an investment and capture all benefits and pay all costs, i.e., the beneficiaries pay to the government an amount equal to the benefits received and the government pays all costs. Individuals who incur costs and those who receive benefits are therefore left indifferent to their preinvestment state. This assumption simply transfers all benefits and costs to the government, and the outcome of the investment will affect government disbursements and receipts. Given that the general taxpayer finances government expenditures, a public investment can be considered an investment in which each individual taxpayer has a very small share.

For precision, suppose that the government undertook an investment and that returns accrue to the government as previously described. In addition, suppose that in a given year the government were to have a balanced budget (or a planned deficit or surplus) and that taxes would be reduced by the amount of the net benefits if the returns are positive, and raised if returns are negative. Therefore, when the government undertakes an investment, each taxpayer has a small share of that investment with the returns being paid through changes in the level of taxes. By undertaking an investment the government adds to each individual's disposable income a random variable which is some fraction of the random variable representing the total net returns. The expected return to all taxpayers as a group equals expected net benefits.

Each taxpayer holds a small share of an asset with a random payoff, and the value of this asset to the individual is less than its expected return, assuming risk aversion. Stated differently, there is a cost of risk bearing that must be subtracted from the expected return in order to compute the value of the investment to the individual taxpayer. Since each taxpayer will bear some of the cost of the risk associated with the investment, these costs must be summed over all taxpayers in order to arrive at the total cost of risk bearing associated with a particular investment. These costs must be subtracted from the value of expected net benefits in order to obtain the correct measure for net benefits. The task is to assess these costs.

Suppose, as in the previous section, that there is one commodity, and that each individual's utility in a given year is a function of his income defined in terms of this commodity and is given by $U(Y)$. Further, suppose that U is bounded, continuous, strictly increasing, and differentiable. The assumptions that U is continuous and strictly increasing imply that U has a right and left derivative at every point and this is sufficient to prove the desired results; differentiability is assumed only to simplify presentation. Further suppose that U satisfies the conditions of the expected utility theorem.

Consider, for the moment, the case where all individuals are identical in that they have the same preferences, and their disposable incomes are identically distributed random variables represented by A. Suppose that the government were to undertake an investment with returns represented by B, which are statistically independent of A. Now divide the effect of this investment into two parts: a certain part equal to expected returns and a random part, with mean zero, which incorporates risk. Let $\bar{B} = E[B]$, and define the random variable X by $X = B - \bar{B}$. Clearly, X is independent of A and $E[X] = 0$. The effect of this investment is to add an amount $\bar{B}$ to government receipts along with a random component represented by X. The income of each taxpayer will be affected through taxes and it is the level of these taxes that determines the fraction of the investment he effectively holds.

Consider a specific taxpayer and denote his fraction of this investment by s, $0 \leq s \leq 1$. This individual's disposable income, given the public investment, is equal to $A + sB = A + s\bar{B} + sX$. The addition of sB to his disposable income is valued by the individual at its expected value less the cost of bearing the risk associated with the random component sX. If we suppose that each taxpayer has the same tax rate and that there are n taxpayers, then $s = 1/n$, and the value of the investment taken over all individuals is simply $\bar{B}$ minus n times the cost of risk bearing associated with the random variable $(1/n)X$. The central result of this section of the paper is that this total of the costs of risk bearing goes to zero as n becomes large. Therefore, for large values of n the value of a public investment almost equals the expected value of that investment.

To demonstrate this, we introduce the function

$$W(s) = E[U(A + s\bar{B} + sX)] \quad (0 \leq s \leq 1) \tag{14}$$

In other words, given the random variables A and B representing his individual income before the investment and the income from the investment, respectively, his expected utility is a function of s which represents his share of B. From (14) and the assumption that U' exists, it follows that

$$W'(s) = E[U'(A + s\bar{B} + sX)(\bar{B} + X)] \tag{15}$$

Since X is independent of A, it follows that $U'(A)$ and X are independent; therefore

$$E[U'(A)X] = E[U'(A)]E[X] = 0$$

so that

169

$$W'(0) = E[U'(A)(\bar{B} + X)]$$
$$= \bar{B}E[U'(A)] \tag{16}$$

Equation (16) is equivalent to the statement

$$\lim_{s \to 0} \frac{E[U(A + s\bar{B} + sX) - U(A)]}{s} = \bar{B}E[U'(A)] \tag{17}$$

Now let $s = 1/n$, so that equation (17) becomes

$$\lim_{n \to \infty} nE\left[U\left(A + \frac{\bar{B} + X}{n} \right) - U(A) \right] = \bar{B}E[U'(A)] \tag{18}$$

If we assume that an individual whose preferences are represented by U is a risk averter, then it is easily shown that there exists a unique number, $k(n) > 0$, for each value of n such that

$$E\left[U\left(A + \frac{\bar{B} + X}{n} \right) \right] = E\left[U\left(A + \frac{\bar{B}}{n} - k(n) \right) \right] \tag{19}$$

or, in other words, an individual would be indifferent between paying an amount equal to $k(n)$ and accepting the risk represented by $(1/n)X$. Therefore, $k(n)$ can be said to be the cost of risk bearing associated with the asset B. It can easily be demonstrated that $\lim_{n \to \infty} k(n) = 0$, i.e., the cost of holding the risky asset goes to zero as the amount of this asset held by the individual goes to zero. It should be noted that the assumption of risk aversion is not essential to the argument but simply one of convenience. If U represented the utility function of a risk preferrer, then all the above statements would hold except $k(n) < 0$, i.e., an individual would be indifferent between being paid $-k(n)$ and accepting the risk $(1/n)X$ (net of the benefit $(1/n)\bar{B}$).

We wish to prove not merely that the risk premium of the representative individual, $k(n)$, vanishes, but more strongly that the total of the risk premiums for all individuals, $nk(n)$, approaches zero as n becomes large.

From (18) and (19) it follows that

$$\lim_{n \to \infty} nE\left[U\left(A + \frac{\bar{B}}{n} - k(n) \right) - U(A) \right] = \bar{B}E[U'(A)] \tag{20}$$

In addition, $\bar{B}/n - k(n) \to 0$, when $n \to \infty$. It follows from the definition of a derivative that

$$\lim_{n \to \infty} \frac{E[U\{A + \bar{B}/n - k(n)\} - U(A)]}{\bar{B}/n - k(n)} = E[U'(A)] > 0 \tag{21}$$

Dividing (20) by (21) yields

$$\lim_{n \to \infty} [\bar{B} - nk(n)] = B \tag{22}$$

or $\lim_{n \to \infty} nk(n) = 0 \tag{23}$

The argument in (21) implies that $\bar{B}/n - k(n) \neq 0$. Suppose instead the equality held for infinitely many n. Substitution into the left-hand side of (20) shows that $\bar{B}$ must equal zero, so that $k(n) = 0$ for all such n, and hence $nk(n) = 0$ on that sequence, confirming (23).

Equation (23) states that the total of the costs of risk bearing goes to zero as the population of taxpayers becomes large. At the same time the monetary value of the investment to each taxpayer, neglecting the cost of risk, is $(1/n)\bar{B}$, and the total, summed over all individuals, is $\bar{B}$, the expected value of net benefits. Therefore, if n is large, the expected value of net benefits closely approximates the correct measure of net benefits defined in terms of willingness to pay for an asset with an uncertain return.

In the preceding analysis, it was assumed that all taxpayers were identical in that they had the same utility function, their incomes were represented by identically distributed variables, and they were subject to the same tax rates. These assumptions greatly simplify the presentation; however, they are not essential to the argument. Different individuals may have different preferences, incomes, and tax rates; and the basic theorem still holds, provided that as n becomes larger the share of the public investment borne by any individual becomes arbitrarily smaller.

The question necessarily arises as to how large n must be to justify proceeding as if the cost of publicly borne risk is negligible. This question can be given no precise answer; however, there are circumstances under which it appears likely that the cost of risk bearing will be small. If the size of the share borne by each taxpayer is a negligible component of his income, the cost of risk bearing associated with holding it will be small. It appears reasonable to assume, under these conditions, that the total cost of risk bearing is also small. This situation will exist where the investment is small with respect to the total wealth of the taxpayers. In the case of a federally sponsored investment, n is not only large but the investment is generally a very small fraction of national income even though the investment itself may be large in some absolute sense.

The results derived here and in the previous section depend on returns from a given public investment being independent of other components of national income. The government undertakes a wide range of public investments and it appears reasonable to assume that their returns are independent. Clearly, there are some government investments which are inter-dependent; however, where investments are inter-related they should be evaluated as a package. Even after such groupings are established, there will be a large number of essentially independent projects. It is sometimes argued that the returns from public investments are highly correlated with other components of national income through the business cycle. However, if we assume that stabilization policies are successful, then this difficulty does not arise. It should be noted that in most benefit–cost studies it is assumed that full employment will be maintained so that market prices can be used to measure benefits and costs. Consistency requires that this assumption be retained when considering risk as well. Further, if there is some positive correlation between the returns of an investment and other components of national income, the question remains as to whether this correlation is so high as to invalidate the previous result.

The main result is more general than the specific application to public investments. It has been demonstrated that if an individual or group holds an asset which is statistically independent of other assets, and if there is one or more individuals who do not share ownership, then the existing situation is not Pareto efficient. By selling some share of the asset to one of the individuals not originally possessing a share, the cost of risk bearing can be reduced while the expected returns remain unchanged. The reduction in the cost of risk bearing can then be redistributed to bring about a Pareto improvement. This result is similar to a result derived by Karl Borch. He proved that a condition for Pareto optimality in reinsurance markets requires that every individual hold a share of every independent risk.

When the government undertakes an investment it, in effect, spreads the risk among all taxpayers. Even if one were to accept that the initial distribution of risk was Pareto efficient, the new distribution of risk will not be efficient as the government does not discriminate among the taxpayers according to their risk preferences. What has been shown is that in the limit the situation where the risk of the investment is spread over all taxpayers is such that there is only a small deviation from optimality with regard to the distribution of that particular risk. The overall distribution of risk may be sub-optimal because of market imperfections and the absence of certain insurance markets. The great advantage of the results of this section is that they are not dependent on the existence of perfect markets for contingent claims.

This leads to an example which runs counter to the policy conclusions generally offered by economists. Suppose that an individual in the private sector of the economy were to undertake a given investment and, calculated on the basis of expected returns, the investment had a rate of return of 10 per cent. Because of the absence of perfect insurance markets, the investor subtracted from the expected return in each period a risk premium and, on the basis of returns adjusted for risk, his rate of return is 5 per cent. Now suppose that the government could invest the same amount of money in an investment which, on the basis of expected returns, would yield 6 per cent. Since the risk would be spread over all taxpayers, the cost of risk bearing would be negligible, and the true rate of return would be 6 per cent. Further, suppose that if the public investment were adopted it would displace the private investment. The question is: Should the public investment be undertaken? On the basis of the previous analysis, the answer is yes. The private investor is indifferent between the investment with the expected return of 10 per cent, and certain rate of return of 5 per cent. When the public investment is undertaken, it is equivalent to an investment with a certain rate of return of 6 per cent. Therefore, by undertaking the public investment, the government could more than pay the opportunity cost to the private investor of 5 per cent associated with the diversion of funds from private investment.

The previous example illustrates Hirshleifer's point that the case of evaluating public investments differently from private ones is an argument for the second best. Clearly, if the advantages of the more efficient distribution of risk could be achieved in connection with the private investment alternative, this would be superior to the public investment. The question then arises as to how the government can provide insurance for private investors and thereby transfer the risks from the private sector to the public at large. The same difficulties arise as before, moral hazards and transaction costs. It may not be possible for the government to provide such insurance, and in such cases second-best solutions are in order. Note that if the government could undertake any investment, then this difficulty would not arise. Perhaps one of the strongest criticisms of a system of freely competitive markets is that the inherent difficulty in establishing certain markets for insurance brings about a sub-optimal allocation of resources. If we consider an investment, as does Hirshleifer, as an exchange of certain present income for uncertain future income, then the misallocation will take the form of underinvestment.

Now consider Hirshleifer's recommendation that, in cases such as the one above, a direct subsidy be used to induce more private investment rather than increase public investment. Suppose that a particular private investment were such that the benefits would be a marginal increase in the future supply of an existing commodity, i.e., this investment would neither introduce a new commodity nor affect future prices. Therefore, benefits can be measured at each point in time by the market value of this output, and can be fully captured through the sale of the commodity. Let $\bar{V}$ be the present value of expected net returns, and let V be the present value of net returns adjusted for risk where the certainty rate is used to discount both streams. Further, suppose there were a public investment, where the risks were publicly borne, for which the present value of expected net benefits was P. Since the risk is publicly borne, from the previous discussion it follows that P is the present value of net benefits adjusted for risk. Now suppose that $\bar{V} > P > V$. According to Hirshleifer, we should undertake the private investment rather than the public one, and pay a subsidy if necessary to induce private entrepreneurs to undertake this investment. Clearly, if there is a choice between one investment or the other, given the existing distribution of risk, the public investment is superior. The implication is that if a risky investment in the private sector is displaced by a public investment with a lower expected return but with a higher return when appropriate adjustments are made for risks, this represents a Hicks–Kaldor improvement. This is simply a restatement of the previous point that the government could more than pay the opportunity cost to the private entrepreneur.

Now consider the case for a direct subsidy to increase the level of private investment. One can only argue for direct subsidy of the private investment if $V < 0 < \bar{V}$. The minimum subsidy required is $|V|$. Suppose the taxpayers were to pay this subsidy, which is a transfer of income from the public at large to the private investor, in order to cover the loss from the investment. The net benefits, including the cost of risk bearing, remain negative because while the subsidy has partially offset the cost of risk bearing to the individual investor, it has not reduced this cost. Therefore, a direct public subsidy in this case results in a less efficient allocation of resources.

We can summarize as follows: It is implied by Hirshleifer that it is better to undertake an investment with a higher expected return than one with a lower expected return (see Hirshleifer, 1965). This proposition is not in general valid, as the distribution of risk bearing is critical. This statement is true, however, when the costs of risk bearing associated with both investments are the same. What has been shown is that when risks are publicly borne, the costs of risk bearing are negligible; therefore, a public investment with an expected return which is less than that of a given private investment may nevertheless be superior to the private alternative. Therefore, the fact that public investments with lower expected return may replace private investment is not necessarily cause for concern. Furthermore, a programme of providing direct subsidies to encourage more private investment does not alter the costs of risk bearing and, therefore, will encourage investments which are inefficient when the costs of risk are considered. The programme which produces the desired result is one to insure private investments.

One might raise the question as to whether risk spreading is not associated with large corporations so that the same result would apply, and it is easily seen that the same reasoning does apply. This can be made more precise by assuming there were n stockholders who were identical in the sense that their utility functions were identical, their incomes were represented by identically distributed random variables, and they had the same share in the company. When the corporation undertakes an investment with a return in a given year represented by B, each stockholder's income is represented by $A + (1/n)B$. This assumes, of course, that a change in earnings was reflected in dividends, and that there were no business taxes. Clearly, this is identical to the situation previously described, and if n is large, the total cost of risk bearing to the stockholders will be negligible. If the income or wealth of the stockholders were large with respect to the size of the investment, this result would be likely to hold. Note that whether or not the investment is a large one, with respect to the assets of the firm, is not relevant. While an investment may constitute a major part of a firm's assets if each stockholder's share in the firm is a small component of his income, the cost of risk bearing to him will be very small. It then follows that if managers were acting in the interest of the firm's shareholders, they would essentially ignore risk and choose investments with the highest expected returns.

There are two important reasons why large corporations may behave as risk averters. First, in order to control the firm, some shareholder may hold a large block of stock which is a significant component of his wealth. If this were true, then, from his point of view, the costs of risk bearing would not be negligible, and the firm should behave as a risk averter. Note in this case that the previous result does not hold because the cost of risk bearing to each stockholder is not small, even though the number of stockholders is very large. Investment behaviour in this case is essentially the same as the case of a single investor.

The second case is when, even though from the stockholder's point of view, risk should be ignored, it may not be in the interest of the corporate managers to neglect risk. Their careers and income are intimately related to the firm's performance. From their point of view, variations in the outcome of some corporate action impose very real costs. In this case, given a degree of autonomy, the corporate managers, in considering prospective investments, may discount for risk when it is not in the interest of the stockholders to do so.

Suppose that this were the case and also suppose that the marginal rate of time preference for each individual in the economy was 5 per cent. From the point of view of the stockholders, risk can be ignored and any investment with an expected return which is greater than 5 per cent should be undertaken. However, suppose that corporate managers discount for risk so that only investments with expected rates of return that exceed 10 per cent are undertaken. From the point of view of the stockholders, the rate of return on these investments, taking risk into account, is over 10 per cent. Given a marginal rate of time preference of 5 per cent, it follows that from the point of view of the individual stockholder there is too little investment. Now suppose further that the government were considering an investment with an expected rate of return of 6 per cent. Since the cost of risk bearing is negligible, this investment should be undertaken since the marginal rate of time preference is less than 6 per cent. However, in this case, if the financing were such that a private investment with a 10 per cent expected rate of return is displaced by the public investment, there is a loss because in both cases the risk is distributed so as to make the total cost of risk bearing negligible. The public investment should be undertaken, but only at the expense of consumption.

THE ACTUAL ALLOCATION OF RISK

In the idealized public investment considered in the last section, all benefits and costs accrued to the government and were distributed among the taxpayers. In this sense, all uncertainty was borne collectively. Suppose instead that some benefits and costs of sizeable magnitudes accrued directly to individuals so that these individuals incurred the attendant costs of risk bearing. In this case it is appropriate to discount for the risk, as would these individuals. Such a situation would arise in the case of a government irrigation project where the benefits accrued to farmers as increased income. The changes in farm income would be uncertain and, therefore, should be valued at more or less than their expected value, depending on the states in which they occur. If these increases were independent of other components of farm income, and if we assume that the farmers' utility were only a function of his income and not the state in which he receives that income, then he would value the investment project at less than the expected increase in his income, provided he is risk averse. If, however, the irrigation project paid out in periods of drought so that total farm income was not only increased but also stabilized, then the farmers would value the project at more than the expected increase in their incomes.

In general, some benefits and costs will accrue to the government and the uncertainties involved will be publicly borne; other benefits and costs will accrue to individuals and the attendant uncertainties will be borne privately. In the first case the cost of risk bearing will be negligible; in the second case these costs may be significant. Therefore, in calculating the present value of returns from a public investment a distinction must be made between private and public benefits and costs. The present value of public benefits and costs should be evaluated by estimating the expected net benefits in each period and discounting them, using a discount factor appropriate for investment with certain returns. On the other hand, private benefits and costs must be discounted with respect to both time and risk in accordance with the preferences of the individuals to whom they accrue.

From the foregoing discussion it follows that different streams of benefits and costs should be treated in different ways with respect to uncertainty. One way to do this is to discount these streams of returns at different rates of discount ranging from the certainty rate for benefits and costs accruing to the government and using higher rates that reflect discounting for risk for returns accruing directly to individuals. Such a procedure raises some difficulties of identification, but this problem does not appear to be insurmountable. In general, costs are paid by the government, which receives some revenue, and the net stream should be discounted at a rate appropriate for certain returns. Benefits accruing directly to individuals should be discounted according to individual time and risk preferences. As a practical matter, Hirshleifer's suggestion of finding the marginal rate of return on assets with similar payoffs in the private sector, and using this as the rate of discount, appears reasonable for discounting those benefits and costs which accrue privately.

One problem arises with this latter procedure which has received little attention. In considering public investments, benefits and costs are aggregated and the discussion of uncertainty is carried out in terms of these aggregates. This obscures many of the uncertainties because benefits and costs do not in general accrue to the same individuals, and the attendant uncertainties should not be netted out when considering the totals. To make this clear, consider an investment where the benefits and costs varied greatly, depending on the state of nature, but where the difference between total benefits and total costs was constant for every state. Further, suppose that the benefits and costs accrued to different groups. While the investment is certain from a social point of view, there is considerable risk from a private point of view. In the case of perfect markets for contingent claims, each individual will discount the stream of costs and benefits accruing to him at the appropriate rate for each time and state. However, suppose that such markets do not exist. Then risk-averse individuals will value the net benefits accruing to them at less than their expected value. Therefore, if net benefits accruing to this individual are positive, this requires discounting expected returns at a higher rate than that appropriate for certain returns. On the other hand, if net benefits to an individual are negative, this requires discounting expected returns at a rate lower than the certainty rate. Raising the rate of discount only reduces the present value of net benefits when they are positive. Therefore, the distinction must be made not only between benefits and costs which accrue to the public and those which accrue directly to individuals, but also between individuals whose net benefits are negative and those whose benefits are positive. If all benefits and costs accrued privately, and different individuals received the benefits and paid the costs, the appropriate procedure would be to discount the stream of expected benefits at a rate higher than the certainty rate, and costs at a rate lower than the certainty rate. This would hold even if the social totals were certain.

Fortunately, as a practical matter this may not be of great importance as most costs are borne publicly and, therefore, should be discounted using the certainty rate. Benefits often accrue to individuals, and where there are attendant uncertainties it is appropriate to discount the expected value of these benefits at higher rates, depending on the nature of the uncertainty and time-risk preferences of the individuals who receive these benefits. It is somewhat ironic that the practical implication of this analysis is that for the typical case where costs are borne publicly and benefits accrue privately, this procedure will qualify fewer projects than the procedure of using a higher rate to discount both benefits and costs.

NOTES

1 J. Hirshleifer (1965, 1966) and Hirshleifer, J.C. de Haven and J.W. Milliman (1960, pp. 139–50).
2 For this point of view, see P.A. Samuelson and W. Vickrey (1964).
3 For this point of view, see O. Eckstein (1961) and S. Marglin (1963).
4 Hirshleifer (1965, pp. 523–34); (1966, pp. 268–75).
5 Hirshleifer (1966, pp. 270–5).
6 Hirshleifer (1966, pp. 270–5).
7 Hirshleifer (1966, p. 270).
8 For a discussion of this problem see M.V. Pauly (1968) and Arrow (1968).
9 For a basic statement of the state-preference approach, see Arrow (1964).
10 J. von Neumann and O. Morgenstern (1964), and Hirshleifer (1965, pp. 534–6).

11 The following argument was sketched in Arrow (1966, pp. 28–30).
12 Hirshleifer (1965, pp. 323–34).

REFERENCES

Arrow, K.J. (1964), 'The role of securities in the optimal allocation of risk-bearing', *Review of Economic Studies*, 31: 91–6.

(1966), 'Discounting and public investment criteria', in A.V. Kneese and S.C. Smith (eds.), *Water Research*, Johns Hopkins Press.

(1968), 'The economics of moral hazard: further comment', *American Economic Review*, 58: 537–8.

Borch, K. (1960), 'The safety loading of reinsurance', *Skandinavisk Aktuarietid-Skrift*, pp. 163–74.

Eckstein, O. (1961), 'A survey of the theory of public expenditure', and 'Reply', in J.M. Buchanan (ed.), *Public Finances: Needs, Sources and Utilization*, Princeton University Press, pp. 493–504.

Hirshleifer, J. (1965), 'Investment decision under uncertainty: choice-theoretic approaches', *Quarterly Journal of Economics*, 79: 509–36.

(1966), 'Investment decision under uncertainty: applications of the state preference approach', *Quarterly Journal of Economics*, 80: 252–77.

Hirshleifer, J., J.C. de Haven and J.W. Milliman (1960), *Water Supply: Economics, Technology and Policy*, University of Chicago Press.

Marglin, S. (1963), 'The social rate of discount and the optimal rate of investment', *Quarterly Journal of Economics*, 77: 95–111.

Pauly, M.V. (1968), 'The economics of moral hazard: comment', *American Economic Review*, 58: 531–7.

Samuelson, P.A. and W. Vickrey (1964), 'Discussion', *American Economic Review Proceedings*, 59: 88–96.

von Neumann, J. and O. Morgenstern (1964), *Theory of Games and Economic Behavior*, 2nd edn, Wiley.

5

INCOME DISTRIBUTION:

Allowing for income distribution

R. Layard and A.A. Walters

1 CRITERIA FOR A WELFARE IMPROVEMENT

We often need to compare different economic states, none of which may be optimal. For example, if one is doing a cost–benefit analysis of a public motorway project, one wants to compare social welfare in two 'states of the world': state 0, where the motorway is not built, and state 1, where the motorway is built and the money to build it is raised in some specified fashion. This is called *cost–benefit analysis* because in comparing state 0 with state 1 we want to assess the additional benefits generated by the project minus the alternative benefits which would have been available but have been lost due to the project (i.e., the costs of the project). In principle one can do a cost–benefit evaluation of the effects of any action, be it private (getting married?) or public (subsidizing food?). How?

The action of shifting from state 0 to state 1 is to be judged by its effects on the happiness of all those affected. One can imagine two main possible types of outcome:

1   Someone gains and no one loses (or no one gains and someone loses).
2   Someone gains but someone else loses.

The Pareto criterion

Case 1 is illustrated by the move from P^0 to P^1 (figure 5.1(a)). Whatever one's social welfare function (provided it is benevolent), this must be an improvement. The jargon describes such a change as a *Pareto improvement*.

> A Pareto improvement is a social change from which at least one person gains and nobody loses, i.e., $\Delta u^i > 0$ (some i) and $\Delta u^i \geq 0$ (all i).

If the move from P to P^1 is a Pareto improvement, we can say that P^1 is Pareto superior to P^0. Notice the relation between the concept of Pareto improvement,

This chapter previously appeared in R. Layard and A. Walters (1978), *Microeconomic Theory*. We would like to thank McGraw-Hill Inc. for their kind permission to reproduce it here.

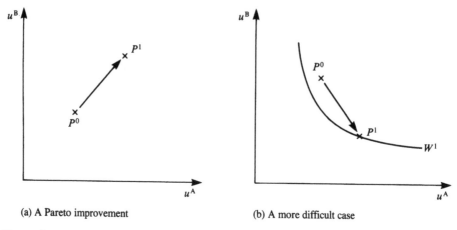

(a) A Pareto improvement   (b) A more difficult case

Figure 5.1 Welfare changes

which describes a change from one state to another, and the concept of Pareto optimality, which describes a state. We can formulate the relation as follows.

A Pareto-optimal state is one from which no Pareto improvement is possible.

A general criterion

Unfortunately in the real world most changes hurt someone (case 2), and if we were only willing to undertake Pareto improvements we should spend much of our time in suspended animation. For the Pareto criterion does not provide a complete ranking of all states. It only orders states in which one utility bundle dominates the other. It says nothing for example about the choices in figure 5.1(b). Is A's gain of sufficient importance to outweigh B's loss (perhaps B is a dangerous criminal who would be locked up if the move to P^1 were made)? To get a complete ordering of social states we have to invoke our welfare function $W(u^A, u^B)$ and this speedily tells us that in figure 5.1(b), P^0 is to be preferred.
Since $W = W(u^A, u^B)$ we have

$$\Delta W = W_{u^A} \Delta u^A + W_{u^B} \Delta u^B \quad \text{approximately}$$

The change is an improvement if $\Delta W > 0$. (Put like this, a Pareto improvement is a special case where ΔW must be positive because both Δu^A and Δu^B are non-negative and one of them is positive.) If enough points like P^0 and P^1 were compared and a move made whenever $\Delta W > 0$, we should ultimately reach the optimum, or bliss point.

However, the approach is not operational so far. For practical policy purposes we need to measure the changes in individual welfare not in units of utility but in units of some numeraire good, and then to attach social value to increments in the numeraire good accruing to different members of society. For this purpose we multiply and divide each term on the right-hand side by the marginal utility of the numeraire good (y) to the individual concerned, so that we obtain

$$\Delta W = W_{u^A} u_y^A \frac{\Delta u^A}{u_y^A} + W_{u^B} u_y^B \frac{\Delta u^B}{u_y^B} \tag{1}$$

We now have for each individual the following two terms:

1    $\Delta u / u_y$ measures his actual change in utility divided by the change in utility that would be produced by one extra unit of y. It thus indicates approximately how many units of y would have produced the same change in utility as he actually experienced. It also indicates approximately how many units of y he might be willing to pay to bring about the change from state 0 to state 1. We shall leave the question of exact measures of individual welfare change and simply assume that all measures give the same answer, which we shall denote by Δy.

2    $W_{u^A} u_y^A$ (or $W_{u^B} u_y^B$) measures the social value of an extra unit of y accruing to A (or B), or what one may call the weight attaching to a marginal unit of his y.

For any action we then simply tabulate Δy for each of the individuals affected and then assign our own ethical weights to each individual's income (or leave this to the politicians). Suppose the value were as follows:

Person	Δy^i	Weight^i
A (rich)	200	1
B (poor)	− 100	3

The change would be undesirable since, using the previous formula

$$\Delta W = 1(200) + 3(-100) = -100 < 0$$

The Kaldor criterion

Here a purist might leave the matter. However, one might well ask: Why not pursue this project and at the same time make A give to B 100 units of y? Then you would have a Pareto improvement. The answer is of course that, if the policy consisted of the project *plus* compensation, the table above would not represent the policy. Instead we should have:

Person	Δy^i
A	100
B	0

and this would pass the test. But if compensation is not actually going to be paid, we can only claim that the project offers a *potential* Pareto improvement. There is no ethical basis for the notion that a project should be done if and only if it leads to a potential Pareto improvement. However, this test has great importance in drawing attention to the waste that can result if productive projects have to be rejected on equity grounds, and we shall therefore discuss the test at some length. It was originally proposed by Kaldor, and we shall refer to it as the *Kaldor criterion.*[1]

> A Kaldor improvement is a change from a given output-mix distributed in a given way to another output-mix which would enable the gainers to compensate the losers while continuing to gain themselves. Since the compensation need only be hypothetical, a Kaldor improvement offers only a potential Pareto improvement.

One should note straightaway that the criterion is explicitly more limited than the general approach offered by the ethical welfare function. For example, if a costless transfer were made between a rich person and a poor one, there would be neither an improvement nor otherwise on the Kaldor criterion. For the criterion is only meant to be used to judge between output mixes. The argument is that we should think separately about production and distribution. Production decisions should maximize the size of the cake, and distributional policy should ensure that it is divided fairly. But the two types of decision should be taken independently. The argument is wrong for at least three reasons.

Critique of the Kaldor criterion

First, the concept of cake is not clear if there is more than one type of cake. One may not be able to decide which of two output mixes is efficient unless one simultaneously settles the question of distribution. The efficient output mix is chosen by a single person using his indifference map and setting his marginal rate of substitution (MRS) equal to the marginal rate of transformation (MRT). By analogy, in the many-person case we might be able to do the same thing using a community indifference map. Each community indifference curve (CIC) would show the locus of (x, y) combinations which could maintain all individuals at fixed levels of utility, assuming always that any given (x, y) bundle was efficiently consumed. However, normally there will be more than one community indifference curve through each point in (x, y) space. Consider, for example, point (x^2, y^2) in figure 5.2. Many different efficient utility mixes (u^A, u^B) can be obtained from that bundle of goods, depending on the distribution of income. Further, the locus of the community indifference curve will depend on which utility mix we take. Take, for example, the utility mix (u^{A0}, u^{B0}), corresponding to the distribution of (x^2, y^2) shown at S. We now want to find all the other (x, y) combinations which are just able to yield (u^{A0}, u^{B0}). To do this we can imagine ourselves holding 0^A steady and thus holding steady A's indifference curve for u^{A0}. At the same time we move 0^B, thus shifting B's indifference map; but we do this in such a way that B's indifference curve for u^{B0} remains tangential to A's indifference curve for u^{A0}. This takes 0^B, for example, to a point such as (x^0, y^0). This point is another point on the community indifference curve for (u^{A0}, u^{B0}). It is intuitively clear that the slope of the community indifference curve at (x^2, y^2) equals the slope of the individual indifference curves at S, where (x^2, y^2) was allocated between the two consumers. The reason is that if one starts to move 0^B along the community indifference curve towards (x^0, y^0), the direction in which 0^B moves is governed by and equal to the slope of the individual indifference curves which are being held tangential to each other.[2]

> A community indifference curve is a locus of (x, y) points which make it just possible to achieve a given utility bundle (u^{A0}, u^{B0}). The slope of the curve equals the marginal rate of substitution of y for x (which is the same for all citizens).

Clearly more than one community indifference curve can pass through a given point (x^2, y^2). Suppose we redistribute this output mix in favour of A. Let us move to point T with utilities (u^{A1}, u^{B1}). At this point in our particular example the relative value of x is much higher. If we now draw a community indifference curve for (u^{A1}, u^{B1}), it would pass through (x^2, y^2) all right but would have a much steeper slope than the previous community indifference curve. These two intersecting curves are shown in figure 5.3. In such a case there is no unambiguous ranking of the social output, independent of distribution.

For the same reason, the Kaldor criterion can yield the paradoxical result that a move from state 0 to state 1 is an improvement, and so is a move from state 1 to state 0. Suppose in figure 5.3 we start at (x^0, y^0) distributed to generate (u^{A0}, u^{B0}). We then move in state 1 to outputs (x^1, y^1) and utilities (u^{A1}, u^{B1}). The move is a Kaldor improvement if (x^1, y^1) can give the original utilities (u^{A0}, u^{B0}), for, if so, it must be possible for the gainers from the move to compensate the losers. Thus the test is whether (x^1, y^1) lies to the north-east of the original community indifference curve. If it does, compensation can be effected, with some of x and/or y left over to make the gainers better off. In figure 5.3 this criterion is satisfied. But having reached state 1, we now ask if state 0 was not better. A move from state 1 to state 0 is a Kaldor improvement if (x^0, y^0) is sufficient to provide (u^{A1}, u^{B1}). It is. Consequently, moves in both directions are Kaldor improvements. The attempt to separate production issues from distributional issues has failed.[3]

How serious is this problem? It would not arise if redistribution of a given output mix (x^2, y^2) produced no change in the relative value of x and y. Suppose we start from S in figure 5.2. We are in a money economy, and each consumer is maximizing utility subject to a money budget constraint. We now increase the money income of A and reduce that of B by the same amount, while we hold prices constant. Suppose that out of each additional dollar A buys a units of x and β units of y, and also that for each dollar that B loses B reduces consumption of x by a units and of y by β units. Then, as income is transferred from B to A there

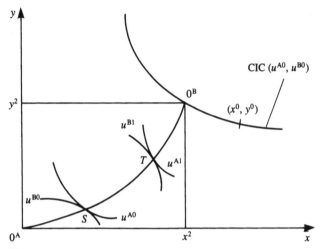

Figure 5.2 The community indifference curve: product space

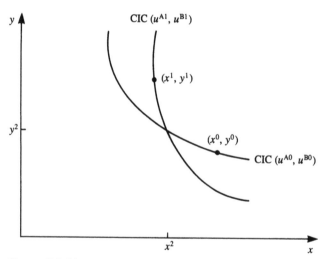

Figure 5.3 Kaldor improvements galore

is no need for any change in relative prices to ensure that the total supply of x and y is demanded. So the efficiency locus must be a straight line and the marginal rate of substitution remains constant as we move along it. In this case the slope of the community indifference curve does not change as redistribution proceeds. So the condition for a unique set of community indifference curves is that the marginal propensity to buy each good out of additional income must be the same for all individuals at any given set of relative prices. For many limited problems such as a cost–benefit analysis of a motorway, this may be a reasonable working assumption, though for the analysis of large tax changes and so on, the problems may be more serious.

This brings us to a second and more fundamental objection to the Kaldor approach. The reasoning behind the criterion is this: If the standard optimality conditions are satisfied and there are lump sum transfers, the social value of each person's dollar will be equal. Expenditure on x (or y) by A has the same social value as expenditure on x (or y) by B

$$W_{u^A} u_y^A = W_{u^B} u_y^B$$

Therefore our general welfare criterion simplifies to

$$\Delta W^* = \frac{\Delta u^A}{u_y^A} + \frac{\Delta u^B}{u_y^B} = \Delta y^A + \Delta y^B$$

However, this only holds if optimality can be achieved by means of lump-sum transfers.

> A lump-sum transfer is one in which neither the loser nor the gainer can affect the size of the transfer by modifying his behaviour.

But lump-sum transfers are impossible. Let us suppose the tax collector can only observe an individual's earnings. He then either taxes them if they are high or subsidizes them if they are low. But this will induce a substitution effect away from work. And that is the fundamental problem of redistribution. More redistribution requires higher marginal rates of tax, and higher marginal tax rates imply ever increasing efficiency losses. After a point the gain in equity from increasing the tax rate will be more than offset by the efficiency cost. At that point we have the optimal tax structure, and it will not embody a 100 per cent marginal tax rate. So inequality will remain. And, on the assumptions we discuss below, this means that the social value of a dollar given to a rich person will be less than the social value of a dollar given to a poor one (weight ^{rich} < weight^{poor}). This is so, even though the distribution of income is the best we can make it, given the constraint that lump-sum transfers are impossible and transfers are effected via the income tax.

> If lump-sum transfers are impossible and social welfare is maximized through an optimal income tax, the social value of each person's dollar will not be identical.

If we now have a project which confers benefits in lump-sum form, it might not be worth doing even if it benefited the rich more than it hurt the poor (e.g., building a motorway through a slum). But it would still be important to notice the cost (in terms of the unweighted $\Sigma \Delta y^i$) of not being able to make lump-sum transfers.

So far we have assumed that society is already arranged so as to maximize the project evaluator's ethical welfare function. A third case against using the Kaldor approach would arise when the evaluator did not agree with the welfare function implicit in the existing distribution of income. It will often happen in any state, however monolithic, that individuals (or local governments) can influence actions in directions that are inconsistent with the values of the central government. If they do not agree with the central government, they should presumably pursue what they believe in.[4]

2 THE MEASUREMENT OF WELFARE COST

Despite the shortcomings of the Kaldor criterion, it is often useful to measure the effects of a change on the total value of output, independently of the distribution of output. One reason is that it is often difficult to know exactly who the gainers and losers are. Even if we do, we can always think of our final choice as depending on the tradeoff between effects on total output and on inequality (see below).[5]

So how are we to measure the effect of a policy on total output (measured in terms of y), i.e., on the unweighted sum of Δy^i? Suppose, for example, that in figure 5.4 we started at P^0, i.e., (x^0, y^0) and then introduced a subsidy on x matched by an equal yield tax on y. This would move us to P^1, i.e., (x^1, y^1). What is the net cost of the move in terms of y? There are two natural questions to ask:

1   If we start from (x^0, y^0), what loss of y would have the same effect on utility as the actual move to (x^1, y^1)?

2   If we start from (x^1, y^1), what gain in y would have the same effect on utility as returning to (x^0, y^0)?

To simplify matters we shall make an assumption that ensures that the answer to both questions is the same. The assumption is that x is a good for which, at any particular set of prices, each consumer demands a given amount that does not vary with income. In other words, the income elasticity of demand for the good is zero. This means that for any particular individual the indifference curves are vertically parallel. Once we know his consumption of x, we know his MRS_{yx}, since this depends only on x and does not vary with y. The assumption also means that, since both individuals have the same marginal propensity to consume x out of additional income (a propensity of zero), community indifference curves are unambiguously defined and are vertically parallel to each other.[6] So what is the net cost of moving from P^0 to P^1 in figure 5.4? Clearly it is the distance $P^1 R$, since with this much more y both consumers could be restored to their original utility.

Exactly the same analysis can be presented in terms of an alternative diagram, in which x is on the horizontal axis as before, but the vertical axis has, not total units of y, but units of y per unit of x. This is in fact the familiar diagram of supply and demand, except that the vertical axis has units of a numeraire good y per unit of x rather than units of money per unit of x. It is vital to understand the relation between this 'per-unit' diagram and the 'total' diagram above it.

Consider first the transformation curve in the total diagram. Its slope measures MRT_{yx}. In the per-unit diagram MRT_{yx} is measured by a distance above the horizontal axis. Since the transformation curve becomes absolutely steeper as x increases, the height of MRT_{yx} in the per-unit diagram rises with x.

Suppose now that we want to evaluate the absolute change in y along the transformation curve, as x increases from x^0 to x^1. If we use the total diagram, we

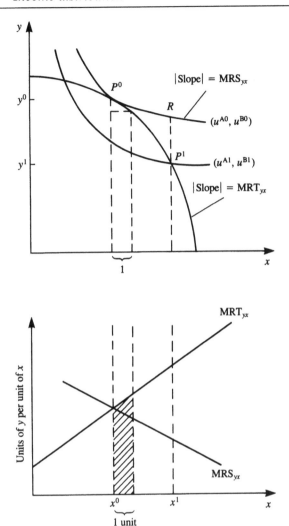

Figure 5.4 Welfare cost of a subsidy

take the difference in the vertical heights of P^0 and of P^1; i.e., we take $(y^0 - y^1)$. If we use the per-unit diagram, we take the area under the MRT_{yx} curve between x^0 and x^1. To see this, revert to the total diagram. Starting at P^0, commence the descent of the hill towards P^1. First move one unit in the horizontal direction, i.e., from x^0 to $x^0 + 1$. How far have you moved down in the vertical plane? Clearly, $- dy/dx$; so the slope measures the descent per-unit movement in a horizontal direction. Now move on one more unit in the horizontal direction. Again you descend $- dy/dx$. Each time the slope must, of course, be evaluated at the point where you are. The total loss of height between P^0 and P^1 is the sum of all the short slopes you have traversed. So, if x were a discrete variable taking only integer values, we should have a loss of height of

$$|\Delta y| = \sum_{x=x^0}^{x^1} \text{MRT}_{yx}(x)$$

where $\text{MRT}_{yx} = -dy/dx$. This expression has a clear counterpart in the per-unit diagram. The loss of y as x rises from x^0 to $x^0 + 1$ is shown by the shaded area under the MRT curve. As x rises from x^0 to x^1 the loss of y is the whole area under the curve from x^0 to x^1. We, of course, expect quantities of y to be measured by areas in the per-unit diagram, since this diagram has dimensions of y/x on the vertical axis and x on the horizontal axis: the product of the two is thus in units of y.

Let us get back to economics. We are saying nothing more than that the cost of increasing x from x^0 to x^1 is the sum of the marginal cost of each unit from x^0 to x^1. Since x is not in fact a discrete variable, a more satisfactory expression is the integral[7] that corresponds to our earlier summation

$$|\Delta y| = \int_{x^0}^{x^1} \text{MRT}_{yx}(x)dx = \text{cost of } x^1 \text{ over and above } x^0$$

This tells us the amount of y that has to be given up if x is increased from x^0 to x^1.

But how much y are people willing to give up? In the total diagram this is measured by the difference in the vertical heights of P^0 and of R. In the per-unit diagram, MRS_{yx} measures the absolute slope of the community indifference curve. As x rises, it falls, since the indifference curve becomes flatter – the relative value of x falls. For reasons identical to those given on the cost side, the vertical difference between P^0 and R in the total diagram is by definition equal to the area under the MRS_{yx} curve in the per-unit diagram

$$|\Delta y| = \int_{x^0}^{x^1} \text{MRS}_{yx}(x)dx = \text{willingness to sacrifice for } x^1 \text{ over and above } x^0$$

The welfare loss resulting from the move is the difference between the actual cost of the move and the cost people are willing to bear

$$\text{Welfare loss} = \int_{x^0}^{x^1} [\text{MRT}_{yx}(x) - \text{MRS}_{yx}(x)]dx$$

This formula is perfectly general.

But let us remind ourselves of what it measures. The welfare cost is the sum of individual net losses (losses minus gains). Conversely, the sum of net gains could be called the 'welfare gain'. How does this relate to our previous measurement of welfare change

$$\Delta W = \text{weight}^A \, \Delta y^A + \text{weight}^B \, \Delta y^B$$

Quite simply it is the same, provided $\text{weight}^A = \text{weight}^B = 1$. When economists talk about 'welfare costs and gains', they are making this assumption more often than not. The reader must decide whether they are doing so by reference to the context.

The welfare cost of a move from x^0 to x^1 is

$$\text{Welfare loss} = \int_{x^0}^{x^1} [\text{MRT}_{yx}(x) - \text{MRS}_{yx}(x)]dx$$

This may be positive or negative. A negative welfare cost implies a potential Pareto improvement; and a positive cost, the reverse. The welfare cost is the unweighted sum of individual losses (gains being negative losses).

Talking loosely, one might say that, if moving from x^0 to x^1 involves a welfare cost, x^1 is a less efficient output than x^0, though strictly, an output mix is either efficient or not and it is a figure of speech to say that one output mix is less efficient than the other, if neither is efficient.

In a competitive economy with no technological externalities MRT_{yx} is given by the supply price of x and MRS_{yx} by the demand price of x. However, if there are income effects in supply or demand for x, we should need to measure welfare change using the 'compensated' demand and supply surves.

In a full analysis, however, we should always want to allow for the fact that a policy with positive net losses may still help someone. For example, food subsidies financed by taxes on manufacturers will benefit landowners in a closed economy. Even though the landowners could not compensate the other members of society for their losses, the change might be considered desirable in a country of small peasant proprietors. It could never be as good a way of supporting landowners as a lump-sum tax transfer, nor (if all factors are in fixed supply) as an income tax transfer. But it might yet be better than competitive equilibrium, even though the welfare cost appears as positive. To decide this we need to use some specific welfare function rather than the completely general one used so far.

3 THE SOCIAL WELFARE FUNCTION AND THE EQUITY–EFFICIENCY TRADEOFF

What, if anything, can we say about the desirable properties of a social welfare function such as $W(u^A, u^B)$? This is really a philosophical problem, but economists cannot avoid philosophical problems if they want to think about normative issues.[8]

First, a word about individual utility. For the positive problem of explaining individual behaviour, it is sufficient to assume that an individual has a preference ordering over all possible 'states of the world'. Suppose we use the vector x^i to describe the level of all relevant variables in state i. If individual A can rank all vectors x^i, we can represent his or her preference ordering by a utility function $u^A(x)$.[9] Any utility function will do, so long as, whenever A prefers i to j, we have

$$u^A(x^i) > u^A(x^j)$$

So if one specific function which does the trick is $v(x)$, any strictly increasing monotonic transformation of v must also do the trick. In other words, let $f(\ )$ be a function of a single variable which increases as that variable increases. Then $f[v(\mathbf{x})]$ will be as satisfactory a utility indicator as $v(\mathbf{x})$, because it maintains the same ranking of the various bundles $\mathbf{x}$. This is what is meant by saying that the utility function is purely 'ordinal' – it simply provides a numerical representation of the preference ordering.

Does such information on preferences provide enough information for making policy prescriptions? It would be very surprising if one could say whether one situation was better than another, just from knowing the preferences of each individual for the two states. For example, if a cake were to be divided between A and B, A might prefer the division whereby A get three-quarters of the cake to the division whereby A only gets one-half; but B might have the opposite ordering. We could hardly expect to say which situation was actually preferable unless we could in some way compare the needs of A and B.

Arrow's impossibility theorem

This idea is obvious from common sense, but it has been made familiar to economists as a result of the work of Arrow, who asked: Can there exist sensible rules which would tell us how to rank different states of the world from an ethical point of view if the only information we have relates to individual preferences? Suppose there are three possible states of the world, 1, 2 and 3 and three people, A, B and C, and we know the order in which the states lie in each individual's preferences. For example A's ordering might be (from highest to lowest) states 1, 2, 3; B's might be states 2, 3, 1; and C's might be states 3, 1, 2. Thus in tabular form we could write the ordering over vectors $\mathbf{x}^i$ as

	Person		
Order	A	B	C
1	$\mathbf{x}^1$	$\mathbf{x}^2$	$\mathbf{x}^3$
2	$\mathbf{x}^2$	$\mathbf{x}^3$	$\mathbf{x}^1$
3	$\mathbf{x}^3$	$\mathbf{x}^1$	$\mathbf{x}^2$

The question then is: What is the ethical ordering of $\mathbf{x}^1$, $\mathbf{x}^2$ and $\mathbf{x}^3$? This is a special case of a wider question: Is there any general rule which can rank social states and is based only on the way these states are ranked by individual members of society?

In answer to this wider question Arrow showed that there could be no such rule which would also satisfy four eminently reasonable requirements.[10]

1   *Pareto rule.* If everyone prefers x^1 to x^2, then x^1 is preferable.[11] Similarly for any other pair (x^i, x^j).

2   *Independence of irrelevant alternatives.* Whether society is better off with x^1 or x^2 should depend only on individual preferences as between x^1 and x^2 and not also on individual preferences for some other vector, for example, x^3. Similarly for any other pair (x^i, x^j).

3   *Unrestricted domain.* The rule must hold for all logically possible sets of preferences.

4   *Non-dictatorship.* We do not allow a rule whereby the ethical ordering is automatically taken to be the same as one particular individual's preferences, irrespective of the preferences of the others.

To put the matter another way, the only rule which satisfies 1 to 3 is the rule which makes one person a dictator.

A famous example of an ethical rule which does not work is the principle of majority voting. For example, given the above preferences, a vote between the states of the world 1 and 2 would give $W(x^1) > W(x^2)$ since A and C would vote for 1 and only B would vote for 2. Similarly, $W(x^2) > W(x^3)$ and $W(x^3) > W(x^1)$. The social ordering is thus

x^1

x^2

x^3

x^1

This, of course, is not a social ordering at all: it does not satisfy the basic need for *transitivity*, that if x^1 is preferred to x^2 and x^2 to x^3, then x^1 is preferred to x^3. The reason for this circularity in the outcome of the voting is of course that there is much diversity of preferences among the voters. However, Arrow's analysis went much further than this particular example, and he was able to show that no rule could exist that would satisfy the four criteria and produce a social ordering based solely on individual orderings.

So, to make ethical judgements, we need more information. In fact, we must be able in some way to compare the experiences (utilities) of different people: our welfare function must contain independent variables that are comparable. In addition these variables must enter into the function in a way that is symmetrical. Let us first look more closely at the question of symmetry and then return to comparability.

Symmetry

A fundamental principle of most modern ethical systems is the principle of impartiality (or anonymity). 'Do as you would be done by' means that, in judging what A ought to do in a situation affecting A and B, it ought to make no difference if one is A or B. Thus the welfare function should have the property that welfare is the same whether $u^A = 10$ and $u^B = 20$ *or* $u^A = 20$ and $u^B = 10$. In other words, in a two-person world the welfare function must have the property that $W(10, 20) = W(20, 10)$. Such a function is called *symmetric*: all the variables enter into it in the same way, so that the function value is invariant when individual values are permuted.

Comparability of levels of utility

We now return to comparability. What degree of comparability is needed? This depends on our answer to the following question. Suppose we know who is the most miserable person alive and we have a policy that will benefit that person but make millions of others less happy (say, releasing from prison a notorious rapist). Would we necessarily support such a policy? According to the Harvard philosopher Rawls, the answer is yes.[12] If we agree with him, we evaluate every policy by the welfare of the most miserable person. In terms of information, this policy requires only that we can compare the *levels* of utility of different people in different situations.[13]

Comparability of unit changes in utility

However, most people would only be willing to see millions suffer if there were some substantial gain to the most miserable person. And we agree with them. In other words, we consider there is some ethical tradeoff between more happiness for some and less happiness for others. To resolve policy problems, we must therefore be able to measure in a comparable way the changes in happiness accruing to different people. *A fortiori* we must, for a given individual, be able to compare the magnitude of that person's change in happiness in moving from state 1 to state 2 with the change in happiness in moving from state 2 to state 3. This property is equivalent to saying that an individual's happiness can be measured on a *cardinal* scale. So, to repeat, we need measures of changes in utility that are both cardinal and inter-personally comparable.

The tradeoff between A's happiness and B's

But there remains the question of the tradeoff between the gains in happiness accruing to some and the losses accruing to others. Bentham, whose utilitarianism provided the initial impetus to utility theory, believed that the changes in happiness should simply be added up. If the net gain was positive, the policy should be followed. Thus according to him

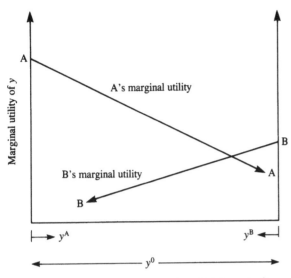

Figure 5.5 The additive utilitarian division of y^0

$$W = u^A + u^B$$

and

$$\Delta W = \Delta u^A + \Delta u^B$$

A policy is good if the simple sum of happiness is increased. To Bentham it made no difference whether the gainer was already happier than the loser, provided that his gain was bigger than the loser's loss.

This approach had some fundamental implications. Imagine a two-person, one-good world with a total y^0 that can be distributed in any way without affecting its total (an unrealistic assumption, as we have said earlier). Suppose too that everybody has the same utility of income function $u(y)$ and that the marginal utility of income diminishes with income. The Benthamite problem is now

$$\max W = u(y^A) + u(y^0 - y^A) \qquad u' > 0 \qquad u'' < 0$$

and the solution $u'(y^A) = u'(y^B)$ implies that $y^A = y^B$. This argument has been regularly used in support of equality.

However, additive utilitarianism has another implication less attractive to egalitarians. Suppose B is a cripple and from any given amount of y obtains half the happiness A would get from the same y. In other words, if $u^A = u(y^A)$, then $u^B = \tfrac{1}{2}u(y^B)$.

We now have

$$\max W = u(y^A) + \tfrac{1}{2}u(y^0 - y^A)$$

The solution is indicated in figure 5.5. The cripple is an inefficient happiness machine and gets less y than A does and even less happiness.

193

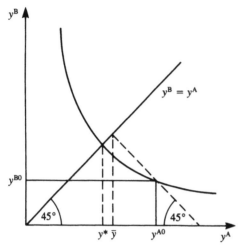

Figure 5.6 The Atkinson measure of equality

This seems hardly fair. So we want a social welfare function in which less value is given to additional units of happiness the higher the original level of happiness. In other words, we need a symmetric welfare function $W(u^A, u^B)$ that is strictly quasi-concave in the individual utilities, so that the happier A is relative to B, the less socially valuable is an addition to A's happiness compared with an addition to B's. Fairly obviously, this approach cannot be applied in any very exact way. We do not know individual utility functions. But where one knows the people concerned well, one would usually be willing to make judgements about 'how upset' or 'how pleased' they would be by particular events and how much 'it matters' if they are helped or disadvantaged. However, there are other cases when we simply cannot resolve these questions, but, even so, it is important to be clear about how we should proceed if we could.

Economic inequality and the equity–efficiency tradeoff

Economic policy usually affects so many people that some fairly crude assumptions are needed. For many purposes it may be adequate to assume that everybody has the same utility of income function $u(y)$. If this utility function is concave (diminishing marginal utility of income), then the new welfare function $W(y^A, y^B)$ is symmetric and strictly quasi-concave.[14] (See figure 5.6.) Thus if A is richer than B, any transfer of income from A to B (with total income constant) raises welfare. This condition is known as the *principle of transfer* and seems a reasonable requirement of any welfare function. The more egalitarian one is, the more the iso-welfare curves of the function approach right angles. By contrast, if one is indifferent to distribution, the curves are straight lines ($W = y^A = y^B$) and one simply maximizes the gross national product, i.e., follows the Kaldor criterion.

It would be convenient to be able to distinguish between the equity and efficiency effects of a policy in a way that embodied an explicit tradeoff between equity and efficiency. Atkinson's equality measure provides such an approach.[15] Let equally-distributed-equivalent income ($y*$) be that income which, if everybody had it, would generate the same level of welfare as the present distribution of income. So, by the definition of $y*$

$$W(y*, y*) = W(y^A, y^B) = W$$

$y*$ is shown on figure 5.6 and must be less than the average income $\bar{y}$, unless there is complete equality. The equality measure is now defined as

$$E = \frac{y*}{\bar{y}}$$

Now clearly social welfare increases if $y*$ increases. But

$$y* = E\bar{y}$$

So we have defined equality E in such a way that social welfare increases if $\bar{y}$ increases proportionately more than E falls or vice versa. An increase in $\bar{y}$ is of course a potential Pareto improvement, but we have now derived a framework for saying whether such an improvement is big enough to outweigh any adverse distributional effects. We can also say whether an inefficient policy of equalization is justified.[16]

To make any of this operational, we must be willing to use some specific welfare function satisfying the preceding criteria. That most commonly used is[17]

$$W = \frac{1}{a} y^{A^a} + \frac{1}{a} y^{B^a} = \frac{1}{a} \sum_{i=A,B} y_i^a \qquad a < 1 \qquad a \neq 0$$

If $a < 0$, W is negative, but it still rises as y^A or y^B rises. The smaller a, the more egalitarian the criterion. As $a \to -\infty$, social welfare comes to depend solely on the income of the poorest person, as Rawls argues it does. In other words, the iso-welfare curves become right angles. By contrast, if $a = 1$, we are indifferent to distribution and measure social welfare by the simple sum of y^A and y^B.

The corresponding equality measure is then, if n is the number of people

$$E = \frac{\left(\sum_i y_i^a / n \right)^{1/a}}{\bar{y}}$$

As a measure of inequality we can take $1 - E$, which, being explicitly related to a social welfare function, is probably preferable to the more traditional Gini coefficient. The latter is half the absolute mean difference in incomes between each pair of individuals, relative to mean income.[18] It can be graphed by plotting a Lorenz curve, showing on the y axis the percentage of total earnings earned by each poorest x per cent of the population (see figure 5.7). The Gini coefficient is then the area A divided by the area A + B.

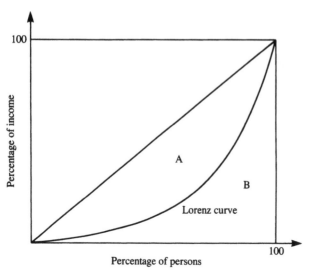

Figure 5.7 The Lorenz curve

When a dollar is transferred from a richer person to a poorer one, the Lorenz curve shifts upwards,[19] so the Gini coefficient falls. Thus the Gini coefficient (like the Atkinson index) satisfies the principle of transfer applied to equality measures: distribution 2 is more equal than distribution 1 if it can be arrived at by starting with distribution 1 and then transferring money income from rich to poor. In fact, for a given total income, any Lorenz curve that lies wholly inside or along another can be got from the first by a process of transfer from richer to poorer. Thus, of two non-intersecting Lorenz curves distributing a given total income, we prefer that lying to the north-west of the other. (This is saying no more than that such a distribution is preferable, given *any* strictly quasi-concave and symmetric welfare function.)

However, in practice Lorenz curves often cross each other. In such cases the Atkinson index is to be preferred to the Gini coefficient since the latter is not based on a satisfactory social welfare function.[20] However, the Atkinson index depends crucially on the value assumed for a. Values typically taken vary between $-\frac{1}{2}$ and -2, but they can have no fully scientific basis, since they embody personal ethical assumptions. Their merit is that they do this in a systematic way.

So, briefly, what have we learned? It is impossible to judge between two alternative economic states without using an ethical welfare function. For any particular welfare function there is an allocation of resources which maximizes welfare for given tastes, technology and endowments. On certain assumptions this allocation will be reached by the free-market mechanism, provided that the distribution of income is made right by lump-sum transfers. If this is done, other economic policies can, for practical purposes, be judged in terms of efficiency without reference to their distributional effects, by using the Kaldor criterion.

However, in fact, lump-sum transfers are impossible, so that at the welfare maximum the social value of a poor person's dollar will exceed that of a rich one's. Thus the equity aspects of policies have always to be considered as well as their efficiency aspects.

NOTES

1 N. Kaldor (1939), 'Welfare propositions of economics and interpersonal comparisons of utility', *Economic Journal*, 49 (September): 549–51. A slightly different criterion was later proposed by J.R. Hicks (1940), 'The valuation of the social income', *Economica*, 7 (May): 105–24.
2 Mathematically, the slope of the community indifference curve is

$$\frac{d(y^A + y^B)}{d(x^A + x^B)} = \frac{dy^A + dy^B}{dx^A + dx^B}$$

But, since the indifference curves of A and B have the same slope

$$\frac{dy^A}{dx^A} = \frac{dy^B}{dx^B}$$

So

$$dy^A dx^B = dx^A dy^B$$

giving

$$dy^A dx^B + dy^B dx^B = dx^A dy^B + dy^B dx^B \qquad \text{(from adding } dy^B dx^B)$$

Hence

$$\frac{dy^A + dy^B}{dx^A + dx^B} = \frac{dy^B}{dx^B} = \frac{dy^A}{dx^A}$$

3 As a partial attempt to salvage the criterion, Scitovsky proposed that state 1 should be counted superior to state 0 only if the move from 0 to 1 was a Kaldor improvement *and* the move from 1 to 0 was not a Kaldor improvement. If this double test was not satisfied and if the corresponding double test for the superiority of 0 over 1 was also not satisfied, the states could not be compared (see T. Scitovsky (1941), 'A note on welfare propositions in economics', *Review of Economic Studies*, 9: 77–88).
4 On the problems of the individual decision maker in a world where he does not control all policy variables, see A.K. Sen (1972), 'Control areas and accounting prices: an approach to economic evaluation', *Economic Journal*, 82 (325 suppl.): 486–501.
5 On the measurement of welfare cost see A.C. Harberger (1971), 'Three basic postulates for applied welfare economics', *Journal of Economic Literature*, 9(3): 785–97.
6 At any given p_x/p_y, the total demand for x from A and B is given irrespective of their incomes. Thus there is a unique relation of MRS_{yx} and x.
7 This corresponds to the following identity, when $y = f(x)$

$$f(x^0) - f(x^1) \equiv \int_{x^0}^{x^1} -f'(x)dx$$

8 The best introduction to the issues discussed in this section is A.K. Sen (1970), *Collective Choice and Social Welfare*, Edinburgh, Oliver and Boyd.

9 This assumes his ordering is not lexicographic.

10 K.J. Arrow (1970), *Social Choice and Individual Values*, Edinburgh, Oliver and Boyd, 1970, 2nd edn, see also A.K. Sen (1977), 'On weights and measures', *Econometrica*, 45. Sen shows that a similar result holds even if individual preferences are already known, as in the table above, and as is assumed in the so-called Bergson–Samuelson welfare function. Thus, given similar assumptions to Arrow's, a Bergson–Samuelson welfare function based only on individual orderings is impossible.

11 This is weaker than the normal version of the Pareto criterion by which x^1 is preferred to x^2 if at least someone prefers x^1 and no one prefers x^2.

12 J. Rawls (1971), *A Theory of Justice*, New York, Oxford University Press.

13 The most miserable person is not a dictator since we do not know in advance who will be the most miserable.

14 This follows from the symmetry and strict quasi-concavity of the original welfare function, which specified welfare in terms of the individual utilities.

15 A.B. Atkinson (1970), 'On the measurement of inequality', *Journal of Economic Theory*, 2: 244–63.

16 In a more general model changes in individual incomes ought to be measured in terms of compensating variation. These should include welfare changes induced not only by income changes but also by change in liberty or fraternity accompanying any enforced increase in economic equality.

17 As $a \to 0$ the function tends to

$$W = \log_e y^A + \log_e y^B$$

18 That is

$$\frac{1}{2n^2 \bar{y}} \sum_{i=1}^{n} \sum_{j=1}^{n} |y^i - y^j|$$

Note that each person's income enters into $2n$ pairs of incomes, n times when the individual appears as i and n times when he appears as j.

19 If the recipient is at the ith percentile and the donor at the jth percentile, the curve shifts up over the range between the ith percentile and the jth percentile on the horizontal axis.

20 The Gini coefficient can also be written

$$G = 1 + \frac{1}{n} - \frac{2}{n^2 \bar{y}} (y_1 + 2y_2 + \ldots + ny_n)$$

where y_1 is the income of the richest person, y_2 of the next richest, and so on. Thus it corresponds to a welfare function in which the weights attaching to individual incomes depend only on the ranking of incomes and not their size.

6

THE COSTS AND BENEFITS OF ANALYSIS:

Project appraisal and planning twenty years on

I.M.D. Little and J.A. Mirrlees

In the late 1960s there was considerable development of methods for applying social cost–benefit analysis to investment in developing countries. In the 1970s, these methods began to be applied. From 1974 to 1982 there were massive public-sector investment booms in many of the developing countries. It appears that much of this investment yielded little or nothing. Were the methods flawed in principle? Were they ignored? And if so, why? Was the possible effect of project appraisal swamped by unforeseen events that rendered potentially valuable investments useless? We do not provide definitive answers to these questions, but we hope to contribute to their answers by discussing the current state of the theory of project appraisal and the current practice and influence of social cost–benefit analysis, particularly within the World Bank.

1 REFLECTIONS ON THE PRINCIPLES OF PROJECT APPRAISAL

In our book (Little and Mirrlees, 1974) we provided a method for social investment decisions. In brief, we proposed the following techniques:

Measuring the values of outputs (benefits) and inputs (costs) with shadow prices
Using border prices as shadow prices for traded inputs and outputs, or – in cases where demand or supply is not independent of price – using the marginal revenue or cost to the country in foreign exchange, as a first approximation
Where possible, using costs, themselves measured at shadow prices, as shadow prices for non-traded inputs
Using conversion factors, estimated separately for a number of different broad categories of inputs and outputs, to calculate shadow prices from market prices for most minor inputs and outputs
Using as shadow wage rates (SWRs) market wage rates discounted by a conversion factor estimated from an overall study of the economy, and depending in particular on a judgement that public income is more valuable at the margin than private income

This chapter previously appeared in *Proceedings of the World Bank Annual Conference on Development Economics 1990*. We would like to thank The World Bank for their kind permission to reproduce it here.

199

In cases where no other rule is applicable, using a standard conversion factor
(SCF) to deduce the shadow price from the market price, to be estimated by
comparing (domestic) market prices with border prices for traded goods,
and others for which a sound estimate of the shadow price is available

Estimating the private and public parts of the net (social) costs and income of the
project, so that private income and costs could be discounted relative to
public income and costs, and giving a low weight to private profit income

Basing the shadow prices used on forecasts of border prices and market prices,
not usually on their current values

Discounting net social profits so calculated by means of an accounting rate of
interest (ARI) that is high (or low) enough to be expected to ration investment projects in the whole economy to the funds available – a rate that could
well vary over time – but in no case using a discount rate less than the rate
available for investment in international capital markets

Allowing for uncertainty only to the extent that the profitability of the project
was expected to be correlated with the general state of the economy

In the case of large projects, allowing for changes in prices brought about by their
introduction, and estimating the incremental value of outputs and inputs by
'surplus' calculations

Converting all external effects of the project to numerical terms by making some
estimate of the cost or value in terms of public income and including them
directly in the calculation of the present social value of the project.

These features of the method proposed had grown out of wide debate and
discussion among economists. Other studies of cost–benefit analysis which
reflected that debate in their own way differed in some respects, but there was
much in common.[1] We attempted to provide a systematic procedure that would
correct all the important distortions. The method we proposed is not a theoretical ideal. It was intended to be practical, and therefore it simplifies and approximates. Even so, some aspects have been found hard to implement. In later
sections we discuss implementation. The present section deals with some aspects
of these methods, particularly the more controversial features.

An extensive literature in the last twenty years has subjected the methods, or at
least some of the principles embodied in them, to critical analysis.[2] Arising from
that, there are some respects in which expansion, development or revision of
these procedures seems to us to be warranted. But to a large extent we stand by
them.

Traded goods

Much of the literature on methods of social cost–benefit analysis has concentrated on the issue of optimal shadow prices under perfect certainty. Squire

(1989), in the *Handbook of Development Economics*, concludes that the literature has shown that the border price principle for traded goods is quite robust.

In the case of a small country, for which border prices are essentially independent of the amounts imported and exported, quite weak assumptions are sufficient to justify the border price principle. When price varies with the amount of trade, it is not exactly right to use marginal revenues and costs. This was pointed out in Little and Mirrlees (1974, p. 229), but it has tended to be neglected. A more extensive treatment has been given in Bhagwati and Srinivasan (1978). The point is that the change in exports, say, affects not only the price received by the country in world markets but also the prices received by domestic producers and paid by domestic consumers, for these prices are generally linked – by taxes, or by the workings of price control systems – to the world price. These changes in market prices involve changes in the welfare of consumers and the actions of producers that ought not to be neglected. The calculations required in principle are similar to those required for the correct pricing of non-traded factors of production. The attractive idea that one could look only to the external environment when estimating shadow prices is not justified – or, at least, it is not exactly justified.

This is only one example of the widespread effects that should in principle be estimated to calculate shadow prices. Although it is reasonable – in the absence of a good applicable model of the economy – to guess that these hard-to-trace effects would not much modify a first approximation based on marginal foreign revenue alone, that is a guess, warranting at least testing in plausible models.

Non-traded goods

A major simplifying idea behind the shadow pricing methods suggested is that given an estimate of the shadow wage rate and an estimate of the accounting rate of interest, it would be possible to calculate shadow prices for many non-traded goods on the basis of input–output data, describing costs of production. This is based on a general principle that the shadow price for a commodity produced under competitive conditions and constant returns to scale is equal to its average cost, calculated using the shadow prices of the inputs into its production (including labour and capital).[3]

Granted the often reasonable approximations of constant returns and competitive conditions, this social cost principle seems common sense, but there is a hidden difficulty – one that has struck economists who consider economies in which the number of traded goods appears to exceed the number of non-traded goods and factors – too many equations chasing too few unknowns.

The difficulty can best be brought out by contemplating a strikingly unsatisfactory, but not unrealistic, state of affairs. Suppose that two private producers are producing the same commodity, using only labour as an input, and one of them is more efficient than the other. Suppose also that subsidies are provided to the less efficient, so that in fact both firms operate. Costs of production in the two firms are different, when measured using shadow prices. Therefore, the social cost principle does not give an unambiguous rule for calculating the relationship between output and input shadow prices.

The analysis of Diamond and Mirrlees (1976) assumed that equilibrium was unique. This is a common assumption, but it is not always warranted. In the situation described, we can only say that the appropriate output shadow price depends on what will actually happen when demand for the product changes. Marginal social cost should be calculated, but what that is depends on the shares of the two firms in the change in aggregate output. There is no good reason to expect marginal cost to be equal to average cost in this case.

The main areas in which these considerations are relevant is when import substitution is subsidized or when quantitative controls are used to achieve the same effect. Then the border price principle is correct when trade can be expected to adjust to changed demand. Otherwise, economic theory cannot predict how much domestic production will be allowed to supply. The project appraiser has to guess what will be allowed to happen. The appraiser should also make recommendations about sources of supply and point out the possible impact on the value of the project. The right answer to the project question may not be yes or no, but rather 'only if these inputs are imported instead of being produced domestically'.

The social cost rule is incomplete in the sense that it does not enable appraisers to calculate theoretically satisfactory shadow prices for all goods. Sieper (1981) and others have found relatively simple rules that may sometimes be used for calculating the shadow prices for non-traded goods in some of the more difficult cases (for the main results of Sieper's unpublished paper, see Squire, 1989). The last resort is to derive the shadow price from the market price by applying a standard conversion factor based on comparisons of shadow and market prices for commodities (such as traded goods) where the shadow price has been satisfactorily estimated. Despite the weakness, we believe that our proposals take good care of the major distortions. In the simplest terms, our rule would not permit projects making cars at a greater foreign exchange cost than by direct purchase abroad.

Another aspect of the social cost procedure has drawn comment (see, for example, Srinivasan, 1982). It is essential for applying the principle that there be some means of making prior estimates of shadow wage rates and discount rates. We proposed basing these on simple macroeconomic models, and calculations of that kind have been done for one or two countries. (In other cases, estimates of conversion factors for other countries have been used, and the ubiquitous 10 per cent accounting rate of interest does not derive from any serious model.) There is no economic theorem that says that the strategic shadow prices calculated in this way are, in some sense, best unbiased estimators; nor is it easy to conceive how such a theorem could be formulated. As with other features of practical welfare economics, the recommendation to use simple macroestimation is essentially intuitive.

Income differences

The presumption that public income is more valuable than private income has been challenged. That presumption forms the basis for arguments that the shadow wage rate should be a substantial proportion of actual wage rates (after adjusting from market prices to shadow prices for consumption goods).

The reasons for it were, first, that government could use additional revenues for further socially profitable investment to a greater extent than private income earners; second, that there are administrative costs to raising tax revenue; and, third, that raising tax revenue creates distortions. The first consideration is weak for countries in which public income seems to be spent on, or diverted to, many objects of little value. The second is not very large. The third argument, which is emphasized by Squire (1989), seems to need further analysis.

Claims about the cost of public funds in developed countries that are based merely on the existence of distorting taxes are invalid. In any economy there are distorting taxes on labour and commodities. Revenue is rightly raised that way, because discriminating lump-sum taxes are not possible. In many economies there are also elements of the tax system, such as income tax allowances, that approximate a uniform lump-sum subsidy. If that uniform subsidy is at an optimal level, then a public expenditure that brings about equal income increases for a representative sample of people is just as valuable as a project that increases public income by the same amount. That is because one can be transformed into the other, at the margin, without distortion. Projects that augment private incomes, however, generally do so differentially, though not necessarily benefiting the rich more than the poor. Taking the usual view of the relationship between income and welfare, private income changes accruing to those above mean income levels are worth less than public income changes; but in the opposite case, they are worth more.

The above argument may not be very relevant for developing economies, where scarcely any policy tools approximating a uniform subsidy exist. Typically, a reduction in government income or rise in expenditure would be offset by an increase in the 'inflation tax', or, after some delay, by taxes on consumer goods, reductions in other public services, or indeed a cutback in investment. Again, a judgement on the relative value of public and private income turns, in part, on a welfare judgement of the relative value of income to people with different incomes.

When changes accrue to those of average incomes, a useful guide is the Ramsey model of an economy with identical individuals and all government revenue raised by taxes proportional to sales and purchases of commodities (that is, no tax allowances or general subsidies). For such an economy, plausible speci-fications of consumer preferences yield a 20 to 40 per cent premium for public over private income. (One attempt to estimate this for the US economy is Ballard, Shoven and Whalley, 1985.) When private income accrues to those with incomes much above the income of the average taxpayer (often quite a low income level in developing countries), its value relative to public income is correspondingly lower.

Uncertainty

It has been argued that careful project appraisal is worth little when uncertainty about the project and about the environment within which it will operate is great. Project appraisal is costly, and the benefits of better decisions could fail to justify that cost. But it is by no means clear that the benefits of improved decisions are slight in a *very* uncertain environment. We have considered this question and find that there can be a reduction in the value of appraisal because of general uncertainty. But in principle it remains considerable.

One can think of cost–benefit analysis as the elimination of error – not all error, but some of the error implicit in decisions by hunch or apparent financial profitability. A theory of these matters is sketched in the appendix. It is shown, using a plausible simple model, that in the context of project appraisal, we should expect some reduction in the value of appraisal when general uncertainty is greater. A simple rule of thumb for judging the benefit is developed. It says that the value of a system of project appraisal is (at least) 10 per cent of the standard deviation of the errors removed by appraisal, multiplied by the ratio of that standard deviation to the standard deviation of errors not removed. In section 3 below we discuss some evidence suggesting that the ratio of these standard deviations is around unity. The variation in observed rates of return is very great. It is not implausible to suppose that the standard deviation of errors removed by appraisal is at least a quarter of the mean net value of projects. With good appraisal it ought to be much more. On that basis, one can claim that appraisal is worth at least 2 per cent of the mean net value of projects appraised.

In our book on project appraisal, we recommended allowing for uncertainty by subtracting from the expected value of net social profitability of the project in any year an amount equal to $A \cdot \text{cov}(P, Y)/\text{E}(Y)$, where $\text{cov}(P, Y)$ is the covariance between social profit P and national income Y, $\text{E}(Y)$ is the mean expected value of national income, and A is a measure of risk aversion known as the coefficient of relative risk aversion, for which we suggested the value 2. Another way to express this is to suggest that the net value of a project in a year be taken as

$$E(P)(1 - A \cdot r \cdot \text{CVP} \cdot \text{CVY}) \qquad (1)$$

where r is the correlation coefficient between the project's social profits and national income, CVP is the coefficient of variation (ratio of standard deviation to mean) for social profit, and CVY is the coefficient of variation for national income. The justification for these rules is provided in the appendix.

Estimating these correlation coefficients and variances and means is a matter of skill, requiring training, not least in the concepts and judgements of appropriate values in well-specified examples. Frequently there would be very little data to go on. One could use data for similar industries in similar countries where there is more relevant experience. The task is essentially equivalent to the use of 'beta coefficients' by financial managers, and it is as hard or easy as that.

Some allowance for uncertainty should be made, though it seldom is. The appropriate allowance can be substantial, especially in the later years of a project. But for most countries, the coefficient of variation for national income is not very large, looking forward for a decade or so, if one may be guided by time series; and therefore in most cases the allowance for uncertainty is not a large adjustment in the value of the project. It should be noted that the allowance could take the form of an increase in the value of the project, if it were negatively correlated with national income.

In our book we also pointed out that allowance should sometimes be made for inflexibility, for the cost of irreversible commitments in projects, though we claimed that such an adjustment should seldom be required. We probably understated the importance of this consideration (see Henry, 1974, for an analysis). In a sense, the issue of flexibility is the desirability of continuing appraisal during the life of the project. At the time of initial investment appraisal, the project can develop in many ways; and some projects have more possibilities of development and adjustment than others. The more flexible projects are worth more for that reason. How much more they are worth depends on how much, and when, flexibility is expected to be exercised.

Because of discounting, flexibility that can occur only after decades (as in the choice between projects that are long lived and ones that are not quite so long lived) is not likely to be worth a great deal. Flexible response to variations in prices may well be exercised before many years have passed. Granted the great uncertainty in many prices, such flexibility may be of considerable value. The specific rules we listed in our book neither draw attention to this nor provide rules of thumb for evaluating it. In principle, flexibility is already valued in the estimation of expected profit, because the probability distributions of social profit for various more or less flexible projects or programmes should have been compared, allowing for the response of the project to varying circumstances. But project reports seldom if ever allow for responsive alteration in production, such as closing (temporary or permanent) or expansion. They should.

At least they should when it could be important. But this seems to be a difficult and costly task. For a substantial price, consultants will construct a model and do a computer simulation of many alternative futures. It may contain many fairly arbitrary assumptions, and it may ignore shadow pricing, which is likely to be quantitatively even more important. In large projects, where flexibility could be substantial in the first two decades, it may be worth attempting such an analysis, but the appraiser needs to keep close track of just what possibilities are being simulated. This is an area in which it is too easy to make spurious claims which add to the apparent value of the project.

Appraisal incentives

This last line of thought brings us to the question of the environment within which project appraisal itself may operate. Appraisers – like workers, managers, and politicians – have their incentives, and they may be expected to respond to them. Space allows little systematic discussion here. The obvious difficulty is that appraisers will be judged on the number of 'good' projects they find relative to the numbers others find. More and more often, as a system of appraisal operates, the standards on numbers of projects found will be based on past performance, and it will not be surprising if arguments and analysis are shaded to continually increase that number. As we discuss below, such a phenomenon appears to have occurred in the World Bank. We have no doubt it has also occurred elsewhere.

The difficulty is that the obvious basis for incentives – comparison of appraisals with results – is almost impossible to use, because of the great length of time that elapses between initial recommendation and final results. And if comparison is used, the reappraisal process could be corrupted. There are other possibilities: independent reappraisal of randomly selected projects shortly after the original appraisal, or explicit grading of project appraisals by quality, as judged by independent inspectors, paying attention not only to analytical method and conformity to standard procedures but also to checking the empirical basis of the appraisal. If good project appraisal warrants expenditure of resources, as we argue in the appendix and in section 4, so does good appraisal of appraisal. We do not argue for any further levels of appraisal, though that raises an interesting question.

2 THE RISE AND FALL OF COST–BENEFIT ANALYSIS IN THE WORLD BANK AND THE STATE OF THE ART ELSEWHERE

During the 1970s there was a remarkable development of both the methodology and the use of shadow pricing in estimating the true national value of projects in economies in which, primarily because of government taxes and controls, the allocation of resources was distorted. This happened first because of an increasing realization of the degree of these distortions, and second because of a desire to apply systematic decision procedures where previously there had been haphazard action and arbitrary plans. We would claim that our development of a method by which a set of consistent shadow prices could be estimated had some part in it (Little and Mirrlees, 1969; Dasgupta, Marglin and Sen were also devising guidelines for project appraisal; see UNIDO (UN Industrial Development Organization), 1972). Within two or three years most donor agencies and a few developing countries were using some simple version of the methodology. But among donor or lending agencies the methods were most fully used and further developed by the World Bank (the first major demonstration of how to estimate a full set of shadow prices was by Scott; see Scott, MacArthur and Newbery, 1976). The World Bank's own version of the methodology was published in Squire and van der Tak (1975). This methodology incorporated 'social' prices whereby consumption was weighted according to the income of the consumer. If such distributional weights were not used, then the shadow prices were (tendentiously) called 'efficiency' prices. Efficiency pricing was based on the remarkable and extreme presumption that a dollar's worth of consumption had the same social value to whomsoever it accrued. Efficiency prices were also based on the presumption that all kinds of income and all uses of income were equally valuable. Our book (Little and Mirrlees, 1974), which also incorporated distributional weights, was published at about the same time. But it is important to note that Little and Mirrlees (1969), which did not use distributional weights, had not assumed that all *uses* of income were equally valuable. As in UNIDO (1972), investment was presumed to be worth more than consumption. In Little and Mirrlees (1974) the numeraire was changed to uncommitted government income, which was also presumed to be worth more than average consumption.

A battle raged in the World Bank during the 1970s about whether social prices should be used. Formally, the 'social price brigade' won, in that guidelines on the use of distributional weights were actually incorporated in the *Operational Manual* in 1980. In practice, we believe, they were hardly ever used except in an experimental manner in a few cases. But aside from this battle, there was a good deal of debate, interest and research. Guidelines flowed from the Central Projects Department under Warren Baum, which also ran a long series of workshops. With or without distributional weights, a fairly full set of sectoral conversion factors and shadow wage rates was estimated by staff members or consultants for nearly twenty countries. The use of the foreign exchange numeraire became standard practice in the World Bank and remains so.

Multiple conversion factors are an important, indeed essential, feature of the Little–Mirrlees and Squire–van der Tak methodologies. We suppose that they were used for the countries for which they were estimated. Shadow pricing in the World Bank reached its apogee around 1981. Yet, inspection of a sample of completion reports of projects approved in the 1970s suggests that the Squire–van der Tak system was far from being fully adopted, either intensively or extensively. Many country economists were still unconvinced, either because they were overworked or lazy or because they were genuinely unsure of the usefulness or validity of the system. At the same time, there have always been senior World Bank staff members who have remained suspicious of economic analysis, especially when it conflicts with their hunches about what is good for development – whether it be integrated rural development, afforestation or steel plants.

In the 1980s there was a decline in the use of shadow pricing at the Bank. In terms of interest, attention, guidance, supervision and research, the decline is steep. The change in actual working practice may be less dramatic. We say this partly because the Bank, even at the apogee, had been less than thoroughly permeated by the Squire–van der Tak methodology, and partly because it is difficult to describe the present state. This difficulty stems from the fact that there is no longer a Central Projects Department, offering common advice and exercising common quality control over project appraisals. We do not know whether regions now diverge significantly, but we guess probably not (or not yet, anyway).

There have always been sectoral differences, particularly in the case of power (but also telecommunications and water supply), and these remain. The benefit of power is generally taken to be measured by what it is sold for. This must often yield an underestimate of benefit, where tariffs are controlled at low levels. We were told during interviews we conducted at the World Bank in the process of writing this paper that the World Bank's loans are made conditional on tariffs being raised (though such conditions are not always fulfilled) if this is required to show a 10 per cent return. In fact we found one appraisal report of a hydro-electric project in which the benefit was reckoned to be the cost of power from a thermal project (based on imported oil); the benefit was thus grossly over-estimated, because the World Bank grossly overestimated the future price of oil. We have mentioned this methodological divergence because we return below to the proper appraisal of power and other non-traded goods projects.

However difficult they are to make, some general propositions as to present practice are essential, although we have not made sufficient inquiries to be sure they are altogether correct. We believe the following:

Social pricing, using distributional weights, has been abandoned.

No distinction is made between public and private income, or between the uses of income – whether saved or invested.

Sectoral conversion factors are rarely if ever calculated and used.

Shadow wage rates are not systematically used or estimated.

The values of non-traded goods are mostly converted to border values by a single standard conversion factor. To put this in another way, there is seldom if ever any attempt to estimate the actual foreign exchange consequences of using or producing particular non-traded goods. It is also equivalent to saying that the relative prices of non-traded goods are assumed to be undistorted (except perhaps that taxes may be subtracted).

If the above propositions are correct, they amount to saying that apart from the cutoff economic rate of return, only one shadow price – a standard conversion factor or shadow exchange rate – is used (and it is unclear how this is estimated, or whether it is estimated in the same way for different countries). This is probably not very different from the practice in the 1960s, when shadow exchange rates were used (and even shadow wage rates) when required to make the rate of return good enough. The only important improvement may be some greater use of border prices for tradable goods. It is doubtful whether the World Bank can now be said to have a standard methodology. It is certainly not that of Squire and van der Tak (or of Little and Mirrlees, or even of UNIDO).[4]

Before speculating about the reasons for this withering, we briefly survey the situation in the regional banks and other donor agencies, and in developing countries. Here, nothing much seems to have changed in the past ten to fifteen years. There was no buildup of interest and development of the methodology similar to that in the World Bank, nor consequently any subsequent withdrawal. Those adopting in the mid 1970s a limited version of Little–Mirrlees, whether directly or following the World Bank, include the Asian Development Bank (ADB), the Inter-American Development Bank (IDB), the Overseas Development Administration (ODA) in the United Kingdom, and the Kreditanstalt für Wiederaufbau in Germany. Japan also claims to follow the World Bank. France and the European Commission still use the 'effects method', despite its errors, as pointed out by Balassa (1976). Other countries seem to follow no particular methodology, or hardly use cost–benefit analysis at all. The Canadians and the British agree, however, that most consultants are familiar with the World Bank methodology and use it (and the British add that they are required to do so).[5]

The IDB is still active in calculating national parameters using input–output methods. Current work apparently includes estimates for Colombia, Panama and Venezuela. But we do not know what use in practice is made of them. Apart possibly from the IDB, the British ODA seems to be the most persistent upholder of the principles adopted in the mid 1970s. It also appears to be more convinced of the practical value of the methodology than other agencies. A third edition of the ODA's *Appraisal of Projects in Developing Countries* (ODA, 1988) retains guidelines for the calculation of sectoral and other conversion factors, for shadow wages, for the incorporation of different values for saving and investment, and for the use of distributive weights. Although the latter two adjustments are rarely used, examples are given of the careful calculation and use of multiple conversion factors.

Information on the state of the art in developing countries is spotty. Chile, partly inspired by Harberger (1972), has a well-developed system of appraisal operating at all government levels. In India, the project appraisal division of the Planning Commission continues to operate, but it appraises only about one-third of public-sector projects. Lal (1980) worked out a full set of national parameters, but practice has degenerated to the use of a single shadow exchange rate which never changes. The Development and Project Planning Centre, University of Bradford, has recently on request calculated national parameters for Ethiopia and Jamaica. Work has begun on China and Sri Lanka.[6] Squire (1989) reports on the basis of information from World Bank staff members that (of twenty-seven countries surveyed) Côte d'Ivoire, Ethiopia, Republic of Korea, Pakistan, Philippines, Sierra Leone, Thailand and Yugoslavia undertake project appraisals using shadow prices (how rigorously is not clear). Personal information suggests that Malaysia should be added to the positive list.

We here mention some reasons for the rather poor penetration, because they differ from reasons applicable to the World Bank and other lending agencies. Public projects derive from ministries or other agencies with departmental, sectoral or regional interests (not to speak of personal, monetary or political interests, which also sometimes intrude). Only the central government and the ministries of planning or finance can at best be expected to look to the national interest. Some conflict is inevitable and essential, because project proponents do not welcome central control, which constrains the extent to which they can make projects serve their own purposes.

Even financial control has proved difficult in many countries, and soft budgeting has resulted in the subsidization of many decentralized agencies. So a central system of project appraisal must always be unpopular, and therefore it needs strong political backing at the highest level. This may be lacking for many reasons, among them the fact that at least until very recently many planners and politicians in developing countries sensed that the methods proposed would conflict with the import-substituting industrialization policies that were at the heart of their development philosophy.

3 SOME REASONS FOR THE DECLINE OF INTEREST IN SHADOW PRICES AND COST–BENEFIT ANALYSIS IN THE WORLD BANK

The decline proclaimed in the title of this section assumes that the general propositions of the previous section are not very far from the truth. If so, it is a shattering indictment, because a shadow price is the marginal effect on social welfare of any quantity change. Shadow prices are fundamental to the evaluation of policy changes, not merely investment projects. This is well recognized in the normative theory of taxes and subsidies, but it also applies to the evaluation of quantitative controls – quotas and rationing.

Shadow prices and cost–benefit analysis are inseparable. Sometimes actual prices coincide with their shadow values, as if on the equator in the midday sun. Only then is financial analysis also cost–benefit analysis. For public-sector projects and enterprises, a decision has to be made about pricing. A good guideline is to make prices coincide as nearly as possible with their shadows, which requires knowledge of the shadows. Sometimes, however, it is impossible or obviously undesirable to charge at all – for example, in the case of most roads. But the shadows are still required to plan the roads.

It is sometimes argued that the thrust of policy should be to get the prices right, and it is suggested that this is an argument for forgetting about, or at least deemphasizing, shadow prices. To the extent that activities are private, and there is no price or profit control, this is feasible and may be desirable. But in the public sector, or whenever there is public regulation, getting the prices right implies knowing the shadow prices.

Less room for project analysis? The growth of non-project, health and education loans

Despite the importance of our introductory remarks, cost–benefit analysis and shadow pricing are closely associated with investment projects, in the normal narrow sense of the word *project*. The decline of interest may thus be related partly to the relative decline of project lending. Structural adjustment loans and other non-project loans – such as those to development finance corporations – account for an increasing proportion of World Bank lending. There may also be no identifiable project in the case of sectoral adjustment loans. In the case of loans for health and education, no economic rate of return (or present value) is estimated; shadow pricing is still relevant for cost effectiveness, but we do not know whether it is used. In a few countries – such as Brazil – World Bank lending now includes almost no projects to which cost–benefit analysis can be applied. Nevertheless, overall, there are still a great many projects, and, furthermore, sectoral adjustment loans also lend themselves to analysis that makes use of shadow prices. The growth of forms of lending other than straight project loans has probably caused a diversion of attention out of proportion to their relative importance.

Institutional reasons

The World Bank is a relatively unsuitable and unstable institution for time-consuming and dedicated quality control (via technical and economic appraisal at all stages) of the investments it finances.

Ironically, in the 1970s, when the World Bank's Central Projects Department was trying to engineer an improvement in economic analysis, its president, Robert McNamara, was presiding over a huge increase in the volume of lending, which put pressure on country and project staff to get enough projects approved. There is no doubt that this created tension. When the pressure is on to get the money out, it is not surprising that demands for more complex analysis are unwelcome. Worse than this, project analysts would never get promoted if they were honestly compelled to report unfavourably on several projects. Promotion would come from writing good reports that would help steer the project through the processes of approval, and not from improving projects or improving project selection. Economic rates of returns (ERRs) on projects became more and more optimistic, without justification. No one we have spoken to denies that the incentives facing the staff worked towards a deterioration in the quality of project work or asserts that this was a trivial matter; it is well known as the 'McNamara effect'. It parallels what was happening in the commercial banks.

The present situation is not very different. The World Bank is again under pressure to lend, because of the debt crisis. The debt crisis has in turn arisen largely because the massive lending from 1974 to 1982 was matched by investments that turned out to have very low or negative returns. Almost all developing countries raised the share of investment in gross national product (GNP) in this period, some by a great deal, and the increase was predominantly in the public sector. The World Bank was not immune from promoting or supporting some very bad investments, for which its own price projections were partly responsible.

The reorganizations of the World Bank in the 1980s have clearly contributed to the decline of cost–benefit analysis. There is now no Central Projects Department to promote common methods and to exercise quality control. Regionalization need not, of itself, have had this result. But it has. There is now no fully independent watchdog over the quality of project work. We have the impression of widespread deterioration. This is not only in economic analysis. Fewer resources are apparently devoted to project work. There is, we are told, less continuity and expertise in project teams than earlier on. Technical, financial and institutional analysis may all have suffered. Obviously economic analysis would not be immune.

New concerns

New concerns may have complicated the project analyst's task. There was a new emphasis in the 1970s on projects that would benefit the poor directly. Cost–benefit methods were adapted to make the poverty impact quantifiable and to integrate it into the cost–benefit analysis. That this has been rejected reduces the work load, for it is difficult to trace the beneficiaries of a project and assess their wealth. Yet we gather that for some kinds of projects, the analyst is still expected to do this (only, having done so, the analyst must not apply weights to these differential benefits – it could be argued that this is incurring the costs of the analysis without the benefits). Now the development of women has been added as a project concern. Surely this is an irrelevant consideration in most projects. Then there is the environment. All effects of a project – including on the development of women and the environment – that might seriously affect its value should always be considered and quantified if possible. But there is a cost to insisting that in all cases the appraiser should be seen to have spent considerable resources on trying to identify kinds of consequences that are unlikely to be of any importance. This is not to say that apparently remote environmental damage may not be large and important. In some areas, the specialist's assessment of these magnitudes is much to be desired.

Sustainability has come to be used in recent years in connection with projects. This is more of a buzzword – probably derived from the environmental lobby – than a genuine concept. It has no merit. Whether a project is sustainable (forever? – or just for a long time?) has nothing to do with whether it is desirable. If unsustainability were really regarded as a reason for rejecting a project, there would be no mining, and no industry. The world would be a very primitive place. In defence of sustainability, it will be said that the concept has drawn attention to some often disregarded reasons for project failure. But it seems much better to detail what these reasons are.[7]

We were told in our discussions with World Bank staff that on occasion the same analyst would give a project a high ERR but would say it was unsustainable. Of course a reason for this could be that sustainability was irrelevant, as with the possibly rapid extraction of an ore body. But this is not what was meant. What was meant was that the same analyst could give a project a high ERR but could also say that it would probably fail (that is, end up with a low *ex post* return). This could arise because the project analyst, wearing the hat of ERR analyst (rightly), thinks that it is up to him to take account only of limited kinds of risk – for example, that future prices will be worse for the project than predicted, or that agricultural response has been overestimated. The analyst does not, in writing a project report, assess such risks as that the dictator will be shot and the subsequent economic management will be so muddled that a major slump will be unavoidable, or even that the economic administration will deteriorate to the extent that the project will be starved of funds for recurrent costs. He is also probably in no position to assess whether the country is overborrowing or planning more investment than it can possibly handle efficiently.

It appears that the 'division' of labour is as it should be. The project appraiser should make it clear which risks have been taken into account and which have not. The appraiser or some other person familiar with the political and macro-economic situation of the country (or maybe the administration of a sector) may comment that no project in that country (or sector) is at present likely to succeed, whatever the calculated ERR.

Methodological defects

We have been considering some institutional reasons for the decline of cost–benefit analysis. But cost–benefit analysis, or the World Bank's version of it, may have been its own worst enemy. The methodology may have been unsound. We discussed this in section 1 of this paper. There was some sniping from theoretical perfectionists over the years. This may have reduced its acceptability, but probably only among those already disposed to attach a high value to comprehensive countrywide planning. Little–Mirrlees methods have stood up to intensive theoretical discussion remarkably well, and on balance the large outpouring of theory consequent on the original publication of Little and Mirrlees (1969) has confirmed the correctness of the author's original intuitions.

The other way in which the methods could have been self-defeating is that they were too complex, so that the simplifications we have described may have been both inevitable and all to the good. This argument is best examined after reviewing the evidence provided by the World Bank's Operations Evaluation Department (OED). Here, we will remark only that simplification and theoretical soundness are not good bedfellows.

4 EVIDENCE FROM WORLD BANK DATA ON THE VALUE OF COST–BENEFIT ANALYSIS

The World Bank's annual review of evaluation results for 1988 gives some information on nearly 2,000 projects approved in the period 1968–80 and subsequently evaluated. The World Bank's OED provides original appraisal ERRs and reestimated economic rates of return (RERRs) on more than 1,000 projects approved in the period 1968–80, together with figures for original and completed costs and expected and actual gestation periods. Gerhard Pohl and Dabrarko Mihaljek (1989) have analysed these OED data, and this section draws on their work.[8]

RERRs are taken from project completion reports usually made by those responsible for the project, which could lead to bias. They will normally allow for known changes in capital cost and any known changes in the mix of inputs and outputs. But actual experience of operation either will be limited to a short period or will be non-existent. Changes in price predictions also will be fed in. The difference between the ERRs and the RERRs is mainly a difference of expectation. The methodology of the estimation of the ERR will not normally be changed. Obviously, the RERR is very far from being postmortem ERR.

To the extent that resourses permit, the OED conducts an 'audit' on top of the project completion reports and ranks projects as 'satisfactory' or 'unsatisfactory'. In the case of projects with calculated RERRs, there is in most cases a coincidence of an unsatisfactory rating and a RERR of less than 10 per cent. But there are exceptions, in which a project with a high RERR is deemed unsatisfactory. In such cases it is clear that the OED does not believe the RERR. But it does not have the resources to make an independent estimate, so the incredible RERR is recorded.

Over the years 1968–80, there was a remarkable and continuous rise in appraisal ERRs. They averaged 17 per cent in 1968 and 29 per cent in 1980. There was no similar trend in average RERRs for projects approved in that period, which, apart from the years 1970 and 1980, were in the range 13 to 17 per cent.[9] As a result, a large gap between ERRs and RERRs has arisen and has excited some attention. It casts some doubt on the objectivity and stability of appraisal, there being no reason to think that investment possibilities were rapidly improving. The rise in appraisal ERRs was common to all regions and sectors but was most marked in Asia and Africa; and sectorally in agriculture and rural development and in transport and tourism. We do not know to what extent the apparent euphoria was genuinely felt, or to what extent it was due to the McNamara effect.

The RERRs of 1968–80 were calculated over the period from 1974 to 1988, with an average lag between approval and reappraisal of nine years. One would expect the RERRs to be importantly affected by the year of reappraisal, particularly by the euphoria that may have continued until mid 1982. After that, the reappraisers' expectations of project performance would surely have been scaled down, in view of the difficulties in which most developing countries found themselves, and all sectors would have been affected. Almost no projects approved before 1971 were evaluated in 1983 or later:

Year of approval	Percentage of projects evaluated after 1982
1971	16
1972	23
1973	35
1974	66
1975	86
1976	90
1977	92
1978	96
1979	98
1980	98

All other things being equal, one would expect, with scaled down expectations and with the rising proportion of reappraisals done after 1982, falling RERRs, especially for the projects approved from 1973 to 1976. The data do show low RERRs (13 per cent) for projects approved between 1973 and 1976, but they then rise (to about 16 per cent) for the projects with 1977, 1978 and 1979 vintages. We leave the reader with this puzzle. We do not have figures for appraisal ERRs in the 1980s.

The proportion of unsatisfactory projects is of interest, as are average RERRs. As we have seen, an unsatisfactory rating usually coincides with a RERR of less than 10 per cent, but not invariably so. The average percentage of unsatisfactory operations among those approved in the period 1968–73 was 15 per cent. In the period 1974–9, it was 23 per cent. This deterioration occurred in all regions except Europe, the Middle East and North Africa. It would be of interest to know whether this can be accounted for by a shift to more difficult sectors (agriculture and rural development) and regions (Africa), or whether there was some general deterioration in project identification and appraisal, again possibly resulting from the McNamara effect.

We turn to Pohl and Mihaljek's (1989) analysis. They regress RERRs on a number of independent variables, including ERRs. Except for regional and sectoral dummies, few of these variables are significant. The simplest equation of all, regressing RERR on ERR alone, gives a coefficient of 0.44 for ERR, which is highly significant, explaining 19 per cent of the variance. Sectoral dummies for transport and urban projects are significant and raise the yield by 7 to 9 percentage points compared with agriculture. Regional dummies are also significant. Asian projects are better than Europe, the Middle East, North Africa and Latin America, whereas Sub-Saharan Africa trails badly. But of course project appraisers know which region and what sector they are in. The coefficient for the appraisal ERR is hardly affected.

The essential findings of the analysis, relevant to assessing the benefits of cost–benefit analysis, are that there was an unjustified rise in revealed optimism about project returns in the 1970s; and that the ERR is a highly significant explanatory variable for RERRs, with a coefficient of 0.44, but it explains only about 20 per cent of the variance ($R^2 = 0.19$).

The main conclusion drawn by Pohl and Mihaljek (1989, p. 32) is that 'cost–benefit and rate-of-return calculations seem to be most useful in the case of large and capital-intensive investment projects. A sufficiently high minimum rate of return criterion, say 10 per cent, will help to screen out large and capital-intensive projects with potentially low rates of return. But further refinements in the methodology, such as allowing for distorted prices resulting from overvalued exchange rates, while intellectually appealing, do not seem to make much difference in practice.'

This conclusion is far from clear. Taken literally, it seems to suggest that all shadow pricing is futile and that even financial rates of return should be calculated only for large, capital-intensive projects. Worse, there is nothing in the analysis reported above that has any bearing on the conclusions. There was no analysis relevant to the question of whether refinement of method would improve ERRs (that is, make them better predictors of RERRs), or of whether such improvement would justify its cost.

Pohl and Mihaljek (1989, p. 32) do say that 'this was also brought out by an analysis of industrial projects for which both financial and economic rates of return were available. Appraisal of financial rates of return were just as good a predictor of *ex post* economic rates of return as *ex ante* economic rates of return. The adjustments for price distortions seemed to make little difference, at least for projects that had been accepted for World Bank financing.'

For this a statement is hardly enough: supporting evidence needs to be closely considered. It is hard to believe that one can do as well aiming at the wrong target. If so, it seems to be unnecessary to take thought at all. Pohl and Mihaljek's final twelve words should be noted. For industrial projects, the main point of shadow pricing is to spot projects in which financial returns are misleading, say, because of protection. If some of these are successfully rejected, there will be a bias towards some coincidence of financial returns and ERRs.

Taking the figures for pre- and post-project evaluations at face value, it is important to appreciate what the apparently low incidence of association between them is saying. A linear regression of the RERR on the ERR is not appropriate, or at least it is not to be interpreted in the way one might usually interpret a regression coefficient. To interpret the statistical results reported by Pohl and Mihaljek (1989) we need a properly specified underlying model.

A simple plausible model is that the *ex ante* and *ex post* estimates of rates of returns are attempts to assess the true value of the project, both subject to additive errors (multiplicative would be better, but Pohl and Mihaljek have used additive, and we are interpreting their results). We can interpret the regression as revealing the value that is common to the two observations. Write C for the common element of the two evaluations. It is subject to errors u and v, independent of one another, and of C. We then have ERR $= C + u$; RERR $= C + v$.

The regression coefficient of the RERR on the ERR is cov(RERR, ERR)/var(ERR), where cov is covariance and var is variance. With this additive model, that is equal to var(C)/[var(C) + var(u)]. The regression coefficient therefore shows the proportion of total variability that is due to the common element.

At least that would be correct if the error, u, were independent of the common element, C. It is not. The common element is made up of the true value of the project and any source of error common to the two appraisals. Because the worst observations in the first round, having rates of return below 10 per cent, are (largely) rejected, there is a negative covariance between the common value and the error u (assuming that the mean return in all projects assessed is above the cutoff value). The regression coefficient is then var(C)/[var(C) + var(u) + cov (C, u)]. This means that the regression coefficient actually underestimates the ratio of the common variance to the error variance.

We are interested in the variance of the true value of the project and the extent to which it seems to be picked up by these observations. We cannot directly tell how much of the common element is the true value and how much is the common sources of error. Because many sources of error (such as utilization estimates and prices) changed greatly between the two evaluations, we believe that the true value is a rather substantial part of the common value. All in all a regression coefficient of 0.44 for ERR, when regressing RERR on ERR alone in Pohl and Mihaljek's simplest equation, suggests that the variance of the true value of the project may be nearly as large as the variance of error in an evaluation.

The 'proportion of the variance explained' in the regression equation is the product of that regression coefficient and the corresponding one for RERRs. Even allowing for the selection bias, it appears that errors in the reevaluation may not be much less than errors in the initial evaluation. It should be appreciated that the low proportion of variance explained is in fact a compound of the error magnitude at the two evaluations. It is not surprising that it is as low as 20 per cent. That is not in itself evidence of a particularly low common element.

These errors in the project appraisals are substantial, but they are not immense. Taken literally, they are quite good news for the users of project appraisals. We show in the appendix on uncertainty that the value of project appraisal can be measured roughly by taking 10 per cent of the standard deviation of true project values, times the ratio of that standard deviation to the standard deviation of measurement errors. If the two standard deviations are of about the same magnitude, as seems to be implied by this data, the value of project appraisal is truly substantial.

Several considerations suggest that the data may considerably understate the precision with which projects can be appraised. First, we should not pay excessive attention to the average divergence. Given the World Bank's selection methods, it makes no difference if a project yielding 20 per cent was appraised at 40 per cent. Excessive optimism is likely to be important only if it pushes a bad project over the 10 per cent barrier. One would hope that around that level, appraisals would have been done with greater care. We believe that the association between ERRs and RERRs is greater around these low appraisal levels. More generally, the simple model we have used to interpret the data gives too much weight to outliers.

The data suggest some further observations, comparing the World Bank's experience of evaluations with that of the countries for which they are done. Improving the World Bank's portfolio may not improve that of the country. There is the problem of fungibility between project funds and the general budget. The value of project aid has often been called into question over the past forty years. Despite this long history, we do not know of any empirical work devoted to ascertaining first what difference is made to a country's investment by the involvement of donors and lending agencies in project preparation and selection. We do not know how many projects are effectively invented by the World Bank (and whether these were particularly successful or unsuccessful); we do not know what happened to projects the World Bank rejected; and we do not know whether, if carried out, the projects had high or low returns.

It has been repeated ad nauseam that economic appraisal at a late stage very rarely stops a project. It must be applied early on to stop work on the project or to effect improvements in the design of a project that will finally go ahead. If one asks whether such improvements are made – and we have asked this question of a few people in the World Bank, in ODA, and in India's Project Appraisal Division of the Planning Commission – one is always told that they are. But there is no way of assessing the magnitude of this benefit of the appraisal process, which is already incorporated in reported ERRS and helps the borrower even if fungibility were complete.

Thus we do not know to what extent the high average RERRs on World Bank projects are achieved because the World Bank improves projects or invents good projects, and to what extent they come simply from skimming the cream from the country's own proposals (nor do we know whether the World Bank helps the country to achieve a higher-yielding portfolio by convincing it not to go ahead with unpromising ventures the World Bank rejects).

There is a lot we do not know. There is no doubt, however, that the World Bank's average RERR is high for the projects of the 1970s – about 16 per cent. Of course, as we have pointed out, RERRs are not true *ex post* rates, which may be significantly lower. Even if the true return is several percentage points lower, it would still be above the real foreign borrowing rate (an ERR calculated using border prices and conversion factors for non-traded goods will be a good approximation to the foreign exchange yield). This is more than one can say for total investment in many, if not most, developing countries. Because almost all did use their borrowing to support or raise the ratio of investment to GNP, there would be no debt crisis if total investment had yielded even half that of the World Bank – financed investments.

India is a country with no debt crisis because it did not borrow commercially until recent years. India engineered no foreign-debt-supported public investment boom, as did many other countries in which the rise in investment was so rapid that it can only have been hastily planned and executed. But, in work in progress, Joshi and Little (1990) have calculated nevertheless that the return on public-sector investment in India over the period 1974–5 to 1984–5 was no more than 6 per cent.[10] The average RERR (both weighted by size of project and unweighted) over roughly the same period for projects in India was very high, about 23 per cent (negative returns arbitrarily put at minus 5 per cent).[11]

This makes India one of the great stars for World Bank-financed investments, although it is not only Joshi and Little who find the returns to investment in India to be low. It is also notable that the apparent high performance of World Bank investments is not attributable to the World Bank having avoided agriculture, which has low returns in other countries. More than half the projects are agricultural, and even in value terms they amount to about a third of World Bank-financed investment in India, with average returns about as high as in other sectors.

RERRs may be grossly overestimated, the World Bank may be very good at creaming off projects, or the World Bank is very good at creating or improving projects. It is clearly of great importance for World Bank policy to know how much weight to give to these different possibilities. We cannot tell. But if the World Bank is good at discovering and improving projects (and rejecting poor projects in countries with limited alternative sources of finance), then there is a strong case for the World Bank to do all it can to teach countries to improve their selection of investments, or to make its influence felt over a greater value of investments than it actually helps to finance (this should be possible in the case of sectoral loans). But whatever the value of the World Bank's involvement in projects, including economic appraisal, it remains true that cost–benefit analysis would be much more effective if done in the country. It can then be applied to all large projects, and there is no problem of fungibility.

We have very briefly reviewed above what little we know of the use of cost–benefit analysis for public-sector investments in developing countries. In most it is non-existent, and in only a very few is it better than rudimentary. There is, of course, more to planning public-sector investment than project appraisal (in Little and Mirrlees, 1974, we did try to show how the two can, and should, be integrated). From this wider perspective also it seems that in only a minority of developing countries is there any coherent and rational control over ministries and other public agencies, with the result that far more projects get started than can be financed without interruption.

The World Bank does not seem to have played a leading role in the promotion of rational public-investment planning. Yet there would appear to be room for the World Bank to have a considerable beneficial influence. It is surely an essential part of continuous (sustainable) structural adjustment that public-sector investments be well chosen. This applies both at the most central level, where inter-sectoral choices are required, and at sectoral levels, whether or not sectoral adjustment loans are being made.

For the World Bank to have such an influence it must have – and be understood to have – the necessary skills. These include a thorough understanding of cost–benefit analysis and shadow pricing. They also include experience of the control of public expenditure.

The declarations of ignorance in this section suggest the need for research on how far the World Bank's activities improve the productivity of investment in the borrowing countries. Because examination of rejected project proposals and what happened to them is essential, and very many projects need to be examined, a deeper analysis than the OED has the resources for is warranted. A pilot study of one cooperative country (if such can be found) could throw much light on the possible value of a wide-ranging study.

5 THE COSTS OF COST–BENEFIT ANALYSIS

We have discussed the benefits of cost–benefit analysis in general, and of shadow pricing in particular, at some length. What are the costs?

No one suggests that industrial or other 'commercial' projects should be approved without even a financial analysis. Nor does anyone suggest that any old road should be approved without a traditional estimate of its benefits in terms of expected vehicle cost savings, time savings and traffic generation; nor that an irrigation or settlement project be approved without some estimate of the value of the extra crops expected to be produced.

What more is required for an economic rate of return? For traded goods it is now generally accepted that border prices are to be used. But this is little or no extra work, because the future international prices of such goods will be needed in any case for a financial analysis. Otherwise present practice merely involves multiplying some of the rows by the standard conversion factor (SCF), adding up, and recalculating the ERR and present value – a few minutes' work at most for the project analyst on a personal computer. The country economist supplies the SCF. This could take some time if conscientiously done, but, knowing how often it has been 'calculated' as 0.8, the economist may get away with this and just write a memo saying 'SCF = 0.8'.

The benefits, as we have argued above and argue again in the appendix, are immensely greater than the costs of applying these procedures. They would justify much more extensive work, both on national parameters and on the specifics of the individual project. This cost–benefit analysis at least seems to give a very clear answer. It is less easy to generalize about the value of refining the appraisal (as opposed to the use of simplifications and often justifiable shortcuts) and about the loss from cutting short an analysis when important aspects have not been adequately allowed for.

6 THE TRADE-OFF BETWEEN COMPLEXITY AND RELIABILITY

Here, we comment briefly on the value of refining calculations at both the national and the sectoral or project level.

National parameters

How sophisticated should be the analysis that goes into the calculation of national parameters, such as discount rate and shadow wage rates? There is no very short answer. Most of the national parameters calculated by the World Bank are out of date. The IDB and the Development and Project Planning Centre, Bradford University, have calculated recent sets for a number of countries, whether for their own use or at the country's request (the introduction of Little and Mirrlees's methods to China with a set of national parameters is still a victim of Tiananmen Square). Where do the priorities lie? Given the World Bank's policy of using a single accounting rate of interest, unvarying by country and time, there may seem to be little point in estimating this parameter. (The rate is almost always 10 per cent, but 12 per cent is used for a few cases.) Yet, in theory, variations should be one of the main responses to changing external or exogenous conditions. There is a case for more serious attention to these issues.

The shadow wage rate, or the conversion factor from which it is derived, is a parameter that can vary substantially by region, and for which local information specific to the project should influence the figure used. Here, we consider its estimation at the national level.

Employment is one way in which the benefits of a public-sector project 'leak' into the private sector. This arises when the increased demand for labour raises wages or when the wage paid is above the supply price of labour. Part of the resultant increased private income is a cost to the economy if, as we have insisted, it is worth less than public income. Given this, the calculation of a shadow wage (the real cost of employing someone) becomes very complicated. It is hard to estimate not only the loss of output elsewhere but also the increase in private income.

Regarding modern-sector urban wages, there is a consensus that the shadow wage is probably not very different from the wage paid, despite the presence of a wage gap between the 'organized' and 'informal' sectors. Given that modern-sector projects are also capital intensive, it is reasonable to assume that the actual wage is as good an approximation of the shadow wage as can be found.

Research in recent years has tended to suggest that rural labour markets, and informal-sector markets generally, are active and that the wage paid is probably close to the marginal product. With some large-scale agricultural projects, however, wages in the area may well be raised, with some loss of producers' surplus and some gain in private incomes. Some agricultural projects have foundered as a result of lack of knowledge of, or enquiry about, labour supply conditions. Such effects as those suggested above certainly need to be investigated, whether or not they are formally used to quantify a shadow wage rate (SWR).

Sectoral costs and benefits

Specific conversion factors for the use of important non-traded goods were regarded as an essential part of the Little–Mirrlees or Squire–van der Tak methodologies. But we also need to consider the numeraire value of the outputs of projects in these sectors. We take power as an example, mention transport and construction more briefly, and must bypass the important subject of irrigation for lack of space. Public utilities (defined as public enterprises for whose output little or no charge is made) present special problems.

Power

Perhaps the most important non-traded good is power. The World Bank has power projects in most countries, and power is an input into all other projects – occasionally a very large input.

We have seen that the output of power projects was never normally valued in the Squire–van der Tak manner. This was reasonable. It would be absurd to calculate an ERR for every power station financed. The ideal procedure is to obtain agreement with the country on an appropriate tariff system. Normally this will be based on long-run marginal cost (LRMC) at accounting prices. When the tariff is in place, demand at those prices must be estimated and should be satisfied (obviously by the least-social-cost mode). Sectoral loans can then be made, and there is no need to calculate a power conversion factor for other projects. There is an equilibrium, and the price is already 'right'. Unfortunately, things get more complex when there is serious excess supply or demand at a price equal to LRMC (which still needs to be calculated). There may then be a good case for charging less or more than LRMC, as the accounting price diverges from LRMC for several – even many – years. When there is excess demand, as in India, the value of power is its marginal product, not its marginal cost. However, the stipulation of serious excess supply or demand at a price equal to LRMC at least makes it clear whether any investment in power is justified.

Construction and transport

A construction conversion factor may be desirable on the ground that construction enters importantly into many projects, and that it may be very labour intensive. If the latter is the case, a lot in turn depends on whether SWRs should be used. This could make a construction conversion factor significantly different from (lower than) the SCF.

Construction is of course virtually the only input into road programmes, which are a large component of World Bank lending in several countries. Sectoral lending seems to make good sense for roads, where a component of an ongoing programme that can be separately and validly assessed may be impossible to identify. As with power, the World Bank may then want to assure itself that road programmes are designed and assessed according to its own guidelines (noting that roads are public utilities to the extent that there is little or no cost recovery; see below). It would then and only then be willing to lend on a sectoral, and not a project, basis.

Transport costs also enter into almost all projects. Although transport is non-traded, its use may have quite large foreign exchange implications, making a special conversion factor desirable.

The extent to which multiple conversion factors should be calculated by the World Bank depends on the country (how distorted are the relative prices of non-traded goods?), on the sectoral composition and size of the World Bank's lending programmes, and on the extent to which the country itself is willing to adopt good cost–benefit analysis on a sectoral (even if not a countrywide) basis. If a set of consistent conversion factors calculated by input–output procedures is not available, the project analyst can often make a good guess at one that is particularly relevant, by back-of-the-envelope methods.

Public utilities

Public utilities are special. Their costs are (generally) borne by the public sector, whereas a large part of the benefit accrues to the private sector.[12] A transfer to the private sector occurs when, as often happens with electricity, gas and water supply, there is no full cost recovery.

We have argued that public income in most developing economies is worth more than private income because of the administrative costs of taxation and the absence of anything even approximating a general lump-sum subsidy, so that taxation is necessarily distorting at the margin in the relevant sense. These considerations are sometimes strengthened when most saving comes through the public budget. The argument for assigning a greater weight to public than private income holds even if no distributional weights are acknowledged. In brief, increasing the public-sector deficit is costly, and projects that do increase it should be penalized.

As we have already mentioned, differential weighting of public and private income is ignored in cost–benefit analysis done by the World Bank and other agencies. We would urge that the fiscal effect of all projects should be estimated and included in appraisal reports. As far as possible, this should include indirect effects, such as changes in tax payments by recipients of additional income. If that is done, it will be clear how the present value of a project can depend on the way it is financed. Public utility pricing policy and project appraisal results are inseparable. If, as we suspect, public income can have a much greater value than private income, the impact of pricing on the value of the project could be very substantial. Estimation of the administrative and distortional costs of taxation in developing countries is a matter on which more research would be valuable.

7 CONCLUSIONS

Social cost–benefit analysis is not as widely, as well, or as effectively practised as its expected net value might lead one to hope and expect. We have covered, or at least touched on, many aspects of its theory, practice and effects. We have claimed that much in the rules we collected and prescribed in 1969 and 1974 has survived analytical scrutiny, that these procedures are capable of being used effectively, and that many important aspects of them have been neglected by project evaluators. We have found that the extent to which they are used and have real influence is not great, even in the World Bank. We have examined some of the data appearing to show considerable randomness in the evaluations performed within the World Bank. We went on to consider the bearing of the very considerable uncertainty that has been shown to attend project appraisal upon the value of the appraisal activity itself. We argue that the value is indeed probably diminished by that uncertainty but is nevertheless very large.

In aggregate, much of the investment in developing countries has had very low returns. This is evident in the low growth of many of these countries during the 1980s. Project appraisal is an essential part of the business of avoiding these mistakes in the future. Good project appraisal is done by people with their own incentives, within organizations that wittingly or not set these incentives. Both environments of project appraisal, the intellectual and the political-organizational, are keys to the quality of selection overall. This needs to be most seriously considered by those who manage and create these environments.

APPENDIX: UNCERTAINTY AND PROJECT APPRAISAL

One can regard project appraisal as a reduction in uncertainty, that is to say, acquisition of information. The value of information has been studied in the literature.[13] Here we apply it to the making of decisions. The process of appraisal is selection among several possibilities, each of uncertain value. Suppose, for example, that there are two projects. Their true values are x and y. Suppose, for definiteness, that $x > y$. Appraisal will yield apparent values $x + A$ and $y + B$, where the random variables A and B are the errors that remain after appraisal. Before appraisal, uncertainty is even greater: their values seem to be $x + A + C$ and $y + B + D$, where C and D are further error terms. Assume that all four error terms have zero mean; that amounts to saying that there is no identifiable bias in the relative evaluations for the two projects.

Without appraisal, the larger of $x + A + C$ and $y + B + D$ determines the choice. The wrong choice (y rather than x) is made if and only if $A + C - B - D < y - x$: that is, writing M for the random variable $(A - B)$ and N for the random variable $(C - D)$, the wrong choice is made when

$$M + N < y - x \tag{A.1}$$

Similarly, if project appraisal is used, the wrong choice is made when

$$M < y - x \tag{A.2}$$

M and N – like A, B, C, and D – have zero means. For simplicity, assume that M and N are independent random variables, with single-peaked density functions (for example, normal or lognormal random variables).

The chance of the wrong choice is less when there is project appraisal because

$M + N$ is a more dispersed random variable than M, and $y - x$ is negative – that is, less than the mean of both M and N. We want to estimate the magnitude of the reduced chance of error. Using an expected-utility representation of the value of projects when there is uncertainty, we can write $u(x)$ and $u(y)$ for the utility of the two projects. Then the value of project appraisal is $u(x) - u(y)$ times the reduction in the probability of error.

This reduction in the probability of error is

$$P(M + N < y - x) - P(M < y - x) \tag{A.3}$$

where P denotes the probability of the event described. This expression can be written using distribution functions F and G for the random variables M and N; so the second term in equation (A.3) is $F(y - x)$, and the first is

$$\int_{-\infty}^{\infty} P(M < y - x - n)g(n)dn \quad \text{or} \quad \int_{-\infty}^{\infty} F(y - x - n)g(n)dn \tag{A.4}$$

where $g = G'$ is the density function for N. The whole expression (A.3) therefore can be written as follows

$$\int_{-\infty}^{\infty} F(y - x - n)g(n)dn - F(y - x) \tag{A.5}$$

We can get some impression of the magnitude of this expression from an approximation. Suppose that the variance of N is small; call it σ^2. Then the reduction in the probability of error is approximately

$$\tfrac{1}{2}\sigma^2 F''(y - x) = \tfrac{1}{2}\sigma^2 f'(y - x) \tag{A.6}$$

where f is the density function for M. Unfortunately, this is a good approximation only when σ is small relative to the variance of N. The value of this project appraisal is therefore measured roughly by

$$\tfrac{1}{2}\sigma^2 f'(y - x)[u(x) - u(y)] \tag{A.7}$$

The expression σ^2 measures the information provided by the project appraisal, because it measures the uncertainty that is removed by the appraisal. The expression f' is positive when $x > y$, because we are on the left-hand side of the probability distribution. The expression f' is greatest when $x - y$ is neither close to zero nor very large and when noise – the degree of general uncertainty not removed by appraisal – is small. Reasonably enough, appraisal is not very valuable when the difference between the projects is small, nor is it valuable when the difference is very great (relative to noise). For given projects, the value of the appraisal is also smaller the greater is noise; greater noise means that f increases less steeply to its maximum at $y - x = 0$.

To assess the magnitude of the expected value of doing project appraisal, we can make two more special assumptions: that $u(x)$ is simply x, and that noise is distributed normally with standard deviation τ. Furthermore, we can calculate

226

the maximum value of project appraisal (as $y - x$ varies). This is an upper estimate of the value, but the value is fairly close to its maximum over a substantial range of values.

It is easiest to calculate this maximum for the low σ^2 approximation, equation (A.7). The maximum value of equation (A.7) is

$$0.147 \frac{\sigma^2}{\tau} \tag{A.8}$$

where the constant is $1/[\sqrt{(2\pi)e}] = 0.14676$. This actually overstates the maximum. When σ^2 is not small, some mathematical manipulation shows that the value of appraisal is

$$(x - y)\left[F\left(\frac{y - x}{\sqrt{r^2 + 1}}\right) - F(y - x)\right] \ldots \tag{A.9}$$

where r is σ/τ, the ratio of the two standard deviations. Numerical calculations of this formula yield the following table of maximum appraisal values as σ/τ varies:

σ/τ	Maximum appraisal value/σ
0.5	0.069
1.0	0.119
1.5	0.149
2.0	0.164

The maximum occurs at a value of $y - x$ in the middle of the likely range of true values.

The limited evidence available, discussed in section 3, suggested that the ratio of the standard deviations might be about unity for the class of appraisals we are interested in, although with competent analysis it ought to be substantially greater than that. This yields a simple yardstick for the value of appraisal as something like 10 per cent of its standard deviation – a very substantial amount considering that, even for small investment decisions, the standard deviation for the present value of the project would usually be many millions of dollars.

Allowance for uncertainty

In Little and Mirrlees (1974), we provided a simple formula for estimating the impact of uncertainty on the value of a project

$$V = E(X) - A \frac{\text{cov}(X, Y)}{E(Y)} \tag{A.10}$$

where X is the (random) social profit value of the project, Y the (random) level of national income, E( ) denotes the expected value of the indicated variable, cov( )

the covariance of the two variables, and A is the coefficient of relative risk aversion. The derivation (Little and Mirrlees, 1974, section 15.8, p. 331) is only indicated. Although something like the formula is well known in decision theory and the theory of asset values, it may be useful to provide a clearer argument. It will be shown that the project should be undertaken if V in equation (A.10) is positive (to a first approximation).

The formula is based on a simplified view of a project and an economy. The value of national income Y to the economy is taken to be $E[u(Y)]$ for a utility function u. A project equivalent to an uncertain change X in national income is worth doing if

$$v = E(u(Y + X)) - E[u(Y)] > 0 \tag{A.11}$$

Assume that X is going to be small relative to Y, whatever happens. Granted that, we can approximate both terms in equation (A.11) by a Taylor expansion around the expected value of Y, $E(Y)$. We have

$$\begin{aligned} u(Y + X) &\approx u[E(Y)] + u'[E(Y)][Y - E(Y) + X] \\ &\quad + \tfrac{1}{2}u''[E(Y)][Y - E(Y) + X]^2 \\ u(Y) &\approx u[E(Y)][Y - E(Y)] + \tfrac{1}{2}u''[E(Y)][Y - E(Y)]^2 \end{aligned} \tag{A.12}$$

Taking expectations, and writing σ_X^2 and σ_Y^2 for the variances of X and Y, we find that

$$\begin{aligned} E[u(Y + X)] &\approx u[E(Y)] + u'[E(Y)]E(X) \\ &\quad + \tfrac{1}{2}u''[E(Y)]\{\sigma_Y^2 + 2\mathrm{cov}(Y, X) + \sigma_X^2 + [E(X)]^2\} \\ E[u(Y)] &\approx u[E(Y)] + \tfrac{1}{2}u''[E(Y)]\sigma_Y^2 \end{aligned} \tag{A.13}$$

After subtraction, we obtain an expression for the increase in expected utility from introducing the project

$$v \approx u'[E(Y)]E(X) + \tfrac{1}{2}u''[E(Y)]\{\sigma_X^2 + [E(X)]^2 + 2\mathrm{cov}(Y, X)\} \tag{A.14}$$

These approximations neglect further terms, among which are, for example, a term $1/2u''' \cdot E(X)\sigma_Y^2$. This could well be larger in magnitude than the terms $1/2u''\{[E(X)]^2 + \sigma_X^2\}$, included in equation (A.13). But all of these will be small relative to the terms in $E(X)$ and $\mathrm{cov}(Y, X)$. The main part of the approximation therefore reduces to

$$v \approx u'[E(Y)]E(X) + u''[E(Y)]\mathrm{cov}(Y, X) \tag{A.15}$$

The coefficient of relative risk aversion is defined for any expected utility level, y, as

$$A(y) \approx \frac{-yu''(y)}{u'(y)} \tag{A.16}$$

Here, we define A more particularly as the value of the coefficient at $E(Y)$. Then, equation (A.16) may be written

$$v \approx u'[E(Y)]\left[E(X) - A\,\frac{\text{cov}(Y,X)}{E(Y)}\right] \tag{A.17}$$

The right-hand side of equation (A.17) is $u'[E(Y)]V$, where V is the expression (A.10). Therefore the criterion, do the project if $v > 0$, is approximately the same as the criterion, do it if $V > 0$. This shows the validity of the formula given in equation (A.10).

The correlation coefficient r between X and Y is defied by

$$\text{cov}(X, Y) = r(\sigma_X \sigma_Y) \tag{A.18}$$

where σ_X, σ_Y are, by our earlier definition, the standard deviations of X and Y. Therefore, the expression in equation (A.14) is also equivalent to the more intuitive form given in the equation on page 204,

$$V \approx u'[E(Y)]E(X)\left\{1 - Ar\,\frac{\sigma_X}{E(X)}\,\frac{\sigma_Y}{E(Y)}\right\} \tag{A.19}$$

The expression in braces is a multiplier, applied to the expected value of net profit, to adjust for uncertainty.

NOTES

The authors wish to acknowledge discussions with economists in the World Bank and with J.D. MacArthur, J.M. Healey and J. Wilmshurst.

1 See, for example, the famous UNIDO Guidelines (UNIDO, 1972), written by Dasgupta, Marglin and Sen; work by international trade theorists, much of it presented in Corden (1974); a notable series of studies by Arnold Harberger, collected in Harberger (1972); other work collected or referred to in the useful collection by Layard (1972); and an earlier formulation of our own, Little and Mirrlees (1969).

2 Two recent surveys (Drèze and Stern, 1987; Squire, 1989) give accounts of the literature, particularly on shadow pricing.

3 A general theorem with this consequence was proved formally in Diamond and Mirrlees (1976).

4 In a recent Development Assistance Committee review of *Project Appraisal Criteria and Procedures* (Development Assistance Committee, OECD (1987) [87], 11), the methodology used by the World Bank is described as being that of Squire and van der Tak. Presumably the World Bank supplied this information, but it seems to be more of a travesty than the truth.

5 These observations are based mainly on Development Assistance Committee, OECD (1987); interviews with the United Kingom ODA staff; and hearsay (for the ADB and IDB).

6 We are indebted to J.D. MacArthur for this information.

7 Sustainability is also described as a 'central notion' in the extraordinarily vapid document, *Principles for Project Appraisal*, Development Assistance Committee, OECD (1988).

8 Note that in many cases, the so-called economic rates of return are really modified financial rates of return. That is true for power, telecommunications, water supply (and possibly some other sub-sectors). It is important to remember this limitation in the following discussion.

9 We have no explanation for the high average RERR of 21 per cent in 1970. We distrust the high figure for 1980 (24 per cent), because relatively few projects approved in that year have been evaluated, and because there is a tendency for good projects to have short evaluation lags. We do not know how negative rates of return that could approach infinity are reckoned. From Pohl and Mihaljek (1989) it appears they may all be counted as minus 5 per cent. In view of this arbitrariness, it would be useful to know the median rates.

10 Joshi and Little's work is a draft chapter, entitled 'Macroeconomic Management, Investment and Growth in India, 1960–61 to 1984–85', of a contribution to the World Bank research project on macroeconomic policy and growth. The calculation is made at market, not shadow, prices. Recalculation at shadow prices would raise the yield insofar as the benefits from public-sector investments are not reflected in public-sector value added. This may be considerable. An offset, however, is that a good deal of public-sector industrial value added would be even less than it is if calculated at shadow prices. It should be noted that similar calculations for total manufacturing investment (public and private) show returns of about 10 per cent.

11 The averages are taken over a total of sixty-eight Indian projects evaluated by the OED for the period 1974–87 for which an RERR was calculated. Lipton and Toye (1990) also found an average RERR of about 23 per cent on thirty-three projects for which the OED provided them with evaluation documents.

12 This section owes much to Squire (1989).

13 See particularly Gould (1974), which studies the influence of greater uncertainty about what is initially unknown on the value of finding out about it. The question of assessing the value of information quantitatively is not considered, nor is the influence of greater ambient uncertainty on the value of information. In the analysis below, we note particularly the importance of this last issue.

REFERENCES

Balassa, Bela (1976), 'The "effects method" of project evaluation', *Oxford Bulletin of Economics and Statistics*, 38(4): 219–31.

Ballard, C.L., John B. Shoven and John Whalley (1985), 'General equilibrium computations of the marginal welfare costs of taxes in the United States', *American Economic Review*, 75: 128–38.

Bhagwati, J.N. and T.N. Srinivasan (1978), 'Shadow prices for project selection in the presence of distortions: effective rates of protection and domestic resource costs', *Journal of Political Economy*, 86(1): 97–116.

Corden, W. Max (1974), *Trade Policy and Economic Welfare*, Oxford, Clarendon Press.

Development Assistance Committee, OECD (1987), *Review of Project Appraisal Criteria and Procedures* (87)11, Paris.

(1988), *Principles for Project Appraisal*, Paris, OECD.

Diamond, Peter A. and James A. Mirrlees (1976), 'Private constant returns and public shadow prices', *Review of Economic Studies*, 43: 41–7.

Drèze, Jean and Nicholas H. Stern (1987), 'The theory of cost–benefit analysis', in A. Auerbach and M. Feldstein (eds.), *Handbook of Public Economics*, Amsterdam, North-Holland.

Gould, J.P. (1974), 'Risk, stochastic preference and the value of information', *Journal of Economic Theory*, 8: 64–84.

Harberger, Arnold C. (1972), *Project Evaluation: Collected Papers*, London, Macmillan.

Henry, C. (1974), 'Option values in the economics of irreplaceable assets', *Review of Economic Studies*, 41(S): 89–104.

Joshi, V. and I.M.D. Little (1990), 'Macroeconomic management, investment, and growth in India 1960–61 to 1984–85', Oxford University, Processed.

Lal, Deepak (1980), *Prices for Planning: Towards the Reform of Indian Planning*, London, Heinemann.

Layard, Richard (ed.) (1972), *Cost–Benefit Analysis: Selected Readings*, Harmondsworth, Penguin.

Lipton, M. and J. Toye (1990), *Does Aid Work in India? A Country Study of the Impact of Official Development Assistance*, London, Routledge.

Little, I.M.D. and James A. Mirrlees (1969), *Manual of Industrial Project Analysis, vol. II*, Paris, OECD Development Centre.

(1974), *Project Appraisal and Planning*, London, Heinemann.

ODA (Overseas Development Administration) (1988), *Appraisal of Projects in Developing Countries*, 3rd edn, London, HMSO.

Pohl, Gerhard and Dabrarko Mihaljek (1989), 'Project evaluation in practice: uncertainty at the World Bank', Economic Advisory Staff, World Bank, Washington, DC, Processed.

Scott, M.F.G., J.D. MacArthur and D.M.G. Newbery (1976), *Project Appraisal in Practice*, London, Heinemann.

Sieper, E. (1981), 'The structure of general equilibrium shadow pricing rules for a tax-distorted economy', unpublished paper, Department of Economics, Australian National University, Canberra, Processed.

Squire, Lyn (1989), 'Project evaluation in theory and practice', in Hollis Chenery and T.N. Srinivasan (eds.), *Handbook of Development Economics, vol. II*, Amsterdam, North-Holland.

Squire, Lyn and H.G. van der Tak (1975), *Economic Analysis of Projects*, Baltimore, MD, Johns Hopkins University Press.

Srinivasan, T.N. (1982), 'General equilibrium theory, project evaluation, and economic development', in M. Gersovitz *et al.* (eds.), *The Theory and Experience of Economic Development*, London, Allen & Unwin.

UNIDO (UN Industrial Development Organization) (1972), *Guidelines for Project Evaluation*, Project Formulation and Evaluation Series, no. 2, New York, United Nations.

PART II

HOW TO VALUE THINGS

7

TIME SAVINGS:
Research into the value of time

The MVA Consultancy, Institute for Transport Studies at Leeds University,
Transport Studies Unit at Oxford University

1 THE NEOCLASSICAL THEORY OF TIME ALLOCATION

1.1 Introduction

There are a number of separate strands which need to be brought together in order to develop a theoretically sound basis for time valuation in transport appraisal. The classical theory of consumer behaviour needs to be adapted for the time allocation problem and for a range of other characteristics peculiar to transport. The outcome has to be a model which can be empirically estimated in the transport context; this leads on to a formulation in terms of the 'random utility' theory of discrete choice, and the underlying techniques which will allow us to identify, as far as possible, the sources of variation in our samples.

1.2 Direct and indirect utility

The classical economic theory of the consumer is based on the concept of a rational man ('homo economicus') who derives utility from the consumption of commodities and attempts to maximize this utility subject to his available resources. A typical mathematical statement of this problem (following, for instance, Deaton and Muellbauer, 1980) would be to take x as a quantity vector of commodities, with an associated price vector p, and a total disposable income Y, whence we have

$$\text{Max } U(x) \quad \text{subject to} \quad p \cdot x \le Y \tag{1.1}$$

Under appropriate assumptions about the form of the function U, which we will not discuss here, the solution can be obtained by setting up the Lagrangean L as

$$L = U(x) + \lambda(Y - p \cdot x) \tag{1.2}$$

We would like to thank HMSO for their kind permission to reproduce this chapter in this book.

235

differentiating with respect to x and λ, and setting to zero, which gives the first-order conditions

$$dU/dx_i = \lambda \cdot p_i \qquad (i = 1, n) \tag{1.3a}$$

and

$$Y = p \cdot x \tag{1.3b}$$

The utility function U, when viewed as a function of the quantities of commodities chosen, is known as a direct utility function, and effectively assumes fixed prices and incomes. However, as a result of the maximization process, it is possible to solve for x in terms of p and Y. Then, by substituting in the original function, we obtain the *indirect* utility function, viewed in terms of prices and income. This represents the maximum utility attainable for given price and income conditions.

Considerable confusion can be caused by these two kinds of utility once we depart from the rigour associated with the classical theory of microeconomics, and it is therefore important to make the distinction at the outset, even though in practice we will see that there are certain kinds of 'hybrid' whose status is not clear. As a general rule, a utility function is direct when its arguments are commodities, and it is indirect when its arguments are prices and income.

1.3 Consumer behaviour and the allocation of time

The general discussion of time allocation within the utility framework has an extensive history, and it is not our intention to review it in any detail. For a reasonably complete review of work in this field, the reader is directed to Bruzelius (1979).

Our approach will be similar to that set out in Bruzelius, in that we will base it on a modified version of the model suggested by DeSerpa (1971, 1973). This involves including time spent in various activities in the direct utility function.

We thus assume that an individual's utility is composed of a vector of commodities x, plus a vector of time spent in various activities, t. One of these activities is assumed to be work, and for convenience we shall distinguish this element as t_w. Thus we have $U(x, t, t_w)$.

We now introduce various kinds of constraints into the maximization problem. Firstly, we have budget constraints. The total expenditure $(p \cdot x)$ cannot exceed the available income, which can be represented as $w \cdot t_w + y$, where w is the wage rate (here assumed constant regardless of time worked, and, by implication, *net* of tax) and y is the amount of income available from non-work sources. In addition, the total time spent in activities cannot exceed the total time available, T. It is open to us to exclude from T certain essential requirements (e.g., sleeping, essential eating, etc.) as we wish; note that the choice of T (e.g., twenty-four hours) implies certain units: e.g., the amount of income from other sources, y, must be commensurate with the period assumed.

Most models of time allocation, having their roots in neoclassical theory, assume that working hours are infinitely flexible, and can be freely varied by the consumer. Since this is an extremely unrealistic assumption, we shall add a slightly more realistic constraint – that it is necessary to work a minimum number of hours, t_w^* (again commensurate with the assumptions about T).

We now make allowances for the fact that for certain activities (of which travelling to work is a good example), individuals are compelled to spend more time than they would ideally wish. This notion is basically due to DeSerpa (1971), and he describes it as the 'technological constraints'. In DeSerpa's model, each commodity has associated with it a minimum time requirement, assumed to be proportional to the amount consumed; the constraints then imply that the time spent on consuming an amount x_i must be at least as great as the time requirement.

There are conceptual problems in formulating these requirements for consumption time, but they turn out to be essentially irrelevant: all that is required is to acknowledge the possibility of minimum time requirements. Given our choice of period T, we will therefore simply assume that each element t_i in the time vector has associated with it a minimum t_i^* (which may, of course, be zero); if required, these t_i^* could be taken as functions of further properties of the system, etc. Here they act as exogenous constraints in exactly the same way as the minimum working hours hypothesis.

We are now in a position to set out our model as a maximization problem subject to a number of constraints. For clarification, we include in square brackets after each constraint the associated Lagrangean multiplier.

$$\text{Max } U(x_1, x_2, \ldots, x_m, t_1, t_2, \ldots, t_n, t_w) \tag{1.4}$$

subject to

$$
\begin{aligned}
w \cdot t_w + y \geq p \cdot x \quad & [\lambda] \\
T \geq \Sigma t_i + t_w \quad & [\mu] \\
t_w \geq t_w^* \quad & [\phi] \\
t_i \geq t_i^* \quad & [\psi_i], \quad \text{all } i
\end{aligned}
$$

λ can be shown to be the marginal utility of an additional unit of income. Corresponding interpretations exist for the remaining Lagrangean multipliers. Thus μ is the marginal utility for having an additional unit of time available (by, for example, reducing the time requirements for essential activities, such as sleep); ϕ is the marginal utility of *decreasing* (note the change of sign) the minimum working hours required, and the ψ_i are the marginal utilities of decreasing the time requirements of each activity i. The way in which they are defined ensures that none of the Lagrangean multipliers can have values less than zero; this is the basic Kuhn–Tucker result.

We can now draw an important distinction between those activities for which the minimum time requirements *are* binding and those for which they are not. In the latter case, individuals are freely willing to commit more time to these activities than is strictly required. In the spirit of DeSerpa's (1971) classification (based on Tipping, 1968), we shall refer to these activities as 'pure leisure activities', and to those activities where the time constraints do bind as 'intermediate activities'. It is clear that with this definition, most types of travelling will be an intermediate activity. For the sake of notational convenience, we may assume that the first r activities are intermediate.

We now proceed with the first-order conditions for a maximum. The Lagrangean is formulated as

$$L = U(x,t,t,t_w) + \lambda \cdot (w \cdot t_w + y - p \cdot x) + \mu \cdot (T - \Sigma t_i - t_w)$$
$$+ \phi \cdot (t_w - t_w^*) + \Sigma \psi_i \cdot (t_i - t_i^*) \tag{1.5}$$

Differentiating with respect to x, t and t_w gives

$$\partial U / \partial x_i - \lambda p_i = 0 \tag{1.6a}$$

$$\partial U / \partial t_j - \mu + \psi_j = 0 \tag{1.6b}$$

$$\partial U / \partial t_w + \lambda w - \mu + \phi = 0 \tag{1.6c}$$

We now introduce a concept – the 'marginal valuation of time spent in activity j'. This is the ratio of the marginal utility of time in activity j to the marginal utility of income. Combining equations (1.6b) and (1.6c) by eliminating μ gives

$$\frac{1}{\lambda} \frac{\partial U}{\partial t_j} = w + \frac{1}{\lambda} \frac{\partial U}{\partial t_w} + \phi / \lambda - \psi_j / \lambda \tag{1.7}$$

From this it can be seen that for the marginal valuation of time in activity j to be equal to the wage rate (after tax), the sum of the last three terms on the right-hand side of equation (1.7) would have to be zero. In fact, earlier theoretical results based on tradeoffs between work and leisure assumed that each of the three terms was individually zero, in other words no disutility from work, no minimum working hours, and no minimum time constraints.

A more useful way of viewing this marginal valuation of time in activity j is as follows: dividing equation (1.6b) by λ, we have

$$\frac{1}{\lambda} \frac{\partial U}{\partial t_j} = \mu / \lambda - \psi_j / \lambda \tag{1.8}$$

Now when $\psi_j = 0$, because the time constraint does not bind, we have the result that the marginal valuation of time in activity j is equal to μ / λ. Some commentators have referred to this value as the 'resource value of time', since it represents the consumer's willingness to pay to have the total time budget increased (though we note that a relaxation of the time budget constraint is not, of course, feasible in reality). Thus for all 'pure leisure' activities, the marginal valuation of time is equal to the resource value, at the optimum. This could either be because consumers are genuinely indifferent as to which leisure activity they are partaking of, implying a *constant* marginal valuation of time, or because they have rearranged their allocation of time to leisure activities so that the marginal valuations are all equal. In this latter case, there may be physical constraints (in space and time) or indivisibilities which impede such a rearrangement, so that the full value of leisure time cannot be realized. This 'constrained transferability of time' is a difficult element to incorporate formally within the model, but it must be borne in mind.

Now the essential point that must be appreciated is that while we have shown that 'pure leisure' time has a value (i.e., the 'resource' value), in that utility is derived from it, there is no value, *at the margin*, to a saving in leisure time. Any time saved in one leisure activity can only be used in another leisure activity, and will have the same valuation. Thus the consumer will not be prepared to pay to save (pure) leisure time, since he cannot increase his utility by so doing.

We have been careful to refer to the *marginal valuation* of time in an activity, rather than the value of it, in order to avoid this confusion. While leisure time has a non-zero marginal valuation, the *value of saving leisure time* is zero. The next step is to observe that for intermediate activities, the marginal valuation of time in the activity is less than the resource value, and indeed for most kinds of travelling will be negative. It is clear from equation (1.8) that the difference between the marginal valuation of time spent in an intermediate activity i and the resource value is ψ_i/λ. By reducing the amount of time spent in activity i and transferring it to leisure, it is possible to increase utility, by a unit amount equal to the difference between the marginal valuations of time spent in the activity and time spent in leisure. Hence ψ_i/λ represents the value of saving time in activity i and transferring it to leisure (what Truong and Hensher (1985) refer to as 'the value of transferring time'). It is this concept which is conventionally referred to as the 'value of time' in transport appraisals.

Hence our empirical interest is centred on the values of ψ_i/λ, and in terms of the theory we have set out here, these values are never negative, and are non-zero every time the consumer is forced to spend more time in an activity than he would ideally wish. Note that the concept of the resource value of time turns out to be of purely theoretical interest. We may mention in passing that the reason why some commentators have suggested that the value of time saved should be equal to the resource value is because they have assumed that the marginal valuation of time spent in non-leisure activities is zero. By rewriting equation (1.8) we derive the fundamental property of time value

Value of saving time in activity i $\qquad\qquad (\psi_i/\lambda)$

$= $ Resource value of time $\qquad\qquad\qquad (\mu/\lambda)$

$-$ Marginal valuation of time spent in activity i $\qquad \dfrac{1}{\lambda}\dfrac{\partial U}{\partial t_i}$ $\qquad$ (1.9)

In most transport problems, the marginal valuation of time is expected to be negative, because travel time contributes to disutility.

1.4 Random utility theory

Having set out the basic theory on which time valuations can be based, we now go on to explain the statistical framework of discrete choice theory, since in practice the possibilities of empirical measurement are almost entirely confined to situations involving choices between two or more alternatives.

One again, there is a large literature on this subject (see, for example, Domencich and McFadden, 1975). Suppose that an individual has to choose between a number of mutually exclusive alternatives $i = 1, \ldots, n$. For each alternative we can define the conditional (indirect) utility U_i which will be the maximum utility he can attain if he chooses alternative i. Then we postulate that he will choose that alternative for which U_i is the greatest. Note that U_i does not merely represent the utility of option i, but takes account of possible foregone utility in other consumption or other activities because of the time and money resources needed to consume alternative i. It is the incorporation of these 'budget' effects that shows that we are dealing with *indirect* utility.

From the modelling point of view, we aim to specify a formula for U_i in terms of the attributes of alternative i, together with other general effects. However, we recognize that in part the choice will be made on the basis of factors which we may be able neither to recognize nor measure. Thus we write

$$U_i = V_i + \epsilon_i \tag{1.10}$$

where ϵ_i is an error term, which introduces a stochastic element into the utility function. It then becomes possible to speak of the *probability* that alternative i is chosen, as a function of the relative values of $V_i (i = 1, \ldots, n)$, which is termed the 'representative utility', and the assumed distribution of the stochastic elements. This allows a link between the observed distribution of choices and the utility formulation, so that given an appropriate assumption about the form of ϵ_i, V_i can be specified, typically as a linear expression in elements such as time and cost, weighted by coefficients which are estimated so as to satisfy some statistical criterion.

As Domencich and McFadden (1975) show, the assumption that the set of ϵ_i are independently and identically distributed with a standardized Weibull distribution (having a standard deviation of $\pi/\sqrt{6}$) leads to the well-known multinomial logit model, which has the form:

$$p_i = \exp(V_i)/\Sigma \exp(V_j) \tag{1.11}$$

where p_i is the probability that i is chosen out of all the available alternatives j. Although this assumption is in fact quite restrictive as a general model of choice, it has many attractive features which have accounted for its widespread use.

Where such a model is calibrated on individual observations, it is standard practice to calibrate by means of maximum likelihood; when the data are more aggregate, it is possible to perform transformations which permit the use of weighted least squares estimation.

It turns out that the assumptions that the error terms for each alternative are (a) independent and (b) identical (i.e., of the same variance) are much more restrictive than the assumption (c) that the distribution is Weibull, and various ways of relaxing these assumptions have been developed without losing too much of the simplicity of the logit formulation. However, in the particular case of binary choice, these two assumptions no longer have force, since it is then possible to redefine the problem in terms of *differences* in utility. Hence while the use of the logit approach in problems of multiple choice requires caution, in binary choice problems it is unexceptionable.

Whether the model is estimated by regression analysis or by Maximum Likelihood (ML), statistics are available to test goodness-of-fit and model specification. In both cases, a variance–covariance matrix of the coefficients is available (in the ML case, this is only asymptotically valid), which not only allows tests as to whether individual coefficients are significantly different from zero, but also allows tests of significant difference between coefficients and tests of significance for ratios of coefficients, using the approximation formula for the variance of a function of random variables. In addition, global statistics are available to assess rival models, provided one is 'nested' within the other (that is, can in some sense be viewed as a restricted version of the other). For ML estimation, this is done by means of the likelihood ratio test: if model 1 is nested within model 2, and L_1 and L_2 are the values of the respective log-likelihood functions, then it can be shown (e.g., Fienberg, 1978) that the statistic

$$2 \cdot (L_2 - L_1)$$

is distributed as χ^2 with degrees of freedom equal to the number of coefficient restrictions applied to model 2 to convert it to model 1. A corresponding test, based on the F-statistic, is available for models estimated by regression methods.

The general practice in model development (see for example Gunn and Bates (1982)) would be to reject calibrated models with variables whose coefficients were indistinguishable from zero, and to apply the principles of parsimony, so that a more complicated model structure would have to be justified with reference to its improvement to goodness-of fit. However, these rules should not be adhered to slavishly, particularly when there are good theoretical reasons for accepting model forms which are only marginally inferior by these criteria.

1.5 A tentative formulation for travel choices

Given that the basic theory and the model formulations both relate to the concept of utility, it is perhaps surprising that little effort is apparent in the literature to relate functional form to the a priori requirements of microeconomic theory. As Bruzelius (1979; p. 151) says: 'the reasons for including variables other than time requirements and cost in the generalized cost functions are unclear; reference is simply made to the fact that the statistical properties of the model are improved'.

In fact, it was not until 1978 that the question of whether, and how, income and price should be entered into the specification of the utility functions for discrete choice models was rigorously treated by Train and McFadden (1978). In the course of developing their argument, they propose a straightforward model for the journey to work with a tradeoff between income (dependent on hours worked) and leisure. A discrete choice is provided by different modes, with differing associated times and costs. Although they do not explicitly refer to such terms, it is clear from the working that the 'representative utility' of the discrete choice model is an *indirect* utility function, thereby justifying the inclusion of price and income variables.

By assuming various alternative functional forms for the direct utility function, they investigate whether there are a priori requirements for the way in which price and income are incorporated in the indirect utility function. Their conclusions were that the theory offers no clearcut guidelines as to the correct way to enter income and price terms. More recently, Truong and Hensher (1985) have set out a simple derivation of one model form based on a version of the DeSerpa model, and we will follow the lines of their work.

Since our attention is on travel time, we will simplify the basic model set out in equation (1.4) by distinguishing only the following elements in the utility function:

x will be the quantity of a generalized consumption 'good',
q will be the time spent in a generalized activity,
t_i, c_i, $i = 1, \ldots, n$ will be respectively travel times and costs associated with alternative, mutually exclusive, choices (of, for instance, mode or route for a specified journey).

Then the direct utility function is $U(x, q, t_1, \ldots, t_n)$ which is to be maximized subject to

$$y \geq px + \Sigma \delta_i c_i \quad [\lambda] \tag{1.12a}$$

$$T \geq q + \Sigma \delta_i \cdot t_i \quad [\mu] \tag{1.12b}$$

$$t_i \geq t_i^* \quad [\psi_i] \tag{1.12c}$$

The elements δ_i are dummies indicating which choice is made: δ_i is 1 if i is chosen, 0 otherwise. By assumption, only one of them can be non-zero. The minimum time requirement constraints only apply to the chosen alternative; thus in the Lagrangean the appropriate elements are multiplied by δ_i as well. Note that for strict consistency all elements should be commensurate with the time period T.

The Lagrangean is written as

$$L = U(x, q, t_1, \ldots, t_n) + \lambda(y - px - \Sigma\delta_i \cdot c_i)$$
$$+ \mu(T - q - \Sigma\delta_i \cdot t_i) + \Sigma\psi_i \cdot \delta_i(t_i - t_i^*) \tag{1.13}$$

The first-order conditions for a maximum are thus

$$\partial U/\partial x = \lambda p \tag{1.14a}$$

$$\partial U/\partial q = \mu \tag{1.14b}$$

$$\partial U/\partial t_i = \mu \cdot \delta_i - \delta_i \cdot \psi_i \tag{1.14c}$$

It is reasonable to assume that both the time and money budget constraints are binding.

We can obtain an approximation for the indirect utility function as follows. Firstly, approximate the direct utility function to the first order as

$$U \simeq a + \frac{\partial U}{\partial x} \cdot x + \frac{\partial U}{\partial q} \cdot q + \Sigma \frac{\partial U}{\partial t_i} \cdot t_i \tag{1.15}$$

Now substitute the first-order maximization conditions.

$$U \simeq a + \lambda px + \mu q + \Sigma\delta_i(\mu - \psi_i) \cdot t_i \tag{1.16}$$

Now substitute the total time and money budget constraints.

$$U \simeq a + \lambda(y - \Sigma\delta_i \cdot c_i) + \mu T - \Sigma\delta_i \psi_i t_i \tag{1.17}$$

This is an approximation to the indirect utility function. The *conditional* indirect utility functions, according to which alternative i is chosen, are given (approximately) by

$$U_i \simeq a + \lambda(y - c_i) + \mu T - \psi_i t_i \tag{1.18}$$

Since the terms a, λy and μT are independent of the alternative, they may be dropped from consideration, and we derive the simplest form for the deterministic element of the random utility model for the choice between the alternatives

$$V_i = -\lambda c_i - \psi_i t_i \tag{1.19}$$

On the basis of the previously outlined theory, the ratio of ψ_i to λ, i.e., the ratio of the time and cost coefficients in the discrete choice model, can be interpreted as the value of saving time spent in travel alternative i.

The indirect utility function in (1.19) is linear but it is quite possible to consider utility specifications which are not only non-linear in cost and time, but also include interaction between cost and time (see, for example, Hensher and Truong, 1985). However, as a useful simplification, we have assumed throughout that the utility function is *separable* in terms of the variables cost and time.

When we come to apply such a model to a sample population, it is reasonable to expect that the coefficients λ and ψ_i will vary across individuals, not least because both time and money constraint will vary, as well as because of random taste variations. This discussion therefore suggests that in order to take account of this variation within the population, it would be prudent to *segment* the model according to the characteristics of the individuals and their journey conditions.

2 THE BEHAVIOURAL THEORY OF TRAVEL CHOICE

2.1 Modal considerations

Time valuation is affected by the comfort and convenience of the mode used, in addition to the time and cost attributes, and the higher values for walking and waiting time have been justified on this basis. Comfort and convenience is a 'catch-all' description for a wide range of mode-specific and situation-specific attributes such as the amount of physical and mental effort, protection from weather, vibration, noise, overcrowding, safety, exposure to violence and intimidation, etc.

There are two ways in which we can take these effects into account:

(i)   by isolating explicitly the effects of these 'comfort' factors, enabling purer values of time to be produced but necessitating separate values of comfort; or

(ii) implicitly incorporating within the values of time those factors which are experienced in proportion to time.

For a variety of reasons (the principal of which is that the effects of interest are largely time related), the first approach was not considered tractable and we have chosen to obtain overall values of time for different modes. Avoiding the quantification of comfort introduces two important considerations. Firstly the comfort level for each 'mode' we choose to define must be reasonably similar and, when applying values of time in the future, we need to take account of any comfort changes within a 'mode'.

Secondly, different modes make it easier or more difficult to engage in other activities while travelling, with the inclination to do so varying by person and group type, journey purpose and time of day (for example, people using rail are more likely to sleep on journeys home in the evening and read the paper in the morning). There tends to be a minimum time required to undertake some of these activities, as well as requirements such as adequate lighting, space, etc.

The extent to which useful activities can be performed in the course of travel is particularly significant for business travel (we have in mind here particularly the 'briefcase' traveller). The assumptions inherent in the current convention for valuing travel in the course of work (that all travel time occurs in business hours;

no work is undertaken during travel; and that none of the work 'lost' during travel is made up by employees in their own time) are most suspect for this type of travel.

2.2 The alternative uses of time saved/lost

Travel time savings (or losses) may be used for more or less travel, or be spent on a number of other activities. There are a wide variety of ways in which time may be used but, very broadly, most time budget studies distinguish between four groups (other than travel):

(i)   subsistence activities (sleeping, eating, personal care),
(ii) household tasks (domestic activities, shopping, child care, etc.),
(iii) paid work/education,
(iv) social/recreational/leisure activities.

Group (iii) activities are largely institutionally determined (although wives, for example, may have a choice of full-time, part-time or no paid employment). Of the remainder, subsistence activities appear to be the most stable, between groups, across countries and over time. These reflect physiological needs that have to be met by all individuals; conversely, time spent on groups (ii)–(iv) show marked variation between person type (notably working men, working women, housewives and the retired) because they are associated with different roles, linked to life-cycle stages.

In general, one would expect that a small time saving (or loss) would be tacked on to, or taken from, an adjoining activity but that a more substantial change would provide an opportunity to add a new activity to the programme or require that one be removed.

For business travel, it is incorrect to assume that the opportunity cost of time is necessarily equivalent to the employee's wage rate (plus overheads) for two reasons. Firstly, as we have already seen a proportion of travel time is likely to be used productively. Secondly, much of the longer distance business travel market involves travelling in time that would normally be regarded as the employee's own: this time may not be directly paid for by the employer. Indeed, in some cases the opportunity cost to the employer may be virtually zero. A large proportion of business travel is undertaken by employees whose jobs are often defined in terms of completing specific duties rather than the fulfilment of a fixed number of hours' work.

Hensher (1976a) argued that the valuation of business travel time should include the cost of that time to the traveller as well as to the employer and in this respect the precise timing of the trip is of crucial importance. If travel takes place in normal working hours, then time spent by the traveller should have zero personal opportunity cost (because this time would already have been allocated to work). There will be an effect on the personal utility of the traveller, however, depending on whether his disutility of travel is greater or smaller than that of his normal work routine.

Where travel takes place in time perceived by the traveller to be his own, we must also consider the opportunity cost to the traveller associated with the competing alternative uses that could be made of that time. Competition for time will be stronger at certain times of the day than at others. It will often be the case that the traveller will be compelled to adjust his normal daily routine to accommodate business travel, and that, in many cases, the daily routines of other household members will also be disrupted.

2.3 The effect of reliability on travel choices

Empirical evidence has generally found that time spent waiting (for public transport) and walking is more highly valued than time spent in-vehicle. However, as the review by the Bureau of Transport Economics (1982) shows, the variability for waiting time values is greater than that for walking time (*ibid.*, table 8.4). While reluctance towards walking can be expected to vary primarily with age and infirmity, geographical and climatic conditions (thus is generally related to 'effort'), waiting time values seem to depend on two distinct aspects. One is the pleasantness or otherwise of where the waiting takes place, while the second is the uncertainty of when the service will arrive.

It is commonly assumed in transport appraisals that average waiting times will be equal to half the headway, which implies that passengers arrive at random. For very frequent services this is probably a reasonable assumption, but once headways become more extended, this will normally be an overestimate of actual waiting time. Recent work by Bowman and Turnquist (1981) attempts to model expected waiting time as a function of headway and reliability (in terms of the ability of the service to keep to schedule). As might be expected, for any given scheduled headway, and particularly where this headway is large, it is only with very unreliable services that arrivals tend towards randomness; when the service is reliable, waiting times can be very low, though there is an observed safety margin of, say, two minutes to cater for errors in clock time, etc.

Similar remarks apply to interchange. The difference is that there is, in the first place, a probable fixed disutility 'penalty' associated with the inconvenience of having to transfer between services/modes, and secondly, the traveller cannot avoid the scheduled gap between the arriving and departing services (though there may be the possibility of undertaking other activities during this time).

On the tentative hypothesis (supported by qualitative evidence) that waiting, etc., due to unreliability is more highly valued than that due to scheduling, it seems possible that an *increase* in interchange time accompanied by an improvement in time keeping could be seen as a benefit. This could not be reflected within existing appraisal methods. A comparable argument can be applied to car travel in congested conditions.

The implications of this argument are that even if we could better predict the expected waiting time, along the lines of the method in Bowman and Turnquist, using frequency and reliability data, the value to be attached to such an estimate would still itself depend on the separate components of headway and reliability. We note that, irrespective of waiting effects, service frequency has implications for time valuation, since less frequent services will place more constraints on travellers because of the 'constrained transferability of time'. Ultimately, the answer lies in distinguishing the two components explicitly and evaluating each component in its own right.

Earlier empirical studies based on revealed preference (RP) which have obtained values for waiting time have been based either on the actual waiting time experienced on a specific day, or on the 'usual' waiting time. In either case, it seems acceptable to interpret this as 'expected waiting time', but without further information about the headways and reliability of the service being faced, we cannot deduce anything about the relative influences of these two factors. There is an implied tradeoff between the two factors, for a given expected wait time. Insofar as the two aspects are differently valued, we may expect major variations in the disutility of (expected) waiting time, depending on the actual service.

2.4 Punctuality

Although there may well be some disutility attached to the pure uncertainty of not knowing how long a journey may take, we can plausibly assume that the major factor is the requirement for punctuality in some form. Punctuality implies that there exist certain 'deadlines', which may be more or less strict, by which time a journey, or a leg of a journey, must be completed, and that additional disutility is incurred when this is not achieved. In some cases the disutility is purely psychological, whereas in other cases, actual cost may be incurred (as when wages are docked for late reporting, or when a connection is missed and the fare is not refundable).

While such deadlines are commonly experienced in everyday life, it is quite difficult to incorporate them into the utility theory which we have developed here, and they lead to rather asymmetrical behaviour.

2.5 Journey frequency

Another important aspect which will determine whether people are willing to accept increased costs in order to avoid missing a deadline is the relation of such extra costs to the overall budget, and this will depend on journey frequency.

Although this effect is allowed for within the utility framework set out above, by means of the time period for which the budgets are valid, it is not made explicit. The high cost of an infrequent journey needs to be seen in relation to the accumulated cost of frequent journeys over a given period, and in this way its effect can easily be dissipated. Although the same might appear to be true of time, the unique feature of time whereby it cannot, with trivial exceptions, be transferred from one period to another, militates against it.

Another possibility is that infrequent trips have specific cost budgets allocated to them (as in the case of holiday trips, for instance), and that these budgets may be less binding. Whatever the explanation, it seems plausible that infrequent and irregular trips may manifest higher values of time than frequent ones like the journey to work.

2.6 Non-linearities in the utility function

We now return to the theoretical structure in order to explore the implications of less restrictive functional forms for utility. When we developed a simple form of the indirect utility function suitable for a discrete choice problem, the first-order approximation ensured that the value of time was constant (at least for any given segmentation). In other words, the rate of tradeoff between money and time was constant regardless of the amount of time or money being expended. Although this is a reasonable approximation when we are dealing with small changes, there are many cases where it may be too restrictive. In this section, we consider what further insights utility theory has to offer in this respect.

In our application of random utility theory, we deal with indirect utility functions. It is possible to construct iso-(indirect) utility functions, in terms of travel expenditure in money and time, which have a formal resemblance to indifference curves. Since increases in time or money expenditure detract from the maximum utility that can be obtained with a given budget, the corresponding properties for these 'indifference curves' is that they should be concave to the origin, and that (indirect) utility decreases, the further we move from the origin. We can illustrate this by means of figure 7.1, which is consistent with approaches by Goodwin (1981) and Hensher and Truong (1985).

Although figure 7.1 can be interpreted in many ways, it is convenient to consider it as referring to a particular journey by a particular mode (e.g., travelling to work by train), and assume that there is some notional budget (not necessarily binding) for this journey in terms of 'acceptable' cost and time. Then, if we have strict concavity, as illustrated, a number of useful results are immediately obtained. The value of time is given by the (negative) slope of the curve at any point in the (cost, time) plane. As cost increases towards the boundary of acceptability, the value of time falls, because travellers are increasingly unwilling to incur further money expenditure. Conversely, as time increases towards the boundary of acceptability, the value of time increases.

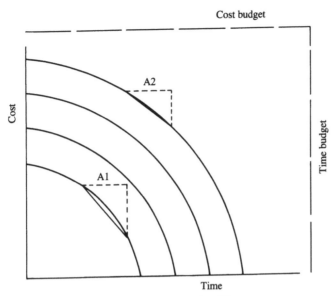

Figure 7.1 Lines of equal (indirect) utility

Next consider two individuals, at the points A1 and A2, where we may assume that, because of home location, individual 2 has a longer and more expensive journey to work than individual 1. Suppose now that both individuals are faced with a time increase of x minutes; what reduction in cost would leave them with the same utility? Clearly, the answer is obtained by moving along the indifference curve until the time coordinate is equal to the existing journey time plus x minutes; the change in cost indicates the amount by which they would require compensation. The slope of the line joining the two points is an indication of the (non-marginal) value of time. Provided only that the indifference curves are reasonably 'parallel', the slope will be lower for individual 2, since the change in his travel time is proportionately less. These kinds of effects cannot be dealt with using linear indirect utility functions, which imply constant value of time.

Another property which follows from the assumption of strict concavity is that individuals will need to be compensated more for an increase in travel time of x minutes than they will be prepared to pay to save x minutes off their existing journey time. Thus, once we move away from purely marginal changes, the value of time may vary according to whether an individual is experiencing a 'gain' or a 'loss'.

While all this appears perfectly plausible, and would seem to counsel against the use of linear forms, the major problem is to know what non-linear formulation is appropriate. As Hensher and Truong (1985, p. 256) point out: 'it is . . . necessary to decide what appropriate functional form is to be used in representing the individual's preference system, and what sort of restrictions are to be imposed on the functional form to guarantee "rational" results from an economic viewpoint'.

In practice, we will use fairly simple deviations from the constant value of time formulation, including piecewise linear functions; we will not impose a priori restrictions of concavity, etc., but we will reject model forms which, when calibrated, violate these restrictions.

None of this, however, relates to the issue of small time savings. The notion that small time savings should have low or zero value is in fact incompatible with the utility theory as expressed here, though this does not mean, of course, that it is implausible! A zero value would entail that the indirect 'indifference curve' would have to be parallel to the time axis over small sections. Possible rationales are either that the savings are not perceived, or that, even if perceived, they are too small to be converted into other useful activities. It appears that any insight which can be thrown on this problem will have to come from outside the utility framework.

2.7 Further discussion on the issue of perception

As far as car costs are concerned, Bruzelius (1979, p. 146) comments: 'it is widely believed that the motorist underestimates his true costs for a journey. This may be regarded as an instance of perceptual error since the underestimation may be due to the fact that the driver perceives his costs, which are actually non-fixed, as fixed when deciding on a journey.'

The general experience is that it is difficult to obtain reported values for car costs which can sensibly be used in model estimation. Work by Quarmby (1967) and Daly and Zachary (1977) has proxied car cost by distance and then converted the coefficient into cost units: these and other studies have suggested a value which corresponds closely with an estimate based on fuel cost only.

These studies have been able to obtain results because of the presence of other modes within the choice set, where the costs are easier to estimate (though it should be noted that increasingly there are related problems due to season tickets, travelcards, etc.). However, when analysing route-choice problems within the car mode, there is no cost yardstick on which we can rely, unless we can make use of more directly perceived costs, such as parking (see, for example, Metcalf and Markham (1974)) or tolls (for example Atkins (1983), Thomas and Thompson (1970)).

Reporting bias becomes a major issue in revealed preference analysis when we make use of reported values. It is plausible to expect that rejected alternatives will be less accurately reported than chosen alternatives, partly because information may be out of date, but more importantly because respondents may be tempted to 'justify' their choice by downgrading rejected alternatives. This issue has been extensively discussed (see, e.g., Golob, 1979; Thomas, 1968; and Gwilliam, 1984) but no firm conclusions can be drawn.

To the extent that reported values for rejected alternatives are systematically biased, rather than being randomly misperceived, two things may occur within model estimation. In the first place, the level of explanation in the model may be unrealistically high, because the (biased) data allow the model to distinguish between chosen and rejected alternatives more successfully than it could if unbiased values were used: the consequences will be that the level of error will be underestimated, and the accuracy with which the coefficients are estimated will be overestimated. In addition, the results themselves may be biased.

These problems, which relate specifically to the relative trustworthiness of chosen and rejected alternative attributes, are not encountered with engineering data, which is in general neutral to the choice made. However, engineering estimates are much cruder and lose a large amount of the individual variation which can enhance the accuracy of disaggregate estimation. Bruzelius (1979, p. 147) concludes: 'Unfortunately there is not much solid evidence available, but there appears to be a belief in the profession that reported data are preferable.'

The final issue under this heading concerns application. Given that we have derived a value of time on some suitable definition, to what kind of time should we apply such a value? For example, if people misperceive the actual duration of waiting time by a factor of 2, so that they tend to report a wait of ten minutes as one of twenty minutes, their value of 'perceived' time is half their value of 'true' time. If then, as a result of a transport improvement, we predict a decrease in 'engineering' waiting time of x minutes, how do we value this?

In principle, the solution is clear: the times should be corrected before they are valued. In practice, the relationship between the various types of measurement is far from being understood.

2.8 Habit, delays and inertia

In this section we deal with three aspects of the dynamic process of choice. Consideration of this is necessary as a counterbalance to the implicit assumption during the theoretical development that choices are made on the basis of perfect information and that there is no cost (disutility) associated with change. Neither of these assumptions is inherently plausible.

Quite apart from the psychological factors which may predispose people to remain with a particular choice in the face of subsequent changes in travel conditions, there are institutional factors which will prevent the kind of instantaneous adjustment which the theory envisages. These are, *inter alia*, the commitment to fixed costs, such as a car or season ticket, and the costs associated with obtaining up-to-date information. Empirical evidence suggests that choices tend to be reevaluated primarily in the light of major changes, such as changes of residence or workplace, changes in household formation and acquisition of first or subsequent cars.

A particular consequence of this is that individuals will be much less sensitive to changes in rejected travel possibilities than in the mode or route habitually used. If no reevaluation has taken place for some time, it may be quite erroneous to attempt to explain a choice on the basis of currently observed travel attributes, using cross-sectional models.

It would appear that this particular problem is circumvented by the use of reported data. To the extent that individuals report times and costs, etc. as they were at the last reevaluation, the issues of delays and misinformation can be ignored within the context of value of time estimation (they continue, of course, to have serious implications for forecasting).

However, the direct habit or inertia effects which are characterized by a bias towards the existing situation cause major problems for revealed preference (RP) analysis. Essentially they imply that the utility of any particular alternative depends on whether it is currently being chosen or not. It is this which leads to the non-reversibility phenomenon, as demonstrated in Goodwin (1977). Since the calibration of an RP model relies on using the estimated utility to explain the choice of alternative, it would clearly be circular if the estimate of utility depended on the choice. One possible way of dealing with the problem is to calibrate an RP model on data collected at more than one point in time as is done in Hensher and Johnson (1981).

2.9 The theory of value of time over time

Values of time are often assumed to grow at the same rate as national income, which implies a constant proportional relationship. However, the theoretical treatment has shown that there is no reason to expect a strict and simple relationship between the value of time and money income at any point in time, and this would appear to apply *a fortiori* to the value of time at different points in time. In this section we discuss this issue in some detail.

In the context of the values used in project evaluation, Beesley and Dalvi (1973) has set out five sources of possible change in 'the value of time at the work–leisure margin', namely:

1 the time budget available may change;
2 the onerousness of work or the pleasurability of consumption may change;
3 the price of the consumption goods with which time is associated or the effort with which time devoted to working is associated, may change;
4 the time required for a given unit consumption or production activity may change;
5 consumers' tastes may change, either due to the changes of individual tastes or by the replacement of one set of consumers by a succeeding generation.

On the *time budget available* it is argued that increasing availability of labour-saving devices, as well as time-saving investments in the transport sector, would militate to reduce the value of time over time.

The *onerousness of work* might be expected to decline over the years as working conditions continue to improve and automation removes the worst forms of tedium in work. Beesley argues that this will lead to an increased willingness to work both on the part of existing and new workers. The partial effects of this are to militate towards a reduction of non-working time and hence an increase in its value. It is interesting to note, however, that the same effect would point to a change in the ratio between the value of the marginal product of labour – and hence of working time as conventionally valued – due to an increased willingness to work at a given wage rate giving a diminishing marginal product and the increased value of non-work time due to its increasing scarcity.

Increased utility of leisure could occur both because of innovation in ways of using leisure time and also from increasing educational resources of individuals. Beesley argues that ways to use leisure pleasurably will proliferate and that this will be a force raising leisure time values. There does appear to be an element of uncertainty here, however. Leisure activities generate utility through varying combinations of time and purchased inputs. Innovation in leisure pursuits could be either time saving or resource input saving. If they were the former (e.g., the electric buggy which halves the time taken for a round of golf) it is conceivable that the marginal utility of income would increase by more than the marginal utility of time spent in the leisure activity and consequently the value of time would fall. The trend in tastes for leisure is argued by Beesley to have moved in the direction of increasing the value of leisure time as the traditional work ethic appears to have been weakened. He also cites the evidence of growing social approval for not working which will continue to raise the measured value of non-working time.

The conclusions reached by Beesley on the factors affecting the value of leisure time over time are worth quoting verbatim. 'Viewed independently, time budgets and the net effects of the prices of leisure and work activities will reduce the measured values. Falling disutility of work, and innovations in leisure activities will increase time values.'

By quoting contrary directions of movement, without being able from a priori reasoning to attribute any values to these effects, Beesley is arguing that there is uncertainty even about the direction of the change in the value of leisure time over time. Given this uncertainty, he argues that a more sensible attitude would be to adopt a zero trend value. What is clear is that he has produced a very strong set of arguments against the a priori presumption that the value of non-working time should increase over time broadly in step with the level of GDP per capita.

2.10 Distributional effects

There is an immense literature and controversy over distribution, and we cannot do more than touch on the question. However, since the use of values of time in scheme appraisal has distributional implications, the subject cannot be totally ignored.

The current appraisal method implicitly assumes that measured losses in economic welfare may be subtracted from measured gains, so that it is in general sufficient to consider net effects. Net gains are then aggregated over the whole population at the current conventional values. No sophisticated reasoning on the validity of inter-personal comparisons of welfare is involved.

The only direct concession to distributional effects in current UK practice is the 'equity' value of time which is applied to the evaluation of time savings that accrue outside the course of work. This practice has arisen in the specific context of income-related values of time, and two rather separate arguments have been adduced, along the following lines:

(a) to use income-related values of time would result in a shift in public resources towards higher-income groups, without any corresponding increase in contributions by them;

(b) the evidence that behavioural values of time are related to income is ambiguous, and in any case information about the variation in incomes of road users is inadequate.

Both these arguments are legitimate, though the underlying problem remains unsolved: if higher-income people genuinely value their time savings more, then a government which wanted to follow market signals should allow this to be reflected in evaluation. Any distributional effects would ideally have to be compensated for by optimal lump-sum transfers.

Some of the more important distributional effects of changes in transport facilities may emerge through the subtle and tortuous procedures of the urban land market (see for example Nelson, 1977 and Muth, 1969). It is generally accepted that land values are strongly related to accessibility, particularly accessibility to jobs, and that there is a compensating relation between land costs and transport costs. This basic relationship is perturbed when an area is made more accessible as a result of transport improvements, thereby reducing overall transport costs (including costs associated with time), and a new equilibrium is reached in terms of higher land prices. To a considerable extent, given the relative inflexibility of supply and demand in the housing market, such an increase represents windfall gains to existing owners of land, who will tend to be higher-income households.

3 TOWARDS A RESEARCH PROGRAMME

3.1 Statistical requirements

Having developed the utility model framework, we are in a position to articulate our data requirements more carefully. We are looking for data relating to choices which will be rich enough to allow us to identify the most important contributors to variability in values of time, by means of relatively straightforward utility specifications, and applying segmentation techniques. This has implications for both sample size and design.

In a review paper, Harrison (1974) identifies nine conditions for the accurate measurement of values of time in the context of choice models. In our context there are four which specially command our attention:

(a)   The variables considered relevant must not be too closely correlated
(b)   The variables affecting choice must show a fair amount of variation in the sample
(c)   The sample analysed must show a reasonable proportion choosing each of the relevant options
(d)   As a check on validity, the proportion of choices explained by the analysis must be high.

These conditions, in particular the first one, are sufficient to rule out a number of the more readily observable situations. For instance, the sample requirements in order to obtain values of time within a reasonable confidence interval using an aggregate destination choice model (e.g., a gravity model) are quite impractical, as demonstrated in Gunn, Mackie and Ortuzar (1980), because travel cost and travel time are so highly correlated at the zone-to-zone level. It is not by accident that most successful empirical research hitherto has been based on disaggregate mode choice for the journey to work.

It is possible to develop a theoretical approximation for the variance of the estimated value of time as a function of properties of the sample, in a way which not only validates conditions (a)–(c) above, but also suggests sampling strategies which can reduce this variance. Nevertheless, the practical implications remain serious. Knowing what kind of observations are of most use for estimation does not obviate the problem of how to locate or identify such observations.

In order to appreciate the design problem, it is instructive to consider in more detail the simple case of binary choice between coach and train, in which we assume the only variables of relevance are the costs (c) and time (t) differences. This example is taken from Bates (1983).

The model, then, can be represented as

$$\Delta U = a - \lambda \Delta c - \psi \Delta t + \Delta \epsilon \tag{3.1}$$

where, arbitrarily, we define differences as 'coach–train'. The equation $\Delta U = 0$

represents a line in the $(\Delta c, \Delta t)$ plane, as shown in figure 7.2(a), the actual location and slope of the line being determined by the (unknown) values of a, λ and ψ. If the size of $\Delta\epsilon$ is small, relative to the contributions of the 'deterministic' part of the utiity function, then it will be approximately the case that any observation on one side of the line will choose one alternative, and any observation on the other will choose the other. Thus, the modelling process can be seen as one of *choosing* a line which will segment the population as accurately as possible into those choosing coach and those choosing train.

Consider now the data illustrated in figure 7.2(b). Here the observations have been plotted according to their values of $(\Delta t, \Delta c)$ and have also been coded – T for those who actually chose train, and C for those who chose coach. It is clear that these data provide virtually no help in estimating the line which segments the coach-choosers from the train-choosers. Each respondent has chosen the 'dominant' alternative – the one which is favoured on the basis of all the attributes, so that there is no evidence of a tradeoff between cost and time, which is essential if we are to deduce the slope of the line.

The situation is not much better in figure 7.2(c), though here there is some evidence of a possible tradeoff. It is however only those observations near the line which make any significant contribution to the estimation. Thus it may be appreciated that what is required to calibrate a satisfactory model is not to have clearly separated population groups with distinct choices, but to have as many 'marginal' choosers as possible, i.e., respondents who might change their choice given a small change in their actual Δc and Δt, as is illustrated in figure 7.2(d).

In passing, we should note that the theory of random utility models requires that there should be a certain number of observations on the 'wrong' side of the line – for example, people who choose one option although it appears inferior taking only the deterministic elements of utility into account. It is the location of such points that allows the scale of the random element to be determined (or rather, since in the logit model the scale is fixed by assumption, allows the relative size of the deterministic elements, as measured by their coefficients, etc., to be determined relative to the random element). The more 'irrationals' there are and the more widely spread away from the line they are located, the smaller will be the contribution from the deterministic component of utility, and the less is explained by the model. On the other hand, in a situation where there are no irrational observations, the random element tends to zero weight relative to the deterministic component, which in practical estimation terms leads to infinite coefficients with associated computing problems.

While careful survey design could alleviate some of the problems, we might find it very difficult and costly to estimate a satisfactory model on the basis of revealed preference (RP) data once we moved away from the journey to work mode choice context. To make any progress, especially in the inter-urban and private non-commuting travel contexts, it is necessary to consider the use of hypothetical questions, and two approaches are potentially useful: these are the

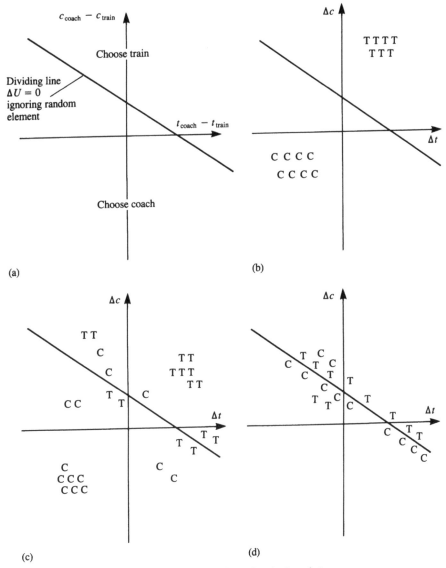

Figure 7.2 Hypothetical illustration of mode choice date

'Transfer Price' (TP) and 'Stated Preference' (SP) methods. We now discuss these methods.

3.2 The use of hypothetical questions

Some commentators have used the generic term Stated Preference to encompass all forms of hypothetical questions aimed at eliciting measures of preference, and both approaches which we are considering here would fall under such a definition. Ultimately, it is possible to modify the two approaches until they blur into each other. However, we have chosen to retain our terminology, whereby TP explicitly refers to the respondent's current situation, whereas SP offers a series of alternatives in which the variables of interest are systematically changed.

Transfer Price, which was first proposed in the context of Value of Time estimation by Lee and Dalvi (1969, 1971) and later used, in a slightly modified form, by Hensher (1976a, b), is the more straightforward of the two approaches. As should be clear from the preceding discussion, the successful application of the RP approach relies essentially on having a high proportion of observations for which the value ΔU (in the binary case: the generalization to multiple alternatives is quite simple) is small, relative to the magnitude of the random element. But in many observed situations, this is patently not the case. The TP approach aims to elicit an estimate of ΔU more or less directly, by means of questions like: 'By how much would the cost of your chosen alternative have to rise in order for you to switch to your rejected alternative?'

A number of variants of this question have been proposed by various different researchers. In essence, however, subject to certain assumptions, the value given can be taken as an estimate of the utility difference between the chosen and rejected alternatives, expressed in given units (in this case, in money units). This in theory allows a gradation among the sample according to the perceived relative disadvantages between alternatives, and the ensuing metric can be directly calibrated to time and cost differences, etc., using least squares methods.

The theoretical work discussed above shows clearly that the information content available from a given sample is generally greatly increased, on the assumption that the reported TP is a reasonable estimate of ΔU (possibly scaled). However, the usefulness of this approach depends crucially on the respondent's ability to comprehend the question and provide a metric which is meaningful.

The Stated Preference approach is more complicated; it is a distillation of techniques which have been widely used in market research but until recently have had very little application within transport.

The approach is to design a set of hypothetical alternatives based on a limited number of attributes assumed to be of relevance, and then to obtain some response to the alternatives. The two most common types of response are (a) rating, where using for instance a five- or seven-point semantic scale, alternatives are assessed, or possibly compared on a pair-wise basis, and (b) ranking, where the alternatives are placed in order of preference. In the case of rating, it is usual to treat the response variable (after appropriate transformations) as a direct estimate of utility; in the case of ranking, a common approach is to extend the multinomial logit discrete choice theory by means of the 'exploded logit' method which appears to have been first used by Beggs, Cardell and Hausman (1981). Because most SP analyses have treated the multiple observations obtained from each respondent as independent, there remains some controversy about the validity of the estimated variances of the coefficients; they are likely to be underestimated, and this 'repeated measurements' problem needs to be borne in mind. However, even allowing for this the implications are that SP can produce results with acceptable confidence limits from greatly reduced sample sizes.

It is only fair to say that there existed considerable scepticism about both these approaches, relative to the more orthodox RP approach (which of course has itself been widely criticized). It was clear that if the study was to make extensive use of either of these 'hypothetical' methods, some validation would have to be carried out. It was appreciated that in rigorous scientific terms nothing could be learnt from a single experiment: even if two methods gave answers that could in some way be described as 'the same', this could not be construed as proof. In the circumstances, an attractive approach was to obtain a data set which was suitable for calibration using both RP data and data obtained from hypothetical questions. This we proceeded to do.

Our initial preference was for the Transfer Price approach, as being relatively simple to administer and to analyse, and having some history within value of time research. For both methods the crucial question really turns on the respondent's ability to take the method seriously and to give responses which truly reflect his underlying preferences. Bonsall (1983) has discussed the general question of biases in response to hypothetical questions, and distinguishes four types:

(i) affirmation bias, which results from a tendency of respondents to agree with the interviewer or analyst;
(ii) unconstrained response bias, which occurs when the respondent fails to consider all the negative aspects of a possible change in, say, mode;
(iii) rationalization bias, which in some sense is the opposite effect, where the respondent has a selective blindness towards the relative disadvantages of the currently chosen option;
(iv) policy response bias, where the respondent deliberately biases his response with the intention of influencing a policy decision.

Although attempts were made to avoid such biases, it is very likely that some will be present in the data.

With SP, on the other hand, the nature of the task usually makes it much more difficult for the respondent to introduce purposive biases into his response. Possible exceptions are 'lexicographic' response, threshold effects (e.g., the respondent may deliberately downgrade all alternatives which imply a fares increase) and, perhaps, a credibility effect (where the respondent downgrades options considered infeasible). The more important question in this case is whether the respondent is able to perform the task – there is now considerable experience within the market research field as to the practical limitations in terms of the number of alternatives, number of attributes defining an alternative, number of levels for each attribute, etc. A useful review is provided by Cattin and Wittink (1982); a general conclusion is that the more the hypothetical situations depart from the respondent's practical experience, the less reliable the response will be.

The results of the TP experiment are reported in Broom *et al.* (1983) and Gunn (1984). We were not able to convince ourselves that the responses given were sufficiently reliable to allow the method to be used. A crucial element in reaching this decision was the very low correlation between the utility differences that could be calculated on the basis of the RP model and the reported TP values, which indicated that the variation in TP could not be taken as a reliable metric of relative preferences.

The results of the SP approach are reported in Bates (1984), and the results were sufficiently encouraging to convince both ourselves and the Department that SP techniques would be a legitimate tool to use in those contexts where revealed preference was not a feasible option.

3.3 The advantages and disadvantages of SP

In this section, we discuss the case for Stated Preference techniques more fully, in the light of the theoretical issues which have been raised. There are two strong reasons for adopting the SP approach: (i) perception and (ii) the effect on travel choice of habit.

With respect to *perception*, a number of the problems are avoided when using SP data. We can dispense with the link between reported data and perceived values, since the attribute values are provided directly by the experiment. Further, we can probably ignore most of the confounding effects which influence the relationship between true and perceived values. We are still left with the link between true and engineering values, which is of course a modelling problem outside the choice dimension, and with the existence of constraints on the choice itself, of which we may not be aware. The potential price which we pay for this improvement, of course, is that the reported *response* may be unreliable, for reasons already discussed.

Turning to the effect of *habit*, there is no way within the RP approach in which we can estimate the size or distribution of the habit effect, which for a given individual may well, of course, depend on the actual duration of the habit. However, it is possible in theory to investigate this within both the TP and SP approaches. Unfortunately, the effect is confounded with that of self-selectivity.

The work by Broom *et al.* (1983) on Transfer Price did reveal an apparent habit effect which was quite large; however, subsequent work by Gunn (1984) suggests that the effect is in line with what would be expected on the basis of the self-selectivity argument. Correct interpretation of the habit effect is important for TP, since the methodology itself relates to a change of travel alternative. For SP, on the other hand, it appears less important, since some, if not all, of the comparisons will be carried out *within* a given travel alternative.

On balance, we judge that with SP the potential bias due to habit is minimized, but it should be borne in mind that the responses given can only strictly be interpreted as an indication of preferences at the time when the questions were asked. It is not sensible to suggest that the responses include the longer-term equilibrium effects which would apply after lags have worked their way through: evidence adduced by McKenzie and Goodwin (1985) suggests that the time involved may lie between three and ten years.

There is a further important practical issue relating to experimental design for Stated Preference. Clearly, if attributes are only included in a design at two levels, it is not possible to test for non-linearity (though of course non-linear forms can be fitted based on a priori reasoning). When more than two levels are included, the standard approach is to fit piecewise linear functions, which will often suggest suitable functional forms. However, it is not generally possible to fit polynomial functions with any efficiency to such data, unless the experiment has been specifically designed with a particular form in mind, because the correlation between first and higher-order terms will be extremely high. Hensher and Truong (1985) give an example of a suitable design on the assumption of a quadratic utility function, and their approach can be generalized, at the price of some complexity.

Although the amount of validation is not large, we have sufficient confidence in the SP approach to propose using it in contexts such as leisure travel which are not in general amenable to the RP method. Whatever form of data is collected, the analysis follows similar lines – we postulate a random utility model, in which certain key coefficients are segmented in a way suggested by theoretical considerations.

As a consequence of these considerations, empirical results derived within this study are based on both RP and SP data, analysed within the general framework of random utility models. In some cases, the same set of respondents has been used to provide both RP and SP data, and the results can be compared.

4 EMPIRICAL RESULTS

4.1 Introduction

We now set out the main empirical results from the surveys carried out within the project, with the aim of demonstrating to what extent it is possible to support the hypotheses set out above. Our particular concern is to identify the sources of variation in values of time due to income, type of journey, and personal and household characteristics.

As well as referring to our own data, we also draw on the work of other contributors. This presents certain problems, however, since while there is a considerable volume of published results (of which useful reviews are given in Bruzelius (1979) and BTE (1981)), variations in exchange rates and purchasing power between countries makes it difficult to convert to a common base. Many of the studies have calculated overall values to time as a percentage of the average wage rate, which to some extent ameliorates the problem. However, we have reservations about this approach, as it implies a proportional relationship between values of time and income which, as we shall see below, cannot be substantiated.

We have largely confined ourselves to empirical studies carried out in the United Kingdom. We emphasize that this is not in any way to suggest that there is some inherent superiority about these studies over those carried out in other parts of the world; indeed there are major contributions from the USA and Australia, in particular, as is clear in the references cited above.

The main empirical studies which we shall refer to are as follows (all are mode choice studies of the journey to work):

1   Quarmby (1967). The main data set represents the choice between car and bus in the Leeds area. These data were subsequently reanalysed by LGORU.
2   LGORU. The earlier study (Rogers, Townsend and Metcalf (1970)) collected data comparable with that of Quarmby from three more British cities (Leicester, Liverpool and Manchester). At a later stage (Davies and Rogers (1973)) these were combined with the Quarmby data, and supplemented with data for London, which had a wider range of modal choice. Unfortunately, some of the later results are difficult to reconcile, as we shall note below.
3   Daly and Zachary (1977). This was also under the auspices of LGORU, and had a sample from seven provincial cities with a choice between car and public transport (mainly bus).
4   Ortuzar (1980). This data set, from the Garforth corridor in Leeds, involved the choice between car driver, car passenger and several public transport options.

We will merely draw out the most important conclusions of our own work.

4.2 An overall view

The first thing that is necessary in order to compare results obtained from different surveys is to correct for inflation; this has been done by means of the Retail Price Index. The base for all values is June 1985.

Table 7.1 sets out the results, stratified by mode (including walking and waiting) and purpose. Results obtained within our study are boxed. In addition, for comparison purposes, the Department's recommended values are included at the bottom of each box to which they apply; it will be recalled that these values relate to income levels in 1979 although the price base has been adjusted.

For commuting trips, the values for car drivers range between 1.6 p./min. and 5.2 p./min., leaving out the LGORU result. For rail the range is slightly

Table 7.1 *Values of in-vehicle time (mid 1985 prices, pence per min.)*

	Car	Rail	Coach	Bus	Walk	Wait
Commuting	5.2 Tyne RP 3.6 Tyne SP 3.7 WY RP (5.5 LGORU) 1.7 Ort RP 1.9 Daly RP 1.6 Quarmby	4.0 N Kent SP 3.6 N Kent RP 2.4 WY RP 1.7 Ort RP 2.8 Daly RP	4.0 N Kent SP 3.6 N Kent RP	(5.5 LGORU) 2.4 WY RP 1.7 Ort RP 2.8 Daly RP 1.6 Quarmby	(12.7 LGORU) 2.2 NK SP 3.1 NK RP 5.5 WY RP 5.9 Ort RP 2.6 Daly RP 4.5 Quarmby	(16.8 LGORU) 2.7 NK SP 9.1 NK RP 3.1 WY RP 9.6 Ort RP 9.8 Daly RP 4.5 Qmby
	1.8	1.8	1.8	1.8	3.7	3.7
EB Employer's Business	4.5 Tyne SP 11.5 driv 9.2 pass	12.4		7.7		
Leisure	3.7 Tyne RP 4.5 Tyne SP 3.8 LD SP	5.9 LDSP	4.0 LD SP	1.25 Urban SP	2.5 Urban SP	5.8 Urban SP
	1.8	1.8	1.8	1.8	3.7	3.7

narrower (1.7 to 4.0), and for bus (again leaving out the LGORU result) of a generally lower order (1.6 to 2.8). The only available result for coach comes from the North Kent survey, where no significant difference between coach and rail was found with the RP data; for the SP data, no specific analysis along these lines was carried out, but preliminary results suggested similar values for the two groups of *users*.

Almost all studies which have examined the issue have found walking time to be valued more highly than in-vehicle time (though this is not true of North Kent, nor of Daly and Zachary). The range of values, however, apart from LGORU is not greatly different from those for car and rail, though it is generally higher than that for bus – the in-vehicle mode with which it would be most usually associated.

The results for waiting time are more variable, and this distinction *vis-à-vis* walking time has been confirmed in the international comparison given in BTE (1981, 36). With the exception of the North Kent SP result, where the waiting times offered in the experiment were very low relative to the overall journey time, all studies reveal values that are higher than (public transport) in-vehicle times, in some cases substantially so. The greater variability is likely to be associated with differences in the component aspects of frequency and reliability, as discussed in sections 2.3 to 2.5.

To summarize, while the range and accuracy of these results is far from ideal, a general pattern does emerge, whereby in-vehicle values for car and rail (and, on the limited evidence, coach) are of the same magnitude, of the order of 3 p./min., bus values are lower, of the order of 2 p./min., walking time values of the order of 4 p./min. and waiting times rather higher.

Turning briefly to leisure purposes, where the evidence relies entirely on our own analysis, we find values for car and coach of roughly the same order as for commuting, while the rail value is rather higher. For urban bus travel, the value is very low, indeed lower than any other result in the table. The ratios of walking and waiting time to in-vehicle time (based on the urban bus SP study) are approximately 2 and 4 respectively. Note that the waiting time value refers to 'expected waiting time', based on an application of the formula given by Bowman and Turnquist (1981).

Apart from the statistical errors which we have already referred to, the variation in the central values set out in table 7.1 must be largely due to modal specification and sample characteristics (including, of course, location and date of survey): the estimation methods are generally comparable, as, with slightly more reservation, are the data definitions. It is of interest and concern, however, that if we leave aside the waiting and walking values, the apparent ranking of values of time by mode is diametrically opposite to any comfort effects which we would expect to be the chief determinant of inter-modal differences.

We can conjecture that long-distance rail is likely to be the most comfortable, followed by coach (at any rate, the kind of coach services included in our long-distance surveys), then car driver, then urban rail (which accounts for all the commuting results) and finally urban bus. Our expectations are that people will be more willing to pay for time savings, other things being equal, as the travelling conditions become less comfortable, though evidence concerning the possible magnitude of such an effect is sparse. While it might be a small effect, it does not seem plausible that it in fact operates in the reverse direction! The most likely explanation resides in the composition of the various samples, and in particular, a possible self-selectivity effect.

4.3 Variation in values of time with income

While in earlier work on time valuation, there was considered to be some theoretical justification for a connection between values of time and the wage rate, we have shown that the primary reason for anticipating a relationship is the declining marginal utility of income. The theory does not offer any guidance as to the form of the relationship, other than to suggest that values of time will increase with income.

Early empirical work produced values of in-vehicle time which were generally found to be about 20–30 per cent of the wage rate, though it may be noted that there is little explanation of how the sample 'wage rate' was derived, and within the various data items required (household or personal income, gross or net, conversion from annual to hourly figures, etc.) there is considerable room for manoeuvre! While this convergence (see Bruzelius, 1979, and BTE, 1981, for more detail) is impressive, the empirical evidence for a direct relationship with income is surprisingly weak.

We now illustrate, in figure 7.3, the relationships between values of time and income for all the surveys considered by us in which a positive relationship has been found. Again all values have been converted to the June 1985 base, though the actual points along the income axis are in many cases the results of judicious guesswork. In addition it should be noted that for the North Kent survey, income was collected on a personal basis, so that this result is not compatible with the other surveys.

If anything is apparent from figure 7.3, it is that the relative positions for different modes illustrated in table 7.1 are broadly maintained across the income range, and that the relationship with income is (with the sole exception of the Quarmby results) less than proportionate – in other words the best fitting line for any one survey has a positive intercept on the 'value of time axis'. The implication is therefore that the proportion tends to decline as income increases. On the other hand, the base values are considerably higher than the 20–30 per cent suggested in the earlier evidence cited above. Without getting embroiled in the income definition problem, we may note that for the lowest income group (c. £3,500 p.a. which implies, on the basis of an 1,800 hour working year and a single worker household, an income of 3.24 p. per working minute), most of the surveys

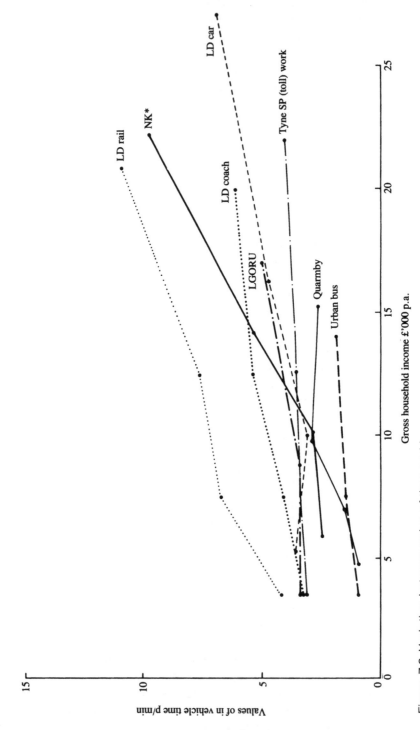

Figure 7.3 Variation between value of time and income

*For the North Kent Survey, income is related to persons, not households

suggest a value of about 3.5 p./min.! Comparable figure for high income levels (say £20,000 p.a.) give an income of 18.5 p. per working minute, with estimated values of time in the range 4–10 p./min. No allowance has been made for tax in these calculations.

It would be quite wrong to attach too much importance to these figures. In addition, we must point out that, as well as the self-selectivity argument, there are factors other than income which may account for the variation illustrated in figure 7.3. However, we may conclude that (a) we have clearly demonstrated the existence of an income relationship, which has never been done before with any conviction, (b) the value of time as a proportion of income is a decreasing function of income, rather than a constant as has hitherto been assumed, and (c) it seems intrinsically unlikely that the variation due to income can explain the general level of modal variation in table 7.1, which tends to confirm the existence of self-selectivity (indeed, the modal variation plotted in figure 7.3 supports this).

REFERENCES

ACTRA [Advisory Committee on Trunk Road Assessment] (1978), Report of the Committee, HMSO, London.

Atkins, S.T. (1983). 'The value of travel time: an empirical study using route choice, PTRC summer annual meeting, Paper N11.

(1984), 'Why value travel time? The case against', *Journal of the Institution of Highways and Transportation*, July 1984, pp. 2–7.

Bates, J.J. (1983), 'Stated preference techniques for the analysis of transport behaviour', World Conference on Transport Research, Hamburg.

(1984), 'Values of time from stated preference data', PTRC Summer Annual Meeting, Brighton, Paper H2.

(1985), 'Sensitivity to level of service: evidence from stated preference work', 1985 International Conference on Travel Behaviour, Noordwijk, Netherlands.

(1987), 'Measuring travel time values with a discrete choice model – a note', *Economic Journal*, 97.

Bates, J.J. and M. Roberts (1983), 'Recent experience with models fitted to stated preference data', PTRC Summer Annual Meeting, Brighton, Paper N8.

Becker, G.S. (1965), 'A theory of the allocation of time', *Economic Journal*, 75: 493–517.

Beesley, M. E. and Q. Dalvi (1973), The Journey to Work, Cost Benefit and Cost Effectiveness, Allen & Unwin.

Beggs, S., N.S. Cardell and J. Hausman (1981), 'Assessing the potential demand for electric cars', *Journal of Econometrics*, (16): 1–9.

Bonsall, P. (1983), 'Transfer price data – its definition, collection and use', 2nd International Conference on New Survey Methods in Transport, Hungerford Hill, NSW, Australia; also in Ampt, E.S., A.J. Richardson and W. Brog (eds.) (1985), *New Survey Methods in Transport*, Utrecht, VNU Science Press.

Bowman, L.A. and M.A. Turnquist (1981), 'Service frequency, schedule reliability and passenger wait times at transit stops', *Transportation Research*, 15A: 465–71.

Bradley, M.A., P.A. Marks and M. Wardman (1986), 'A summary of four studies into the value of travel time savings', PTRC Summer Annual Meeting, Brighton, Stream M.

Broom, D., S.R. Lowe, H.F. Gunn and P.M. Jones (1983), 'Estimating values of time: an experimental comparison of transfer price methods with the revealed preference approach', PTRC Summer Annual Meeting, Brighton, Paper N10.

Bruzelius, N. (1979), *The Value of Travel Time*, London, Croom Helm.

BTE [Bureau of Transport Economics] (1981), *The Value of Travel Time Savings in Public Sector Evaluation*, Canberra, Australian Government Publishing Service.

Cattin, P. and D.R. Wittink (1982), 'Commercial use of conjoint analysis: a survey', *Journal of Marketing*, 46: 44–53.

Chapman, R.G. and R. Staelin (1982), 'Exploiting rank ordered choice set data within the stochastic utility model', *Journal of Marketing Research*, 19: 288–301.

Cosslett, S.R. (1981), 'Efficient estimation of discrete choice models', in C. Manski and D. McFadden (eds.), *Structural Analysis of Discrete Data with Econometric Applications*, MIT Press.

Crittle, F.J. and L.W. Johnson (1980), *Basic Logit (BLOGIT) – Technical Manual*, Australian Road Research Board Technical Manual ATM no. 9, Victoria, Australia.

Daly, A.J. and S. Zachary (1975), 'Commuters' values of time', Report T55, Local Government Operational Research Unit, Reading.

(1977), 'The effect of free public transport on the journey to work', Transport and Road Research Laboratory Supplementary Report SR 338, Crowthorne, Berkshire.

Davies, A.L. and K.G. Rogers (1973), 'Modal choice and the value of time', Report C143, Local Government Operational Research Unit, Reading.

Deaton, A. and J. Muellbauer (1980), *Economics and Consumer Behaviour*, Cambridge University Press.

Department of Transport (1976), *Transport Policy*, London, HMSO.

(1976, continuing) 'Highways Economics Note 2', APM Divison.

(1982), 'Urban public transport subsidies: an economic assessment of value for money', Summary Report and Technical Report, EcLRT Division.

DeSerpa, A.J. (1971), 'A theory of the economics of time', *Economic Journal*, 81: 828–45.

(1973), 'Microeconomic theory and the valuation of travel time: some clarification', *Regional and Urban Economics*, 2: 401–10.

Domencich, T.A. and D. McFadden (1975), *Urban Travel Demand: A Behavioural Analysis*, Amsterdam, North-Holland.

Festinger, L. (1957), *A Theory of Cognitive Dissonance*, Stanford University Press.

Fienberg, S.E. (1978), *The Analysis of Cross-Classified Categorical Data*, Cambridge, MA, MIT Press.

Fowkes, A.S. (1986), 'The UK Department of Transport Value of Time project: results for North Kent commuters using revealed preference methods', *International Journal of Transport Economics* (June).

Fowkes, A.S. and M. Wardman (1985), 'The logit model, and the consequences of inter-personal taste variations', UTSG Annual Conference, Birmingham.

Goldschmidt, J. (1977), 'Pedestrian delay and traffic management, transport and road research laboratory', Supplementary Report SR 356, Crowthorne.

Golob, T.F. *et al.* (1979), 'Attitude-behaviour relationships in travel demand modelling', *Proceedings of Third International Conference on Behavioural Travel Modelling*, Croom Helm, London.

Goodwin, P.B. (1974), 'Generalized time and the problem of equity in transport studies', *Transportation*, 3: 1–24.

(1977), 'Habit and hysteresis in mode choice', *Urban Studies*, 14: 95–8.

(1978), 'On Grey's critique of generalized cost', *Transportation*, 7: 281–95.

(1981), 'The usefulness of travel budgets', *Transportation Research*, 15A: 97–106.

Grey, A. (1978a), 'The generalized cost dilemma', *Transportation*, 7: 261–80.

(1978b), 'Has generalized cost any benefit?', *Transportation*, 7: 417–22.

Gunn, H.F. (1983), 'Generalized cost or generalized time', *Journal of Transport Economics and Policy*, 17(1).

(1984), 'An analysis of transfer price data', PTRC Summer Annual Meeting, Brighton, Paper H1.

Gunn, H.F. and J.J. Bates (1982), 'Statistical aspects of travel demand modelling', *Transportation Research*, 16A: 371–82.

Gunn, H.F., P. Mackie and J. de D. Ortuzar (1980), 'Assessing the value of travel time savings – a feasibility study on Humberside', Working Paper 137, Institute for Transport Studies, University of Leeds.

Gwilliam, K.M. (1984), 'The objectives and effects of transport subsidies', ECMT Round Table 67, Paris.

Harrison, A.J. (1974), *The Economics of Transport Appraisal*, Croom Helm, London.

Harrison, A.J. and D.A. Quarmby (1969), 'The value of time in transport planning: a review', 6th Round Table, European Conference of Ministers of Transport, Paris.

Henley, D.H., I.P. Levin, J.J. Louviere and R.J. Meyer (1981), 'Changes in perceived travel cost and time for the work trip during a period of increasing gasoline cost', *Transportation*, 10(1): 23–34.

Hensher, D.A. (1972), 'The consumer's choice function: a study of traveller behaviour and values', unpublished PhD Thesis, School of Economics, University of New South Wales, Sydney.

(1976a), 'The value of commuter travel time savings: empirical estimation using an alternative valuation model', *Journal of Transport Economics and Policy*, 10: 167–76.

(1976b), 'Valuation of commuter travel time savings: an alternative procedure', in I.G. Heggie (ed.), *Modal Choice and the Value of Travel Time*, Oxford, Clarendon.

Hensher, D. A. and C. W. Johnson (1981). *Applied Discrete Choice Modelling*, London, Croom Helm.

Hensher, D.A. and J.J. Louviere (1983), 'Identifying individual preferences for international air fares: an application of functional measurement theory', *Journal of Transport Economics and Policy*, 17(3): 225–46.

Hensher, D.A. and T.K. Truong (1985), 'Valuation of travel time savings – a direct experimental approach', *Journal of Transport Economics and Policy*, 19(3): 237–61.

Horowitz, J. (1981), 'Sampling, specification and data errors in probabilistic discrete-choice models', Appendix C in D.A. Hensher and L.W. Johnson, *Applied Discrete Choice Modelling*, London, Croom Helm.

Hunt, E.K. and J. Schwartz (1972), *A Critique of Economic Theory*, Harmondsworth, Penguin Books.

IAURP (Institut d'Amenagement et d'Urbanisme de la Region Parisienne) (1969), 'Choix du Moyen de Transport par les Usagers', *Cahiers de l'IAURP*, 4–5, Paris.

Johnson, L. and D.A. Hensher (1982), 'Applications of multinomial probit to a two-period panel data set', *Transportation Research*, 16A(5–6): 457–64.

Kocur, G., T. Adler, W. Hyman and B. Aunet (1982), 'Guide to forecasting travel demand with direct utility assessment', United States Department of Transportation, Urban Mass Transportation Administration, Report no. UMTA-NH-11-0001-82-1, Washington DC.

Lancaster, K.J. (1969), *Mathematical Economics*, New York, Macmillan.

Lee, N. and M.Q. Dalvi (1969), 'Variations in the value of travel time', *Journal of the Manchester School of Economics and Social Studies*, 37: 213–36.

(1971), 'Variations in the value of travel time: further analysis', *Journal of the Manchester School of Economics and Social Studies*, 39: 187–204.

Louviere, J.J. (1978), 'Psychological measurement of travel attributes', in D.A. Hensher and M.Q. Dalvi (eds.), *Determinants of Travel Choice*, Teakfield.

(1981), 'Psychological contributions to understanding individual traveller behaviour', in K.P. Burnett and J.J. Louviere (eds.), *Transportation Geography*, New York, V.N. Winston & Sons.

Louviere, J.J. and D.A. Hensher (1981), 'Demand for international air travel: behavioural models of preference and choices with particular emphasis on the impact of alternative fare structures', Bureau of Transport Economics Occasional Paper 46, Australian Government Publishing Service, Canberra.

Mackinder, I.H. (1979), 'The predictive accuracy of British transportation studies – a feasibility study', Transport and Road Research Laboratory Supplementary Report 483, Crowthorne.

McIntosh, P.T. and D.A. Quarmby (1970), 'Generalized costs and the estimation of movement costs and benefits in transport planning', Department of Transport MAU Note 179, London. Also available in Highway Research Record 383 (1972), pp. 11–26.

McKenzie, R.P. and P.B. Goodwin (1985), 'Dynamic estimation of public transport demand elasticities: some new evidence', PTRC Summer Annual Meeting, Brighton, Paper J17.

Marks, P.A. (1986), 'Value of service, level changes for long distance rail and coach travellers', Institute of Transport Studies Working Paper 226, University of Leeds.

Marks, P.A., A.S. Fowkes and C.A. Nash (1986), 'Valuing long distance business travel time savings for evaluation: a methodological review and application', PTRC Summer Annual Meeting, Transportation Planning Methods Seminar, Brighton.

Mathews, P.J. and P.C. Baguley (1979), 'The assessment of traffic operations at dual-carriageway roadworks', PTRC Summer Annual Meeting, Warwick, Paper P21.

Metcalf, A.E. and J. Markham (1974), 'Recent findings on the value of time', CIE Economics Unit Research Paper 3, Dublin.

Michaels, R.M. (1974), 'Behavioural measurement: an approach to predicting travel demand', Transportation Research Board Special Report no. 149, pp. 51–7.

Muth, R.F. (1969), *Cities and Housing*, Chicago, University of Chicago Press.

Nelson, J.P. (1977), 'Accessibility and the value of time in commuting', *Southern Economic Journal*, 43: 181–96.

Ortuzar, J. de D. (1980), 'Modal choice modelling with correlated alternatives', unpublished PhD Thesis, University of Leeds.

Peacock, A. and C. Rowley (1975), *Welfare Economics: A Liberal Restatement*, London, Martin Robertson.

Quarmby, D.A. (1967), 'Choice of travel mode for the journey to work: some findings', *Journal of Transport Economics and Policy*, 1: 1–42.

Rogers, K.G., G.M. Townsend and A.E. Metcalf (1970), 'Planning for the work journey', Report C67, Local Government Operational Research Unit, Reading.

Searle, G. (1978), 'Generalized costs: fool's gold or useful currency', *Transportation*, 7: 297–9.

Self, P. (1972), *Econocrats and the Policy Process*, London, Macmillan.

Stopher, P.R. (1969), 'A probability model of travel mode choice for the work journey', Highway Research Record 283, pp. 57–64.

Thomas, T.C. (1968), 'The value of time for passenger cars: an experimental study of commuters' values', Stanford Research Institute, Menlo Park.

Thomas, T.C. and G.I. Thompson (1970), 'The value of time saved by trip purpose', Stanford Research Institute, Menlo Park.

Tipping, D.G. (1968), 'Time savings in transport studies', *Economic Journal*, 78: 843–54.

Train, K. and D. McFadden (1978), 'The goods/leisure tradeoff and disaggregate work trip mode choice models', *Transportation Research*, 12: 349–53.

Truong, T.K. and D.A. Hensher (1985), 'Measurement of travel time values and opportunity cost from a discrete-choice model', *Economic Journal*, 95: 438–51.

Wardman, M. (1986a), 'Route choice and the value of motorists' travel time – theoretical and methodological issues', Institute for Transport Studies Working Paper 223, University of Leeds.

(1986b), 'Route choice and the value of motorists' travel time – empirical findings', Institute for Transport Studies Working Paper 224, University of Leeds.

Watson, P.L. and P.R. Stopher (1974), 'The effect of income on the usage and valuation of transport modes', Proceedings of the 15th Annual Meeting, Transportation Research Forum, vol. 15.

8

SAFETY AND THE SAVING OF LIFE:
The theory of equalizing differences

Sherwin Rosen

1 INTRODUCTION

The theory of equalizing differences refers to observed wage differentials required to equalize the total monetary and non-monetary advantages or disadvantages among work activities and among workers themselves. The basic idea originates in the first ten chapters of Book I of *The Wealth of Nations*, which is unsurpassed for the depth and breadth of analysis as well as for clarity of exposition. It remains the fundamental reference work on the subject. The topic is important for both theoretical and empirical reasons. On the conceptual level it can make legitimate claim to be *the* fundamental (long-run) market equilibrium construct in labour economics.[1] Its empirical importance lies in contributing useful understanding to the determinants of the structure of wages in the economy and for making inferences about preferences and technology from observed wage data.

As a framework of analysis, equalizing or compensating wage differentials has found its most widespread use as a theory of supply of workers to labour activities that are differentiated by various attributes – working environments, worker skills and other job requirements. In one important class of problems these attributes refer to non-pecuniary, consumption by-products of work. Activities that offer favourable working conditions attract labour at lower than average wages, whereas jobs offering unfavourable working conditions must pay premiums as offsetting compensation in order to attract workers. Measurable job attributes on which compensating wage differentials have been shown to rise empirically include: (i) onerous working conditions, such as risks to life and health, exposure to pollution, and so forth; (ii) inter-city and inter-regional wage differences associated with differences in climate, crime, pollution and crowding; (iii) special work-time scheduling and related requirements, including shift work, inflexible work schedules, and possible risks of layoff and subsequent unemployment; and (iv) the composition of pay packages, including vacations, pensions and other fringe benefits as substitutes for direct cash wage payments. Another

This chapter previously appeared in O. Ashenfelter and R. Layard (1986), *Handbook of Labour Economics*, vol. I. We would like to thank Elsevier Science Publishers, B.V. for their kind permission to reproduce it here.

important class of problems identifies work environments with investment rather than with consumption. This includes acquired skills necessary to perform different types of work, empirically associated with formal schooling require- ments and on-the-job training. It also includes prospects for unusual lifecycle success or failure associated with the variance of possible outcomes in alternative career choices. The first class of problems is (loosely) associated with the indus- trial, interfirm, and regional wage structure, and the second is associated with the occupational wage structure, though there are interactions between the two.

A basic analytical symmetry leads to another, less common development of the theory as one of demand for workers with alternative traits and productive characteristics. At its most elementary level, these ideas lie behind the 'efficiency units' interpretations of heterogeneous labour inputs that is useful in produc- tivity theory and growth accounting. A much richer theory is obtained if more general and complex substitutions between productive traits of various workers are entertained, though this entire area is not yet completely understood.

This account stresses both supply and demand. It is shown that market clearing in this type of problem has a fundamentally different character than in most economic models of markets. The main point of contact with standard theory is the role of prices in achieving market equilibrium. The main point of difference is that the equilibrium achieves a matching and sorting function of allocating or assigning specific workers to specific firms. In contrast to the standard market paradigm, where the identities of traders is immaterial to final outcomes and indeed is the ultimate source of efficiency of a decentralized competitive market system, with whom and for whom one works is generally of considerable importance for achieving efficient labour allocations. Getting the most out of the resources that are available requires matching the proper type of worker with the proper type of firm: the labour market must solve a type of marriage problem of slotting workers into their proper 'niche' within and between firms. Herein lies the source of my assertion concerning the fundamental nature of this equilibrium construct for labour economics.

In the general analysis to follow, a labour market transaction is viewed as a tied sale in which the worker simultaneously sells (rents) the services of his labour and buys the attributes of his job. These attributes are fixed for any one job, but may vary from job to job. Hence, the worker exercises choice over preferred job attributes by choosing the appropriate type of job and employer. On the other hand, employers simultaneously buy the services and characteristics of workers and sell the attributes of jobs offered to the market. The characteristics of a particular worker are fixed, but may differ among workers. An acceptable match occurs when the preferred choices of an employer and an employee are mutually consistent; when the worker finds the employer's job attributes to be the most desirable and the employer finds the worker's productive characteristics to be the most desirable, both among all feasible choices.

The actual wage paid is therefore the sum of two conceptually distinct transactions, one for labour services and worker characteristics, and another for job attributes. The positive price the worker pays for preferred job activities is subtracted from the wage payment. The price paid by employers to induce workers to undertake onerous tasks takes the form of a wage premium, a negative price for the job, as it were. The observed distribution of wages clears both markets over all worker characteristics and job attributes. In this sense the labour market may be viewed as an implicit market in job and worker attributes. The resulting market equilibrium associates a wage with each assignment. The set of wages and the measurable attributes and characteristics associated with all such assignments are the equalizing differences observed in the market. Such associations underlie virtually all empirical estimates of wage functions estimated in actual data, and have become a focal point of modern research in labour economics. The theory of equalizing differences is helpful in interpreting these regressions and shows what inferences can be made from them concerning the preferences of workers and the technologies of firms.

The next section sketches the theory in the simplest possible case of binary choice over job consumption attributes. Before turning to that task, it should be pointed out that both the theory and applications of equalizing differences are based on the assumption of perfect information on both sides of the market. Hence, this theory (or any other) cannot possibly explain all wage variation in some specific set of data, even in the absence of measurement error.[2] The search for a job and investment in information is in many ways a search for the type of allocations described here. Hence the theory must be considered as one of longer run tendencies and of equilibrium behaviour in the steady state of a more complex dynamic process.

2 EQUALIZING DIFFERENCES FOR WORK-RELATED CONSUMPTION

The pure theory and its empirical consequences are best illustrated by an example in which different types of jobs offer two different levels of some disamenity. The first rigorous analytical statement of a model of this type is found in Friedman and Kuznets (1954, chapters 3 and 4, plus appendix) restated and summarized in Friedman (1962). It is the basis on which virtually all subsequent work has proceeded.

To focus on essentials, consider a labour market in which workers are pro-ductively homogeneous (thus sorting by worker characteristics is ignored for the time being) with two types of jobs. Let D be an index of job type, with $D = 0, 1$. Jobs of type 1 are associated with some disamenity, whereas jobs of type 0 are not. To be specific, think of the disamenity as airborne particulates at the worksite. Then type 1 jobs are 'dirty' (some particulates) and type 0 jobs are 'clean' (no particulates). An external observer ideally would organize the data as follows. First, each job is classified by type, with a value of 1 or 0 assigned to each based on some objective measurements, such as meter readings of dust or other pollutants. Second, wages w_1 and w_0 paid to workers on each type of job, as well as the number of workers employed in each is recorded. Third, specific data associated with each worker – such as non-earned income, other measures of wealth, family status, age and other demographic variables – and data associated with each firm – such as firm size, type of industry, capital intensity and so forth – are also observed. The analytical task is to construct an econometrically implementable structural model that describes how the data are generated, and which identifies the underlying behavioural relationships. The rules of this game follow the standard procedures of modern economics: both workers and firms are capable of making choices and these choices are rational and privately optimal. Rational decision making defines the behavioural structure, i.e., the demand and supply curves for each type of job.

It is possible to view these supply and demand relationships in either of two equivalent ways. Firms demand employees to work on the particular job type offered while workers supply labour to particular job types. Alternatively, workers may be viewed as demanding a particular type of job amenity, and firms may be viewed as supplying it. Clearly, both views achieve the same answer, and I shall go back and forth between them whenever it is convenient. This equivalence is due to the fact that the implicit market for the consumption attribute may itself be viewed in two equivalent ways. When the $D = 1$ job is used as the benchmark, it is natural to think of an implicit market for amenable attributes. Taking the clean job as benchmark lends itself more readily to thinking in terms of the supply and demand for labour on the disamenable job. In fact it is always possible to renormalize any analysis and speak of markets for amenities (goods) rather than disamenities (bads).[3] I normalize on the type 0 job in what follows, just because, following Smith, it is the usual practice.

2.1 Preferences, opportunities and worker choices

Preferences of a worker are defined over two types of consumption goods and can be represented by a utility function $u = u(C, D)$, where u is the utility index, C is market consumption goods purchased with money, and D is the tied consumption indicator of a job. For a given value of C it is natural to assume that $u(C, 0) \geq u(C, 1)$. Thus, D shifts conventional preferences and $D = 1$ is not preferred to $D = 0$, other things equal. The utility function allows an exact calculation of how much income or market consumption the worker must be compensated to undertake the less preferred job. Let C_0 be market consumption when $D = 0$. Given C_0, define C^* as the consumption level required to achieve the same utility on a $D = 1$ type job as C_0 guarantees on the $D = 0$ job. Then C^* satisfies $u(C^*, 1) = u(C_0, 0)$. Since $D = 1$ is never preferred at the same consumption level to $D = 0$, other things equal, it follows that $C^* \geq C_0$. Now define the difference

$Z = C^* - C_0$ as the compensating variation for $D = 1$ compared with $D = 0$. It is the additional compensation necessary to make the worker indifferent between the two types of jobs at a given utility index. To put it in yet another way, Z is the minimum supply or reserve price to the disamenable job.[4] Sometimes it is called a 'shadow' price.

It is useful to think of utility $u(C, D)$ as defined over two continuous variables rather than over a continuous and a discrete one. Treat D as a cardinal measure, such as parts per million (ppm) particulates, even though the actual choices (for now) are qualitative. Then, for example, $D = 1$ refers to some particular level, say 10 ppm, and $D = 0$ refers to some lower level, say 0 ppm, and $u(C, D)$ can be regarded as a conventional description of preferences in which D is a 'bad' rather than a good. Assume $u(C, D)$ is a quasi-concave, so the worker's indifference curves are convex. The definition of Z (and Z') is shown in figure 8.1. The curve is an indifference curve and Z and Z' are measured by the vertical distance ab.

Competitive labour markets and binary choices imply that labour market opportunities are completely described by exactly two points in the (w, D) plane. The clean job offers point $(w_0, 0)$ and the dirty one offers $(w_1, 1)$. If the market is competitive we know that the worker takes these numbers as given, take it or leave it. Information on wages and working conditions (w_i, D_i) is presumably found by 'comparison shopping' among alternative types of jobs.[5] If the worker also is exogenously endowed with a source of non-earned income (possibly zero) denoted by y, the consumption opportunity set is described by points c and d in figure 8.1. Working on job type 0 commands $C_0 = y + w_0$ units of market consumption goods and $D = 0$ units of job related consumption; whereas working on job type 1 commands $C_1 = y + w_1$ units of market consumption and $D = 1$ units of the job disamenity. Define $\Delta W = (w_1 - w_0)$ as the *market equalizing difference*. Then the $D = 1$ job offers ΔW additional units of market consumption for worse working conditions. It is the implicit market price of dirt.

A worker chooses the job type that maximizes utility: $D = 1$ is chosen if $u(\Delta W + C_0, 1) > u(C_0, 0)$ and $D = 0$ is chosen if $u(\Delta W + C_0, 0) < u(C_0, 0)$. The worker is indifferent between the two if utility is the same. The rule is illustrated in figure 8.1. As illustrated, point c lies above the indifference curve through d so $D = 1$ is the preferred choice. If ΔW had been small enough so that c had fallen below the indifference curve through d, then $D = 0$ would have been the preferred choice; and of course c and d would have been indifferent had they fallen on the same indifference curve.

Figure 8.1 suggests an alternative way of characterizing the worker's choice, which turns out to be more convenient and more powerful than the direct utility calculation. That $D = 1$ is preferred in the figure is clearly the same thing as saying that ΔW exceeds Z. Here ΔW is just the vertical distance between points c and b, and the indifference curve shows that the worker requires Z units of

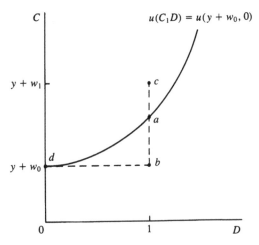

Figure 8.1

additional consumption to be compensated for $D = 1$ over $D = 0$. If the market offers more than this increment, then $\Delta W > Z$ and utility is larger on the dirty job. A surplus value or rent is gained by the worker in the bargain. Clearly, workers choosing $D = 1$ do not necessarily inherently prefer that type of work. Rather, the wage difference is sufficiently large to buy off their distaste for it. On the other hand, if $Z > \Delta W$ the opportunity cost of the better job in terms of market consumption foregone is less than the willingness to pay for it, so $D = 0$ is the preferred alternative. The worse job does not offer sufficient compensation to be attractive. Consequently, choices are completely described by the rule

$$\text{choose } D = 1 \text{ or } D = 0 \text{ as } \Delta W \gtrless Z \tag{1}$$

Ties ($\Delta W = Z$) are broken by a random device, such as flipping a coin.

2.2 Market supply

The supply of labour to each type of job is defined as the number of applicants, given the relative wage prospects offered by each. Market supply functions are found by varying relative wages and determining how choices respond, according to the individually rational behaviour rule (1). Given w_0 and w_1, each individual applies to the job for which utility is maximized, so the total number of workers applying for job type D are all those for whom utility is largest there. Varying one or both of the wages and calculating how choices are affected is the conceptual experiment which maps out the market supply curves of workers to job types.

Given the equivalence between the reservation wage rule (1) and the direct utility calculation, it is clear that w_1 and w_0 need not be considered separately for ascertaining whether a worker chooses job type 0 or 1. The difference ΔW is a sufficient statistic for the problem: any combination of w_0 and w_1 which leads to the same value of ΔW leads to the same individual choices. Similarly, Z is a complete representation of preferences for this problem. Given the size of the labour force choosing between $D = 0$ and $D = 1$, *relative* market supply conditions are completely characterized by calculating the number of workers for whom $\Delta W > Z$ and calculating the number for whom $\Delta W < Z$. It is worth emphasizing that the differential ΔW is the relevant market price available to all workers independently of their preferences.[6] Though ΔW is the same for all workers, Z is a personal taste variable which generally varies from person to person, depending on their own circumstances and inherent preferences. It is convenient to describe differences in preferences among workers parametrically for analysis. Define $g(Z)$ as the density, in the sense of a probability density function, of tastes in the population of workers making choices and define $G(Z)$ as the cumulated density. Then for a given value of ΔW, all those choosing job type 1 satisfy the condition $\Delta W > Z$, and the fraction of workers who apply for $D = 1$ must be

$$N_1^s = \int_0^{\Delta W} g(Z)dz = G(\Delta W) \tag{2}$$

The remaining fraction of workers apply for jobs of type 0. These are persons for whom $\Delta W < Z$, so

$$N_0^s = \int_{\Delta W}^{\infty} g(Z)dz = 1 - G(\Delta W) \tag{3}$$

Relative market supplies partition the distribution $g(Z)$ and assign workers to job types according to tastes. Figure 8.2 illustrates equations (2) and (3) for a given value of ΔW. Relative supply to $D = 1$ jobs is the area under $g(Z)$ to the left of ΔW – this is equation (2). Relative supply to $D = 0$ is the area to the right of ΔW – this is equation (3). The supply functions themselves sweep out the distribution of preferences $g(Z)$. To see this, consider a small increase in ΔW. Then the partition moves slightly to the right of what is shown in figure 8.2. All those who previously found it optimal to choose $D = 1$ certainly find it optimal to do so at a higher wage. However, those who were indifferent or had a slight net preference for $D = 0$ now find the balance tipped in favour of $D = 1$ instead: the choice condition (1) for this extensive margin of workers flips from $Z > \Delta W$ to $Z < \Delta W$. Finally, those who have very strong preferences against $D = 1$ do not find the increase in wages large enough to change their minds: they remain in $D = 0$. These are all persons whose Z lies further out in the right-hand tail of $g(Z)$.

This formulation is very general in accommodating virtually all possibilities for how preferences might be distributed among workers. The following cases are instructive.

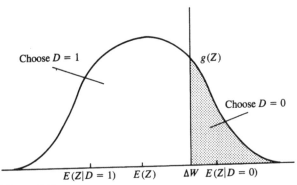

Figure 8.2

Case 1

Workers have identical reservation prices Z. Then their preferences are identical and the distribution $g(Z)$ is degenerate with a point of mass at the common value of Z and no mass elsewhere. Since $g(Z)$ is a spike, the relative supply functions $G(\Delta W)$ and $1 - G(\Delta W)$ are step functions, with one step. Supply to $D = 1$ is infinitely elastic at a value of ΔW equal to the common reservation wage Z and is completely inelastic for wages either above or below it.

Case 2

The distribution $g(Z)$ is discrete over k specific values of Z, say $Z_1, Z_2, \ldots, Z_k$. Then there are k distinct types of worker preferences in the population, with proportion $G(Z_j)$ having reservation prices of Z_j or less. This is an immediate generalization of case (1). The supply curve to $D = 1$ is also a step function, but it has k steps rather than one step.

Case 3

Increasing the number of values of k in case (2) and passing to the limit of a dense continuous set of subjective valuations of attributes leads to a continuous density for $g(Z)$, as depicted in figure 8.2. If $g(Z)$ is unimodal and roughly symmetrical on either side of the mode, then the supply curve to $D = 1$ has a logistic shape when viewed from the vertical axis. There is rising supply price throughout.

Case 4

$g(Z)$ may be a mixture of discrete and continuous components. An important practical case is when a non-trivial fraction of workers are neutral towards the attribute, with $Z = 0$, and the rest are continuously distributed over $Z > 0$: a mass of workers place no value at all on dirty working conditions and are inherently indifferent to dirt while other workers have definite distaste for dirt. Such a density would appear similar to the one in figure 8.2 with the addition of a point of mass or spike at $Z = 0$. In that case the supply curve to $D = 1$ types of jobs begins with a flat, infinitely elastic section at $\Delta W = 0$, for the fraction of workers with $Z = 0$; and is increasing thereafter to induce workers who dislike the job to choose it.

Comparing Case 1 above with the rest, these examples illustrate the general point that the elasticity of supply to $D = 1$ is decreasing in the variance or spread of the distribution $g(Z)$.

2.3 Technology, opportunities and firm choices

Firms must choose the job type offered to the market. This choice depends on the nature of technology, which in turn determines the relevant internal supply prices of each type of job. The optimal decision then depends on comparing relative internal supply prices with market wage opportunities and costs. The basic idea in the dirt example is that a firm can spend resources to clean up its work environment, within limits dictated by technology. The cost of doing so is compared with the wage savings on labour costs available from the fact that w_1 generally exceeds w_0. If labour cost savings exceed the cost of cleaning, the optimal strategy is to offer $D = 0$ type jobs to the market; while if cleaning costs exceed wage savings the firm chooses to offer $D = 1$ jobs to the market. In this way it is possible to characterize the firm's choice by a reservation price rule analogous to equation (1). This general logic extends to virtually any type of attribute.

It is natural to think of the firm as engaging in a form of joint production, in which it sells a conventional good to the market and simultaneously sells a non-market good to its workers (an early development along these lines is found in Thompson (1968)). Denote the market good by x and the non-market good by D, as above. Taking $D = 1$ as a benchmark, think of particulates at the worksite as a natural byproduct of x production. For example, the production of steel (x) involves smoke (D). However, production possibilities between x and D are not necessarily rigid because the firm may be able to use resources to reduce D to smaller levels. These possibilities take several forms: supplying workers with equipment and clothing that reduces exposure to pollutants, purchasing more expensive but cleaner capital, and using larger proportions of labour time to clean up the work environment as opposed to direct production of market goods. All these factors may be summarized in a joint production function $F(x, D, L) = 0$, where x and D are outputs and L is labour input. Assume $F_x > 0$, $F_D < 0$, and $F_L < 0$. Define the marginal rate of transformation between x and D by $-F_D/F_x$. Then the production possibilities curve in the (x, D) plane is an increasing function of D. Its slope gives the marginal costs of reducing D in terms of x foregone.[7] Comparing marginal cost with wage opportunities determines whether $D = 1$ or $D = 0$ is the optimal choice.

An immediate and elementary but important implication is that $D = 1$ must be productive if dirty jobs are ever observed in the market. For if workers demand a wage premium to work on disagreeable jobs then a firm would never find it in its self-interest to offer such jobs unless there were compensating advantages to its profitability. The production function $F(\cdot)$ shows that this benefit is extra market output x. Consequently, it is necessary that $-F_D/F_x$ is positive for at least one firm if $D = 1$ type jobs are ever observed in the market. Given that the marginal rate of transformation $-F_D/F_x$ is positive for at least some firms, its magnitude clearly depends on the particular circumstances of production. For some types of work it may be very large indeed. In these cases the costs of making jobs more amenable may be extremely large. An example might be underground mining. There are virtually no circumstances under which such jobs are 'pleasant'. On the other hand, the marginal rate of transformation may be very small in other lines of work, for example office workers in insurance companies.

Let us analyse a specific linear technology which lends itself to a development similar to that used for workers. Suppose

$$x = a_1 L, \qquad \text{if } D = 1,$$

$$x = a_0 L, \qquad \text{if } D = 0 \tag{4}$$

Define $B = a_1 - a_0$. Then imposing the restriction $B > 0$ incorporates the idea that $D = 1$ is productive in the sense discussed above: the efficiency of labour in x production is larger when resources are not used for cleaning up the work environment. In fact B represents the relevant marginal cost per worker of producing clean worksites in terms of foregone output x. The relevant marginal labour cost per worker to the firm's profits of providing clean jobs rather than dirty ones is just the wage difference ΔW. The firm chooses the alternative with the smallest cost. Therefore the firm's decision rule must be

$$\text{choose } D = 1 \text{ or } D = 0 \text{ as } B \gtreqless \Delta W \tag{5}$$

If B exceeds ΔW the foregone costs of cleaning exceed the incremental labour costs of providing clean jobs, so $D = 1$ is the best choice. But if ΔW exceeds B, the cleaning costs are smaller than the wage premium of providing dirty jobs and $D = 0$ is the preferred choice.

2.4 Market demand

The demand for workers in each type of job is a function of relative wage rates, other factor prices, demand conditions for output, and so forth. It is found by aggregating the choice rules discussed above over employers. For this exercise the

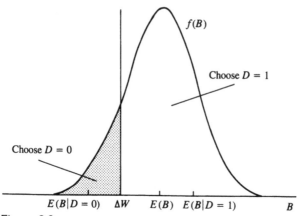

Figure 8.3

size of each firm is taken as given.[8] From the development above, the two numbers B and ΔW are sufficient statistics for this problem. Let B be distributed among firms according to profitability density $f(B)$, with cumulated density function $F(B)$, where the densities are taken to incorporate the size of each firm as well as its technology. Thus, for example, $F(B)$ indicates the fraction of potential jobs in the market for which firm technology is B or less (if all firms were the same size this would just be the fraction of firms with B or less). Since a firm offers $D = 1$ or $D = 0$ according to (5), the fraction of $D = 1$ jobs offered to the market must be the sum over all firms for whom $B > \Delta W$, or

$$N_1^d = \int_{\Delta W}^{\infty} f(B)\mathrm{d}B = 1 - F(\Delta W) \tag{6}$$

The fraction of $D = 0$ jobs offered must be the remainder of the distribution.

Relative supplies of job types partition the distribution of technology $f(B)$, as shown in figure 8.3. The number of dirty jobs offered to the market is the area under $f(B)$ to the right of ΔW, which just depicts eq. (6). The number of clean jobs offered to the market is the area under $f(B)$ to the left of ΔW. The number of jobs offered is equivalent to the demand for workers in each job type. Therefore, the demand function for workers in $D = 1$ jobs sweeps out the distribution of technology. Suppose ΔW rises a little in figure 8.3. Then all firms offering $D = 0$ jobs continue to do so. Firms with values of B slightly above the old value of ΔW were previously offering $D = 1$ jobs, but were close to indifferent to offering $D = 0$ and now find the balance tipped in favour of supplying $D = 0$ jobs. Firms for whom cleaning costs are very large continue to offer dirty jobs. The job market would show an expansion of amenable job offerings and a contraction of disamenable ones: the partition in figure 8.3 moves to the right.

As was true of supply, this formulation accommodates a wide variety of distributions $f(B)$. For example, if all firms have the same technology the distribution degenerates to a spike and the market demand function is a downward step function with the height of the step given by the common value of B. A little experimentation will show that market demand for workers in $D = 1$ jobs is decreasing in the spread or variance of the underlying distribution of technology $f(B)$, similar to the results for worker discussed above.

2.5 Market equilibrium and selection

Market equilibrium is defined by equality between demand and supply for workers on each type of job. This involves two things. First, the level of wages w_1 and w_0 must adjust so that the total number of workers seeking positions equals the number of positions to be filled. The principle of substitution is at work here. On the one hand, increases in the level of wages in a particular labour market increases supply by attracting job seekers from other markets and from new entrants into the labour force. On the other hand, an increase in wages reduces the amount of labour demanded through both capital–labour substitution and product substitution due to produce price changes. Second, the wage differential ΔW and the relative demand for workers in $D = 0$ jobs is increasing in ΔW and the relative demand for workers in $D = 1$ jobs is decreasing in ΔW, so the standard stability conditions for market equilibrium are met and the equilibrium is unique. In equilibrium ΔW adjusts to make the partitions in figures 8.2 and 8.3 conform to each other: the area under $g(Z)$ to the left of ΔW in figure 8.2 equals the area under $f(B)$ to the right of ΔW in figure 8.3.

It is an immediate consequence of this construction that workers and firms are systematically matched or assigned to each other in market equilibrium. Workers found on $D = 1$ jobs have the smallest distastes for D and firms offering $D = 1$ employment have the largest costs of cleaning up their work environments. Hence there is a tendency towards negative assortative matching in equilibrium.[9] Workers with larger than average values of Z are systematically found in firms with smaller than average values of B and conversely. It is precisely this feature of the labour market which distinguishes this class of problems from the standard market paradigm.

This important result may be stated more formally as follows. Let $E(Z) = \int Zg(Z)dZ$ be the population average of Z over all workers making choices and let $E(B) = \int Bf(B)dB$ be the mean of B over the entire population of firms. Write $E(x|y)$ as the conditional expectation of random variable x, given some particular value of the variable y. Here the relevant conditioning variables are $D = 0$ or $D = 1$, and the relevant random random variables are Z and B.[10] Looking only at workers found on $D = 1$ jobs, the choice rule (1) implies $E(Z|D = 0) \geq E(Z)$ and $E(B|D = 0) \leq E(B)$: workers choosing clean jobs have larger than average distastes for dirt, and firms offering clean jobs have smaller than average cleaning costs.

The difference between the conditional and unconditional expectations is called a *selectivity bias* and is a convenient measure of the extent to which workers or firms found in any given job classification depart from a random sample of all workers in all firms. If there is any heterogeneity in the underlying populations, workers and firms are systematically sorted and selected among classes of jobs according to the choice rules (1) and (5), and the observations are stratified by the complex of factors that make decisions differ among the agents. Selection and stratification are ubiquitous in economics and the market for job amenities is perhaps the most elementary example of it. It should be noted that selectivity effects are the rule in virtually all spatial allocation problems. Here 'space' is not geographical, but rather a point in the 'space of job characteristics'.

Systematic selection and stratification have important consequences for the inferences that can be drawn from data about underlying tastes and technology in the population. For example, it is a common practice to survey workers at their worksites and ask them questions about what aspects of their jobs are most important to them. These surveys typically find that wages and other pecuniary considerations are not at the top of the list, and that other, non-pecuniary factors are more prominent in workers' responses. A tempting interpretation of such findings is that wages do not influence labour supply decisions to different types of jobs: in a word, that supply is inelastic. Yet this analysis suggests that considerable care must be taken in drawing such inferences from qualitative survey responses.

It is clear from figure 8.2 that if workers differ by tastes for work-related consumption then the average reservation price for workers on each job type may differ markedly from the market wage difference ΔW. Another way of saying this is that the allocation of workers to job types typically generates significant amounts of economic rent, defined as the excess return over that required to change a decision. In figure 8.2 the average person choosing $D = 1$ is far from the margin of indifference and would maintain the same choice even if ΔW changed substantially. The same thing holds true for the average worker who chose $D = 0$. The difference between the reservation wage and the actual wage is the rent earned in a person's current choice. In fact the rent earned by the average person in $D = 1$ is given by $\Delta W - E(Z|D = 1)$, and the average rent for people found in $D = 0$ is $E(Z|D = 0) - \Delta W$. If these numbers are large, the typical survey respondent would identify non-monetary considerations as more important to his job choice than wages because a change in relative wage would not affect the decision of the average person in each job category. The caution required in going from this observation to the conclusion that relative supply is inelastic is that inferences about averages don't necessarily carry over to margins: it is the weight of people at the margin of choice – the number who are close to indifferent between the two types of jobs – that determines the supply response. The relationship between averages and margins in turn depends on how tastes are distributed in the underlying population.

To illustrate some of the issues, let us work through the case where Z is normally distributed in the worker population. Write $Z = \bar{Z} + v$, where v is a normal variate with mean zero and variance σ^2. $\bar{Z}$ is the unconditional (population) mean of Z. Define $\phi(x)$ as the standard normal density and write $\Phi(x)$ as the cumulative density. The proportion of workers, n_1, found in $D = 1$ jobs is, from (1)

$$n_1 = \text{Prob}(Z \le \Delta W) = \text{Pr}(\bar{Z} + v \le \Delta W) = \text{Pr}(v \le \Delta W - \bar{Z})$$
$$= \text{Pr}\left(\frac{v}{\sigma} \le \frac{\Delta W - \bar{Z}}{\sigma}\right) = \Phi\left(\frac{\Delta W - \bar{Z}}{\sigma}\right) \tag{7}$$

The fraction of workers found in $D = 1$ jobs at relative wage ΔW is the ordinate of the cumulated standard normal evaluated at $(\Delta W - \bar{Z})/\sigma$. Differentiating (7) with respect to ΔW and converting to an elasticity yields

$$\epsilon_1 = \frac{\Delta W}{n_1} \frac{dn_1}{d(\Delta W)} = \left(\frac{\Delta W}{\sigma}\right)\left[\phi\left(\frac{\Delta W - Z}{\sigma}\right) \bigg/ \phi\left(\frac{\Delta W - \bar{Z}}{\sigma}\right)\right] \tag{8}$$

Given ΔW, we may calculate the average value of Z among all workers found on $D = 1$ jobs. This is the conditional expectation

$$E(Z|D = 1) = E(\bar{Z} + v|\bar{Z} + v \le \Delta W) = \bar{Z} + E(v|v \le \Delta W - \bar{Z})$$
$$= \bar{Z} + \sigma E\left(\frac{v}{\sigma}\bigg|\frac{v}{\sigma} \le \Delta W - \bar{Z}\right)$$
$$= \bar{Z} - \sigma\phi\left(\frac{\Delta W - \bar{Z}}{\sigma}\right) \bigg/ \Phi\left(\frac{\Delta W - \bar{Z}}{\sigma}\right) \tag{9}$$

The first two equalities in (9) follow from choice rule (1) and the definition $Z = \bar{Z} + v$, while the third and fourth equalities follow from well-known properties of the normal distribution. The ratio of ordinates Φ/ϕ is called Mill's ratio, named after the statistician who first tabulated it in the 1920s. The difference between the unconditional mean of Z and the conditional mean in (9) is the 'selectivity bias'. Call it S_1. Then, from (9)

$$S_1 = \sigma\phi\left(\frac{\Delta W - \bar{Z}}{\sigma}\right) \bigg/ \Phi\left(\frac{\Delta W - \bar{Z}}{\sigma}\right) \tag{10}$$

S_1 is a precise measure of the extent to which preferences of people found on $D = 1$ jobs differ from the average among workers in all jobs. It is clear from the formula and from the construction in figure 8.2 that S_1 is increasing in the variance of preferences in the entire population. Finally, define $\Delta W - Z$ as the rent earned by a person who chooses $D = 1$. Then average rent accruing to all workers found on $D = 1$ jobs must be, from (9) again

$$R_1 = \Delta W - E(Z|D = 1) + \sigma\left[\frac{\Delta W - \bar{Z}}{\sigma} + \frac{\phi(\cdot)}{\Phi(\cdot)}\right]$$

Average rent among $D = 1$ workers is an increasing function of the standardized wage differential and also of the variance of preferences. Of course, similar expressions may be found for workers choosing $D = 0$ jobs, and also among firms offering both types of jobs.

Now in this particular example there is a partial restriction between ϵ_1, S_1 and R_1 because they all depend on the inverse Mill's ratio ϕ/Φ. For example, as σ^2 goes to zero S_1 and R_1 also converge to zero and ϵ_1 goes to infinity because population heterogeneity vanishes. At the opposite extreme, ϵ_1 goes to zero and S_1 and R_1 grow very large as σ^2 grows very large, i.e., as heterogeneity of preferences grows large. So indeed at these extremes qualitative survey responses do indicate something about supply elasticities. However, for intermediate values of σ^2 the situation is less clear. In fact we have, from (8) and (10), $\epsilon_1/S_1 = (\Delta W/\sigma^2)$. The relationship between ϵ_1 and S_1 depends on the variance σ^2 and the typical survey response gives us little information about variances. In fact the variance of response among workers found on each job category gives us only indirect evidence on σ^2 in the whole population because of the qualitative nature of these responses and because both groups of workers are censored samples of the population.

While this example has the virtue of lending precision to calculations, readers should be cautioned that there is no particular reason to expect preferences to follow the normal distribution rather than some other one. The general point remains that information on conditional averages does not necessarily convey much information about decision makers near the margin of choice, which determines the responsiveness of supply to relative wage movements. There is no good substitute for direct estimates of supply elasticities.

In fact most of the empirical work in this area has been devoted to establishing the magnitude of the market equalizing difference ΔW in a variety of cases. Usually this is done on cross-section data for individual workers, where the wage of a worker is related to the type of job on which the person is found and to a host of other factors such as union status, race, sex, education, and experience that serve as proxies for other forces that are known to affect wages. The immediate goal of this work is to ascertain whether and to what extent the labour market provides implicit compensation for non-pecuniary attributes of work. However, it is tempting and natural to extend these estimates to other uses. For example, in the specific problem under discussion, the estimated equalizing difference for dirty jobs may assist in evaluating the monetary benefits of pollution abatement programmes in the economy at large. The selection aspects of market equilibrium help delimit the possibilities for extrapolating labour market estimates to programme evaluation.

The potential for using market estimates of compensating wage differentials for policy evaluation lies in the logic of cost–benefit analysis itself: benefits are valued according to a 'willingness to pay' criteria, which in turn is closely related to the idea of compensating variations (the Z's) underlying the structure of worker's choices in the labour market. While such things as pollution are not directly marketed, the labour market acts as an implicit market because ΔW has the ready interpretation of a price or valuation on the disamenity. However, this price does not give a complete picture of valuations because it is a precise reading only for the set of workers who are close to the margin of choice, and as we have seen this may be much different from the average value in the population, depending on the dispersion of preferences. The logic of revealed preferences shows the difficulty. Given ΔW we know that all people in $D = 1$ jobs value D no more than ΔW; otherwise they could not have chosen that type of work. We also know that people found on the $D = 0$ job must place a value of at least ΔW and possibly greater on D; otherwise they would have chosen to work on dirty jobs rather than on clean ones. This is just another way of saying that rents and selection effects may exist in the market allocation of workers to jobs. But from knowledge of ΔW alone it is not possible to make inferences on the extent of such rents.[11]

Nonetheless, the estimated value of ΔW may provide a bound on the typical person's valuation of D in certain circumstances. For example, suppose the fraction of workers found in $D = 1$ jobs is fairly small. Then from figure 8.2 it follows that the average worker would be willing to pay at least as much as ΔW for pollution abatement elsewhere, since such workers now 'pay' ΔW by accepting the $D = 0$ job rather than the $D = 1$ job. Consequently ΔW serves as a lower bound on willingness to pay in this case. That such information can be fairly limited is easily illustrated. Suppose some workers have no preferences against D; that is, their Z is zero. If the market equilibrium is such that these workers are sufficiently numerous to occupy all $D = 1$ jobs, then we know that the market equalizing difference ΔW is zero, and knowing that the valuation of the typical person exceeds zero does not tell us anything that we didn't already know. Rees (1976) has stressed this point. Only if the market valuation ΔW is significantly sizeable does the method provide helpful information.

By this time it almost goes without saying that similar statements apply to firms. The market price ΔW gives us some information on cleaning costs (job related pollution abatement) of firms. The cost of cleaning must be at least ΔW for those firms offering $D = 1$ jobs; and it must be at most ΔW for firms offering $D = 0$ jobs. This type of inference has not been used much in project evaluation, perhaps because costs of projects tend to be easier to calculate than benefits and firm's cost functions for work related attributes may be substantially different than elsewhere in the economy.

NOTES

Financial support from the National Science Foundation is gratefully acknowledged.

1 It is also central to urban economics and to virtually all economic problems involving product differentiation and spatial considerations, e.g., see Samuelson (1983) for an

elegant description of Von Thunen's theory of spatial equilibrium, which is closely related to Smith.

2 The well-known exchange between Rottenberg (1956) and Lampman (1956) is relevant here. Also see Reder (1963). In light of much subsequent research on the determinants of wages it seems fair to add the point that search, information costs, and other omitted factors sustain significant wage variability among measurably identical jobs and workers. To put it in another way, the R^2 in the typical wage regression is not large. In extremely micro-oriented data the signal-to-noise ratio is very small and it may be difficult to detect the effects under discussion. Less detailed data, e.g., from a broadly based worker survey rather than one from workers in a small number of firms in a particular local labour market, have the virtue of reducing the noise and increasing the signal. In any event, many empirical estimates of equalizing differences now appear in the literature, so there is no need to argue in the abstract.

3 The point is similar to the analysis of labour supply in that it is only a matter of convenience whether the analysis is cast in terms of the demand for leisure (a good) or in terms of a supply of labour (a 'bad').

4 Corresponding to the discussion above, norming on $D = 1$ leads to a development in terms of the equivalent variation Z', defined by $u(C_1, 1) = u(C_0 - Z', 0)$. It is well known that $Z = Z'$ when both are evaluated at the same utility index; otherwise they differ by an income effect. More subtle distinctions can be made, such as the difference between Marshallian and Hicksian variations, but that is immaterial for present purposes. Some very interesting implications of these distinctions in the context of equalizing differences for health risks are presented in Cook and Graham (1977), but their analysis is applicable to a broader class of problems than risks to life.

5 In the language of search theory it is easiest to think of job amenities as 'search goods' rather than 'experience goods' though no doubt much labour mobility at early ages is better described as experience goods.

6 Notice that the size of the labour force is taken as given in this exercise and the problem is to allocate a given number of workers between job types. Fixing the number of workers to be assigned is what justifies working with ΔW alone. The total number of people to be allocated is a function of the absolute level of real wages w_1 and w_0, in the conventional manner of labour supply. A general equilibrium model is required to determine the level of wages in each market. Those details are ignored here because it is obvious that there are no difficulties in establishing the existence of an equilibrium.

7 It is straightforward to include other resource inputs such as capital and materials. Had we chosen to measure the job characteristic in terms of cleanliness (a good) rather than dirtiness, the production possibilities frontier would have been a more conventional downward-sloping curve rather than an upward-sloping one.

8 Of course, a full general equilibrium analysis would determine the size distribution of firms as part of the problem, but that is taken as exogenous here. Think of what follows as an examination of the cross-section of firms in the market at the equilibrium size distribution.

9 Since firms do not directly care about workers' tastes and workers do not directly care about firms technologies, the *matching* is not perfectly rank order in Z and B, nor is it

unique since any worker with $Z < \Delta W$ will find any firm for which $B > \Delta W$ acceptable and vice versa.

10 These variables are random in the sense of $f(B)$ and $g(Z)$. It bears repeating that this randomness is induced by population heterogeneity, *not* by stochastic preferences or stochastic technology.

11 It is clear that nothing can be learned about the structure of preferences in a single cross-section because the price ΔW is the same for all people in the sample. However, a probit or logit analysis of individual choices would indicate variables that affect selection. For example, the partial effect of wealth and earnings potential (skill) increases the propensity to choose the more amenable job due to the usual income (and substitution) effects [Weiss (1976)]. Some inferences about the structure of preferences can be made if time series data are available so that changes in ΔW are observed. Then there are supply shifters in (2) and demand shifters in (6) so the problem may be modelled and estimated by the usual simultaneous equations methods.

REFERENCES

Cook, P. and D. Graham (1977), 'The demand for insurance and protection: the case of irreplaceable commodities', *Quarterly Journal of Economics*.

Friedman, M. (1962), *Price Theory: A Provisional Text*, Chicago, Aldine.

Friedman, M. and S. Kuznets (1954), *Income from Independent Professional Practice*, New York, NBER.

Lampman, R. (1956), 'On choice in labor markets: comment', *Industrial and Labor Relations Review*.

Reder, M. (1963), 'Wage structure: theory and measurement', *Aspects of Labor Economics*, New York, NBER.

Rees, A. (1976), 'Compensating wage differentials', in A. Skinner and T. Wilson (eds.), *Essays on Adam Smith*, Cambridge.

Rottenberg, S. (1956), 'On choice in labor markets', *Industrial and Labor Relations Review*.

Samuelson, P. (1983), 'Thunen at two hundred', *Journal of Economic Literature*.

Thomson, E. (1968), 'The perfectly competitive production of collective goods', *Review of Economics and Statistics*.

Weiss, Y. (1976), 'The wealth effect in occupational choice', *International Economic Review*.

9

SAFETY AND THE SAVING OF LIFE:
The economics of safety and physical risk

M.W. Jones-Lee

The terms 'safety' and 'risk' are at the same time commonplace, evocative and somewhat obscure. As a result, it is hardly surprising that each of these terms has come to be used in a variety of subtly different ways, both in everyday language and in more technical discussion. It would therefore seem appropriate to begin by explaining precisely what is to be meant by 'safety' and 'physical risk' in the present context. It is also important to be clear from the outset about the sense in which the argument that follows will attempt to provide an 'economic' analysis of these phenomena.

In this chapter 'safety' refers exclusively to the safety of human life and constitutes the degree of protection from – or more accurately, attenuation of – physical risk. The latter is, in turn, the extent of an individual's exposure to the possibility or chance of death or injury during a specified period of time. In much of what follows, physical risk will be described in terms of one or another kind of *probability*, in which case safety and physical risk become straightforward obverses of one another in that the former denotes the probability of surviving a forthcoming period (or avoiding a particular kind of injury during it) while the latter is the probability of dying during the period (or incurring the injury).

Turning to the question of how economics comes to feature centrally in a discussion of safety and physical risk, it is essential to appreciate that improved levels of safety can normally be achieved only at the cost of a curtailment in some of the other desirable ways in which a society might make use of its scarce resources. Crudely put, the more a society spends on safety, the less will be available for, say, education, housing and the arts, or, in the last analysis, the manufacture of television sets and the brewing of pints of beer. Given that – other things being equal – most people prefer lower rather than higher levels of exposure to the risk of death or injury, it follows that the individual or social choice of an optimal level of safety in any particular context has a significant *economic* dimension in that it is a decision concerning the appropriate tradeoff, or balance, between competing uses of scarce resources.

The following examples help to illustrate the form that this tradeoff might take.

This chapter previously appeared in M.W. Jones-Lee (1989), *The Economics of Safety and Physical Risk*, Oxford, Basil Blackwell.

1   Research in transport engineering suggests that installation of overhead lighting on all stretches of motorway in the UK could be expected to reduce personal injury accident rates by more than 10 per cent. The resource costs of installing such lighting, however, would be substantial – currently in the region of £20,000 per kilometre on a six-lane dual-carriageway – and would therefore entail a significant reduction in expenditure on some of the other investment projects that might be funded by the transport budget, such as the construction of new ringroads or motorways. To what extent would the installation of overhead lighting be justified?

2   Estimates of the adverse health effects of different doses of ionizing radiation have been derived from studies of various groups exposed to such radiation. Although experts are not in universal agreement about the precise nature of these effects, it appears that, even at very low doses, more exposure to radiation means more risk of contracting cancer or passing on genetic defects. At the same time, additional protective devices – designed to reduce or mitigate the effects of radiation – could be installed in nuclear power plants or in diagnostic radiotherapy units, *but at a cost*. Given that this additional cost would ultimately be reflected in, say, higher electricity prices or reduced health service facilities, is the introduction of these additional protective devices warranted?

3   Before the UK Committee on the Safety of Medicines will recommend that a new drug may be licensed for general use, it currently requires the drug to be tested on a relatively small sample of patients. While these tests can clearly be expected to detect the more prevalent adverse effects of a new drug, they are much less likely to detect effects that tend to occur only in a small proportion of cases. One way round this problem would be to conduct an extensive 'post-marketing surveillance' of any new drug during the period immediately following its introduction to general use. Such a surveillance, however, would involve considerable cost, a substantial proportion of which would undoubtedly fall upon the National Health Service. Would the increased likelihood of detecting any harmful effects of new drugs justify this additional cost?

4   In many developing countries road accidents have reached alarming proportions during recent years and have become a source of considerable concern to aid agencies, politicians and transportation planners. There is little doubt that this toll of death, injury and damage could be reduced, but again only at a significant cost to societies that are in some cases already seriously impoverished.

These are just a few of the ways in which countries at all stages of economic development face the economic problem of choosing between safety and other desirable ways of utilizing scarce resources. This chapter is about such choices. It does not purport to provide clear-cut and unequivocal answers to the many difficult questions involved, but is instead an attempt to lay bare and shed light upon the central issues. While the questions considered are in many cases uncomfortable and the way in which they are addressed may seem to some people to be callous and distasteful, it remains the author's firm conviction that they are questions of such importance that a humane society simply cannot afford to set them aside or to leave their resolution to chance.

1 POSSIBLE PROCEDURES FOR TAKING ACCOUNT OF SAFETY EFFECTS IN PUBLIC-SECTOR ALLOCATIVE DECISION MAKING

In decisions involving risk to human life it is tempting to suppose that one should always be guided by the old maxim, 'safety first'. Matters are not quite so straightforward, however. Certainly, if the risk of death or injury to the children in a primary school could be significantly reduced at the cost of installing one or two fire-resistant doors, then few of us would have much doubt that the cost would be worth incurring. But suppose, instead, that the safety improvement was very small (say a one in a million reduction in the annual risk of death), applied to only a few people (e.g., the half dozen victims of a very rare disease) and would be so costly that, if undertaken, it would preclude or delay the installation of equipment vital to the relief of suffering on the part of many hundreds of people. It is then not at all obvious that the safety improvement should be undertaken.

How might a humane decision maker in the public sector sensibly approach the problem of resource allocation and project appraisal when variations in safety are involved? On the assumption that he has access to reasonably reliable estimates of the safety effects of the various projects under consideration, one can identify six broad avenues of approach that the decision maker might reasonably adopt. In particular, he could:

1   Ignore the estimates on the grounds that safety effects are, for one reason or another, incommensurable with the other costs and benefits of public-sector projects.
2   Rely upon informal judgement in weighing safety effects against other costs and benefits.
3   Use safety standards or targets. This would involve the prespecification of 'acceptable' levels of risk in various contexts. Projects that failed to meet the safety standards would be rejected out of hand and those that met the standards would then be accepted or rejected on the basis of their other costs and benefits.
4   Use cost effectiveness analysis. Basically, cost-effectiveness analysis seeks to maximize the extent of achievement of a given goal or objective (such as safety improvement) within a predetermined budget or, equivalently, to minimize the cost of achieving a particular goal.
5   Define and estimate monetary values of safety improvement and costs of risk so that safety effects can be incorporated directly into standard procedures

of economic appraisal, such as cost–benefit analysis or social welfare maximization.

6   Employ a decision analysis approach. Essentially, this involves the identification of the decision maker's main objectives and priorities and the subsequent estimation of the structure and parameters of a so-called 'multi-attribute utility function' for the decision maker. The primary purpose of this approach is not so much to turn decision making into a formulaic mechanical procedure as to facilitate decisions concerning complex issues by providing the decision maker with an ordered structure and framework within which to assemble and analyse a wide diversity of information.

In subsequent sections, the first five approaches will be considered and evaluated in greater detail. For a discussion of the decision analysis approach, see Jones-Lee (1989) chapter 5.

2 THE 'NO ANALYSIS' APPROACH

While it cannot be denied that safety effects are inherently different in kind from many of the other benefits and costs of the typical public-sector project, it is also incontrovertibly the case – as noted in the introductory section – that safety competes with other desirable goals in the allocation of a society's scarce resources. Given this fact, it is a central contention of the argument developed here that safety effects *cannot* be ignored if anything remotely resembling an efficient and equitable allocation of resources is to be achieved. It is as true of safety effects as of any of the other potential consequences of public-sector projects that if they are ignored in the course of project appraisal then, to the extent that these effects are beneficial, they will tend to be *under*provided, and, if harmful, *over*provided. Thus, however awkward and uncomfortable it may be to take account of safety effects, it is essential that some attempt should be made to do so. This assertion would be qualified only if randomness in the allocation of resources was held to be desirable per se, or if the resource cost of analysing safety effects was itself prohibitive in relation to their potential impact.

3 INFORMAL JUDGEMENT

Primae facie, reliance upon the informal judgement of the project planner or relevant politician in decisions that affect individual safety has much to commend it. Clearly this approach avoids the pitfalls of simply ignoring safety effects while at the same time avoiding the difficult and contentious problems of devising more formal methods of evaluation. In general it has the appeal of civilized circumspection in the face of complex moral issues. This seems to be the kind of consideration John Broome (one of the most vigorous critics of the approach advocated later in this chapter) had in mind when he wrote:

They [decisions concerning safety] are normally made, like other hard decisions, by a political process. My alternative is to continue in that way and try to improve the process. When the questions are ones that have no unique right answer, as I believe these are, it is the process we must concentrate on, not its conclusion. Above all, we need to keep vividly in the decision-makers' imaginations just what they are deciding about: people's lives. If they come to think they have a neat and correct way to reduce lives to money and lump them in with other goods, then they will be hiding from themselves the real difficulty of their responsibilities. (Broome, 1983b, p. 13)

The most obvious objection to reliance upon informal judgement in the assessment of safety effects is that the process of reasoning that underpins the judgement is typically not open to scrutiny and critical evaluation, so that there is normally no way of detecting and reversing suspect judgements. Furthermore, reliance upon informal judgement will almost certainly lead to inconsistency in the treatment of safety effects both between different decision makers and on the part of a given decision maker in relation to different projects. This problem of inconsistency can best be illustrated by reference to the concept of an 'implicit value of safety', or, more graphically, an 'implicit value of life'. In order to introduce this concept suppose that a decision maker must choose one of two mutually exclusive projects, which for simplicity we take to have identical capital costs but which differ in their anticipated effects upon safety and other benefits. In particular, suppose that costs and benefits are as specified in table 9.1. A decision maker who chooses project A instead of project B reveals an 'implicit value of life' of less than £100,000 in that, by rejecting B in favour of A, he implicitly reveals that he does not regard the additional three lives saved under B as being 'worth' the loss of £300,000 in other benefits relative to A. Conversely, selection of project B would reveal an implicit value of life of *at least* £100,000.

By examining past decisions for and against projects with potential safety effects it is therefore possible to place upper and lower bounds on implicit values of life. Other things being equal, consistency of past decisions requires that these implicit values should have a broadly similar order of magnitude. However, evidence from both the UK and the USA indicates widely divergent implicit values of life from past decisions affecting safety. For example, in the UK implicit values range from less than £1,000 per life (from a decision not to legislate for the child-proofing of drug containers) to more than £20,000,000 per life (from high-rise apartment safety standards). One obvious implication of this sort of inconsistency is that a straightforward transference of resources from high-rise apartment safety to child-proofing of drug containers would, on balance, save lives at no additional resource cost overall. Empirical evidence therefore tends to confirm the a priori expectation that leaving the evaluation of safety effects to informal judgement is likely to lead to inconsistency and consequent inefficiency in the allocation of scarce resources.

While dealing with the concept of implicit values of life and safety, it is also worth remarking that *any* decision for or against a project with potential safety effects necessarily places an upper or lower bound on the relevant implicit value.

Table 9.1 *Costs and benefits of two mutually exclusive projects*

	Capital cost	Expected reduction in fatalities	Other benefits
Project A	£500,000	2	£550,000
Project B	£500,000	5	£250,000

Thus those who, for whatever reason, object to the idea of placing explicit values on life and safety must nonetheless face the fact that in this sort of decision making some sort of implied valuation is literally unavoidable.

4 SAFETY STANDARDS

Like reliance upon informal judgement, the use of safety standards seems at first sight to be a simple and straightforward way of taking account of effects on physical risk in public-sector decision making. Unfortunately, safety standards suffer from two very serious deficiencies. First, their use begs the vitally important question of the criteria by which the standards are to be set in the first place (just how safe is 'safe'?). Second, there is the related problem that rigid adherence to such standards allows no account to be taken of the *cost* of meeting them. Once again this is likely to lead to serious inconsistencies between implicit values of life and safety in different contexts and hence inefficiency in the allocation of scarce resources. To see how, consider the following simple example. Suppose that the government of a small country is reviewing its policy concerning safety on inter-urban public transport. The country's two major cities are linked by parallel train and bus services with annual passenger loadings of 10 million and 5 million passenger-km respectively. Currently, the annual fatality rate for the railway is 1 death per 10^6 passenger-km while that for the bus service is four deaths per 10^6 passenger-km. The annualized cost of reducing each of these accident rates to various levels has been estimated to be as in table 9.2.

In the event, the government decides to impose a uniform safety standard of 0.8 fatalities per 10^6 passenger-km on each of the two modes, bringing train fatalities down to 8 per annum and bus fatalities down to 4 per annum at an aggregate annualized cost of £1,000,000 (i.e., £40,000 for the railway plus £960,000 for the buses).

If we now consider the value of avoidance of one fatality implied by the situation on the railways, we discover that this must be less than £25,000 because the government is apparently unwilling to spend an additional £25,000 per annum to reduce the annual railway fatalities from eight to seven. By contrast, the implicit value of avoidance of one fatality on the buses lies between £180,000

Table 9.2 *The cost of reducing fatalities on two transport modes*

Railway route			Bus route		
Fatality rate per 10^6 pass.-km	No. of fatalities p.a.	Annualized cost (£000)	Fatality rate per 10^6 pass.-km	No. of fatalities p.a.	Annualized cost (£000)
1.0	10	—	4.0	20	—
0.9	9	15	3.0	15	80
0.8	8	40	2.0	10	250
0.7	7	65	1.4	7	420
0.6	6	100	1.2	6	600
0.5	5	200	1.0	5	780
0.4	4	400	0.8	4	960
0.3	3	700	0.6	3	1,150

(the additional annualized cost of reducing bus fatalities from five to four) and £190,000 (the additional cost of reducing bus fatalities from four to three).

Clearly, then, the imposition of a uniform safety standard involves a serious inconsistency of valuation. Suppose, however, that the government could be persuaded to abandon its uniform safety standard and simply transfer £360,000 of its annual safety budget from buses to trains, thereby effectively equating the implicit value of life on the two modes at approximately £200,000. Certainly, the accident rate on the buses would rise from 0.8 to 1.2 fatalities per 10^6 passenger-km but the train rate would fall from 0.8 to 0.4, implying a reduction in the overall transport fatalities from 12 to 10 per annum.

The government's insistence upon the use of a safety standard and the consequent inconsistency in the implicit value of life can therefore be viewed as effectively costing the country two lives per annum. One objection to this line of reasoning is that equalizing the implicit value of life would result in a situation that was *unfair* to bus passengers in that they would be exposed to a higher fatality rate than users of the railway. However, it is not at all clear that fairness in this context is synonymous with equalization of fatality rates. Given that people are, by and large, free to choose which of the two modes to travel on, it would seem more plausible to argue that fairness requires that, at the margin, the resources devoted to avoiding one fatality should be equalized on the two modes (i.e., that the implicit value of life should be the same for each mode). All things considered, the use of safety standards would therefore seem likely to lead to an allocation of scarce resources that is not only inefficient (in the sense that it does not minimize the number of fatalities for a given overall expenditure on safety) but is also inequitable.

Finally, it seems natural in a section dealing with safety standards to consider the closely related concept of an 'acceptable' level of risk. While some writers use the term in a careful and qualified (though I believe potentially misleading) way, others have implied that there will exist levels of risk (or, more accurately, *increments* in risk) that are sufficiently small as not to warrant concern and hence are 'acceptable'. In this sense, acceptability is absolute: increments in risk below a certain level are acceptable; those above are not. But of course if risk is undesirable per se, then no rational individual would willingly accept an increment in risk, however, small, unless there were some corresponding benefit. The central question is then how large the offsetting benefit needs to be to compensate for a given increment in risk, so that the whole issue of acceptability of risk becomes equivalent to the kind of approach discussed in section 6.

5 COST-EFFECTIVENESS ANALYSIS

Basically, cost-effectiveness analysis seeks to maximize the extent of achievement of a given beneficial goal within a predetermined budget or, equivalently, to minimize the expenditure required to achieve a prespecified goal. In particular, and in marked contrast with cost–*benefit* analysis, no attempt is made to place a *monetary value* upon the beneficial goal. Clearly, then, this kind of analysis would be appropriate if (a) a decision maker's overall safety budget was predetermined and (b) the sole effect of the various projects under consideration was to improve levels of safety. What cost-effectiveness will *not* do is to give any indication of the appropriate size of the safety budget; nor will it resolve the problem of project selection whenever different projects provide more than one kind of beneficial effect with the mix of benefits differing between projects. In such circumstances one requires some common unit in which to aggregate the various benefits and this is precisely what cost-effectiveness analysis cannot do. As an example of the way in which the latter difficulty might manifest itself, consider a situation in which a budget of £1,000,000 must be expended on one of two mutually exclusive projects, each of which precisely exhausts the budget but which would have the mixes of safety effects and other benefits shown in table 9.3

Given that the budget is predetermined, it might seem that the appropriate way to proceed is by comparing the *net cost* (capital cost minus other benefits) per serious injury avoided for each of the two projects. For project A this would be £1 while for project B it would be £2. Project A would therefore seem to be the more cost-effective. Does this mean that project A should be adopted? Anyone who is tempted to answer in the affirmative should simply note that rejection of project B in favour of A would be tantamount to treating the additional nine serious injuries avoided under B as being not worth the loss of £19 of other benefits – a conclusion that most people would surely find unacceptable.

In fact, it appears that what is required in a decision such as this is some means of aggregating safety effects with other benefits in order to arrive at an overall

Table 9.3 *Costs and benefits of two mutually exclusive projects*

	Capital cost (£)	Expected number of serious injuries avoided	Present value of other benefits (£)
Project A	1,000,000	1	999,999
Project B	1,000,000	10	999,980

benefit figure for each project so that a direct comparison can be undertaken. One very obvious and direct way of doing this would be to confront squarely and explicitly the question of how to define and estimate monetary values of safety improvement and costs of increased risk. While it is not surprising that this is the kind of approach that has tended to appeal to economists, it is almost inevitable that in matters as sensitive as life, death and injury there should be no immediately obvious and universally acceptable way of defining and measuring monetary costs and values, so that in consequence a variety of different methods have been proposed. These various approaches to the costing of risk and valuation of safety are described in section 6. Broadly speaking, the different approaches break down into those that are pursuant of a national output maximisation objective and those that seek to maximise social welfare.

6 THE EXPLICIT COSTING OF RISK AND VALUATION OF SAFETY

6.1 Output-based definitions

The output-based concept that has been most commonly employed in the safety field is the so-called 'gross output' or 'human capital' definition in which the major component of the cost of a fatality is treated as the discounted present value of the victim's future output (or income) extinguished as a result of his or her premature demise. Allowances are typically made for non-marketed output (such as housewives' services) and for various 'direct' economic costs such as damage, medical costs and so on. The value of preventing a fatality is correspondingly treated as the cost avoided. To give an idea of the sort of orders of magnitude that emerge under this definition, for developed economies such costs and values are typically in the region of £100,000–£200,000 in 1987 prices. The obvious objection to this way of defining cost and value in the present context is precisely that it focuses exclusively upon output effects and takes no account of the fact that most people value safety principally for its own sake rather than for its capacity to preserve current and future levels of national output. In short, people value safety mainly because of their aversion to death and injury per se rather than because of their concern to preserve productive resources and maintain future levels of gross national product. In an attempt to meet this criticism some advocates of the gross output approach have recommended the addition of a more or less arbitrary allowance for the 'pain, grief and suffering' of victims and their dependents, relatives and friends. However, the fact that the allowance is effectively arbitrary largely vitiates this attempt to rescue the gross output approach.

A now largely discredited variant of the output-based approach is that in which the discounted present value of the victim's future consumption is subtracted from discounted future output to arrive at a so-called 'net output' figure. The net output approach thus provides a measure of the narrow, purely economic impact of the death or injury of an individual on the rest of society. The objection to the net output approach is, fairly obviously, that it will treat the death of anyone past retirement age as a negative cost (i.e., as a benefit) to the rest of society – a conclusion that is understandably repugnant to the majority of people.

6.2 Social welfare definitions

Turning to costing and valuation procedures based upon the social welfare maximization objective, two separate but related strands of thought can be identified. Basically, the question is whether one approaches the definition of values of safety and costs of risk from the essentially pragmatic perspective of conventional social cost–benefit analysis or within the somewhat more elegant but arcane context of maximization of a so-called 'social welfare function'. As it happens, the prescriptions of cost–benefit analysis are precisely those that would emerge from maximization of a social welfare function in a particular special case, so that it is no surprise that the two approaches lead to broadly similar conclusions concerning the definition of values of safety and costs of risk.

The underlying prescriptive premise of conventional social cost–benefit analysis is that public-sector allocative decisions should reflect, as far as possible, the preferences and wishes of those who will be affected by the decisions. This immediately raises the question of how such preferences and wishes are to be 'measured', for want of a better term. One possibility would be to proceed on the traditional democratic principle of 'one person, one vote'. However, quite apart from the fact that this would be an administratively extremely cumbersome and costly way to settle particular allocative or investment decisions in the public sector, according each person one vote in the allocative decision-making process would fail to take account of differences in people's *strength* of preference for one as opposed to another use of society's scarce resources. Plainly, what is needed is a variant of the 'one person, one vote' principle which will reflect the strength of individual preferences, bearing in mind the constraints imposed by the overall scarcity of resources. To this end, social cost–benefit analysis effectively replaces the question 'would you vote in favour of undertaking investment scheme X rather than scheme Y?' by the question 'How much would you personally be willing to pay to have scheme X undertaken rather than scheme Y?'. The answer to this question, if truthfully given, will clearly be an indication of the individual's strength of preference for scheme X relative to scheme Y, conditioned by considerations of resource scarcity via his or her income constraint.

The most obvious objection to this procedure is that it replaces the principle of 'one person, one vote' with that of 'one pound, one vote' and, as such, inevitably gives the rich more votes in the allocative decision-making process than the poor. There are, broadly speaking, three ways in which advocates of cost–benefit analysis have responded to this criticism.

1   If one takes the view that income and wealth are optimally distributed, then it is quite appropriate that those with a greater command over resources should have a potentially more significant impact on the way they are allocated.

2   If, by contrast, one takes the view that income and wealth are *not* optimally distributed, then the appropriate way to effect a redistribution is not by tampering with the results of cost–benefit analysis (by, for example, deflating the willingness to pay of the rich and inflating that of the poor), but, rather, by direct redistributional measures using taxes and transfers.

3   Because redistributional taxes and transfers are politically infeasible, individual willingness to pay should indeed be deflated or inflated using appropriate 'distributional weights' which, for those of more egalitarian persuasion, will clearly tend to be inversely related to income or wealth.

Whichever of these stances is adopted, the important point to appreciate is that the fundamental input to cost–benefit analysis is, in all cases, *individual willingness to pay*. A conventional analysis will simply aggregate this over all affected individuals and treat the result as the total 'benefit' of a project, whereas an analysis with explicit distributional weights will clearly employ a weighted aggregate.

What does all this entail for the valuation of safety and costing of risk? Quite simply, it means that if values of safety and costs of risk are to be used in cost–benefit analysis – whether of the conventional or 'distributionally weighted' variety – then what is required in the first instance is information concerning individual willingness to pay for safety improvement, or requirement of compensation for increased risk. Often, though not always, the variations in safety – whether beneficial or harmful – will be quite small. Suppose for the time being that these variations in risk can be described in terms of changes in probability. To focus matters, consider changes in the probability of death during a forthcoming period and in addition suppose that death is a 'homogeneous' event (i.e., at this stage we will not distinguish between various ways of dying). Denoting changes in the probability of death during a forthcoming period for each of n individuals owing to a particular investment project by δp_i $(i = 1, \ldots, n)$ and their marginal rates of substitution of wealth for probability of death by m_i ($i = 1, \ldots, n$), the aggregate willingness to pay (or required compensation) V will for δp_i small be well approximated by

$$V = - \sum_i m_i \delta p_i \tag{1.1}$$

Now consider the case in which, for all i

$$\delta p_i = - \frac{1}{n} \tag{1.2}$$

so that in particular $\Sigma_i \delta p_i = -1$.

In this case all individuals are afforded an equal improvement in safety which reduces the expected number of lives lost during the forthcoming period by precisely one. Such a safety improvement is said to involve the avoidance of one 'statistical death' or the saving of one 'statistical life'. Substituting from equation (1.2) into (1.1) it then follows that for the purposes of a conventional cost–benefit analysis the value of saving one statistical life (or, more succinctly, the 'value of statistical life') is given by

$$V = \frac{1}{n} \sum_i m_i \tag{1.3}$$

i.e., by the arithmetic mean of m_i taken over the affected population.

It might be objected that this argument depends crucially on the condition embodied in (1.2). However, it turns out that it is a straightforward matter to generalize the analysis to accommodate *unequal* variations in individual risk. For example, it follows from the definition of covariance that

$$\text{cov}(m_i, \delta p_i) = \frac{1}{n} \sum_i m_i \delta p_i - \frac{1}{n^2} \sum_i m_i \sum_i \delta p_i \tag{1.4}$$

Hence, if we again consider the saving of one statistical life, so that $\Sigma_i \delta p_i = -1$, though the δp_i are not necessarily equal, then from (1.1) and (1.4)

$$V = \frac{1}{n} \sum_i m_i - n \, \text{cov}(m_i, \delta p_i) \tag{1.5}$$

Thus, V again depends upon the arithmetic mean of m_i but now also contains a term reflecting the way in which δp_i varies with m_i across the affected population. In fact, it seems likely that for most safety improvements δp_i and m_i will be uncorrelated so that the expression for V simplifies to precisely that given in (1.3).

Having examined the implications of the precepts of conventional social cost–benefit analysis for the definition of values of safety and costs of risk, let us now turn to the closely related but somewhat more general perspective of maximization of a utilitarian social welfare function. A great deal has been written about social welfare functions, but the basic idea is to make 'social' choices (i.e., choices affecting more than one person in society) in such a way as to maximize an index of social welfare, W, where the latter depends only upon the well-being of the individuals that make up society. As such, social welfare maximization is clearly based upon the utilitarian tradition of 'consequential-ism', whereby alternative courses of action are judged exclusively by their consequences (rather than by, say, the way that they measure up to other ethical precepts such as the desirability of protecting rights, telling the truth and so on). A further sense in which social welfare maximization is characteristically utilitarian is that consequences are assessed solely in terms of individual well-being or 'welfare' (this has been referred to as 'welfarism' (Sen and Williams, 1982, pp. 3–4)). As well as its inherent consequentialist and welfarist character, social welfare maximization is usually taken to embody three further features. First, it is normally (though not invariably) held that individuals are the best judges of their own well-being so that the individual welfare indices ω_i are identified with one or another real-valued utility representation u_i of individual preferences. In addition, writing $W = f(u_1, u_2, \ldots, u_n)$, it is normally taken that $\partial f / \partial u_i > 0$ $(i = 1, \ldots, n)$. This is often referred to as the 'Paretian' value judgement and is tantamount to the prescription that if one person prefers arrangement A to arrangement B and no one prefers B to A then A is to be recommended. Finally, it is often, though again not always, assumed that it is appropriate to treat f as linear in individual utilities with, in particular

$$W = \sum_i a_i u_i \qquad a_i > 0 \ (i = 1, \ldots, n) \tag{1.6}$$

In fact, Harsanyi (1955) has shown that provided individual and social choices under certainty and uncertainty obey a limited number of apparently quite appealing conditions and if (somewhat less plausibly) individual and social probability judgements coincide, then the social welfare function *necessarily* takes the form shown in (1.6) with the u_i being individual cardinal von Neumann–Morgenstern utilities (von Neumann and Morgenstern, 1947).

Furthermore, given Harsanyi's postulates, social choices under uncertainty will be taken so as to maximize the mathematical expectation of W, which, given (1.6), is equivalent to maximizing $\sum_i a_i Eu_i$ where Eu_i denotes the mathematical expectation of utility for the ith individual.

What, then, would maximization of a social welfare function of the type specified in (1.6) imply for the definition of values of safety and costs of risk? Consider a highly simplified situation in which individual expected utility can be written as

$$Eu_i = (1 - p_i)u_i(w_i) \tag{1.7}$$

where p_i is the probability of death during the forthcoming period for the ith individual and w_i is his wealth. Suppose in addition that p_i depends upon public expenditure on safety, s, and that this expenditure is financed by individual lump-sum taxes t_i. Choice of an optimal level of s and taxes t_i $(i = 1, \ldots, n)$ can then be written as the following constrained social welfare maximization problem

$$\max_{s, ti} \sum_i a_i(1 - p_i)u_i(w_i - t_i) \text{ subject to } s = \sum_i t_i$$

A little algebraic manipulation of the first-order conditions for a constrained maximum yields the following result

$$c = \frac{1}{n} \sum_i m_i - nc \, \text{cov}\left(m_i, \frac{\partial p_i}{\partial s}\right) \tag{1.8}$$

where

$$c = -\left(\sum_i \frac{\partial p_i}{\partial s}\right)^{-1}$$

and can therefore be interpreted as the marginal social cost of saving one statistical life and

$$m_i = \frac{u_i}{(1 - p_i)du_i/dw_i}$$

is, as above, the ith individual's marginal rate of substitution of wealth for probability of death in the context of the simplified expected utility model given in (1.7). Thus, to the extent that a social optimum requires that the marginal social cost of saving one statistical life should be equated with the marginal value of doing so, the result given in (1.8) indicates that the value of statistical life, at the margin, is given by

$$V = \frac{1}{n} \sum_i m_i - nc \, \text{cov}\left(m_i, \frac{\partial p_i}{\partial s}\right) \tag{1.9}$$

Clearly then, in this case constrained social welfare maximization leads to an expression for the value of statistical life that is very similar to that given by the cost–benefit analysis approach and is indeed identical to it if m_i and $\partial p_i/\partial s$ are uncorrelated across individuals.

6.3 Other approaches to the explicit costing of risk and valuation of safety

In addition to the explicit costing and valuation procedures so far considered, at least four other methods have been proposed for defining and estimating costs of risk and values of safety. While each of the proposed methods has a superficial appeal, it transpires on closer examination that all are seriously deficient whether viewed from the narrow perspective of national output maximization or in the wider context of maximization of social welfare. The four methods are as follows:

1   The 'life insurance' method, in which the cost of death or injury (and the value of their avoidance) is directly related to the sums for which people typically insure their lives or limbs.
2   The 'court award' method, in which the sums awarded by the courts in damages for death or injury are treated either as indicative of an individual's loss of future output or as some more nebulous reflection of the cost that society associates with death or injury.
3   The 'implicit public-sector valuation' method, in which the values of life and safety implicitly reflected in *past* public-sector decisions (as discussed in section 3) are treated as indicative of the appropriate level at which to set explicit costs and values for *future* decisions.
4   The 'valuation of life in terms of value of time' method, in which the value of remaining life expectancy for an individual is defined as the aggregate value of time for the individual over his or her remaining life expectancy.

As a means of approximating a 'gross output' value of safety or cost of risk (appropriate to the national output maximization objective) the life insurance method would be satisfactory only if people tended to hold life insurance in an amount that fully covered their human capital or held injury insurance in an amount that would reflect the output loss due to injury. This seems highly improbable to say the least. In fact, it seems altogether more likely that those who hold life insurance will do so in such a way as to cover the expected financial requirements of their dependants so that if such cover is an approximation to anything it is 'net' rather than 'gross' output. Having said this, it must be admitted that in the case of injury insurance it is conceivable that the typical cover might give a rough indication of anticipated gross output losses. However, by no stretch of the imagination could any kind of insurance cover be held to reflect an individual's willingness to pay for his own safety or that of those he cares for (which, it will be recalled, is the appropriate basis for defining costs and values relevant to the social welfare maximization objective). Individuals who place very high values on their own safety might quite rationally hold no life insurance whatsoever (e.g., the bachelor with no relatives or dependants). Equally, people who place little or no value on their own continued survival, per se, may hold quite large amounts of life insurance (e.g., the potential suicide who is nonetheless concerned to ensure the continued financial well-being of his family and dependants). All in all then, the sums for which people typically insure their lives or limbs would seem to give little if any guide to the appropriate level at which to set the gross output or willingness-to-pay based costs of risk or values of safety. Nor, for that matter, do they appear to be relevant to any other conceivably sensible way of defining such costs and values.

Turning to court awards, the position is somewhat more complicated. Essentially, the potential relevance of court awards for the estimation of either output- or social welfare-based costs of risk and values of safety depends upon the underlying legal principles that can be held to determine whether or not a particular plaintiff is entitled to damages in any given case and, if so, in what amount. As Atiyah points out:

most lawyers see the primary function of awards of damages for injury and fatal accidents, as compensatory alone. Indeed, in the UK it has for many years been emphatically stated by judges that the functions of the civil law are not penal or deterrent. English judges do not seem to regard damage awards as incentives to greater safety, perhaps partly because the great majority of damage awards are paid for by insurance companies, and English lawyers are sceptical of the extent to which the incentive effect of the law still operates when this is the case. In other countries it may be that the courts do not adopt quite the same extreme posture that English judges do. Even in other Commonwealth countries (which usually follow English legal traditions) it would, I think, be found that there is a greater willingness to believe that damage awards have a minor or subsidiary role as deterrents, and this is certainly true also of the US. But even in these countries no lawyers would doubt that the primary purpose of damage awards is compensatory. (Atiyah, 1982, p. 188)

Given this state of affairs, the central question therefore concerns the way in which the courts in different countries construe the term 'compensation'. In fact, interpretations appear to vary quite widely. In the case of fatal injuries, for example, in the UK the dependants of the deceased can expect to recover damages for wrongful death only in an amount reflecting their share of the imcome that the deceased would have earned had he or she survived, and not for any 'subjective' losses such as grief and suffering. In the USA, by contrast, compensating awards for subjective losses to surviving dependants can be very large indeed. For non-fatal injuries, however, the English courts *will* make awards for subjective losses but only to the injured party and again in an amount typically substantially less than in comparable cases in the USA.

As in the case of life insurance, it would therefore seem that, in the UK at least, court awards for wrongful death might give some indication of the appropriate level of 'net output' based costs and values but are essentially irrelevant to the gross output or willingness-to-pay definitions. For non-fatal injuries in the UK, and in all cases in the USA, the presence of apparently more or less arbitrary awards for 'subjective' losses, varying substantially in magnitude between the two countries, renders the relevance of such awards to any definition of cost or value essentially undecidable. Only if one argues (as indeed some have), that such awards are a true reflection of the cost that 'society' associates with death or injury would there seem to be any justification for treating the awards as indicative of the approriate level at which to set costs of risk or values of safety. Such an argument seems somewhat tenuous, to say the least.

The objection to the 'implicit public-sector valuation approach' is fairly obvious. Quite apart from the huge variation in implicit public-sector values already noted, it is clearly no answer to the question 'How ought public sector bodies to define and measure costs of risk and values of safety in future allocative decisions?' to advocate that one should simply employ the costs and values implicit in past decisions. In fact, such a procedure would be legitimate only if one were convinced that past decisions had been based on appropriately defined costs and values, and few of us would, one suspects, carry such a conviction, especially in view of the wide disparities evident in implicit public-sector values.

The valuation of life in terms of value of time method can similarly be disposed of fairly briefly. Values of leisure time, for example, are essentially *relative* valuations – willingness to pay to do as one pleases with a marginal hour of time rather than spend it travelling on a bus or a train or whatever. Multiplying such a value by remaining hours of life expectancy therefore gives no indication whatsoever of either an individual's gross output or his marginal rate of substitution of wealth for physical risk. Indeed, to the extent that a value of leisure time is a marginal value, it is rather hard to imagine what interpretation to give to its product with remaining life expectancy – it could hardly be construed as an individual's willingness to pay to do as he pleases for the rest of his life rather than spend it travelling! Turning to values of working time, these are usually based upon gross of tax wage rates and can therefore be viewed as indicative of an individual's marginal productivity. Multiplying such a value by the remaining expectation of *working* hours would therefore give an approximation to an individual's gross output. However, multiplying by remaining life expectancy would clearly substantially overestimate gross output and would certainly give no indication whatsoever of an individual's willingness to pay for safety.

7 EMPIRICAL ESTIMATES

Basically, two types of approach have been employed in the empirical estimation of individual marginal rates of substitution of wealth for physical risk – and hence willingness-to-pay based values of statistical life. These have been described as the 'revealed-preference' (or 'implicit value') and 'questionnaire' (or 'contingent valuation') approaches. Essentially, the revealed-preference approach involves the identification of situations in which people actually do explicitly or implicitly trade off wealth or income against the risk of death or injury. The most obvious source of such data is the labour market where, *ceteris paribus*, riskier jobs can be expected to carry clearly identifiable wage premia as compensation for risk. In fact, the majority of revealed-preference studies conducted to date have been of this type and are commonly referred to as 'compensating wage differential' or 'hedonic price' studies. Other kinds of revealed-preference study have been based upon data concerning the time–inconvenience–safety tradeoffs involved in car seat-belt use, the fuel–time–safety tradeoff involved in motorway speed decisions, house price–air pollution tradeoffs, the purchase price and maintenance costs of domestic smoke detectors and the frequency of car tyre replacement.

In marked contrast with the revealed-preference studies, those based on the questionnaire approach involve asking a sample of individuals more or less directly about their willingness to pay – or required compensation – for various hypothetical changes in risk.

Clearly, the revealed-preference approach has the advantage of being based upon real rather than hypothetical choices. However, the compensating wage differential approach, in particular, has the major disadvantage that wage rates depend on many other factors besides risk, so that it is necessary to control for these factors in order to isolate the pure wealth–risk tradeoff. This is typically done by regressing wage rates on various explanatory variables, including measures of risk. Clearly, the reliability of any estimate derived in this way depends (a) upon the quality of the regression analysis and the avoidance of, in particular, specification errors and omitted variables bias and (b) the nature and quality of workers' *perceptions* of job risks. (Thus, for example, if the value of statistical life is defined in terms of individual marginal rates of substitution of wealth for subjective probability of death, then it would clearly be inappropriate to base an empirical estimate of this value on wage premia for 'objectively' measured job risk if the latter diverged significantly from workers' perceptions of this risk.)

Another fairly obvious limitation of the revealed-preference approach is that it produces highly aggregated results – market equilibrium wage premia for risk – and is inherently incapable of generating estimates at the individual level.

While the questionnaire approach clearly suffers from the hypothetical nature of the tradeoffs that it presents to subjects, it does avoid some of the major difficulties encountered in the revealed-preference studies. Thus, with appropriate design of the questionnaire, one can in principle go directly to the wealth–risk tradeoff without the necessity to control for other variables as in the wage differential studies. Furthermore, the questionnaire approach facilitates direct investigation of the relationship between subjective and objective probabilities. Finally, and perhaps most significantly, the questionnaire approach yields estimates of *individual* valuation of safety, thereby allowing the researcher to make inferences about the way in which the latter varies with income, age, social class and so on. It is also a straightforward matter to compute values of statistical life with various distributional weighting schemes, an exercise that would, incidentally, be extremely difficult – if not impossible – under the revealed-preference approach.

On balance, then, it seems that there are pros and cons associated with both the revealed-preference and questionnaire approaches. In the author's opinion, neither approach is inherently superior and, indeed, they are almost certainly best viewed as essentially complementary rather than competing estimation procedures.

It has to be admitted that, as in so many other areas of economic analysis, the addition of empirical flesh to theoretical bones is far from straightforward and empirical work in this field has certainly produced estimates that lack the precision and reliability one would ideally wish for. However, this difficulty is almost certainly endemic to the study of human behaviour and one should not be surprised to encounter it in fairly acute form in a context as complex, contentious and emotive as this.

In fact, reactions to the plethora of empirical estimates appear to fall into one of two categories. Sceptics take the view that the variation in these estimates raises such serious doubts about their individual and collective reliability as to render them virtually worthless as a source of information about the 'true' magnitude of marginal rates of substitution and hence values of statistical life.

Alternatively, one can set about the difficult (and, admittedly, somewhat speculative) task of trying to identify the reasons for the large differences in the empirical estimates – and of evaluating their relative reliability – so as to be able to make an informed judgement about the appropriate order of magnitude of values of statistical life for use in public-sector decision making. It is the author's firm conviction that this more positive approach to the evidence is markedly preferable on philosophical, scientific and practical grounds. This conviction is reinforced by the fact that those government agencies (both in the UK and elsewhere) that have explicitly or implicitly rejected the willingness-to-pay estimates have thereby been driven to a position in which decisions concerning the allocation of resource to safety improvement are either based on procedures that are demonstrably flawed or employ the 'gross output' definition of the cost of risk and the value of safety, which is by now almost universally regarded as being seriously deficient.

Before proceeding to compare and evaluate the different empirical estimates of willingness-to-pay based values of statistical life, it is clearly desirable that they should all be converted to a common currency and year. Accordingly, table 9.4 summarizes the results of the various revealed-preference studies, with all values converted to pounds sterling, in March 1987 prices, and rounded to the nearest £10,000, while table 9.5 summarizes the questionnaire results. The reader should be warned that, while many individual studies produced a variety of estimates, with one or two exceptions these have been distilled into a single 'representative' figure for each study, either by taking the particular author's preferred estimate or by a straightforward process of averaging. The only case in which this was not done was for Frankel (1979) in which the estimates differed by more than an order of magnitude.

The first thing to notice about the figures summarized in tables 9.4 and 9.5 is that, in spite of the fact that the estimates have been converted to a common currency and year, there remain considerable differences between them. In fact, the various estimates can usefully be thought of as falling within one of four broad intervals, namely less than £250,000, between £250,000 and £500,000, between £500,000 and £1,000,000, and more than £1,000,000. The numbers and percentages of the estimates in each of these intervals are given in table 9.6.

Taken at face value, therefore, the empirical evidence summarized in tables

Table 9.4 *Revealed-preference estimates of the value of statistical life (£-sterling, 1987)[a]*

Author(s)	Nature of study	Estimated value of statistical life
Thaler and Rosen (1973)	Compensating wage differentials (USA)	420,000
Smith, R.S. (1973)	Compensating wage differentials (USA)	7,950,000
Melinek (1974)	Compensating wage differentials (USA)	990,000
Melinek (1974)	Time–inconvenience–safety tradeoff in use of pedestrian subways (UK)	400,000
Ghosh *et al.* (1975)	Motorway time–fuel–safety tradeoff (UK)	400,000
Smith, R.S. (1976)	Compensating wage differentials (USA)	2,470,000
Jones-Lee (1977)	Wealth–safety tradeoff involved in frequency of tyre replacement (UK)	1,883,000
Viscusi (1978a)	Compensating wage differentials (USA)	2,590,000
Veljanovski (1978)	Compensating wage differentials (UK)	4,550,000
Dillingham (1979)	Compensating wage differentials (USA)[b]	400,000
Blomquist (1979)	Time–inconvenience–safety tradeoff in use of car seat-belts (USA)	400,000
Brown (1980)	Compensating wage differentials (USA)[c]	1,270,000
Dardis (1980)	Purchase of domestic smoke detectors (USA)	280,000
Needleman (1980)	Compensating wage differentials (UK)	130,000
Olson (1981)	Compensating wage differentials (USA)[d]	5,260,000
Portney (1981)	House price–air pollution tradeoff (USA)	150,000
Marin and Psacharopoulos (1982)	Compensating wage differentials (UK)	1,910,000
Smith, V.K. (1983)	Compensating wage differentials (USA)	600,000
Arnould and Nichols (1983)	Compensating wage differentials (USA)	410,000
Ippolito and Ippolito (1984)	Cigarette smokers' responses to health-hazard information (USA)	390,000
Weiss *et al.* (1986)	Compensating wage differentials (Austria)	3,250,000
	Mean	1,720,000
	Median	600,000

Notes:

[a] With the exception of Jones-Lee (1977), Dardis (1980) and Portney (1981), all estimates are for 'self-only' risks and do not include an allowance for willingness to pay for others', as well as own, safety. Portney's estimate is based on the aggregate risk of death from pollution-induced disease to all members of a household together with the assumption that all household members' safety is valued equally. This can therefore be viewed as an average value of own and relatives' lives. To the extent that the risks in the Jones-Lee and Dardis studies applied to all the occupants of a motor car or household, then the estimates from these studies will presumably reflect an additional willingness to pay for other people's safety. These studies will therefore, if anything, tend to overestimate the value of statistical life of 'self-only' risks.

[b] Estimate given is for the blue-collar sample only.

[c] Estimate given is for regression *excluding* individual-specific intercepts.

[d] Estimate given is for regression *excluding* risk interaction variables.

Table 9.5 *Questionnaire estimates of the value of statistical life (£-sterling, 1987)*

Author(s)	Nature of study	Estimated value of statistical life
Acton (1973)	Small non-random sample survey (n = 93) of willingness to pay for heart attack ambulance (USA)	50,000
Melinek *et al.* (1973)	Non-random sample survey (n = 873) of willingness to pay for domestic fire safety (UK)	250,000
Melinek *et al.* (1973)	Non-random sample survey (n = 873) of willingness to pay for hypothetical 'safe' cigarettes (UK)	80,000
Jones-Lee (1976)	Small, non-random sample survey (n = 31) of willingness to pay for airline safety (UK)	8,250,000
Maclean (1979)	Quota sample survey (n = 325) of willingness to pay for domestic fire safety (UK)	2,480,000
Frankel (1979)	Small, non-random sample survey (n = 169) of willingness to pay for elimination of small airline risk (USA)	11,700,000
Frankel (1979)	Small, non-random sample survey (n = 169) of willingness to pay for elimination of large airline risk (USA)	50,000
Jones-Lee *et al.* (1985)	Large, random sample survey (n = 1,150) of willingness to pay for transport safety (UK)	1,860,000
	Mean	3,090,000
	Median	1,060,000

9.4–9.6 seems to suggest that, if a 'true' value of statistical life exists, then it is very unlikely to be much less than £500,000 in 1987 prices and may, indeed, be well in excess of £1,000,000. However, these conclusions should be qualified by two considerations. In the first place, as was remarked earlier, individual marginal rates of substitution – and hence values of statistical life – will almost certainly differ from one cause of death to another, so that it may not be appropriate to attempt to extract a single figure from a set of estimates obtained from studies related to different causes. Second, it is clear that some of the estimates in tables 9.4 and 9.5 deserve to be regarded as being inherently more reliable than others. To take the author's own work, for example, it is plainly the case that by virtually all the relevant criteria (e.g., sample size, quality of survey design, intelligibility of questions, existence of built-in consistency checks and so on) the Jones-Lee *et al.* (1985) study is markedly superior to its 1976 predecessor.

Table 9.6 *Numbers and percentages of all estimates of the value of statistical life in various intervals*

	Number	Percentage
Less than £250,000	5	17.3
Between £250,000 and £500,000	9	31.0
Between £500,000 and £1,000,000	2	6.9
More than £1,000,000	13	44.8

Given this, it is clearly important to apply some sort of weighting scheme to reflect differences in quality and reliability before attempting to derive any kind of point estimate from the various results.

As far as variation in the value of statistical life with different causes of death is concerned, one would certainly expect the extent of aversion to risks from, say, nuclear power – and hence the values of statistical life for such risks – to be significantly greater than for more familiar and better understood risks, such as those encountered in transport or in the non-nuclear workplace. However, if one sets aside the more controversial, emotive and poorly understood sources of risk, there seem to be good grounds for expecting that values of statistical life would show at least a broad correspondence across different causes of death. If this conjecture is correct, then it seems to be quite legitimate, at least as a first approximation, to seek a single, summary value of statistical life for all commonplace 'everyday' risks of quick and (one assumes) painless death. Almost without exception, the risks to which the estimates in tables 9.4 and 9.5 relate appear to fall within this category.

Assessment of the relative reliability of the different estimates is clearly a highly judgemental matter, but there do seem to be some rather obvious sources of bias that can be attributed to particular studies or types of study. For example, in their excellent review, Violette and Chestnut (1983) suggest that the compensating wage differential studies, as a group, probably suffer from four major potential sources of bias, namely (a) the quality of workers' perceptions of job-related risks, (b) workers' attitudes and aversion to job-related risks, (c) the extent to which wage–risk premia reflect risks of non-fatal as well as fatal injury and (d) the omitted-variables problem. Of these, Violette and Chestnut argue that the first two factors will tend to bias estimated values of statistical life in a downward direction, while the third and fourth will have the opposite effect. In particular, workers who underestimate risk will tend to gravitate to more dangerous jobs and vice versa, so that actual wage differentials will be smaller than they would be if perceptions were 'correct'. Furthermore, if workers in the occupations that formed the basis for these studies were atypically sanguine about physical risk compared with the overall population, then again one would expect values of safety based on their required wage premia to be biased downwards. While Violette and Chestnut's comments relate exclusively to the US studies, this point would seem to apply with particular force to Needleman's (1980) UK study which, it will be recalled, focused upon construction workers. By contrast, if wage premia reflect compensation for risks of non-fatal as well as fatal accidents, then the bias in treating premia as exclusively for the latter is clearly in the upward direction. Finally, to the extent that wage premia are, in fact, paid in compensation for factors that are additional to job risk but are both positively correlated with risk *and* omitted from the specification of wage equations, then again the consequent bias in estimated values of statistical life will be un-ambiguously upward.

Another limitation of the US compensating wage differential studies identified by Violette and Chestnut concerns the quality of the risk data sets employed in these studies. In general, these either broke down risks insufficiently finely (as in the case of the Bureau of Labour Statistics data) or focused on more hazardous occupations and failed adequately to distinguish between job-related and other risks (as with the Society of Actuaries data set). In this sense, the Marin and Psacharopoulos (1982) study, based on a fairly fine occupational classification covering a wide range of occupations and using the job-specific ACCRISK concept, must be judged markedly superior. It is also worth remarking that when Marin and Psacharopoulos employed the conceptually inferior GENRISK measure (which, like the Society of Actuaries data, conflated work-related and other risks), the estimated value of statistical life fell substantially, paralleling the tendency for those US studies based on BLS data (which focused exclusively on work-related risks) to produce much larger estimates than studies that used the Society of Actuaries data.

As far as the other revealed-preference studies are concerned, with the exception of Dardis (1980), these all involved relatively complex or indirect tradeoffs and the extraction of estimated values of statistical life required a number of rather restrictive, not to say precarious, assumptions. These estimates should therefore probably be treated with some caution.

Of all the empirical studies, however, undoubtedly the most controversial are those based upon the questionnaire approach. In the first place, most of these studies employed relatively small, non-random samples. Second, questions posed were of very variable quality. Third, there was little, if any, attempt to probe respondents in order to shed light upon the underlying rationale for responses. Finally, by their very nature, such studies produce estimates that are questionable, if only because they are derived from responses to hypothetical questions rather than from observations of real choices.

In the author's view, the studies that are least vulnerable to these criticisms are those of Acton (1973), Maclean (1979) and Jones-Lee et al. (1985). Though modesty inhibits expression of the judgement, the last of these would seem to deserve the most serious attention, if only because of the relative sophistication

Table 9.7 *Numbers and percentages of the more reliable estimates of the value of statistical life in various intervals*

	Number	Percentage
Less than £250,000	1	6.3
Between £250,000 and £500,000	4	25.0
Between £500,000 and £1,000,000	1	6.3
More than £1,000,000	10	62.4

of the sampling procedure employed and because the questions related to familiar kinds of risk and involved fairly straightfoward scenarios. Inevitably, also, this study was able to benefit from many of the lessons learned in earlier surveys of this type.

All things considered, then, the more reliable estimates are probably those given by the compensating wage differential studies (with the possible exceptions of those by Melinek and Needleman) together with Dardis's study and the questionnaire surveys of Acton, Maclean and Jones-Lee *et al.* Focusing upon these estimates, their mean and median are, respectively, £2,230,000 and £1,890,000, while the numbers and percentages of the estimates in the various intervals are given in table 9.7.

Finally, if one is to attempt to identify a sub-set of the *most* reliable estimates, then the following would seem to be serious candidates for inclusion in this category:

1   Estimates derived from those compensating wage differential studies for the USA that employed BLS data since these, in contrast with the studies using Society of Actuaries data, concerned work-related rather than general risks.
2   The Dillingham (1979) compensating wage differential estimate for the USA, which also used work-related risk data.
3   The compensating wage differential estimates given by Veljanovski (1978) and Marin and Psacharopoulos (1982) for the UK and by Weiss *et al.* (1986) for Austria, all of which were based upon data concerning accidents at work.
4   The Dardis (1980) revealed-preference estimate based on smoke detector purchases, which involves a simple and direct wealth–risk tradeoff.
5   The Jones-Lee *et al.* (1985) questionnaire estimate which was based upon a large, random sample survey involving questions concerning familiar, every-day risks.

The mean and median of the most reliable estimates are, respectively, £2,830,000 and £2,470,000, while the numbers and percentages of these estimates in the various intervals are given in table 9.8.

The results given in tables 9.7 and 9.8 therefore indicate that, if anything, an

Table 9.8 *Numbers and percentages of the most reliable estimates of the value of statistical life in various intervals*

	Number	Percentage
Less than £250,000	0	0.0
Between £250,000 and £500,000	2	18.2
Between £500,000 and £1,000,000	1	9.1
More than £1,000,000	8	72.7

attempt to weight the different estimates for relative reliability is likely to reinforce substantially the earlier conclusions concerning the appropriate magnitude of the value of statistical life for 'everyday' risks, such as those encountered in transport or in the workplace. Indeed, given the empirical evidence assembled to date it is very difficult to resist the conclusions that (a) the value of statistical life for more commonplace risks almost certainly exceeds £250,000, (b) it is highly probable that the value is at least £500,000 and (c) a respectable case can be made for a value of over £1,000,000.

The last of these conclusions seems all the more persuasive when one bears in mind that the two most recent and comprehensive empirical studies for the UK (namely those of Marin and Psacharopoulos, 1982; and Jones-Lee *et al.*, 1985) both produce estimates in the region of £1,900,000 in 1987 prices in spite of the fact that one study used the revealed-preference approach while the other was based on the questionnaire method. Furthermore, these two estimates are for 'self-only' risks and include no allowances for the 'direct' economic effects of safety improvement, such as avoided police and medical costs as well as losses of net output. If values of statistical life are augmented to reflect concern for other people's safety as well as direct economic effects, then figures in excess of £2,000,000 in 1987 prices could well be warranted. Lest the reader should be tempted to regard this as being an outrageously large number, it should be borne in mind that, given the willingness-to-pay definition of the value of statistical life, use of such a figure in the transport context would be tantamount to assuming that motorists would, on average, be willing to pay about £20 per annum for a 10 per cent reduction in the risk of being killed in a car accident. That, surely, is not *so* outrageous.

REFERENCES

Acton, J.P. (1973), 'Evaluating Public Programs to Save Lives: The Case of Heart Attacks', Research Report R-73-02. Santa Monica, Rand Corporation.
(1976), 'Measuring the monetary value of life saving programs', *Law and Contemporary Problems*, 40: 46–72.

Arnould, R.J. and L.M. Nichols (1983), 'Wage-risk premiums and workers' compensation: a refinement of estimates of compensating wage differential', *Journal of Political Economy*, 91: 332–40.

Atiyah, P.S. (1982), 'A legal perspective on recent contributions to the valuation of life', in M.W. Jones-Lee (ed.), *The Value of Life and Safety: Proceedings of a Conference held by the Geneva Association*, Amsterdam, North-Holland, pp. 185–220.

Bergstrom, T.C. (1974), 'Preference and choice in matters of life and death', in J. Hirschleifer, T. Bergstrom and E. Rappaport (eds.), *Applying Cost-Benefit Concepts to Projects which Alter Human Mortality*, UCLA-ENG-7478. Los Angeles, School of Engineering and Applied Sciences, University of California, Appendix 1.

(1982), 'Is a man's life worth more than his human capital?', in M.W. Jones-Lee (ed.), *The Value of Life and Safety: Proceedings of a Conference held by the Geneva Association*, Amsterdam, North-Holland, pp. 3–26.

Blomquist, G. (1979), 'Value of life savings: implications of consumption activity', *Journals of Political Economy*, 87: 540–58.

(1981), 'The value of human life: an empirical perspective', *Economic Enquiry*, 19: 157–64.

(1982), 'Estimating the value of life and safety: recent developments', in M.W. Jones-Lee (ed.), *The Value of Life and Safety: Proceedings of a Conference held by the Geneva Association*, Amsterdam, North-Holland, pp. 27–40.

Broome, J. (1978), 'Trying to value a life', *Journal of Public Economics*, 9: 91–100.

Brown, R.A. and C.H. Green (1981), 'Threats to health and safety: perceived risk and willingness-to-pay', *Social Science and Medicine*, 15: 67–75.

Dardis, R. (1980), 'The value of life: new evidence from the marketplace', *American Economic Review*, 70: 1077–82.

Dehez, P. and J.H. Drèze (1982), 'State-dependent utility, the demand for insurance and the value of safety', in M.W. Jones-Lee (ed.), *The Value of Life and Safety: Proceedings of a Conference held by the Geneva Association*, Amsterdam, North-Holland, pp. 41–65.

Dillingham, A.E. (1979), 'The Injury Risk Structure of Occupations and Wages', Ph.D. Dissertation, Cornell University.

(1980), 'The relationship between estimates of wage premiums for injury risk and the measurement of injury risk: results from one population', Illinois State University, Department of Economics.

Drèze, J.H. (1962), 'L'utilité sociale d'une vie humaine', *Revue Française de Recherche Opérationelle*, 22: 139–55.

(ed.) (1974a), *Allocation under Uncertainty: Equilibrium and Optimality*, London, Macmillan.

(1974b), 'Axiomatic Theories of Choice, Cardinal Utility and Subjective Probability: A Review', J.H. Drèze (ed.), *Allocation under Uncertainty: Equilibrium and Optimality*, London, Macmillan, pp. 3–23.

(1981), 'Inferring risk tolerance from deductibles in insurance contracts', *The Geneva Papers on Risk and Insurance*, 6: 48–52.

(1987), *Essays on Economic Decisions under Uncertainty*, Cambridge University Press.

Fischer, G.W. (1979), 'Willingness to pay for probabilistic improvements in functional health status: a psychological perspective', in S.J. Mushkin and D.W. Dunlop (eds.), *Health: What is it Worth?* Elmsford, NY, Pergamon Press.

Fischer, G.W. and J.W. Vaupel (1976), 'A lifespan utility model: assessing preferences for consumption and longevity', Working paper, Durham, NC: Center for Policy Analysis, Institute of Policy Sciences and Public Affairs, Duke University.

Frankel, M. (1979), 'Hazard opportunity and the valuation of life', Mimeo, University of Illinois at Urbana-Champaign.

Ghosh, D., D. Lees and W. Seal (1975), 'Optimal motorway speed and some valuations of time and life', *Manchester School*, 43: 134–43.

Harsanyi, J.C. (1955), 'Cardinal welfare, individualistic ethics and interpersonal comparisons of utility', *Journal of Political Economy*, 83: 309–21.

(1982), 'Morality and the theory of rational behaviour', in A. Sen and B. Williams (eds.), *Utilitarianism and Beyond*, Cambridge University Press, pp. 39–62.

Ippolito, P.M. and R.A. Ippolito (1984), 'Measuring the value of life saving from consumer reactions to new information', *Journal of Public Economics*, 25: 53–81.

Jones, G.H. (1946), *Road Accidents*, Report submitted to the Minister of Transport, London, HMSO.

Jones-Lee, M.W. (1969), 'Valuation of reduction in probability of death by road accident', *Journal of Transport Economics and Policy*, 3: 37–47.

(1974), 'The value of changes in the probability of death or injury', *Journal of Political Economy*, 82: 835–49.

(1975), 'Optimal life insurance: comment', *Journal of Finance*, 30: 902–3.

(1976), *The Value of Life: An Economic Analysis*, London, Martin Robertson; Chicago, University of Chicago Press.

(1977), 'Some empirical rigor mortis: an empirical procedure for estimating the value of life from tyre replacement data', Paper presented at the SSRC Health Economists' Study Group, University of Newcastle upon Tyne, July.

(1978), 'The value of human life in the demand for safety: comment', *American Economic Review*, 68: 712–16.

(1979), 'Trying to value a life: why Broome does not sweep clean', *Journal of Public Economics*, 12: 249–56.

(1980a), 'Human capital, risk aversion and the value of life', in D.A. Currie and W. Peters (eds.), *Contemporary Economic Analysis*, vol. 2, London, Croom Helm, pp. 285–321.

(1980b), 'Maximum acceptable physical risk and a new measure of financial risk aversion', *Economic Journal*, 90: 550–68.

(1981), 'The value of non-marginal changes in physical risk', in D.A. Currie, D. Peel and W. Peters (eds.), *Microeconomic Analysis*. London, Croom Helm, pp. 233–68.

(1983), Letter to the Editor, *The Financial Times*, 22 August.

(1984a), 'Natural disasters: a comparison of alternative methods for evaluating preventive measures', *The Geneva Papers on Risk and Insurance*, 9: 188–205.

(1984b), 'The valuation of transport safety', in *Proceedings of the Annual Transportation Convention, Pretoria*, vol. G. Pretoria, National Institute for Transport and Road Research, 1–14.

(1987a), 'The political economy of physical risk', *Journal of the Society for Radiological Protection*, 7: 33–44.

(1987b), 'The economic value of life: a comment', *Economica*, 54: 397–400.

(1987c), 'Valuation of safety', *Public Money*, 7: 14.

(1987d), 'Evaluating Safety Benefits', in A. Harrison and J. Gretton (eds.), *Transport UK 1987*. Newbury, Policy Journals, 87–92.

(1989), *The Economics of Safety and Physical Risk*, Oxford, Basil Blackwell.

Jones-Lee, M.W. (ed.) (1982), *The Value of Life and Safety: Proceedings of a Conference held by the Geneva Association*, Amsterdam, North-Holland.

Jones-Lee, M.W. and A.M. Poncelet (1982), 'The value of marginal and non-marginal multiperiod variations in physical risk', in M.W. Jones-Lee (ed.), *The Value of Life and Safety: Proceedings of a Conference held by the Geneva Association*, Amsterdam, North-Holland, pp. 67–80.

Jones-Lee, M.W., M. Hammerton and V. Abbott (1983), 'The value of transport safety: results of a national sample survey', Report to the UK Department of Transport.

(1987), *The Value of Transport Safety: Results of a National Sample Survey*. Newbury, Policy Journals.

Jones-Lee, M.W., M. Hammerton and P.R. Philips (1985), 'The value of safety: results of a national sample survey', *Economic Journal*, 95: 49–72.

Kahneman, D. and A. Tversky (1979), 'Prospect theory: an analysis of decision under risk', *Econometrica*, 47: 263–91.

Kahneman, D., P. Slovic and A. Tversky (eds.) (1982), *Judgement under Uncertainty: Heuristics and Biases*, Cambridge University Press.

Keeney, R.L. (1980a), 'Evaluating alternatives involving potential fatalities', *Operational Research*, 28: 188–205.

(1980b), 'Equity and public risk', *Operations Research*, 28: 527–34.

(1980c), 'Utility functions for equity and public life', *Management Science*, 26: 345–53.

(1982), 'Evaluating mortality risks from an organisation perspective', in M.W. Jones-Lee (ed.), *The Value of Life and Safety: Proceedings of a Conference held by the Geneva Association*, Amsterdam, North-Holland, pp. 217–27.

Keeney, R.L. and H. Raiffa (1976), *Decisions with Multiple Objectives*, New York, Wiley.

Linnerooth, J. (1976), 'Methods for evaluating mortality risk', *Futures*, 8: 293–304.

(1979), 'The value of human life: a review of the models', *Economic Inquiry*, 17: 52–74.

(1982), 'Murdering statistical lives . . .? in M.W. Jones-Lee (ed.), *The Value of Life and Safety: Proceedings of a Conference held by the Geneva Association*, Amsterdam, North-Holland, pp. 229–61.

Maclean, A.D. (1979), 'The Value of Public Safety: Results of a Pilot-scale Survey', London, Home Office Scientific Advisory Branch.

Marin, A. (1983a), 'Your money or your life', *The Three Banks Review*, 138: 2–37.

(1983b), Letter to the Editor, *The Financial Times*, 23 August.

(1988), The cost of avoiding death – nuclear power, regulation and spending on safety', *The Royal Bank of Scotland Review*, 157: 20–36.

Marin, A. and G. Psacharopoulos (1982), 'The reward for risk in the labor market: evidence from the United Kingdom and a reconciliation with other studies', *Journal of Political Economy*, 90: 827–53.

Melinek, S.J. (1974), 'A method of evaluating human life for economic purposes', *Accident Analysis and Prevention*, 6: 103–14.

Melinek, S.J., S.K.D. Woolley and R. Baldwin (1973), 'Analysis of a Questionnaire on Attitudes to Risk', Fire Research Note 962. Borehamwood: Joint Fire Research Organisation.

Miller, G.A. (1956), 'The magical number seven plus or minus two: some limits on our capacity to process information', *Psychological Review*, 63: 81–97.

Miller, T.R., K.A. Reinert and B.E. Whiting (1984), 'Alternative Approaches to Accident

Cost Concepts: State of the Art', Report prepared for the Federal Highway Administration, US Department of Commerce, Washington, DC, Granville Corp.

Needleman, L. (1976), 'Valuing other people's lives', *Manchester School*, 44: 309–42.

— (1980), 'The valuation of changes in the risk of death by those at risk', *Manchester School*, 48: 229–54.

— (1982), 'Survival discount rates', mimeo, University of Waterloo.

Olson, C. (1978), 'Trade Unions, Wages, Occupational Injuries and Public Policy', Ph.D. Dissertation, University of Wisconsin.

— (1981), 'An analysis of wage differentials received by workers on dangerous jobs', *Journal of Human Resources*, 16: 167–85.

Portney, P.R. (1981), 'Housing prices, health effects and valuing reductions in risk of death', *Journal of Environmental Economics and Management*, 8: 72–8.

Sen, A. and B. Williams (1982), *Utilitarianism and Beyond*, Cambridge University Press.

Smith, R.S. (1973), 'Compensating wage differentials and hazardous work', Technical Paper No. 5: Office of Policy Evaluation and Research, Department Labour.

— (1976), *The Occupational Safety and Health Act: Its Goals and Its Achievements*, Washington, American Enterprise Institute.

— (1979), 'Compensating wage differentials and public policy: a review', *Industrial and Labor Relations Review*, 32: 339–52.

Smith, V.K. (1983), 'The role of site and job characteristics in hedonic wage models', *Journal of Urban Economics*, 13: 296–321.

Smith, V.K. and W.H. Desvousges (1987), 'An empirical analysis of the economic value of risk changes', *Journal of Political Economy*, 95: 89–114.

Thaler, R. and S. Rosen (1973), 'The value of saving a life: evidence from the labour market', University of Rochester Graduate School of Management Working Paper No 7401. Also in N.E. Terleckyj (ed.), *Household Production and Consumption*, New York, National Bureau of Economic Research, pp. 265–301.

Veljanovski, C. (1978), 'The economics of job safety regulation: theory and evidence: part I – the market and the common law', mimeo, Centre for Socio-Legal Studies, University of Oxford.

Violette, D.M. and L.G. Chestnut (1983), 'Valuing Reductions in Risk: A Review of the Empirical Estimates', Report to the Economic Analysis Division, US Environmental Protection Agency. Boulder, CO, Energy and Resource Consultants Inc.

Viscusi, W.K. (1978a), 'Labor market valuations of life and limb: empirical evidence and policy implications', *Public Policy*, 26: 359–86.

— (1978b), 'Health effects and earnings premiums for job hazards', *Review of Economics and Statistics*, 60: 408–16.

— (1980), 'Imperfect job risk information and optimal workmen's compensation benefits', *Journal of Public Economics*, 14: 319–37.

Von Neumann, J. and O. Morgenstern (1947), *Theory of Games and Economic Behavior*, Princeton, Princeton University Press.

Weiss, P., G. Maier and S. Gerking (1986), 'The economic evaluation of job safety: a methodological survey and some estimates for Austria', *Empirica-Austrian Economic Papers*, 13: 53–67.

Zeckhauser, R. (1975), 'Procedures for valuing lives', *Public Policy*, 23: 419–64.

Zeckhauser, R. and D. Shepard (1976), 'Where now for saving lives?', *Law and Contemporary Problems*, 40: 4–45.

10

THE ENVIRONMENT:

The environment and emerging development issues

Partha Dasgupta and Karl-Göran Mäler

Environmental resources are of minor importance to poor countries ... They play an insignificant role in the process of economic development ... Such resources are luxury goods and they loom large in public consciousness only when incomes are high ... Environmental resources are only a rich country's preoccupations .. They are a mere diversion created by economists not sensitive to the true needs of the poor in poor countries ...

These sentences will seem at once strange and recognizable. They will seem strange because today we all like to admit that the ideas they express aren't true. At the same time, they will be recognizable to anyone who has delved into the literature on development economics and looked for environmental issues in it. Even were we to search through the vast body of writings on development planning, not to mention the one on investment criteria, we would be hard put to discover any sign of environmental resources. Official development does not yet acknowledge their existence, in that you won't find them in any recognized survey article, or text or treatise on the subject.

To cite only a few instances, Drèze and Stern (1987) and Stern (1989) are surveys of cost–benefit analysis and development economics, respectively. The former, a ninety-page article, contains precisely one sentence on the subject of non-renewable and renewable resources (and it is to tell readers where to go if they wish to learn about such matters); and the latter, an eighty-eight-page article, also contains a single sentence (and this also tells readers where to go should they wish to learn about such matters). A third example is provided by the two-volume *Handbook of Development Economics* (Chenery and Srinivasan (eds.), (1988), which simply has no discussion of environmental resources and their possible bearing on development processes. The disconnection of academic development economics from a central aspect of the lives of people about whom development economics revolves would appear to be pretty much complete. Environmental resources appear in this literature about as frequently as rain falls on the Thar.[1]

Despite this neglect, something like a literature on the environment and

This chapter previously appeared in *Proceedings of the World Bank Annual Conference on Development Economics 1990*. We would like to thank The World Bank for their kind permission to reproduce it here.

economic development is now emerging.[2] In this paper we will therefore try and place this small literature in perspective and develop what appears to us to be some of the themes with the greatest research potential; those which have at the same time implications for policy in poor countries. This will enable us also to apply economic theory to obtain new insights into the allocation and management of environmental resources. We want to do this by providing a framework of thought which will encourage the reader to view environmental resources as *economic goods*. This will no doubt seem a banal intention, but it is remarkable how much of current writing on the environment displays an innocence of this point of view. Our approach is based on the conjecture that until environmental resources become a commonplace furniture of economic thinking and modelling, they will continue to be neglected in the design of policy and in the implementation of policy. Periodic 'affirmative actions' on the environment is not the right way of going about things.

Now there are several routes we can follow for the purpose of introducing our subject. Here, we will pursue one which is perhaps less popular today than it used to be: it is to seek a unifying principle concerning the 'technology of production' of environmental goods and services. In other words, we will start by viewing the matter from the purely *ecological* side of things. Later, we will view the subject from the *institutional* end. They are complementary avenues of enquiry. Both need to be covered, but it is pretty much a matter of indifference along which one we start.

1 ENVIRONMENTAL RESOURCES AND THEIR PHYSICAL CHARACTERISTICS

Environmental problems are almost always associated with resources which are regenerative – we could call them *renewable natural resources* – but which are in danger of exhaustion from excessive use.[3] The earth's atmosphere is a paradigm of such resources. Under normal courses of events the atmosphere's composition regenerates itself. But the speed of regeneration depends upon the rate at which pollutants are deposited into it, and it depends upon the nature of the pollutants. (Smoke discharge is clearly different from the release of radioactive material.) Now, in talking of a resource we need first of all a way of measuring it. In the case in hand we have to think of an atmospheric *quality* index. The net rate of regeneration of the stock is the rate at which this quality index changes over time. This will depend upon the nature and extent of the pollutants which are discharged, and it will also depend upon the current index of quality; that is, the current level of stock. These are immensely complex, ill-understood matters. There is a great deal of synergism associated with the interaction of different types of pollutants in the atmospheric sink.[4] But the analytical point we are making here remains valid.

Animal, bird, plant and fish populations are also typical examples of renewable natural resources, and there are now a number of studies which address the reproductive behaviour of different species under a wide variety of 'environmental' conditions, including the presence of parasitic and symbiotic neighbours. Land is also such a commodity, for the quality of arable and grazing land can be maintained by careful use. Overuse, however, impoverishes the soil and eventually produces a wasteland.[5]

Underground basins of water often have a similar characteristic. The required analysis, however, is a bit more problematic in that we are concerned both about its quality *and* quantity. Under normal circumstances an aquifer undergoes a self-cleansing process as pollutants are deposited into it. (Here, the symbiotic role of different forms of bacteria, as in the case of soil and the atmosphere, is important.) But the effectiveness of the process depends, as always, on the nature of pollutants (e.g., the type of chemicals) and the rate at which they are discharged. Furthermore, many aquifers are recharged over the annual cycle. But if the rate of extraction exceeds the recharge rate the water table drops, thereby raising extraction costs. In fact aquifers display another characteristic. On occasion the issue isn't one of depositing pollutants into them. If, as a consequence of excessive extraction, the groundwater table is allowed to drop to too low a level, then in the case of coastal aquifers there can be salt-water intrusion, resulting in the destruction of the basin.[6]

These examples suggest that a number of issues in environmental economics are within the subject matter of capital theory.[7] But there are added complications, among which is the fact that the impact on the rate of regeneration of environmental resources of a wide variety of investment decisions is not fully reversible, and in some cases quite irreversible.[8] In this, limited sense, issues concerning what is usually labelled 'pollution' can be studied in the same, general sort of way as those concerning animal, bird, plant and fish populations, aquifers, forests and soil quality. This provides us with a unified way of thinking about matters. It allows us to use insights we draw from a study of one class of environmental resources when studying another. It forces us to pay attention to the intertemporal structure of economic policies.

If this were all, life would have been relatively simple. But it isn't all. We will argue presently that admitting environmental resources into economic modelling ushers in a number of additional, potent complications for development policy. They arise out of the fact that for poor people in poor countries, such resources are often *complementary* to other goods and services. So an erosion of the environmental resource base can make certain categories of people destitute even while the economy on average is seen to be growing.

There is thus an intellectual tension between aggregate concerns (such as, for example, the greenhouse effect; or the appropriate mix of resources and manufactured capital in aggregate production) which sweep across regions, nations and continents, and those (such as, for example, the decline in firewood or water availability) that are specific to the needs and concerns of poor people of as small a group as a village community. This tension should be borne in mind. Environmental problems present themselves in the form of different images to different people. At this stage of our understanding it would be a wrong research strategy to try and put them all together into one large basket. In the following two sections we will ignore the detailed, institutional features which surround the use of *local* environmental resources and study the inter-temporal nature of environmental policy in terms of aggregate considerations. This will allow us to discuss in a simple manner the link between measures of net national product and rules for social cost–benefit analysis of investment activity. As a byproduct, it will enable us to talk briefly about a matter which is much discussed today (namely, *sustainable development*) and which a decade and a half ago was shown to be the implication of a wider, richer inquiry going under a different name (namely *optimal development*). We will pick up the institutional trail in section 3.

2 DETERMINANTS AND CONSTITUENTS OF WELL-BEING AND NET NATIONAL PRODUCT

It is as well to remember that the kinds of resources we are thinking of here are on occasion of direct use in consumption (as with fisheries), on occasion in production (as with plankton, which serves as food for fish species), and sometimes in both (as with drinking and irrigation water). Their stock, as we noted earlier, is measured in different ways, depending on the resource: in mass units (e.g., biomass units for forests, cowdung and crop residues), in quality indices (e.g., water and air quality indices), in volume units (e.g., acre-feet for aquifers) and so on. When we express concern about environmental matters we in effect point to a decline in their stock. But a decline in their stock, *on its own*, is not a reason for concern. This is seen most clearly in the context of exhaustible resources, such as fossil fuels. To not reduce their stocks is to not use them at all, and this is unlikely to be the right thing to do.

To be sure, this is not the case with renewable natural resources, since we could in principle limit their extraction and use to their natural regeneration rate and thus not allow their stocks to decline. But this too may well be the wrong thing to do, in that there is nothing sacrosanct about the stock *levels* we have inherited from the past. Whether or not policy should be directed at expanding environmental resource bases is something we should try and *deduce* from considerations of population change, inter-generational well-being, technological possibilities, environment regeneration rates and the existing resource base. The answer cannot be pulled out of the air. That it can is a common misconception. Here is a recent example of this:

We can summarize the necessary conditions for sustainable development as constancy of the natural capital stock; more strictly, the requirement for non-negative changes in the stock of natural resources, such as soil and soil quality, ground and surface water and their quality, land biomass, water biomass, and the waste-assimilation capacity of the receiving environments. (Pearce, Barbier and Markandya, 1988, p. 6.)

The passage involves a 'category mistake', the mistake being to confuse the *determinants* of well-being (e.g., the means of production) for the *constituents* of well-being (e.g., health, welfare and freedoms). But leaving that aside, the point is not that sustainable development, even as it is defined by these authors, is an undesirable goal. It is that thus defined it has negligible information-content. (We are not told, for example, what stock levels we ought to aim at.) This is the price that has to be paid for talking in terms of grand strategies. The hard work comes when one is forced to do the ecology and the economics of the matter.[9]

So then, information about stocks on their own is not a sufficient statistic for well-being. What we are after are present and future well-being and methods of determining how well-being is affected by policy. And it is not an accident that the index which, *when properly computed*, can be used towards this end is *net national product* (NNP).

Defining net national product

Net national product is held in ill repute today.[10] It is often thought that it is even in principle incapable of reflecting aggregate inter-generational well-being. This belief is not correct. Subject to certain technical restrictions, for any conception of the social good, and for any set of technological, transaction, information and ecological constraints, there exists a set of *shadow* (or *accounting*) prices of goods and services. These prices, when used in the estimation of net national product, ensure that small projects which increase this index are at once those which increase the social good.[11] A great many of these accounting prices will be *person*, or *household specific*. Put more generally, they will be *agent-relative*, to reflect the fact that needs and incomes differ along gender, age, caste or ethnic lines, and that many of the exchanges which take place in poor agrarian and pastoral societies are *non-anonymous*; that is, such exchanges take place in *personalized* or *named markets*.[12]

These considerations bring out the intellectual tension we spoke of earlier. The point is that in practice it is impossible to take all this into account in one grand measure of real net national product. The thing to do is to improve on our current ways of doing things and capture these concerns in a piecemeal fashion. This is the approach we will take here.

Current estimates of net national product are based on biased sets of prices. They are biased in that the prices that are imputed to environmental resources *on site* are usually zero, even though we know that their accounting prices are positive. Thus, the social profits of projects which degrade the environment are lower than the profits that are actually imputed to them. This means in turn that wrong sets of projects are chosen. In particular, resource-intensive projects look better than they are in fact.

One can go further. The bias would be expected to extend itself to the prior stage of research and development. When environmental resources are under-priced, there is little incentive for agencies to develop technologies which econo-mize on their use. Now, the extent of the distortion created by this underpricing will vary from country to country. Quite obviously, poor countries cannot compete with rich nations in the field of basic research. They have to rely on the flow of new knowledge produced in advanced industrial economies. Despite this, poor countries need to have the capability for basic research. This is because the structure of their shadow prices is likely to be quite different, most especially for non-traded goods and services. Even when it is publicly available, basic know-ledge is not necessarily *useable* by scientists and technologists unless they them-selves have a feel for basic research. Basic knowledge shouldn't simply be taken off the shelf. Ideas developed in foreign lands ought not merely be transplanted to the local economy. They need to be adapted to suit local ecological conditions. This is where estimating shadow prices (and more generally, creating incentives which correspond to these shadow prices) can be of considerable help. Adapt-ation is itself a creative exercise. Unhappily, it is often bypassed. The foreign technology is simply purchased and installed with little by way of modification. There is great loss in this.

This leads to the question how we should value environmental resources on site; or, in other words, what are their shadow prices on site. It also leads to the question how we should measure net national product once we have estimated shadow prices. As it happens, this latter question has a precise answer. How we should define NNP is therefore not a matter of opinion, it is a matter of fact.

The theory of inter-temporal planning tells us to choose current controls (for example, current consumptions and the mix of current investments) in such a way as to maximize the current-value Hamiltonian of the planning problem. As is now well known, the current-value Hamiltonian is the sum of the flow of current well-being and the shadow value of all the net investments currently being undertaken. (Thus, the planning exercise generates the entire set of inter-temporal shadow prices.[13]) It is possible to show that the current-value Hamiltonian measures the return on the *wealth* of an economy, measured in terms of well-being (see appendix I). The theory also tells us that if the objective of planning (that is, the inter-generational index of well-being) is stationary, then along the optimal programme the Hamiltonian remains constant through time.[14]

This provides us with the necessary connection between the current-value Hamiltonian and net national product. NNP is merely a linearized version of the current-value Hamiltonian, the linearization amounting to representing the current flow of well-being by the shadow value of all the determinants of current well-being. In the simplest of cases, where current well-being depends solely on current consumption, real net national product reduces to the *sum* of the social (or shadow) value of an economy's consumptions and the social (or shadow) value of the changes in its stocks of real capital assets.

The Hamiltonian calculus in fact implies something more. It implies also that along an optimal programme real net national product at any date is the maximum consumption the economy can enjoy at that date were it made a condition that consumption be never allowed to fall. In short, net national product at any date along an optimal programme is the maximum sustainable consumption at that date. This was not seen immediately as an implication of the mathematical theory of programming, although it should have been transparent from the work of Arrow and Kurz (1970) and Solow (1974). So a proof was provided by Weitzman (1976) in the context of economies which are capable of sustaining a steady economic state, and it was extended to the context of economies with exhaustible resources in Dasgupta and Heal (1979, pp. 244–6) (see also Solow, 1986).

Now 'changes in capital stocks' means changes in *all* capital stocks: manufactured capital as well as natural resources. As of now, we know of no country which tries to account for environmental resource changes in its national income accounting. As we noted earlier, the effect on estimated growth rates could be significant were countries to do this, since it is entirely possible that growth in *per capita* gross national product is currently being achieved in a number of poor countries via a deterioration of its environmental resource base. Growth in NNP over the recent past may well have been negative in a number of countries which are judged to have enjoyed positive growth.[15]

By way of illustration of how this can be, consider as an extreme case a country which lives ('optimally') simply by exporting its exhaustible resources and importing consumption goods with the export revenue. Assume too that resources are costless to extract, and that other than extraction there is no domestic production. Net national product in this country, when correctly measured, would be *nil*. No matter that its current consumption may be high, the social value of the rate of disinvestment would exactly match the shadow value of its consumption rate. Furthermore, being exhaustible, exports must eventually go to *zero*, and so consumption must eventually go to zero. Such an economy can't manage a positive, sustainable consumption path. It is this fact which is reflected in NNP, when correctly measured. However, we would not know any of this from conventional national income accounts. NNP in this economy, as conventionally measured, could be large, and would even be seen to be rising were the rate of disinvestment to be stepped up. (See Dasgupta and Heal, 1979, pp. 244–6.)

The national elaborations of these ideas are still not quite as well known as they ought to be. Thus, in a recent World Bank volume, El Sarafy and Lutz (1989, p. 2) write: 'It does not make sense to incorporate expenditures incurred to redress some or all of the negative consequences of production and consumption activities in the stream of income generated by economic activity. It has therefore been proposed that such outlays should not be counted as final expenditure, as is currently the case, rather as intermediate expenditure.'

The prescription is not necessarily correct: it all depends upon whether such expenditures are for the purposes of redressing a flow of environmental damage or for enhancing stocks of environmental resources. To take an example, expenditures for liming lakes to counter the flow of acid rains maintain environmental quality. Were this not to be included in final demand, increased liming (which increases well-being) would be recorded as a decline in NNP. Similarly, capital expenditures (for example, the construction of stack-gas scrubbers, sewage treatment plants, solar energy equipment) should also not be deducted from estimates of net national product: for they go to augment the durable-capital base. On the other hand, those expenditures which go to enhance resource bases, such as forests, get reflected in the value of changes in resource stocks. In order to avoid double counting, such expenditures therefore, should be excluded from NNP computations.

The general moral is that before writing down an expression for NNP it is best to express in a formal model the characteristics of the activities being undertaken in the economy under study. What passes for intermediate expenditure and what does not will be reflected in the Hamiltonian, and one can then readily construct the formula for the country's NNP, and one can simultaneously obtain the system of shadow prices. The procedure is a shade pedantic. But it provides a safeguard against mistakes. In appendix I we provide a formal account of this.

How does uncertainty in future possibilities affect the evaluation of NNP? We will avoid any further technicalities here. (But see appendix II for a rigorous development of the ideas described below.) The interesting case to consider is one where there are discrete but random events in the future. (An example is the harnessing of nuclear fusion; more generally, unanticipated technological break-throughs. Alternatively, the example could be the discovery that some genetic material has high medicinal value, or that the biosphere behaves in an unantici-pated way.) The shadow prices of existing capital assets will reflect such future possibilities (e.g., that the shadow value of fossil fuels will plummet with the discovery of cheap, alternative energy sources). If market prices do not reflect these shadow prices (as indeed, mostly they do not), they are in need of correction; and this can in principle be done by taking into account option values, to be discussed below. Furthermore, the discovery can be expected to affect the value of all then existing stocks of capital. It follows that current NNP should be adjusted for this change in value.

All this reasoning is relevant only from the vantage point of the period before the occurrences of the events in question. When, at some random future date a discovery is made, the economy enters a new regime, and NNP has now to be recomputed. In fact, NNP undergoes a discrete change, to capture the fact that prior to the discovery, the event was only a possibility, but that after the discovery it is a realized event.

Difficulties associated with the estimation of shadow prices and real net national product are compounded by the fact that unlike computers and tractors, environmental resources often affect current well-being directly as stocks, and not merely as service flows. (An exception is noise pollution.) Fisheries and aquifers are useful not only for the harvest they provide (this is the flow); as a stock they are directly useful, because harvesting and extraction costs are low if stocks are large. Tropical forests are beneficial not only for the timber they may supply (this is the flow of service); as a stock they prevent soil erosion and, in the case of large tropical forests, help maintain a varied genetic pool and contribute substantially to the recycling of carbon dioxide. To take another example, transportation costs (in particular caloric costs) for women and children would be less were the sources of firewood not far away and receding. Likewise, air and water quality have direct well-being effects; (it is, let us remember, the concentration of pollutants which is relevant here). This has an implication for the current-value Hamiltonian, and therefore for real net national product (see appendix I).

Estimating shadow prices

The prior question, of how we should estimate shadow prices for environmental resources, is a complex one. But it is not uniformly complex. For commodities like irrigation water, fisheries and agricultural soil, there are now standard techniques of evaluation. These techniques rely on the fact that such resources are inputs in the production of tradable goods.[16] For others, such as firewood, and drinking and cooking water, the matter is more complex. The fact remains, though, that even these are inputs in production; specifically, inputs in *household* production. And this provides us with a method for estimating their shadow prices. To obtain them we will need to have an estimate of household production functions. In some cases (as with fuelwood) the resource input is a substitute for a tradable input (for example, kerosine); in others (as with cooking water) it is a complement (sometimes a weak complement) to tradable inputs (for example food grain). Such information is in principle obtainable. They allow the analyst to estimate shadow prices.[17]

The approach we have outlined above (the 'production function approach') allows one to capture only the 'use-value' of a resource, and its accounting price may well exceed this. Why? The reason is that there are additional values embodied in a resource stock. One additional value, applicable to living resources, is their 'intrinsic worth' *as* living resources. (We plainly don't think that the value of a blue whale is embodied entirely in its flesh and oil, or that the value of the 'game' in Kenyan game parks is simply the present-value of tourists' willingnesses-to-pay!) It is pretty much impossible to get a quantitative handle on 'intrinsic worth', and so the right thing to do is to take note of it, keep an eye on it and call attention to it whenever the stock is threatened.

There is another source of value which is more amenable to quantification. It arises from a combination of two things common to environmental resources: uncertainty in their *future* use-values and irreversibility in their use. (Genetic materials in tropical forests provide a prime example.) The twin presence of uncertainty and irreversibility implies that even were the aggregate well-being function neutral to risk, it would not do to estimate the shadow price of an environmental resource solely on the basis of the expected benefit from its future use. Irreversibility in its use implies that preservation of the stock has an additional value, the value of extending one's set of future options. Future options have an additional worth precisely because with the passage of time more information is expected to be forthcoming *about* the resource's use-value. (This additional worth is often called an *option value*.) The shadow price of a resource is the sum of its use-value and its option value (see Arrow and Fisher, 1974; Henry, 1974; Fisher and Hanemann, 1986; Dasgupta, 1982; Mäler, 1989).

As we noted earlier, environmental resources *in situ* are mostly regarded free in current economic exercises even while their shadow prices are positive. As we have also noted above, this leads to biases in policy and to biases in the design and installation of new technology. Recall also that even at the prior level of research and development they lead to biases, for there is little incentive for agencies to develop technologies which economize on the use of environmental resources. Indeed, an entire debate, whether *economic* and *environmental* considerations are in contra-position, is a misplaced one. They *are* when economic calculations are biased. They would be consonent with each other if environmental resources were to be put on par with the kinds of goods and services which occupy the attention of economists most of the time.

3 MARKETS AND THEIR FAILURE

All this has been from what one might call the operations-research side of things. It is an essential viewpoint, but it is a limited viewpoint. By way of its complement is the institutional side, with all its attendant difficulties. Indeed, it is the institutional side which has most often been the starting gate for environmental economics. Particular emphasis is placed upon the fact that *markets* for these goods either don't exist, or are prone to malfunctioning when they do exist.[18] As we noted earlier, by markets one should not necessarily mean price-guided institutions. By markets we mean institutions which make available to interested parties the opportunity to negotiate courses of actions. And by malfunctioning markets we mean circumstances where such opportunities are not present (because, say, property rights are unspecified), or where they are exploited at best partially (because, say, the bargainers don't know each other well; see Farrell, 1987), or where they are somewhat one-sided. (This often one-sidedness of opportunities means that we are thinking of distributional issues as well, and not merely those bearing on efficiency.)

Nowhere is this generalized form of market failure more common than in those hidden interactions which are *unidirectional*; for example, deforestation in the uplands, which often inflict damages on the lowlands. As always, it pays to concentrate first on the assignment of property rights before seeking remedies. The common law, if one is permitted to use this expression in a universal context, usually recognizes polluters' rights, not those of the pollutees. Translated into our present example, this means that the timber merchant who has obtained a concession in the upland forests is under no obligation to compensate farmers in the lowlands. If the farmers wish to reduce the risk of heightened floods, it is they who have to compensate the timber merchant for reducing the rate of deforestation. Stated this way, the matter does look morally bizarre, but it is how things are. Had property rights been the other way round, one of *pollutees'* rights, the boots would have been on the other set of feet, and it would have been the timber merchant who would have had to pay compensation to farmers for the right to inflict the damages which go with deforestation. However, when the cause of damages is hundreds of miles away and when the victims are thousands of impoverished farmers, the issue of a bargained outcome *usually* does not arise.[19] Thus, judged even from the viewpoint of efficiency, a system of polluters' rights in such an example would be disastrous.[20] We would expect excessive deforestation. Stated in another way, the private cost of logging would in this case be lower than its social cost.

Now when the social costs of production of environmental goods are higher than their private costs, resource-based goods may be presumed to be *underpriced* in the market. Quite obviously, the less roundabout, or less distant, is the production of the final good from its resource base, the greater is this underpricing, in percentage terms. Put another way, the lower is the value-added to the resource, the larger is the extent of this underpricing of the final product. We may then conclude that countries which export primary products do so by subsiding them, possibly at a massive scale. Moreover, the subsidy is paid not by the general public via taxation, but by some of the most disadvantaged members of society: the sharecropper, the small landholder, or tenant farmer, the forest dweller, and so on. The subsidy is hidden from public scrutiny; that is why nobody talks of it. But it is here. It is real. We should be in a position to estimate them. As of now, we have no such estimates.

Matters are usually quite different for economic and ecological interactions which are *reciprocal*, such as for example the use by several parties of a piece of grazing land. Many of the production and exchange contracts we see in poor agrarian and pastoral societies over the use of such resources are explicit ones, and their compliance is enforced by means of elaborate rules, regulations and fines.[21] However, many contracts are merely *implicit*, the obligations they entail having often been codified over the years in the form of *social norms*, and the associated *social sanctions* on occasion imposed upon those in violation of such norms, and on occasion even upon those who fail to impose sanctions upon those in violation of such norms, and on rare occasions upon those who fail to impose sanctions upon those who fail to impose sanctions upon those in violation of such norms, and so forth.[22] Thus, the fact that a piece of environmental property is not in private (or government) hands does not mean at all that there is institutional failure. The anthropological literature is replete with studies of communities that have developed elaborate patterns of monitoring and control over the use of what are today called *common property resources.*[23]

Economic analysis is thought by some to have implied that common property resources can only be managed through centralized coordination and control; where by 'centralized' we mean the government, or some agency external to the community of users. (Referring to the problem of the commons in the theoretical literature, Wade (1987, p. 220), in a much-cited article, writes 'The prevailing answer runs as follows: when people are in a situation where they could mutually benefit if all of them restrained their use of a common-pool resource, they will not do so unless an external agency enforces a suitable rule.' And he proceeds to describe enforcement mechanisms in his sample of villages which do not rely on external agencies.) This is simply not so. The theory of games has unravelled the variety of institutional mechanisms (ranging from taxes to quantity controls) which can in principle support desirable allocations of common property resources. The theory makes clear, and has made clear for quite some time, that enforcement of the agreed-upon allocation can be carried out by the users themselves. In many cases this may well be the most desirable option. As always, monitoring, enforcement, information and transaction costs play a criticial role in the relative efficacy of these mechanisms, and we will have something to say about this in what follows. (For a formal, mathematical account, and an informal discussion of the possibilities implied by the formal analysis, see Dasgupta and Heal, 1979, chapter 3, sections 4–5.) The confirmation of theory by evidence on the fate of different categories of common property resources is a pleasing success of modern economic analysis.[24]

4 PUBLIC FAILURE AND THE EROSION OF LOCAL COMMONS

There is a vast difference between *global* and *local* commons. The open seas are common property resources, as are usually village ponds. As economic analysis makes clear, what are problems for the former are by no means problems for the latter. However, it is the global commons, and popular writings on them (for example, the influential article by Hardin, 1968), which have shaped popular images of *all* common property resources. This has been most unfortunate. It is unfortunate because, unlike global commons, the source of the problems associated with the management of local commons is often not the users, but other agencies. The images which are invoked by 'the tragedy of the commons' are mostly not the right ones when applied to local commons. The point is that local commons (such as village ponds and tanks, pastures and threshing grounds, watershed drainage and riverbeds, and sources of fuelwood, medicinal herbs, bamboo, palm products, resin, gum and so forth) are in no society open for use to *all*. They are open only to those having historical rights, through kinship ties, community membership, and so forth. Those having historical rights-of-use tend, not surprisingly, to be very protective of these resources. Local commons are easy enough to monitor, and so their use is often regulated in great detail by the community; as we noted earlier, either through the practice and enforcement of norms, or through deliberate allocation of use. (See, for example, Wade, 1987.)

It is not difficult to see why common property resources matter greatly to the poorest of the rural poor in a society, nor therefore, to understand the mechanisms through which such people may well get disenfranchised from the economy even while in the aggregate it enjoys economic growth.[25] If you are steeped in social norms of behaviour and understand community contractual obligations, you do not calculate every five minutes how you should behave. You follow the norms. This saves on costs all round, not only for you as an 'actor', but also for you as 'policeman' and 'judge'. It is also the natural thing for you to do if you have internalized the norms. But this is sustainable so long as the background environment remains pretty much constant. It will not be sustainable if the social environment changes suddenly. You might even be destroyed. It is this heightened vulnerability, often more real than perceived, which is the cause of some of the greatest social tragedies in contemporary society. For they descend upon people who are in the best of circumstances acutely vulnerable.

Since they are confirmed by economic theory, the findings of case studies are almost certainly not unrepresentative. They suggest that privatization of village commons and forest lands, while hallowed at the altar of efficiency, *can* have disastrous distributional consequences, disenfranchising entire classes of people from economic citizenship.[26] They also show that *public ownership* of such resources as forest lands is by no means necessarily a good basis for a resource allocation mechanism. Decision makers are in these cases usually far removed from site (living as they do in imperial capitals), they have little knowledge of the ecology of such matters, their time horizons are often short, and they are in many instances overly influenced by interest groups far removed from the resource in question.

All this is *not at all* to suggest that rural development is to be avoided. It is to say that resource allocation mechanisms which do not take advantage of dispersed information; which are insensitive to hidden (and often not so hidden) economic and ecological interactions (that is, general equilibrium effects); which do not take the long view; and which do not give a sufficiently large weight to the claims of the poorest within rural populations (particularly the women and children in these populations) are going to prove environmentally disastrous. It appears then, that during the process of economic development there is a close link between environmental non-degeneration and the well-being of the poor, most especially the most vulnerable among the poor. Elaboration of this link has been one of the most compelling achievements at the interface of anthropology, economics and nutrition science.

Information concerning the ecology of local commons is often dispersed, and is usually in the hands of the historical users. There are exceptions of course, but as a general rule this makes it desirable that the local commons be protected as commons and that decisions regarding local commons be left in the hands of the users themselves. This is because the local commons will almost certainly remain the single source of essential complementary goods for poor people for a long while yet. To be sure, it is essential that governments not only provide infrastructural and credit and insurance facilities, it is essential also that they make new information concerning technology, ecology and widening markets available to the users. But there is little case for centralized *control*. Quite the contrary, there is a case for facilitating the growth of local, community decision making, in particular decision making by women, who are for the most part the main users of such resources. The large, often fragmented literature on local common property resources is beginning to offer us an unequivocal picture that during the process of economic development the protection and promotion of environmental resources would be best served were a constant public eye kept on the conditions of the poorest of the poor in society. Environmental economics and the economics of destitution are tied to each other in an intricate web. We should not have expected it otherwise.

5 INTERNATIONAL FAILURE AND THE EROSION OF GLOBAL COMMONS

Global commons pose a different type of problem. The impossibility of establishing adequate property rights to the atmosphere, to watersheds and to large bodies of water, such as the oceans, are a cause of inefficiencies in the allocation of resources. In the case of the atmosphere (for example, over the matter of global warming), there isn't even the option of 'voting with one's feet'. Furthermore, future generations are not directly represented in today's forum for decision making. Their interests are included only indirectly through transactions between different coexisting generations. Thus, the inefficiencies and inequities involved are not merely static ones, they are inter-generational ones as well.[27] From this it follows that the international community needs consciously to design systems which improve upon existing resource allocation mechanisms.

The most complicated international environmental problems are, like the local commons, characterized by reciprocal externalities, that is, those where most countries contribute to environmental damages and they also suffer from them.

Emissions of greenhouse gases are an instance of this. A central problem is that while reciprocal, countries do not 'contribute' to the damages in equal amounts. Thus, for a cooperative outcome to be achievable, some financial transfers will be necessary, if only in an implicit manner. Several such systems suggest themselves, debt relief for the preservation of the Amazon being the one which has most frequently been talked about.

This is not to say that agreements cannot be reached without side payments; it is only to say that they will tend to be less efficient. Barrett (1990) has argued, for example, that one should not expect all countries to sign the Montreal protocol on emissions of chlorofluorocarbons (CFCs). (The protocol involves no side payments.) If an equilibrium exists, it can only involve *some* countries signing the protocol. The reason is that were only a few countries to sign the protocol, national benefits from further reduction in CFC emission would be high. This would induce more countries to sign. However, were many countries to sign the protocol, national benefits from further reduction would be small, and it would then not be worth a country's while to sign the agreement.[28]

Direct (side) payments among countries for solving environmental problems have not been so common. When made, side payments have tended to be non-pecuniary; for example, trade and military concessions (see Krutilla, 1966; Kneese, 1988). Very recently, an agreement has been reached on reducing the production and use of CFCs in developing countries. This has involved the creation of an international fund for technological transfers to these countries. It is a most promising development, and it needs to be studied carefully for the purposes of further development.

One broad category for allocation mechanisms well worth exploring in the international context involves making the global commons quasi-private. The basic idea, which originated in Dales (1968), is similar to the principle currently being experimented with in the USA. The idea, if extended to the international sphere, would have the community of nations set bounds on the *total annual* use of the global commons, such as the atmosphere, have it allocate an initial distribution of *transferable national rights* which add up to the aggregate bound, and allow the final allocation among different users to be determined by competitive markets.[29]

To give an example, consider the emission of greenhouse gases. Suppose it is desired by the community of nations that emissions should be reduced to a prescribed global level. Units of the various gases would then be so chosen that all gases have the same (expected) effect on global climate. In other words, at the margin the emission of one unit of any one gas would have the same (expected) climatic effect as the emission of one unit of any other gas. The scheme would allow countries to exchange permits for one gas for permits for any other. Countries would receive an initial assignment of marketable permits. As is well known, this scheme has informational advantages over both taxes and quantity controls on individual emissions.[30] Furthermore, were the permits to refer to *net* emissions (i.e. net of absorption of carbon dioxide by green plants), the scheme would provide an incentive for countries with fast-growing tropical rain forests to earn export revenue by encouraging forest growth and then selling permits to other countries. The scheme also has the advantage that the necessary side payments required to induce all (or most) countries to participate in the agreement can be made through the initial distribution of emission permits. Countries which do not expect severe damages from global warming would also wish to participate were they to be provided initially with a sufficient number of permits (or rights).

The sticking point will clearly be over reaching an agreement on the initial distribution of permits among nations.[31] But the point to make here is that if the bound which is set on annual aggregate greenhouse emissions is approximately optimal, it is always possible to distribute the initial set of rights in such a way that *all* countries have an incentive to join the scheme. For this reason one cannot overemphasize the fact that there are large potential gains to be enjoyed from international cooperation; a scheme involving the issue of marketable permits in principle offers a way in which all nations can enjoy these gains. The argument that 'national sovereignty' would be endangered is in fact no argument, for the point about global commons is precisely that they are beyond the realm of national sovereignty.

6 SUMMARY

In this article we have tried to present a perspective of what we take to be the central emerging issues at the interface of environmental and development concerns. The fact that for such a long while environmental and development economics have had little to say to each other is a reflection of these academic disciplines, it does not at all reflect the world as we should know it. Poor countries are for the most part agrarian and pastoral, and it is but natural that the bulk of society in these lands depends crucially on renewable natural resources. One of the sobering lessons of the international development experience has been that the magnitudes of poverty and destitution have proved singularly resistant to reduction in many parts of the globe. It is beyond our competence to try and explain this, but there is growing evidence that acute poverty and environmental degradation are closely linked in most poor countries. We have argued that the poor in resource-exporting countries are very likely subsidizing these exports. A reasonable rule of thumb for the 'environmentalist' would therefore be to keep a constant eye on the poorest of the poor. Their activities (for example, migration patterns of communities, time-use patterns of poor women) are often a good signal of the state of the environment. By the same token, it is fatuous to talk and write about poverty and development unless we simultaneously study the fate of environmental resources under alternative resource allocation mechanisms. The separation of environmental and development economics has proved to be enormously costly in terms of lost hopes and wasted lives.

We have argued that local and global common properties pose quite different problems, that environmental damages at the local level have often been inflicted upon such communities (possibly unwittingly) by outside agencies – very often by their own governments. There are countries where information about the environmental resource base is almost wholly absent. If environmental resources are to be brought in line with other capital assets they must as a minimum enter national income accounting. In this paper we have presented an outline of how to go about doing this in a meaningful way. We would imagine that it is the global commons which will occupy the international stage in the immediate future, as evidence accumulates on the mechanisms underlying their degradation. We have presented the bare bones of a resource allocation mechanism in which countries receive marketable permits for the use of the global commons and in which all nations have an incentive to participate.

APPENDIX I

In this appendix we present what we hope is a canonical model involving consumption and accumulation with environmental effects.[32] Our aim is to display the connection between shadow prices, rules for project evaluation and national income accounting in a context which is simple, but which has at the same time sufficient structure to allow us to obtain a number of prescriptions we alluded to in the text, especially in section 2. In order to keep to what for our purposes in this article are essential matters, we will ignore the kinds of 'second-best' constraints (including disequilibrium phenomena) which have been the centre of attention in the literature on project evaluation, as for example in Dasgupta, Marglin and Sen (1972) and Little and Mirrlees (1974).

We consider an economy which has a multi-purpose, man-made capital good whose stock is denoted by K_1. If L_1 is the labour effort combined with this, the flow of output is taken to be $Y = F(K_1, L_1)$, where $F(\cdot)$ is an aggregate production function.[33] The economy enjoys in addition two sorts of environmental resource stocks: clean air, K_2, and forests, K_3. Clean air is valued directly, whereas, forests have two derived values: they help keep the atmosphere (or air) 'clean', and they provide fuelwood, which too is valued directly (for warmth or for cooking). Finally, we take it that there is a flow of environmental amenities, Z, which directly affects aggregate well-being.

Forests enjoy a natural regeneration rate, but labour effort can increase it. Thus we denote by $H(L_2)$ the rate of regeneration of forests, where L_2 is labour input for this task, and where $H(\cdot)$ is, for low values of L_2 at least, an increasing function. Let X denote the rate of consumption of fuelwood. Collecting this involves labour effort. Let this be L_3. Presumably, the larger is the forest stock the less is the effort required (in calorie requirements, say). We remarked on this in section 4. We thus assume that $X = N(K_3, L_3)$, where $N(\cdot)$ is an increasing, concave function of its two arguments.

Output Y is a basic consumption good, and this consumption is also valued directly. However, we take it that the production of Y involves pollution as a byproduct. This reduces the quality of the atmosphere both as a stock and as a flow of amenities. We assume however that it is possible to take defensive measure against both these ill effects. Firstly, society can invest in technologies (e.g., stack-gas scrubbers) which reduces the emission of pollutants, and we denote the stock of this defensive capital by K_4. If P denotes the emission of pollutants, we have $P = A(K_4, Y)$, where A is a convex function, decreasing in K_4 and increasing in Y. Secondly, society can mitigate damages to the flow of amenities by expending a portion of final output, at a rate R. We assume that the resulting flow of amenities has the functional form, $Z = J(R, P)$, where J is increasing in R and decreasing in P.

There are thus four things that can be done with output Y: it can be consumed (we denote the rate of consumption by C); it can be reinvested to increase the stock of K_1; it can be invested in the accumulation of K_4; and it can be used, at rate R, to counter the damages to the flow of environmental amenities. Let Q denote the expenditure on the accumulation of K_4.

Now, the environment as a stock tries to regenerate itself at a rate which is an increasing function of the stock of forests, $G(K_3)$. The net rate of regeneration is the difference between this and the emission of pollutants from production of Y. We can therefore express the dynamics of the economy in terms of the following equations

$$dK_1/dt = F(K_1, L_1) - C - Q - R \tag{1}$$

$$dK_2/dt = G(K_3) - A(K_4, F[K_1, L_1]) \tag{2}$$

$$dK_3/dt = H(L_2) - X \tag{3}$$

$$dK_4/dt = Q \tag{4}$$

$$X = N(K_3, L_3) \tag{5}$$

and

$$Z = J\{R, A(K_4, F[K_1, L_1])\}. \tag{6}$$

The current flow of aggregate well-being, W, depends positively upon aggregate consumption, C; the output of fuelwood, X; the flow of environmental amenities, Z; and the quality of the atmospheric stock, K_2. However, it depends negatively upon total labour effort, $L = L_1 + L_2 + L_3$. (As noted in the text, labour effort could be measured in caloric terms.) We thus have $W(C, X, Z, K_2, L_1 + L_2 + L_3)$.

Stocks of the four types of assets are given at the initial date; the instantaneous control variables are C, Q, R, X, L_1, L_2 and L_3; and the objective is to maximize the (discounted) sum of the flow of aggregate well-being over the indefinite future. We take well-being to be the numeraire. Letting p, q, r and s denote the (spot) shadow prices of the four capital goods, K_1, K_2, K_3 and K_4 respectively, and letting v be the imputed marginal value of the flow of environmental amenities, we can use equations (1)–(6) to express the current-value Hamiltonian, V, of the optimization problem as

$$V = W(C, N(K_3, L_3), Z, K_2, L_1 + L_2 + L_3) + p[F(K_1, L_1) - C - Q - R]$$
$$+ q[G(K_3) + A(K_4, F[K_1, L_1])] + r[H(L_2) - N(K_3, L_3)] + sQ$$
$$+ v[J\{R, A(K_4, F[K_1, L_1])\} - Z \tag{7}$$

Recall that the theory of optimum control instructs us to choose the control variables at each date so as to maximize (7).[34] Writing by W_C the partial derivative of W with respect to C, and so forth, it is then immediate that along an optimal programme the control variables and the shadow prices must satisfy the conditions: (i) $W_C = p$; (ii) $W_X N_2 + W_L = rN_2$; (iii) $W_Z = v$; (iv) $W_L = [qA_2 - vJ_2 - p]F_2$; (v) $W_L = -rdH(L_2)/dL_2$; (vi) $p = vJ_1$; and (vii) $p = s$.[35]

Interpreting these conditions is instructive, for they tell us what kinds of information we need in order to estimate shadow prices. (We are not going to write down the inter-temporal 'arbitrage conditions' which these shadow prices must also satisfy, since we won't be using them.) But for our purposes, the point to note is that we can immediately derive the correct expression for net national product (NNP) from expression (7). It is the linear support of the Hamiltonian along the optimal programme. In order to keep the expression for net national product from becoming overtly cumbersome, let us denote by $\mathbf{O}^*$ the *vector* of all the non-price arguments in the Hamiltonian function along the *optimal* programme at any given date. Thus, $\mathbf{O}^* = (C^*, Z^*, Q^*, R^*, K_1^*, K_2^*, K_3^*, K_4^*, L_1^*, L_2^*, L_3^*)$. It follows from taking the Taylor expansion around $\mathbf{O}^*$ that the linear support of the Hamiltonian is

$$V(\mathbf{O}^*) + W_C C^* + W_X X^* + W_Z Z^* + W_{K_2} K_2^* + W_L(L_1^* + L_2^* + L_3^*)$$
$$+ pdK_1^*/dt + qdK_2^*/dt + rdK_3^*/dt + vdK_4^*/dt. \tag{8}$$

Now, for evaluating a marginal project $V(\mathbf{O}^*)$ is irrelevant, as it is a constant term. We may as well then drop it. In this case, NNP in the optimizing economy, measured in well-being numeraire, is the remaining term of expression (8), namely:

$$NNP = W_C C + W_X X + W_Z Z + W_{K_2} K_2 + W_L(L_1 + L_2 + L_3)$$
$$+ pdK_1/dt + qdK_2/dt + rdK_3/dt + vdK_4/dt.[36] \tag{9}$$

However, for international comparisons $V(\mathbf{O}^*)$ is of interest, since countries differ in the stocks of capital they hold. In this case NNP should be measured on the basis of expression (8).[37] Now, it is possible to show that:

$$V(\mathbf{O}^*) = \delta(pK_1^* + qK_2^* + rK_3^* + vK_4^*) \tag{10}$$

where δ (> 0) is the rate at which the flow of aggregate well-being is discounted. This means that the Hamiltonian measures the sum of the social returns on all of society's capital assets. In short, it is a measure of society's wealth. (See Solow, 1986.)

Notice that all resources and outputs are valued at the prices which sustain the optimum programme.[38] To highlight the points we want to make here, we have chosen to work with a most aggregate model. Ideally, (income) distributional issues will find reflection in the aggregate well-being function. These consider- ations can readily be translated into the estimates of shadow prices. (See Das- gupta, Marglin and Sen, 1972).

Let us suppose that we are involved in the choice of projects. A marginal project is a perturbation to the optimal programme. It can be expressed as a ten-vector $(dC, dX, dZ, dL_1, dL_2, dL_3, dI_1, dI_2, dI_3, dI_4)$, where $I_i = dK_i/dt$, $(i = 1, 2, 3, 4)$; and dC, and so on, are small changes in C, and so forth. A marginal project has no effect on the fourth term on the right-hand size of (9). (For the purposes of social cost–benefit analysis we could, therefore, simply ignore this term when estimating NNP.) Along an optimal programme the social profitabi- lity of the last project is nil, that is, its contribution to NNP is nil. This follows from the fact that the controls are chosen so as to maximize expression (7). All this is well-known, and our purpose here is to obtain some additional insights. A scrutiny of expression (9) tells us that:

(a) Were wages to equal the marginal ill-being of work effort, wages would not be part of NNP. Put in other words, the shadow wage bill ought to be deducted from gross output when we estimate NNP. However, if labour is supplied inelastically, it is a matter of indifference whether the wage bill in this optimizing economy is deducted from NNP. On the other hand, were we to recognize a part of the wage bill as a return on the accumulation of human capital, that part *would* be included in NNP.

(b) Current defensive expenditure, R, against damages to the flow of environ- mental amenities should be included in the estimation of final demand. (See the third term in expression (9).) Moreover, investments in the stock of environmental defensive capital should also be included in NNP. (See the final term of expression (9).) Now, expenditures which go towards enhanc- ing the environment find expression in the value that is imputed to changes in the environmental resource stock. We may conclude therefore that this change should not be included in estimates of NNP. (Notice the absence of sQ in expression (9).)

(c) The value of *changes* in the environmental resource base (K_2 and K_3) should be included in NNP. However, anticipated capital gains (or losses) are not part of NNP.

APPENDIX II

In this appendix we will present a sketch of the arguments which are involved in the definition of net national product when there are random events in the future that are expected to have an effect on the value of the then existing capital assets. As an example, we could imagine the discovery and installation of cleaner production technologies which make existing abatement technologies less valuable. For simplicity of exposition, we will assume that such discoveries are uninfluenced by policy; for example, research and development policy. (R&D policy can easily be incorporated.)[39]

It is most striking to consider discrete events. Thus imagine that at some random future date, *T*, an event occurs which is expected to affect the value of the then existing stocks of capital. We consider the problem from the vantage point of the present, which we denote by $t = 0$. Let us assume that there is a (possibly subjective) probability density function, π', over the date of occurrence. (We are thus supposing for expositional ease that the event *will* occur at some future date.) From this we may define the cumulative function Φ'.

We take it that the social good is reflected by the expected value of the sum of the discounted flow of future well-being. Were the event in question to occur at date *T*, the economy in question would enter a new production and ecological regime. In what follows we continue to rely on the notation which was developed in appendix I. As is proper, we now proceed to work backwards. Thus, let K_i^T (with $i = 1, 2, 3, 4$) denote the stocks of the four assets at date *T*. Following an optimal economic policy subsequent to the occurrence of the event would yield an expected flow of aggregate well-being. This flow we discount back to *T*. This capitalized value of the flow of well-being will clearly be a function of K_i^T. Let us denote this by $B(K_1^T, K_2^T, K_3^T, K_4^T)$. It is now possible to show that until the event occurs, the optimal policy is to pretend that the event will never occur, and to assume that the flow of aggregate well-being is given, not by $W(\cdot)$, as in appendix I, but by $(1 - \Phi')W(\cdot) + \pi' B(\cdot)$. We may therefore conclude from the analysis of appendix I that NNP at any date prior to the occurrence of the event is given by the expression

$$\text{NNP} = (1 - \Phi)[W_C C + W_X X + W_Z Z + W_{K2} K_2 + W_L(L_1 + L_2 + L_3)$$
$$+ p dK_1/dt + q dK_2/dt + r dK_3/dt + v dK_4/dt]$$
$$+ \pi[B_{K1} K_1 + B_{K2} K_2 + B_{K3} K_3 + B_{K4} K_4]. \tag{11}$$

(As in appendix I, we are suppressing the time index for clarity.) Notice that if the event is not ever expected to occur, then $\pi' = 0$ for all *t*, and consequently, $(1 - \Phi') = 1$ for all *t*. In this case expression (11) reduces to expression (9). Note also that no marginal economic activity can affect the terms within the second pair of square brackets at date *t*. It follows that we could drop these terms from estimates of NNP. Now, were we to do this, expression (11) would *look* the same as expression (9). But their *values* would not be the same. This is because the shadow prices (for example, p, q, r and s) appearing in expression (11) assume quite different values from those in expression (9). This is because future possibilities hypothesized in this model economy are quite different from those assumed in the model economy of the previous appendix. And finally, we should note that the shadow prices appearing in expression (11) are Arrow–Debreu contingent commodity prices.

NOTES

1 On the other hand, environmental economics as an autonomous subject has developed rapidly in recent years. Much work has been done both at the analytical and empirical levels on the valuation of environmental resources (see for example Johansson, 1987, 1990) and on the identification of appropriate environmental policy instruments (see for example Tietenberg, 1990). However (and this is the point we are making in the text), both these sets of questions have been discussed in the context of western industrial democracies. We will confirm later in this article that the context matters very much in the field of environmental economics.

2 The incorporation of environmental resources into social cost–benefit analysis for development planning was attempted in Dasgupta (1982). Earlier treatises on social cost–benefit analysis in poor countries, such as Little and Mirrlees (1969, 1974) and Dasgupta, Marglin and Sen (1972), contain no discussion of these issues. Readers wishing to study environmental economics should consult Ulph (1989) for a review of a number of texts and treatises written over the past fifteen years or so.

3 There are exceptions of course, such as perhaps the Ozone layer. But nothing is lost in our ignoring these exceptions here. We also recognize that minerals and fossil fuels aren't renewable. Excepting for some remarks in section 2 we are ignoring non-renewable resources here for reasons of space. For an account of what resource allocation theory looks like when we include exhaustible resources in the production process, see Dasgupta and Heal (1979).

4 An excellent treatise on these matters, as on the science of other environmental matters, is Ehrlich, Ehrlich and Holdren (1977).

5 The symbiotic relation between soil quality and vegetation cover is, of course, at the heart of the current anxiety over sub-Saharan erosion.

6 For instances of these occurrences, see Dasgupta (1982) and C.S.E. (1982, 1985).

7 This is very much the spirit of the exposition in Clark (1976).

8 As always, one shouldn't be literal. A very slow rate of regeneration produces a strong flavour of irreversibility.

9 The theory of optimal development in economies with environmental resources was developed over fifteen years ago and it produced a series of sharp prescriptions, much sharper than the recent literature on sustainable development. An implication of the theory of optimal development were rules for social cost–benefit analysis of investment projects. See, for example, Mäler (1974), *Review of Economic Studies* (Symposium on Exhaustible Resources), Dasgupta and Heal (1979), Dasgupta (1982) and Lind (ed.) (1982).

10 In what follows, we will be concerned only with the *real* value of net national product.

11 The technical restrictions amount to the requirement that both the set of feasible allocations and the social ordering reflecting the social good are convex. The assumption of convexity is dubious for pollution problems, as was illustrated in Starrett's classic article (see Starrett, 1972). Nevertheless, in a wide range of circumstances it is possible to separate out the 'non-convex' sector, estimate net product for the 'convex' sector, and present an estimate of the desired index as a combination of the real net product of the convex sector and estimates of stocks and their changes in the non-convex sectors. This is a simple inference from the work of Weitzman (1970) and Portes (1971).

12 We are borrowing the latter terminology from Hahn (1971). As an example of a named market, consider the Hindu *jajmani* system, which supports a set of mutual economic obligations between landowners (peasant masters) and low-caste families. (See, for example, Wiser, 1936; Epstein, 1967; Bowes, 1978.) We are not suggesting that such personalized markets are efficient, even when we take account of existing transaction and informational costs. Nor are we suggesting that they lead to equitable allocations. The outcomes are often the result of implicit bargaining among people with vastly different bargaining strengths. See below in the text. See also Dasgupta (1993) for further discussion.

13 The current-value Hamiltonian will in general also contain terms reflecting the social cost of breaking any additional constraint that happens to characterize the optimization model. But we are avoiding such technicalities in the text.

14 In saying this we are suitably normalizing the relevant variables. Thus in particular, if there is no future discounting, no continual technical change, and no population change, then the Hamiltonian does indeed remain constant through time along the optimal programme. The best economics treatment of all this is still Arrow and Kurz (1970).

15 See the calculations in Repetto and others (1989). Suggestions that conventional measures of net national product should be augmented by measures of *net nature product* (see the interesting work of Agarwal and Narain, 1989) are prompted by this concern and are perfectly consistent with what we are saying in the text. By net nature product Agarwal and Narain mean a measure of net changes in the environmental resource base. The correct measure of NNP is, of course, the sum of conventional NNP and net nature product. It is this aggregate which we are elaborating upon in the text. For *tactical* reasons it may well be desirable to present valuations of changes in the environmental resource base separately from net national product figures. But we are concerned in the text with analytical issues. For this reason we are discussing an overall measure of NNP.

16 See, for example, Brown and McGuire (1967) for irrigation water; Clark (1976), Cooper (1975) and Dasgupta (1982) for fisheries; and Repetto and others (1989) for soil fertility.

17 See Schecter and others (1989) and Mäler (1990c). We should note, however, that applied work in this area has shied away from production in poor households in poor countries. There is an urgent need for research in this field. See section 4 below.

18 Mäler (1974), Baumol and Oates (1975) and Dasgupta (1982) start with this viewpoint, and then move to ecological matters.

19 The qualification is important, since community leaders, non-government organi-

zations and a free Press have been known to galvanize activity on behalf of the relatively powerless. In recent years this has happened on a number of occasions in India in different sets of contexts. The most publicized one has been the Chipko Movement, which involved the threatened disenfranchisement of historical users of forest products. This was occasioned by the State claiming its rights over what was stated to be 'public property' and then embarking on a logging programme. The connection between environmental protection and civil rights is a close one. There is absolutely no question that political and civil liberties are instrumentally useful for environmental protection. See Dasgupta (1990) and Dasgupta and Weale (1990) for a cross-country statistical investigation of the link between civil and political liberties and socio-economic performance.

20 The classic on this subject, Coase (1960), had an argument proving the neutrality of the assignment of property rights on allocative efficiency. Coase's theorem requires stringent assumptions, including the little-noticed one that there are only two parties involved. With more than two parties matters are different, for Shapley and Shubik (1969) and Starrett (1973) have shown that an economy can fail to possess a core allocation if there are polluters' rights over *private bads*, such as household garbage. In their examples a core allocation, however, *does* exist with pollutees' rights.

21 In the current literature see, in particular, Feder and Noronha (1987), Wade (1987, 1988), Hecht, Anderson and May (1988), Agarwal and Narain (1989), Chopra, Kadekodi and Murty (1989) and Ensminger (1990).

22 By a social norm we mean a generally accepted injunction to follow a specified behavioural strategy. Social norms are internalized by people up to a point, so that the infinite chain of meta-norms we have just mentioned in the text is not required for sustaining reciprocity and cooperation. See in particular Wiser (1936), Polanyi (1944, 1977), Goody (ed.) (1973), Scott (1976), Chambers, Longhurst and Pacey (eds.) (1981), Cashdan (ed.) (1989) and a fine, analytical discussion by Elster (1989). We are not suggesting that social norms are efficient, nor that they are necessarily equitable. In fact, inefficiencies and inequities abound. (See, for example, Popkin, 1979; Beteille (ed.), 1983; Iliffe, 1987; Elster, 1989.) We are merely asserting that they exist, and that they support outcomes which wouldn't prevail in their absence. Aumann (1981), Fudenberg and Maskin (1986) and Abreu (1988) provide a formal basis for seeing how norms can be sustained even when people have not internalized them, and how they can be both inefficient and inequitable. The required analysis makes use of the theory of repeated games. See Dasgupta (1991, 1993) for an elementary exposition.

23 See the references in the previous two notes.

24 Game theoretic analyses of common property resources have almost invariably concentrated on the case of large numbers of users, where each user contributes a tiny amount to environmental degradation, but where the total effect, by virtue of the large numbers involved, is substantial. Repetto (1988) confirms that it is this class of cases, and *not* instances of large investment projects, which provides most of the bases of environmental degradation in poor countries.

25 A formal account of the processes through which this can occur is developed in Dasgupta (1989).

26 For alternative demonstrations of this theorem, see Cohen and Weitzman (1975) and Dasgupta and Heal (1979, chapter 3).

27 See Mäler (1990a) for a more detailed discussion of these issues.

28 So far as we are aware, a prior issue, whether the game in question possesses an equilibrium, has not been studied.

29 See Tietenberg (1980, 1990) for reviews of the experience that has been accumulated with such schemes in the United States. See also Dasgupta (1982) and Mäler (1990b) for mathematical formalizations of these schemes under varying environmental circumstances. The motivation behind these formalizations is that they enable us to calculate the efficiency gains realizable by such resource allocation mechanisms. At the international level, over the atmospheric commons, the proposal has been put forward explicitly in a recent paper by Dorfman (1989).

30 See Dasgupta, Hammond and Maskin (1980) for a formal analysis of optimal incentive schemes for pollution control.

31 How a national government allocates the nation's rights among agencies within the country is a different matter.

32 The model is adapted from Mäler (1974) and Dasgupta (1982). For notational simplicity we won't attach an index for time, t, to any of the variables, unless its absence will prove to be confusing.

33 In what follows we assume that all functions satisfy conditions which ensure that the planning problem defined below is a concave programme. We are not going to spell out each and every such assumption, because they will be familiar to the reader. For example, we assume that $F(\cdot)$ is concave.

34 Notice that we have used equation (5) to eliminate X, and so we are left with six direct control variables.

35 F_2 stands for the partial derivative of F with respect to its second argument, L_1; and as mentioned earlier, $L = L_1 + L_2 + L_3$. We have used this same notation for the derivatives of $N(\cdot)$, $J(\cdot)$ and $A(\cdot)$.

36 We may divide the whole expression by W_C to express NNP in aggregate consumption numeraire. It should also be recalled that by assumption W_L is *negative*.

37 We are grateful to Martin Weale for this point. See Weale (1990).

38 One could alternatively think of a sequence of policy reforms, and to use shadow prices defined at the existing structure of production. Given that the planning programme is by hypothesis concave, a sequence of such moves would take the economy ultimately to the optimum. For a simplified exposition of the connection between these two modes of analysis (reforms and optimization), see Dasgupta (1982, chapter 5).

39 The analysis which follows builds on Dasgupta and Heal (1974) and Dasgupta and Stiglitz (1981). However, these earlier pieces did not address the measurement of NNP, and it is this which is our present concern.

REFERENCES

Abreu, D. (1988), 'On the theory of infinitely repeated games with discounting', *Econometrica*, 56(2): 383–96.

Agarwal, A. and S. Narain (1989), *Towards Green Villages*, New Delhi, Centre for Science and Environment.

Agarwal, B. (1989), 'Rural women, poverty and natural resources: sustenance, sustainability and struggle for change', *Economic and Political Weekly*, 24(43): WS46–66.

Arrow, K.J. and A. Fisher (1974), 'Preservation, uncertainty and irreversibility', *Quarterly Journal of Economics*, 88(2): 312–19.

Arrow, K.J. and M. Kurz (1970), *Public Investment, the Rate of Return and Optimal Fiscal Policy*, Baltimore, Johns Hopkins University Press.

Aumann, R. (1981), 'Survey of Repeated Games', in M. Shubik (ed.), *Essays in Game and Theory and Mathematical Economics*, Mannheim, Wissenschaftsverlag, Bibliographisches Institut.

Barrett, S. (1990), 'The problem of global environmental protection', *Oxford Review of Economic Policy*, 61(1): 68–79.

Baumol, W. and W. Oates (1975), *The Theory of Environmental Policy*, Englewood Cliffs, NJ, Prentice Hall.

Beteille, A. (ed.) (1983), *Equality and Inequality: Theory and Practice*, Delhi, Oxford University Press.

Binswanger, H. (1988), 'Brazilian Policies that Encourage Deforestation in the Amazon', World Bank Environment Department No. 16.

Bowes, P. (1978), *Hindu Intellectual Tradition*, New Delhi, Allied Publishers.

Brown, G. and C.B. McGuire (1967), 'A Socially Optimum Pricing Policy for a Public Water Agency', *Water Resources Research*, 31(1): 33–44.

Cain, M. (1983), 'Fertility as an Adjustment to Risk', *Population and Development Review*, 9(4): 688–702.

Cashdan, E. (ed.) (1989), *Risk and Uncertainty in Tribal and Peasant Economies*, Boulder, CO, Westview Press.

Chambers, R., R. Longhurst and A. Pacey (eds.) (1981), *Seasonal Dimensions to Rural Poverty*, London, Francis Pinter.

Chen, L.C. (1983), 'Evaluating the Health Benefits of Improved Water Supply through Assessment of Nutritional Status in Developing Countries', in B. Underwood (ed.), *Nutrition Intervention Strategies in National Development*, New York, Academic Press.

Chenery, H. and T.N. Srinivasan (eds.) (1988), *Handbook of Development Economics*, vols. 1 and 2, Amsterdam, North-Holland.

Chopra, K., G.K. Kadekodi and M.N. Murty (1989), *Participatory Development: People and Common Property Resources*, New Delhi, Sage Publications.

Clark, C.W. (1976), *Mathematical Bioeconomics: The Optimal Management of Renewable Resources*, New York, John Wiley.

Coase, R. (1960), 'The problem of social cost', *Journal of Law and Economics*, 31(1): 1–44.

Cohen, J.S. and M.L. Weitzman (1975), 'A Marxian view of enclosures', *Journal of Development Economics*, 1(4): 287–336.

Cooper, R. (1975), 'An economist's view of the oceans', *Journal of World Trade Law*, 9: 347–77.

C.S.E. (1982, 1985), *The State of India's Environment*, New Delhi, Centre for Science and Environment.

Dales, J.H. (1968), *Pollution, Property and Prices*, Toronto, University of Toronto Press.

Dasgupta, P. (1982), *The Control of Resources*, Oxford, Basil Blackwell; Cambridge, MA, Harvard University Press; Delhi, Oxford University Press.

(1989), 'The allocation of hunger', Walras-Bowley Lecture, Econometric Society. Published as 'The economics of destitution', in *Advanced Lectures in Quantitative Economics*, vol. II, A. de Zeeuw (ed.), London: Academic Press.

(1990), 'Well-being and the extent of its realization in poor countries', *Economic Journal*, 100 (Supplement): 1–32.

(1991), 'The environment as a commodity', *Oxford Review of Economic Policy*, 6(1): 51–67. To be republished in A. Stevenson and D. Vines (eds.), *Information Strategy and Public Policy*, Oxford, Basil Blackwell.

(1993), *The Economics of Destitution*, STICERD, London School of Economics.

Dasgupta, P., P. Hammond and E. Maskin (1981), 'On imperfect information and optimal pollution control', *Review of Economic Studies*, 47(4): 854–60.

Dasgupta, P. and G. Heal (1974), 'The optimal depletion of exhaustible resources', *Review of Economic Studies*, 41 (Symposium on the Economics of Exhaustible Resources): 3–28.

(1979), *Economic Theory and Exhaustible Resources*, Cambridge University Press.

Dasgupta, P., S. Marglin and A. Sen (1972), *Guidelines for Project Evaluation*, New York, United Nations.

Dasgupta, P. and J. Stiglitz (1981), 'Resource depletion under technological uncertainty', *Econometrica*, 49(1): 85–104.

Dasgupta, P. and M. Weale (1990), 'On the measurement of well-being', mimeo, Department of Economics, Stanford University.

Dorfman, R. (1989), 'Protecting the global environment: an immodest proposal', mimeo, Department of Economics, Harvard University and World Institute for Development Economics Research.

Drèze, J. and N.H. Stern (1987), 'The theory of cost benefit analysis', in A.J. Auerbach and M. Feldstein (eds.), *Handbook of Public Economics*, vol. 2, Amsterdam, North-Holland.

Ehrlich, P., A. Ehrlich and J. Holdren (1977), *Ecoscience: Population, Resources and the Environment*, San Francisco, W.H. Freeman.

El Sarafy, S. and E. Lutz (1989), 'Introduction', in Y.J. Ahmad, S. El Sarafy and E. Lutz (eds.), *Environmental Accounting for Sustainable Development*, Washington, DC, World Bank.

Elster, J. (1989), *The Cement of Society: A Study of Social Order*, Cambridge University Press.

Ensminger, J. (1990), 'Co-opting the elders: the political economy of state incorporation in Africa', *American Anthropologist*, 92(2).

Epstein, T.S. (1967), 'Productive efficiency and customary systems of rewards in rural south India', in R. Firth (ed.), *Themes in Economic Anthropology*, London, Tavistock Pubications.

F.A.O. (1987), *Fifth World Food Survey*, Rome, Food and Agricultural Organization.

Farrell, J. (1987), 'Information and the Coase theorem', *Journal of Economic Perspective*, 1(2): 113–30.

Feder, E. (1977), 'Agribusiness and the elimination of Latin America's rural proletariat', *World Development*, 5: 559–71.

(1979), 'Agricultural resources in underdeveloped countries: competition between man and animal', *Economic and Political Weekly*, 14(30–2): 1345–66.

Feder, G. and R. Noronha (1987), 'Land rights systems and agricultural development in sub-Saharan Africa', *World Bank Research Observer*, 2(2): 143–70.

Fernandes, W. and G. Menon (1987), *Tribal Women and the Forest Economy*, New Delhi, Indian Social Institute.

Fisher, A. and M. Hanemann (1986), 'Option value and the extinction of species', *Advances in Applied Micro-economics*, 4.

Fudenberg, D. and E. Maskin (1986), 'The folk theorem in repeated games with discounting and with incomplete information', *Econometrica*, 54(3): 533–54.

Goody, J. (ed.) (1973), *The Character of Kinship*, Cambridge University Press.

Hahn, F.H. (1971), 'Equilibrium with transaction costs', *Econometrica*, 39(3): 417–40.

Hardin, G. (1968), 'The tragedy of the commons', *Science*, 162: 1243–8.

Hecht, S. (1985), 'Environment, development and politics: capital accumulation and the livestock sector in Eastern Amazonia', *World Development*, 13(6): 663–84.

Hecht, S., A.B. Anderson and P. May (1988), 'The subsidy from nature: shifting cultivation, successional palm forests, and rural development', *Human Organization*, 47(1): 25–35.

Henry, C. (1974), 'Investment decisions under uncertainty: the irreversibility effect', *American Economic Review*, 64(4): 1006–12.

Iliffe, J. (1987), *The African Poor*, Cambridge University Press.

Jodha, N.S. (1980), 'The process of desertification and the choice of interventions', *Economic and Political Weekly*, 15.

    (1986), 'Common property resources and rural poor in dry regions of India', *Economic and Political Weekly*, 21.

Johansson, P.-O. (1987), *The Economic Theory and Measurement of Environmental Benefits*, Cambridge University Press.

    (1990), 'Valuing environmental damage', *Oxford Review of Economic Policy*, 61(1): 34–50.

Kneese, A.V. (1988), 'Environmental stress and political conflicts: salinity in the Colorado River', mimeo, Resources for the Future.

Krutilla, J. (1966), 'The International Columbia River Treaty: an economic evaluation', in A.V. Kneese and S. Smith (eds.), *Water Research*, Baltimore, Johns Hopkins University Press.

Kumar, S.K. and D. Hotchkiss (1988), 'Consequences of deforestation for women's time allocation, agricultural production, and nutrition in hill areas of Nepal', *International Food Research Institute*, Research Report No. 69.

Lind, R. (ed.) (1982), *Discounting for Time and Risk in Energy Policy*, Baltimore, Johns Hopkins University Press.

Little, I.M.D. and J.A. Mirrlees (1969), *Manual of Industrial Project Analysis in Developing Countries, 2: Social Cost–Benefit Analysis*, Paris, OECD.

    (1974), *Project Appraisal and Planning for Developing Countries*, London, Heinemann.

Mahar, D. (1988), 'Government policies and deforestation in Brazil's Amazon region', World Bank Environment Department Working Paper No. 7.

Mäler, K.-G. (1974), *Environmental Economics: A Theoretical Enquiry*, Baltimore, Johns Hopkins University Press.

    (1989), 'Environmental resources, risk and Bayesian Decision Rules', mimeo, Stockholm School of Economics.

    (1990a), 'International environmental problems', *Oxford Review of Economic Policy*, 6(1): 80–108.

    (1990b), 'The acid rain game, 2', mimeo, Stockholm School of Economics.

(1990c), 'The valuation of environmental resources', mimeo, Stockholm School of Economics.

Nerlove, M. and A. Meyer (1990), 'Endogenous fertility and the environment: a parable of firewood', mimeo, University of Pennsylvania.

Nerlove, M., A. Razin and E. Zadka (1987), *Household and Economy: Welfare Economics of Endogenous Fertility*, New York, Academic Press.

Pearce, D., E. Barbier and A. Markandya (1988), 'Sustainable development and cost–benefit analysis', Paper presented at the Canadian Environment Assessment Workshop on Integrating Economic and Environment Assessment.

Polanyi, K. (1944), *The Great Transformation*, New York, Holt, Rinehart and Winston.

(1977), *The Livelihood of Man*, New York, Academic Press.

Popkin, S.L. (1979), *The Rational Peasants: The Political Economy of Rural Society in Vietnam*, Berkeley, CA, University of California Press.

Portes, R. (1971), 'Decentralized planning procedures and centrally planned economies', *American Economic Review*, 61 (Papers and Proceedings): 422–9.

Repetto, R. (1988), 'Economic policy reform for natural resource conservation', World Bank Environment Department Paper No. 4.

Repetto, R. *et al.* (1989), *Wasting Assets: Natural Resources in the National Income Account*, Washington, DC, World Resources Institute.

Schecter, M., M. Kim and L. Golan (1989), 'Valuing a public good: direct and indirect valuation approaches to the measurement of the benefits from pollution abatement', in H. Folmer and E. van Ierland (eds.), *Valuation Methods and Policy Making in Environmental Economics*, Amsterdam, Elsevier.

Scott, J. (1976), *The Moral Economy of the Peasant*, New Haven, Yale University Press.

Shapley, L. and M. Shubik (1969), 'On the core of an economic system under externalities', *American Economic Review*, 59(4): 678–84.

Solow, R.M. (1974), 'Intergenerational equity and exhaustible resources', *Review of Economic Studies*, 41 (Symposium on the Economics of Exhaustible Resources): 29–45.

(1986), 'On the intergenerational allocation of exhaustible resources', *Scandinavian Journal of Economics*, 88(2): 141–56.

Starrett, D.A. (1972), 'Fundamental non-convexities in the theory of externalities', *Journal of Economic Theory*, 4(1): 180–99.

(1973), 'A note on externalities and the core', *Econometrica*, 41(1): 179–84.

Stern, N.H. (1989), 'The economics of development: a survey', *Economic Journal*, 99(3): 597–685.

Tietenberg, T.H. (1980), 'Transferable discharge permits and the control of stationary source air pollution: a survey and synthesis', *Land Economics*, 56: 391–416.

(1990), 'Economic instruments for environmental regulation', *Oxford Review of Economic Policy*, 61(1): 17–33.

Ulph, A. (1989), 'A review of books on resource and environmental economics', *Bulletin of Economic Research*, 42(3): 219–28.

Wade, R. (1987), 'The management of common property resources: finding a cooperative solution', *World Bank Research Observer*, 2(2): 219–34.

Weale, M. (1990), 'Environmental statistics and the national accounts', mimeo, University of Cambridge.

Weitzman, M.L. (1970), 'Optimal growth with scale economies in the creation of over-head capital', *Review of Economic Studies*, 37(4): 555–70.

(1976), 'Welfare significance of national product in a dynamic economy', *Quarterly Journal of Economics*, 90(1): 156–62.

Wiser, W.H. (1936), *The Hindu Jajmani System*, Lucknow, UP, Lucknow Publishing House.

11

EXHAUSTIBLE RESOURCES:

Resource depletion, research and development and the social rate of discount

Partha Dasgupta

INTRODUCTION

Imagine a planner undertaking an inter-temporal optimization exercise. He is morally at ease with the objective function and he is confident that he has captured all technological and institutional constraints accurately. These institutional constraints consist of, among other things, the responses of the private sector to the planner's decisions. The extent to which the planner can exercise control in the economy can be great or small, depending on the economy in question. Assume next that there is no uncertainty. It is of course well known that if an optimum exists, then under certain circumstances (for example, the objective function is concave and the constraint sets are convex) it can be decentralized, in the sense that there exists a system of inter-temporal *shadow prices* which, if used in investment decisions, can sustain the desired programme.[1] Let the planner choose a good as the numeraire. The shadow own rate of return on the numeraire is usually called the *social rate of discount*. It is the percentage rate at which the present-value shadow price of the numeraire falls at any given instant. Thus, let s_t denote the present-value shadow price of the numeraire at t (that is, the amount of numeraire at $t = 0$ to be paid for a unit of the numeraire to be delivered at t along the decentralized optimal programme). Then, assuming continuous time and a differentiable shadow price, $-\dot{s}_t/s_t$ is the social rate of discount at t. Its precise value will depend on the commodity chosen as the numeraire since, except for some unusual circumstances, *relative* shadow prices of goods will change over time.

The introduction of uncertainty leads to no formal difficulties. A commodity is characterized not only by its physical characteristics and the date, but also by the state of nature; that is, one now has contingent commodities (see Arrow, 1953, 1971; Debreu, 1959). The shadow prices emerging from an optimization exercise are present-value contingent prices. The social rates of discount can now be defined analogously.

In this paper, I shall analyse the structure of such inter-temporal shadow prices

This chapter previously appeared in R. Lind *et al.* (1982), *Discounting For Time and Risk in Energy Policy*. We would like to thank Resources for the Future, Washington, DC for their kind permission to reproduce it here.

using models that accommodate exhaustible natural resources. In doing this I shall explore the sensitivity of optimal programmes to certain key parameters reflecting a planner's preferences; namely, the felicity discount rate and the elasticity of marginal felicity. The next section and the discussion of resource depletion will be concerned with a world in which there is no uncertainty. In the section on uncertainty, technical change, and innovation, I shall discuss technological innovation viewed as an uncertain event. From each of these exercises one will be able also to obtain criteria for social benefit–cost analysis of investment, be it investment in fixed capital or in R&D.

A GENERAL ARGUMENT

Begin by supposing time to be discrete: $t = 0, 1, \ldots$. There are compelling moral arguments to justify the inclusion of all future times in the exercise. There are also technical advantages in considering an infinite horizon. I shall therefore do so.[2] Since my idea here is to explore production possibilities in a finite earth, it is reasonable to postulate a constant population size. I assume that individuals in any given instant are treated identically, either because they are identical or, if they are not, because the planner chooses to do so. To be specific, I shall suppose that consumption at time t is divided equally among the individuals at t. Let me then normalize and set the population size at unity. Let C_t be aggregate consumption at time t, and let $\{C_t\}$ denote an infinite consumption sequence $(C_0, C_1, \ldots, C_t, \ldots)$. Denote by $\mathcal{F}$ the set of *feasible* consumption sequences. This set will be specified in detail later.

Now let $W(\{C_t\}) \equiv W(C_0, C_1, \ldots, C_t, \ldots)$ represent the objective function of the planner. It is often called the planner's *social welfare function*. For the moment I do not specify its form but instead suppose only (a) that it is a real-valued function defined over $\mathcal{F}$, and (b) that it is strictly concave and twice differentiable. The planner's problem is then

$$\underset{\{C_t\} \in \mathcal{F}}{\text{maximize}} \ W(\{C_t\}), \tag{1}$$

That is, the problem is to locate those consumption sequences from $\mathcal{F}$ that maximize W. Assume for the moment that a solution to expression (1) exists.

Let us now suppose that W is increasing in each of its arguments; that is, that W is Paretian.[3] I come now to the notion of efficient consumption sequences: $\{C_t\} \in \mathcal{F}$ is efficient if there exists no feasible sequence $\{C_t'\}$ such that $C_t' \geq C_t$ for all $t \geq 0$, and $C_t' > C_t$ for at least one t. Since W is by assumption Paretian, we know in advance that an optimum consumption sequence is efficient. Efficiency is here a necessary condition for optimality. We now need a set of conditions that, in conjunction with the requirement of efficiency, will enable us to locate an optimal consumption sequence. In undertaking this task it will be useful to define a new term.

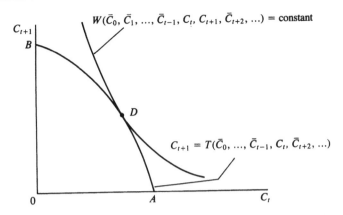

Figure 11.1

Let $\{C_t\}$ be a feasible consumption sequence. We shall call that rate at which it is found just desirable to substitute consumption at some period t for that in the next period $(t+1)$, *the consumption rate of interest* between t and $t+1$. We denote that rate by ρ_t; it is a welfare term. It is useful to consider the factors that might influence the consumption rate of interest. One might argue that ρ_t should be positive if $C_{t+1} > C_t$, the argument being that an extra bit of consumption at time t is more valuable than the same extra bit at $t+1$, since individuals will, in any case, have more consumption at $t+1$. One might then wish to have ρ_t roughly proportional to the rate of growth of consumption, or in any case, an increasing function of it. One may feel that ρ_t ought to depend on the level of consumption at time t as well. On the other hand, it may not seem reasonable to have ρ_t depend significantly on consumption rates at times far away from t.

There is a second reason why ρ_t may be positive. We might undervalue consumption at $t+1$ as compared with consumption at t simply because $t+1 > t$. The point is that one may wish to take into account the possibility of extinction. This component of ρ_t is usually referred to as the *rate of pure time preference*, or alternatively, the *rate of impatience*.

The rate ρ_t is a pure number per unit of time. In traditional terminology, it is the marginal rate of indifferent substitution between consumption at time t and consumption at $t+1$ less unity. More formally, consider $W(\bar{C}_0, \bar{C}_1, \ldots, \bar{C}_{t-1}, C_t, C_{t+1}, \bar{C}_{t+2}, \ldots)$, where the bar denotes that these quantities are kept fixed. In figure 11.1 we can plot in the (C_t, C_{t+1}) plane the *social indifference curve*, given by

$$W(\bar{C}_0, \bar{C}_1, \ldots, \bar{C}_{t-1}, C_t, C_{t+1}, \bar{C}_{t+2}, \ldots) = \text{constant} \qquad (2)$$

If W is strictly concave, equation (2) defines a strictly convex curve. We have defined ρ_t as the negative of the slope of equation (2) minus one. Thus, from equation (2) we have

$$\frac{\partial W(\{C_t\})}{\partial C_t} dC_t + \frac{\partial W(\{C_t\})}{\partial C_{t+1}} dC_{t+1} = 0$$

yielding

$$p_t \equiv \frac{-dC_{t+1}}{dC_t} - 1 = \frac{\partial W(\{C_t\})/\partial C_t}{\partial W(\{C_t\})/\partial C_{t+1}} - 1 \tag{3}$$

Notice that in general, p_t depends on all the arguments of W. But as we have seen, it may appear approximate to have p_t depend only on C_t and C_{t+1}. This will be the case if W assumes the 'utilitarian' form

$$W(\{C_t\}) = \sum_{t=0}^{\infty} u(C_t)/(1 + \partial)^t, \quad \partial > 0 \tag{4}$$

We are assuming here that the infinite sum exists. Then since $\partial W(\{C_t\})/\partial C_t = u'(C_t)/(1 + \partial)^t$, we have

$$p_t = \frac{u'(C_t) - u'(C_{t+1})/(1 + \partial)}{u'(C_{t+1})/(1 + \partial)} \tag{5}$$

When we come to discuss the utilitarian optimum in the following sections, we shall make use of equation (5). But, for the moment, I concentrate on the more general form, equation (3). Since an optimum consumption sequence is efficient, we are concerned only with efficient sequences. Thus suppose $\{C_t\} \in \mathcal{F}$ is efficient. Now suppose that consumption is reduced at time t by ϵ, where ϵ is a small positive number. Let $h(\epsilon)$ (≥ 0) be the maximum increase in consumption that is possible at $t + 1$ without lowering consumption at any other date. Suppose next that

$$\lim_{\epsilon \to 0} \frac{h(\epsilon)}{\epsilon}$$

exists. We now define

$$r_t \equiv \lim_{\epsilon \to 0} \frac{h(\epsilon)}{\epsilon} - 1$$

as the *social rate of return on investment* during $(t, t + 1)$. It will be noted that r_t depends in general on t and, in particular, on the efficient sequence along which it is being computed. Now consider a set of efficient consumption sequences expressed as

$$C_{t+1} = T(\bar{C}_0, \ldots, \bar{C}_{t-1}, C_t, \bar{C}_{t+2}, \ldots)$$

where, again, the bar denotes that these quantities are kept fixed. If $\mathcal{F}$ is convex, T is a concave curve. It has been drawn as AB in figure 11.1.

Figure 11.1 indicates that if consumption at all dates other than t and $t + 1$ are held fixed at their 'barred' values, then in choosing between points on curve AB, we cannot do better than to choose D, the point at which $p_t = r_t$. The condition tells us that the marginal rate of transformation between consumption at dates t and $t + 1$ must equal the marginal rate of indifferent substitution.

Let us now generalize the above argument. First make the rather innocuous assumption that consumption along an optimal programme is positive throughout (though possibly tailing off to zero in the long run). Assume that W is strictly concave. Let $\{C_t\}$ denote an efficient programme, and let r_t denote the social rate of return on investment along it. Suppose $\mathcal{F}$ is convex. Then for a large class of cases a necessary and sufficient condition for this programme to be optimal is that

$$r_t = \rho_t \quad \text{for all } t \tag{6}$$

It will be useful to restate condition (6) explicitly in the language of social benefit–cost analysis. Suppose that the left-hand side of equation (6) were to fall short of the right-hand side at any date. Now one marginal unit of consumption at time t can be transformed into $1 + r_t$ units at $t + 1$. But this will fall short of $1 + \rho_t$, the number of units of extra consumption at $t + 1$ that will compensate for the loss of a unit of consumption at t. It follows that social welfare could be increased by consuming somewhat more at that date and, consequently, investing just that much less. In the language of benefit–cost analysis, the rate of return r_t on marginal investment being less than the rate ρ_t at which it is socially desirable to discount the next period's consumption makes this alteration an improvement. When this marginal adjustment is made (that is, a neighbouring programme is chosen), presumably r_t is increased (since $\mathcal{F}$ is convex) and ρ_t is reduced (since W is concave). These marginal adjustments are made until the two rates are equal. Similarly, if the left-hand side of equation (6) exceeds its right-hand side at any date along an efficient programme, a reverse argument comes into play and social welfare could be improved by consuming somewhat less at that date. In terms of benefit–cost analysis this marginal investment is worth carrying out, since the return on the investment exceeds the rate at which it is judged desirable to discount the next period's consumption. If this marginal investment is made (that is, a neighbouring programme is chosen), r_t decreases and ρ_t increases. These marginal adjustments are made until the two rates are equal.

The necessity of condition (6) for a programme (consumption sequence) to be optimal is, therefore, clear. The sufficiency of condition (6) for an efficient programme to be optimal can be proved for a large class of economies, of which the economies are to be discussed in the following sections on resource depletion and uncertainty are special cases.

Now suppose that aggregate consumption is chosen as the numeraire. Then what we have called the consumption rate of interest is the social rate of discount.

This is about as far as one can go in general terms. In the next two sections I shall specify $\mathcal{F}$ and W in more details to analyse optimal programmes in the light of different ethical beliefs.

RESOURCE DEPLETION IN A UTILITARIAN WORLD

In the following discussion, it will prove convenient to work with continuous time. I shall suppose that the planner's preferences can be represented by the continuous-time formulation of equation (4). Thus

$$W = \int_0^\infty e^{-\delta t} u(C_t) dt \tag{7}$$

In addition, I suppose

$$\delta \geq 0,\ u'(C) > 0,\ u''(C) < 0,\ \lim_{c \to 0} u'(C) = \infty,\ \text{and}\ \lim_{c \to \infty} u(C) = 0 \tag{8}$$

I have qualified the term 'utilitarian' advisedly. There are several distinct moral frameworks that can be appealed to in order to justify equation (7), of which classical utilitarianism is one.[4] Since I shall not wish to appeal to classical utilitarianism, it will be appropriate to refer to $u(\cdot)$ as the *felicity function*.[5] The term δ then is the felicity discount rate. The assumptions (8) need no detailed comment. The first three are standard. So is the fourth, which ensures the avoidance of zero consumption at any date along the optimum. The fifth assumption will allow one to keep the exposition tidy and to discuss an important limiting case, namely, $\delta = 0$.

Return to equation (5). In the continuous-time formulation, it reads as

$$p_t = - \frac{\frac{d}{dt}[e^{-\delta t} u'(C_t)]}{e^{-\delta t} u'(C_t)} \tag{9}$$

or

$$p_t = \delta - \frac{u''(C_t)\dot{C}_t}{u'(C_t)}$$

Denote $\eta(C_t)$ as the *elasticity of marginal felicity*. That is,

$$\eta(C_t) = - \frac{u''(C_t)C_t}{u'(C_t)}, \quad (> 0).$$

Then equation (9) becomes

$$p_t = \delta + \eta(C_t)\dot{C}_t/C_t \tag{10}$$

The above is the consumption rate of interest at time t along the programme $\{C_t\}$. Thus, suppose $\delta = 0.02$, $\eta(C_t) = 2.5$, and $\dot{C}_t/C_t = 0.04$. Then $p_t = 0.12$ (or 12 per cent per-unit time). But for my purposes here this is not a useful numerical exercise. We want to make the consumption rate of interest endogenous to the analysis. Thus the programme $\{C_t\}$ cannot be given in advance of the analysis. Suppose then that $\{C_t^*\}$ is the optimum programme. The consumption rate of interest along the programme can then be computed from equation (10). It is the social rate of discount if consumption is the numeraire. If, instead, felicity is chosen as the numeraire, then δ is the social rate of discount. Unless $\dot{C}_t^*/C_t^* = 0$ the two discount rates will not be equal.

Consider a feasible perturbation of the optimal programme $\{C_t^*\}$. I write it as $\{\Delta C_t\}$. It is a marginal investment project. Since the perturbation is around the optimal programme, social welfare will not change. Thus, taking a first-order Taylor approximation, we have

$$\int_0^\infty e^{-\delta t} u'(C_t^*)\Delta C_t dt = 0 \tag{11}$$

The term $e^{-\delta t} u'(C_t^*)$ is the present-value shadow price of a unit of consumption if felicity is the numeraire. Equation (11) says that the marginal investment project has zero present value of net social benefits. But

$$\int_0^\infty e^{-\delta t} u'(C_t^*)\Delta C_t dt = \int_0^\infty e^{-(\delta t - \log u'(C_t^*))}\Delta C_t dt$$

$$= \int_0^\infty e^{-\delta t}\cdot \exp\left(\int_0^t \frac{d}{d\tau}\{\log u'(C_\tau^*)\}d\tau\right)\Delta C_t dt$$

$$= \int_0^\infty \exp\left(-\int_0^t p_\tau d\tau\right)\Delta C_t dt = 0 \tag{12}$$

The last expression in equation (12) is the present value of the marginal investment project computed on the understanding that aggregate consumption is the numeraire.

I turn now to a description of $\mathcal{F}$ that I shall be interested in. The model is familiar.[6] The stock of a single non-deteriorating, homogeneous commodity, K_t, in conjunction with a flow of an exhaustible resource, R_t, can reproduce itself. Let Y_t denote output of this homogeneous commodity. I assume that $Y_t = F(K_t, R_t)$, where F is strictly concave, strictly increasing, twice differentiable, and homogeneous of degree less than unity. In this section, I suppose an absence of technical progress. For ease of exposition, suppose that the exhaustible resource can be extracted costlessly. Let S_t denote the resource stock at time t. A *feasible programme* $[K_t, S_t, R_t, C_t]$ is one that satisfies the following condition

$$\dot{K}_t = F(K_t, R_t) - C_t$$

$$S_t = S_0 - \int_0^t R_\tau d\tau \tag{13}$$

$$K_t, S_t, R_t, C_t \geq 0 \qquad \text{and } S_0 \text{ and } K_0 \text{ given.}$$

This condition defines the set of feasible consumption programmes, $\mathcal{F}$. Since I am trying to focus attention on the impact of exhaustible resources on production and consumption possibilities, I have kept my feasible set very large. Condition (13) provides that any programme that is technologically feasible is institutionally feasible. Joseph Stiglitz, in this volume, analyses various plausible institutional constraints and their implications for the social rate of discount. By contrast, I am considering, in this and the following section, an untarnished economy. I shall be looking at what is called the 'first best'.

Since the optimum programme is efficient, it will be useful to characterize efficient programmes first. Let $[K_t, S_t, R_t, C_t]$ be an efficient programme, and for simplicity of exposition, suppose that $R_t > 0$ for all t along it. As in the previous section, let r_t denote the social rate of return along it. It is then well known that the programme must satisfy the following two conditions[7]

$$\dot{F}_{R_t}/F_{R_t} = r_t \tag{14}$$

and

$$\lim_{t \to \infty} S_t = 0 \tag{15}$$

Condition (14) is referred to as the Hotelling rule (1931) in honour of the man who noted it first. If output (consumption) is the numeraire, F_{R_t} is the spot shadow price of the exhaustible resource along the efficient programme under consideration. The left-hand side of equation (14) is then the shadow rate of return on holding the resource as an asset. This must equal the shadow rate of return on holding the homogeneous consumption good. But it is possible to satisfy equation (14) and at the same time throw away a part of the resource stock. This cannot be efficient, and condition (15) ensures that this does not happen.

Now, for the economy described in condition (13), it is simple to show that $r_t = F_{K_t}.$[8] Thus equation (14) can be written as

$$\dot{F}_{R_t}/F_{R_t} = F_{K_t} \tag{16}$$

Equations (15) and (16) are conditions that an efficient programme (with $R_t > 0$ for all t) must satisfy. They are not, in general, sufficient. But it can be shown that they form a pair of necessary *and* sufficient conditions if the production function is of the Cobb–Douglas form, that is, $F(K, R) = K^{a_1} R^{a_2}; (a_1, a_2, 1 - a_1 - a_2 > 0).$[9]

Certain special forms of F deserve scrutiny now. Consider the class of *constant-elasticity-of-substitution* (CES) production functions, which can be written as

$$F(K, R) = [a_1 K^{(\sigma - 1)\sigma} + [a_2 R^{(\sigma - 1)\sigma} + (1 - a_1 - a_2)]^{\sigma(\sigma - 1)} \tag{17}$$

with $0 < \sigma < \infty$ and $\sigma \neq 1$

The case $\sigma = 1$ corresponds to the Cobb–Douglas form.

The question arises whether feasible consumption can be bounded away from zero or whether it must tend to zero in the long run. Notice that if $\sigma < 1$, then average output per unit of resource flow is a declining function of resource flow and is bounded above. Hence, feasible consumption must tend to zero. The economy must decay in the long run. It is doomed. If $\sigma > 1$, then $F(K,0) > 0$ for $K > 0$; that is, resource flow is not even necessary for production. The resource enters into production in an interesting way if F is of the Cobb–Douglas form. It can be shown that if $a_2 \geq a_1$, then feasible consumption must tend to zero, but that if $a_1 > a_2$, it is feasible to have consumption bounded away from zero and, in particular, that it is possible to have unbounded consumption by allowing capital accumulation to take place at a stiff rate in initial years.[10] Since this last point will be demonstrated later in this section, I shall not go into it now. But these considerations suggest that analytically exhaustible resources pose an interesting problem for the Cobb–Douglas economy. It is for this reason that I shall concentrate on such an economy later on. Optimal planning in a more general CES world has been discussed in Dasgupta and Heal (1974).[11]

But for the moment let me return to the more general world defined by condition (13). The planning problem consists of obtaining the feasible programme that will maximize equation (7). The situation may be regarded as one in which the government chooses two functions, C_t and R_t. The rates of consumption and resource extraction could then be regarded as the *control variables*. The time profiles of the stocks of the composite commodity and the exhaustible resource would then follow from equations (13). The terms K_t and S_t are usually referred to as *state variables* in this formulation. At this stage we shall not inquire into the conditions under which an optimum programme exists. It will become clearer later that we shall need further assumptions to ensure that the planning problem we have posed has an answer.

Assume then that an optimum programme exists. A question of interest is whether along an optimum the resource is exhausted in finite time or whether it is spread out thinly over the indefinite future. It is not desirable to exhaust the resource in finite time if either (a) the resource is necessary for production (that is, $F(K,0) = 0$ or (b) the marginal product of the resource (or equivalently, its average product) is unbounded for vanishing resource use (that is, $\lim_{R \to 0} F_R (K,R) = \infty$).[12] To economists, condition (b) would be rather obvious. If the resource at the margin is infinitely valuable for zero rate of use, it would clearly be sub-optimal to exhaust it in finite time and have no resource left for use after the exhaustion date. It would prove desirable to spread the resource thinly over the indefinite future. However, if condition (a) is satisfied, but not (b), the result is not that obvious, though perhaps to observers who are not economists it is the more transparent condition. But recall that by assumption the durable capital good can be eaten into. By assumption, gross investment in fixed capital can be negative. Therefore, one can have positive consumption at all times despite an absence of the resource. This is why condition (a) on its own is not readily transparent. But one can see why the result comes out the way it does. Suppose (a) holds. If the resource is exhausted in finite time, there is no production after the date of exhaustion. Subsequent generations will be forced to consume out of the remaining stock of the durable commodity. It would be a cake-eating economy, the social rate of return on investment would be nil, and savings would have no productivity. It is this feature that could be avoided were the resource not to be exhausted in finite time. By assumption, investment is productive ($F_K > 0$) so long as production continues. But if condition (a) holds, one can have production only if $R > 0$.

If, however, neither (a) nor (b) holds, it can be shown that along an optimum programme the resource is exhausted in finite time (Dasgupta and Heal, 1974). The resource is neither necessary for production nor infinitely valuable at the margin at vanishing rates of use. The idea roughly is to use up the resource early in the planning horizon to raise the levels of consumption during the initial years while fixed capital is accumulated. Production is then maintained even after the resource is exhausted.

We have now a necessary and sufficient condition under which it is desirable to spread the resource over the indefinite future. Along an optimal programme $R_t > 0$ if, and only if, either condition (a) or condition (b) holds. Since this is obviously the interesting case, we shall assume in what follows that the production function satisfies either condition (a) or condition (b).

Since an optimum programme is inter-temporally efficient, it must satisfy the conditions (14) and (15). We know that along an efficient programme $r_t = F_{K_t}$. Using this fact and equation (9) in the optimality condition (6) yields

$$\frac{\eta(C_t)\dot{C}_t}{C_t} + \delta = F_{K_t} \tag{18}$$

Equation (18) is widely referred to in the literature as the Ramsey rule.[13] It is a special case of the rather general optimality condition (6). Its virtue lies in its simplicity. The condition brings out in the simplest manner possible the various considerations that may appear morally relevant in deciding on the optimum rate of accumulation. We now analyse the set of conditions that have been obtained.

Equations (16) and (18) together imply

$$F_{K_t} + \frac{u''(C_t)C_t}{u'(C_t)}\left(\frac{\dot{C}_t}{C_t}\right) - \delta = \dot{F}_{R_t}/F_{R_t} + \frac{u''(C_t)C_t}{u'(C_t)}\left(\frac{\dot{C}_t}{C_t}\right) - \delta = 0$$

Integrating this yields

$$e^{-\delta t}u'(C_t)F_{R_t} = \lambda(>0), \ldots \tag{19}$$

where λ is a constant.[14] The economy being discussed in this section possesses three commodities – felicity, aggregate output and the exhaustible resource. Let felicity be the numeraire. Then in the language of shadow prices, $u'(C_t)$ is the spot price of output (consumption). Consequently $u'(C_t)F_{R_t}$ is the spot price of the resource. It follows that $e^{-\delta t}u'(C)F_{R_t}$ is the present-value price of the resource. The term δ is the own rate of interest on felicity. It should be obvious that this must be constant along an optimum programme. But the shadow spot price of the resource in terms of output is F_R, and this rises to infinity at the rate F_K.

As I have mentioned earlier, equation (16) holds throughout an optimal programme if, and only if, either condition (a) or condition (b) holds. At least one of these conditions is met by the class of all CES production functions so long as the elasticity of substitution is finite (see equation (17)). If $\sigma > 1$, the resource is not necessary for production (that is, condition (a) is not satisfied) but condition (b) is met.[15] If $0 < \sigma < 1$, then while condition (b) is not satisfied, the resource is necessary for production (that is, condition (a) is met). For the Cobb–Douglas case ($\sigma = 1$), both (a) and (b) are satisfied. In what follows, we shall work with the Cobb–Douglas form because, as I have argued earlier, this provides the most interesting possibilities for the resource problem.

Necessary and sufficient conditions for a feasible programme to be optimal are that it be efficient and that it satisfy the Ramsey rule. For a programme to be efficient, it is necessary that conditions (14) and (15) are satisfied. Moreover, we have noted that if the production function is of the Cobb–Douglas form, conditions (14) and (15) are together also sufficient for a programme to be inter-temporally efficient. It follows that in a world with a Cobb–Douglas technology, equations (14), (15), and (18) form a set of necessary and sufficient conditions for a feasible programme to be optimal. If an optimal programme exists, it will be characterized by these equations. If an optimal programme does not exist, no feasible programme will satisfy them all at the same time. The three equations will be inconsistent with the requirement that the programme be feasible.

It will prove immensely helpful to specialize further and suppose that η, the elasticity of marginal felicity, is a constant. The greater the value of η, the more concave the felicity function. This will imply in turn what would be termed a more egalitarian inter-temporal consumption policy.

Let $F(K_t, R_t) = K_t^{a_1} R_t^{a_2}$, and assume that $a_1 > a_2 > 0$. Naturally, $1 - a_1 - a_2 > 0$. By assumption, $\lim_{C \to \infty} u(C) = 0$. Consequently $\eta > 1$, and so

$$u(C) = -C^{-(\eta - 1)}$$

Recall that I have claimed that if $a_1 > a_2$, it is feasible to have consumption bounded away from zero. This means that it is possible to have constant positive consumption. In what follows, I shall denote by $\bar{C}_{\max}$ the maximum constant consumption level the economy is capable of providing.

Positive felicity discounting: $\delta > 0$

One might expect that an optimal programme would exist if $\delta > 0$. This is in fact the case (Dasgupta and Heal, 1974). Here we shall characterize it in broad terms.

Rewrite equation (18) for the present model as

$$\dot{C}_t/C_t = \frac{a_1 K_t^{a_1-1} R_t^{a_2} - \delta}{\eta} \tag{20}$$

Feasibility dictates that $R_t \to 0$. Since $\delta > 0$, the only way one can ensure that $\dot{C}_t/C_t$ is non-negative in the long run is that $K_t \to 0$ as well. But if $K_t \to 0$, then $Y_t \to 0$, and hence $C_t \to 0$. Consequently equation (20) implies that $C_t \to 0$. A positive rate of impatience, no matter how small, implies that it is judged optimal to allow the economy to decay in the long run, even though it is feasible to avoid decay. This is true no matter how large a value of η we choose to express our values. A positive rate of pure time preference tilts the balance overwhelmingly against generations in the distant future. This alone is a powerful result; it indicates that utilitarianism, with a positive rate of impatience, can recommend what can be regarded as ethically questionable policies. The welfare criterion does not recommend sufficient capital accumulation in the early years to offset the declining resource use inevitable in later years. Since the optimum is efficient, consumption at some interval must exceed $\tilde{C}_{max}$. It can be shown that the consumption profile will have at most one peak; the lower the value of δ, the further away in the future is the peak. In figure 11.2 a typical optimum consumption path (with $\delta > 0$) is contrasted with the inter-generational max–min consumption policy, $C_0 = \tilde{C}_{max}$.

Of course, later generations (should they exist) suffer incredibly as a result of the initial profligacy under the utilitarian programme. They are far worse off than they would be under the max–min policy.[16]

The Ramsey rule (20) suggests that the effect of a large value of η is to flatten the consumption path somewhat, the dive towards zero consumption being that much postponed. It is interesting to note that the two parameters reflecting ethical values, η and δ, play somewhat dissimilar roles. In a loose sense, the larger the value of η, the more egalitarian the distribution of consumption (and felicities) across generations.[17] This makes sense if one recollects that the effect of a large η on the felicity function is to impose more curvature on it, as figure 11.3 shows. There are benefits to be had in keeping consumption for a long while within the region in which the felicity function makes a sharp turn. The effect of δ is quite different and its consequence is a discrimination against future felicities. A positive δ results in generations of the distant future receiving very little capital. Their consumption rates are nearly zero.

Much of our attention has been focused on the substitution of augmentable capital for exhaustible resources in production. With this in mind, we can write condition (16) in a simple form. It will enable us to interpret the manner in which fixed capital ought to substitute for resource use along optimal programmes in general. Define $\tilde{R}_t$ as $\tilde{R}_t = R_t^{(1-a_2)/a_1}$. One is then measuring the resource use in a new system of units ($\tilde{R}_t$ is a monotonically increasing function of R, and $\tilde{R} = 0$ when $R = 0$; $\tilde{R} = \infty$ when $R = \infty$). Now $F_R = a_2 K^{a_1} R^{a_2-1} = a_2 K^{a_1} \tilde{R}^{-a_1}$. Moreover,

$$F_K = a_1 \times K^{a_1-1} R^{a_2} = a_1 \frac{Y}{K}.$$

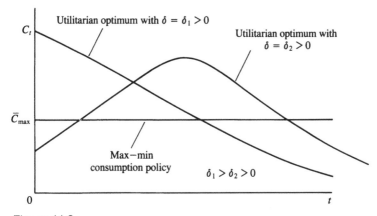

Figure 11.2

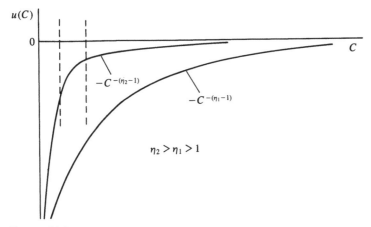

Figure 11.3

Using this term in equation (16) yields

$$a_1(\dot{K}_t/K_t - \dot{R}_t/\tilde{R}_t) = a_1 \frac{Y}{K}$$

Let $Z_t = K_t/\tilde{R}_t$, and let $x_t = Y_t/K_t$ denote the output capital ratio. Then the above equation reduces to

$$\dot{Z}_t/Z_t = x_t \tag{21}$$

This is an appealing condition. It says that the greater the output capital ratio, the greater the percentage rate at which it is desirable to substitute fixed capital for the resource in use. Stating it another way, the more valuable is fixed capital in production (at the margin or on average; it does not matter), the greater is the speed with which fixed capital ought to substitute for the resource in use. It ought to be emphasized that equation (21) is a condition that efficient paths must satisfy. Its validity does not rest on the utilitarian formulation of the optimality criterion that we have been analysing in this section.[18]

We are interested in the optimum rate of resource depletion. Return once again to our general optimality condition (19). (It is that $e^{-\delta t}u'(C_t)F_{R_t} = \lambda > 0$.) For the special case at hand (that is, isoelastic felicity function $u(C_t) = -C_t^{-(\eta-1)}$, $\eta > 1$, and Cobb–Douglas production function) this becomes

$$(\eta - 1)a_2 e^{-\delta t} C_t^{-\eta} R_t^{-(1-a_2)} K_t^{a_1} = \lambda$$

for $u'(C_t) = (\eta - 1)C_t^{-\eta}$ and $F_R = a_2 K^{a_1} R^{a_2-1}$.

This is written more conveniently as

$$C_t/K_t = e^{-(\delta/\eta)t}((\eta - 1)a_2/\lambda)^{1/\eta} K_t^{-(1-a_1/\eta)} R_t^{-(1-a_2)\eta} \tag{22}$$

But observe that equation (21) and the fact that $\tilde{R}_t = R_t^{(1-a_2/\eta)/a_1}$ imply[19]

$$\dot{C}_t/K_t = Y_t/K_t - \dot{K}_t/K_t = -\frac{(1-a_2)\dot{R}_t}{a_1 R_t} \tag{23}$$

From equations (22) and (23) we now obtain

$$\left(\frac{1-a_2}{a_1}\right)\dot{R}_t/R_t = -[(\eta - 1)a_2/\lambda]^{1/\eta}(e^{-(\delta/\eta)t}) K_t^{(a_1/\eta - 1)} R_t^{-(1-a_2)/\eta} < 0 \tag{24}$$

It follows that R_t declines monotonically along the optimal program.

Equation (24) is an equation in $\dot{R}_t$. We can now express the equation for capital accumulation, condition (13), as

$$\dot{K}_t = K_t^{a_1} R_t^{a_2} - C_t$$

Now use equation (22) to obtain

$$\dot{K}_t = K_t^{a_1} R_t^{a_2} - e^{-(\delta/\eta)t}[(\eta - 1)a_2/\lambda]^{1/\eta} K_t^{a_1/\eta} R_t^{-(1-a_2/\eta)} \tag{25}$$

Equations (24) and (25) are equations in $\dot{K}_t$ and $\dot{R}_t$. With $\delta > 0$, the pair is non-autonomous in time. We have argued that both $C_t \to 0$ and $K_t \to 0$ in the long run. And of course $R_t \to 0$. Consequently $Y_t \to 0$. The economy is allowed to decay in the long run. It can be shown that $F_K \to \delta a_2/(1 - a_1 + a_2(\eta - 1)) < \delta$. Consequently,

$$g_C \equiv \dot{C}_t/C_t \to \frac{-\delta}{\eta}(1 - a_2)/(1 - a_1 - a_2 + \eta a_2) < 0.$$

It is also possible to demonstrate that $g_S \equiv \dot{S}_t/S_t \to -\delta(1 - a_1)/(1 - a_1 + a_2$ $(\eta - 1))$.[20] Consequently, $R_t/S_t \to \delta(1 - a_1)/[1 - a_1 + a_2(\eta - 1)]$. Suppose that $\eta = 2$, $\delta = 0.02$, $a_1 = 0.25$, and $a_2 = 0.05$. Then $R_t/S_t \to 0.02$; about 2 per cent of the then existing stock ought to be extracted in the long run. In other words, about 50 years of resource supply at the then current rates of extraction ought to be available in the long run. Moreover, with those parameters the optimum rate of consumption will be declining in the long run at about 1.2 per cent per annum; while the consumption rate of interest will approach a figure of about 1.2 per cent per annum.

No felicity discounting: $\delta = 0$

The interesting special case is $\delta = 0$. Equations (24) and (25) are then autonomous differential equations. Figure 11.4 depicts their phase paths. Path GH is the locus of points at which $\dot{K}_t = 0$. It is obtained from equation (25) by setting $\delta = 0$ and $\dot{K}_t = 0$. The equation for path GH is

$$K = ((\eta - 1)a_2/\eta)^{1/a_1(\eta - 1)} R^{-(1 + a_2(\eta - 1))/a_1(\eta - 1)} \tag{26}$$

Anywhere to the right of GH, $\dot{K}_t > 0$, and anywhere to the left of GH, $\dot{K}_t < 0$. As Equation (24) makes clear, there is no corresponding locus along which $\dot{R}_t = 0$. $\dot{R}_t < 0$ at all points. Now recall that K_0 and S_0 are given as initial conditions; but R_0 has to be chosen optimally. If R_0 is chosen too low (say the initial point chosen lies to the left of GH), both $\dot{K}_t < 0$ and $\dot{R}_t < 0$. Capital will be decumulated at a rate that increases as R_t decreases (see equation (25)). The entire stock of fixed capital will be consumed in finite time, and the programme will not be feasible. Indeed, as figure 11.4 makes clear, if the initial point chosen lies slightly to the right of path GH (say, the path $A'B'$), the corresponding trajectory $A'B'$ will reach a maximum value for the capital stock and will then turn down. Capital will be consumed from then on, and, as R_t decreases, the rate of consumption increases. Fixed capital will be consumed in finite time. There is then a critical phase path AB that approaches path GH asymptotically as $R \to 0$. Any path to the left of AB eventually turns down and runs out of capital in finite time. But along path AB, $K_t \to \infty$. If an optimum exists one suspects it is this path.[21] If R_0 is chosen too high (that is, the initial point chosen lies to the northeast of path AB, say on path $A''B''$), R_t remains too large in the sense that the integral of resource use will exceed the initial stock. Such a path is infeasible.

It remains to confirm that AB is the optimal path. To do this, it would be convenient if we were able to obtain the equation representing path B in an explicit form. For very low values of R, path AB has the same functional form as path GH since it approaches GH asymptotically. Let us suppose that path AB has the functional form

$$K = \Pi R^{-(1 + a_2(\eta - 1))/a_1(\eta - 1)}, \quad \text{with } \Pi > 0 \tag{27}$$

We now need to verify that this equation satisfies the optimality conditions for some value of Π. If it does, it will yield the value of Π as well. Differentiate equation (27) with respect to time. This yields

$$\dot{K}_t = \frac{- \Pi(1 + a_2(\eta - 1))}{a_1(\eta - 1)} R^{-(1 + (a_1 + a_2)(\eta - 1))/a_1(\eta - 1)} \dot{R}_t \tag{28}$$

Now use equations (27) and (28) to eliminate K_t and $\dot{K}_t$ from equation (25). This gives us an equation in $\dot{R}_t$. Now eliminate $\dot{R}_t$ between this and equation (24). This yields

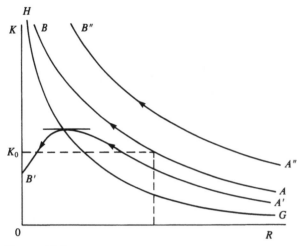

Figure 11.4

$$\Pi = (\eta/(\eta - 1)(1 - a_2))^{\eta/a_1(\eta-1)}((\eta - 1)a_2/\lambda)^{1/a_1(\eta-1)} \tag{29}$$

We have thus shown that the trajectory defined by equations (27) and (29) satisfies the optimality conditions. Our hunch was correct. Equation (27) does indeed denote path AB, with the value of Π being given by equation (29). We can now use equation (27) in equation (24) to eliminate K_t and reduce it to a differential equation depending solely on R_t. This in turn is readily integrable. I omit details here, but it can be checked that the integral is

$$R_t = (R_0^{1-\mu} + Mt)^{1/1-\mu} \tag{30}$$

where $M > 0$ and

$$\mu = \frac{(a_1 + a_2)(\eta - 1)^2 + (1 + a_2)(\eta - 1) + (1 - a_1)}{a_1(\eta - 1)\eta} > 1 \tag{31}$$

Simple manipulation shows that $\mu > 1$ if and only if $(a_1 - a_2) + (1 - a_1 - a_2)\eta + a_2\eta^2 > 0$, which is true by assumption.

From this it follows that

$$\frac{1}{1 - \mu} = -\frac{a_1(\eta - 1)\eta}{a_2(\eta - 1)^2 + (\eta - 1)(1 + a_2 - a_1) + (1 - a_1)} < 0$$

If the integral of the extraction function (30) is to converge, it is necessary and sufficient that

$$\frac{1}{1 - \mu} < -1;$$

or $\mu < 2$. From equation (31) it follows that this is so if and only if

$$\eta > \frac{1 - a_2}{a_1 - a_2} (> 1).$$

We have therefore demonstrated by construction that if

$$\eta > \frac{1 - a_2}{a_1 - a_2},$$

there is a feasible programme that satisfies the optimality conditions (15),(16), and (18), even though $\delta = 0$. Therefore this programme is optimal. We have yet to describe the movement of consumption along the optimum. Using equation (27) in equation (22) yields

$$C_t = \Pi^{a_1/\eta} R_t^{-1/(\eta-1)} ((\eta - 1)a_2/\lambda)^{1/\eta} \tag{32}$$

Since R_t is monotonically declining (equation (30)), consumption along the optimal path is monotonically increasing. Moreover, since $R_t \to 0$, it follows that $C_t \to \infty$. As a final check, notice that $C_t^{-(\eta-1)}$ is proportional to R_t (equation (32)). Therefore, the felicity integral along this programme does indeed converge. Notice further that since $K_t \to \infty$, $F_K \to 0$. It follows that the consumption rate of interest tends to zero in the long run along the optimum programme. If the consumption good is chosen as the numeraire, this means that the social rate of discount, while positive throughout, declines to zero in the long run.

Now, it follows from equation (30) that $\dot{C}_t/C_t \to 0$, (that is, while consumption increases to infinity, its long-run rate of growth declines to zero). We shall presently confirm that optimum consumption is a fixed proportion of optimum gross national product. Therefore, the long-run rate of growth of optimum GNP is also zero. The behaviour of the long-run resource utilization ratio is simple to work out, because equation (30) implies that R_t/S_t is proportional to $(R_0^{1-\eta} + Mt)^{-1}$. Consequently $R_t/S_t \to 0$. A vanishing fraction of a vanishing resource stock is all that is required to sustain the unbounded increase in output and consumption. When $a_1 > a_2$, exhaustible resources pose no threat whatsoever.

We can describe the optimal programme also in terms of the savings ratio required to sustain it. Using equation (27) in the production function implies that aggregate output (GNP) along the optimum is given by

$$Y_t = \Pi^{a_1} R_t^{-1/(\eta-1)}$$

and, consequently, using equation (32) implies that

$$C_t/Y_t = \left(\frac{(\eta - 1)a_2}{\lambda}\right)^{1/\eta} \Pi^{-(\eta-1)a_1/\eta} = \frac{(\eta - 1)(1 - a_2)}{\eta} < 1 - a_2$$

or, to state it another way

$$s_t = \dot{K}_t/Y_t = 1 - C_t/Y_t = \frac{1 + a_2(\eta - 1)}{\eta} > a_2 \tag{33}$$

The savings ratio along the optimal programme is constant and exceeds a_2.

To see what orders of magnitude may be involved, let $a_1 = 0.25$ and $a_2 = 0.05$. Then we need $\eta > 95/20$. Suppose that $\eta = 5$, in which case $s_t = 24$ per cent. This is a high rate of savings, though not unduly high.

We can characterize fully the optimal programme for different values of η. We have argued that for $\delta = 0$ it is required that

$$\eta > \frac{1 - a_2}{a_1 - a_2}$$

Now

$$\frac{d}{d\eta}\{1 + a_2(\eta - 1)\}/\eta\} < 0, \quad \lim_{\eta \to \infty}\left(\frac{1 + a_2(\eta - 1)}{\eta}\right) = a_2$$

$$\lim_{\eta \to (1 - a_2)/(a_1 - a_2)}\left(\frac{1 + a_2(\eta - 1)}{\eta}\right) = a_1$$

Equation (33) tells us that if we ignore the case

$$\eta = \frac{1 - a_2}{a_1 - a_2},$$

the optimal savings ratio falls from a_1 to a_2 as η rises from

$$\frac{1 - a_2}{a_1 - a_2}$$

to ∞. All this squares with one's intuition and merges beautifully with the max–min consumption policy. The point is that the larger η is, the more egalitarian is the underlying preference ordering. One knows in advance that the limiting case of $\eta \to \infty$ will yield the max–min consumption policy; that is, the maximum constant consumption programme $C_t = \bar{C}_{max}$ (see Hardy, Littlewood and Polya (1934), and Arrow (1973)). A crude method of confirming this is to let η go to infinity in equation (32). In this case, the equation says that C_t is constant along the optimum programme and, since the optimum is efficient, this constant level must be $\bar{C}_{max}$. In fact, $\bar{C}_{max}$ can be computed explicitly in terms of the technological coefficients a_1 and a_2 and the initial stocks K_0 and S_0. This was one of the tasks undertaken by Robert Solow (1974) in his important contribution on the question of Rawlsian savings in a world such as I have been discussing here. As one would expect, the larger a_1, K_0, and S_0 are, the larger $\bar{C}_{max}$ is. Here I am approaching the max–min policy as a limiting case of utilitarianism. Thus if $(1 - a_2)/(a_1 - a_2) < \eta < \infty$, the utilitarian optimum is characterized by unbounded consumption in the long run, while the consumption rate of interest falls monotonically to zero (since $\dot{K}_t > 0$, and $\dot{R}_t < 0$, and therefore $\dot{F}_K < 0$ and $F_K \to 0$). But the larger is η, the more delayed is the rise in consumption to infinity. Earlier generations consume less than $\bar{C}_{max}$ (so that later generations may benefit

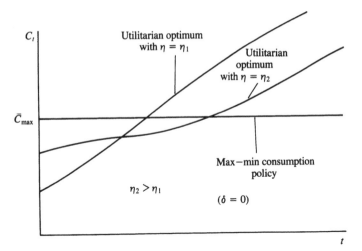

Figure 11.5

from the higher rate of capital accumulation); but the greater is η, the closer are the initial rates of consumption to $\bar{C}_{max}$, and consequently the further delayed is the date at which consumption under utilitarianism reaches the level $\bar{C}_{max}$. That is, the utilitarian optimum consumption path becomes flatter as η is raised in value (see figure 11.5). In the limiting case, $\eta = \infty$, the utilitarian solution merges with the max–min programme.

The arguments leading to the characterization of the utilitarian optimum suggest strongly that for $\delta = 0$, an optimum does not exist if $\eta < (1 - a_2)/(a_1 - a_2)$. This is indeed the case. The point is that even though the economy is capable of unbounded consumption, it is not productive enough to allow consumption to rise to infinity at a rate fast enough for the felicity integral to converge to a finite number. All feasible programmes yield consumption paths that lead the felicity integral to diverge to $-\infty$. No optimum policy exists. That is, no feasible programme satisfies the three optimality conditions (15), (16), and (18) simultaneously.

Let me summarize the results obtained in this section. If $\delta > 0$ and $\eta > 1$, a utilitarian optimum exists. Consumption and output along the optimum decline to zero in the long run. The larger the value of η (or, correspondingly, the smaller the value of δ), the more delay there is before consumption is allowed to approach zero. The optimum consumption path can have at most one peak in the future. If δ is large, optimum consumption is monotonically declining; there is no peak in the future. If δ is small, consumption rises initially, attains a peak, and then declines to zero in the long run. If $\delta = 0$, a utilitarian optimum exists only if $\eta > 1(1 - a_2)/(a_1 - a_2)$. Output and consumption increase monotonically without bound along the optimum programme. Earlier generations consume less than $\bar{C}_{max}$ with a view to allowing later generations to enjoy high rates of consumption. The savings ratio along the optimum is constant throughout. The larger the value of η, the flatter the optimum consumption path. In the limiting case, $\eta = \infty$, the utilitarian optimum coincides with the max–min (constant consumption) programme. If $\eta \leq (1 - a_2)/(a_1 - a_2)$ and $\delta = 0$, no utilitarian optimum exists (see figures 11.2 and 11.3).

CONCLUSIONS

Quite apart from any of the details that one might find interesting, the main morals that have emerged from the foregoing analysis would seem to me as follows.

A sentence such as, 'It is wrong to use positive discount rates in investment decisions, since this biases against the claims of future generations', is based on a misunderstanding. First, one has to make clear what good has been chosen as the numeraire, and second, optimum discount rates are arrived at from an optimization exercise, and one's appraisal of inter-generational equity ought to be caught in the formulation of the objective function. In general, the latter may be too opaque in that the implications of a seemingly innocuous objective function may be unpalatable. This can happen because the set of feasible actions often is not well understood, as I noted in the discussion of resource depletion in a utilitarian world. It is here that exercises in optimum planning play such a useful role. They illuminate the implications of differing ethical beliefs. But the point remains that as a primitive concept, the social rate of discount is not very useful. Working with an additive, separable form of the social welfare function (equation (7)), we noted that in a model of capital accumulation and resource depletion, the optimal long-run rate of consumption depends very sensitively on whether one discounts future felicity. If the felicity discount rate is positive (no matter how small), consumption in the long run tends to zero along the optimal path, even when it is feasible to avoid decay in consumption. If, on the other hand, the felicity discount rate is nil, then when an optimum exists, it is characterized by an evergrowing rate of consumption with unbounded consumption in the long run. But in either case, the consumption rate of interest (that is, the social rate of discount, when consumption is chosen as the numeraire) is positive throughout and, for the model discussed in the section on resource depletion in a utilitarian world, equals the marginal product of capital.

Working with the class of iso-elastic felicity functions, the sensitivity of the optimum consumption profile to the choice of the elasticity of marginal felicity was analysed in the section on resource depletion in a utilitarian world. With a zero discount rate on future felicity, the effect of a larger value of this elasticity was found to be a flatter consumption profile, implying a more egalitarian distribution of consumption. In the limit, as the elasticity tends to infinity, the optimum consumption profile merges with the maximum constant consumption the economy is capable of providing. This last result is precisely what intuition would suggest.

The last section (which is omitted in this edition) presented a model of endogenous technical change under uncertainty. The model was aimed at capturing the kinds of argument that one feels are relevant when debating on programmes designed to increase the probability of major technological innovations, such as the arrival of a clean breeder reactor or controlled nuclear fusion. Rules for social benefit–cost analysis in such a world were derived, and it was found that the Ramsey rule of the previous section (equation (18)) is modified to the extent of having an additional term, which can be interpreted as a risk premium (see equations (45) and (46)). This term contains, among other things, the conditional probability of success. It is as though one pretends that the innovation will never occur and then proceeds to set the consumption rate of interest at a level exceeding the sure rate of return on investment, the difference being this risk premium. I discussed the limiting case of an infinite elasticity of marginal felicity and concluded with the conjecture that under certain parametric specifications of the R&D process, infinite risk aversion is not an argument for not undertaking R&D. If the conjecture is correct, then the intuition behind it must be that in not undertaking R&D, one is ensuring that the innovation will not be made, and an extreme risk averter will not wish to accept that.

NOTES

Note: Because the participants of the conference were from different professions, Robert Lind, the conference chairman, instructed me to avoid appealing to control theory and to discuss the main issues in a non-technical manner. The introduction and the presentation of my general argument are non-technical and are concerned with the relationship between optimum aggregate planning and social benefit–cost analysis in general, and with the role of social rates of discount in particular. The discussions of resource depletion, uncertainty, and technical change are more technical and are concerned with a model of capital accumulation, resource depletion and investment in research and development. In the concluding section, I summarize what I take to be the main morals emerging from the analysis. The presentation of the material in the discussion of resource depletion is based on chapter 10 of Dasgupta and Heal (1979). I am most grateful to Geoffery Heal, Robert Solow and Joseph Stiglitz, who have sharpened my understanding of these matters through our conversation and correspondence over the past several years.

1 These are often called 'accounting prices' or 'dual variables'.
2 These arguments have been discussed at length in Koopmans (1966), Chakravarty (1969), Arrow and Kurz (1970) and Dasgupta and Heal (1979).
3 This is, of course, not the usual definition of a Paretian social welfare function, but I am sure no confusion will arise in my defining it here in this manner.

4 These frameworks have been discussed at length in Dasgupta and Heal (1979, chapter 9).

5 The terminology is that of Gorman (1957). Arrow and Kurz (1970) use this terminology in their book.

6 See, for example, Dasgupta and Heal (1974, 1979), Solow (1974) and Stiglitz (1974).

7 Here $F_R = \partial F/\partial R$, $F_k = \partial F/\partial K$, and so forth. For a proof, see, for example, Dasgupta and Heal (1974, 1979), Solow (1974), and Stiglitz (1974).

8 See, for example, Dasgupta and Heal (1979, chapter 7).

9 See Stiglitz (1974) and Mitra (1975). Technically, the point is that the present value of the capital stock tends to zero along any path that satisfies condition (16). Capital overaccumulation cannot then take place if condition (16) is obeyed. What can happen is an underutilization of the resource and this is ruled out by condition (15).

10 See also Solow (1974), Stiglitz (1974) and Dasgupta and Heal (1979). Recall that I have been supposing fixed capital to be non-deteriorating, and the question arises how depreciation affects this result. It is easy to show that feasible consumption must tend to zero in the Cobb–Douglas economy (with no technical change) in the presence of exponential decay. This form of depreciation is therefore embarrassing for the discussion that follows, but it is highly unrealistic as well. Economists continually postulate it in growth models for the analytical advantages it affords. There is little else to commend it. On the other hand, if fixed capital depreciates linearly in time, our claims in the text regarding the Cobb–Douglas economy go through. Likewise, if depreciation of fixed capital is proportional to gross output, our claims obviously go through. But such considerations rather complicate the notation. Depreciation will therefore be ignored here. I am grateful to Robert Dorfman for pointing out in his discussion of this paper the need for considering the question of depreciation.

11 In his discussion of this paper, Tjalling Koopmans expresses doubts about the legitimacy of using CES production functions for the problem at hand. My own justification for concentrating attention on CES functions is not that I think they are a good approximation for the resource problem, but that they expose in an illuminating manner the nature of the problem. Patently, what is of interest in a world with no technical advance is the asymptotic property of the elasticity of substitution, σ, as the capital/resources flow ratio rends to infinity. Thus, suppose $\sigma = \sigma(K/R)$. Then if $\lim_{(K/R)\to\infty} \inf \sigma(K/R) > 1$ the resource is inessential. It is essential if $\lim_{(K/R)\to\infty} \sup \sigma(K/R) < 1$. For analytical purposes, restriction to CES functions is therefore not misleading.

12 This is proved in Dasgupta and Heal (1974) under somewhat different technological conditions.

13 Frank Ramsey (1928) pioneered the theory of optimum inter-temporal planning.

14 As one would imagine, the numerical value of λ is chosen so as to satisfy the resource constraint,

$$\int_0^\infty R_t dt = S_0$$

15 The resource is infinitely valuable at the margin for a vanishing rate of utilization.

16 To put the matter rather dramatically, notice that $u(C_t) \to -\infty$ as $C_t \to 0$. Nevertheless, the implication of $\delta > 0$ is that, viewed from the present instant (that is, $t = 0$),

this is not only not disastrous, but desirable. But if δ reflects the possibility of future extinction, the probability that generations in the distant future will exist will also tend to zero.

In his comments on this paper, James Sweeney noted that this result depends crucially on the assumption that there is no technical change. Indeed, this will be confirmed in the following discussion of uncertainty, technical change, and innovation. But suppose the more conventional form of continuous technical progress. To be specific, suppose that

$$Y_t = e^{\beta t} K_t^{a_1} R_t^{a_2} \text{ (with } \beta, a_1, a_2, 1 - a - a_2 > 0)$$

Then as Stiglitz (1974) and Garg and Sweeney (1977) have shown, the optimal programme has the property that $C_t \to 0$ if $\delta > \beta/a_2$ and $C_t \to \infty$ if $\delta < \beta/a_2$. The point is that the 'origin' shifts. But the moral remains that δ is a crucial parameter. At any event, it is difficult to entertain the idea of continuous technical progress (see Tjalling Koopmans' discussion in Lind *et al.* (1982) [see p. 349 fn.], on the probability of continuous technical progress).

17 The precise sense in which this is true has been discussed well in Atkinson (1970).

18 One can in fact cast equation (16) in a form similar to equation (21) for the class of CES production functions in general. The elasticity of substitution plays a key role in such an equation. For details, see Dasgupta and Heal (1974).

19 Equation (21) says that $\dot{K}_t/K_t = \dot{R}_t/\tilde{R}_t = Y_t/K_t$. But $\dot{\tilde{R}}_t/\tilde{R}_t = (1 - a_2)/a_1 \dot{R}_t/R_t$ and $C_t = Y_t - K_t$. These yield equation (23).

20 For proofs of these assertions, see Dasgupta and Heal (1974) and Stiglitz (1974).

21 We say 'if' because we are now considering the case $\delta = 0$.

REFERENCES

Arrow, K.J. (1953), 'Le Role des Valeurs Boursières pour le Répartition la Meilleur des Risques', *Econometrie*, Paris.

(1971), *Theory of Risk Bearing*, Chicago, Markham.

(1973), 'Some ordinalist–utilitarian notes on Rawls' Theory of Justice', mimeo, Harvard University.

Arrow, K.J. and M. Kurz (1970), *Public Investment, the Rate of Return and Optimal Fiscal Policy*, Baltimore, Johns Hopkins University Press for Resources for the Future.

Atkinson, A.B. (1970), 'On the measurement of inequality', *Journal of Economic Theory*.

Chakravarty, S. (1969), *Capital and Development Planning*, Cambridge, MIT Press.

Dasgupta, P. and G.M. Heal (1974), 'The optimal depletion of exhaustible resources', *Review of Economic Studies*, Symposium.

(1975), 'Resource depletion and research and development', mimeo, London School of Economics.

(1979), *Economic Theory and Exhaustible Resources*, James Nisbet and Cambridge University Press.

Dasgupta, P., G.M. Heal and M.K. Majumdar (1977), 'Resource depletion and research and development', in M. Intrilligator (ed.), *Frontiers of Quantitative Economics*, North-Holland.

Debreu, G. (1969), *Theory of Value*, New York, Wiley.

Garg, P. and J. Sweeney (1977), 'Optimal growth with depletable resources', mimeo, Stanford University Press.

Gorman, W.M. (1957), 'Convex indifference curves and diminishing marginal utility', *Journal of Political Economy*.

Hardy, G.H., J.E. Littlewood, and G. Polya (1934), *Inequalities*, Cambridge University Press.

Hotelling, H. (1931), 'The economics of exhaustible resources', *Journal of Political Economy*.

Kamien, M. and N. Schwartz (1978), 'Resource depletion and optimal innovation', *Review of Economic Studies*.

Koopmans, T.C. (1966), 'On the concept of optimal economic growth', in *Econometric Approach to Development*, Illinois, Rand McNally.

Mitra, T. (1975), 'Efficient growth with exhaustible resources in an open neoclassical model', mimeo, University of Illinois at Chicago Circle.

Ramsey, F. (1928), 'A mathematical theory of saving', *Economic Journal*.

Solow, R.M. (1974), 'Intergenerational equity and exhaustible resources', *Review of Economic Studies*, Symposium.

Stiglitz, J.E. (1974), 'Growth with exhaustible resources: efficient and optimal paths', *Review of Economic Studies*, Symposium.

Yaari, M. (1965), 'Uncertain lifetime, insurance, and the theory of the consumer', *Review of Economic Studies*, 32: 137–50.

PART III

CASE STUDIES

12

REGULATION AND DEREGULATION:

Enhancing the performance of the deregulated air transportation system

Steven A. Morrison and Clifford Winston

In a dramatic break with past policy, the US commercial air transportation system was deregulated in 1978. Although deregulation was initially popular, primarily because it led to lower fares, public uneasiness has recently set in.[1] Airport congestion and flight delays, increased concerns with safety, and rising fares in less competitive markets have all been attributed to the change in the regulatory environment. But, deregulation is only one among many influences on the air transportation system. Equally influential are technological change, macroeconomic performance and public policies besides those having to do with economic regulation. Because all these influences are inter-dependent, each must operate in accord with the others or the system can become disrupted.

This paper focuses on improving the air system by aligning public policy regarding mergers, airport pricing and investment, and safety with the traffic volumes and patterns that exist under deregulation. We argue that the failure to bring these policies into line with the air system as it has evolved over the past ten years has generated the current dissatisfaction with the system and hampered the long-run performance of deregulation. Using an empirical model of air travellers' preferences, we analyse the economic effects of recent airline mergers. Sections on the effects of efficient pricing, optimal runway investment at airports and evaluating air safety management in the deregulated environment are omitted from this edition. We conclude that the mismanagement of the regulatory transition in air transportation should motivate architects of deregulation in other industries to establish transitional advisory bodies. The cost of establishing such bodies is small; the benefits could amount to preventing the return of regulation.

AIR TRAVELLER PREFERENCES

Traveller preferences are estimated here with a disaggregate airline carrier choice model. We constructed a random sample of air passenger round-trips with a

This chapter previously appeared in *Brookings Papers on Economic Activity: Microeconomics* (1989). We would like to thank The Brookings Institution for their kind permission to reproduce it here.

single destination taken in the third quarter of 1983. We identified each traveller's choice of carrier and routing and, using the *Official Airline Guide*, constructed every possible carrier-routing-fare class alternative. For some markets there were hundreds of alternatives.

The passenger is assumed to select the carrier and routing (for example, American Airlines, non-stop) that maximizes utility. The choice is influenced by the carrier's fare, service time, safety record, reputation and promotional offerings. The traveller's fare class choice is assumed to be exogenous; that is, travellers choose a fare class based on their income, prior planning and so on and then select a carrier and routing. We use the average fare for the chosen fare class and routing; high fares should decrease the likelihood of a carrier being selected. The dimensions of service time included are total travel time, transfer time, on-time performance and schedule delay. On-time performance is defined by the Department of Transportation as the percentage of a carrier's flights arriving within fifteen minutes of the scheduled arrival time. Schedule delay is the difference between the traveller's desired departure time and the closest available departure time and is a function of the carrier's flight frequency and load factor.[2] On-time performance should have a positive influence on carrier choice; the other dimensions of service time should have negative influences. The impact of carrier safety is captured by a dummy variable that indicates whether the carrier was involved in a fatal accident during the preceding six months. Involvement in such an accident should have a negative influence on carrier choice. Promotional and reputation effects are captured by a hub dummy, a major carrier classification dummy, available frequent flier mileage and number of cities served and passenger complaints. Airlines that are major carriers or that have a hub at a passenger's origin or destination enhance their reputations and increase the likelihood that travellers will select them. A carrier's reputation and likelihood of selection are negatively related to its volume of complaints. Finally, the extent of a carrier's network and its available frequent flier mileage are promotional advantages that have positive influences on carrier selection.

Air traveller choices are represented by the multi-nominal logit model.[3] Parameter estimates are presented in table 12.1. The coefficients have their expected signs and are precisely estimated. The fare and service time coefficients are especially important to our analysis. A quantitative sense of their plausibility can be shown by calculating the values of time implied by the model (table 12.2).[4] The value of time reflects travellers' opportunity cost and utility or disutility of travel. We find air travellers have a high value of travel time, nearly $35 an hour, and an even higher value of transfer time. The latter value reflects the disutility to air travellers of the time spent walking through terminals and waiting at their departure gate to make a connection. Both estimates are broadly consistent with previous research. The estimated value of schedule delay may seem surprisingly low, but it is plausible because most air travellers plan ahead and can make productive use of the time spent before their actual departure time even if it

Table 12.1 *Multi-nomial logit airline choice model estimates[a]*

Explanatory variable	Coefficient[b]
Average fare for chosen fare class (dollars)	− 0.0291
	(0.0018)
Travel time (minutes)	− 0.0165
	(0.0016)
Schedule delay (minutes)	− 0.00145
	(0.00015)
Transfer time (minutes)	− 0.0194
	(0.0029)
Accident dummy (1 if carrier involved in fatal accident within past six months; 0 otherwise)	− 2.264
	(0.208)
Percentage of flights on time	0.0353
	(0.0067)
Complaints per 100,000 enplanements	− 0.1309
	(0.0287)
Hub dummy (1 if origin or destination is carrier's hub; 0 otherwise)	0.7460
	(0.1774)
Frequent flier miles awarded times number of cities (domestic and foreign) served by carrier (thousands)	0.0104
	(0.0018)
Major carrier dummy (1 if carrier is a major; 0 otherwise)	− 0.4737
	(0.1358)

Notes:
[a] Dependent variable is *choice* of air carrier and routing.
[b] Standard errors are in parentheses. Number of observations is 3,593; log likelihood at zero is − 8273; log likelihood at convergence is − 1732.
Sources: Fares for chosen alternatives are from US Civil Aeronautics Board, *Ticket Dollar Value Origin and Destination Data Bank.* Fares for non-chosen alternatives, all travel times, and transfer times are from the July, August, and September 1983 *Official Airline Guide.* The variables needed to construct schedule delay (frequency and passengers and seats per flight) are from CAB Service Segment Data. The accident dummy is based on National Transportation Safety Board reports. Percentage of flights on time is from CAB, *Schedule Arrival Performance.* Data for on-time performance are from late 1981 because collection of these data ceased after the air traffic controllers strike and did not resume until 1987. Complaints are from the Department of Transportation. Because this variable is expected to have a lagged effect we used 1981 data. Use of 1983 data actually strengthened the variable's effect. Airlines provided information on their hubs and frequent flier mileage programmes. Carriers' cities served and classification are from the 1983 Department of Transportation, Federal Aviation Administration and Civil Aeronautics Board, *Airport Activity Statistics of Certificated Route Air Carriers,* and Department of Transportation, Office of Aviation Information, 'Points with Scheduled Commuter Air Service, December 1983', table 9 (computer printout).

Table 12.2 *Air-travellers' values of time*

Item	1983 dollars per hour	Fraction of wage
Value of travel time	34.04	1.70
Value of transfer time[a]	73.96	3.70
Value of schedule delay	2.98	0.15

Note: [a] Because travel time includes transfer time, the value of transfer time is obtained as the sum of the individual travel time and transfer time marginal rates of substitution.
Source: Authors' calculations from table 12.1.

differs from their desired departure time. The delay would have a high value to those travellers who change travel plans or do not plan and simply show up at the airport to catch the earliest available flight. Unfortunately previous research cannot be relied upon to evaluate our finding. Finally, travellers place some value on carriers' on-time performance records; a 1 percentage point change is valued at $1.21 per round trip. Thus if the most unreliable carriers improved their on-time performance by 25 percentage points, thereby becoming the most reliable carriers, that would almost have the same value to travellers as an hour reduction in travel time.

The value placed by travellers on the remaining effects is also revealing. The disutility that travellers attach to a carrier recently involved in a fatal accident is $77.72 per round trip, roughly the same as an additional hour of transfer time. This high value shows that the market provides strong incentives for carriers to set and maintain high safety standards. Few carriers could absorb such a disadvantage for long and remain financially solvent. Traveller complaints are less important. The average monetary loss in reputation from complaints is about $14 per round trip. Competitive advantages conferred by frequent flier pro- grammes, a hub, and a major classification are worth $32.01, $25.66 and $16.26 per round trip.[5] These advantages pose entry barriers that prevent airline markets from being perfectly contestable.[6] A computer reservation system (CRS) is also believed to be a source of competitive advantage. We found, however, that ownership of a CRS had an insignificant effect on carrier choice.

Our findings suggest some useful policy perspectives. Because travellers place such a high premium on service time, some passengers could benefit even if improvements necessitate higher fares. A useful approach to reduce travel time is to price the use of scarce runway capacity at airports efficiently so as to reduce congestion. Airline mergers that reduce transfer time by eliminating connections that require changing airlines (inter-lining) also provide traveller benefits. Merged carriers could also benefit travellers by offering a larger network and consolidated frequent flier mileage and, if they are not already, by becoming major carriers. Such benefits, however, must be weighed against fare increases due to reduced competition. The strong push of market forces for high safety standards suggests that air safety policy should be designed to reinforce rather than replace market forces.

THE ECONOMIC EFFECTS OF MERGERS

The success of airline deregulation can largely be attributed to the competition it unleashed. The benefits it has produced could therefore be eroded if competition is restrained. It has been widely alleged that the recent spate of airline mergers has succeeded in curbing competition by enabling carriers to develop 'fortress' hubs where they can raise fares without fear of entry. Such fare increases are commonly blamed on the change in the regulatory environment – that is, on deregulation. Such a view of the situation, however, ignores the change in government merger policy during the 1980s. The change coincided with, but was not the result of, deregulation. During the regulated era, merger requests were almost always denied except when the merger was designed to keep one of the carriers from going bankrupt. During deregulation the authorities have been more lenient; just since 1986 the Department of Transportation has approved eight mergers.

Judging the merits of the changed merger policy – and the mergers that have been approved under it – requires knowing its effect on airline travellers. In this section we evaluate both price and non-price effects of six mergers approved during 1986–7 on travellers' welfare. Specifically, we analyse the mergers of American Airlines and Air California, USAir and Piedmont Airlines, USAir and Pacific Southwest Airlines, Delta Airlines and Western Airlines, Northwest Orient Airlines and Republic Airlines, and Trans World Airlines and Ozark Airlines. We do not address the carriers' various motives for merging or how their profits were affected.

The effect of the six mergers on travellers' welfare has been mixed: half the mergers have reduced it, and, assuming that frequent flier mileage continues to be provided and continues not to be subject to tax, half have improved it. If the benefits and costs of frequent flier mileage were eliminated, the mergers would reduce travellers welfare. Furthermore, the mergers have largely foreclosed any opportunity to integrate the air transportation system more effectively, thus undermining deregulation's long-run performance.

A simple framework for analysing airline mergers

Our carrier choice model provides a basis for analysing the impact of a merger on travellers' welfare because it controls for the key price and non-price variables that are likely to be affected. Based on the model, the change in welfare, formally called the compensating variation (*CV*), can be approximated as

$$CV \simeq -\frac{1}{\lambda}(\bar{V}_f - \bar{V}_o)$$

where $\bar{V}_o$ is the travellers' average utility before the merger, $\bar{V}_f$ is the travellers' average utility following the merger, and λ is a conversion factor to put the results in monetary units.[7]

Because of the linear specification of the travellers utility function, (weighted) average utility is equal to utility evaluated at the weighted average values for each of its components.[8] This, combined with our implementation of the compensating variation formula, means that utility change, and thus welfare change, is a linear function of the *changes* in the weighted average values of its components. Calculating the effects of mergers is thus greatly simplified, because we need only to obtain or estimate values of those variables likely to be affected by a merger. The result is that our approximation does not take into account the substitution (that is, change in choice probabilities) that accompanies the change in the attribute of a choice alternative. In addition, we do not account for mode shifts or destination shifts in response to mergers. Not taking these effects into account means that net benefits are understated.

The variables in our model that contribute to utility change are average fare, transfer time, travel time, schedule delay, major carrier dummy, hub dummy, and frequent flier miles and cities served.[9] As explained below, their initial 1983 (weighted average) values are used to calculate pre-merger utility, and their estimated post-merger values are used to calculate post-merger utility.[10]

Sample

The demand model used to evaluate the effect of mergers on air travellers is based on round trips with the same initial and final points and a single destination. Accordingly, for each of the six mergers evaluated, we selected a random sample of 115 routes on which at least one of the merger partners provided some form of service (direct, on-line connect, or inter-line connect). The data extracted for each of the sampled origin-destination routes included the routings (that is, carriers and connecting points) and the number of passengers who selected that routing.

Fares

Beginning with Elizabeth Bailey and John Panzar, a large literature has developed that estimates the impact of airline competition on deregulated fares.[11] A basic specification that has emerged is that average fare on a route is influenced negatively by the number of actual and potential competitors on that route, and is influenced positively by route distance and the presence of a slot-controlled airport at the origin or destination.[12] Using a random sample of 112 routes, we estimate such a relationship, defining an actual competitor as one offering direct or on-line connecting service and a potential competitor as one serving the origin and destination airports but not the route. Our specification captures the notion that the fewer the actual competitors, the greater the impact of an additional one.

It has been argued that fares are higher, because of market power, when the origin or destination is a carrier's hub. We included hub dummy variables to account for this effect. An airport was considered a hub if one or more airlines serving the route hubbed at the origin or destination.[13] We capture the impact of network coverage and promotional offerings on fares by including the average number of frequent flier miles awarded and cities served. As in the demand model, the effect is specified interactively; the costs and benefits of this aspect of mergers are thus evaluated in a consistent way. Finally, route density dummies were included to account for the effects of traffic density.

The results are presented in table 12.3. All coefficients have the expected sign and have adequate statistical reliability. Based on this equation, if a merger were to reduce actual competitors from two to one (without changing the number of potential competitors or the hub variables), the average round-trip fare on the route would increase about 9 cents a mile, or $89 when evaluated at the mean sample distance of 983 miles. If the number of actual competitors were reduced by one from an initial level greater than two, fares would increase less than 1 cent a mile, or about $6 at the mean distance. If the merger affected the hub dummies, fares would go up 3–9 cents a mile ($32–$93) depending on the circumstances.[14] Mergers that decrease by one the number of potential competitors would add an additional $3 to fares. In percentage terms (evaluated at the average fare in the sample), the effect of losing an actual competitor ranges from 2 per cent to 32 per cent with no hub effects, and up to 55 per cent when hub effects come into play. These predictions are reasonably similar to other models.

The fare equation also indicates that an increase in the average number of frequent flier miles awarded and cities served increases fares. Although the magnitude is not statistically precise, it is plausible and suggests that, with competition held constant, merged carriers will recoup some but not all of the value to travellers of the network and promotional benefits of mergers in higher fares.[15]

In implementing the fare component of utility change, average pre-merger fare was calculated based on the number of actual competitors, potential competitors, and hub locations in 1983. Post-merger fares were calculated based on the changes that the merger caused in the explanatory variables.[16] For example, where both merger partners served a route before the merger, the merger would reduce the number of actuals by one while leaving potentials unchanged. Actuals

Table 12.3 *Round-trip fare regression estimates*[a]

Explanatory variable	Coefficient[b]
One-way great circle distance (miles)	0.4839
	(0.0592)
One-way great circle distance squared (tens of thousands of miles squared)	− 0.5674
	(0.0896)
Number of actual competitors on the route if actuals is 2 or less, 2 otherwise, interacted with distance	− 0.0905
	(0.0241)
Number of actual competitors greater than 2 on the route if actuals is 3 or more, 0 otherwise, interacted with distance	− 0.0062
	(0.0021)
Dummy variable (1 if the number of actual competitors is 1 and the origin or destination is a hub for a major carrier that serves the route, 0 otherwise), interacted with distance	0.0946
	(0.0886)
Dummy variable (1 if the number of actual competitors is 2 or more and the origin or destination is a hub for a major carrier that serves the route, 0 otherwise), interacted with distance	0.0327
	(0.0117)
Number of potential carriers on the route (carriers serving the origin and the destination but not the route), interacted with distance	− 0.0026
	(0.0021)
Average number of (one-way) frequent flier miles awarded times cities served	0.00025
	(0.00025)
Slot dummy (1 if the origin or destination is Washington National Airport [DCA], 0 otherwise)	9.1999
	(22.1071)
Slot dummy (1 if the origin or destination is Kennedy International Airport [JFK], 0 otherwise)	32.2650
	(25.2609)
Slot dummy (1 if the origin or destination is LaGuardia Airport [LGA], 0 otherwise)	52.1567
	(32.9722)
Slot dummy (1 if the origin or destination is Chicago O'Hare Airport [ORD], 0 otherwise)	76.0575
	(21.1712)
Non-hub–small hub dummy (1 if the route involves a non-hub and a small hub, 0 otherwise)	82.0854
	(41.6439)
Non-hub–medium hub dummy (1 if the route involves a non-hub and a medium hub, 0 otherwise)	15.3948
	(56.0104)
Non-hub–large hub dummy (1 if the route involves a non-hub and a large hub, 0 otherwise)	47.0871
	(26.3551)
Small hub–medium hub dummy (1 if the route involves a small hub and a medium hub, 0 otherwise)	91.7666
	(30.1034)
Small hub–large hub dummy (1 if the route involves a small hub and a large hub, 0 otherwise)	98.6893
	(19.2535)
Medium hub–medium hub dummy (1 if the route involves two medium hubs, 0 otherwise)	110.2812
	(39.8927)
Medium hub–large hub dummy (1 if the route involves a medium hub and a large hub, 0 otherwise)	34.3480
	(17.0427)
Large hub–large hub dummy (1 if the route involves two large hubs, 0 otherwise)	31.7839
	(15.6989)

Notes:
[a] Dependent variable is average round-trip fare.
[b] Standard errors are in parentheses. Number of observations is 112; $R^2 = 0.89$.
Source: Authors' calculations.

remain unchanged when only one of the merger partners serves the route, although potentials could decrease by one or remain unchanged. If neither of the merger partners served the routes pre-merger (recall that an actual competitor provides direct or on-line connecting service) but provided inter-line connecting service, the merger could increase the number of actual competitors and possibly reduce potential competition. Hubs before the merger were the actual hubs of the major carriers in 1983. We assumed that post-merger hubs were the union of the hubs operated by each of the merger partners in 1983. Finally, in constructing the frequent flier–cities served effect on fares, actual cities served in 1983 were used in the pre-merger calculation. Post-merger cities served were the actual number of cities served by the merger partners after the merger.

Travel time and transfer time

From the sample that we used to estimate the carrier choice model, we estimated transfer time and travel time equations. The results were (standard errors in parentheses):

$$\text{Transfer time (minutes)} = \underset{(0.23)}{83.09} \ (\textit{Number of inter-line connections})$$
$$+ \underset{(0.26)}{65.95} \ (\textit{Number of on-line connections}).$$
$$R^2 = 0.73; \ 3{,}593 \text{ observations}$$

Thus if an end-to-end merger changes one inter-line connection to an on-line connection, transfer time falls by the difference between the two coefficients, about seventeen minutes.

$$\text{Travel time (minutes)} = \underset{(0.23)}{19.23} + \underset{(0.004)}{1.204} \ (\textit{Transfer time})$$
$$+ \underset{(0.0003)}{0.1516} \ (\textit{Distance}) + \underset{(0.14)}{46.36} \ (\textit{Stops}).$$
$$+ \underset{(0.33)}{24.45} \ (\textit{Connections}).$$
$$R^2 = 0.96; \ 3{,}593 \text{ observations}$$

Using these two equations, we calculated pre-merger transfer time and travel time based on the routings in the merger samples. Post-merger values of these variables were constructed by assuming that whenever the two merger partners provided inter-line connecting service, that same (connecting) service was now on-line, saving seventeen minutes in transfer time and twenty minutes in travel time. No other possible time effects were captured.

Table 12.4 *Weekly one-way frequency regression estimates*[a]

Explanatory variable	Coefficient[b]
Constant	26.1348
	(19.8704)
One-way great circle distance	− 0.0193
	(0.0084)
Number of actual competitors on the route if actuals is 1 or 2,	14.8685
0 otherwise	(13.2183)
Number of actual competitors on the route if actuals is 3 or more,	22.8018
0 otherwise	(4.1064)
Number of actual competitors on the route if the origin or destination	3.0909
is a hub for a major carrier that serves the route, 0 otherwise	(3.0135)

Notes:
[a] Dependent variable is total weekly one-way frequency on each route.
[b] Standard errors are in parentheses. Number of observations is 112; $R^2 = 0.54$.
Source: Authors' calculations.

Schedule delay

We estimated a frequency equation using the same sample that we used to estimate the fare equation. The dependent variable is total weekly one-way frequency on each route; the explanatory variables are distance, number of actual competitors on the route (one variable for two or fewer actual competitors, another for three or more), and a hub-actual competitor interaction term. The results are presented in table 12.4. All coefficients have the expected sign (actual competitors have a positive effect on frequency, distance has a negative effect), and exceed their standard errors. Using this equation, we calculated schedule delay assuming an average load factor (before and after merger) of 0.65 and seats per flight equal to 166 (both figures are average values for 1983). A merger that reduces actual competition on a route by one carrier will decrease flight frequency by some fifteen to twenty-three flights a week, depending on the number of actual competitors.

Major carrier variable

The major carrier variable, the fraction of passenger-miles (that is, market share) on a route provided by major carriers, would not be affected by two of the mergers (Delta-Western, Northwest-Republic) because each of the partners was a major before the merger. The other four cases involved a major merging with a non-major – creating a larger major, and thus increasing the market share of majors on some routes.

Hub variable

The hub variable is the fraction of passengers who fly on routes on which one of the merger partners operates a hub at the origin or desination. The hubs pre-merger were the actual hubs of the merger partners in 1983. Post-merger hubs were the union of the pre-merger hubs of the merger partners. A merger would increase this variable if, before the merger, one of the partners had a hub at the origin or destination of a route but did not serve the route. In all other cases this variable would be unaffected by the merger.

Frequent flier miles and cities served

Before the merger this variable is the weighted average of frequent flier miles times cities served for each of the merger partners. After the merger it is the weighted average of frequent flier miles times cities served by the new merged carrier. Cities served pre-merger is defined as actual cities served in 1983 by each of the merger partners. Post-merger cities served is the number of cities actually served by the partners post-merger.

The effect of a merger on this variable is best illustrated by an example. Suppose carrier A (serving 75 cities) merges with carrier B (serving 85 cities), with the combined carrier serving 110 cities. Passengers who flew on airline A before the merger will now generate 47 per cent $[(110/75) - 1]$ more frequent flier miles times cities served; passengers who flew on B pre-merger will generate 29 per cent more frequent flier miles times cities served.

The merger thus benefits travellers by enabling the merged carrier to offer service to more cities. The cities' value, pre- and post-merger, is enhanced by frequent flier programmes, but it is assumed that the merger has not led to additional frequent flier enhancement. As indicated by the fare equation, there is a partially offsetting cost in higher fares due to the increase in cities. And if additional frequent flier enhancement were included as a benefit, it should be controlled for in the fare equation as a cost. We are thus consistent in neglecting both the benefits and costs of this effect, which, on net, is probably small.

Findings

The economic effects of the mergers on travellers are presented in table 12.5. Half the mergers reduce welfare, and half increase it, with aggregate annual effects ranging from $-\$75$ million to $+\$71$ million. Cumulatively, the mergers have a modest impact on travellers' welfare, raising it by roughly $70 million annually. The per passenger effects of each merger are also small, on average always less than $2.50.

The effects of the mergers generally consist of a welfare loss from increased fares coupled with a welfare gain from increased frequent flier mileage and cities served. The expansion of a major carrier is a significant source of benefits in the USAir–Piedmont merger. As shown in table 12.6, the benefits from increased frequent flier mileage and cities served are critical. If frequent flier benefits and costs were eliminated, the mergers would lower annual welfare by approximately $335 million in aggregate. Taxing frequent flier mileage (benefits and costs are assumed to fall by one-third) would cause the aggregate effect of the mergers to become negative $67 million.

The anti-competitive effects of each merger depend on how potential and actual competition are affected and on hub formation. As shown in table 12.7, actual and potential competition are not affected in a large percentage of the routes involved in the American Airlines–AirCalifornia and USAir–Pacific Southwest Airlines mergers, so that per passenger fare losses in those cases are fairly small. A substantial number of routes in the other mergers experience a loss in potential competition, and roughly 12–25 per cent of routes experience a loss in actual competition. In those cases, with the exception of TWA–Ozark, fare losses are greater.

Discussion

Most discussions of the recent airline mergers have focused on their effects on fares. We have found that when non-price effects are included in the evaluation, three of the mergers have improved travellers welfare. Although we have not quantified them, carriers' operating efficiencies derived from the mergers add to this positive aspect of mergers.

A major concern raised by our findings is that the mergers' offsetting positive effect on travellers is heavily dependent on airlines' continuing their promotional activities. If frequent flier programmes are eliminated, the mergers' effect on travelers is negative. On the other hand, without frequent flier programmes airline markets would be more contestable.

More worrisome is the impact of the mergers on deregulation. Anti-competitive effects of mergers have already eroded benefits from fare deregulation; more important, the restructuring of carriers' networks has virtually eliminated the possibility of continued progress in achieving an optimal configuration of carrier competition.[17] Our earlier study found that welfare under deregulation fell short of the optimal level by $2.5 billion (1977 dollars).[18] The source of this gap was insufficient competition on medium- to low-density routes; competition on high-

Table 12.5 *Economic effects of airline mergers*

Effect[a]	American Airlines–Air California	USAir–Piedmont	USAir–Pacific Southwest Airlines	Delta–Western	Northwest–Republic	Trans World Airlines–Ozark	Total
	Total annual value (millions of 1983 dollars)						
Change in fares due to decreased competition	− 13.40	− 80.88	− 90.81	− 104.51	− 101.31	− 32.04	− 422.95
Change in fares due to additional cities served	− 26.49	− 47.35	− 20.63	− 139.97	− 83.64	− 33.37	− 351.45
Change in travel time (including transfer time)	0.00	0.02	0.00	0.00	0.10	0.06	0.18
Change in schedule delay	− 0.54	− 2.15	0.35	− 2.53	− 2.16	− 1.21	− 8.24
Change in frequent flier mileage and cities served	97.72	67.52	28.32	310.38	171.63	78.37	753.94
Change in major dummy	11.27	41.08	7.23	0.0	0.0	17.26	76.84
Change in hub dummy	2.39	9.03	0.20	1.61	5.47	0.00	18.70
Total	70.96	− 12.73	− 75.33	64.98	− 9.91	29.05	67.02
	Value per passenger (1983 dollars)						
Change in fares due to decreased competition	− 0.41	− 2.45	− 2.75	− 2.07	− 2.58	− 1.09	− 1.94
Change in fares due to additional cities served	− 0.77	− 1.44	− 0.62	− 2.76	− 2.14	− 1.14	− 1.61
Change in travel time (including transfer time)	0.00	0.00	0.00	0.00	0.00	0.00	0.00
Change in schedule delay	− 0.02	− 0.07	0.01	− 0.05	− 0.06	− 0.04	− 0.04
Change in frequent flier mileage and cities served	2.83	2.05	0.86	6.13	4.38	2.67	3.42
Change in major dummy	0.33	1.25	0.22	0.00	0.00	0.59	0.35
Change in hub dummy	0.07	0.27	0.00	0.03	0.14	0.00	0.09
Total	2.05	− 0.39	− 2.28	1.28	− 0.25	0.99	0.27

Note: [a] Positive indicates an improvement.
Source: Authors' calculations.

Table 12.6 *Economic effects of mergers under varying assumptions about benefits and costs from frequent flier mileage and cities served*[a] *(millions of 1983 dollars)*

Assumption	American Airlines-Air California	USAir-Piedmont	USAir-Pacific Southwest Airlines	Delta-Western	Northwest-Republic	Trans World Airlines-Ozark	Total
Full benefits from frequent flier mileage and cities served (base case)	70.96	− 12.73	− 75.33	64.98	− 9.91	29.05	67.02
Benefits from frequent flier mileage and cities served fall by one-third	47.21	− 19.45	− 77.89	8.18	− 39.24	14.05	− 67.14
No benefits from frequent flier mileage and cities served	− 0.28	− 32.90	− 83.03	− 105.43	− 97.89	− 15.94	− 335.47

Note: [a] The change in the costs of frequent flier mileage and cities served, originally based on the fare equation, is assumed to be proportional to the change in benefits.
Source: Authors' calculations.

Table 12.7 *Effects of mergers on actual and potential competition[a] (percentage of routes affected)*

Assumption	American Airlines– Air California	USAir– Piedmont	USAir– Pacific Southwest Airlines	Delta– Western	Northwest– Republic	Trans World Airlines– Ozark
No change in actual and potential competition	91.3	50.0	95.5	67.5	36.5	59.1
No change in actual competition; decrease in potential competition	5.2	30.7	3.6	19.3	37.4	15.7
Decrease in actual competition; no change in potential competition	3.5	18.4	0.0	12.3	25.2	19.1
Increase in actual competition; decrease in potential competition	0.0	0.0	0.0	0.0	0.9	2.6
No change in actual competition; increase in potential competition	0.0	0.9	0.9	0.9	0.0	1.7
Increase in actual competition; no change in potential competition	0.0	0.0	0.0	0.0	0.0	1.7

Note: [a] A potential carrier serves the origin or the destination, or both, but not the route.
Source: Authors' calculations.

density routes was adequate. Mergers have not diminished competition on high-density routes enough to threaten to erase deregulation's benefits, but by substantially foreclosing the possibility of increased competition on low- to medium-density routes, mergers have made it even less likely that deregulation will reach its full potential.

To be sure, public policy towards mergers is not designed with this concern in mind. If the net benefits are found to be positive, as they were in half the cases analysed here, then the affirmative decisions have arguably served the public interest. There is unfortunately no legal channel whereby the Department of Transportation could have forced TWA to acquire, for example, Eastern instead of Ozark because such a merger would generate greater social benefits.

Policy can still minimize the costs of mergers while promoting competition. Promotion of entry by foreign carriers, which would certainly require reciprocal foreign entry rights to American carriers, and prevention of airport gate and slot monopolization are two constructive steps in this direction. A third, taxation of frequent flier mileage, could actually raise travellers' welfare and provide revenues to the government by lowering entry barriers. A final, if controversial, step would be to broaden the concept of anti-competitive effect in any future merger evaluations to incorporate the long-run opportunity cost of network consolidation. Public policy has failed deregulation by not doing so in recent merger cases.

LEARNING FROM THIS ASSESSMENT

Public policy towards airline mergers, airport capacity utilization, and air safety has not been responsive to the changes in the air transportation system brought by deregulation and has consequently lowered social welfare in the long run. The costs of these policy failures have been magnified because each has had adverse effects on other aspects of the system: mergers have strengthened individual carriers' control of major airports, making it easier for them to block pricing innovations that could curb congestion; failure to deal with congestion effectively has jeopardized safety and has led to limits on operations that reduce competition; mismanagement of air safety has increased congestion and led to calls to decrease airport activity, thus hurting competition.

What can be learned from this assessment? First, practical solutions to the problems at hand present themselves. The policy changes we have proposed constitute the foundations of a plan for Samuel Skinner, the new secretary of transportation. In particular, future merger decisions should be based on a broader and longer-run view of the effects of mergers on network development and competition. To help minimize the impact of previous decisions on competition, the secretary should take the lead in promoting foreign carrier entry and reciprocal agreements with other countries. Such a reform would not only enhance domestic competition, but perhaps pave the way for deregulation of international flights. The secretary should also remove any legal obstacles to and promote the use of airport congestion pricing. In addition, pricing 'innovations' should be applied to all carriers with the objective of regulating the use of scarce runway capacity during peak periods. It should not be applied just to one type of carrier (general aviation), as was recently the case at Boston's Logan Airport. Although the policy at Logan probably increased net welfare, it was politically insensitive and thus jeopardized the introduction of more beneficial types of congestion pricing. Finally, the secretary should recognize that the Federal Aviation Administration's objectives could be better achieved if it were an independent agency. The Department of Transportation should not oppose a separation of responsibilities.

Beyond the matter of practical solutions to existing problems, it is important to explain why policy that compromised the performance of the deregulated air system was formulated. Given that Congress passed the deregulation legislation and still supports it, and that the FAA and DOT are administered by appointees made by a pro-deregulation administration, it is difficult to see how legislative and bureaucratic interests would be served by policies that on balance harm air system performance. Local governmental interests may partially explain why airports have not strongly advocated efficient tolls; but this behaviour cannot be easily extended to the national level, especially when such tolls could lower federal spending.

Our explanation is that errors in forecasting deregulation's long term effects on traffic volumes and patterns are responsible for the counter-productive policies. Deregulation's architects did not foresee the need to establish an advisory body that would be responsible for guiding the air system's transition to a stable deregulated equilibrium. The agencies assigned specific tasks misjudged deregulation's effect on their area of responsibility.[19]

The Airline Deregulation Act of 1978 quickly phased the Civil Aeronautics Board out of existence. (Coincidentally, its complete elimination on January 1, 1986, just preceded the appearance of major problems in the air system.) Specific responsibilities were parceled out to the FAA and DOT. The FAA, whose long-standing responsibility for safety was not affected by deregulation, acknowledged that it was 'caught unprepared and underestimated the changes deregulation would bring'.[20] DOT, taking over the CAB's responsibility for evaluating mergers, had no long-run vision of the industry and simply passed on the administration's sympathies.[21] DOT's approach towards congestion and delays amounted to coaxing carriers to limit operations and to report on-time performance.[22]

Although it is understandable that architects of deregulation believe that it is necessary to eliminate all vestiges of regulation quickly, if only to make it difficult to reregulate, such zeal may prove counterproductive in the long run. The reputation of airline deregulation and the performance of the air system have been harmed by policies that could have been avoided had provisions been made for an advisory body responsible for guiding the air system's transition.[23] A forceful advocate in the policy-making arena was needed to point out existing policies' incompatibilities with deregulation and to articulate the need for greater caution in judging the anti-competitive effects of mergers, for congestion pricing at airports, and for an adaptive and visionary FAA.

Fortunately, it is not too late for other industries to learn from the air experience. Because it is probably too late to form a transitional advisory body for surface freight transportation, the Interstate Commerce Commission should not be forced to close its doors. It can still help the freight transportation system in its transition to full deregulation by promoting policies towards captive railroad shippers and collective ratemaking that are compatible with unregulated competition. As deregulation evolves in telecommunications, banking, and natural gas, an advisory body should be established to manage a transition in these industries that promotes the goals of deregulation.[24]

Despite the overwhelming evidence that airline deregulation has produced significant gains for society, ineffective management of the regulatory transition has provided an opening for advocates of reregulation. Proponents of deregulation have great incentives to prevent this from happening elsewhere.

NOTES

We are grateful to Robert Hahn, Richard Johnson, Joan Winston, and the conference participants for their comments and to Leslie Siddeley and Carol Evans for research assistance.

1 The overall decrease in fares is documented in John R. Meyer and Clinton V. Oster, Jr (eds.) (1981), *Airline Deregulation: The Early Experience*, Boston, Auburn House; Elizabeth E. Bailey, David R. Graham, and Daniel P. Kaplan (1985), *Deregulating the Airlines*, MIT Press; and Steven Morrison and Clifford Winston, *The Economic Effects of Airline Deregulation*, Brookings, 1986.

2 Following George W. Douglas and James C. Miller III (1979), *Economic Regulation of Domestic Air Transport: Theory and Policy* (Brookings), schedule delay (*SD*) is calculated empirically as

$$SD = 92 F^{-0.456} + \frac{12010}{F} \cdot P^{0.5725} \cdot (S - P)^{-1.79}$$

where F is daily flight frequency, P is passengers per flight and S is seats per flight.

3 The multi-nominal logit choice probabilities are given by

$$Prob_i = \exp V_i(\beta, X_i) / \sum_{j=1}^{J} \exp V_j(\beta, X_j)$$

where $Prob_i$ is the probability of selecting carrier-routing combination i, V_i is the mean utility of alternative i, which is a function of parameters denoted by β and explanatory variables denoted by X. Because the traveller often had hundreds of carrier-routing alternatives to choose from, estimation was performed by using a sub-sample of the choice set that consisted of ten alternatives including the chosen alternative. Daniel McFadden, 'Modelling the Choice of Residential Location', in Anders Karlgvist *et al.* (eds.) (1978), *Spatial Interaction Theory and Planning Models*, Studies in Regional Science and Urban Economics 3, New York, North-Holland, pp. 75–96, has shown that, predicated on the assumption that the multi-nominal logit model is correct, this sampling procedure results in consistent estimates of multi-nominal logit parameters. We tested for possible violations of the independence from irrelevant alternatives property associated with the multi-nominal logit model applying a test suggested by Kenneth A. Small and Cheng Hsiac (1985), 'Multi-nominal Logit Specification Tests', *International Economic Review*, 26 (October): 619–27. We constructed choice sets composed of different random samples of ten and five alternative carrier-routing combinations. In all cases, we could not reject the null hypothesis of a multi-nominal logit structure.

4 These values represent the marginal rate of substitution of money for various components of time spent in travel. They are calculated by forming the ratio of the time and fare coefficients. We attempted to estimate different time coefficients for first class and other travellers, whose value of time might be expected to differ. Our attempts proved unsuccessful largely because all passengers' service time is the same regardless of any differences in the price paid for the trip.

5 The estimate of the value of frequent flier mileage for a round trip is based on an average of seventy-six cities served, which yields a value of a frequent flier mile of 2.7 cents. The average round-trip distance in our sample is 1,179 miles, which gives the round-trip value in the text. (The value of a city for the mean number of frequent flier miles is 42 cents.)

6 Steven A. Morrison and Clifford Winston (1987), 'Empirical implications and tests of the contestability hypothesis', *Journal of Law and Economics*, 30 (April): 53–66, statistically reject perfect contestability in airline markets, and Michael E. Levine (1987), 'Airline competition in deregulated markets: theory, firm strategy, and public policy,' *Yale Journal on Regulation*, 4 (Spring): pp. 393–494, includes an institutional discussion of why perfect contestability is not attainable in these markets. The role of travel agents in creating entry barriers is likely to be picked up by the hub dummy.

7 The exact formula for the *CV* is given by

$$CV = -\frac{1}{\lambda}\left[\log \sum_{i=1}^{n}\exp(V_i)\right]_{V_o}^{V_f}$$

where V_i is the utility associated with carrier-routing i and n is the number of carrier-routing alternatives. The approximation given in the text is obtained by taking a Taylor's expansion of the exact formula and dropping higher-order terms. The approximation's accuracy obviously depends on the degree of variation among carrier-routing utilities, which should not be too great. The value of λ in the formula is obtained (by Roy's Identity) from the fare coefficient in the choice model.

8 The weights are equal to the fraction of passengers who selected a particular alternative.

9 Because of the difficulty of modelling a merger's effect on accidents, on-time performance and complaints, we assume that these variables are unaffected by mergers.

10 Thus, variables that were initially dummy variables in the carrier choice model take on values between zero and one.

11 Elizabeth E. Bailey and John C. Panzar (1981), 'The contestability of airline markets during the transition to deregulation', *Law and Contemporary Problems*, 44 (Winter): 125–45.

12 A change in average fare can be interpreted as reflecting absolute changes in fare levels or a change in the percentage of discount fare seats available.

13 Defining an airport as a hub if only one airline serving the route hubbed at the origin or destination did not produce any estimation improvements.

14 This would occur if the origin or destination was already a hub for one of the major carriers serving the route and the merger reduced the number of actual carriers to one (in which case this hub effect alone would cause fares to rise about $61). The hub effect would also come into play if, for example, carrier A (but not carrier B) serves the route and the origin or destination is a hub for carrier B. If the number of actual competitors serving the route remaining after merger were more than two, the hub effect alone would cause fares to increase about $32. If the resulting carrier had a monopoly on the route, fares would increase about $93 because of the hub effect.

15 Assuming the same round-trip distance (1,179 miles) and number of cities (seventy-six) in the demand calculation (note 5), a frequent flier mile raises average fare 0.9 cents (compared with the 2.7 cent valuation by travellers) and an additional city served raises average fare 14 cents (compared with the 42 cent valuation by travellers).

16 An alternative approach would be to use changes in actual fares. This was not pursued because investigations of actual pre- and post-merger fares in specific markets revealed that, even for a short time span, changes in actual fares are idiosyncratic, reflecting other effects besides mergers.

17 It is important to bear in mind that even with the mergers, the percentage of travellers on carriers that have more than a 70 per cent market share was greater in 1978 than in 1987; conversely, the percentage of travellers on carriers with less than a 30 per cent market share is greater in 1987 than in 1978. See Air Transport Association (1988), *Airline Deregulation 10 Years Later: What Has It Done for the Consumer?* (October).

18 Morrison and Winston, *Economic Effects of Airline Deregulation*, pp. 58–9. This finding and the following argument should be qualified as evaluating optimal welfare independent of whether it could actually be attained.

19 Dennis Sheehan and Clifford Winston (1987), 'Expectations and automobile policy', in Clifford Winston and Associates, *Blind Intersection? Policy and the Automobile Industry* (Brookings), argue that congressional misperceptions of the effects of various legislation hurt the welfare of automobile consumers and producers. Similarly, Michael E. Levine (1981), 'Revisionism revised? Airline deregulation and the public interest', *Law and Contemporary Problems*, 44 (Winter): 179–95, argues that airline regulation was imposed by a Congress that, while attempting to act in the public interest, made a mistake.

20 Statement by Bob Buckhorn, FAA spokesman, quoted in Laura Parker (1988), 'FAA Controller Work Force Back to Prestrike Strength', *Washington Post*, October 2.

21 To be sure, one could make a case that these sympathies were consistent with the plausible *ex ante* benefit–cost evaluation.

22 One could also argue that this was the best policy DOT could pursue given their authority.

23 The members of this transitional advisory body could have been drawn from the CAB, other areas of government, industry and academia. It would have been important that those people taken from the CAB not promote their agency's regulatory interests, but contribute to the advisory body's goal of managing a smooth regulatory transition. The 'usual group of suspects' (Alfred Kahn, Elizabeth Bailey, Michael Levine) could easily have met this criterion for membership.

24 This body should be bipartisan, with a finite lifetime. One option, to ensure its independence from an administration's political pressures (either anti- or blindly pro-deregulation), would be a congressionally chartered body with an automatic sunset provision. This body's mandate would be strategic thinking about the long-term effects of deregulation, anticipating how and where these effects would stress the evolving equilibrium. Its task would be to formulate contingency plans and policy advice, not to manage the industry's daily operations.

13

PRICING:

Pricing and congestion: Economic principles relevant to pricing roads

David M. Newbery

1 INTRODUCTION

The road network is a costly and increasingly scarce resource. For the UK the Department of Transport (1989a) calculates that total road expenditures (capital and current) or 'road costs' averaged £4.34 billion per year at 1989/90 prices for the period 1987/8–1989/90. Public expenditure on roads has been fairly stable recently, increasing by about 6 per cent in real terms between 1982/3 and 1988/9, but with no strong trend (Department of Transport, 1989b, tables 1.18, 1.22, 1.23). From the 24.6 million vehicles registered, road taxes of £12.7 billion were collected (including the £1.4 billion car tax), or 2.9 times the Department's figures for 'road costs'. In 1987 15.1 per cent of consumers' expenditure was on transport and vehicles, and 11.3 per cent was on motor vehicles alone. Clearly, road transport is of major economic significance. Car ownership per 1,000 population in the UK appears to be catching up on the rates in the larger European countries and is now about 83 per cent of French and Italian levels, 73 per cent of West German levels. Over the decade 1979–89 the number of private cars increased from 14.3 million to 18.5 million, or by 29 per cent. From 1978–88, the number of total vehicle-km driven rose from 256 billion to 363 billion or by 42 per cent. As the length of the road network increased rather less, the average daily traffic on each km of road rose by 34 per cent over the same decade on all roads and by 52 per cent on motorways. Traffic on major roads in built up areas (i.e. those with a speed limit of 40 mph or less) increased by 13 per cent (Department of Transport, 1989b, tables 2.1, 2.3).

As road space is a valuable and scarce resource, it is natural that economists should argue that it should be rationed by price – road users should pay the marginal social cost of using the road network if they are to be induced to make the right decisions about whether (and by which means) to take a particular journey, and, more generally, to ensure that they make the correct allocative decisions between transport and other activities. If road users paid the true social cost of transport, perhaps urban geography, commuting patterns, and even the

This chapter previously appeared in the *Oxford Review of Economic Policy*. We would like to thank Oxford University Press for their kind permission to reproduce it here.

sizes of towns would be radically different from the present. The modest aim here is to identify these social costs, provide rough estimates of their magnitude for Britain, and hence identify the major policy issues.

One way to focus the discussion is to ask how to design a system of charges for road use. The problem of designing road charges can be broken down into various sub-problems. First, what is the marginal social cost (that is, the extra cost to society) of allowing a particular vehicle to make a particular trip? Part will be the direct cost of using the vehicle (fuel, wear and tear, driver's time and so forth) and will be paid for by the owner. This is the private cost of road use. Other costs are social: some will be borne by other road users (delays, for example), some by the highway authority (extra road maintenance), and some by the society at large (pollution and risk of accidents). These are called the *road use costs* – the social costs (excluding the private costs) arising from vehicles using roads. It seems logical to attempt to charge vehicles for these road use costs, so as to discourage them from making journeys where the benefits are less than the total social costs (private costs plus road use costs). The first task, therefore, is to measure these road use costs.

The second question is whether road users should pay additional taxes above these road use costs. One argument is that road users should pay the whole cost of the highway system, not just the extra cost of road use, either to be 'fair' in an absolute sense or to achieve parity or equity with, say, rail users (in those rare countries where the railway is required to cover its total costs without subsidy). Another argument is that the government needs to raise revenues and some part of this revenue should be collected from road users, since to exempt them would be to give them an unreasonable advantage over the rest of the population. Both arguments appeal either to the desire for equity or fairness, or to the need for efficiency in the allocation of resources (road versus rail), or both.

Relevant principles of taxation

The modern theory of public finance provides a powerful organizing principle for taxing and pricing. Under certain assumptions policies should be designed to achieve production efficiency, with all distortionary taxes falling on final consumers. Broadly, the conditions for this result, set out formally in Diamond and Mirrlees (1971), are (a) that production efficiency is feasible and (b) that any resulting private profits are either negligible or can be taxed away. The feasibility condition would be satisfied if the economy were competitive and externalities could be corrected or internalized.

The theory has immediate implications for road charges and taxes. Road users can be divided into two groups: those who transport freight, which is an intermediate service used in production, and those who drive their own cars or transport passengers, who enjoy final consumption. Freight transport, which is roughly and conveniently synonymous with diesel using vehicles, should pay the road use costs to correct externalities and to pay for the marginal costs of maintenance. Additional taxes (comprising the *pure tax element*) on (largely gasoline using) passenger transport can be set, using the same principles that guide the design of other indirect taxes. We shall show below that one would expect a close relationship between road use costs and total road expenditures. There is no logical reason to attribute the taxation of passenger transport to the highway budget, since it is a component of general tax revenue. But if all road taxes and charges are taken together, there are good reasons to expect that they will exceed total highway expenditure. In short, in a well-run country no conflict need arise between the goals of designing an equitable and efficient system of road use charges and taxes and the desire to cover the highway system's costs.

The theory provides a useful framework for the study of road user charges. The first step is to identify the road use costs. The second is to see what methods are available for levying charges and how finely they can be adjusted to match these costs. The third step is to examine how far these methods have repercussions outside the transport sector and, where these occur, how to take them into account. These three steps will suffice for freight transport. For passenger transport, one other step is needed: to determine the appropriate level for (and method of levying) the pure tax element.

2 QUANTIFYING THE SOCIAL COSTS OF ROAD USE

Vehicles impose four main costs on the rest of society – accident externalities, environmental pollution, road damage and congestion. Accident externalities arise whenever extra vehicles on the road increase the probability that other road users will be involved in an accident. To the extent that accidents depend on distance driven and other traffic these accident costs can be treated rather like congestion costs. Newbery (1988a) argued that accident externalities could be as large as all other externality costs taken together, and are thus possibly of first-order importance. There are two reasons for this high estimate, both disputed. The first is that the figure critically depends on the value of a life saved or the cost of a life lost. If one bases this on apparent willingness to pay to reduce risks, then the cost per life saved might be between £650,000 and £2 million at 1989 prices, based on the survey results of Jones-Lee, reported in this volume. The lower figure is over double that originally used by the Department of Transport, who based their earlier estimates on the expected loss of future earnings of a representative victim. Apparently the Department of Transport has been persuaded of the logic behind the willingness-to-pay approach, and now uses a figure of £500,000.

The second reason is that, in the absence of convincing evidence, the estimate assumed that the number of accidents increased with the traffic flow as the 1.25

power of that flow. (That is, if the traffic is twice as heavy, the risk of an accident happening to each car is increased by 19 per cent. Compare this with the number of pairwise encounters between vehicles, which rises as the square of the flow.) This in turn means that one-quarter of the cost of mutually caused accidents is an uncharged externality, even if each driver pays the full cost of the accident to him. (To the extent that society pays through the NHS, these individual costs are borne by society and attributable as part of 'road costs'. The Department of Transport includes direct costs. It might argue that their earlier valuation of life was based on the lost earnings which might have to be made good through the social security system to survivors.) Note that it is important to relate the accident rate to traffic levels in order to identify the size of the externality. Indeed, one might argue from the fact that the accident rate has fallen as traffic has increased that this 1.25 power law is invalid, and that at best there is no relationship between traffic and the accident rate. If so, then there would be no externality between motor vehicles (other than that already counted in the cost falling on the NHS). This would be the case if one took seriously the explanation of 'risk compensation', according to which road users choose a desired level of perceived risk with which they are comfortable – too little risk is boring, too much is frightening. Improvements in road safety then induce compensating increases in risk taking, while deteriorating road conditions (ice, snow, heavier traffic) induce more caution. Of course, one should be wary of using time series information about accident rates as road improvements are continuously undertaken to improve road safety. The relationship between the accident rate and traffic should be derived from a properly estimated cross-section analysis.

Jones-Lee (1990) does indeed assume that the accident *rate* (i.e. the risk of an accident per km driven) is independent of the traffic flow, from which it follows that there is no externality between motor vehicles (except those caused by the system of social and health insurance). He also assumes that the probability of any vehicle having an accident involving a pedestrian or cyclist is constant per km driven, in which case it follows that the accident rate experienced by cyclists and pedestrians is proportional to the number of vehicle km driven. If this is the case, then motor vehicles do impose an externality on non-motorized road users (though not on other motorists), which Jones-Lee calculates to be quite large – perhaps 10–20 per cent of total road costs. Of course, we remain relatively uncertain about the relationship between accidents to other road users and traffic. It has been remarked that not so long ago children were allowed to play in the street, and cycle or walk unaccompanied to school. The number of accidents to such children was quite high. Now it is so obviously insane to allow such activities that the number of accidents may have fallen with the increase of traffic. Of course, the accident externality is still there, though hidden in the form of the extra costs of ferrying children to school, and not allowing them to play or cycle unsupervised.

The main problem therefore lies in identifying the relationship between traffic and accidents – in the words of the US Federal Highway Cost Allocation Study 'Quantitative estimation of accident cost and vehicle volume relationships, however, has not yet proved satisfactory . . .' (US Federal Highway Authority, 1982). Given the huge costs involved and the potential gains from lowering accident rates, identifying such relationships should have overwhelming research priority.

Similarly, pollution costs share many of the same features as congestion costs (and tend to occur in the same places). Where they have been quantified (for the US) they appear to contribute less than 10 per cent of total road costs. They are normally dealt with by mandating emission standards, and by differential taxes on the more polluting fuels (for example, by having higher taxes on leaded petrol). A new European Directive on vehicle emissions, known as the Luxembourg Agreement, will be implemented in the UK. This mandates NO_x levels of half the current limit, and reductions in hydrocarbon releases of three-quarters, at an estimated cost to the motorist of £800 million or about 4 per cent of motoring costs (Department of the Environment, 1989). Provided the pollution costs are reflected in fuel taxes, and the requirement to meet emissions standards, these costs will have been satisfactorily internalized. One should, however, be rather cautious about mandating stringent emissions standards without a careful cost–benefit analysis. Crandall *et al.* (1986, pp. 114–15) estimate that the programme costs for the US of the more stringent 1984 emissions standards might be about $20 billion per year with a replacement rate of 10.5 million cars, which is several times the rather optimistic estimates of the potential benefits of reducing pollution. (Safety regulations in contrast, though expensive, seem to have been justified on cost–benefit criteria.) Some of these issues are discussed further in Newbery (1990).

Road damage costs

These are the costs borne by the highway authority of repairing roads damaged by the passage of vehicles, and the extra vehicle operating costs caused by this road damage. The damage a vehicle does to the road pavement increases as the fourth power of the axle load, which means that almost all damage is done by heavy vehicles such as trucks. Increasing the number of axles is a potent method of reducing the damaging effect of a vehicle – doubling the number of equally loaded axles reduces the damage to one-eighth its previous level. Consequently most highway authorities closely regulate the axle configuration and maximum legal axle loads. Increasing the road thickness dramatically increases the number of vehicles that can be carried before major repairs are required – doubling the thickness increases this number by 2 to the power 6.5 or so (Paterson, 1987). Consequently the most damaging and therefore costly combination is a heavy vehicle on a thin road.

The theory which allows these costs to be quanitified is set out in Newbery (1988a, b). The road damage costs of a vehicle will be proportional to its damaging power (and will be measured in terms of Equivalent Standard Axles, or ESAs). Britain, in common with most advanced countries, follows a condition-responsive maintenance strategy in which the road is repaired when its condition reaches a pre-determined state. In such cases, the road damage costs will be equal to the average annual costs of maintaining the road network in a stable state, multiplied by the fraction of the road deterioration caused by vehicles as opposed to weather, allocated in proportion to ESA-miles driven. The fraction of total costs allocated to vehicles will depend on the climate, the strength of the road, and the interval between major repairs, and the formula is given in (Newbery 1988a, b). In hot dry climates it will be between 60 and 80 per cent, while in freezing temperate climates the proportion will be between 20 and 60 per cent, the lower figures corresponding to more stringent maintenance criteria or lower traffic volumes. For Britain, Newbery (1988a) argued that the appropriate fraction was 40 per cent. If maintenance is condition-responsive then it is not necessary to charge vehicles for the damage they indirectly do to subsequent vehicles which experience increased operating costs on the damaged pavement – on average the condition of the pavement will remain unchanged.

It is simple to update the road damage costs given in Newbery (1988a) using the latest estimates of road track costs provided in Department of Transport (1989a, table 5). The total cost identified is £785 million, or 8.7 p/ESAkm. The allocable fraction is 0.4, giving £314 million or 3.5 p/ESAkm. As such, road damage costs are a small fraction of total road costs. To provide a quick estimate of how large a fraction, table 13.1 updates the results for 1986 to 1990 from Newbery (1988a, table 2). There the value of the road network was estimated at £50 billion excluding land. Updated to 1990 prices this is £62 billion, to which annual capital expenditure of £2 billion brings it to £70 billion. The cost of land is estimated at 14 per cent of this, to give a total of £80 billion. In Newbery (1988a) the rate of interest on this capital value was taken to be the then Test Discount Rate of 5 per cent real, and if this figure is again used, then interest on the value of the road network would be £4,000 million, compared to the actual capital expenditure of only £1,921 million. Recently the Test Discount Rate has been revised upward to 8 per cent real (presumably reflecting the perceived higher real rate of return in the rest of the economy), and at this rate the interest costs would rise to £6,400 million.

There is little logic in combining current and capital expenditures as the Department of Transport does in estimating 'road costs', and table 13.1 only includes imputed interest at the two different rates of 5 per cent and 8 per cent. It will be seen that allocable road damage costs amount to 3.5–5 per cent of total road costs, and are thus essentially negligible (which is not to deny that it is important to charge them appropriately to heavy goods vehicles.

This estimate is quite close to that for 1986 of 3.5 per cent given in Newbery

Table 13.1 *Road costs at 1989/90 prices (£ million)*

Cost category	Annual average	
	5% TDR	8% TDR
Interest on capital	4,000	6,400
(Capital expenditure)	(1,921)	
Maintenance *less* costs attrib. to pedestrians	2,093	2,093
Policing and traffic wardens	327	327
Total road costs	6,420	8,820
of which attributable to		
road damage costs	314	314
Gross vehicle mass	495	495
VKT	225	225
Balance attributable to PCU	4,884	7,284
PCU km (billion)	375 billion km	
Cost per PCU km pence/km	(1.30 p/km)	(1.94 p/km)

Notes: Figures are annual averages for the years 1987/88 to 1989/90. TDR: Test Discount Rate; VKT: vehicle km travelled. Costs attributable to Gross vehicle mass and VKT taken from Department of Transport (1989a), adjusted in the same way as those given in Newbery (1988a, table 5).
Source: Department of Transport (1989a).

(1988a). Even if repair costs currently allocated by the UK Department of Transport in proportion to Gross Vehicle Weight are included (and the theoretical justification for so doing is rather unclear) the figure only rises to 9–13 per cent (depending on the choice of the TDR). Small *et al.* (1988) estimate that pavement costs, including construction and periodic resurfacing, are less than 16 per cent of road costs in their simulations of an optimized US road system, and road damage charges would only account for 2 per cent of total charges. Far and away the largest element (again, ignoring accident costs, which might also be very large) are the congestion costs.

Congestion costs

These arise because additional vehicles reduce the speed of other vehicles, and hence increase their journey time. The standard way of calculating the short-run marginal congestion cost (MCC) of an extra vehicle in the traffic stream starts by postulating a relationship between speed (v kph) and flow (q vehicles or PCU/h) where PCU are passenger car units, a measure of the congestive effect of different vehicles in different circumstances (e.g., higher for heavy lorries on steep hills than on the level). If the travel cost per km of a representative vehicle is

$$c = a + b/v \qquad (1)$$

where b is the cost per vehicle hour, including the opportunity cost of the driver and occupants, then the total cost of a flow of q vehicles per hour is $C = cq$. If an additional vehicle is added to the flow, the total social cost is increased by

$$\frac{dC}{dq} = c + q\frac{dc}{dq} \qquad (2)$$

The first term is the private cost borne by the vehicle and the second is the marginal externality cost borne by other road users.

The next step is to establish the speed–flow relationship, $v = v(q)$ and here one must be careful to pose the right question. Engineers designing particular sections of the road network are concerned with flow at each point, and most of the relationships estimated are of this form. They show that traffic flow is heavily influenced by junctions, where additional traffic enters or disrupts the smooth flow, and it is possible for the speed flow relationship to be backward bending, as in figure 13.1.

The curve is to be interpreted as follows. As traffic increases above q the speed is given by points such as A, B. As traffic nears the capacity of the link, k, at the point C, the flow changes to a condition of stop-start, and traffic flow through the bottleneck drops, to a point such as D, associated with a lower speed. This is an unstable situation, and as flow falls, so the traffic leaving the bottleneck will accelerate, and eventually clear the blockage. At that time, the speed will jump back up to point A (further details are given in Newbery (1987) and Hall *et al.* (1986)).

Useful though this relation is for road design, it is not what is wanted for estimating the cost of congestion, where we need a measure of the total extra time taken by the remaining traffic to complete their planned journeys, not their speed at a particular point on the road network. The Department of Transport, when planning roads to alleviate congestion, uses formulas estimated by the Transport and Road Research Laboratory, and reported in Department of Transport (1987). These are based on 'floating car' methods in which the observing vehicle remains in the traffic stream for a period of time, and hence gives a better estimate of the average relationship between speed and flow. They find a reasonably stable linear relationship of the form

$$v = a - \beta q \qquad (3)$$

where q is measured in PCU/lane/hr. The estimated value of β for urban traffic is

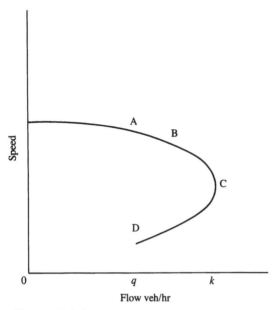

Figure 13.1 Speed flow relationship for a link

0.035. This agrees closely with a careful study of traffic flows within zones of Hong Kong, reported in Harrison *et al.* (1986), itself commissioned as part of Hong Kong's road pricing experiment.

This linear relationship can be used to quantify the average and marginal costs of traffic and hence to determine the MCC. Figure 13.2 below gives this relationship for suburban roads at 1990 prices, based on the estimated COBA 9 formula. The left-hand scale gives the speed associated with the traffic flow, and on such roads average speeds rarely fall below 25 kph, so the relevant part of the diagram is to the left of that speed level. Another, quite useful way of representing this limitation is to suppose that the demand for using suburban roads becomes highly elastic at this level, an idea pursued further below.

In some ways a better measure of the congestion relationship is given by the marginal time cost (MTC) in vehicle-hours per vehicle km, which can then be multiplied by the current value of the time use of the vehicle, b in (1). From (3), the MTC is just $\beta q/v^2$. Given data for q and v, the MTC can be estimated.

Newbery (1988a, table 1) estimated these costs for Britain for the year 1985. Rather than repeat the rather time-consuming calculations reported there, the following short-cut has been adopted. If m is the MCC as a function of q, and if Δq is the increase in traffic over some period, then the revised estimate of the MCC is $m + dm/dq \cdot \Delta q$. The factor by which to scale up the original estimates of MCC can be found from the above equations and is

$$\left(1 + \frac{2\beta q}{v}\right)\frac{\Delta q}{q} \tag{4}$$

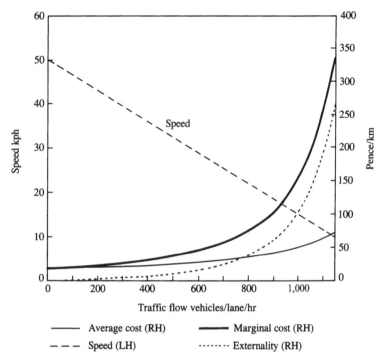

Figure 13.2 Average and marginal cost of trips (urban non-central roads, 1990 prices)

The results of this updating procedure is given in table 13.2. If anything, the estimate will be on the low side, as the relationship is very non-linear. If some roads have an above average increase in traffic while others have a below average increase, then taking the average increase $\Delta q/q$ will underestimate the average of the costs on each road.

Table 13.2 shows in a vivid way the great variation in marginal congestion costs by time of day and location. Urban central areas at the peak have an *average* congestion cost of 10 times the average over all roads, and more than 100 times that the average motorway or rural road.

The table shows that the average congestion cost is 3.4 p/PCUkm, and, given the 375 billion PCUkm driven from table 13.1, if road users were to be charged for congestion, the revenue collected would have been £12,750 million. If we add to this sum the road damage costs (£314 million), the amounts allocated according to Gross Vehicle Mass (£495 million), and VKT (£225 million), all taken from table 13.1, then the appropriate level of road charges should yield £13,784 million. Total road taxes were £12,700 million, or 92 per cent the required level. Congestion charges would amount to 92 per cent of the total appropriate road charge.

It is interesting to compare these estimates with those given in Newbery (1988a). The estimated congestion charges for Britain for 1986 were £6,203

Table 13.2 *Marginal time costs of congestion in Great Britain, 1990*

	MTC (veh h/ 100 PCU km)	VKT fraction	MCC p/PCU km	Index of MCC
Motorway	0.05	0.17	0.26	8
Urban central peak	5.41	0.01	36.37	1070
Urban central off-peak	4.35	0.03	29.23	860
Non-central peak	2.36	0.03	15.86	466
Non-central off-peak	1.30	0.10	8.74	257
Small town peak	1.03	0.03	6.89	203
Small town off-peak	0.63	0.07	4.20	124
Other urban	0.01	0.14	0.08	2
Rural dual carriageway	0.01	0.12	0.07	2
Other trunk and principal	0.04	0.18	0.19	6
Other rural	0.01	0.11	0.05	1
Weighted average			3.40	100

Source: Updated from Newbery (1988a, table 1).

million out of the total appropriate charge (excluding accident costs) of £7,033 million, or 88 per cent. The figures are high as the amount of time wasted is so high, though the costs are frequently ignored by highway authorities, as they are entirely borne by highway users. The Confederation of British Industries has calculated that traffic congestion costs the nation £15 billion a year, or £10 a week on each household's shopping bill (*The Times*, May 19, 1989). This figure is comparable to the £13 billion for the appropriate congestion charge calculated above, though the question of how best to measure the true social cost of congestion is discussed more fully below.

Small *et al.* (1988) cite evidence that suggests congestion costs are also high in the US. Thus average peak-hour delays in crossing the Hudson River to Manhattan have roughly doubled in the past ten years, while congestion delays in the San Francisco Bay Area grew by more than 50 per cent in just two years. In 1987 63 per cent of vehicle-miles were driven on inter-state highways at volume to capacity ratios exceeding 0.8, and 42 per cent on other arterials. Although their study does not quantify the congestion costs they suggest figures of some tens of billions of dollars annually – a figure which squares with the evidence in the next paragraph.

The correct charge to levy on vehicles is equal to the congestion costs they cause (in addition to other social costs like damage costs). If roads experience constant returns to scale, in that doubling the capital expenditure on the road creates a road able to carry twice the number of vehicles at the same speed, and if the roads are optimally designed and adjusted to the traffic, then it can be shown that the optimal congestion charge would recover all of the non-damage road costs (Newbery, 1989). These include interest on the original capital stock, as well as the weather-induced road damage costs not directly attributable to vehicles, and other maintenance expenditures, collectively identified as 'road costs attributable to PCU' in table 13.1. The available evidence supports constant returns to scale or possibly rather mildly increasing returns, of the order of 1.03–1.19. (This always surprises highway engineers, who *know* that it does not cost twice as much to double the capacity of a highway, as many costs – embankments, etc. – are fixed, and the capacity of a two-lane divided highway is considerably greater than of a one-lane divided highway. But most capacity increases are needed in congested urban areas where the costs of land acquisition can be extremely high. The econometric estimates pick this factor up. See Keeler and Small, 1977; Kraus, 1981.) If we take the estimates as supporting constant returns, then the result is directly applicable, and provides a useful benchmark against which to judge the estimated congestion charges. If we assume increasing returns to scale, then road charges would not cover road costs of an optimal road network.

In 1986 the estimated average congestion charge was 1.42 times as high as the road costs attributable to PCU, suggesting either that the road network was inadequate for the level of traffic, or that the correct rate of interest to charge was higher than 5 per cent real. (At 8 per cent the ratio was only 1.0.) The corresponding ratio for 1990 is 2.82 (or 1.75 at 8 per cent interest). In short, if roads were undersupplied in 1986, they are becoming critically scarce as traffic volumes increase faster than road space is supplied. Notice that assuming that there are increasing returns to capacity expansion strengthens the conclusion that roads are undersupplied.

3 CHARGING FOR ROAD USE

Ideally, vehicles should be charged for the road use cost of each trip, so that only cost-justified trips are undertaken. In practice it is not too difficult to charge for road damage, which is largely a function of the type of vehicle and the extent to which it is loaded. Ton-mile taxes as charged by some of the States of the US can approximate the damage charge quite closely, provided they are made specific to the type of vehicle. Vehicle specific distance taxes would be almost as good, provided axle loading restrictions were enforced. Fuel taxes are moderately good in that they charge trucks in proportion to ton-miles. As they charge different types of vehicles at (almost) the same ton-mile rate, they must be supplemented by vehicle specific purchase taxes or licence fees and combined with careful regulation of allowable axle configurations and loadings (Newbery *et al.* 1988; Newbery 1988c).

The more difficult task is to charge for congestion, which varies enormously depending on the level of traffic, which in turn varies across roads and with the time of day, as table 13.2 shows dramatically. The most direct way is to charge an amount specific to the road and time of day, using an 'electronic numberplate' which signals to the recording computer the presence of the vehicle. The computer then acts like a telephone exchange billing system, recording the user, the time and place and hence the appropriate charge, and issuing monthly bills. The cost per numberplate is of the order of $100, or perhaps one quarter of the cost of catalytic converters which are now mandatory for pollution control in many countries. Such systems have been successfully tested in Hong Kong (Dawson and Catling, 1986) but there was initially some pessimism at the political likelihood that they would ever be introduced (Borins 1988). The stated objection was that the electronic detectors could monitor the location of vehicles and hence would violate the right to privacy. This objection may be valid in a society suspicious of (and not represented by) its government, though evidence suggests that this is not likely to be much of a problem in Europe (ECMT, 1989). The objection could be levied against telephone subscribers once itemized bills are introduced, and the objection can be overcome in much the same way by the use of 'smart cards', rather like magnetic telephone cards. The electronic licence plate would be loaded with the smart card and would debit payments until exhausted. Only thereafter would the central computer monitor and bill for road use.

A more plausible explanation for the lack of success in Hong Kong may have been that it was not clear to car owners that the new charges (which were quite high, of the order of $2–3 per day) would replace the existing and very high annual licence fee. Faced with a doubling of the cost of road use commuters understandably objected. But the whole point of charging for road use by electronic licence plates is to replace less well-designed road charging schemes, such as fuel taxes and licence fees. The proposition that needs to be put to the public is that in exchange for the entire system of current road taxes (fuel taxes in excess of the rate of VAT, the special car purchase tax, and the licence fee), road users will be charged according to their use of congested road space, at a rate which for the average road user will be roughly the same. (For the UK this is still just about feasible on the figures given above, at least if the pure tax element on private motorists is allowed to fall to zero.) As more than half the road-using population drive less than the average number of miles in congested areas, this should command majority support.

An alternative method of selling the use of electronic licence plates might be to offer rebates for tax on fuel used (at the estimated rate per km, or on production of receipts) and to waive the licence fee for those installing the licence plates. This might be necessary as an interim measure when their use is confined to major urban centres, notably London. It is noticeable that despite the claim by Channon as Minister of Transport that the Government had no plans to introduce road pricing because of the perceived public hostility, that hostility seems to be diminishing, at least in London. A recent opinion survey conducted by the

Metropolitan Transport Research Unit showed 87 per cent in favour of some form of traffic restraint, and 53 per cent in favour of a fixed charge to drive into Central London. Charging per mile was widely supported, and 48 per cent said they would use public transport if such charges were introduced (*The Independent*, January 26, 1990).

Until road pricing is introduced, alternative and less satisfactory methods of charging are necessary. One such is selling area licences which grant access to congested zones such as city centres during rush hours. This solution has been used in Singapore for over a decade, with considerable success. Heavy parking charges and restricted access may also be effective to varying degrees (World Bank, 1986). At the moment, however, the only way to charge vehicles for the congestion they cause is in proportion to the distance they drive, by fuel taxes and/or vehicle purchase taxes (which approximate reasonably well to distance charges for heavily used vehicles, but less well for automobiles). Such taxes, combined with access charges (area licences, or even annual licences) achieve the desired effect of charging road users on average for congestion, but do little to encourage them to drive on less congested roads or at less busy times of the day (or, indeed, to take public transport instead). In Britain, the estimates above suggest that road taxes might usefully be increased somewhat. It is worth remarking that there are clear advantages in raising such corrective taxes to their efficient level, as they allow other distortionary taxes, which incur deadweight losses, to be reduced.

4 MEASURING THE COSTS OF CONGESTION

So far we have avoided discussing the actual cost of congestion in Britain, and instead calculated the revenue that would be generated if vehicles were to be charged for the congestion they caused. Figure 13.3 shows how the equilibrium demand for trips is established in the absence of such charges. If road users pay only the private costs of the trip, their costs are given by the average cost schedule, which meets the demand schedule at point C. At that point the willingness to pay by the marginal road user is equal to the cost of the trip. The efficient congestion charge would be an amount BD, which, if levied, would cause demand to fall to the level associated with point B. The revenue then raised would be ABDE, and this is the amount referred to above as the revenue attributable to the congestion charge. In the figure it would amount to £600 per lane hour. But is this the correct measure of the congestion cost? Consider various alternative measures. One measure frequently cited in newspaper accounts of the cost of congestion is the extra costs involved in travelling on congested rather than uncongested roads. This might be measured as FC times FH, the excess of the average actual cost over the cost on a road with zero traffic. On the figure this would amount to £530 (per lane hour). But this is an unrealistic

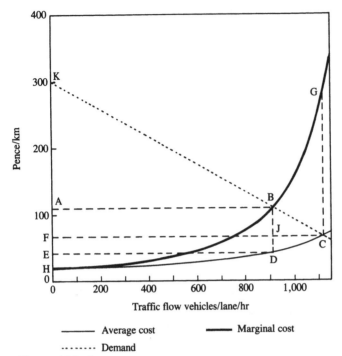

Figure 13.3 Cost of congestion (urban non-central roads, 1990 prices)

comparison, as it would be uneconomic to build roads to be totally uncongested. Instead one might compare the costs of the excessive congestion at point C in excess of those which would be efficient, at point D. These extra costs might be measured as CF times EF, or £270. This is not satisfactory either, as fewer trips would be taken at the efficient level of charges. A better alternative is the loss in social surplus associated with excessive road use. The efficient social surplus associated with point B is the consumer surplus triangle KBA, plus the tax revenue ABDE. The social surplus associated with point C is just the triangle KCF, and the difference is the rectangle FJDE *less* the triangle BCJ, or £198. This is also equal to the area of the standard deadweight loss triangle BCG. In this case the deadweight loss is equal to one third of the revenue measure.

There is one important case in which the revenue measure accurately measures the deadweight loss, and that is where the demand for trips becomes perfectly elastic beyond its inter-section with the marginal social cost schedule at point B. In this case there is no gain in consumer surplus in moving from the efficient level of traffic to the equilibrium level, and hence the loss is just equal to the foregone tax revenue. Put another way, by not charging the efficient toll in this perfectly elastic case, the government foregoes revenue but the consumer makes no gain. In crowded urban areas this is a plausible situation. The equilibrium level of traffic is found where the marginal road user is indifferent between using a car or some alternative – public transport, or walking. Thus traffic speeds in London

410

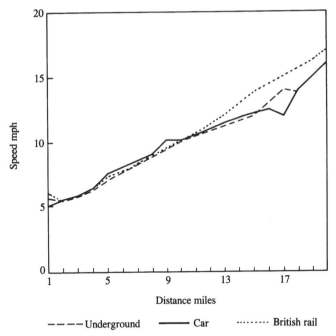

Figure 13.4 Equilibrium trip speed (average door-to-door speed, Central London)

are about the same as they were in the nineteenth century, and the time taken to get to work (or, more properly, the total perceived cost) for many commuters is no better by road than alternatives. Figure 13.4, which is taken from a graph in *The Times*, December 5, 1988, itself based on work by Martin Mogridge, illustrates this graphically for central London. The average door-to-door time taken between points in central London is remarkably similar for all three modes of transport, so car speeds in equilibrium are determined by the speeds of alternative public transport.

In such circumstances, the social costs of congestion may even be understated by the revenue measure. Consider the situation portrayed in figure 13.5. Initially demand is GC and equilibrium is established at C with commuting costs of OF. But if road users were charged an amount BD the same road users would switch to public transport, reducing demand for private road use. This increased demand for public transport would, after appropriate investment and expansion, lead to an improved frequency of service, while the reduced traffic would lead to a faster public transport service, lowering the costs of travel. Given this lower public transport cost, the demand for private transport would fall from GC to GD, and the willingness to pay for private commuting would fall, from the level OF to OA for the marginal commuter. In this case charging the congestion tax would yield tax revenue (a social gain) while reducing the cost of commuting (an additional consumer gain). The tax foregone thus understates the cost of the congestion.

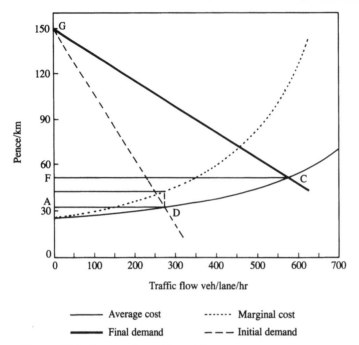

Figure 13.5 Congestion with public transport (urban central areas, 1990 prices)

5 COST–BENEFIT ANALYSIS OF ROAD IMPROVEMENTS

The average road tax paid by vehicles per km is now somewhat below the average efficient level. On roads of below average congestion, vehicles may be overcharged, but in urban areas they are certainly undercharged, in many cases by a large margin. Faced with growing congestion, one natural response is to increase road capacity. Figure 13.6 illustrates the pitfalls in simple-minded cost–benefit analysis. If the road capacity is doubled, then the average and marginal cost schedules will move from 'before' to 'after'. The initial equilibrium will be at B, where demand is equal to the initial average cost (AC), and traffic will be BG. If the AC is lowered to E, then the apparent cost-saving is GBEF, to be compared with the cost of the improvement. But the lower AC will induce increased traffic and the new equilibrium will be at point D, not E. The benefit will be GBDH, which may be significantly lower.

Figure 13.7 shows that where traffic increases come from previous users of public transport, as in figure 13.4, the effect of the road 'improvement' may be to increase traffic volumes but to raise average costs, making everyone worse off, and adding negative value. It is hard to escape the conclusion that as journey speeds in London are now below their level at the turn of the century, before the introduction of the car, much of the road investment has been self-defeating.

The situation is radically changed when road users pay the efficient congestion

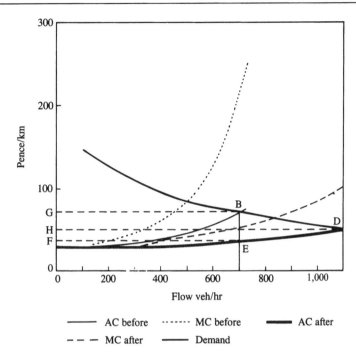

Figure 13.6 Cost–benefit of road improvements

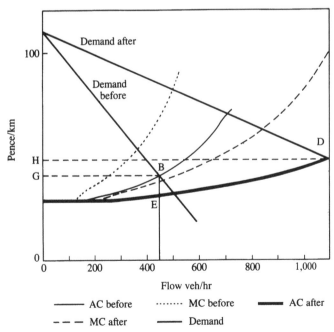

Figure 13.7 Perverse road improvement

413

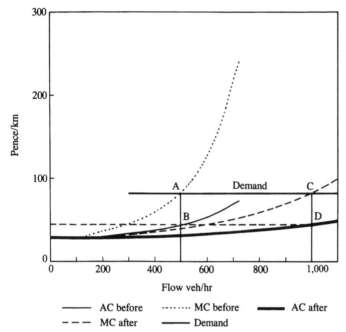

Figure 13.8 Road improvements with charges

charge. Consider figure 13.8, in which the demand for trips is perfectly elastic along AC, and congestion charges at the rate AB (marginal cost *less* average cost) are levied by means of an electronic numberplate. If road capacity is expanded, but the charge maintained, then the social gain is the increase in the revenue collected, ACDB, which can be compared with the cost. If there are constant returns to capacity expansion and the road improvement is self-financing, it is justified. This is another application of the proposition that with constant returns to road expansion, congestion charges will recover the costs of the road investment. If there are increasing returns to expansion, then expansion may still be justified even if it is not self-financing – one should compare the marginal expansion costs with the marginal benefit measured by the increased revenue.

The implications of this are clear – without road pricing, road improvements may yield low or even negative returns, but with efficient pricing, not only are improvements easy to evaluate, they should also be self-financing, at least if there are constant or diminishing returns to expansion, as is likely in congested areas.

6 PRICING PUBLIC TRANSPORT

If private road users are significantly undercharged for using the road in urban areas, then commuters face the wrong relative prices when choosing between public and private transport. If it is hard to raise the price of private driving, why not lower the price of public transport to improve the relative price ratios? There are a number of problems with this proposal. First, it is hard to compute the second-best public transport subsidies given the great variation of congestion costs by time of day and location. Second, the subsidies have to be financed by taxes which have distortionary costs elsewhere. (Note that congestion charges would reduce the distortionary costs of the tax system.) Third, subsidies to public transport appear to be rather cost-ineffective. Few motorists are attracted off the road into private transport, with much of the increase in public transport use coming from those previously not using either mode.

There are also political economic problems with operating public bus companies at a loss – there is a temptation to ration them and lower the quality, thus defeating the purpose of making them more attractive to commuters. It becomes more difficult to gain the benefits of deregulation and privatization. It may just lead to rent-dissipation by the supplier of public transport – as seems to have happened to some extent when the London Underground was heavily subsidized. The same applies to subsidizing rail travel – it becomes unattractive to expand capacity if this just increases the size of the loss.

A more promising approach is to make private transport relatively less attractive and public transport more attractive, by improving the quality of the latter, possibly at the expense of the former. Bus-lanes which reduce road space to other road users have this effect, as would electronic signalling which gave priority to public transport at traffic lights. Banning private cars from congested streets during the working day has a similar effect. Arguably the greatest obstacle to overcome is that of making private road users aware of the true social costs of their road use. Table 13.2 reveals that *average* congestion charges of 36 pence/km would be appropriate in urban centres at the peak, and 30 pence/km during the off-peak, with higher charges appropriate on roads with higher volume and/or lower speeds. Figure 13.2, which is plotted for 1990 costs for suburban areas, shows that, when traffic speeds have fallen to 20 kph, then congestion charges of 50 pence/km are in order. It is hard to make public transport 50 pence/km cheaper than its unsubsidized level, and thus it is more productive to think of ways of raising the cost of private transport at congested periods, or directly reducing its level.

It was argued above that road pricing gives rise to sensible cost–benefit rules for road improvements. The same is also true for other transport investments, especially in public transport and that most capital intensive form, rail transport. If road users paid the full social cost of road use, then there would be every reason to charge users of public transport the full social marginal cost, including congestion. It is unlikely that there are economies of scale in peak-period road or rail use in London, or in peak-period bus use in other cities, and this would lead to fares that would cover the full operating costs, including interest on capital. It would therefore again be easier to apply commercial criteria to investment in public transport, and, indeed, there would no longer be a strong case for keeping these services in the public sector.

7 CONCLUSION

Road pricing is the best method of dealing with congestion, and would have far-reaching implications for the viability and quality of public transport, for the finance of urban infrastructure, and ultimately for the quality of life. The average road charge might not need to increase above current levels, for if roads were correctly priced, demand for the use of the most congested streets would fall, and with it the efficient charge to levy. Current road taxes are heavy and yield revenue greater than the average cost of the current road system. In equilibrium, with efficient road pricing and an adequate road network, one would expect road charges to be roughly equal to road costs, so either road charges would fall below current tax levels, or substantial road investment would be justified, and possibly both.

A shift to road pricing would cause a fall in the cost of driving in non-urban areas, and an increase in the cost of urban driving. In the medium run the quality of urban public transport would improve, and the average cost of urban travel by both public and private transport might fall below current levels. Energy consumption would increase, as there would no longer be any reason to have heavy fuel taxes (other than those needed to reflect the costs of pollution, and this problem is arguably better addressed by mandatory emissions standards). A shift to road pricing matched by offsetting adjustments to other taxes to raise the same total tax revenue is unlikely to be inflationary, both because the average road tax/charge would be almost unchanged, and because any increase in charge leading to higher travel costs could be matched by lower taxes on other goods, leading to a fall in those elements of consumer expenditure.

Similarly, the impact on the distribution of income is likely to be slight and probably favourable. Urban private travel costs would rise, at least in the short run, and urban public transport quality-adjusted costs may fall (depending on how rapidly any subsidies were phased out, and how quickly the increased demand for public transport translated into more supply at higher average quality). Rural transport costs would fall. As urban car owners are richer than average, and users of public transport are poorer, the redistribution should be favourable. The government would have to decide on the fate of the car tax (which raised £1.4 billion in 1989/90), and which is a fairly progressive form of indirect tax, being levied at an *ad valorem* rate on the purchase price. Its logic as a method of rationing access to road space would disappear, but it could be retained as a pure consumer tax if it were thought to be justifiable on redistributive grounds.

REFERENCES

Borins, Sandford F. (1988), 'Electronic road pricing: an idea whose time may never come', *Transportation Research*, 22A(1): 37–44.

Crandall, R.W., H.K. Gruenspecht, T.E. Keeler and L.B. Lave (1986), *Regulating the Automobile*, Washington, DC, Brookings.

Dawson, J.A.L. and L. Catling (1986), 'Electronic road pricing in Hong Kong', *Transportation Research*, 20A (March): 129–34.

Department of the Environment (1989), *Environment in Trust: Air Quality*.

Department of Transport (1987), *COBA 9*, Department of Transport, London.

   (1989a), *The Allocation of Road Track Costs 1989/90*, Department of Transport, London.

   (1989b), *Transport Statistics Great Britain 1978–88*, Department of Transport, London.

Diamond, P.A. and J.A. Mirrlees (1971), 'Optimal taxation and public production, I: productive efficiency', *American Economic Review*, 61: 8–27.

Jones-Lee, M.W. (1990) 'The value of transport safety', *Oxford Review of Economic Policy*, 6 (Summer).

   (1994), 'Safety and the saving of life: The economics of safety and physical risk', this volume.

Hall, F.L., B.L. Allen and M.A. Gunter (1986), 'Empirical analysis of freeway flow density relationships', *Transportation Research*, 20A (March): 197–210.

Harrison, W.J., C. Pell, P.M. Jones and H. Ashton (1986), 'Some advances in model design developed for the practical assessment of road pricing in Hong Kong', *Transportation Research*, 20A: 135–44.

ECMT (1989), European Conference of Ministers of Transport Round Table 80, *Systems of Infrastructure Cost Coverage*, Economic Research Centre, Paris, OECD.

Keeler, T. and K.A. Small (1977), 'Optimal peak-load pricing, investment and service levels on urban expressways', *Journal of Political Economy*, 85(1): 1–25.

Kraus, Marvin (1981), 'Scale economies analysis for urban highway networks', *Journal of Urban Economics*, 9(1): 1–22.

Newbery, D.M.G. (1987), 'Road user charges and the taxation of road transport', *IMF Working Paper WP/87/5*, International Monetary Fund, Washington, DC.

   (1988a), 'Road user charges in Britain', *The Economic Journal*, 98 (Conference 1988): 161–76.

   (1988b), 'Road damage externalities and road user charges', *Econometrica*, 56(2): 295–316.

   (1988c), 'Charging for roads', *Research Observer*, 3(2): 119–38.

   (1989), 'Cost recovery from optimally designed roads', *Economica*, 56: 165–85.

   (1990), 'Acid rain', *Economic Policy*, 11 (October).

Newbery, D.M., G.A. Hughes, W.D.O. Paterson and E. Bennathan (1988), *Road Transport Taxation in Developing Countries: The Design of User Charges and Taxes for Tunisia*. World Bank Discussion Papers, 26, Washington, DC.

Paterson, W.D.O. (1987), *Road Deterioration and Maintenance Effects: Models for Planning and Management*, Baltimore, Johns Hopkins University Press for World Bank.

Small, K.A., C. Winston and C.A. Evans (1988), *Road Work: A New Highway Policy*, Washington, DC: Brookings.

US Federal Highway Authority (1982), *Final Report to the Federal Highway Cost Allocation Study*, Washington, DC, US Government Printing Office.

World Bank (1986), *Urban Transport*, Washington, DC.

14

PUBLIC TRANSPORT:

The allocation of urban public transport subsidy

Stephen Glaister

Local public transport in England has been in decline since the mid 1950s. In the 1970s it ran into steadily increasing deficit. It was a topic of dispute in parliament with the Transport Act 1980, which abolished the severe quantity-licensing restrictions on express (long-distance) coach services, and made it somewhat easier for new operators to obtain licences to compete with established operators on stage carriage (local) bus services. At about that time, some of the metropolitan counties and the Greater London Council (GLC) formulated explicit policies of increasing subsidies to their services. This precipitated a bitter and continuing dispute over the powers and responsibilities of local and central government, the criteria by which subsidy should be judged and the extent and method by which services should be given financial assistance.

This chapter presents estimates of the economic benefits, narrowly defined, of subsidy to public transport in the English metropolitan areas. The chapter shows how the estimates can be used to address the allocation of a total budget between different spending authorities. The full technical details are to be found in Department of Transport, 1982.

ECONOMIC PHENOMENA INVOLVED

If there are no resource costs involved in the greater use of a transport facility, then there will always be a net advantage in reducing the charges for its use. This must be so, since the traffic generated obtains the benefit of use and there are no extra resource costs by assumption. If a bus or rail service is provided at a generous service level which is taken as fixed, so that the average load factor is low then such a situation is created: one will win benefits by reducing fares so as to fill the empty vehicles. However, such a policy is not neutral in its impact on users as against funders of the requisite extra subsidy. In fact, with demand elasticities substantially less than unity, as is typically the case, the benefits to generated traffic will be small relative to the cash benefits to those who would

This is an abridged version of the paper with the same title which first appeared in LeGrand and Robinson (ed.), *Privatisation and the Welfare State*, Allen and Unwin (London, 1984).

have used the service both before and after the reduction. The latter receive a straightforward cash transfer.

This raises the question of whether service levels have been set appropriately. If fares could always be reduced at no resource cost, then there would be an efficiency case for no charges at all. In practice, as fares fall, load factors rise. Each vehicle has to accommodate more boardings and so its speed falls, operating costs rise and existing passengers suffer increased times in the vehicle. More importantly, the probability that the first vehicle to arrive at a stop will be full, will increase and so effective passenger waiting times will increase. This relationship has the property that increasing load factors have little effect when load factors are low, but they inflict severe penalties if the average bus load factor rises much above one half. An additional effect on users is the disbenefit of crowding as load factors increase. The 'load factor effect' thus provides the fundamental link between fares policy and service level policy without which it is impossible to discuss the balance sensibly. The results are sensitive to the details of the particular functional form used and this is an area where more research would be particularly helpful.

The 'second best' congestion pricing argument is well known. Because of congestion, the user of a private vehicle imposes costs on other users that he does not take into account when deciding whether to travel on the basis of the cost he himself faces: the marginal social cost of his trip exceeds the private cost. In these circumstances, some net benefits can be created by reducing fares somewhat, providing that this will encourage some car users to transfer to public transport.

This argument is greatly complicated by the fact that buses can themselves constitute an important source of road congestion. This is the case in central London. Thus, if bus services are expanded in order to accommodate more diverted car users, there is a danger that traffic congestion will actually be made worse.

Another effect that has turned out to be important in practice is the 'system economy of scale effect' first pointed out by Mohring (1972). If demand were to double and services were to be doubled in response, then waiting times would approximately halve. This would be a benefit to the passengers using the services before the expansion: the new users create a benefit external to themselves but internal to the system. This is another argument in favour of subsidy in order to achieve economic efficiency.

In London, a change in London Transport policies has implications for British Rail revenues and on user benefits accruing on British Rail. British Rail travel is treated as one of the interdependent modes. In the other metropolitan authorities, the institutional arrangement is different: the passenger transport authority negotiates directly with British Rail for the provision of rail services and finances them. Hence the financial implications for rail service of policy changes are reflected in the overall financial position of the passenger transport executive. As a simplification, it was assumed that outside London any change in bus fares or services would also occur on rail.

There are a number of other effects that many will consider to be important which are not included explicitly. These include: any energy considerations that are not captured adequately in the various vehicle operating cost calculations, accident benefits, the effects of increased subsidies on labour productivity and wage costs, the long-term effects of transport policies on urban form, and the wider, social aspects of the problem. It should also be emphasized that we have accounted the resource cost of £1 of extra subsidy as being £1. This begs a whole set of important questions concerning the existence of distortions elsewhere in the economy, the alternative uses that the funds would have had, and, in particular, the efficiency cost of raising the finance through taxation. These issues are discussed in Glaister (1987).

RELATIONSHIPS IN THE MODEL

The model traces the effects of change in public transport fares and service levels on the transport system in each of the major urban areas. There are five modes: commercial vehicles, private cars (including taxis and motorcyclists), bus, London Transport rail (in London only) and British Rail. A set of changes is specified to fares and service levels, the latter being represented by vehicle-miles run. In response to this, the model estimates a new set of vehicle and passenger flows.

The effects on revenues, costs and hence overall London Transport subsidy are estimated, and there is an account of the assessed gross benefits to each mode in terms of financial savings and valued time savings and of the total savings net of the cost of the additional subsidy.

The demand for each of the modes is assumed to depend on the money cost of the mode (the 'fare'), on the money costs of using competing modes and on the costs of use of all other modes (the user costs). Money costs for commercial vehicle and car users are calculated from the standard Department of Transport operating cost formulae, which relate costs to road speeds: the demand on any one mode depends upon the generalized cost of travel on each of the other modes, generalized cost being defined as the sum of money costs and other user costs represented in monetary unis.

The demand relationships used take the functional form favoured by London Transport in much of their research work. The formulation (semi-log linear) has the property that own-price elasticities of demand are directly proportional to fares levels. There is also a simple implied relationship between fare elasticities, values of time and service quality elasticities. This is convenient since the evidence on fare effects is quite good, but that on service effects is very much poorer. The exceptions to these general principles are that total commercial vehicle-miles are assumed to be constant – although their occupants do, of course, benefit from any time savings due to improvements in traffic speeds. The own-price and service elasticities for private car users are assumed to be zero, and those who do not pay full fares (usually the elderly benefiting from concessionary fares) only respond to, and benefit from, the part of a fares change that they actually face (if any).

The user costs comprise the sum of waiting time, time spent in the vehicle whilst stationary and time spent in the vehicle whilst moving, each converted into money units using the respective values of time. The time values used are those used in other transport evaluations by the Department of Transport.

Waiting times (for the public transport modes only) comprise a simple function of service level through the vehicle headway and a factor to represent the increasing probability that users waiting at stops will encounter full vehicles as the average load factor increases: the 'load factor effect'. A further penalty for increasing levels of discomfort is also included here.

Times spent in vehicles are determined by general road traffic speeds (except rail). Stopped times are determined by passenger boarding times and the number of boardings that occur, which, in turn, are related to the vehicle load. Traffic speeds are determined as a function of traffic flows through speed/flow relationships. Four road types are identified: in the case of London these are central, inner, outer and primary roads. Finally, traffic flows are determined by commercial vehicle flows, private car flows and bus vehicle flows, using the system of 'passenger car unit' equivalent weights.

It will be noted that these represent a simultaneous set of relationships. An equilibrium is a set of values for the variable that is mutually consistent with all of the relationships. If any policy variable is changed, then a new equilibrium is calculated be means of a search procedure. Having found the equilibrium, the following calculations are performed.

Revenues are calculated from demands and fare levels. Costs are calculated from service levels, wage rates and achieved vehicle speeds (because, if vehicles move faster, a given annual total of vehicle-miles can be provided at lower cost). Subsidy is calculated as cost net of revenue. Being a claim on public funds, changes in grant in respect of concessionary fares are treated as being a component of change in total subsidy. In principle, wage rates could be calculated on the assumption that there is an upward sloping supply of labour – that higher wage rates would have to be paid if more drivers were required in order to run more services. This has been the experience of many operators until relatively recently, but they can now recruit as much labour as they require at the going wage. The results quoted in this paper assume this to be the situation; that is, they assume an infinitely elastic labour supply.

In general, any policy change will cause the set of money costs and service qualities on all modes facing the user of any given mode to change. This will cause a general redistribution of demand between modes and this causes some diffiulties of principles in estimating the economic benefits of the change. The resolution of the difficulties adopted in this study is founded on the principles first suggested by Hotelling (1938) and Hicks (1956).

RESULTS

Table 14.1 gives some of the characteristics of the areas. Note that tables 14.2 and 14.3 list the authorities by increasing levels of subsidy per head (table 14.3, column 1).

A calculation is performed to find the extra net social benefit that would be earned at the margin by using £1 extra subsidy to change each one of the policy variables in turn, holding the others constant. These shadow prices on the policy variables are central to the assessment of the optimality of the balance between fares and services, the balance of expenditure levels between authorities and the rate of return to subsidy in general. The shadow prices at the 1980/1 levels (1982/3 in London), which are shown in table 14.2, illustrate the principle. They indicate that, at the margin, £1 of subsidy spent on reducing bus fares in London is estimated to yield £2.12 gross benefit or £1.12 net of the extra subsidy. But using it to reduce London Underground fares would yield a net benefit of only £0.26, and using it to improve bus services would produce a gross benefit of only £0.37 and hence a net disbenefit of £0.63. The fact that the four shadow prices are not equal suggests that the fares and service levels are out of balance, in the sense that benefits could be created by, say, cutting bus services and using the funds saved to finance cuts in bus fares in such a way as to keep the total subsidy level unchanged. If the four shadow prices have not been equated, then it will always be possible to do better within the same total budget.

Columns 3 and 4 of table 14.2 give the calculated marginal net benefit per pound of extra subsidy spent on each of the policy variables at the base levels (post March 1982 in London and 1980/1 elsewhere). There is wide variation between the areas, with particularly good returns obtainable from reducing London bus fares (fares had been doubled in March 1982) and improving London Underground services. Bus service cuts would be beneficial in West Yorkshire, Manchester and London. Table 14.1 shows that in each of these three cases, average bus load factors are relatively low at eleven or twelve people per bus. Thus the economic benefit calculus reflects the elementary observation that service provision is relatively generous in the three cases. Note also that the shadow price on fares reductions in these three cases is generally high because, if services are to be provided at this level, one may as well reduce fares so as to improve the load factors. In South Yorkshire, where the subsidy per head is the highest outside London (table 14.3, column 1), the return at the margin is close to zero.

Passenger-miles per pound has been promoted by some as a more comprehen-

Table 14.1 *Area characteristics*

Area	Population (million)	'Density' (population per road mile)	Bus fare (£ per mile)	Rail fare (£ per mile)	Bus miles (vehicle miles per capita p.a.)	Rail miles (vehicle miles per capita p.a.)	Bus load	Subsidy/ cost (%)	Bus passenger miles (per capita p.a.)	Commercial vehicles (million vehicle miles per road mile p.a.)	Car trips (million passenger miles per road mile p.a.)	Car trips (passenger miles per capita p.a.)
W. Midlands	2.645	686	0.063	0.05	74	2.0	19	12	532	0.25	2.2	3,206
W. Yorkshire	2.038	461	0.101	0.042	34	1.0	11	30	363	0.11	1.56	3,394
Greater Manchester	2.595	564	0.107	0.061	31	1.7	11	36	338	0.13	1.92	3,397
Merseyside	1.513	599	0.077	0.056	48	3.3	14	46	436	0.12	2.21	3,687
S. Yorkshire	1.302	446	0.027	0.031	38	0.9	16	72	608	0.12	1.72	3,848
London	6.696	5,038	0.128	0.141	25	4.3 (LT)	12	33	{319 (LT bus) 353 (LT rail)	1.31	8.20	1,627

Table 14.2 *Returns at the margin and changes required to equate them*

Area	(1)(2) Passenger miles per £ of subsidy		(3)(4) Net benefit per £ of subsidy		(5)(6) % changes to equate returns		(7) Marginal net benefits if equated
	Fares	Services	Fares	Services	Fares	Services	
W. Midlands	5.93	7.10	0.21	0.41	+ 5	+ 4	0.24
W. Yorkshire	3.17	2.85	0.29	− 0.19	− 24	− 13	0.18
Greater Manchester	3.59	2.28	0.33	− 0.29	− 23	− 17	0.19
Merseyside	5.64	4.82	0.31	0.15	− 6	− 3	0.26
S. Yorkshire	5.79	5.83	0.03	0.03	0	0	0.03
London Bus	6.29	2.92	1.12	− 0.63	− 28	− 31	0.28
London Tube	3.26	4.08	0.26	0.79	− 11	+ 19	

sible criterion than economic benefit. For comparison, columns 1 and 2 of table 14.2 give rates at which public transport passenger-miles could be generated by extra subsidy. There is a relationship with the economic returns, but it is by no means perfect. For instance, South Yorkshire shows a relatively high return on the passenger-miles per pound criterion.

Within each authority, the fact that the shadow price on fares is not generally equal to that on services suggests that benefits could be secured within the same level of subsidy for the authority by juggling fares and services until the shadow prices are equated. The percentage changes required to achieve a balance in each of the areas are shown in columns 5 and 6 of table 14.2. Column 7 shows the rate of economic return to subsidy at the margin, once this balance has been achieved. At this point, one can compare the rates of return across authorities and hence address the question of whether a redistribution of expenditures would be indicated. Until the fares and service balance has been struck, it is difficult to analyse whether there would be a net advantage in reducing expenditures by £1 in, say, South Yorkshire and increasing them by the same amount in Manchester, because the result would depend crucially on whether it would be spent on fares reduction or service improvements.

Table 14.3 shows how the distribution of expenditures per head (shown in column 1) might be changed within the same total, if a variety of criteria for distribution were to be applied. In column 2, marginal net benefits are assumed to be equalized both within and between authorities. In column 4, revenue/cost ratios are equated. In column 5, subsidies per resident are equated.

In column 6, the official guidelines (issued in the White Paper, HMSO, 1982) are reproduced for comparison. Since they add up to somewhat less than the total represented in each of the other columns, figures in parentheses are appended,

Table 14.3 *Subsidy allocations by various criteria*

Area	(1) 1980/1 per capita (£ p.a.)	(2) 1980/1 total (1m. p.a.)	(3) Equal marginal net benefit = £0.224 (£ p.a. per capita)	(4) Equal revenue/cost (64%) (£ p.a. per capita)	(5) Equal subsidy/capita (£ p.a.)	(6) Guidelines[b] 1983/4 (Cmnd 8735) (£ p.a. per capita)	
W. Midlands	13.27	35.11	14.4	15.5	28.8	10.6	(12.3)
W. Yorkshire	14.98	30.52	12.0	18.3	28.8	21.6	(25.0)
Greater Manchester	19.75	51.24	16.6	20.0	28.8	17.7	(20.5)
Merseyside	28.17	46.62	30.7	22.3	28.8	26.4	(30.5)
S. Yorkshire	38.63	50.30	22.4	19.3	28.8	30.7	(35.5)
London	40.87[a]	273.68	45.2	44.1	28.8	32.9	(38.1)
	483.47 [Total]	483.47	483.47 [Total]	483.47 [Total]	483.47 [Total]	418 (483) Totals	

Notes:
[a] 1983/3.
[b] Payment for concessions for elderly and disabled excluded (included elsewhere).

which are the guideline figures grossed up in proportion so as to make them sum to the same total as the others.

In order to obtain an indication of how robust the results are, and to help identify the important points of weakness, we carried out an extensive set of sensitivity tests. Not surprisingly, the valuation of service improvements was shown to be an area of doubt. The information on service elasticities is poor. Outside London, service elasticities at the lower end of the range suggested by research results (0.24–0.43) were used. The effects of modifying them towards the upper end (0.36–0.65) are that: the marginal benefits per pound of subsidy are increased by broadly £0.10 at each level of subsidy; the service cutbacks recommended in some of the areas would be about 10 per cent less (for example, 7 per cent instead of 17 per cent in Manchester); but the comparisons between the counties are not greatly affected. The load factor effect is especially important in London.

Traffic congestion was also shown to be an important element in the evaluation in London but far less significant in the other counties. Outside London, the information on speed/flow relationships and traffic flows on different road types was rather poor, but the assumptions we made would have to be in extreme error to make a difference to these findings. The two most important assumptions underlying congestion in London concern the relation between car use and London Transport fares and service levels, and the speed/flow relationships. Doubling the cross-elasticities and increasing the slopes of the speed/flow relationships by 10 per cent did not greatly change the results.

A significant implication of these observations is that, outside London, most of the benefits from additional subsidies fall to public transport users; the effectiveness of public transport subsidies in reducing traffic congestion is limited. In London, largely because of the number of buses on the roads, balancing of fares and service levels would bring substantial benefits to commercial vehicles and cars. This applies particularly to the central area roads, where a substantial improvement in traffic speeds results. Once a balanced position has been reached, then if subsidies were increased by 50 per cent, for example, about a quarter of the extra benefits would accrue to other road users.

SUMMARY AND DISCUSSION

The study investigated the feasibility of estimating the economic effects of public transport subsidy in several urban areas. In all the metropolitan areas a positive net return to increased subsidy is shown, although this is variable and it is not established that the return is higher than that which could be earned in alternative uses for the funds. In many areas the return to extra subsidy is not as great as the return that could be attained by readjusting fares and service levels so as to obtain a better balance within the same support level. A leading cause of imbalance within areas appears to be overprovision of services, which is reflected in low average load factors. Congestion benefits are persuasive arguments for subsidy only in London. In all areas the predominant effect of fares support is to achieve a cash transfer in favour of those who would have used the services anyway.

It remains to be seen how much more insight can be attained from more complex models. Several of the phenomena involved cannot really be modelled satisfactorily at the aggregate level. It is possible that a more productive way forward would be to concentrate more on the economic and wider social evaluation of specific services, something that has been advocated and shown to be possible by a number of publications. This would throw light on the important and thorny problem of cross-subsidy (and hence on the implications of increased competition). It would encourage those with political responsibilities to take a more explicit view on which kinds of services should be supported. The approach adopted here assumes away the problems of production inefficiencies (failures to produce at lowest cost) and does not address the question of whether subsidy weakens the incentive to eliminate them and to innovate. The study has produced some suggestive evidence of allocative inefficiencies in the imbalance of services in the face of a declining market, but it is likely that the aggregate approach conceals a multitude of sins at the level of the individual bus route. On the other hand, central government will inevitably retain a strategic interest in the allocation of expenditures between areas. If the kind of approach used in this paper is to play any part in this, then it is essential that the amount of special modelling to suit the peculiarities of the individual areas be kept within bounds, in order to preserve an understanding of the sources of the economic differences between them at this level.

REFERENCES

Department of Transport (1982), 'Urban public transport subsidies: and economic assessment of value for money', Summary Report and Technical Report, London, Department of Transport.

Glaister, S. (1987), *Public Transport Subsidy*, Newbury, Policy Journals.

Hicks, J.R. (1956), *A Revision of Demand Theory*, Oxford, Clarendon Press.

HMSO (1982), *Public Transport in Cities*, Cmnd 8735, London.

Hotelling, H. (1938), 'The general welfare in relation to problems of taxation and to railway utility rates', *Econometrica*, 6(3): 242–69.

Mohring, H. (1972), 'Optimisation and scale economies in urban bus transportation', *American Economic Review*, 62(4): 591–604.

15

HEALTH CARE:

QALYs and the equity–efficiency tradeoff

Adam Wagstaff

1 INTRODUCTION

As the volume of research on quality-adjusted life years (QALYs) has increased, concerns have begun to be expressed about the equity implications of this research. Lockwood (1988), for example, has argued that the QALY approach 'is in principle liable to result in forms of allocation that are *unjust* or *unfair*' (Lockwood, 1988, p. 45), emphasis in original. Similar concerns have been expressed by *inter alia* Broome (1988), Harris (1988) and Smith (1987).

That these concerns continue to be expressed despite attempts by advocates of the QALY approach to reassure critics suggests that there has been a misunderstanding either on the part of the critics of the QALY approach or on the part of its advocates. One of the aims of this chapter is to find out the nature of any misunderstanding. More generally the aim of the chapter is to explore the nature of the tradeoff between equity and efficiency in the context of resource allocation via QALYs. To do so clearly requires consideration of the concepts of equity and efficiency. What do advocates of the QALY approach mean by efficiency? What is the concept of equity underlying the QALY approach? Is it at variance with that proposed by the critics of the QALY approach? What is the nature of the tradeoff between efficiency and equity (if any)? How could such a tradeoff be taken into account in resource allocation decisions?

2 EFFICIENCY AS HEALTH MAXIMIZATION

The policy objective underlying the QALY literature is the maximization of the community's health. An individual's 'health' is measured in terms of QALYs and the community's health is measured as the *sum* of QALYs. An individual's QALY score is calculated by weighting each remaining year of his life by the expected quality of life in the year in question. The latter is calculated as a probability-weighted average of the quality-of-life scores associated with each of

This chapter previously appeared in the *Journal of Health Economics*, 10 (1991): 21–41. We would like to thank Elsevier Science Publisher B.V. (North Holland) for their kind permission to reproduce it here.

the possible health states the individual might find himself in. These scores, which are invariant across individuals in the same health states, are measured on a scale ranging from (typically) zero (dead) to one (perfect health). Frequently, they are derived using utility theory in an experimental setting. Thus, writers frequently refer to the quality-of-life score as a *utility score* and to the QALY approach as *cost-utility analysis* (cf., e.g., Torrance, 1986).

Maximizing health is argued to be a natural objective to want to pursue, given a desire to see resources deployed efficiently. As Drummond (1989) puts it, here we are 'concerned with economic efficiency rather than with notions of equity or social justice' (Drummond 1989, p. 71). The goal of health maximization's leads, as Williams (1985) notes, to an inescapable conclusion:

Procedures should be ranked so that activities that generate more gains to health for every £ of resources take priority over those that generate less; thus the general standard of health in the community would be correspondingly higher. (p. 326)

In concrete terms, the calculations of Williams imply that resources in the British National Health Service (NHS) ought to be redeployed towards procedures such as the insertion of pacemakers for heart block, hip replacement and replacement of valves for aortic stenosis, and away from procedures such as kidney transplants and coronary artery bypass grafting for severe angina with one vessel disease.

By identifying efficiency with health maximization, the QALY approach constitutes a departure from traditional Paretian welfare economics. This is no accident. Advocates of health maximization explicitly reject the traditional Paretian value judgements (cf. Williams, 1977, p. 282). Williams (1976) put the case for rejection of the Pareto doctrine in the health care context thus:

If society has explicitly rejected willingness and ability to pay as an appropriate basis for rationing out health care, the problem of vindication surely shifts onto those who persist in using that criterion . . . I would hope to persuade thoughtful scholars that the pure Pareto doctrine, à la Mishan, has outlived its usefulness, and is now merely a *starting point* for work in this field, and which we can safely move beyond in the field of health economics. (p. 13)[1]

Culyer (1989, 1990) suggests that the QALY approach amounts to more than a mere rejection of the Pareto doctrine. Also implicit, he argues, is a rejection of *welfarism*: the view that social welfare depends solely on the welfare (i.e., utility) of the members of the community (cf. Sen, 1979). Building on other work by Sen (1980, 1982), Culyer suggests a schema in which goods (e.g., health care) are viewed as possessing characteristics (e.g., clinical efficacy), which in turn influence the characteristics of people (e.g., being able to feed oneself). It is from these latter characteristics that utility is ultimately derived and it is this that is the focus of welfarism. The QALY approach, by contrast, focuses on the penultimate stage: the characteristics of people. Though utility theory *is* frequently used in the derivation of quality-of-life scores, it is used simply to measure people's health

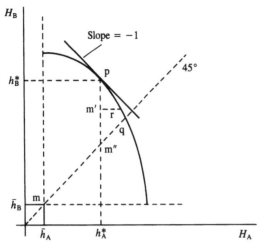

Figure 15.1

rather than the utility they derive from it. That a QALY is not a measure of utility in the welfarist sense becomes obvious when one reflects that the quality-of-life scores used are common to everybody: in resource allocation exercises based on the QALY approach (in contrast to the welfarist approach) two people cannot occupy the same health state and yet experience different utilities.[2]

As a definition of efficiency, health maximization is a good deal stronger than the extra-welfarist counterpart of the Pareto criterion – the traditional welfarist concept of efficiency.[3] The axes of figure 15.1 indicate the health, measured in terms of expected QALYs remaining before death, of two individuals, or *groups* of similar individuals, A and B. In the absence of treatment both A and B would enjoy the same number of QALYs, $\bar{h}_A$ and $\bar{h}_B$. Thus $\bar{h}_A$ corresponds to the shaded area under the no-treatment profile in figure 15.2. Point m in figure 15.1 can therefore be thought of as an *endowment point*.[4] The location and shape of the bowed-out curve in figure 15.1 – the health frontier – depends on the resources available, the capacity of A and B to benefit from health care and the costs to society of that health care; the latter include time and money costs incurred by patients, their family and friends, as well as the costs incurred by the health service. In the case illustrated the resource and technological constraints would allow treatment to be administered which would improve the health (i.e. increase the number of QALYs remaining) of *both A and B*.

The frontier – the slope of which indicates the marginal cost of a QALY to A in terms of QALYs denied to B – is drawn concave to the origin on the assumption that health care is subject to a diminishing marginal product. This can be interpreted either at an individual level (an individual's capacity to benefit at the margin diminishes as more treatment is administered) or at a group level (if the cases are treated in order of capacity to benefit from treatment, the first cases will enjoy a bigger health improvement than the last). The asymmetrical nature of the

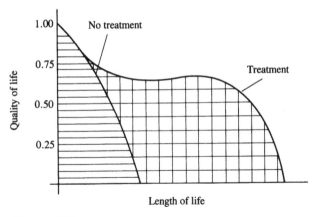

Figure 15.2

frontier in figure 15.1 implies that B can be treated at lower cost than A and/or that B has a greater capacity to benefit from treatment than A.[5]

The community's health (defined as the sum of h_A and h_B) is maximized in figure 15.1 at point p, where the cost of a QALY is the same at the margin for A and B. The movement from point m to point p involves A receiving an additional number of QALYs equal to $h_A^* - \bar{h}_A$: the latter corresponds to the cross-hatched area lying between the treatment and no-treatment profiles in figure 15.2, whilst h_A^* corresponds to the *sum* of the shaded and cross-hatched areas. That health maximization is stronger than the extra-welfarist analogue of the Pareto criterion ought to be obvious from figure 15.1.

3 UTILITARIANISM REDISCOVERED?

The welfarist counterpart of health maximization is, of course, *classical utilitarianism*. The two are *not*, however, the same,[6,7] the difference being that classical utilitarians sought to maximize the sum of *utilities*, whilst advocates of the QALY approach seek to maximize the sum of *QALYs*.[8] The fact that the QALY approach, unlike utilitarianism, is not based on individuals' own valuations of their health, and instead regards a QALY as of equal value to everybody, allows the QALY approach to avoid what many see as an unattractive implication of utilitarianism, namely that resources ought to be distributed away from people who (for whatever reason) place a relatively low value on their health (e.g., the pecuniary benefits of health improvements may be small for persons who are on low wages or are outside the labour force) (cf. Grossman, 1972; Le Grand, 1987, p. 14).

In other respects, however, utilitarianism and health maximization are close bedfellows. Like utilitarianism, health maximization leads to the conclusion that resources ought to be redeployed away from people (or groups of people) who have a low capacity to benefit from treatment. Consider again figure 15.1. Suppose that the costs of treating A and B are the same. Then it follows that the asymmetrical shape of the frontier must stem from the fact that B (who ends up receiving more QALYs than A) has a higher capacity to benefit from health care than A, despite the fact that he starts off with the same health as A.

A closely related point is the similarity between utilitarianism and health maximization in their treatment of the elderly. Suppose that A and B both initially enjoy the same quality of life, but that B is younger and therefore starts off with a higher number of expected QALYs. If A and B are identical in other respects, the impact of medical care on their quality of life will be the same, but the productivity of medical care in terms of QALYs will be higher for B than for A, simply because B is younger. The health frontier is therefore asymmetric as before, but the endowment point is a point such as m' in figure 15.1 rather than m. The frontier therefore shrinks (points on the frontier to the northwest and southeast of m' are now unattainable); B gets all the additional QALYs and A gets none.

Health maximization leads to another notable conclusion, namely that in a fully employed economy resources ought to be redeployed towards people whose output is highly valued and who, as a result of treatment, are able to return to work quickly (cf. Williams, 1981). Suppose in figure 15.1 that the capacity of A and B to benefit from treatment is the same but that B's output is highly valued and therefore the *net* cost to society of treating him is less than that associated with treating B.[9, 10] Health maximization would lead to B receiving more QALYs than A. Unless the highly paid person derives a sufficiently lower utility from health improvements, utilitarianism leads to a similar conclusion.

4 EQUITY IN THE QALY LITERATURE

Despite the differences between utilitarianism and health maximization one is reminded by the previous section of Sen's remark to the effect that utilitarianism is simply concerned with the sum of utilities and is 'supremely unconcerned with the inter-personal distribution of that sum' (Sen, 1973, p. 16).[11]

It would, of course, be untrue to say that the QALY approach is supremely unconcerned with the distribution of QALYs or even that it is unconcerned with distributional matters. As Drummond (1989, p. 71) puts it, the QALY approach does embody 'a kind of equality' by virtue of the fact that a QALY is considered to be worth the same to everybody. Williams (1974a) put the point more forcibly:

The acceptance of the fact that an additional year of healthy life is intrinsically worth, say, £1,000, no matter to whom it accrues, would probably lead to a much finer, humanitarian, and egalitarian health service than we have at present, and does not imply the pursuit of profit rules at all, since my supposed figure of £1,000 is merely a precise expression of what society should be prepared to devote to the cause of increasing expectation of healthy life, irrespective of these financial considerations! (p. 255)

The implication seems to be this: since a QALY is regarded as being of equal value to everybody, the outcome of resource allocation via QALYs is *automatically* equitable irrespective of the degree of inequality involved and the type of person who fares badly.

Culyer (1989) offers a more pragmatic defence of health maximization. He suggests that it may actually be equitable to discriminate against those whose capacity to benefit from medical care is limited. If, in figure 15.1, B really has a higher capacity to benefit from treatment than A, it is unlikely that his health is initially the same. A more plausible assumption might be that B has worse health (and may therefore be expected to be poorer) than A (cf. Culyer, 1989, p. 35). In this case point m lies below the 45° line, so that the difference between the number of QALYs going to A and B is even bigger. Thus in this case the extra resources are going to the person whose health is worse and who happens to be the poorer of the two.

Not all economists, however, feel comfortable with some of the distributional implications of the health maximization approach. Elsewhere Williams has expressed disquiet about the fact that it implies that resources ought, in a fully employed economy, to be redeployed towards those whose output is highly valued (cf. Williams, 1981). Such a conclusion, he argues, runs counter to the egalitarian ethnic underlying the principle that a QALY is to be regarded as being of equal value to everybody.[12] Pereira (1989) has challenged Culyer's pragmatic defence of QALY-maximization, arguing that counterexamples are easy to think of: the greater the capacity of B to benefit from treatment, in figure 15.1, for example, might simply stem from the fact that he or she, being rich, is better nourished and more knowledgeable about health matters (cf. Pereira, 1989, p. 36; Le Grand, 1987, p. 7).

Advocates of the QALY approach have responded to disquiet about the distributional implications of their work by looking again at the notion that a QALY is to be regarded as of equal value to everyone. One possibility currently being explored is that society may want to attach different values to QALYs going to different people. As Culyer (1990) put it:

do we not feel impelled to cherish the life-years of the very young and the very old? . . . do we not feel differently about the person whose poor health is the result of their own reckless or feckless behaviour from the way we feel about the person who is more 'responsible'? . . . (p. 25)

Some preliminary survey results published in Williams (1988) suggest *inter alia* that there may be some support amongst the population for the idea of discriminating in favour of the young (a popular idea with the elderly in the sample!) and against those who have not taken care of their health (an unpopular idea with smokers in the sample!)

Armed with relative valuations such as these, one could, it is argued, then attract a higher weight to QALYs going to some people (e.g., the young) and a lower weight to QALYs going to others (e.g., those who have failed to take care of their health). This ability to allow QALYs to be weighted differently depending on the person concerned has led to the claim that, whatever the prevailing notion of equity, distributional considerations can perfectly easily be integrated into the QALY approach, simply by maximizing a weighted sum of QALYs rather than an unweighted sum (cf., e.g., Culyer, 1989, p. 53). As Culyer (1990) put it, once this has been done,

> is there any distributional concern left that has not been embodied? If not, the maximizers have the day. If so, then we are perhaps at the heart of what it is the egalitarians fear most from the maximizers. But what it is I cannot discern! (p. 25)

Clearly one might raise objections about the survey approach to eliciting views about equity. It is, after all, difficult to distinguish between what people regard as just (or equitable) and what they regard as desirable. The latter will depend not only on what people think is just, but also on their degree of compassion – or 'caring' as it is termed by Culyer (1980) – and on their own selfish interests. Culyer (1980) put the point rather well:

> the source of value for making judgements about equity lies outside, or is extrinsic to, preferences. . . . The whole point of making a judgement about justice is so to frame it that it is (and can be seen to be) a judgement made independently of the interests of the individual making it. (p. 60).

The response by smokers to the question about people taking care of their own health illustrates the point nicely. Though this issue *is* important, it is not my primary concern here. Instead, the next section considers whether the approach proposed in the recent QALY literature – viz. weighting QALYs according to non-health information, such as age, sex, employment status, etc. – really does embody all (or any) of our equity concerns.

5 QALYs AND THE EQUITY LITERATURE

A number of definitions of equity have been proposed and discussed at length in the health economics literature.[13] Two of these bear close similarities to those proposed by critics of the QALY approach, but interestingly none of them gives rise to the notion that society might want to attach different values to QALYs going to different people.

This section considers these definitions of equity. In each case three questions are asked:

(i)   Can the definition of equity provide a basis for determining an equitable allocation of resources?;

(ii) If so, is there a conflict between equity and efficiency (defined in terms of health maximization)?; and
(iii) If there *is* a conflict, can the definition of equity be captured simply by weighting QALYs appropriately in the objective function?

5.1 Equal treatment for equal need

Under this definition equity requires that persons in equal need of health care receive the same treatment, irrespective of personal characteristics that are irrelevant to 'need', such as ability to pay, gender, place of residence, etc. There is, of course, a vertical equity counterpart to this definition.

The idea that need should determine the distribution of health care resources lies at the heart of Lockwood's (1988) critique of the QALY approach. He writes:

justice has something to do with equality, and something to do with giving appropriate weight to certain sorts of moral *claim*. . . . The claim that any patient would plausibly be thought to have on the health services . . . is a function not so much of the amount of *benefit* that the health services are in a position to confer, as of the person's *needs*, in relation to the services' capacity effectively to meet those needs (p. 45, emphasis in original).

He goes on to suggest that there is a potential conflict between the principle 'To each according to what will generate the most QALYs' and the principle (which Lockwood inclines towards) of 'To each according to his need'. A similar view is expressed by Broome (an economist), who suggests that a fair allocation of resources would be based on the premise that 'equal claims demand equal satisfaction, or more generally that claims demand proportional satisfaction' (Broome, 1988, p. 63). In a footnote on the next page he suggests that 'need is one of the most plausible sources of claims' (Broome, 1988, p. 64).

Unfortunately, however, neither Lockwood nor Broome offer any definition of the word 'need' both apparently regarding its meaning as self-evident. This is somewhat surprising in view of the controversy that has surrounded the term. As Culyer *et al.* (1972) put it:

it is difficult to tell, when someone says that 'society needs . . .', whether he means that *he* needs it, society ought to get it in *his* opinion, whether a *majority* of the members of society want it, or *all* of them want it. Nor is it clear whether what it is 'needed' *regardless* of the cost to society. (p. 114)

Williams (1974b) has suggested that what it meant when a person is said to 'need' medical treatment is that the treatment is required in order to reach some desired improvement in health. This interpretation of need requires consideration of (i) the scope for improving the person's health through treatment (a *technical* judgement), and (ii) the extent to which the health improvement is desired (a *social valuation* judgement) (cf. Williams, 1974b, pp. 71–2). This means that one cannot determine how the needs of one person compare with those of another simply by assessing the capacity of each to benefit from treatment. One also has to consider the extent to which society regards the health improvements as desirable. As Culyer (1976) puts it:

Does the individual dying of thirst in the desert 'need' a glass of water? Technically, yes, if he is to live. Normatively, yes only if others agree that he ought to have it. If they do not, he may *want* it as much as it is possible to want anything, but he does not, in our definition, need it (p. 16, emphasis in original).

In other words, in order to establish needs, society has to decide how the health improvements of one person are to be weighed against those of the other. But of course this cannot be done unless society has first decided on the desired levels of *health* of the two individuals.

So, if need is interpreted along the lines suggested by Williams and treatment is therefore regarded simply as an instrument to achieving health improvements, the criterion of equal treatment for equal need cannot *in itself* provide a basis for determining an equitable allocation of resources (cf. Williams, 1988, p. 117). The answer to question (i) above is therefore 'no'.

5.2 Equality of access

Policy statements in Britain and elsewhere make much of the concept of equality of access. The concept of access is, however, often ill-defined in these statements. This confusion is often reflected in the academic literature.[14] However, in Britain at least, there seems to be widespread support amongst economists for Le Grand's (1982) suggestion that access might best be interpreted in terms of the time and money costs that individuals incur in using health care facilities, ideally measured in utility terms.

Mooney (1983), who seems to endorse Le Grand's concept of access, emphasizes that, defined like this, equality of access is all about *equality of opportunity*; whether or not the facility in question is used is immaterial. Frequently it is argued that equality of access should apply only to those in equal need: hence the definition 'equal access for equal need' (cf., e.g., Mooney, 1983). This justifies persons in unequal need facing different access costs, so that, for example, an individual with a minor infection might have to wait longer in a casualty department than a motor accident victim with life-threatening injuries.

It is important to realize that equality of access amongst those in equal need will not guarantee equality of treatment amongst those in equal need (cf. Mooney, 1983, p. 183). The fact that in countries such as the UK government policy tends in practice to involve equalization of expenditures across regions in equal need, even though policy goals tend to be couched in terms of equality of access (cf. Mooney and McGuire, 1987, p. 74), suggests that policymakers realize this and that they may actually be concerned with treatment rather than access. If, however, 'equal access for equal need' *is* regarded as the appropriate equality objective, one runs again into the problem of defining and establishing needs – something that cannot be done until society has first decided what the desired health levels are of the persons concerned. Thus the answer in question (i) above is again 'no'.

5.3 Equality of health

This definition of equity appears to underlie policy documents such as the *Black Report* (Department of Health and Social Security, 1980). It implies that any reduction (increase) in inequality is to be regarded as a good (bad) thing. Thus any movement away from the 45° line in figure 15.1 increases the degree of inequality and is to be regarded as inequitable. The opposite is true of any movement towards the 45° line.[15]

Since the 'equality of health' definition of equity provides a clear statement on the equitable distribution of health, it also provides a clear statement on what constitutes an equitable distribution of health care. One merely has to work back from the desired distribution of health, bearing in mind the current distribution of health, the capacity of individuals to benefit from treatment and the costs of the treatment. Thus in contrast to the definitions of equity considered in the previous two sections, here we are able to answer 'yes' to the first of the questions posed at the beginning of this section.

As can be seen from figure 15.1 the answer to the second question is also 'yes'. The efficient distribution of health is at point p and the equitable distribution with the highest attainable per capita level of health is at q. Health maximization requires that B receive more QALYs than A. The 'equality of health' objective, by contrast, requires that A and B receive the same number of QALYs. A price has to be paid for pursuit of equality; the sum of QALYs is clearly lower than would be the case under health maximization.

In passing it is worth noting that if, as is assumed here, equality of health is interpreted to mean equality of 'expected QALYs remaining', the goal of equalizing health may well not be feasible.[16] This would be the case if point m' were the endowment point. Health maximization would entail giving all the resources to the younger person (B), thereby moving to p. Equity would ideally involve moving to point q, but since this would entail a *reduction* in B's health below its current level, it is not feasible. Point r is the best that can be done from an equity standpoint, so that B receives no treatment at all and A receives all the extra QALYs. These might, of course, take the form simply of an enhanced quality of life rather than any extension of life.

If the equity goal is equality of health, can equity considerations be taken into account simply by weighting QALYs in the health maximizing problem? The answer is 'no'. The reason is that the concern here lies with inequality in the distribution of *health*, not with the question of whether or not A happens to be a compulsive smoker, a parent of a two-year old child, or whatever. If equality of health is the equity objective, *any* allocation of extra QALYs which increases the degree of inequality of health is a bad thing, *irrespective of the non-health characteristics of the individuals concerned* (cf. section 7 below).

5.4 Equity and choice

This is not to say necessarily that non-health characteristics should play no part in distributional considerations. Rather that a concern about them does not stem from a concern about equality. This prompts the question: might weighted health maximization be justified by an appeal to some *other* concept of equity that is not based on the notion of equality?

Of particular interest here is Le Grand's (1984, 1987) concept of equity as equal constraints. He argues that inequality is not necessarily inequitable. One cannot, Le Grand (1984) suggests,

simply observe inequality . . . and thereby judge, *on the basis of that inequality alone*, whether or not an allocation is equitable or inequitable (p. 44, emphasis in original).

He suggests that inequalities *are* inequitable if they reflect inequalities in the constraints people face but are *not* if they simply reflect differences in tastes. Le Grand (1987) gives the example of two people who face the same constraints but have different preferences: their levels of health are different because one is a smoker and the other is not. He then comments:

But this does not seem inequitable. Both were fully aware of the dangers involved; both were unconstrained in their choice by other factors; both have made informed decisions based on their own preferences. The results of these decisions are different, and that is reflected in disparities in their health states; but that is the outcome of their own decision, exercised over the same range of choices, and hence is not equitable. (p. 20)

Viewing equity in these terms would seem on the face of it to provide a promising line of defence for weighted health maximization. Interestingly, however, Le Grand concludes that it would actually be *inequitable* for differences in health-related behaviour to have *any* bearing on the way people are treated by the health care system.

It is arguable whether equity considerations of this kind should play any role in the actual allocation of treatment at the point of use. Rather, they seem to be more appropriately applied to questions of the *finance* of treatment. That is, the question might be not: is it equitable for these particular patients to receive treatment; but, rather, should they receive treatment at the community's expense, or at their own expense? (p. 23)

He then suggests that smokers, for example, should be charged an annual premium to cover the *expected* costs of treatment but should continue to receive the same treatment (or access to treatment) as non-smokers.

The implication of Le Grand's argument is, then, that it might well be equitable for a person's non-health characteristics to influence his rights *vis-à-vis* the health care sector. However, any discrimination ought to be confined to the finance of health care; discrimination in the delivery of health care is not warranted. Once again the answer to the first of the three questions posed at the beginning of the section appears to be 'no'.

6 EQUALITY? OR LESS INEQUALITY?

Of the four definitions of equity examined in the previous section, only the 'equality of health' definition would appear to provide a basis for determining an equitable allocation of health care. But it is not a terribly sensible equity objective[17]: blind pursuit of equality can lead to some rather absurd conclusions. It would, for example, lead to the conclusion that the move from point m in figure 15.1 to point r is unjust, even though *both* A and B are in better health at r and the degree of inequality there is small.

This is *not* to say, however that a concern about the *degree* of inequality in health is to be rejected. Indeed, it is this concern that lies at the heart of Smith's (1987) critique of the QALY literature. Williams (1981) also appeared to be sympathetic to a concern about inequality when, in a discussion about the implications of the 'egalitarian–humanitarian ethic' underlying the QALY approach, he wrote:

> It has frequently been suggested to me in casual conversation . . . that distributional equity dictates that it is better for many people to get a little than for a few people to get a lot (i.e., contradicting the notion that one person getting ten years' additional life expenditure is the same as ten people getting one each). (p. 277)

If the concern about the implications of health maximization for health inequalities is legitimate, but the goal of equality per se is unattractive, how might one proceed?

7 IS A SOCIAL WELFARE FUNCTION THE ANSWER?

One approach suggested by modern welfare economics would be to employ a *social welfare function* (SWF). Given the extra-welfarist orientation of the QALY approach, the SWF would be defined not over utility levels but over *inter alia* the health of the population. This SWF would be constructed so as to reflect an aversion to inequality, but would permit some trade off between inequality and efficiency. The SWF would then be maximized subject to resource and other constraints.

439

7.1 The iso-elastic social welfare function

To illustrate, let us stick with the case of two individuals, or groups of similar individuals, A and B. Then one attractive SWF is the iso-elastic SWF

$$W = [(ah_A)^{1-\tau} + (\beta h_B)^{1-\tau}]^{1/(1-\tau)} \quad \tau \neq 1 \tag{1}$$

Here, W denotes the level of social welfare associated with the health distribution $[h_A, h_B]$.[18] The parameter a indicates the weight to be attached to A's health and β the weight to be attached to B's health. If, for example, A were a young person (or a group of young people) and B an elderly person (or a group of elderly people), society might take a view that a should be larger than β. Alternatively society might wish to adopt the principle underlying the early QALY literature, namely that the identity of the person receiving the QALY is irrelevant to the social value of that QALY. Such a view, which is in effect an *anonymity principle*, would result in a and β being set at the same value.

The parameter τ indicates the degree aversion to inequality in health outcomes. The case where $\tau = 0$ and $a = \beta = 1$ is the case considered in the empirical literature on QALYs to date and the case where $\tau = 0$ but $a \neq \beta$ underlies the recent proposals of Culyer and Williams. In neither case is any aversion to inequality indicated: the difference lies in the slope of the welfare contour. If $\tau > 0$, some aversion to inequality is indicated: with $\tau < \infty$, the contours of the welfare function are convex to the origin and as $\tau \to \infty$ the welfare contour becomes L-shaped with its corner on the 45° line – the so-called *Rawlsian* SWF, since it implies a concern solely with the health of the least healthy person (cf. Rawls, 1972; Atkinson and Stiglitz, 1987, p. 337).[19] Though it is sometimes claimed otherwise (cf., e.g. Barr, 1987, p. 152), equation (1) cannot encompass egalitarianism: if the goal is absolute equality, then all that matters is the distribution of health, not per capita health status; in this case all points along a given ray through the origin give rise to the same level of social welfare and the closer the ray is to the 45° line, the higher is the level of social welfare. Nor can equation (1) capture a less extreme version of egalitarianism where some tradeoff is permitted between 'distance' and the absolute levels of health: in this case the social welfare contours are upward-sloping lines with their corners on the 45° line (cf., e.g., Atkinson and Stiglitz, 1987, p. 341). However, unless the health frontier has some upward sloping parts, the Rawlsian maximin criterion – which *can* be captured by equation (1) – will lead to the same outcome as this family of egalitarian SWFs.

Figure 15.3 shows the implications of aversion to inquality for the choice of point on the health frontier. Health maximization would pick point p out as the best point, whilst the 'equality of health' objective would select point q. The non-linear SWF, by contrast, chooses point s: here there is less inequality than at p, but more inequality than at q. It is also evident that the sum of health statuses

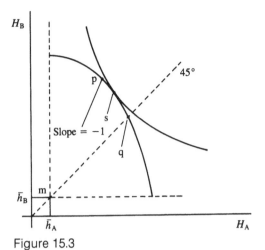

Figure 15.3

is lower at s than at p. Thus the SWF provides an answer to the question posed by Culyer (1990), namely: 'what *is* the acceptable price that one should pay for greater equality?' (Culyer, 1990, p. 24).

7.2 Social welfare maximization and definitions of equity

The attraction of the SWF approach, then, is its ability to capture both efficiency *and* equity considerations. It provides a way of examining the extent to which society wants to accept a lower per capita health status in order to achieve greater equity. The SWF approach also provides the non-technical information required in order to determine *needs*, since it indicates which health improvements are socially desirable. Once the desired distribution of extra QALYs has been established, one can address the technical problem of establishing the least-cost treatments to be used to effect these health improvements.

This raises the issue of whether there might be some conflict between welfare maximization (which reflects one view of equity) and the notion of equal treatment for equal need (which ostensibly reflects another). Consider first the case where A and B start off with the same health (the endowment point lies on the 45° line), have the same capacity to benefit from treatment and can be treated at the same cost (the health frontier is symmetrical about the 45° line). Welfare maximization in this case requires that both A and B receive the same number of extra QALYs and the same amount of health care resources. It is clear that giving A and B *different* amounts of resources would not only violate the principle of equal treatment for equal need, but would also reduce social welfare. This is also true in the more general case where capacities to benefit from treatment differ. In such a case it is quite conceivable that welfare maximization may require that one person gets more extra QALYs than another, yet both require the same amounts of health care resources to achieve their respective health improvements. Differential treatment would again violate the principle of equal treatment for equal need, as well as reducing social welfare. The conclusion is therefore reached that *equal treatment for equal need is actually implied by welfare maximization.*[20]

By contrast, equal access for equal need is not implied by welfare maximization if the SWF is defined over health levels. Welfare maximization identifies persons in equal need, but assigning those in equal need the same access costs will not guarantee that they receive the same treatment (cf. Mooney, 1983, p. 183). Welfare maximization – like 'equal treatment for equal need' – may require differentiation of access costs amongst those in equal need.

8 SOCIAL WELFARE MAXIMIZATION AND RESOURCE ALLOCATION

What implications does acceptance of an aversion towards inequality have for resource allocation via the QALY approach?

8.1 Resource allocation: theory

Health maximization leads, as has been seen, to the rule that resources ought to be deployed so that the marginal cost per QALY is the same across all types of health care activity. As might be expected, social welfare maximization leads to a modification of this rule, namely that the slope of the frontier (the ratio of marginal costs) is to be equated to the slope of the SWF contour. The latter is equal to $(h_A/h_B)^{-\tau}$, where h_A and h_B are the *final* health levels of A and B (i.e., their health *levels after* receipt of any extra QALYs). The latter is the sum of (i) the expected number of QALYs remaining in the absence of treatment (the shaded area in figure 15.2) and (ii) the QALYs that would be gained as a result of treatment (the cross-hatched area in figure 15.2). Since (i) is given, the decision variable in each case is (ii). This affects both the slope of the SWF contour (via its effect on final health) and the slope of the frontier (via its effect on marginal costs).

Note that when $\tau = 0$, i.e., when there is no concern about inequality, the rule reverts to the original rule that the marginal cost per QALY is to be equalized across programmes. In this case the pre- *and* post-treatment levels of health are irrelevant to resource allocation decisions. In the case where there is some concern about inequality, $\tau > 0$ and $(h_A/h_B)^{-\tau}$ is different from one. Here resource allocation decisions cannot be made simply by examining the marginal cost of additional QALYs. Consideration must also be given to (i) the expected health of A and B in the absence of treatment and (ii) the degree to which society is averse to inequality.

8.2 Resource allocation: practice

The implication of the above is that, when allocating resources between health care programmes and between individuals within a given programme, attention needs to be paid both to the degree of inequality implied by each decision and to the importance society attaches to that inequality.

How might the approach suggested be operationalized? To illustrate take the problem of deciding on resource allocation between two health care programmes. Suppose the programmes in question are hip replacements and kidney transplantation. Thus A might represent all persons with hip disease of a given type and severity, and B all persons with kidney disease of a given type and severity. Unless society is indifferent towards inequalities in health, information is required on:

(i)   the prognosis (in terms of QALYs) for a person with a diseased hip in the absence of a hip replacement (the shaded area in figure 15.2);
(ii) the number of people who could benefit from a hip replacement;
(iii) the prognosis (in terms of QALYs) for a person with a diseased kidney in the absence of a kidney transplant (the shaded area in figure 15.2);
(iv) the number of people who could benefit from kidney transplants;
(v)   society's aversion to inequalities in health (i.e., a value for τ); and
(vi) indications of how the marginal cost of a QALYs in each programme changes as the number of cases treated changes.

The product of (i) and (ii) gives the *total* number of expected QALYs that would be enjoyed if hip replacements were not undertaken.

Some of this information is already available. Items (i) and (iii) in the list above have already been calculated in QALY calculations (cf., e.g., Williams, 1985). Two possibilities suggest themselves for items (ii) and (iv); waiting lists (a rather crude and unattractive solution) and survey data (a more promising approach, but one that may require special surveys).[21] In the long term experimental methods might be used to try to elicit values of the inequality aversion parameter τ [item (v)]. In the short term, in the absence of firm guidance from policy makers (or the general public at large), one sensible strategy might be to calculate the optimal allocation of resources for each of several different values of τ. Information on the final item (vi) is currently rather patchy (current figures correspond to a point on a marginal cost curve), but could presumably be generated, perhaps by drawing on the experience of the past and/or that of other countries.

9 CONCLUSIONS

The main negative message to emerge from the foregoing is that health maximization – even in its weighted form – fails to reflect the aversion society apparently feels towards inequalities in health outcomes. The main positive message of the paper is that this aversion *could* be incorporated into resource allocation decisions by using an appropriately specified SWF. Such an approach would allow researchers to capture *both* efficiency *and* equity considerations, by allowing them to take into account how far society is prepared to accept a lower per capita health status in order to achieve greater equality in health outcomes.

Of course, obtaining optimal resource allocations via a SWF would be more burdensome computationally than the health maximization approach. In addition to requiring more information, it would also probably necessitate the use of non-linear programming techniques. But if society *does* take the view that building aversion to inequality into resource allocation decisions is desirable, does it really make sense to continue to force QALYs into the health maximization straitjacket? Might not the extra work entailed in the SWF approach be the price that has to be paid for being in tune with society's views about equity?

NOTES

I am grateful to John Broome, Tony Culyer, Eddy van Doorslaer, Alan Maynard, Alan Williams and an anonymous referee for helpful comments on earlier versions of this chapter. The usual disclaimer applies.

1 It is perhaps worth noting that this rejection of the Pareto value judgement does not imply that quality-of-life scores should not reflect the views of consumers (cf., e.g., Torrance and Feeny (1989). What it *does* imply is that individuals should not be left to decide on their *own* scores and that the rich should not be able somehow to 'buy' higher scores than the poor.

2 Possibly because of the confusing use of the term utility in the QALY literature some have actually criticized the QALY approach for being welfarist. Thus Lockwood (1988) writes: 'what I want to focus on here is the philosophically more fundamental objection that can be levelled against the QALY approach: namely that, precisely *because* it is uncompromisingly welfarist, it is in principle liable to result in forms of allocation that are *unjust* or *unfair*' (p. 45, emphasis in original).

3 Since it is presumably considered unethical to administer health care so as to *impair* health, the extra-welfarist analogue of the potential Pareto criterion would seem a nonsense.

4 Alternatively $\bar{h}_A$ and $\bar{h}_B$ might be interpreted as the expected QALYs remaining if A and B receive medical management rather than surgery (cf. Williams, 1985).

5 This can be seen by noting that the slope of the frontier at q (where health is equally distributed) is greater than 1 in absolute value. In other words, if we abstract from differences in health status and assume that the two individuals have the same health, the cost of an additional QALY is higher for A than for B.

6 Some critics of the QALY approach have suggested otherwise. Smith (1987), in his critique of Williams' (1985) paper on QALYs, writes: 'A cost-effectiveness approach to the allocation of health resources presupposes a simple utilitarian or Benthamite concept of justice' (Smith, 1987, p. 135). Lockwood (1988) also identifies health

maximization with utilitarianism. 'These health-care economists have, it appears, rediscovered utilitarianism. Indeed, the QALY approach has a pleasantly nostalgic air for those familiar with Jeremy Bentham's "felicific calculus"' (Lockwood, 1988, p. 39). Again, the confusion may be due in part to the confusing use of the term utility in the QALY literature.

7 Cf. Culyer (1990) on this point.

8 Recall Culyer's (1990) distinctions noted in section 2.

9 It is not entirely clear from Williams (1981) why time appears to be valued at market prices (i.e., wages) in the case of the employed (cf. Williams, 1981, p. 272). This would seem to run counter to the desire to reject market valuations as a basis for valuations. Nor is it clear why the time of the employed is assigned a positive value (as is the time of housewives), whilst the time of the elderly and mentally handicapped is valued at zero (cf. Williams, 1981, p. 279).

10 Of course, in this case the notion of a fixed budget becomes a bit lazy. The assumption does, however, seem to underlie the QALY approach.

11 Cf. Pereira (1989).

12 Alan Williams has pointed out to me that in his work (cf., e.g., Williams, 1985) he has got round this problem by excluding GNP gains and losses from the calculations. He notes that this can be justified on the grounds that the economy is at less than full employment (a sick person is simply replaced by someone who would have otherwise been unemployed).

13 See, for example, Le Grand (1982, 1987), Mooney (1983) and Mooney and McGuire (1987).

14 On this confusion, see Mooney (1983).

15 Since the objective of equality focuses simply on the distribution of health and not the overall amount of health, this definition of equity has nothing to say about the relative desirability of different points along the 45° line, or indeed along *any* ray through the origin. This means that any move outwards along a ray is neither good nor bad from the standpoint of equity.

16 This is not the only way 'equality of health' might be interpreted. An alternative would be equality of expected QALYs at birth.

17 Indeed many suggest that it is, in any case, rarely stated as a policy objective. On these points see *inter alia* Mooney (1983) and Mooney and McGuire (1987).

18 A similar welfare function underlies Atkinson's (1970) index of inequality (cf. also Deaton and Muellbauer, 1980, pp. 227 ff).

19 For a defence of this interpretation of Rawls' maximum principle in the present context, see Le Grand (1987).

20 One is reminded here of Feldstein's (1976) conclusion that equal taxation of equals is implied by social welfare maximization.

21 In Britain, for example, the annual General Household Survey – the closest survey Britain has to the health interview surveys carried out in many other countries – is very limited in its information on specific health problems.

REFERENCES

Atkinson, A.B. (1970), 'On the measurement of inequality', *Journal of Economic Theory*, 2: 244–63.

Atkinson, A.B. and J.E. Stiglitz (1987), *Lectures on Public Economics*, London, McGraw-Hill.

Barr, N. (1987), *The Economics of the Welfare State*, London, Weidenfeld & Nicolson.

Broome, J. (1988), 'Goodness, fairness and QALYs', in M. Bell and S. Mendus (eds.), *Philosophy and Medical Welfare*, Cambridge University Press, pp. 57–73.

Culyer, A.J. (1976), *Need and the National Health Service*, Oxford, Martin Robertson.

   (1980), *The Political Economy of Social Policy*, Oxford, Martin Robertson.

   (1989), 'The normative economics of health care finance and provision', *Oxford Review of Economic Policy*, 5: 34–58.

   (1990), 'Commodities, characteristics of commodities, characteristics of people, utilities and the quality of life', in S. Baldwin *et al.* (eds.), *The Quality of Life: Perspectives and Policies*, London, Routledge, pp. 9–27.

Culyer, A.J., A. Williams and R. Lavers (1972), 'Health indicators', in A. Schonfield and S. Shaw (eds.), *Social Indicators and Social Policy*, London, Heinemann, pp. 94–118.

Deaton, A. and J. Muellbauer (1980), *Economics and Consumer Behavior*, Cambridge University Press.

Department of Health and Social Security (1980), *Inequalities in health*, DHSS, London.

Drummond, M.F. (1989), 'Output measurement for resource allocation decisions in health care', *Oxford Review of Economic Policy*, 5: 59–74.

Feldstein, M.S. (1976), 'On the theory of tax reform', *Journal of Public Economics*, 6:77–104.

Grossman, M. (1972), *The Demand for Health: A Theoretical and Empirical Investigation*, New York, Columbia University Press.

Harris, J. (1988), 'More and better justice', M. Bell and S. Mendus (eds.), *Philosophy and Medical Welfare*, Cambridge University Press, pp. 75–96.

Le Grand, J. (1982), *The Strategy of Equality*, London, Allen & Unwin.

   (1984), 'Equity as an economic objective', *Journal of Applied Philosophy*, 1: 39–51.

   (1987), 'Equity, health and health care, in: three essays on equity', Discussion paper WSP/23, STICERD, London School of Economics.

Lockwood, M. (1988), 'Quality of life and resource allocation', in M. Bell and S. Mendus (eds.), *Philosophy and Medical Welfare*, Cambridge University Press, pp. 33–55.

Mooney, G. (1983), 'Equity in health care: confronting the confusion', *Effective Health Care*, 1: 179–85.

Mooney, G. and A. McGuire (1987), 'Distributive justice with special reference to geographical inequality in health care', in A. Williams (ed.), *Health and Economics*, London, Macmillan, pp. 68–81.

Pereira, J. (1989), 'What does equity in health mean?', Discussion paper 61, Centre for Health Economics, University of York.

Rawls, J. (1972), *A Theory of Justice*, Oxford University Press.

Sen, A.K. (1973), *On Economic Inequality*, Oxford, Clarendon Press.

   (1979), 'Personal utilities and public judgements: or what's wrong with welfare economics?', *Economic Journal*, 89: 537–58.

(1980), 'Equality of what?' in S. McMurrin (ed.), *The Tanner Lectures on Human Values*, Cambridge University Press, pp. 185–220; reprinted in Sen (1982).

(1982), *Choice Welfare and Measurement*, Oxford, Blackwell.

Smith, A. (1987), 'Qualms about QALYs', *The Lancet*, i: 1134.

Torrance, G.W. (1986), 'Measurement of health state utilities for economic appraisal: a review', *Journal of Health Economics*, 5:1–30.

Torrance, G.W. and D. Feeny (1989), 'Utilities and quality-adjusted life years', *International Journal of Technology Assessment in Health Care*, 5: 559–75.

Williams, A. (1974a), 'The cost–benefit approach', *British Medical Bulletin*, 30: 252–6.

(1974b), 'Need as a demand concept (with special reference to health)', in A.J. Culyer (ed.), *Economic Policies and Social Goals*, London, Martin Robertson, pp. 60–76.

(1976), 'Cost–benefit analysis in public health and medical care: comments on a thesis written by Bengt Jönsson', Report 1976:28, Department of Economics, University of Lund.

(1977), 'Measuring the quality of life in the elderly', in L. Wingo and A. Evans (eds.), *Public Economics of the Quality of Life*, Baltimore, Johns Hopkins Press.

(1981), 'Welfare economics and health status measurement', in J. van der Gaag and M. Perlman (eds.), *Health, Economics and Health Economics*, Amsterdam, North-Holland, pp. 271–81.

(1985), 'Economics of coronary artery bypass grafting', *British Medical Journal*, 291: 326–9.

(1988), 'Ethics and efficiency in the provision of health care', in M. Bell and S. Mendus (eds.), *Philosophy and Medical Welfare*, Cambridge University Press, pp. 111–26.

16

INFRASTRUCTURE:

Water-vending activities in developing countries: a case study of Ukunda, Kenya

Dale Whittington, Donald T. Lauria, Daniel A. Okun and Xinming Mu

Water supply projects in developing countries are traditionally based on either (a) piped systems, with public taps or private household services (or both), or (b) wells with handpumps. Both of these approaches to providing water services have been extensively studied; planning and design manuals for such systems abound. There is, however, a third approach to service delivery which is seldom explicitly recognized or incorporated in design or investment decisions: water vending. Millions of people in villages and cities throughout the developing world are, in fact, already being served by vendors who take water from a source that is available and then deliver it in containers to households or fill household containers from their vehicle tanks.

WATER VENDING

The distribution of water by vendors is expensive, whether the vehicles are powered by people, animals or engines. Households which are served by vendors generally pay more per month for 20–40 litres per capita per day than those directly connected to a piped system who might use as much as 400 litres per capita per day. Households sometimes pay over 10 per cent of their monthly income for vended water, as compared to 1–5 per cent for most piped water systems (Whittington, Lauria and Mu, 1989; Zaroff and Okun, 1984). In addition, vendors sometimes sell water from polluted sources or fouled containers. Water vending can thus be a financial burden and a health threat to millions of people.

Nevertheless, vending is a valuable service for people in urban and rural areas who have no access to piped water; otherwise they would not choose to buy vended water. People moving into slums and squatter settlements on the fringes of rapidly expanding urban areas must often rely on vendors until the piped system is expanded, if ever. In villages traditional water sources may still be available, but people may have sufficient income to afford vended water at least

This chapter previously appeared in the *International Journal of Water Resources Development*, 5. We would like to thank Carfax Publishing Company for their kind permission to reproduce it here.

part of the time and thus obtain some relief from the daily burden of carrying water from a distant source to the household. The principal benefit of water vending to the consumer is thus that it provides a significant saving of time compared to fetching water from other sources.

There are, however, other important social benefits of water vending. Vending is labour intensive. The principal cost of a simple water vending system (i.e. one without motorized vehicles) is typically the labour of the vendors themselves, the social opportunity cost of which may be very low. The capital costs of such water vending systems are much lower than for piped systems and usually require much less foreign exchange. Vending often provides significant employment in communities with few other opportunities (at least in the short term). The technology used in most vending systems is relatively simple and can be maintained locally. Vending operations are also robust; there are typically many vendors, and if the equipment of one breaks down, others still function.

While water vending is ubiquitous in developing countries, it takes many forms and is organized in many different ways. All systems have one or more of three types of vendors:

(1) *Wholesale vendors* obtain water from some source and sell it to distributing vendors.
(2) *Distributing vendors* obtain water from a source or a wholesale vendor and sell it to consumers door-to-door. (In this article we use the term *vendor* alone to refer to a *distributing vendor.*)
(3) *Direct vendors* sell water to consumers coming to the source to purchase water. In Kenya direct vendors sell water from kiosks where the water is dispersed from a distribution system.

An individual can be both a wholesale and a direct vendor, selling to distributing vendors and to customers directly as shown in figure 16.1. A distributing, wholesale or direct vendor may obtain water directly from a source or a piped distribution system. A distributing vendor may in addition use a vehicle to get water from the source directly or from a wholesale vendor. Customers may get water by pipeline, from a distributing vendor, or by walking to a public tap, a direct vendor (kiosk) or a source.

Prices for water may be set competitively or controlled at any of several possible points in a vending system. Any of the three kinds of vendors may be formally or informally organized, or operate independently. The prices distributing vendors receive may be set in a competitive market, while they may buy water from wholesale vendors with monopoly power. Alternatively, wholesale vendors may compete freely, but distributing vendors may be organized to control prices. Water from a public tap is generally free, but, when attended, the direct vendor makes a charge.

Despite the fact that water vendors serve millions of people in cities and villages throughout the developing world and may offer a more convenient

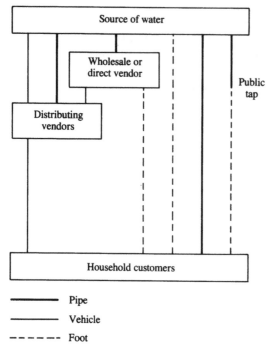

Figure 16.1 Possible water distribution system

service than is available from public handpumps or public taps (although at a high price), water vending has received little attention in the published literature (for exceptions see Adrianzen and Graham, 1974; Antoniou, 1979; Fass, 1982; Suleiman, 1977; and Zaroff and Okun, 1984). Most information is anecdotal. Professionals in the water resources field have ignored water vending in part because its existence is seen as an indication of the failure of water supply institutions to provide an adequate service. Although this is often an accurate assessment of the situation, vending is worthy of study for the following reasons:

(1) Vending will continue to exist in developing countries for the foreseeable future due to severe shortages of capital for piped systems or for wells and handpumps.
(2) Vending may in some circumstances actually prove to be an appropriate technology for a community at a given level of economic and social development because it is typically very reliable.
(3) Information on water vending practices, particularly costs and charges, may be useful for traditional water supply planning decisions.
(4) Vending systems may be improved in quality and economy.

The research reported in the remainder of this paper was initiated in order to take a first step towards providing detailed data on water vending in developing countries.

THE STUDY AREA

Ukunda is a village of about 5,000 people located 40 km south of Mombasa in the Kwale district of Kenya. It is the largest population centre along the Kenyan South Coast between Mombasa and the Tanzanian border. The town lies alongside a paved highway which parallels the coastline and is about 3 km from the ocean. Ukunda's economy is representative of many small provincial centres in Africa which are being rapidly drawn into a national market economy. The economy of Ukunda is, however, heavily influenced by its proximity to the luxury tourist hotels at Diani Beach and Mombasa. Although the economy of the South Coast region is primarily based on agriculture and fishing, many people in Ukunda find jobs in tourist-related activities, particularly during the high season from November to March. This increased economic activity supports a petrol station, a handful of third-class hotels and restaurants, numerous bars and a few handicraft enterprises. There are also a few local offices for government organizations such as the Ministry of Water Development (MWD).

The majority of houses in Ukunda and surrounding villages are constructed of mud with thatched roofs, although corrugated metal roofs and masonry walls are becoming increasingly common. The agricultural areas around Ukunda are heavily populated, with over 200 people per km^2. Over 90 per cent of the population along the South Coast is Wadigo, who are Moslems, but the percentage in Ukunda itself is somewhat less due to substantial in-migration. Education levels in the Kwale district are low; about three quarters of the population has never attended school. Per capita annual income in the region is in the order of US$200, although it is estimated at US$350 in Ukunda.

Rainfall along the South Coast is approximately 1,200 mm per year. The rainy season lasts from April to October. Numerous small streams drain the Shimba Hills 30 km west of the coast; one small river passes 2 km north of the centre of Ukunda on its way to the sea.

Residents of Ukunda have numerous sources of water available in the village without walking to nearby rivers or ponds. The MWD operates a pipeline which was designed primarily to serve the resort hotels on Diani Beach. The source of water for this system is four boreholes 10 km north of Ukunda. The system's capacity is about 4,000 m^3 per day, but it is subject to frequent breakdowns. There are only about fifteen private house connections in Ukunda; most people in Ukunda obtain water from the system by purchasing it from direct vendors who are licensed operators (kiosks) or from distributing vendors who buy water from the kiosks (wholesale vendors). A kiosk is typically a small structure with a corrugated metal roof and walls surrounding a single tap which the operator controls by hand. All of the kiosks are used for direct vending to individuals; some of the kiosks also sell to distributing vendors who then deliver water to both households and small businesses.

The vendors carry water in 20 litre plastic jerricans, transported by either carts or bicycles. The carts have a single axle with two automobile tyres and are pushed by hand similar to a wheelbarrow. Most of the carts carry ten 20 litre jerricans weighing 200 kg. A bicycle outfitted for vending can carry three cans. The carts are more efficient for most types of terrain. The bicycles are used for more distant locations and on slopes which are difficult to reach with a fully loaded cart. The cart wheels are equipped with bells which jingle when the carts are moving, and vendors make most of their sales while pushing their carts through the village looking for customers. The level of service which the vendors provide is quite extraordinary: almost anywhere in Ukunda a person can within minutes hear the bells and hail a vendor. Often several vendors appear.

In addition, six open wells and five handpumps are scattered around the village. There is a long tradition of well ownership in Wadigo communities. Wells are typically dug by wealthier members of the community, but anyone in the community is free to use them without charge. The wells in Ukunda range from shallow to about 30 m deep, and most provide water all year round. Some of the wells in Ukunda are up to 2.5 m in diameter, with finely crafted rock walls. None are equipped with working pulleys; individuals collect water by dropping a 2 litre container into the well.

The handpumps in the community were installed by various donor agencies, and several different brands are used. The handpumps are located in the southern part of Ukunda, generally in less densely populated areas. The donors left various institutional arrangements for collecting funds to maintain the handpumps.

FIELD PROCEDURES

The fieldwork on water vending was conducted in June and July 1986, the rainy season, and consisted of four activities:

(1) observations at kiosks, handpumps and open wells;
(2) interviews with water vendors;
(3) interviews with kiosk owners;
(4) mapping out vendor routes.

Observations at kiosks, handpumps and open wells were conducted over the period from 23 June to 5 July 1986 by seventeen individuals from the community, most with the equivalent of a secondary school education. All were given a day of training estimating volumes of containers and recording information; they were then required to pass a test to ensure that they could record information reliably.

Distributing vendors in Ukunda obtain water only from wholesale vendors at the kiosks; observers assigned to kiosks recorded the time each vendor arrived and departed and the amount of water purchased. Individuals obtain water directly from kiosks, open wells and handpumps; observers at all sources recorded the gender and age (adult/child) of each indivudal collecting water and the amount of water collected. The kiosks opened in the morning about 6.15 a.m. They closed for an hour or two early in the afternoon and then closed in the evening about 6.15 p.m. Source observers stayed at their assigned posts for this entire period. Handpumps were generally locked at night and thus were open for use for roughly the same period each day. Data were taken on 28,783 trips by individuals to collect water and on 3,605 trips by vendors.

Of a total of about eighty-five to ninety water vendors in Ukunda, forty-three were interviewed. The questionnaire addressed the vendor's socioeconomic background, employment history, costs and sales, pricing and other business practices, and future developments in the vending business. Ten of the kiosk owners were interviewed to elicit information on their business and their opinions on water vending.

Some enumerators followed vendors all day and recorded (a) the time, location and volume of each fill up at a kiosk, (b) the time, location and price of each sale, and (c) whether the sale was cash or credit. The enumerator also asked each buyer how much water was purchased on average each week. Over a six-day period vendors were followed for an entire day fifty times, and 887 actual sales were observed.

DESCRIPTION OF THE WATER-VENDING INDUSTRY

All of the vendors were male; their average age was thirty years. For all but one, water vending was a full-time occupation. Most vendors sell water throughout the entire year.

The prices charged for vended water are largely determined by free market forces. The vendors are not organized, and entry into the business is easy. Start-up costs are low because carts with jerricans are available for rent by the week from local merchants for as little as 10 ks (US$1 = 16 Kenyan shillings). The cost of a cart is about 1,000 ks. About 40 per cent of the vendors owned their equipment.

Kiosk owners pay the MWD 0.05 ks per 20 l (US$0.16 per m^3) for piped water. During both the rainy and dry seasons, the vendors buy water from the kiosks for 0.15 ks per 20 litre jerrican (US$0.47 per m^3). During the rainy season 90 per cent of vendors' sales are at the rate of 1.5 ks per 20 litre jerrican (US$4.70 per m^3), increasing to 3 ks in the dry season when the demand for vended water is high because of the hot weather and the fact that, because people are employed in tourist-related activities, they have money to spend and little time for collecting water. The piped water system is unreliable and kiosk owners are without water about two days per week in the dry season. During such times of shortage, water vendors may have to collect water from another town 5 km away, and the price may increase to 6 ks per jerrican. During the rainy season, higher prices are occasionally charged in outlying areas, and regular customers near kiosks some-times receive lower prices. Social pressures among the vendors appear to keep the price from falling much below 1.5 ks. During the dry season a system of zonal pricing is much more developed and widespread. The price increases the farther the distance from the kiosks or from the paved road.

Some vendors have regular customers, highly valued because they provide a steady source of revenue, particularly during the rainy season. Vendors extend credit to regular customers and may charge lower prices. Prices in the rainy season may decrease to 1 ks per 20 litre jerrican for such reliable customers and, during periods of shortage, vendors do not increase the price charged regular customers to the market level.

Slightly less than 20 per cent of the sales observed in this study were made on credit. Most vendor sales to households were for two jerricans. Businesses required larger deliveries. The average vendor made about seventeen sales per day, requiring three to four trips to kiosks daily. Most vendors sell water in a relatively small portion of the village.

Because water vending in Ukunda is highly competitive, a vendor must work hard to be successful. As in many sales operations, there is large variation in individual performance, and it is thus difficult to characterize a typical vendor. Table 16.1 presents a weekly budget for both the rainy and dry seasons for an experienced vendor who rents his cart and jerricans.

There is a marked difference in the profitability of water vending in the rainy and dry seasons. In the dry season the water vendors work more hours per day, the price they receive per jerrican is doubled, and their weekly revenues are two to four times as great. The implicit wage rate in the rainy season is 6 ks/hr, about 50 per cent higher than the market wage rate for unskilled labour. In the dry season the vendors earn about 20 ks/hr. Some vendors voluntarily reported that they are able to save money during the dry season. Net annual income varies from 20,000 to 35,000 ks (US$1,300–2,100), about the average household income in Ukunda.

ANALYSIS OF WATER DISTRIBUTION

Slightly more than 20,000 jerricans (400 m³) were sold weekly in the rainy season. Two of thirteen kiosks supplied almost 50 per cent of the water sold to vendors. Vendors buy most of their water in the morning. After a slack period, activity picks up in the afternoon. The average vendor queue time at a kiosk is about ten minutes, being slightly longer at the busier kiosks. Vendors still prefer these kiosks because their water pressure is reliable and they are well located.

Individuals, as contrasted with vendors, collected about 480 m³ per week in the rainy season: 79 per cent by adult women, 13 per cent by adult men, 7 per cent by female children and 1 per cent by male children. Of the water collected directly by

Table 16.1 *A representative water vendor's weekly budget*

	Rainy season	Dry season
Revenues		
Trips per day	3	3
Cans per trip	10	10
Cans sold per day	30	60
Days worked per week	6	6.5
Cans sold per week	180	390
Average price per can (ks)	1.5	3
Total weekly sales (ks)	270	1,170
Costs		
Water		
Price per can (ks)	0.15	0.15
Cost per week (ks)	27	59
Equipment		
Rental of cart and jerricans (ks)	10	15
Total weekly expenses, excluding own labour (ks)	37	74
Profits per week (ks)	233	1,096
Hours worked per week	37	54
Implicit wage rate (ks/hr)	6	20

individuals, 64 per cent was obtained from kiosks, 18 per cent from handpumps and 18 per cent from open wells.

In all, kiosk owners sold about 700 m³ per week during the study period, over half (57 per cent) being sold to vendors. The kiosks received revenues of about 3,000 ks per week from vendors and about 230 ks per week from individuals. At MWD's rate of 0.05 ks per 20 litres, its revenues from kiosks should have been about 1,800 ks per week. In fact, the owners reported average weekly payments to the MWD totalling about 750 ks. The fact that several kiosk water meters were not functioning may have accounted for this difference. The kiosk owners' aggregate profits per week (not considering labour) were about 4,500 ks (US$280). With thirteen kiosks in operation twelve hours per day, it is clear that kiosk owners are not extracting significant monopoly profits from the existing water vending system in Ukunda.

Water vendors supplied 45% of the total water consumed in Ukunda (excluding the water supplied from the few private connections). Conservatively estimating that weekly expenditures during the dry season are double this level, the annual expenditure by people in Ukunda on vended water is about 2.4 million ks (US$150,000), approximately 480 ks per capita per year (US$30). Of this total,

10 per cent accrues to kiosk owners and 90 per cent to the water vendors working in Ukunda for their labour. An average per capita expenditure of 480 ks per year for vended water is about 9 per cent of the average annual per capita income in Ukunda.

IS VENDING AN APPROPRIATE SYSTEM?

Almost half of the water consumed in Ukunda is purchased from vendors. Those who use vendors enjoy a high level of service; good quality water is delivered to their doorstep on demand. Although vending does not provide a level of service comparable to house connections from a well-run piped distribution system, it is far superior to that available in most rural communities in Kenya.

This high level of service is, however, expensive. The operation of the vending system occupies approximately 100 people full time. Should either the water authority or the local community act to change this situation? Is water vending a 'problem', or is it an appropriate solution the community's water needs? What should government policy be towards water vending such as exists in Ukunda?

Although significant resources are being expended in the operation of the water-vending system, no one is making exorbitant profits. A relatively free market in water exists from the vendor's purchase at the kiosk to the point of delivery. Both the kiosk owners and the water vendors are receiving adequate incomes, but neither is extracting large monopoly rents. There are simply real labour costs involved in hauling 400 m³ of water per week around the village in handcarts. Thus, if the water authority has established a reasonable price to be charged to and by the kiosk owners, there is little economic justification for (a) regulating either the price the distributing vendors charge their customers for water, or (b) licensing the distributing vendors or imposing other restrictions on entry into the vending business.

Although government regulation of vendors does not appear to be justified when there is a competitive market in vended water, improvement of a water system, such as an extension of a piped system, may be. In fact, it is obvious from the data on the magnitude of the money and water flows in the vending system in Ukunda that most people in Ukunda can afford yard taps or even house connections. Even assuming that the existing water system was completely reserved for the beach hotels, the people of Ukunda could build a *totally new system* for an annual per capita cost of about US$10–20 including capital and operation and maintenance costs. Average annual per capita expenses in Ukunda on vended water alone are now about US$30. In situations such as this the information on the water vending system can serve as a useful indicator of a community's ability and willingness to pay for a piped distribution system. The fact that yard taps do not already exist throughout Ukunda indicates an inability on the part of the community or water authority to mobilize resources, not an inability or unwillingness of the population to pay for the cost of the improved service.

In other situations where vending exists, the choice of the appropriate level of service may be more complicated, and a more detailed analysis of the service options will be required. Such an analysis will require an understanding of why households choose different water sources, including vendors. In another article we have examined the determinants of households' water source choice decisions in Ukunda using a discrete choice econometric model (see Mu, Whittington and Briscoe, 1990). In the remainder of this article we assume that it is possible to model households' decisions regarding which water source to use, and we consider the question of whether it is justified to install additional handpumps in a village such as Ukunda which already has a water vending system.

VENDING VERSUS HANDPUMPS

Consider a village with an extensive vending system like that of Ukunda. Should either the water authority or a donor agency install additional handpumps? This decision could arise in Ukunda, for example, if political or institutional constraints made the widespread provision of private connections impossible. Are the benefits of an additional handpump greater than its costs? The benefits of the handpump depend on how many households elect to use it and which sources these households are currently utilizing. It is assumed that the number of households which will choose to use the new handpump can be predicted and that the quantity of water households consume is independent of the source they choose. For purposes of this analysis, the households which will choose to use the new handpump are divided into three groups:

(1) households previously using distributing vendors (Group A);
(2) households previously collecting water from kiosks (Group B);
(3) households previously using open wells or other handpumps (Group C).

For those households previously using distributing vendors (Group A), their principal benefits (not considering health issues) will be the difference between (a) the money they would no longer have to pay vendors and (b) the value of the time which they would have to spend hauling water from the new handpump. For those households previously collecting water from kiosks (Group B), their benefits will be both (a) the money they no longer have to pay kiosk owners and (b) the value of any time saved (or lost) by having the handpump closer to (or farther from) their home than the kiosk. For those households previously using open wells or other handpumps (Group C), their benefits will be the value of the time savings associated with having a new water source closer to their home. Against the benefits to each of these three groups must be weighed both the capital and the operation and maintenance costs of the handpump.

Individuals in the community have both higher and lower levels of service open to them, and the additional handpump thus serves less of a need than if it were the highest level of service available. Viewed from this perspective, it is easy to see why the existence of widespread vending fundamentally alters the investment decision regarding the additional handpump. Vending offers a superior level of service for those individuals who place high value on their time, and they are unlikely to choose the new handpump since they have the alternative of having water delivered to their doorstep. For those people in Group A, the net benefits are likely to be low if they have to spend any significant amount of time collecting water from the handpump. Although they save the money previously spent on vended water, they incur the time costs of hauling water, and the value of their time is high relative to others in the community because they previously chose to buy water from vendors rather than collect it for themselves. For those individuals in Groups B and C, their value of time cannot exceed the price per litre of vended water divided by the time they spend collecting a litre of water; otherwise they would already be buying water from vendors. An upper bound on their benefits can thus be calculated.

The investment analysis suggested above can be best illustrated with some specific numbers:

n_1 = number of households that choose to carry water from the new handpump that currently buy their water from vendors (Group A)

n_2 = number of households that choose to use the new handpump that currently buy their water from kiosks (Group B)

n_3 = number of households that choose to use the new handpump that currently use an open well or another handpump (Group C)

p_1 = price of vended water (US\$/litre)

p_2 = price of water sold at kiosk (US\$/litre)

h_1 = hours per day spent collecting water from the new handpump

h_2 = hours per day spent collecting water from the old source (equal to zero for households currently using vendors)

q = average quantity of water consumed per capita per day in the village (assumed equal for all households)

m = average number of individuals per household

v_1 = value of time spent hauling water for households in Group A

v_2 = value of time spent hauling water for households in Group B

v_3 = value of time spent hauling water for households in Group C

C = annual costs of additional handpump (including capital, operation and maintenance)

The annual net benefits of the additional handpump (*NB*) are given by

$$NB = 365[n_1(p_1 * q * m - v_1 * h_1) + n_2(p_2 * q * m + v_2 * (h_2 - h_1)) + n_3(v_3 * (h_2 - h_1))] - C$$

458

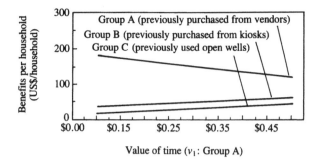

p_1 = US $0.005   price of vended water per litre
p_2 = US $0.0005 price of water sold at kiosk per litre
h_2 = 0.75   hours per day spent collecting water from old source
h_1 = 0.4   hours per day spent collecting water from new handpump
q = 25   litres of water consumed per capita per day
m = 4   average number of individuals per household
v_1 =   value of time of individuals in Group A
v_2 =   value of time of individuals in Groups B and C
$v_1 = 2v_2$

Figure 16.2 Annual benefits per household from the installation of handpumps

The table at the bottom of figure 16.2 presents some values of these parameters characteristic of the situation in Ukunda. The values for individual parameters can be varied and combined in different ways to characterize many villages in developing countries. Figure 16.2 presents the annual net benefits for households in Groups A, B and C for different values of time spent hauling water for households in Group A. For purposes of illustration, the value of time of households in Groups B and C is assumed to be half of that of households in Group A (see Whittington, Mu and Roche, 1989, for empirical support for this assumption).

As the value of time spent hauling water increases, the net benefits of the new handpump to households in Group A decrease, and the net benefits to households in Groups B and C increase, which is evident from the signs of v_1, v_2 and v_3 in the net benefit equation. Because the quantity consumed per capita per day is assumed to be independent of the source, the money savings to households in Groups A and B from the new handpump depend only on the price of water charged by vendors and kiosks respectively, the per capita consumption and the size of the household (and are positively related to all three). The benefits to households in Group A decrease as the time spent collecting water from the new handpump increases. The benefits to households in Groups B and C increase as the *difference* between the time spent hauling water from the old source and the new handpump increases.

Total annual costs (capital and operation and maintenance) of a well and handpump in Ukunda would be in the order of US$500. Thus, if the value of time savings is the primary benefit of the handpump investment (i.e. water quality considerations are not important), the results of these calculations show that a well-located handpump can be very beneficial to households in (a) Group A if their value of time is low and if the distance they have to walk to the new handpump is short, and (b) Groups B and C under most circumstances. If the time savings are significant (e.g. an hour per day), only a relatively small number of households in Groups B and C would be required to justify the investment for most values of time saved and per capita consumption. Only a handful of households in Group A are necessary to justify the investment if the handpump is located very close to them so that the time spent hauling water is minimal (less than thirty minutes per day). The benefits of a handpump to a household in Group A are, however, negative if the household would have to spend an hour per day collecting water and their value of time is greater than US$0.40 per hour.

There is evidence that households using vendors value their time at a higher rate than the current market wage for unskilled labour (US$0.25 per hour; see Whittington, Mu and Roche, 1989). Referring to the information in figure 16.2 on the annual benefits per household *versus* the value of time, it can be seen that at a value of time of US$0.50 per hour annual benefits to households in Group A are on the order of US$110. If households in Groups B and C have average values of time of US$0.25 per hour, their annual benefits are about US$50 and US$30, respectively. It is thus important for the economic justification of the project that any handpumps be located in an area where several households currently using vendors are likely to switch to the new handpump.

These calculations illustrate that as vending becomes more extensive in a village or town and the value of time increases due to increased economic activity and wage employment, the benefits from additional investments in handpumps are likely to decrease. There may, however, still be particular locations where a handpump is needed because the benefits to only a few households may be enough to justify the investment. Similar calculations could be carried out for a comparison between vending and yard taps, although in this case the consumer surplus associated with the increased consumption of water resulting from the installation of yard taps would need to be estimated (Powers, 1978; Churchill *et al.*, 1987).

OTHER INVESTMENT CONSIDERATIONS

There are three other but important aspects of the decision on whether to install additional handpumps in a village where water vending is being practised. The first concerns the dynamic character of water system capacity expansion. Even if the handpump appears to be a good investment using the economic model described above, if incomes in the village are rising it may not be long before the community can afford a piped water system (if it cannot already do so). Because the operation (or expansion) of the vending system does not entail significant capital costs, it is much more flexible and adaptable than a policy of installing additional handpumps. An investment in a handpump needs to provide benefits over an extended period of time in order for its high initial capital costs to be justified, and it therefore may quickly become obsolete. A vending system can potentially play a valuable role in bridging the period from when the community can only afford a few improved sources until incomes are at a level which can support a piped system with private yard taps or house connections. Vending can eliminate the need to overinvest in a system such as handpumps which provides a low level of service.

Second, it is not simply the total average income which determines whether a household can afford the monthly costs generally associated with a house connection from a piped system; the reliability and variation in household income are also important. In Ukunda the incomes of many households are tied to the tourist industry, which is highly seasonal. The water vending system permits households to adjust their water purchases to fit their cash flow situation. Households are not locked into fixed monthly commitments which they are not sure they can pay.

Third, in the investment calculation it is assumed that the price vendors charge for their water is an accurate measure of its social value. As shown in this study, the price of vended water is largely determined by the implicit wage rate associated with the vendors' time. This cost–benefit calculation thus assumes that the opportunity cost of the vendors' time to society is roughly equal to the market wage for unskilled labour (in the rainy season). Whether this is a reasonable assumption depends upon whether in fact the vendors could find other employment if they were not vendors. This is an empirical question, but it is crucial to a proper appraisal of water vending *vis-à-vis* alternative water delivery systems. If the shadow value of labour of water vendors is very low, water vending becomes much more socially attractive. As a first-order approximation, the question of the shadow value of labour depends upon what the roughly 100 people in Ukunda currently engaged in water vending would do if a piped system were installed. In many vending situations they would probably serve another location where piped water is not yet available.

CONCLUSIONS

The findings from this study have important implications for water supply planning in developing countries, not only with respect to water vending, but also with regard to (1) willingness to pay for improved water services, (2) choice of technology, and (3) level of service. First, people in some rural villages are willing and able to pay substantial amounts of money for water, even when traditional sources are readily available. In Ukunda 64 per cent of the water used in the village *in the rainy season* was sold by kiosks to distributing vendors and individuals. Distributing vendors in Ukunda sold more than 45 per cent of the total water consumed in the village. People in Ukunda spend about 9 per cent of their income on vended water.

Second, households are paying much more for vended water than would be necessary to provide and sustain a piped distribution system with yard taps. Such information is important because grants from donor agencies and national governments are not sufficient to meet the huge demands for piped water in developing countries. A survey of vending practices in an area can be a useful indicator of a community's ability and willingness to pay for a piped system.

Third, the case study shows that the prices vendors charge for water are high because hauling water manually is expensive. In Ukunda vendors were making a fair return on their labour and capital investment, but they were not making exorbitant profits. This suggests that government regulation of distributing vendors may not be necessary or advisable.

NOTE

This research was carried out as part of the Water and Sanitation for Health (WASH) project, sponsored by the Office of Health, Bureau for Science and Technology, US Agency for International Development. We would like to thank John Joseph, Samuel Momanyi, Stanislaus K. Mutinda, David Nyamwaya, Robert Roche, Ellis Turner and Makanda David Wafale for their assistance and support during the conduct of this study.

REFERENCES

Adrianzen, T. Blanca and George Graham (1974), 'The high cost of being poor', *Archives of Environmental Health*, 28 (June): 312–15.

Antoniou, James (1979), *Sudan: Khartoum-El Obeid Water Supply Project Urban Poverty Review*, World Bank, Washington, DC.

Churchill, Anthony, A., with the assistance of David de Ferranti, Robert Roche, Carolyn Tager, Alan A. Walters and Anthony Yazer (1987), *Rural Water Supply and Sanitation: A Time for Change*. World Bank Discussion Paper 18. Washington, DC.

Fass, Simon (1982), 'Water and politics: the process of meeting a basic need in Haiti', *Development and Change*, 13: 347–64.

Mu, Xinming, Dale Whittington and John Briscoe (1989), 'Modeling village water demand behavior: a discrete choice approach', *Water Resources Research*.

Powers, Terry A. (1978), 'Benefit–cost analysis of urban water projects', *Water Supply and Management*, vol. 1, Pergamon Press, Oxford, pp. 371–85.

Suleiman, M.S. (1977), *A Study of the Vendor Water Distribution System in Surabaya, Indonesia*, World Health Organization, Geneva.

White, Gilbert F., David J. Bradley and Anne U. White (1972), *Drawers of Water: Domestic Water Use in East Africa*, Chicago, IL, University of Chicago Press.

Whittington, Dale, John Briscoe and Xinming Mu (1987), *Willingness to Pay for Water in Rural Areas: Methodological Approaches and An Application in Haiti*, Field Report No. 213, WASH, USAID, Washington, DC.

Whittington, Dale, Donald T. Lauria and Xinming Mu (1989), *Paying for Urban Services: A Study of Water Vending and Willingness to Pay for Water in Onitsha, Nigeria*, Report INU 40, Infrastructure and Urban Development Department, The World Bank, Washington, DC.

Whittington, Dale, Donald T. Lauria, Daniel A. Okun and Xinming Mu (1988), *Water Vending and Development*, Technical Report No 45, WASH, USAID, Washington, DC.

Whittington, Dale, Xinming Mu and Robert Roche (1989), 'The value of time spent on collecting water: some estimates for Ukunda, Kenya', Report INU 46, Infrastructure and Urban Development Department, The World Bank, Washington, DC.

Zaroff, Barbara and Daniel A. Okun (1984), 'Water vending in developing countries', *Aqua*, No. 5: 289–95.

17

THE ENVIRONMENT:

Assessing the social rate of return from investment in temperate zone forestry

David W. Pearce

1 THE NATURE OF BENEFITS FROM FORESTRY INVESTMENTS

Forestry is a *multiple output activity*. The planting of forests produces a number of *joint outputs and services*. Outputs can be *positive*, taking the form of benefits, or *negative*, i.e., forests may actually reduce the provision of a service compared to the displaced land use, creating a cost. Much depends on exactly where afforestation takes place. Thus:

an afforested area supplies trees as *timber* and as a source of *recreational value*; depending on the 'mix' of trees and the treatments applied to them, in-place *biological diversity* may be increased compared to the number of species and/or total species biomass in the displaced land use;

landscape values may be increased or decreased according to the preferences of those looking at the landscape;

some watershed may be protected by afforestation through the *prevention of soil erosion*. Others may suffer from soil erosion from ploughing and road building activity;

water run-off may be reduced by interception to the point where surrounding areas suffer a *diminution of water supply*, but flood peaks may be reduced once the forest is established;

microclimates may be affected by afforestation, but considerable uncertainty surrounds these impacts;

afforestation may increase the *deposition of airborne sulphur oxides and nitrogen dioxide* in the forested area, but, in so doing, will *reduce the transport of these pollutants* to other areas. This 'acidification stripping' process may then result in increases in *waterborne pollutants* in the forested areas through leaching, and the effects of acidification of soils;

forests act as *carbon sinks*, and hence afforestation can reduce CO_2 emissions to the atmosphere, reducing the 'greenhouse effect';

economic security for the nation may be advanced by afforestation because of reduced costs from interruptions in flows of imported timber;

the decline of *rural communities* may be lessened through afforestation.[1]

464

Other benefits widely attributed to afforestation include the creation or protection of *rural employment* and the *savings of imports*. These impacts are
discussed separately below because they generally will not qualify as allowable
benefits in the sense used in this chapter.

Only some of these outputs or services are *marketed*. Typically, only timber
values are reflected in the assessment of rates of return to plantations. As is well
known, such rates of return frequently fall below conventional 'discount rates'
employed by private or public agencies. Hence afforestation invariably appears
to be 'uneconomic'. However, it is the whole range of outputs that is relevant to
economic assessment. Use of timber values alone to determine investment worth
is in fact a purely *commercial* criterion. Henceforth, we distinguish between
commercial rates of return and *economic* rates of return, the latter encompassing
the value of non-marketed outputs and services and other adjustments considered below.

The benefit of afforestation can be measured as the sum of

timber values
recreational value
landscape value
biodiversity value
watershed protection or damage (and other *ecological function* values)
microclimate
air pollution value (other than CO_2)
water pollution values
'greenhouse' benefit – i.e. value of trees as carbon stores
economic security
community integrity

This conceals an *aggregation problem* because individual components of the
aggregate benefits may be inconsistent with each other. Thus a high timber value
may be inconsistent with a high recreational value. There are *tradeoffs* between
the component values in the benefit equation. This issue needs to be borne in
mind when aggregating benefits. Total benefits are symbolized by *B*.

The *costs* of afforestation (land acquisition, planting costings, maintenance,
thinning, felling etc.), will be symbolized by *K*. If any of the above benefit flows
are actually negative – e.g., if reduced water run-off is a cost rather than a benefit
– then they will appear as such in the benefit side of the equation. That is, benefits
are negative costs, and costs are negative benefits.

The overall comparison is thus between the *benefits* of afforestation and the
costs of afforestation or

Net benefits $= B - K$

ignoring, for the moment, the problem of time.

Afforestation is judged *potentially* worthwhile if $B > K$, and potentially not worthwhile if $B < K$.

It is important to compute B and K *relative to the alternative use of the land*. The same exercise should therefore be carried out for such alternative uses. Typically these will be 'wilderness' or agriculture, but in the case of planned 'community forests', afforestation could be at the expense of derelict land, building or recreational land use.

The cost–benefit approach then justifies afforestation if

$$B_f - K_f > B_a - K_a$$

where 'f' refers to forestry and 'a' to the alternative land use. More strictly, we require this condition to hold in circumstances where 'a' is the highest alternative value of the land: afforestation must be compared to the next best use of the land.

2 MARKET FAILURE AND THE VALUATION OF FORESTRY BENEFITS

The fact that many of the outputs of forests are not marketed means that the use of purely commercial or 'free market' criteria to determine the amount of afforestation will result in an *undersupply* of afforestation *as long as the non-marketed benefits are positive*. This undersupply is an instance of *market failure*. Basically, markets do not supply the 'right' amount of afforestation.[2]

But there are other forms of market failure. We cannot be certain that the use of resources is correctly valued if market prices are used, nor that outputs at market values are correctly valued. For inputs the basic rule is that they should be valued at their *opportunity cost*, that is, what they would have received had they been put to alternative use.

2.1 Labour

In the forestry context the resource that has attracted most attention in this respect is *labour*. Because afforestation tends to take place in rural areas where alternative employment outlets are few, it can be argued that the opportunity cost of forestry labour is very much lower than the wage rates actually paid. They might, for example be rates payable for labour on hill farms, or casual labour in the tourist industry, or, if the alternative to forestry employment is unemployment, the cost could be regarded as near zero. In the cost–benefit equation then, the labour component of K would be costed as this opportunity cost wage, or *shadow wage*.

The use of a shadow wage rate is disputed, and the dispute tends to centre on differing interpretations of how labour markets function. Some economists argue that the economic system functions so that, effectively, all markets 'clear'. There is then full employment in the sense that any new job must always take a worker from somewhere else in the system. In the technical language, there is no *employment additionality*. There may well be *income additionality* in that the forestry job pays more than the job it displaces. Indeed, one would expect this to be the case if people only move jobs for higher rewards. But if there is no employment additionality, it would be wrong to shadow price a forestry job at zero. Its proper shadow price would be the income in the displaced job. Moreover, if we think of afforestation as investment at the margin, tracing through the various transfers of jobs that enable the forestry job to be filled is likely to result in the shadow wage being very close to the actual wage paid.

If, on the other hand, markets do not clear, then the creation of a job in the forestry sector does result in employment additionality, and lower shadow prices are justified.[3]

Rather than evaluate what is in effect a fundamental disagreement in macro-economic theory it seems better to adopt two approaches to labour valuation: (a) adopting the ruling wage rate in forestry, and (b) adopting some fraction of this to reflect a lower wage rate. A 1988 survey of 100 farms in Scotland produced an average of £0.62 per hour as the income from farming.[4] However, non-farm activity was used to supplement the low rates of pay in farming. On average, 1,227 hours per annum were spent in farm activity and 957 hours in non-farm activity. Average farm plus non-farm income was £4,964 per annum. But, if agriculture *alone* was the alternative occupation, then income averaged only £565 per annum, although only 5 per cent of farmers relied on agricultural income alone. Subsidies supplied additional income as did work by other members of the household.

In terms of a 'shadow wage rate' these figures suggest that the maximum rate is around £5,000 per annum, i.e., some two-thirds of the market wage. Depending on location, the shadow rate could be considerably less than this, but we set the shadow wage rate at 0.67 of ruling market rates.

2.2 Imports

The other shadow price that attracts a lot of attention in the forestry literature is the value of timber itself. Timber is an internationally traded good and the relevant shadow price for UK timber is therefore the price that it could secure if exported, or the price that has to be paid on world markets for the imports that would otherwise have to be secured. Since the United Kingdom imports some 90 per cent of its timber needs, international trade is particularly important. The shadow price of timber is thus its *border price*, i.e., its import or export price. Many commentators nonetheless feel that this price, which is the market price in the UK, still understates the true value of afforestation. They argue that the market fails in at least one of the following ways:

(i)   The market fails to anticipate *future scarcity* of timber. Since gestation periods are long, the shadow price to be applied to afforestation now should be the expected real price in, say, thirty years time allowing for future scarcity. This argument has been particularly powerful in the history of both UK policy and in the USA.[5]

(ii) The market fails to reflect the importance of *substituting for imports*. There are two strands to this argument:

    1   The market may not anticipate supply interruptions from trade embargoes, political disruptions of supply, etc.

    2   The value of an avoided import is somehow higher than the market price paid for that import. This is the 'import substitution' argument.

Argument (i) is an argument for *forecasting relative prices*. A number of such forecasting exercises have been carried out for UK forestry.[6] The required adjustment to prices is then relatively simple.

Argument (ii)1 is a legitimate one for shadow pricing timber output. An evaluation of the chances of such embargoes and other supply interruptions suggest that a small increment in prices of 0.2–1.8 per cent to reflect the shadow value of economic security would be justified.[7]

Argument (ii)2 is illegitimate. A UK tree does not have a value higher than its border prices simply because it displaces an import valued at that border price. The theory of comparative advantage explains why import substitution arguments cannot be used to defend afforestation. The essence of the argument is (a) that free trade maximizes the well-being of those taking part in trade, (b) that, from a purely 'nationalist' point of view, protection of a domestic industry may be beneficial *if* the protecting country has monopoly power over the good being traded, and (c) where no such monopoly power exists, any tariff or other protective measure will reduce the volume of a nation's trade, making it worse off. Applied to forestry in the UK, there is no monopoly of timber since the UK is very much a 'price taker', timber prices being determined in world markets. No feasible afforestation programme in the UK could affect world prices. Hence protectionist policies towards forestry in the UK would reduce UK well-being. Subsidizing forestry *on import substitution grounds* is thus illegitimate.

2.3 Land

Valuing land acquisition for afforestation poses a problem because the land in question is typically used for agriculture which is in receipt of various forms of subsidy under the Common Agricultural Policy. That is, actual land prices will not be the same as those which would rule if the various forms of agricultural policy intervention did not take place. One study suggests that if *all forms of support and trade distortion* are removed, agricultural land prices might fall by as much as 46 per cent.[8] If so, land costs for afforestation should be recorded as 0.54 of the actual cost (1986 as the base year).

However, as agricultural support declines over time, agricultural land prices will converge on the free market prices, so the 'shadow price' of land will rise relative to the free market price. Put another way, the multiplier of 0.54 would decline over time. Harvey[9] raises two further caveats to the use of the 0.54 multiplier. First, as land leaves agriculture it is likely to become the subject of an 'amenity' demand, i.e., a demand from people who simply wish to own land for amenity purposes. Hence the 46 per cent price fall figure is likely to be too high. Second, there is an additional form of demand for land to be held in agriculture for amenity reasons. This is akin to an option or existence value (see section 4), and effectively means that *some element of the existing subsidy reflects this value*. It is not clear that this form of value applies equally to afforested land regardless of the form of afforestation. It is likely to be true for broadleaved forests, but less true for coniferous forests. The difference between the *social* value of agricultural land the free market price is further narrowed by these considerations. Accordingly, we suggest an upper limit that the social value of land used in future afforestation is taken to be 0.8 of the market value. Since this figure is likely to be on the high side, and certainly does not allow for the land price effects of any major expansion of forestry, a range of values between the limits of 0.5 and 0.8 is used.

3 BENEFITS AND TIME

Benefits and costs accrue over time. Time plays a particularly important role in afforestation economics because timber can take 30, 50 or 100 years to mature for an optimal rotation, depending on the type of wood, the geographical zone, soil type, etc. Because economics adopts the standpoint that consumer preferences 'matter', preferences for having benefits now rather than later, and preferences for postponing costs rather than suffering them now, mean that benefits and costs are *discounted*. The rate of discount is in fact another shadow price. It is the price of consumption now in terms of consumption in the future.

Discounting is controversial because of its potential for shifting forward in time, frequently to another generation, the costs of actions undertaken for benefit now (e.g., the benefits of nuclear power versus the costs of disposing of radioactive waste). In the forestry context the problem is that the discounting of future benefits means that planting costs now figure prominently in the rate of return calculation while the benefits from a rotation in thirty years time are downgraded significantly. To see this consider a rotation in year 30 yielding, say £100,000 of timber at projected prices. At the current UK 'target' discount rate of 8 per cent, this would be valued at

$$\frac{£100,000}{(1.08)^{30}} \simeq £10,000$$

The application of discounting techniques means that afforestation is potentially justified if

$$\Sigma_t d_t[B_{ft} - K_{ft}] > \Sigma_t d_t[B_{at} - K_{at}]$$

where d_t is the 'discount factor' and is equal to $1/(1 + r)^t$, r is the discount rate, t is time and Σ means 'sum of'.

Various suggestions have been made for *lowering* the discount rate applied to afforestation, primarily because it appears unfairly to discriminate against any investment with a long gestation period.[10] The problem with adjusting discount rates downward is that there is no easily derived rule for the quantitative adjustment that is needed. Moreover, if the rate is lowered for forestry why should it not be lowered for other investments?[11] If all discount rates were lowered then it can be shown that the effect could well be detrimental to the environment, the preservation of which is the main motive for advocating lower rates. The overall detrimental effect comes about because generally lower discount rates would alter the optimal balance between investment and consumption in the economy in favour of investment. In turn if investment is more polluting than consumption, then the net effect is to encourage more environmental decay.[12]

Many of the arguments for lowering discount rates are in fact arguments for *valuing benefits more accurately* and comprehensively. Even then, discrimination against forestry seems to remain. This suggests the possibility of lowering the rate for afforestation but not for other investments. This effectively was the situation in the UK whereby afforestation had to achieve a Treasury-approved rate of return lower than that on other projects – a minimum of 3 per cent overall compared to 5 per cent for other public investments. In 1990 recommended discount rates were 6 per cent on most public investments, with 8 per cent for transport projects. The UK Treasury currently proposes that 6 per cent be used for forestry if non-market benefits are to be included. In the cost–benefit analyses of this chapter we use the 6 per cent rate with a lower 3 per cent rate occasionally being also used for sensitivity purposes.

Note that it would be improper to use the lower rate if it is designed to capture the non-market benefits of afforestation. This is because, as will be seen, the aim here is to derive estimates for the major non-market benefits and to add these to the timber benefits. Making these estimates *and* lowering the discount rate would be double counting. However, the 6 per cent rate applies across the board to UK public services (except transport investments) and, for this reason, it is argued that the 6 per cent rate *and* the integration of non-market benefits is legitimate.

An alternative route is to apply the nation-wide general discount rate to forestry and to introduce a *sustainability constraint*. Although there are many interpretations of *sustainable development* a strong case can be made for interpreting it as non-declining per capita well-being over time, a condition for which is that the stock of overall capital in the economy should also be non-declining. Put more simply, it is a requirement to 'keep capital intact' and is more familiar in business as the need not to 'live off capital'. The precise rationale for this requirement need not detain us here.[13]

In practice the constant capital stock rule could mean two things: maintaining a stock of *all* capital, man made and 'natural'; or maintaining a stock of 'natural' capital, i.e., environmental assets. In the former case it would be legitimate to run down environmental capital (e.g., deforestation would be legitimate) *provided* other forms of capital were built up. In the latter case, the existing stock of environmental assets must not be run down in the aggregate, but there can be substitution within that stock. On the narrower interpretation of sustainability, then, it could be argued that the UK's stock of forest should not be run down. Put another way, afforestation would be justified at least as compensation for loss of forests, but an *expansion* of the stock of land devoted to forestry would require additional arguments. The sustainability argument is further complicated by substitution within the stock of existing environmental assets. Thus, forest stocks might be run down in favour of expanded farming. Two observations are in order. First, what constitutes acceptable substitution depends on *valuation* which is precisely why the approach of 'cost–benefit thinking' has been adopted. Second, in the UK context the issue is generally one of a longer-run decline in land devoted to farming, with afforestation being considered as one of the main alternative uses of some of the released land.

In fact some of the arguments justifying expansion of forestry are already represented in the benefits of afforestation for 'fixing' CO_2 emissions. The sum of benefits does not indicate to whom the benefits and costs accrue. UK forestry investment would typically be evaluated according to the benefits and costs to the *UK*. But the benefit of fixing CO_2 is not confined to the UK. It is a 'global public good'. The sustainability requirement, then, also needs a 'boundary'. If the boundary is the UK, then the only afforestation that would be justified on a sustainability constraint is that which holds the forest stock *in the UK* constant.[14] But if UK afforestation is seen as a contribution to moves to restore the *global* forest stocks, then the picture is rather different. The UK cannot adopt a stance that *any* afforestation is good so long as it compensates for a global loss of forests, but there is an alternative approach which would credit UK forest expansion with the benefits of global CO_2 reduction.

While the Rio Framework Convention on Climate Change, negotiated in 1992, sets short term targets for CO_2 control in industrial countries, longer term targets will have to relate to a warming increase above which the world should not go because of the significant ecological disruption that would otherwise be judged to ensue. The upper limit target rate that is widely suggested is 0.1 Deg C per decade of 'realised warming', together with 2 Deg C absolute increase in temperature above pre-industrial levels.[15] Any target can then be translated into 'allowable' greenhouse gas emissions. On the assumption that non-carbon greenhouse gases are severely curtailed – as the 1990 modifications to the Montreal Protocol on the protection of the ozone layer require – the allowable warming target of 0.1 Deg C per decade appears to correspond to significant reductions in CO_2 emissions below current (1990) levels.[16] A rational international agreement will allow for carbon 'sinks' as the negative of an allowable emission, i.e., the creation of any carbon sink should constitute an 'offset' for any CO_2 emissions of equal amounts. The offset idea is effectively the sustainability constraint – it embodies the underlying requirement that the total of CO_2 emissions should not exceed a fixed annual level.

On this basis, afforestation secures a 'carbon credit' equal in value to the cost of reducing CO_2 emissions by other means, e.g., by substituting non-carbon fuels. This issue is explored further in section 10.

4 THE NATURE OF ECONOMIC VALUE

Given that non-market value is potentially very important in justifying forestry expansion it is worth dwelling briefly on the components of economic value. Although different authors use different systems of classification, the following seems most helpful.[17] Economic values may be divided into:

use values,
non-use values.

In turn, use values can be divided into direct and indirect values. A direct use value would be, for example, timber harvesting and the use of thinnings. Recreational uses of forests is another.[18] An indirect use value would be exemplified by an ecological function, such as watershed protection. Another use value is *option value* which reflects the willingness to pay for afforestation on the grounds that, while not used at present, the option to use the forest is valued.[19]

Non-use values relate to economic values not associated with any direct or indirect use values. Individuals may, for example wish to support afforestation on the grounds that they think forests are valuable even though they will never personally make direct use of them. Motives for these 'existence' and 'bequest' values are debated but may include concern for future generations, the adoption of some 'stewardship' role with respect to nature, conferment of 'rights' to nature, and so on.

Table 17.1 shows the overall classification system. It also indicates the type of valuation methodology that is appropriate for the various components of 'total economic value'. These methodologies are not discussed further here.[20] The following sections are devoted to drawing up a 'balance sheet' for the cost–benefit assessment of forestry expansion.

Table 17.1 *Valuing forest benefits*

| Total economic value | | | | |
Direct use values	Indirect use values	Option values	Existence values	Bequest values
Type of benefits				
T	B	B	B	B
R	W	R	L	
B	M	C		
S	G	L		
L	C			
	A			
	P			
Valuation technique				
Market prices	Avoided damage costs	CVM	CVM	CVM
HPM	Preventive expenditures			
TCM	Value of productivity changes (Replacement costs)			

Notes: TCM = travel cost method
HPM = hedonic pricing method
CVM = contingent valuation method
T = timber
R = recreation
B = biodiversity
S = economic security

C = community integrity
L = landscape
W = watershed/ecosystem function
M = microclimate
G = greenhouse impact
A = air pollution
P = water pollution

5 THE COMPONENTS OF COST–BENEFIT ANALYSIS: TIMBER (T)

This section estimates the value of timber. Table 17.2 summarizes the commercial rate of return and NPV data for afforestation under various yield classes and locations, excluding all grants. Full results are to be found in annex 3 of Pearce (1991).[21]

In the table, various assumptions are made about the shadow price of land. In each case 80 per cent of the market value is used. This is taken to be £3,000 per hectare in the lowlands and £660/hectare in the uplands. If a different view is taken, by arguing that the amenity value factor in agricultural land prices applies

Table 17.2 *Commercial analysis of afforestation (timber benefits only)*
(NPV at £1989/90 hectare, and IRRs) (6% discount rate)

		NPV	IRR
FT1	Semi natural pinewoods/uplands		
	land value = 0.5	− 798	3.2
	land value = 0.8	− 975	3.0
FT2	Semi natural broadleaves/lowlands		
	land value = 0.5	− 2,940	—
	land value = 0.8	− 3,839	—
FT3	Semi natural broadleaves/uplands		
	land value = 0.5	− 1,099	—
	land value = 0.8	− 1,276	—
FT4	Spruce/uplands		
	land value = 0.0	− 4	6.0
	land value = 0.5	− 288	5.4
	land value = 0.8	− 458	5.1
FT5	Community forests	− 3,173	2.6
FT6	Native broadleaves/lowlands		
	land value = 0.5	− 3,384	1.0
	land value = 0.8	− 4,283	0.9
FT7	Pines/lowlands		
	land value = 0.5	− 1,741	3.7
	land value = 0.8	− 2,605	3.2
FT8	Fir, spruce, broadleaves/lowlands		
	land value = 0.0	572	7.1
	land value = 0.5	− 819	5.0
	land value = 0.8	− 1,653	4.3

Notes:
FT = forestry type
LV = 0.5 refers to shadow price of land at 50% of market value, similarity for LV = 0.8
'—' under IRR means a negative IRR.

equally well to forestry land, then the lower factor of 50 per cent of market value might be used (see the discussion in section 2). A shadow price of *zero* may also be applicable in some cases where the alternative value of the land is zero.

A once-for-all premium of 1 per cent on timber prices is assumed to reflect economic security (see section 11 below).

For forest types appropriate to those parts of the country where the shadow price of labour is less than the market wage, the cost of labour is taken to be 67 per cent of its market value (see section 2).

The internal rate of return columns in table 17.2 are perhaps the easiest way of seeing the overall private profitability of timber production. At a 6 per cent discount rate only the following are profitable or marginally profitable:

mixed fir, spruce and broadleaves in the lowlands, assuming land has zero opportunity cost,
spruce in the uplands provided land has a zero opportunity cost.

Timber prices

As noted in section 2.1 timber prices in commercial rate of return calculations should reflect future expectations. Similarly, the relevant price for an evaluation of UK afforestation is the price at which timber is imported to the UK. For this reason, *global* and world *regional* prices are the relevant ones for the evaluation exercise.

Arnold (1991)[22] suggests various estimates of average annual price rises in the USA;

1–1.1 per cent per annum, mostly concentrated after the turn of the century (US Forest Service study). Pulpwood prices rise more slowly than sawlog prices.
0.2–1.2 per cent per annum averaged across sawlogs and pulpwood (Resources for the Future), and perhaps higher with sawlog prices rising faster than pulpwood, if there is a high demand.

Contrary to the USA, the European picture appears to be more one of rising prices for pulpwood and falling prices for coniferous logs. The difference in the price trends in the two regions reflects more intensive application of recycling technology in Europe than the USA, and the consequent more limited scope for further market penetration of recycling. There has also been slower growth in the consumption of European sawn wood. Prices in the two regions are expected to converge. Expected technical changes in the European processing industry and large supplies of roundwood are likely to keep prices down.

Pearce *et al.* survey price projections and conclude that a range of 0–2 per cent per annum in future real prices would embrace all reasonable assessments, and that projections at the lower end of the range are more likely to be realised.[23]

Overall, stable real prices define the lower bound of expected price changes with an upper bound of perhaps 1.5 per cent per annum. Table 2 assumes constant real prices only.[24]

Table 17.3 *Recreational consumer surplus by forest type (£1989)* *(per hectare/year)*

Recreational value	Uplands	Lowlands
Low	3	n.a.
Moderate	30	50
High	n.a.	220
Very high	n.a.	424

6 THE COMPONENTS OF COST–BENEFIT ANALYSIS: RECREATION (R)

Benson and Willis provide estimates of the net benefits to recreationalists of different types of forest plantation.[25] The results are shown in table 17.3. It is a matter of local circumstance as to when recreation benefits are likely to accrue. It is assumed here that there are no benefits until year 16 and that thereafter they continue at the same level until the end of the rotation. *The benefits are 'gross' in the sense that recreational benefits from the alternative use of land are not accounted for.*

While recreational values are not translatable across continents, it would be surprising if they differed very much. Recent work in the USA suggests a present capital value per hectare of forest of around $1,100, i.e., around £690. It is interesting to note that this is consistent with the moderate annual recreational values presented here for the lowlands.[26]

Just as timber prices may rise in real terms over time, so recreational benefits may rise. USA work does suggest rising real values. Walsh surveys the US evidence on the growth of demand for recreation.[27] Land-base recreation is forecast to grow by some 1.0 per cent per annum. The 1 per cent growth rate may in fact be too low for the UK (data from the General Household Survey indicates that all recreational activity surveyed has been growing at 3 per cent per annum (participations per adult per year), while walking has grown at 2 per cent per annum). Adopting a 1 per cent growth rate for the increase in benefits from forest-based recreation is therefore conservative.

The final analysis in section 13 shows the effects of including a rising value of recreational benefits.

7 THE COMPONENTS OF COST–BENEFIT ANALYSIS: WILDLIFE CONSERVATION (BIODIVERSITY) (B)

It is possible to rank desirable forest types in respect of wildlife values. These values are regarded as being a function of 'naturalness', diversity and rarity.

Diversity is typically regarded as being most valuable if it is itself natural. The introduction of Sitka spruce does for example increase diversity, but conservationists tend to regard such gains as being at the expense of natural diversity. Most afforestation tends to increase diversity. The ranking that emerges from one study is: (a) new mixed 'native' woodland, (b) mixed broadleaves and conifers, (c) non-native broadleaves or conifers alone.[28]

Wildlife impacts depend very much on the actual location of any new forest. Of particular value is planting which links existing woodland, making the connected area larger and thus increasing diversity. Of note is the finding that spruce is probably no better or worse than alternative non-native woodlands for wildlife diversity. The assumptions that afforestation displaces low-value agricultural land which, in turn, is regarded as being of low wildlife conservation interest.

8 THE COMPONENTS OF COST–BENEFIT ANALYSIS: WATER RESOURCE IMPACTS (W)

Forests have a number of water-related ecological impacts on the surrounding watershed of forested areas. These are:

impacts on water supply,
impacts on water quality,
impacts on air pollutant deposition,
soil erosion,
fertiliser impacts,
pesticide impacts,
harvesting impacts.

Water supply

Afforestation involves evaporation losses mainly due to canopy interception: 20–50 per cent of incoming rainfall may be intercepted with streamflow reductions of around 15 per cent. At one well studied site, reductions in streamflow of about 15 per cent were recorded where 60 per cent of the site was planted with conifers. Current models predict a loss of flow of 15 per cent in the wet uplands from a 75 per cent afforested catchment. The economic importance of such reduced flows depends on the relationship between supply and demand for water. While some monetary estimates of loss have been made, e.g., in terms of additional water extraction or storage costs to water authorities, and reduced hydropower capacity, the data are not currently in a form that enables valuation of the various areas under discussion. The effects are negligible in the lowlands or will appear as a small cost.

Air/water pollution

Forests 'scrub' air pollutants so that afforestation has the effect of increasing deposition of various pollutants. Some pollutants are absorbed by leaf and stem surfaces; some, such as SO_2 and O_3 are absorbed through the stomata; and the effect on NO_2 and NO appears indeterminate. Co-deposition of NH_3 and SO_2 may produce a significant increase in the deposition of both gases. Deposition varies according to the type of forest. The economic significance is two-fold. By scrubbing the pollutants the forest may prevent them from incurring damage elsewhere, depending on the buffering capacity of the recipient soils. But by concentrating them in the forested area pollutant concentrations in drainage waters are increased. This impacts on acidification and aluminium content. Technically, the correct 'valuation' of this impact would compute the localized damage due to acidification from forests and then *deduct* the damage that would otherwise be done by the emissions that initially arise. That is, forests should not be debited with all acidification damage given that the source of the acidification is, say, power station emissions.

Acidification

Streams draining forested areas on sensitive sites may be more acidic and may contain more aluminium, although long-term studies have so far failed to detect an impact.

Erosion and sedimentation

New planting may cause soil erosion and consequent increased sedimentation of watercourses. Chemical leaching may also occur. Costs to the water industry can be high, with one instance of £180,000 additional costs for a treatment plant to counteract the effects of ploughing for planting in the catchment area. Soil erosion may also be present throughout the rotation. Soil erosion is however common with intensive agricultural systems, and the overall effect may be beneficial.

Fertilisers

Fertiliser run-off from forest treatment appears to be of negligible significance as far as rivers are concerned, but can be important if run-off is to lakes and reservoirs. Impacts are likely to be very site specific and again this is not likely to be bad in areas that were intensively farmed.

Table 17.4 *Summary of water-related ecological impact by areas*

	Uplands	Upland margins	Lowlands
Water loss:			
ecological	—	—	—
economic	—	—	—
Erosion:			
ecological	—	neg	+
economic	—	neg	+
Fertiliser:			
ecological	neg	neg	+
economic	neg	neg	+
Pesticide:			
ecological	neg	neg	+
economic	neg	neg	+
Deposition:			
ecological	+ +	neg	neg
economic	+ +	neg	neg
Harvesting:			
ecological	—	neg	neg
economic	—	neg	neg

Notes:
+ = a benefit
− = a cost compared to alternative land use
net = negligible

Pesticides

Insecticides and herbicides are used on a relatively small scale in forestry but can affect water quality. Herbicide impacts can occur through reduced vegetative cover affecting streamwater chemistry.

Harvesting

Harvesting by clear felling modifies the microclimate, results in a sudden increase in debris and interrupts nutrient cycling. Nitrate in drainage waters may be increased. But there is no evidence that water treatment costs have increased as a result.

Hornung and Adamson conclude that ecological impacts are likely to be site-specific and that there is considerable scope for their mitigation through careful forest management.[29] Impacts by forested area are summarized in table 4. A distinction is made between ecological and economic impacts; significant ecological impacts could occur without them being 'valued' highly, and vice versa. More generally, one would expect them to be similar in magnitude.

9 THE COMPONENTS OF COST–BENEFIT ANALYSIS: LANDSCAPE EVALUATION (L)

Campbell and Fairley assess the role of forests in landscape evaluation.[30] Aesthetic qualities include enjoyment, psychological well-being, child education and development, artistic and creative stimuli and a 'sense of security'. They indicate that there is a general consensus about what constitutes landscape value. These values contribute both to land and property values, and to option and *existence* value (cf. table 17.1) not revealed in market prices. They also argue that the demand for landscape conservation is growing. Landscape value is highest with multi-purpose non-monocultural forests. As with biodiversity, native woodlands are assigned the highest landscape value. Also echoing the biodiversity discussion, landscape value depends critically upon the location and design of forests, so that no general conclusion can be reached about non-site-specific values. Overall, however, the ranking for landscape values would appear to be very similar to that for biodiversity.

10 THE COMPONENTS OF COST–BENEFIT ANALYSIS: GREENHOUSE EFFECT (G)

Trees take carbon dioxide from the atmosphere and fix it in perennial tissue. The CO_2 is eventually released as the wood decays or is burned. Some uses of the wood 'lock up' the carbon for long periods, and this period of lock-up overlaps the next rotation of tree growing so that rates of accumulation of carbon exceed rates of decay. This net gain is not indefinite and is probably around 100 years plus, after which fixation is then matched by decay and there is no further increase in storage. In areas of organic rich soils, an increase in CO_2 output from the soils as a result of increased composition of pre-existing soil organic matter, consequent on drying produced by tree growth, may have to be set against any carbon credit due to carbon fixing in tree biomass.

For a period of at least 100 years, then, afforestation produces a net gain in carbon fixing capacity and hence, a 'carbon credit' is due to afforestation on this basis. Carbon fixing by forests has thus to be seen as a means of postponing global warming. The extent of this effect can be modified by at least two further factors. If timber end-uses are changed then net fixation could be increased, e.g.,

Table 17.5 *Carbon storage in forests* ($C =$ *tonnes CO_2 as carbon*)

		(tonnes C/ha/pa)
Upland:	Sitka spruce	1.7
	Scots pine	1.4
	Birch	1.0
Lowland:	Scots pine	1.7
	Corsican pine	2.7
	Oak	1.5
	Poplar coppice	4.0

by using more timber in durable uses. Second, there may be carbon *losses* from soil if afforestation occurs on peaty soils. These may offset, to some extent, the CO_2 fixation effects of afforestation.

Cannel and Cape provide figures for the equivalent carbon stored by different yield classes.[31] Table 17.5 summarizes the carbon storage figures, allowing for decay in timber products.

What is the value of fixing a tonne of CO_2? There are two approaches that might be used:

the *damage avoided* approach would suggest that a tonne of fixed CO_2 is equal to the avoided damage that would be done if the carbon was not fixed;

the *offset* approach would suggest that the value of carbon fixing is equal to the cost of offsetting CO_2 emissions by investing in CO_2 reduction technology. Since CO_2 removal is not currently feasible, this amounts to saying that the value is equal to the cost of substituting a non-carbon fuel for a carbon fuel at the margin.

Pursuing the damage avoided approach, global warming damage estimates have been produced by Nordhaus and by Ayres and Walter.[32] They are highly speculative but suggest the following figures, per tonne CO_2 (carbon weight) (1990 $):

Nordhaus	$1.2 (minimum)	to	$10 (maximum)
Ayres and Walter	central guess	=	$30–35

Nordhaus' 'medium damage' scenario calculates an optimal reduction in greenhouse gases consistent with a benefit of tonne C of CO_2 reduction of $7, or around £4 per tonne. These figures relate to losses of GNP and Ayres and Walter's figures suggest that other costs may be significantly higher. This conclusion is reinforced by subsequent work.[33] We therefore suggest a value of £8 per tonne CO_2 carbon weight.

Calculating carbon fixing credits for UK forestry

Carbon fixing data were supplied by the Forestry Commission Research Station at Alice Holt. The carbon fixing functions allow for repeated rotations and for a 'typical mix' of end uses of wood. The end uses are significant because once felled, carbon is released from wood, but in varying degrees according to the uses made of wood. The end-use mix assumed here is:

Branches, lop and top	100% to waste, bark and fuel
Small diameter roundwood	51% to pulpwood
	37% to particleboard
	1% to medium density fibreboard
	8% to fencing
	3% to mining
Large diameter roundwood	13% to waste, bark and fuel
	23% to pulpwood
	23% to particleboard
	1% to medium density fibreboard
	14% to pallet and packaging
	19% to fencing
	13% to construction
	5% to mining
	2% to 'other'

A typical 'fixation and decay' curve is shown in figure 17.1.

Since we are not interested in detailed accuracy at this stage, the 'average carbon in fixed form' curves have been approximated by a generalized function of the form

$$F = M(1 - e^{-gt}) \tag{1}$$

where F = average carbon in fixed form – i.e., a moving average of *accumulated* carbon fixation.

To obtain *annual* additions to carbon fixations, we require

$$\frac{dF}{dt} = Mg\, e^{-gt} \tag{2}$$

Equations (1) and (2) are estimated below for this option shown in this figure to illustrate the calculations.

$M = 80$ tc/ha when $F = 60$ tc and $t = 60$. Hence

$$60 = M(1 - e^{-60g}) \qquad \text{from (1)}$$
$$= 80(1 - e^{-60g})$$

Therefore $0.25 = e^{-60g}$ so $g = 2.3$ per cent per annum (i.e., $g = 0.023$).

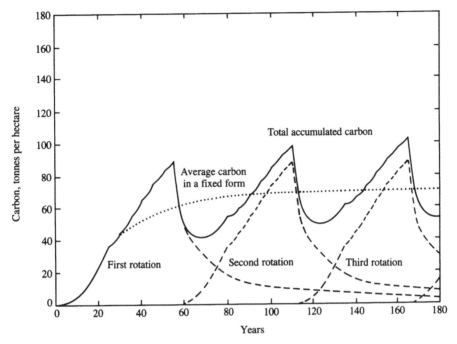

Figure 17.1 Sitka spruce

Substituting in (2) we have

$$\frac{dF}{dt} = 80(0.023)e^{0.023t}$$
$$= 1.84\ e^{-0.023t} \tag{3}$$

Note that dF/dt allows for carbon decay from the first rotation.

These gains need to be *discounted*. At 6 per cent, for example, the right-hand side of equation (3) becomes

$$1.84\ e^{-0.023t}\ e^{-0.06t} = 1.84\ e^{-0.083t}$$

This takes a value of only 0.03 tc/ha for year 50, so virtually all carbon 'credits' are captured by calculating present values up to the time horizon $t = 50$. The present value of this is then

$$PV = \int_{1}^{50} 1.84\ e^{-0.083t} \cdot dt = 20.04$$

Therefore, the relevant carbon credit is 20 tonnes c/ha.

Table 17.6 summarizes the resulting present value of 'carbon credits' – for example, FT1 Semi-natural pinewoods in the uplands is estimated to achieve a PV of carbon fixed of 17.8 tonnes/ha. At £8/tonne this gives a carbon credit of $17.8 \times 8 = £142$.

Table 17.6 *Summary carbon credits (damage approach) (Present values, 6% discount rate £ per hectare)*

Forest type		
FT1	Semi-natural pinewoods/uplands	142
FT2	Semi-natural broadleaves/lowlands	187
FT3	Semi-natural broadleaves/uplands	200
FT4	Spruce/uplands	210
FT5	Community forests	213
FT6	Native broadleaves/lowlands	246
FT7	Pines/lowlands	167
FT8	Fir, spruce, broadleaves/lowlands	254

The offset approach will produce different results. Anderson has made some preliminary estimates of carbon credits for a 'typical' forest and, after allowing for the decay of the wood products, suggests figures of £527–554 per hectare (present value at 6 per cent discount rate).[34] These figures are approximately twice those suggested by the damage avoided approach. In the final summary cost–benefit we use the lower figures, but their conservative nature needs to be borne in mind.

11 THE COMPONENTS OF COST–BENEFIT ANALYSIS: ECONOMIC SECURITY (S)

Markandya and Pearce have evaluated the arguments for ascribing a credit to afforestation on grounds of economic security.[35] Economic security refers to the benefits of avoiding the costs that would be imposed by import supply interruptions such as might occur with a trade embargo. Economic security does not refer to 'import savings'. While it is difficult to estimate the welfare gains from economic security, the Markandya–Pearce work suggests that the border price of timber might be raised by between 0.2 and 1.8 per cent to reflect economic security, depending on demand conditions. Overall, adding 1 per cent to border prices would seem justified. This premium is already allowed for in the timber valuations in table 17.2.

12 THE COMPONENT OF COST–BENEFIT ANALYSIS: COMMUNITY INTEGRITY (C)

Community integrity relates to the value that society puts on the conservation of rural communities. It is not to be confused with the benefits of creating rural *employment* (which may be zero as discussed earlier), but nonetheless has a link with employment. Essentially, some or all of what society spends to create rural employment in sparsely populated areas could be regarded as a reflection of willingness to pay for conserving rural communities and the rural 'way of life'.

13 SUMMARY OF COST–BENEFIT ANALYSIS

We now illustrate how the various *quantified* items in a cost–benefit assignment of afforestation can be brought together. Consider FT1: semi-natural pinewoods in the uplands.

Table 7 allows for timber, recreation and carbon fixing values, but assumes a zero timber real price rise. It does allow for rising recreational values relative to the general price level, and makes various assumptions about shadow wages and land prices. It *omits* the items for landscape (L), biodiversity (B), watershed (W), microclimate (M), non-CO_2 air pollution (A) and community values (C). At present, these have proved too difficult to value.

Assumptions:

1 Land price: 50% and 80% of market value (£600);
2 Labour cost: 67% of market wage rates;
3 Timber price: constant in real terms, with single 1% premium to reflect economic security;
4 Recreation: moderate value for the uplands = £30/ha/yr; low value for the uplands = £3/ha/yr;
5 Carbon: value of fixing one tonne carbon is £8. PV of carbon fixed = 17.8 t/ha; at £8/t, value = £142/ha.

Results:

	NPV at 6% (89/90)	IRR
Timber value only		
land value 50%	− 798	3.2
land value 80%	− 975	3.0
Timber and recreation value		
land value 50% moderate recreational value	− 483	4.1
land value 80% moderate recreational value	− 661	3.8
land value 50% low recreational value	− 768	3.3
land value 80% low recreational value	− 946	3.1
Timber, recreational and carbon-fixing value		
land value 50% moderate recreational value	− 344	4.5
land value 80% moderate recreational value	− 522	4.1
land value 50% low recreational value	− 628	3.7
land value 80% low recreational value	− 806	3.4

Table 17.7. *Representative cost–benefit appraisals (£1989/90 Present values, per ha) (r = 6%, land value = 0.8, shadow wages = 0.67, moderate recreational value)*

Forest type	FT1	FT2	FT3	FT4	FT5	FT6	FT7	FT8
Timber	− 975	− 3,839	− 1,276	− 458	− 3,173	− 4,283	− 2,605	− 1,653
Recreation	314	547	261	268	2,091*	547	412	
Carbon	142	187	200	210	213	246	167	254
Total	− 519	− 3,105	− 815	20	− 869	− 3,490	− 1,962	− 987
IRR%	4.1	0.1	—	6.0	4.8	1.6	3.8	4.9

Note: * high recreational value assumed.

Table 17.8. *Justification for afforestation*

Forest type	Assumptions giving positive NPV at 6 per cent
FT5 Community forests	Very high recreational values
FT4 Spruce/uplands	Moderate recreational values and land values at 0.5 market values
FT8 Fir, spruce, broadleaves/lowlands	High recreational values and land values at 0.8 market values
FT7 Pine in lowlands	Moderate recreational values and land values at 0.5 market values

The remaining costs can be treated similarly and the results are shown in table 17.7.

Further analysis shows that the results in table 17.8 are highly sensitive to assumptions made about land values and recreational values. Thus, FT8 (fir, spruce and broadleaves in the lowlands) shows a 4.3 per cent IRR for timber alone if land is valued at 80 per cent of market prices, but a 7.1 per cent IRR with zero shadow land values. This rises to 16.9 per cent for zero land values, high recreational values and the carbon credit.

Certain conclusions may be drawn from the analysis on the assumption that the net effect of the unquantified items is not significant, or that they cancel each other out. Table 17.8 shows the circumstances in which forest expansion is justified at the 6 per cent discount rate.

Obviously, tradeoffs would be possible. Lower recreational values could be acceptable if the opportunity cost of land was also lower. It is important, however, to relate land price assumptions to the yield class assumptions: higher than assumed yield classes might be obtained, but at the price of more expensive land, and *vice versa*.

It is important to note that the case for justifying an expansion of the forest types in table 17.8 depends also on assumptions about a range of environmental values. So, for example, an expansion of spruce in the uplands might not be justified for poorly designed, monoculture forests where landscape values might be negative, but might be justified where planting would result in well-designed, multi-purpose forests.

On the basis of the analysis above, options other than those listed in table 17.8 do not have an immediate economic justification. These are: native broadleaves managed for timber, semi-natural pinewoods in the uplands, and semi-natural broadleaves in the uplands or lowlands. But it is important to note that these forest types are likely to have benefits which are currently unquantified, especially biodiversity conservation. Semi-natural pinewoods in the uplands, for example, with moderate recreational value and a shadow land price of 0.5, shows an overall quantified negative NPV of £344/ha. Society may well be willing to pay this sum to conserve the associated biodiversity. A similar argument applies to the other forest types.

NOTES

I am indebted to the following for comments on various earlier versions: David Grundy and Tim Rollinson (Forestry Commission, Edinburgh); Arnold Grayson; John Fisher (DoE); Mike Hornung and John Good (ITE); David Harvey and Ken Willis (Newcastle); David Burdekin (Forestry Commission at Alice Holt). Donald Thompson and his team at Forestry Commission Research, Alice Holt kindly supplied diagrammatic material on carbon fixing by plantation type. I am indebted to Dennis Anderson (UCL and World Bank) for discussions on the economic interpretation of the carbon fixing data.

1 The US Forest Service, for example, has as one of its objectives the maintenance of 'community stability'. This is particularly relevant to the many small communities in the west of the USA dependent upon public timber harvesting. For an evaluation of the 'worth' of this benefit see R. Boyd and W. Hyde (1989), *Forestry Sector Intervention: The Impacts of Public Regulation on Social Welfare*, Iowa State University Press, Ames.

2 It must not be concluded from this that some form of public ownership will therefore necessarily produce the 'right' amount. Public ownership could introduce distortions of its own. Other forms of regulatory intervention may also introduce bigger distortions than those induced by market failure. If so, it may be a matter of opting for the 'least distorted' option, an instance of what economists call the 'second best' problem. There are no *a priori* rules for deciding the form of ownership or regulation. It is an empirical matter. For an evaluation of regulatory options for forestry in the USA, using cost–benefit principles, see Boyd and Hyde, *Forestry Sector Invervention*.

3 On employment and income additionality, see I. Byatt (1983), 'Byatt Report on Subsidies to British Export Credits', *World Economy*, vol. 7: 163–78.

4 See J. Dewar (1991), *New Planting Methods, Costs and Returns*, Forestry Commission, Edinburgh, and *Very Small Farms in Scotland: an Economic Study*, SAC Economic Report No. 10, February.

5 See Boyd and Hyde, *Forestry Sector Invervention*.

6 See M. Arnold (1991), *The Long Term Global Demand for and Supply of Wood*, Oxford Forestry Institute, Oxford, mimeo and A. Whiteman (1991), *UK Demand for and Supply of Wood and Wood Products*, Forestry Commission, Edinburgh. See also D.W. Pearce, A. Markandya and I. Knight (1988), *Economic Security Arguments for Afforestation*, A Report to the Forestry Commission, Edinburgh, November; and D.W. Pearce and A. Markandya (1990), 'Economic Security Arguments for Afforestation', Department of Economics, University College London, *mimeo*.

7 See Pearce, Markandya and I. Knight, *Economic Security Arguments* and Pearce and Markandya , 'Economic security arguments'.

8 D. Harvey (1991), *The Agricultural Demand for Land: Its Availability and Cost for Forestry*, Countryside Change Unit, University of Newcastle, Newcastle.

9 Ibid.

10 See E. Kula (1988), *The Economics of Forestry: Modern Theory and Practice*, London, Croom Helm. Kula advocates a modified discounting method in which discount factors are weighted according to the structure of the population in terms of its generations. Thus, a benefit to a generation just starting in year N, say, would have a discount factor of 1, not $1/(1 + r)^N$. This avoids, Kula claims, inter-generational discrimination. The effect is to give higher weight to future costs and benefits than under conventional discounting. For a debate on Kula's methodology see E. Kula (1988), 'Future generations; the modified discounting method', *Project Appraisal*, 3: 85–8; K. Thompson (1988), 'Future generations: the modified discounting method – a reply', *Project Appraisal*, 3(3): 171–2; C. Price (1989), 'Equity, consistency, efficiency and new rules for discounting', *Project Appraisal*, 4(2) (June): 58–65. For an extensive survey of alternative views on the discount rate and its impact on resource and environmental issues, see A. Markandya and D.W. Pearce (1988), *Environmental Considerations and the Choice of Discount Rate in Developing Countries*, Environmental Department, World Bank, Washington, DC.

11 Kula's approach is capable of quantitative estimation using demographic projections of age structure, does effectively lower the discount rate, and would be applied across all investments. See Kula, 'Future generations'.

12 See Markandya and Pearce, *Environmental Considerations*, and for formal proofs see J. Krautkraemer (1988), 'The rate of discount and the preservation of natural environments', *Natural Resource Modelling*, 2(2) (Winter).

13 An intuitive analysis is provided in D.W. Pearce, A. Markandya and E. Barbier (1989), *Blueprint for a Green Economy*, Earthscan, London. The analytical foundations lie in a sequence of arguments:
  1 Sustainable development is about being fair to future generations who should be no worse off than the current generation.
  2 Current activities are giving rise to the potential for future generations to be worse off (e.g., greenhouse effects, ocean pollution, etc.).
  3 Hence future generations must be compensated.
  4 Setting up 'compensation funds' for the future is hazardous.

5 But we can compensate future generations by passing on a stock of capital assets at least equal to the current stock.

6 Such 'constant capital' rules can be demonstrated to produce constant consumption flows over time, a measure of inter-generational fairness.

14 Even this begs the issue of the starting point. Typically, the sustainability requirement operates with its reference point as *now*.

15 See F.R. Rijsberman and R.J. Swart (1990), *Targets and Indicators of Climatic Change*, Stockholm Environment Institute, Stockholm.

16 See Intergovernmental Panel of Climate Change (IPCC) (1990), *Policymakers Summary of the Scientific Assessment of Climate Change*, Working Group 1, May.

17 The approach here follows that of D.W. Pearce and R.K. Turner (1989), *Economics of Natural Resources and the Environment*, Harvester-Wheatsheaf, London. See also D.W. Pearce (1987), *Economic Values and the Environment*, The 1987 Denman Lecture, Department of Land Economy, University of Cambridge.

18 On the value of UK forests for recreational purposes see K. Willis and J. Benson (1989), 'Recreational values of forests', *Forestry*, 62(2): 93–110.

19 Some writers regard option value as a non-use value.

20 See D.W. Pearce and A. Markandya (1989), *Environmental Policy Benefits: Monetary Valuation*, OECD, Paris; and P-O. Johansson (1987), *The Economic Theory and Measurement of Environmental Benefits*, Cambridge University Press.

21 D.W. Pearce (1991), *Assessing the Returns to the Economy and to Society from Investments in Forestry*, Forestry Commission, Edinburgh.

22 See Arnold, *Long Term Global Demand*.

23 D.W. Pearce, A. Markandya and I. Knight (1988), *Economic Security Arguments for Afforestation*, Report to the Forestry Commission, Edinburgh, November.

24 This is in keeping with Sedjo and Lyon's analysis. Only in a 'high demand' scenario do prices rise at 1.2 per cent per annum. See R. Sedjo and K. Lyon (1990), *The Long Term Adequacy of World Timber Supply*, Resources for the Future, Washington, DC.

25 J. Benson and K. Willis (1991), *The Demand for Forests for Recreation*, University of Newcastle, Newcastle.

26 See M.D. Bowes and J.V. Krutilla (1989), *Multiple Use Management: the Economics of Public Forestlands*, Resources for the Future, Washington, DC, Paper 7. The actual value obtained was some $410 per acre at a 7 per cent discount rate, i.e., some $1,000 per hectare, which is consistent with $1,100 per hectare at a 6 per cent discount rate.

27 R. Walsh (1986), *Recreation Economic Decisions: Comparing Benefits and Costs*, Venture, State College PA.

28 See J. Good *et al.* (1991), *Forests as Wildlife Habitat*, Institute of Terrestrial Ecology, Grange-over-Sands, Cumbria.

29 M. Hornung and J. Adamson (1991), *Forestry Expansion: The Impact on Water Quality and Quantity*, Institute of Terrestrial Ecology, Grange-over-Sands, Cumbria.

30 D. Campbell and R. Fairley (1991), *Forestry and the Conservation and Enhancement of Landscape*, Countryside Commission for Scotland, Edinburgh.

31 M. Cannell and J. Cape (1991), *Forestry Expansion: International Environmental Impacts: Acid Rain and the Greenhouse Effect*, Institute of Terrestrial Ecology, Grange-over-Sands, Cumbria.

32 W. Nordhaus (1991), 'To slow or not to slow: the economics of the greenhouse effect',

Economic Journal, 101(407) (July): 920–37. J. Walter and R. Ayres (1991), 'Global Warming: Damages and Costs', and R. Ayres and J. Walter, 'The Greenhouse Effect: Damages, Costs and Abatement', *Environmental and Resource Economics*, 1(3): 237–70.

33 See Metroeconomica Ltd (1991), *Nuclear Power and Greenhouse Gases*, Report to Nuclear Electric, Cheltenham.

34 See D. Anderson (1990), *The Forestry Industry and the Greenhouse Effect*, Report to the UK Forestry Commission and the Scottish Forestry Trust, Edinburgh.

35 Markandya and Pearce, *Environmental Considerations*.

INDEX